Transactions of the RHS (2024), **2**, 1–2
doi:10.1017/S0080440124000112

INTRODUCTION

Welcome

Jan Machielsen

Cardiff University, Cardiff, UK
Email: machielsenj@cardiff.ac.uk

(Received 15 August 2024; accepted 22 August 2024)

Welcome to the second volume of the seventh series of the *Transactions of the Royal Historical Society*. Last year's issue, edited by my predecessors, Harshan Kumarasingham and Kate Smith, marked the beginning of a period of change for our journal. While some of the content in this volume originated from invited lectures given at the Society's London premises, most comprises exciting new material submitted by the Society's fellowship and the wider historical community. All content undergoes double-blind peer review – a process that, as the journal of a learned society, the editorial board and I are working hard to make as transparent, constructive and timely as possible.

As part of this transition, it has been a particular delight – and a tribute to Kate's and Harshan's hard work – to see the new Common Room section of the *Transactions* taking form. This volume shows the Common Room shaping up in precisely the way they foresaw in last year's welcome, as 'an alternative site in which issues pertinent to our discipline can be shared, discussed and collectively worked through'. Through a combination of commissioned and pitched content, the contributions to the Common Room speak eloquently to the wider issues facing our discipline.

This year's virtual 'watercooler moments' cover an extremely broad range of topics. They include reflections on best research practices (such as whether to anonymise our sources), the latest historiographical trends and the difficulties experienced by independent scholars. Other contributions address questions of pedagogy and student well-being in our supposedly 'post-truth' world. Contributions also showcase the value of history in contemporary society, for instance by demonstrating the materiality of wills in the wake of a government consultation. Each is important in a different way, and their variety shows that while historians work on the past, they live in the present. We hope that these pieces will foster further discussion and possibly even fresh contributions in turn.

The year 2024 brought both opportunities and challenges. The *Transactions* and the Society have welcomed Cambridge University Press's move to Open Access, which means that henceforth all publications in our journal will be accessible to everyone without any cost to the author. Our publisher's move to a new funding model is an innovative response to the wider higher education landscape. Yet not all news is good news. A cyber incident at Cambridge University Press in June significantly affected the publication of many journals, including ours, and ultimately caused this year's volume to be delayed. A blocked publication pipeline has also impacted the *Transactions'* visibility, making it more difficult to trail and celebrate our publications.

The work of repositioning the *Transactions* as a leading general journal in the field will continue next year – and beyond. Our central objective has been to increase the visibility of the *Transactions* as a journal that covers the full breadth of human history. Our decision to organise this year's research articles roughly chronologically shows that more work is needed particularly to attract submissions that discuss the premodern past. But if you are reading this, regardless of your subject expertise, we would welcome a submission from you.

Finally, by the time this volume lands in your letterbox, a new co-editor may well be in place. We are moving to a system of staggered appointments, ensuring that there will be continuity as well as change. Next year's welcome will again be co-written.

Cite this article: Machielsen J (2024). Welcome. *Transactions of the Royal Historical Society* 2, 1–2. https://doi.org/10.1017/S0080440124000112

Transactions of the RHS (2024), **2**, 3–38
doi:10.1017/S0080440124000136

ARTICLE

Yangzhou, 1342: Caterina Vilioni's Passport to the Afterlife

Krisztina Ilko

Queens' College, University of Cambridge, Cambridge, UK
Email: ki259@cam.ac.uk

(Received 6 February 2024; revised 22 July 2024; accepted 22 July 2024;
first published online 3 October 2024)

Abstract

The tombstone of an Italian woman, Caterina Vilioni, in Yangzhou (1342) is a rare and important testimony to Christianity in Yuan China. By exploring the visual language and the multicultural geopolitical context of Caterina's funerary monument, this article sheds light on the dynamic processes behind how cultural and religious barriers were negotiated in the premodern Eurasian world. Despite the increasing scholarly interest in the European import of Asian luxury merchandise along the Silk Roads, movement of objects, persons, and ideas the other way around from Europe to Asia is much less explored. Moreover, the expansion of European networks towards the east was written from the perspective of men: friars, diplomats and merchants. Yet, the Yangzhou tombstone directs attention to the overlooked presence of non-elite Christian women in the cosmopolitan port cities of south-east China well before the era of modern global maritime exchange. While previous scholars traced the tombstone to Buddhist and Christian art, I argue that the visual language intentionally projected cultural ambiguity. By comparing it to the Mongol *paiza* (safe conduct pass), this article proposes that Caterina's burial marker functioned as an 'otherworldly passport', which invoked spiritual protection and facilitated the passage between two realms.

Keywords: global Middle Ages; Silk Roads; Venetian mercantile networks; women and religion; Yuan dynasty

In 1951, a late medieval Christian tombstone with Latin inscriptions was discovered during road construction at the South Gate of Yangzhou (扬州市) in current-day Jiangsu province in eastern China (Figures 1 and 2).[1] It survives

---

[1] Francis A. Rouleau, 'The Yangchow Latin Tombstone as a Landmark of Medieval Christianity in China', *Harvard Journal of Asiatic Studies*, 17 (1954), 346–65; Lauren Arnold, *Princely Gifts and Papal Treasures: The Franciscan Mission to China and its Influence on the Art of the West, 1250–1350*

Figure 1. Caterina Vilioni's tombstone, 1342. Granite, h: 58 cm. Yangzhou: Marco Polo Museum. (Photo: Deborah Howard.)

(San Francisco, 1999), 138–46; Deborah Howard, 'Venice and Islam in the Middle Ages: Some Observations on the Question of Architectural Influence', in *Late Antique and Medieval Art of the Mediterranean World*, ed. Eva R. Hoffman (Oxford, 2007), 389–404, at 392, 402, n. 20; Jennifer Purtle, 'The Far Side: Expatriate Medieval Art and its Languages in Sino-Mongol China', in *Confronting the Borders of Medieval Art*, ed. Jill Caskey, Adam S. Cohen and Linda Safran (Leiden, 2011), 167–97; Mengtian Bai, 'Yangzhou Latin Tombstones: A Christian Mirror of Yuan China Society' (Honors Papers, Oberlin College, 2018); Eva Caramello and Romedio Schmitz-Esser,

Figure 2. Copy of Caterina Vilioni's tombstone. Negative reproduction of the facsimile of the original rubbing made in 1951. (Image: Rouleau, 'Yangchow', plate 2.)

in excellent condition, and only the top and the bottom of the grey stone slab have been damaged. The upper half of the funerary monument is decorated with low-carved reliefs depicting the enthroned Virgin Mary and Child

'From Genoa to Yangzhou? Funerary Monuments for Europeans in Yuan China and their Paleographic Analysis', *Medieval Worlds*, 16 (2022), 210–28.

above scenes from the martyrdom of St Catherine of Alexandria. According to the Latin inscription written with Gothic majuscules, the stone slab commemorated the death of Caterina Vilioni, daughter of Domenico Vilioni, in June 1342.[2] While no other surviving written sources attest to the existence of Caterina Vilioni, her funerary monument is a rare and important testimony to the presence of western European Christianity in Yuan China (1271–1368).

Significant recent scholarly interest has sought to understand more fully the integration and perception of foreigners in medieval European cities.[3] The present article turns this concept upside down by investigating European Christians as strangers in one of the largest cities of fourteenth-century east China. Caterina's tombstone was found near to that of her brother, Antonio Vilioni.[4] Theirs are two of only three western Christian tombstones that survive from Yuan China. The mention of their late father as a resident of Yanghzhou on both tombstones demonstrates that their presence was far from transitory. The Vilioni family had been based in the city for some time. As a woman's tomb, Caterina's is of special importance. The expansion of European networks towards the east has been written from the perspective of men: friars, diplomats and merchants.[5] This is hardly surprising, however, since the extant written sources privilege male perspectives. The example of Tamta, an Armenian noblewoman from the circle of Queen Tamar of Georgia whose travel to Mongolia between 1236 and 1245 is only briefly noted in the sources, demonstrates the limited nature of the information that survives about the voyages of female Christians in the Mongol empire, even when they belonged to the top echelons of society.[6] Most often, not even their names were recorded. The wife of the French goldsmith Guillaume Boucher, whom the Mongols forcibly brought to Kharakorum in the 1240s, is described only as 'a Lotharingian woman born in Hungary'.[7] In contrast, Caterina Vilioni's tombstone offers a tangible legacy and opens a unique window onto the presence and patronage of non-elite European Christian women in premodern China.

---

[2] Inscription: 'In the name of the Lord, amen. Here lies Caterina, daughter of the deceased lord Domenico Vilioni, who died in AD 1342, in the month of June.' ('In nomine D[omi]ni amen hic jacet / Katerina filia q[u]ondam Domini / D[omi]nici de Vilionis que obiit in / anno Domini mileximo [a] CCC / XXXX II de mense Junii.') A Chinese seal-script composed of four characters, reminiscent of a collector's mark, was also added at a later point to the left of the original inscription: 'Yin-wei obtained [the pleasure of] seeing [this].' ('Yin-wei huo kuan.') Rouleau, 'Yangchow', 353.

[3] Deborah Howard, *Venice and the East* (New Haven, 2000); Miri Rubin, *Cities of Strangers: Making Lives in Medieval Europe* (Cambridge, 2020).

[4] R. C. Rudolph, 'A Second Fourteenth-Century Italian Tombstone in Yangzhou', *Journal of Oriental Studies*, 13 (1975), 133–6.

[5] Peter Jackson, 'Western European Sources', in *The Cambridge History of the Mongol Empire*, ed. Michal Biran and Hodong Kim (Cambridge, 2023), II, 1070–1114; Gherardo Ortalli, *Dall'Europa a scoprire l'Oriente: da Gengis Khan a Marco Polo* (Rome, 2021).

[6] Anthony Eastmond, *Tamta's World: The Life and Encounters of a Medieval Noblewoman from the Middle East to Mongolia* (Cambridge, 2017), 16, 342–4.

[7] William of Rubruck, 'Itinerarium', in *Sinica Franciscana*, I, ed. Anastasius van den Wyngaert (Florence, 1929), 278.

Caterina's gravestone was first published in an article by the sinologist and Jesuit priest Francis Rouleau shortly after its discovery.[8] More recent work by Lauren Arnold and Jennifer Purtle sought to identify whether certain features of the iconography originated either from Buddhist or from Christian art.[9] In an analogous way, Eva Caramello and Romedio Schmitz-Esser aimed to determine whether the epigraphic features of the inscription were either in line with north Italian practice or defined by the 'influence of Chinese characters'.[10] The present article shifts the attention to the cultural ambiguity of the visual context and argues that numerous features of the imagery were designed to be intentionally ambiguous. These elements were intelligible both for local Chinese and for European Christian viewers, which ultimately helped to contextualise Caterina Vilioni's identity in Yangzhou not only as a stranger, but also as a stranger who had put down roots in this strange land and made it her home. By exploring the visual language and the multicultural geopolitical context of Caterina's tombstone, this article sheds light on the dynamic processes of how cultural barriers were negotiated in premodern Eurasia.

At stake here is how the practice of cultural translation could serve, not as a hindrance to pinpointing the origin of particular features of a composite object, but as a useful interpretative vector in its own right. By examining fifteenth- and sixteenth-century 'Veneto-Saracenic' objects, crafted in Venice with a deliberate attempt to emulate Levantine prototypes, Elizabeth Rodini proposed that we move beyond traditional classifications preoccupied with 'origin' and place of production and instead focus on 'mobility' as a category of value.[11] This approach highlights a problem central to the fledgling field of the Global Middle Ages, in which artefacts are often pigeonholed in inflexible interpretative processes of influence, adaptation and hybridity.[12] The Yangzhou tombstone not only eludes rigid categorisations in the traditional frameworks of stylistic and iconographical analysis but also calls attention to objects which deliberately communicated ambiguous messages. This raises crucial questions both about Caterina's identity and about the potential multi-ethnic and -confessional viewership of her funerary monument.

---

[8] Rouleau, 'Yangchow', 346–65.

[9] Arnold, *Princely Gifts*, 138–46; Purtle, 'The Far Side', 167–97.

[10] Caramello and Schmitz-Esser, 'Funerary Monuments', 210–28.

[11] Elizabeth Rodini, 'Mobile Things: On the Origins and the Meanings of Levantine Objects in Early Modern Venice', *Art History*, 41 (2018), 246–65.

[12] On the emergence and key challenges of the 'global turn' in the medieval period, see Catherine Holmes and Naomi Standen, 'Introduction: Towards a Global Middle Ages', *Past and Present*, 238 (2018), 1–44. The study of material culture, where the present article also intervenes, represents one of the most dynamic approaches towards the Global Middle Ages in recent scholarship: Christina Normore (ed.), *Reassessing the Global Turn in Medieval Art History* (Amsterdam, 2018); Finbarr Barry Flood and Beate Fricke, *Tales Things Tell: Material Histories of Early Globalisms* (Princeton, 2023). For problems with 'influence', see Anna Contadini, 'Threads of Ornament in the Style World of the Fifteenth and Sixteenth Centuries', in *Histories of Ornament: From Global to Local*, ed. Gülru Necipoğlu and Alina Payne (Princeton, 2016), 290–307, at 291. On the critique of 'hybridity', see Finbarr B. Flood, *Objects of Translation: Material Culture and Medieval 'Hindu-Muslim' Encounter* (Princeton, 2009), 1–14.

Indeed, we must consider whether even Chinese Christian beholders would interpret the imagery along the same lines as European Christians.

Looking at Yangzhou through the eyes of Caterina Vilioni therefore broadens our understanding of the presence of both western and native Christians in the Yuan. The intertwined relationship between Buddhism and Islam has attracted much of the scholarly spotlight on religious plurality in east Asia.[13] Christian denominations, however, also gained followers.[14] Previous scholars have analysed in detail the early expansion of the East Syrian Church during the Tang Dynasty (618–907).[15] The early modern and modern Roman Catholic missions spearheaded by the Jesuit brethren in Beijing, Macau, and elsewhere have similarly been extensively studied.[16] Examining the case of a Roman Catholic woman in fourteenth-century Yangzhou will throw much-needed light on the intermittent period between the pre-tenth century and the modern context of the development of Christianity in China.

Religion aside, there is another reason why Caterina's tomb is worthy of our attention. Since she hailed from an Italian mercantile family, her story is also intertwined with medieval trade. Scholars have explored in great depth the ever-increasing demand of late medieval Europeans for luxury goods imported from Asia along the Silk Roads. Sumptuous silk fabrics interwoven with gold thread, such as *panni tartarici* or tatar fabrics are some of the best known facets of this intercontinental luxury trade.[17] The intricate blue-and-white porcelains manufactured in the famous Jingdezhen kilns were also highly prized by the wealthiest layers of European courtly society.[18] Moreover, artistic raw materials such as mother-of-pearl, coconut and exotic seashells also found their ways to the west where they were fashioned into lustrous containers, reliquaries and drinking vessels by local European craftsmen.[19] The trade of perishable

[13] Hyunhee Park, *Mapping the Chinese and Islamic Worlds: Cross-cultural Exchange in Pre-modern Asia* (Cambridge, 2012); Nancy S. Steinhardt, *China's Early Mosques* (Edinburgh, 2015); John W. Chaffee, *The Muslim Merchants of Premodern China* (Cambridge, 2018).

[14] Michael Angold (ed.), *The Cambridge History of Christianity*, v: *Eastern Christianity* (Cambridge, 2006); Nicolas Standaert (ed.), *Handbook of Christianity in China 635-1800* (Leiden, 2001).

[15] R. Todd Godwin, *Persian Christians at the Chinese Court: The Xi'an Stele and the Early Medieval Church of the East* (2018); Samuel N. C. Lieu and Hyun Jin Kim, '"Nestorian" Christians and Manichaeans as Links between Rome and China', in *Rome and China: Points of Contact*, ed. Hyun Jin Kim, Samuel N. C. Lieu and Raoul McLaughlin (2021), 80–107; Matteo Nicolini-Zani, *The Luminous Way to the East: Texts and History of the First Encounter of Christianity with China* (Oxford, 2022).

[16] Liam Matthew Brockey, *Journey to the East: The Jesuit Mission to China, 1579-1724* (Cambridge, MA, 2008); Mary Laven, *Mission to China: Matteo Ricci and the Jesuit Encounter with the East* (2011); R. Po-Chia Hsia, *A Jesuit in the Forbidden City: Matteo Ricci 1552-1610* (Oxford, 2012); Petra ten-Doesschate Chu and Ning Ding (eds.), *Qing Encounters: Artistic Exchanges between China and the West* (Los Angeles, 2015); Lianming Wang, *Jesuitenerbe in Peking. Sakralbauten und transkulturelle Räume, 1600–1800* (Heidelberg, 2020).

[17] David Jacoby, 'Oriental Silks at the Time of the Mongols: Trade and Distribution in the West', in *Oriental Silks in Medieval Europe*, ed. Juliane von Fircks (Riggisberg, 2016), 93–123; Lisa Monnas, *Merchants, Princes and Painters: Silk Fabrics in Italian and Northern Paintings, 1300-1550* (New Haven, 2008).

[18] Anne Gerritsen, *The City of Blue and White: Chinese Porcelain and the Early Modern World* (Cambridge, 2020).

[19] Philippe Cordez, *Schatz, Gedächtnis, Wunder: Die Objekte der Kirchen im Mittelalter* (Regensburg, 2015).

merchandise, such as spices, coconut and plants imbued with medicinal properties, has received particular attention.[20] However, despite all of this interest in the European import of Asian merchandise, movement of objects in the opposite direction, namely from Europe to Asia, is much less explored. Moreover, despite a few famous European travellers such as Marco Polo, it is generally accepted that commerce along the Silk Roads was structured through a chain of middlemen.[21] The presence of the Vilioni family in Yangzhou, however, raises the possibility of more direct routes of exchange between Asia and Europe than is often supposed.

After introducing the development of Christianity in premodern China, this article will focus on three key points. Firstly, it will examine the surviving written sources about the Vilioni family and trace their origins to Venice. This will also facilitate a broader contextualisation of the expansion of north Italian mercantile networks to the East China Sea. Secondly, through an in-depth consideration of the shape, composition and details of the imagery on Caterina's tombstone, I will argue that the visual language intentionally projected cultural ambiguity. By comparing the tomb to Mongol *paiza*, a distinctive form of safe conduct passes, the third and final section will propose that Caterina's burial marker functioned as an 'otherworldly passport', which invoked spiritual protection and facilitated the passage between two realms. Traversing boundaries and tracing movement are therefore key methodological platforms that underpin this study. This passage is manifested both through examining the movement of living flesh and blood bodies across great physical distances and between widely different cultures and societies, and also through the crossing of the supernatural passageways between this world and the next.

Christian objects in premodern China

To illuminate the broader historical and visual setting of the Vilioni tombstone, we should first briefly consider the early development of the Church of the East (whose members are sometimes also called Nestorian Christians), with particular attention to its material legacy.[22] Despite the predominance of Buddhism, Christianity was present in China sporadically by at least the

---

[20] Hugh Cagle, *Assembling the Tropics: Science and Medicine in Portugal's Empire, 1450–1700* (Cambridge, 2018); Elizabeth Lambourn, *Abraham's Luggage: A Social Life of Things in the Medieval Indian Ocean World* (Cambridge, 2018).

[21] Janet Abu-Lughod's scheme, which breaks down the thirteenth-century world into cultural zones, has been a landmark in this respect and is among the most influential works in historical scholarship. Janet Abu-Lughod, *Before European Hegemony: The World System A.D. 1250–1350* (New York, 1989). See also Valerie Hansen, *The Silk Road: A New History* (Oxford, 2012).

[22] On the Church of the East, see Joel Walker, 'From Nisibis to Xi'an: The Church of the East across Sasanian Persia', in *The Oxford Handbook of Late Antiquity*, ed. Scott F. Johnson (Oxford, 2012), 994–1052; Wilhelm Baum and Dietmar W. Winkler, *The Church of the East: A Concise History* (2003). On the term 'Nestorian', see Sebastian P. Brock, 'The 'Nestorian' Church: A Lamentable Misnomer', *Bulletin of the John Rylands Library*, 58 (1996), 23–35; Jack Tannous, *The Making of the Medieval Middle East* (Princeton, 2018), 13–14 n. 9.

seventh century.[23] The appearance of Christianity in Tang China can be set in the broader context of the spread of the religion in Central Asia along the Silk Roads. The Church of the East found fertile soil in Sogdiana in parallel to its Chinese expansion.[24] Moreover, the Uighur Khaghanate in the north accepted Manichaeism as its official religion in the eighth century, which amalgamated certain common devotional threads from Christianity and represented another facet of the same vehicle of Iranian culture and language in Central Asia.[25]

The Xi'an stele erected in a monastery near the Tang imperial city of Chang'an (now Xi'an) in 781 is a key piece of evidence for tracing the early history of Chinese Christianity.[26] The Syriac and Chinese inscriptions commemorate the spread of *jingjiao* (景教) or 'luminous teaching' originating from *Da Qin* (大秦) or 'the west', which is traditionally identified as the Christian faith. The origins of the Christian Church of the East (or East Syrian Church) had close ties with the Sassanian empire.[27] The Xi'an stele narrates the arrival of Alouben from the patriarchate in Seleucia-Ctesiphon and other Syro-Persian missionaries who brought sacred texts and images with them to China in the ninth year of Emperor Taizong (Tai Tsung) in 635.[28] The multivalent cultural connotations are further highlighted by the fact that the donor of the stele was the son of a priest originating from Balkh in Afghanistan.[29]

Further important testimony to the early history of the Syriac Christian Church comes from the Luoyang pillar. After the pillar had disappeared for decades on the black market, its rediscovery in 2006 generated substantial scholarly interest in specialist circles.[30] Luoyang is east of Chang'an and served as an auxiliary eastern capital for most of the Tang dynasty. The octagonal pillar, which resembles Buddhist dhāraṇī pillars, was erected in 829 as a funerary

---

[23] Pénélope Riboud, 'Tang', in *Handbook of Christianity in China 635-1800*, ed. Nicolas Standaert (Leiden, 2001), 1–42; Pier Giorgio Borbone and Pierre Marsone (eds.), *Le christianisme syriaque en Asie centrale et en Chine* (Paris, 2015).

[24] Aleksandr Nymark, 'Sogdiana, its Christians and Byzantium: A Study of Artistic and Cultural Connections in Late Antiquity and the Early Middle Ages' (Ph.D. thesis, Indiana University, 2001), 168–200.

[25] Émile Benveniste, *Études sogdiennes* (Wiesbaden, 1979), 308–14; Hansen, *The Silk Road*, 110.

[26] Godwin, *Persian Christians*; Ken Parry, 'Early Christianity in Central Asia and China', in *Christianity in Asia: Sacred Art and Visual Splendour*, ed. Alan Chong (Singapore, 2016), 28.

[27] Sebastian P. Brock, 'Christians in the Sasanian Empire: A Case of Divided Loyalties', *Studies in Church History*, 18 (1982), 1–19; Antonino Forte, 'Iraniens en Chine. Bouddhisme, mazdéisme, bureaux de commerce', in *La Sérinde, terre d'échanges: art, religion, commerce du Ier au Xe siècle*, ed. Jean-Pierre Drège (Paris, 2000), 181–90.

[28] Riboud, 'Tang', 22–3; Hansen, *Silk Road*, 149.

[29] Samuel N. C. Lieu, 'Epigraphica Nestoriana Serica', in *Exegisti monumenta: Festschrift in Honour of Nicholas Sims-Williams*, ed. Werner Sundermann et al. (Wiesbaden, 2009), 229.

[30] Zhang Naizhu, 'Ba Henan Luoyang xin chutu de yijian Tangdai jingjiao shike', *Xiyu yanjiu*, 1 (2007), 65–73; Luo Zhao, 'Luoyang xin chutu Da Qin jingjiao xuanyuan zhiben jing ji chuangji shi-chuang de jige wenti', *Wenwu*, 6 (2007), 30–48, 48. This pillar is sometimes described as having been unearthed in May 2006. Li Tang, 'A Preliminary Study on the Jingjiao Inscription of Luoyang: Text Analysis, Commentary and English Translation', in *Hidden Treasures and Intercultural Encounters: Studies on East Syriac Christianity in China and Central Asia*, ed. Dietmar W. Winkler and Li Tang (Vienna, 2009), 109–32, at 109. Others, however, pointed out that it was originally found by farmers in a field in 1976 while digging a well. Nicolini-Zani, *The Luminous Way*, 137.

monument of a certain An, a Sogdian Christian woman, and an unnamed deceased uncle of the donor. While the second part of the inscription is a memorial epitaph associated with the funerary context, the first part contains a *sūtra* on the 'Origins of the Da Qin Luminous Religion'.[31] The Luoyang pillar and the Xi'an stele were probably both buried in 845, when all foreign religious institutions including Buddhist ones were attacked. While this was a major blow for Christianity, further evidence attests to the continuation of Christianity throughout the Tang period.

The surviving material is far from being limited to funerary art.[32] Three fragmentary murals representing New Testament scenes were discovered in the early twentieth century in the remnants of what appears to have been a Christian church in Qocho (Gaochang), the ancient oasis city on the northern rim of the Taklamakan Desert in modern-day Xinjiang.[33] The Tang-dynasty wall paintings, probably remnants of a larger Christological cycle, depict *Palm Sunday*, *Repentance* and *Entry into Jerusalem* (lost). Just as remarkable was the discovery of a large ninth-century silk painting in the Dunhuang Caves (Cave 17) in 1906–8.[34] The silk painting shows Christ or a Christian holy figure in a crimson robe with a cross on his chest, wearing a headdress adorned with another cross.[35] The saint raises his other hand in benediction, a gesture similar to the Buddhist *mudra*.[36]

While some material evidence therefore attests to elite patronage for the Tang dynasty, historical or literary sources remain extremely scarce until the Yuan period – Caterina Vilioni's time.[37] Between the thirteenth and fourteenth centuries, all of China was incorporated into the Mongol empire, which stretched at its height from Korea to the Kingdom of Hungary, and from the Siberian steppe to Burma and Iraq.[38] The relative stability brought by the Mongol conquest facilitated increased cultural, social and mercantile interactions across these vast polities, which is often characterised as the 'Pax Mongolica'.[39] The Mongol empire is also known for its religious tolerance.

---

[31] Tang, 'A Preliminary Study', 110.

[32] Ken Parry, 'Images in the Church of the East: The Evidence from Central Asia and China', *Bulletin of the John Rylands Library*, 78 (1996), 143–62.

[33] Albert von Le Coq, *Chotscho Facsimile-Wiedergaben der wichtigeren Funde der ersten königlich preussischen Expedition nach Turfan in Ost-Turkistan* (Berlin, 1913).

[34] Li Tang, 'Christian or Buddhist? An Exposition of a Silk Painting from Dunhuang, China, Now Kept in the British Museum', in *Artifact, Text, Context: Studies in Syriac Christianity in China and Central Asia*, ed. Li Tang and Dietmar W. Winkler (Zurich, 2020), 233–43, at 233.

[35] Yoshirō Saeki, *The Nestorian Documents and Relics in China* (Tokyo, 1951), image between pages 408 and 409.

[36] Li Tang, 'Christian or Buddhist?', 238.

[37] Pierre Marsone, 'Two Portraits for One Man: George, King of the Önggüt', in *From the Oxus River to the Chinese Shores: Studies on East Syriac Christianity in China and Central Asia*, ed. Dietmar W. Winkler and Li Tang (Vienna, 2013), 225–35, at 231.

[38] Michal Biran, 'The Mongol Empire and Inter-civilizational Exchange', in *The Cambridge World History*, V: *Expanding Webs of Exchange and Conflict, 500 CE–1500 CE*, ed. Benjamin Z. Kedar and Merry E. Wiesner-Hanks (Cambridge, 2015), 534–58.

[39] Claus-Peter Haase, 'Von der "Pax Mongolica" zum Timuridenreich', in *Die Mongolen in Asien und Europa*, ed. Stephan Conermann and Jan Kusber (Frankfurt am Main, 1997), 139–60.

The founder of the Yuan dynasty Khubilai Khan (r. 1260–94) and the Il-khanid ruler Hülegü Khan (r. 1256–65), both sons of the Turkic (Keraite) Christian princess Sorghaghtani Beki, were known for their Christian sympathies.[40] In 1289, the so-called Office of the Christian Clergy or *Chongfusi* was established to monitor the Church of the East and other foreign religious communities in China.[41] The *History of the Yuan Dynasty* reports that a certain Jesus the Christian and Interpreter headed the office in 1291.[42] After his death in 1308, his son Elias succeeded him. While we still have only a rudimentary understanding of its organisation and mechanisms, the *Chongfusi*'s objective seems to have reached beyond simply administrating religious groups and probably also involved supervising foreign minorities. Moreover, there were also personal overlaps between the religious minorities. The bilingual Uighur-Chinese tombstone of the Christian Mar Solomon (d. 1313) indicates that he, perhaps in connection with the local religious office, led both the Christian and the Manichean congregations in the major cosmopolitan port city of Quanzhou.[43]

After 1276 a new social policy instituted preferential discrimination for non-ethnic Chinese, which served to consolidate the high social status of the Mongol ruling class.[44] This ranked the people into four classes in descending order: (1) Mongols, (2) non-Mongol, non-Chinese foreigners (*semu ren*), (3) Northern Chinese (*bei ren*), and finally (4) Southern Chinese (*nan ren*).[45] While designed to favour Mongols, the policy also benefited *semu ren*, who quickly assumed important positions of authority in Yuan China. This preferential ethnic discrimination encouraged the arrival of additional foreigners, including Roman Catholic priests, merchants (like the Vilioni) and diplomats from western Europe.

Practically all the documented early travellers are men, either friars or merchants. The Venetian merchant Marco Polo (1254–1324) is one of the most famous examples of European visitors in premodern China. Rustichello da Pisa's *Le Divisament dou monde*, which narrated Marco's travels in Asia along the Silk Roads between 1271 and 1295, became a medieval bestseller across Europe.[46] The Italian Franciscan John of Pian de Carpine (d. 1252) headed an early embassy sent by Pope Innocent IV to the Great Khan.[47] Another famous

---

[40] James D. Ryan, 'Christian Wives of Mongol Khans: Tartar Queens and Missionary Expectations in Asia', *Journal of the Royal Asiatic Society*, 3 ser., 8 (1998), 411–21; Peter Jackson, 'Hülegü Khan and the Christians: The Making of a Myth', in *The Experience of Crusading, ii: Defining the Crusader Kingdom*, ed. Peter Edbury and Jonathan Philips (Cambridge, 2003), 196–213.

[41] Johan Van Mechelen, 'Yuan', in *Handbook of Christianity in China 635–1800*, ed. Standaert, 43–111, at 85.

[42] Ken Parry, 'Early Christianity in Central Asia and China', in *Christianity in Asia: Sacred Art and Visual Splendour*, ed. Alan Chong (Singapore, 2016), 26–31, at 30.

[43] Li Tang, *East Syriac Christianity in Mongol-Yuan China* (Weisbaden, 2011), 60–3.

[44] Purtle, 'The Far Side', 177–8.

[45] *Ibid. Semu ren* has been traditionally interpreted as 'people with coloured eyes', but this should not be understood as a physical description of the appearance of this ethnically diverse group. Instead, it was used as an administrative category: Jonathan Neaman Lipman, *Familiar Strangers: A History of Muslims in Northwest China* (Hong Kong, 1998), 32–3 n. 29.

[46] David Jacoby, 'Marco Polo, his Close Relatives, and his Travel Account: Some New Insights', *Mediterranean Historical Review*, 21 (2006), 193–218, at 193.

[47] John of Pian de Carpine, 'Ystoria Mongolorum', in *Sinica Franciscana*, i, 122.

Franciscan, the Fleming William of Rubruck (1215–70), arrived carrying a letter from King Louis IX of France (r. 1226–70) in Kharakorum around 1254.[48] Several friars also acquired images during their travels for their missionary work. John of Montecorvino (1246/7–c. 1289) had commissioned six pictures with biblical scenes, narrated in Latin, 'Tartar' (*tursicus*, probably Chinese or perhaps Mongolian or Turkish) and Persian.[49] William of Rubruck records that a Parisian goldsmith, Guillaume Boucher, crafted a much-admired silver tree for the court of Möngke Khan in Kharakorum which functioned as a fountain for serving alcoholic refreshments.[50] Boucher also took smaller commissions from the Roman Catholic expatriate community in Kharakorum.[51] He made a 'beautiful silver crucifix, crafted in the French style, which had a silver image of Christ affixed upon it', a silver pyx for the Eucharist and a pan for making communion wafers. Their loss further underscores the importance of Caterina Vilioni's tombstone as a rare tangible piece of evidence of Christian material culture from Yuan China.

The Vilioni family in Yangzhou

Although their roots have been debated in previous scholarship, the Vilioni most likely originated from Venice.[52] Another member of the family, a certain Pietro Vilioni, is recorded as a Venetian merchant who traded in central Asia. Pietro issued his last will in 1263 in the city of Tabriz (modern-day Iran), seat of the Persian Il-khanate in the Mongol empire.[53] According to his will, Pietro was the travelling partner in numerous Venetian *colleganze*, some of which he had contracted with his father, Vitale Vilioni.[54] Pietro imported linen to Persia from Germany, Venice, and Lombardy, as well as Stanforte cloth made in Mechlin. His profits were then reinvested in sugar and small pearls. Pietro's private possessions included a chess and backgammon board made from rock crystal, jasper, silver, gems and pearls, complemented by crystal gaming pieces, a vase, two candelabras, three bowls decorated with rock crystal, a saddle adorned with crystal, jasper, silver, gems and pearls, as well as expensive silk textiles embroidered with silver and gold thread.[55] In the second half of the thirteenth century, Venice had become a leading centre for the production of refined rock crystal objects.[56] Pietro had probably brought the crystal

---

[48] Jackson, 'Western European Sources', 1086.

[49] John of Montecorvino, 'Epistola III', in *Sinica Franciscana*, I, 352; Purtle, 'The Far Side', 190.

[50] William of Rubruck, *Itinerarium*, 276–7.

[51] *Ibid.*, 253.

[52] Rouleau, 'Yangchow', 360–3; Deborah Howard, 'Venice and Islam in the Middle Ages: Some Observations on the Question of Architectural Influence', *Architectural History*, 34 (1991), 59–74, at 61 n. 20.

[53] Critical edition: Alfredo Stussi, 'Un testamento volgare scritto in Persia nel 1263', *L'Italia dialettale*, n.s. 9 (1962), 23–37.

[54] Angeliki E. Laiou, 'Venice as a Center of Trade and Artistic Production in the Thirteenth Century', in *Il Medio Oriente e l'Occidente nell'arte del XIII secolo*, ed. Hans Belting (Bologna, 1982), 11–26, at 19.

[55] Stussi, 'Un testamento volgare', 23–37.

[56] Laiou, 'Venice as a Center', 19–22.

objects with him to Tabriz.[57] A further potential member of the family, a certain Domenico Vilioni (Ilioni), was active in Genoa in 1348. He appears in connection with the merchant Jacopo de Oliverio, who reportedly lived in China for years where he 'quintupled his wealth'.[58] This Chinese connection has led previous scholars to identify this Domenico with Caterina's father.[59] Given that Caterina's father predeceased her and that she herself had passed away in 1342, this possibility can be ruled out.

Caterina's father probably made his living as a merchant. While we do not know his merchandise, the most likely possibilities include textiles, spices, pearls, sugar and rock crystal. These were not only traded by his kinsman Pietro Vilioni in Tabriz, but their circulation between Italy and the eastern shore of China is further attested in contemporary sources. The well-known trading manual *The Practice of Commerce* (*Pratica della mercatura*), composed by the Florentine banker Francesco Balducci Pegolotti and his associates sometime around 1339–40, names Cansay (Hangzhou) and Cambalech (Beijing) as the easternmost destinations of Italian traders.[60] Italian merchants are recorded exporting French textiles to China already by the 1330s.[61] In 1338, Toghon Temür, the last emperor of the Yuan dynasty in China, asked a group of Genoese merchants to obtain gifts for him from the west, including clearly very desirable rock crystals.[62] The burial of Caterina's brother, Antonio Vilioni, in Yangzhou in November 1344 further suggests that, like Pietro and Vitale in the Il-khanate, the Vilioni were part of a larger family enterprise with a base in Yangzhou.[63]

Yangzhou's advantageous geographical position meant that the Vilioni could transport their merchandise either through overland routes or by the sea. While the *Pratica* describes how one could travel from Italy to China primarily by land along the Silk Roads, some evidence suggests that Genoese merchants commanded their own ships in the Indian Ocean.[64] Persia with its two key commercial centres of Ormuz (maritime port) and Tabriz (land) was a gateway where Italian merchants passed towards the Mongol empire.[65] The Genoese merchant

---

[57] Jacoby, 'Marco Polo', 195.

[58] Robert S. Lopez, 'Nouveaux documents sur les marchands italiens en Chine à l'époque mongole, communication du 11 février 1977', *Comptes rendus des séances de l'année: Académie des inscriptions et belles-lettres*, 121 (1977), 455–7; Roberto S. Lopez, *Su e giù per la storia di Genova* (Genoa, 1975), 184.

[59] Lopez, *Su e giù*, 184; Antonia Finnane, *Speaking of Yangzhou: A Chinese City, 1550-1850* (Boston, 2004), 341 n. 8; Thomas Ertl, 'Repercussions from the Far East: A Comparison of the Catholic and Nestorian Presence in China', *Transcultural Studies*, 2 (2015), 38–63, at 41; Hans Ulrich Vogel, *Marco Polo Was in China: New Evidence from Currencies, Salts and Revenues* (Leiden, 2012), 353.

[60] Francesco Balducci Pegolotti, 'Pegolotti's Notices of the Land Route to Cathay', in *Cathay and the Way Thither*, ed. and trans. Henry Yule (4 vols.; 1913–16), III, 146–9.

[61] Luciano Petech, 'Les marchands italiens dans l'empire mongol', *Journal asiatique*, 250 (1962), 549–74, at 557; Eliyahu Ashtor, *Levant Trade in the Middle Ages* (Princeton, 1983), 60.

[62] Laiou, 'Venice as a Center', 19.

[63] Arnold, *Princely Gifts*, 139.

[64] Thomas Sinclair, *Eastern Trade and the Mediterranean in the Middle Ages: Pegolotti's Ayas-Tabriz Itinerary and its Commercial Context* (Abingdon, 2020), 99.

[65] Johannes Preiser-Kapeller, 'Civitas Thauris: The Significance of Tabrīz in the Spatial Frameworks of Christian Merchants and Ecclesiastics in the 13th and 14th Century', in *Politics,*

Tommaso Gentile arrived to Ormuz in 1343, from where he originally intended to sail to China.[66] Since Pietro Vilioni was stationed in Tabriz, it is not unreasonable to propose that the city was an entrepot within a greater mercantile network which connected different members of the Vilioni family and which reached as far as Yangzhou on the shores of the East China Sea.

Yangzhou was the northernmost of the great eastern port cities of China. Functioning as an auxiliary capital of the Tang dynasty, it had served as a major port of entry to China for Arab and Persian traders since the eighth century.[67] Its importance derived from directly connecting this intercontinental commerce from the 'Silk Road of the Sea' through the Grand Canal to the Yuan capital, Cambalech (Beijing).[68] Yangzhou was a major economic hub that possessed a salt monopoly as well as a significant banking and commercial centre, which generated substantial revenues from the sugar, gold, tea, spice, gemstone and textile trade.[69] It was a meeting point of cultures, where people of different languages, religions and ethnicities interacted and lived together. The discovery of a trilingual imperial edict written in Chinese, Persian and Mongolian from around 1400 attests to the city's vibrant cosmopolitanism.[70]

Sophisticated garden culture and ingeniously designed waterscapes were defining features of the urban core.[71] The nucleus of the municipality developed around a fortress erected alongside the Han'gou canal during the Warring States period. Direct access to waterways remained essential throughout the city's history: under the Sui dynasty (581–618) the settlement was renamed to Jiangdu, the 'City of the River'.[72] The Grand Canal became the key waterway during the Tang dynasty, which cut through the municipal centre. During the late Southern Song period, Yangzhou was divided into three main walled districts, two military and one commercial. By 1269, at least four fortresses had been erected.[73] However, these were not sufficiently garrisoned, and the city capitulated to the Mongols without a fight in 1276. This date also signifies a commercial uplift for Yangzhou with the construction of new shipping docks. These were used to build 600 warships for Khubilai Khan's campaign against the Japanese in 1294, as well as to facilitate the expanded salt transport administration.[74] On the other hand, Yangzhou is perhaps best known for its

---

Patronage and the Transmission of Knowledge in 13th-15th Century Tabriz, ed. Judith Pfeiffer (Leiden, 2014), 251–300; Vladimír Liščák, 'Catalan Atlas of 1375 and Hormuz around 1300', *Advances in Cartography and GIScience of the International Cartographic Association*, 1 (2019), https://doi.org/10.5194/ica-adv-1-11-2019.

[66] Ashtor, *Levant Trade*, 61.

[67] Chaffee, *Muslim Merchants*, 42–3.

[68] Steinhardt, *Mosques*, 9.

[69] Vogel, *Marco Polo*, 341; Steinhardt, *Mosques*, 75–6.

[70] Steinhardt, *Mosques*, 52–3.

[71] Wu Jiaxing, Li Baohua and Zhang Xinji, *Yangzhou gugang shi* [History of the Old Port of Yangzhou] (Beijing, 1988); Lucie Olivová and Vibeke Børdahl (eds.), *Lifestyle and Entertainment in Yangzhou* (Copenhagen, 2009).

[72] Lucie B. Olivová, 'Building History and the Preservation of Yangzhou', in *Lifestyle and Entertainment in Yangzhou*, ed. Olivová and Børdahl, 3–36, at 5.

[73] *Ibid.*, 6.

[74] Jiaxing, Baohua and Xinji, *Yangzhou gugang shi*, 85.

sophisticated garden culture, which was underpinned by the wealth of the local mercantile elite.[75]

In addition to numerous Buddhist temples, the Transcendent Crane Mosque in Yangzhou is one of the two earliest mosques in China.[76] This houses the cenotaph of Buhading, a descendant of the Prophet Muhammad, who settled in the city in 1272. Yangzhou was also home to a lively Christian community. William of Rubruck's description of three Nestorian churches, as well as a tombstone excavated in 1981 belonging to Elizabeth, wife of Xindu from Dadu (Beijing), attests that members of the Syriac Church of the East were also present in the city in the fourteenth century.[77] This presence is further attested by the *Yuan dian zhang*, a collection of court decisions from between 1270 and 1322 originally written in Mongol, which reports that a certain Ao-la han, the son of the founder of an Eastern Christian church dedicated to the Cross in Yangzhou, was alive and living in the city in 1317.[78] Yangzhou was also home to a small migrant community of Roman Catholics in the thirteenth and fourteenth centuries. The Franciscan missionary Odoric of Pordenone (1286–1331), who visited Yangzhou personally around 1324, mentioned the presence of a Franciscan convent.[79] Marco Polo's supposed three-year tenure as governor of the city has been heavily debated, but his presence in the city for several years has been generally accepted.[80] Caterina Vilioni and her family therefore must have been part of a small but well-established colony of westerners in Yangzhou, which, as Marco Polo's presence suggests, included Venetian merchants from at least the 1280s onwards. The evidence of a Franciscan convent indicates that this community not only had direct access to Roman Catholic liturgy and mass, but the right to receive proper burial in consecrated soil as well.

The visual ambiguity of Caterina's tombstone

Caterina's tombstone is formed from a single grey stone slab with a cusped top, framed by a simple vegetal pattern around the edges. While the inscription fills the lower half, the upper half is decorated with images. The top is dominated by the enthroned Virgin and Child, paired with two small angels on the left. Below this composition, three scenes form a narrative cycle of the patron saint of Caterina Vilioni, St Catherine of Alexandria, depicting her torture on the wheel, with the corpses of her two tormentors lying in the foreground; Catherine's beheading with a kneeling figure on right; and the deposition of her body by two angels into her tomb. While the subject is clearly Christian,

---

[75] Craig Clunas, *Fruitful Sites: Garden Culture in Ming Dynasty China* (Durham, 1996), 203; Christian de Pee, *Urban life and Intellectual Crisis in Middle-Period China, 800–1100 CE* (Amsterdam, 2022), 62–3.

[76] Nancy S. Steinhardt, *Chinese Architecture: A History* (Princeton, 2019), 115; Steinhardt, *Mosques*, 75–82.

[77] Ertl, 'Repercussions from the Far East', 38–9.

[78] *Cathay and the Way Tither*, ii, 211, n. 2.

[79] Rouleau, 'Yangchow', 351.

[80] *The Travels of Marco Polo*, trans. William Marsden (London, 1818), 485 (bk. 2, ch. 60); Stephen G. Haw, *Marco Polo's China: A Venetian in the Realm of Khubilai Khan* (London, 2006), 3–4.

numerous visual features are closely connected to Buddhist art. Previous scholars traced how decorated psalters and copies of Jacobus de Voragine's famous *Golden Legend* with illuminations of St Catherine served as prototypes for the iconography, while other features derived from local Chinese tradition.[81] This was, however, not a random amalgamation of cosmopolitan imagery. Instead, this article argues that the shape of the slab, the narrative composition and the details of the carvings reinforce the notion that the visual language of the tombstone intentionally projected cultural ambiguity.

It is first worth considering the visual context of Caterina's gravestone among burials of foreigners and members of other religious minorities in east and south-east China. The revised edition of Wenliang Wu's important corpus of religious inscriptions from Quanzhou, another major port city south of Yangzhou, collected more than 600 tombstones from the area belonging to various Islamic, Christian, Manichean, Hindu, Buddhist and local communities.[82] Comparison with this corpus shows that the form and ratio of the Vilioni tombstone is strikingly close to Muslim tombstones from the same period.[83] The slab commemorating in Arabic the death of Amir Sayyid from Bukhara in 1302 and another Chinese–Arabic bilingual stone that quotes from the Qur'an are not only analogous in shape but are similarly adorned with a decorative band running around the edges.[84] Similar Islamic tombstones were discovered in Yangzhou in the vicinity of the South Gate in the 1920s, close to the spot where the Vilioni tombstones were unearthed three decades later. For instance, the slab of a Muslim woman called ʿĀysha Khātūn (d. 724 AH/1324 CE), offers a pertinent example with a finely carved border decorated with floral and vegetal motifs (Figure 3).[85] This popular Islamic form also served as a model for Nestorian Christian funerary monuments from Quanzhou. Many of these are decorated with a pair of angels around a lotus flower, a symbol denoting purity and spiritual awakening in Buddhism, and a cross on top.[86] The same imagery appears on the tombstone of Elizabeth, who died at the age of thirty-three in Yangzhou in May 1317.[87] The trilingual inscriptions on the slab are written in Chinese, Syriac and Uighur, and use two different calendars, namely Chinese and Turkic. On the other hand, not all Nestorian grave markers bore writing: a granite stone from Quanzhou is adorned with a single yet majestic image of a crowned angel spreading his four wings above the whirling clouds on which he is seated

---

[81] Arnold, *Princely Gifts*, 138–46; Purtle, 'The Far Side', 167–97.

[82] Wenliang Wu, revised by Youxiong Wu, *Quanzhou zongjiao shike* [Religious inscriptions of Quanzhou] (Beijing, 2005).

[83] Wu, *Quanzhou zongjiao shike*, pls. 4, 7, 9, 15. One of these dates to as early as 1212. Rudolph, 'Fourteenth-Century Italian Tombstone', 133.

[84] Wu, *Quanzhou zongjiao shike*, pl. 44.1; pl. A92.1.

[85] Masaki Mukai, '"Muslim Diaspora" in Yuan China: A Comparative Analysis of Islamic Tombstones from the Southeast Coast', *Asian Review of World Histories*, 4 (2016), 231–56, at 236.

[86] Wu, *Quanzhou zongjiao shike*, pl. B21.2.

[87] Ertl, 'Repercussions from the Far East', 38–9; Shimin Geng, Hans-Joachim Klimkeit and Jens Peter Laut, 'Eine neue nestorianische Grabinschrift aus China', *Ural-altaische Jahrbücher*, n.s. 14 (1996), 164–75, pl. 1.

Figure 3. Tombstone of 'Āysha Khātūn, 724 AH/1324. Granite. Yangzhou: Transcendent Crane Mosque. (Photo: Deborah Howard.)

cross-legged.[88] Besides the Vilioni siblings, the only other Roman Catholic tombstone that survives from Yuan China is that of the Franciscan friar Andrew of Perugia, who served as the third of five bishops of Quanzhou from 1323 until his death in 1332.[89] While the Latin text written with Gothic majuscules is similar to the Vilioni inscriptions, the imagery follows the Nestorian template of a lotus borne aloft by a pair of angels.[90]

The brief, although finely carved, inscription on Caterina's tombstone is not specific enough to locate its precise point of inspiration. The palaeographical evidence, namely the shape of the letters and the ligature (the typology of the letter connections), shows similarities to fourteenth-century northern Italian epigraphy.[91] Caramello and Schmitz-Esser have recently argued that the inscription was carved by an experienced Franciscan stonecutter, sent from Italy by the pope to aid John of Montecorvino.[92] However, this theory can hardly be substantiated due to a lack of evidence, especially in light of the already demonstrated presence of European lay craftsmen in Yuan China.

The scheme of the inscription is not unusual for funerary monuments across western Christendom, and in particular northern Italy.[93] For instance, the epitaph of Visconte Malaspina made in Verona in 1362 follows the same formula, only in this case a son instead of a daughter is commemorated.[94] A similar 'hic iacet' (here lies) formulation can be found on two fourteenth-century tombstones of Italians discovered near Ephesos.[95] Whoever drafted Caterina's inscription was thus familiar with the western European tradition. The word *mileximo* (thousand) may offer a further clue to the family's Venetian roots, since the use of 'x' for a voiceless 's' is characteristic of the Venetian dialect.[96] If Caterina had died in Venice or its overseas possessions, she could have expected a very similar script and epigraph. But could this mean that the slab was made elsewhere? Elizabeth Lambourn has convincingly

---

[88] John Guy, 'Quanzhou: Cosmopolitan City of Faiths', in *The World of Khubilai Khan: Chinese Art in the Yuan Dynasty*, ed. James C. Y. Watt (New York, 2010), 159–78, at 174, fig. 199.

[89] Purtle, 'The Far Side', 180.

[90] Inscription: 'HIC [IN PATER FILII ET SPIRITUS SANCTI] SEPULTUS EST. ANDREAS PERUSINUS [DE VOTUS EPISCOPALUS CAYTON] ORDINUS [FRATRUM MINORUM ... IESU CHRISTI] APOSTOLUS ... [IN MENSE ... A.D.] M [CCC XX] X II.' Wu, *Quanzhou zongjiao shike*, 373; Jennifer Purtle, 'The Production of Painting, Place, and Identity in Song-Yuan (960–1279) Fujian' (Ph.D. thesis, Yale University, 2001), 642–5.

[91] Caramello and Schmitz-Esser, 'Funerary Monuments', 210–28.

[92] *Ibid.*, 222, 225.

[93] Inscription transcribed and translated in n. 2.

[94] Inscription: 'HIC JACET BISCONT.FIL/IVS.DI MARCHIONIS.SPI/NETE QVI OBIIT IN ANNO/ D[omi]NI. M.CCC.LXII. I[n]DIT[i]O[n]E/Q...T...CIMA.DIE III OCT/OBRIS ...'. London, Victoria & Albert Museum, Acc. N. 191-1887. John Pope-Hennessy, *Catalogue of Italian Sculpture in the Victoria and Albert Museum* (1964), 369, no. 392.

[95] Ergün Laflı, Maurizio Buora and Denys Pringle, 'Four Frankish Gravestones from Medieval Ephesos', *Anatolian Studies*, 71 (2021), 171–84, at 174–6.

[96] Caramello and Schmitz-Esser, 'Funerary Monuments', 222. It should also be noted that the use of *mileximo* is not limited to Venetian evidence. For instance, a Lombard source from 1200 is cited by Arthur Kingsley Porter, *Lombard Architecture, Monuments-Mizzole-Voltorre*, (New Haven, 1917), III, 78.

demonstrated that Muslim tombstones in the same period were exported along seaborne routes across the Indian Ocean littoral at great distances, from the ports of Mogadishu and Kilwa in east Africa to eastern Java.[97] The formulaic Latin inscription notwithstanding, it is clear that Caterina's tomb embarked on no such journey. The unique visual features and the shape of the slab firmly pinpoint the place of production of Caterina's tomb in Yangzhou.

Where the Christian iconography is concerned, we can only compare Caterina's gravestone to that belonging to her brother, Antonio, from 1344 (Figure 4).[98] Above the Latin inscription, this slab depicts Christ the Judge, surrounded by two angels holding a processional cross and a lance.[99] Below, the opening of the tombs at the Last Judgment is represented on the right, while St Anthony of Egypt with a woman and a child, possibly the Virgin and Child (although without halos), appear on the left. The slab of Caterina differs from her brother's in three striking ways: it provides a narrative, it prioritises holy women (the Virgin and St Catherine), and, more specifically, it pays particular attention to a female saint associated with the 'east' in the medieval western imagination, St Catherine of Alexandria.

The patron saint of Caterina was one of the most popular virgin saints and a mainstay of medieval hagiography. A convert to Christianity, she was allegedly condemned to death by the pagan Roman emperor Maxentius in the fourth century. After various attempts to torture her – including breaking her body on a wheel – were divinely frustrated, she was ultimately beheaded. According to the Greek *typikon*, a set of rules composed by abbot Symeon of Sinai in 1214, her body was deposited by angels in the monastery on Mount Sinai.[100] The abbreviated cycle on Caterina Vilioni's tombstone composed of three images of Catherine's torture, decapitation and burial follow the iconographical tradition already established in the western canon. The late thirteenth-century vita icon in the Museo Nazionale in Pisa and the Getty Museum's altarpiece by Donato and Gregorio d'Arezzo from around 1330 (Figure 5) both include these three scenes, among others.[101] In both cases, the scenes are shown separately. In contrast, Caterina's tombstone presents the narrative in a continuous manner. This fluidity, as well as the distinctly linear carving style, are features shared with Buddhist art in the Yuan period,

---

[97] Elizabeth Lambourn, 'Carving and Communities: Marble Carving for Muslim Patrons at Khambhāt and around the Indian Ocean Rim, Late Thirteenth-Mid-Fifteenth Centuries', *Ars Orientalis*, 24 (2004), 99-133.

[98] Arnold, *Princely Gifts*, 139-40.

[99] Inscription: 'IN NOMINE DÑI AMEN HIC JACET ANTONIUS FILI Q(U)NDAM DÑI DOMENICI DE VILIONIS QUI MIGRAVIT IN ANNO DÑI M CCC XXXX IIII DE MENSE NOVEMBRIS.' Purtle, 'The Far Side', 180 n. 39.

[100] Alexei A. Dmitrievskii, *Opisanie liturgicheskikh rukopisei* (3 vols.; Kiev, 1895-1917; repr. Hildesheim, 1965), III, 411; Nancy P. Ševčenko, 'The Monastery of Mount Sinai and the Cult of St Catherine', in *Byzantium: Faith and Power (1261-1557): Perspectives on Late Byzantine Art and Culture*, ed. Sarah T. Brooks (New York, 2006), 118-37, at 118-20.

[101] Helen C. Evans (ed.), *Byzantium: Faith and Power* (New York, 2004), 485-7, no. 296; Roberto Bartalini, 'Da Gregorio e Donato ad Andrea di Nerio: vicende della pittura aretina del Trecento', in *Arte in terra d'Arezzo: Il Trecento*, ed. Aldo Galli and Paola Refice (Florence, 2005), 11-40, at 11-18, fig. 2.

Figure 4. Antonio Vilioni's tombstone (detail), 1344. Facsimile of the rubbing of the granite tombstone. Yangzhou: Marco Polo Museum. (Image: Wikimedia Commons.)

Figure 5. Donato and Gregorio d'Arezzo, St Catherine and scenes from her life, c. 1330. Tempera and gold leaf on panel, 107 × 174 cm. Los Angeles: The J. Paul Getty Museum, 73.PB.69. (Photo: The J. Paul Getty Museum.)

exemplified by the 1340s prints of *The Lotus Sūtra* (*Miaofa lianhua jing*) from Quanzhou.[102] On the other hand, small-scale artworks from western Europe starting from the 1340s also developed a tendency that favoured the reduction and compression of the visual programme, which draws further attention to the ambiguity of the free-flowing yet compact narrative of the Vilioni slab. A petite ivory diptych with a Saint Catherine cycle (*c.* 1350) condenses the beheading and the transfer of the body into a single scene, placed above the torture on the wheel.[103] This object serves as an especially close analogy to the tomb's abbreviated narrative. It is indeed possible that a small and highly mobile object of private devotion was used as a potential model for the gravestone's imagery.

While they together act out a Christian narrative, the half-naked kneeling figure of St Catherine, the exotic clothing of the executioner and the kneeling man wearing a loose robe at the edge of the execution scene each diverge from western iconography in highly revealing ways. First of all, the kneeling figure has been identified by Rouleau and Arnold as a Franciscan friar, and, most recently, by Caramello and Schmitz-Esser as Domenico Vilioni, 'the father and commissioner of the work, holding the deceased child in his hand'.[104] Since Domenico is mentioned as *quondam* or deceased in the inscription, the latter possibility can be excluded. Moreover, his clean-shaven head and the voluptuous folds of his tunic resemble a Buddhist monk more closely than a Franciscan friar, whose habit would have been cinctured with a cord.[105] The occasional inclusion of Buddhist monks in the wall paintings of Yuan tombs reinforces this argument. On the west wall of an octagonal tomb chamber from 1309 at Hongyucun in Shanxi, a deceased couple is depicted (Figure 6).[106] While the husband looks at their three sons, the wife's gaze is directed towards a Buddhist monk. Therefore, regardless of who the kneeling figure was meant to represent on Caterina's tombstone, his portrayal in the guise of a Buddhist monk immediately forged a visual connection with Yuan funerary art.

Secondly, despite St Catherine generally being depicted fully clothed in western images, she is visualised semi-naked during her martyrdom on the gravestone. Comparable figures, however, appear in woodblock prints, such as the one representing the execution Dou E in a Yuan play written by Guan Hanqing (*c.* 1210–*c.* 1298).[107] Shane McCausland fittingly argued that

---

[102] Purtle, 'The Far Side', 182.

[103] Toronto, Art Gallery of Ontario, AGOID.29117. For an image, see https://ago.ca/collection/object/agoid.29117 (accessed 22 July 2024).

[104] Rouleau, 'Yangchow', 356; Arnold, *Princely Gifts*, 144; Caramello and Schmitz-Esser, 'Funerary Monuments', 220.

[105] Michael F. Cusato, '*Cucullus non facit monachum*? The Controversy over the Franciscan Habit in the Early Fourteenth Century', in *Loyalty in the Middle Ages: Ideal and Practice of a Cross-Social Value*, ed. Jörg Sonntag and Coralie Zermatten (Leiden, 2015), 361–403.

[106] Han Binghua and Huo Baoqiang, 'Shanxi Xingxian Hongyucun Yuan Zhida er nian mu bihua' [Murals in the Yuan tomb, dated Zhida 2 (1309), at Hongyucun, Xing county, Shanxi province]', *Wenwu*, 11 (2011), 40–6.

[107] Shane McCausland, *The Mongol Century: Visual Cultures of Yuan China, 1271-1368* (Honolulu, 2015), 94–6.

Figure 6. Tomb mural with deceased couple flanked by their three sons and a Buddhist monk and his attendant, 1309. Mural. Tomb at Hongyucun, Xing county, Shanxi province. (Photo: Wikimedia Commons.)

the unclothed back of Dou E recalls Buddhist judgment scenes, where the punishment is carried out on similar semi-nude bodies.[108] The silk painting by Lu Zhongyuan (active *c.* 1271–1368) envisions the torture of men and women, clad in loincloths, on the orders of one of the Ten Kings of Hell.[109] The disrobed figure of St Catherine awaiting execution on the Yangzhou slab thus probably reflected this firm association between the disrobed body and punitive mutilation in Yuan visual culture.

In contrast to these tormented characters, however, St Catherine wears a crown. This attribute is not uncommon in western iconography, as demonstrated by the ivory diptych discussed above. However, in contrast to the latter western exemplar, the Yangzhou tombstone showcases a headpiece that recalls the shape of Buddhist tiaras, like the one on a late Yuan porcelain of the head of a bodhisattva in the Metropolitan Museum of Art.[110]

Finally, the belted tunic of the executioner, paired with a wide-rimmed wind hat and tall boots, identify him as a contemporary Mongol soldier. Similarly fashionable figures appear in a silk painting depicting the hunt of

[108] *Ibid.*

[109] *Ibid.* On the *sūtra* of the Kings of Hell, see Stephen F. Teiser, '"Having Once Died and Returned to Life": Representations of Hell in Medieval China', *Harvard Journal of Asiatic Studies*, 48 (1988), 433–64, at 450–2.

[110] New York, Metropolitan Museum of Art, Accession Number: 38.56.9. For an image see https://www.metmuseum.org/art/collection/search/42492 (accessed 5 July 2024); Suzanne G. Valenstein, *A Handbook of Chinese Ceramics* (New York, 1989), 136, fig. 132.

Khubilai Khan from around 1280, attributed to the Chinese court artist Liu Guandao (1258–1333).[111] Shifting the attention from court painting to more widely accessible works, comparable figures are often featured in woodblock prints accompanying fourteenth-century *pinghua* or popular novels. The historical fiction *The Plain Tale of the Three Kingdoms* (*Sanguozhi pinghua*), printed in 1321–3, includes numerous scenes populated with such soldiers (Figure 7).[112] Various figures in the encyclopaedia *Shilin Guanji*, printed in the 1330s, also offer analogies.[113]

Other features, however, are less decisively identified. The layered yet shallow tomb of St Catherine is not unlike the one depicted in the d'Arezzo altarpiece. However, this form is also close to Muslim tombs from the Yuan dynasty, such as the multi-layer cenotaph of Buhading in Yangzhou (Figure 8).[114] Moreover, the angels are represented in a manner similar to late medieval European examples such as the illumination of the Belles Heures of duc de Berry (Figure 9).[115] In both cases, the legs of the angels are covered by their robes. Yet similar figures also appear in Chinese art, such as the winged creatures on the murals from the sixth century in the Dunhuang caves, namely Mogao Cave 285 (Figure 10).[116]

The top of Caterina's tombstone is occupied by one of the most central images of Christianity, the enthroned Virgin and Child. The frontal side of a roughly contemporary red marble sarcophagus that bears the arms of the Sanguinacci family, probably originating from the Veneto around 1300, is decorated with a similar image (Figure 11).[117] However, in contrast to the robust throne of the Italian Madonna, on the Yangzhou tombstone Mary is sitting on a squat little chair similar to stools common in contemporary China.[118] Moreover, the haloed figure of the Virgin Mary is remarkably similar to Guanyin (觀音).[119] Originally a male figure in the Buddhist pantheon, this bodhisattva became a popular female deity in thirteenth-century China as the child-giving (*songzi*) Guanyin. She sometimes appears with a child on her lap, and her head is often framed by the moon in a manner that is strikingly reminiscent of the Virgin Mary's halo (Figure 12).

---

[111] Joyce Denney, 'Textiles in the Mongol and Yuan Period', in *The World of Khubilai Khan*, ed. Watt, 243–67, at 252.

[112] For the historiographical context of this copy, see Robert E. Hegel, 'A Plain History of the Chronicles of the Three Kingdoms', *East Asian Publishing and Society*, 9 (2019), 99–124.

[113] Bai, *Yangzhou Latin Tombstones*, 36.

[114] Steinhardt, *Mosques*, 81.

[115] Arnold, *Princely Gifts*, 143.

[116] Wu Hung, *Spatial Dunhuang: Experiencing the Mogao Caves* (Seattle, 2023), 12. See also Neville Agnew (ed.), *Conservation of Ancient Sites on the Silk Road: Proceedings of the Second International Conference on the Conservation of Grotto Sites, Mogao Grottoes, Dunhuang, People's Republic of China, June 28–July 3, 2004* (Los Angeles, 2010), 4, fig. 1.3.

[117] Lisbeth Castelnuovo-Tedesco and Jack Soultanian, *Italian Medieval Sculpture in the Metropolitan Museum of Art and the Cloisters* (New York, 2010), 147–9.

[118] New York, Metropolitan Museum of Art (MMA), Acc. n. 2015.500.1.31.

[119] Arnold, *Princely Gifts*, 140–3; Jeremy Clarke, *The Virgin Mary and Catholic Identities in Chinese History* (Hong Kong, 2013), 21–6.

Figure 7. Soldiers dressed in Mongol fashion, *The Plain Tale of the Three Kingdoms* (*Sanguozhi pinghua*) composed in the Song and Yuan, printed in 1321–3. (Tokyo: National Diet Library. Photo: National Diet Library.)

Figure 8. Tomb of Buhading, 1275. Granite. Yangzhou: Transcendent Crane Mosque. (Photo: Wikimedia Commons.)

Figure 9. Angels transporting St Catherine's body, The *Belles Heures* of Jean de France, duc de Berry, 1405–1408/1409. Tempera, gold, and ink on vellum, 23.8 × 17 cm. New York: The Metropolitan Museum of Art, 54.1.1a, b, fo. 20r. (Photo: The Metropolitan Museum of Art, Open Access.)

The cross, a central symbol of Christianity, appears three times on the Vilioni slab, integrated in the imagery as well as the text. The Christ Child's halo is inscribed with it, and it frames the inscription both at the beginning and at the end. Besides the previously mentioned Xi'an stele and Luoyang pillar, the cross is the most common feature of thirteenth- and fourteenth-century eastern Christian tombstones from Quanzhou and elsewhere. The

Figure 10. Flying apsara, 535–57. Mural. Dunhuang: Mogao Cave 285. (Photo: Wikimedia Commons.)

Figure 11. Sarcophagus with Virgin and Child and the arms of the Sanguinacci Family, *c.* 1300. Red limestone, 82.6 × 223.5 × 94 cm. New York: The Metropolitan Museum of Art, 18.109. (Photo: The Metropolitan Museum of Art.)

symbol, however, was also not limited to monumental art nor funerary sculpture. Hundreds of small, flat bronze plaques survive from northern China from the Yuan dynasty, which are usually termed as the 'Ordos

Figure 12. Zhang Yuehu, Guanyin, late 1200s. Hanging scroll, ink on paper, 104 × 42.3 cm. Cleveland: The Cleveland Museum of Art, 1972.160. (Photo: The Cleveland Museum of Art.)

Crosses' as well as 'Nestorian Crosses'.[120] The loop on their back indicates that they were attached to clothing or worn on the body. Scholars have proposed that they served talismanic, apotropaic purposes.[121] The occasional traces of red ink, combined with the purposeful abstention from repetition of the visual features, however, suggest that they were more likely used as seal matrices, in which case the unique design of each piece was for security purposes.[122] In either case, the crosses' direct association with Christians is uncertain. Most feature a Syrian or Maltese cross as their central theme, but this is combined with Buddhist symbols, animal motifs (especially birds) and various geometric patterns.[123] For instance, an exemplar from the Royal Ontario Museum resembles a swastika, a common motif which represents light rays and good fortune in Buddhist art (Figure 13).[124] The Ordos Crosses thus project a similar meshing of Christian and Buddhist designs to that of the Vilioni slab. Moreover, they highlight that the shape of the cross was present across a broad spectrum of Yuan material culture, which was not necessarily limited to a strictly Christian context.

No surviving written sources document Caterina Vilioni's life, nor does the taciturn funerary inscription reveal her age, marital status, or whether she was born at or migrated to Yangzhou. Yet, the tombstone itself offers invaluable evidence to understand better her complicated identity. The ambiguous features we have explored highlight the presence of a variety of visual echoes in the imagery of Caterina's gravestone. The shape, composition and details of the imagery of the tombstone functioned in combination to communicate intentionally ambiguous messages associated with Buddhist, Christian and even Islamic traditions to a diverse audience. The heterogeneous visual language of Caterina's funerary monument therefore exhibits a sort of cultural mixing which some scholars would characterise as 'hybridity'.[125] This frequently employed framework for cross-cultural art historical analysis, which prioritises the syncretic aggregation of discrete cultural forms, however, fails to elucidate fully the complex social and cultural processes of displacement

---

[120] Florian Knothe, 'Chinese Bronze Crosses: A Jingjiao Phenomenon of the Middle Ages', *Orientations*, 46 (2015), 60–3; Jian Andrea Chen, 'Investigation of the Idea of Nestorian Crosses, Based on F. A. Nixon's Collection', *QUEST: Studies on Religion & Culture in Asia*, 2 (2017), 3–24, https://hub.hku.hk/bitstream/10722/293960/1/content.pdf?accept=1 (accessed 5 July 2024).

[121] Louis Hambis, 'A propos des sceaux-amulettes 'Nestoriens', *Arts Asiatiques*, 3 (1956), 279–86.

[122] Frederick S. Drake, 'Nestorian Crosses and Nestorian Christians in China under the Mongols', *Journal of the Royal Asiatic Society Hong Kong Branch*, 2 (1962), 11–25, at 14.

[123] Florian Knothe, 'Crosses of the Church of the East', in *Christianity in Asia: Sacred Art and Visual Splendour*, ed. Alan Chong (Singapore, 2016), 33–5, at 33.

[124] On an analogous example from Hong Kong: Parry, 'Images in the Church of the East', 158–9. The swastika can also be associated with the seal of the Buddha's heart. Xiaojing Yan, 'The Confluence of East and West in Nestorian Arts in China', in *Hidden Treasures and Intercultural Encounters*, ed. Winkler and Tang, 383–92, at 388.

[125] Hybridity assumes purity, a highly problematic concept: Carolyn Dean and Dana Leibsohn, 'Hybridity and its Discontents: Considering Visual Culture in Colonial Spanish America', *Colonial Latin American Review*, 12 (2003), 5–35; Annie E. Coombs and Avtar Brah, 'Introduction: The Conundrum of Mixing', in *Hybridity and its Discontents: Politics, Science, Culture*, ed. Annie E. Coombs and Avtar Brah (London, 2000), 1–16.

Figure 13. Ordos Crosses, tenth–fourteenth centuries. Cast bronze. Toronto: Royal Ontario Museum, Bishop William C. White Collection. (Photo: author.)

behind this object's creation. Instead of arguing through a binary system of influence and reception, acknowledging the porous nature of cross-cultural artefacts is key. By drawing on 'cultural ambiguity' as a more useful category of analysis, my approach shifts the emphasis from the geographic points of origins to an appreciation of the mobility of these multicultural features as well as the process of their displacement.[126]

While Caterina's tombstone communicated different messages to different audiences, the ambiguity of the visual language also consistently signalled a certain sense of displacement. Its meaning was never fixed, nor was it a question of either–or. For a Muslim merchant trading in Yangzhou, the shape and ornamental patterns would have seemed familiar from Islamic funerary monuments, while the imagery and inscription appeared entirely foreign. A fourteenth-century Buddhist would have recognised the figures and objects represented in the St Catherine narrative but would have found their religious significance incomprehensible. As for Christian observers, a convert from Yangzhou, a member of the Church of the East and a European visitor would have all perceived the imagery through very different lenses.

---

[126] For similar methodological approaches on translation and displacement, see Flood, *Objects of Translation*, 5. For a similar use of mobility as a category of analysis but in a western Eurasian context, see Rodini, 'Mobile Things', 247–65. Transcultural and transmaterial approaches have also received increased prominence: Vera-Simone Schulz, 'Transkulturelle Objektgeschichten: Islamische Artefakte in europäischen Kirchenschätzen und über diese hinaus', in *Islam in Europa 1000–1250*, ed. Claudia Höhl, Felix Prinz and Pavla Ralcheva (Regensburg, 2022), 47–54.

Even if the viewer would not have been able to locate the parent cultures of the extraneous features, they would have certainly recognised their evident displacement. In this sense, the Yangzhou tombstone prompts art-historical scholarship to engage in more nuanced ways with similar objects in the vast 'grey area' that lies between exotic and exoticizing objects.[127] Instead of perpetuating the preoccupation with sources of origins, the peripatetic visual repertoire of Caterina's tombstone thus highlights the importance of recognising not only the outcomes but also the processes of cultural translation and artistic displacement as effective vectors of interpretation on their own.

Otherworldly passport

So far we have seen that displacement played an important part in formulating the visual language of the funerary monument. Continuing on this path, this section will explore the role of the tombstone as a physical marker which signalled Caterina's migration between this life and the next.

The cusped shape of Caterina's tomb and the combination of inscriptions on the lower half with images on the upper half offer a template analogous to a contemporary Mongolian passport or *paiza* (Figure 14).[128] The name derives from a Persian reading of the Chinese *paizi* (tablet) which refers to the format of these passes. Sources written in the Mongolian language mention them as *gerege* meaning 'that which bears witness', and they were traditionally carried in tandem with a decree that explained the reasons behind the privileges the *paiza* conferred.[129] As tablets of authority, the *paizas* were issued by the Khan and they allowed envoys, diplomats, office holders and foreign travellers to pass across borders easily. They could also empower their bearers to requisition resources. Baohai Dang has divided *paizas* into four basic categories: postal-road tablets, passes for officers (e.g. commanders and diplomats), night travel/patrol and lucky charm.[130] Higher-level *paizas* were typically made of metal, most often iron, although the ones crafted for more elite owners were sometimes moulded from or inlaid with silver and gold. For instance, the four tablets that Marco Polo, his father and his uncle received from Gaigatu, Il-Khan of Persia (r. 1291–5) were made of gold.[131] The Beijing-born

---

[127] On the dichotomy between exotic and exoticizing, see Rodini, 'Mobile Things', 248; Contadini, 'Threads of Ornament', 290–1.

[128] Baohai Dang, 'The Paizi of the Mongol Empire', *Zentralasiatische Studien*, 31 (2001), 31–62; James C. Y. Watt, 'Notes on Artistic Exchanges in the Mongol Empire', in *The Legacy of Genghis Khan: Courtly Art and Culture in Western Asia, 1256–1353*, ed. Linda Komaroff and Stefano Carboni (New York, 2002), 62–73, at 67–9; Sheila S. Blair, 'A Mongol Envoy', in *The Iconography of Islamic Art: Studies in Honour of Robert Hillenbrand*, ed. Bernard O'Kane (Edinburgh, 2007), 45–60, at 50–4.

[129] Christopher P. Atwood, 'Mongol Messenger's Badge (Paiza or Gerege) in Pakpa Script: Signs of Authority in the Mongol Empire', Project Himalayan Art, Rubin Museum of Art, 2023, http://rubinmuseum.org/projecthimalayanart/essays/mongol-messengers-badge-paiza-or-gerege-in-pakpa-script (accessed 3 June 2024). On the Mongolian etymology, see also Gerhard Doerfer, *Türkische und mongolische Elemente in Neupersischen*, (Wiesbaden, 1965), II, 239–41; Francis Woodman Cleaves, 'Daruya and Gerege', *Harvard Journal of Asiatic Studies*, 16 (1953), 237–59, at 255–9.

[130] Baohai Dang, 'The Paizi', 31.

[131] Jacoby, 'Marco Polo', 203.

Figure 14. Paiza (Mongol safe conduct pass), late thirteenth century. Iron with silver inlay, 18.1 × 11.4 cm. New York: The Metropolitan Museum of Art, 1993.256. (Photo: The Metropolitan Museum of Art.)

diplomat and monk Rabban Bar Ṣawma also received a similar *paiza* when Arghun Khan dispatched him as the leader of an Il-khanid embassy to western Europe in 1286.[132]

Another extant *paiza* issued by Abdullah Khan of the Golden Horde (r. 1362–70) is an oblong silver tablet.[133] *Paizas* made in the Yuan period were instead typically cast in a pear-shape format, called in Chinese *yuanfu* or round tallies.[134] An exemplar in the National Museum of Mongolia in Ulaanbaatar authorised its holder to go about at night.[135] In addition to the

---

[132] Morris Rossabi, *Voyager from Xanadu: Rabban Sauma and the First Journey from China to the West* (Los Angeles, 2010), 99; *The Monks of Khubilai Khan*, trans. E. A. Wallis Budge (London, 1928), 50.

[133] N. Ts. Münküyev, 'A New Mongolian P'ai-Tzu from Simferopol', *Acta Orientalia Academiae Scientiarum Hungaricae*, 31 (1977), 185–215, at 203; Dang, 'The Paizi', 32.

[134] Dang, 'The Paizi', 39; Atwood, 'Mongol Messenger', n. p.

[135] Cai Meibiao 'Yuandai yuanpai liangzhong zhi kaoshi', *Lishi yanjiu*, 4 (1980), 124–32, at 130; Igor De Rachewiltz, 'Two recently published P'ai-tzu discovered in China', *Acta Orientalia Academiae Scientiarum Hungaricae*, 36 (1982), 413–17, at 415; Dang, 'The Paizi', 34, 51, fig. 6.

multilingual inscriptions, a serial number in Chinese ('Di 50') was also implemented, which functioned as a security device to limit the circulation of these sought-after passes.[136] In an analogous attempt in the Il-Khanate, Ghazan Khan (r. 1295–1304) cancelled all old *paizas* and issued new ones, which contained the names of their bearers and were to be returned at the end of service.[137] These passes thus also signalled the status and the identity of their owners.

The hooks or holes on top enabled the travellers to wear the *paiza* as a pendant or to fix it onto their clothing. They were inscribed with instructions to permit safe passage to their carriers. The 'Phags-pa script of a late thirteenth-century silver-inlayed iron *paiza* from China recalls the following warning: 'By the strength of Eternal Heaven, an edict of the Emperor [Khan]. He who has not respect shall be guilty' (Figure 14).[138] Enhanced with an animalistic mask on the top, similar to the decoration of Tibetan mirrors for reflecting evil, this *paiza* also provided protection on a spiritual level.[139] This apotropaic function might explain why a Yuan talisman was crafted in the form of a tiger-head *paiza*.[140] The Vilioni tombstone acted in an analogous vein by heralding the identity of its owner through the inscription, while invoking the help of Caterina's two heavenly protectors through the imagery. Therefore, in similar way to a *paiza* in the earthly realm of the Mongol empire, the tombstone signalled the hope of safe passage to the otherworld.

The images on Caterina Vilioni's tombstone also evoke associations with two different physical locations, both in the vicinity of Egypt. The first one is Sinai, where the angels allegedly transported the body of St Catherine after her decapitation. The Eastern Orthodox monastery on Mount Sinai had been built in the sixth century on the site where God spoke to Moses from the Burning Bush.[141] As Nancy P. Ševčenko demonstrated, its connection to St Catherine appears in the written sources first in Rouen in France, and even there relatively late, only in the eleventh century, although it subsequently spread rapidly.[142] Due to the enormous popularity of St Catherine in western Europe, Sinai became a major pilgrimage destination for Latin pilgrims in the thirteenth and fourteenth centuries. While after the Council of Florence in 1438–9 and the Ottoman conquest of Constantinople in 1453 the monastery became less hospitable for western travellers, the creation of Caterina Vilioni's tombstone falls precisely in the peak period of Latin pilgrimage to St Catherine's remains on Sinai. Therefore, this image recalled an important *locus sanctus* of western Christianity and ushered the attention to the parallel

[136] Chinese: 'Di zi wushi hao'. Dang, 'The Paizi', 34.

[137] Christopher P. Atwood, *Encyclopedia of Mongolia and the Mongol Empire* (New York, 2004), 433–4.

[138] Watt, 'Artistic Exchanges', 67–9. Online catalogue of the Metropolitan Museum of Art, https://www.metmuseum.org/art/collection/search/39624 (accessed 5 July 2024).

[139] Online catalogue of the Metropolitan Museum of Art, https://www.metmuseum.org/art/collection/search/39624.

[140] Dang, 'The Paizi', 33, 45, 50, fig. 5.

[141] Dmitrievskii, *Opisanie liturgicheskikh rukopisei*, III, 411.

[142] Ševčenko, 'The Monastery of Mount Sinai', 124–5.

between the actual grave of Caterina Vilioni in Yangzhou and the sepulchre of her holy patron, St Catherine of Alexandria in the Sinai.

On the other hand, the scenes from the martyrdom of St Catherine are set in the ancient city of Alexandria. A gateway to the east, this place had special importance for Venetian merchants from both an economic and a symbolic point of view. Although the main commercial centre of the Mamluk empire was Cairo, its chief Mediterranean port was Alexandria.[143] Due to the unstable and aggressive interactions between the Christian and Islamic worlds during the crusades, direct access to the much sought-after eastern merchandise deposited in the main warehouses in Cairo was intentionally prohibited.[144] Instead, European merchants from the *dār al-ḥarb* (Land of War) were limited to conducting their trade in Alexandria and Damietta alone. Moreover, Alexandria also became a crucial point of reference in the sacred geography of the Venetian empire. St Mark, the apostle and first bishop of Alexandria, became the patron saint of Venice. This relationship was codified by a *furtum sacrum* in 828–9, when two Venetian merchants, Bruno di Malamocco and Rustico di Torcello, smuggled out his bodily remains from Alexandria and transferred them to Venice. Deborah Howard and Thomas Dale have drawn attention to the ongoing Venetian efforts to promote this sacred connection between Venice and Alexandria.[145] For instance, in a mosaic of the atrium of San Marco, the burial of St Mark in Alexandria appears as if it were happening under the thirteenth-century *verde antico* ciborium in the apse of the basilica di San Marco itself.[146] The promotion of Venice as a 'new Alexandria' in turn also helped to emphasise and in a way justify the rapidly expanding mercantile empire of Venice in the broader Mediterranean. Thus, the reference to Alexandria on Caterina's tombstone could also communicate the link between the Vilioni family and its ancestral homeland, Venice.

Yet, Caterina's tombstone not only referenced spiritual travel, but also attested to the increased patterns of crossing geographical boundaries in a more mundane sense. One might recognise two final themes which Yuan *paizas* and Caterina's 'otherworldy passport' share: mobility and a sense of foreignness. Firstly, both can be perceived as tangible mementos of mobility. The most basic type of *paiza* was used for accessing the *jam*, the impressive post-road system of the Mongol empire, which under Khubilai Khan

---

[143] Abraham L. Udovitch, 'Medieval Alexandria: Some Evidence from the Cairo Genizah Documents', in *Alexandria and Alexandrianism: Papers Delivered at a Symposium Organized by the J. Paul Getty Museum and the Getty Center for the History of Art and the Humanities and held at the Museum, April 22-25* (Malibu, 1996), 273–84, at 279.

[144] David Jacoby, 'Between Venice and Alexandria: Trade and the Movement of Precious Metals in the Early Mamluk Period', *Mamluk Studies Review*, 21 (2018), 115–38; Sarah M. Guérin, 'Avorio d'ogni Ragione: The Supply of Elephant Ivory to Northern Europe in the Gothic Era', *Journal of Medieval History*, 36 (2010), 156–74, at 164.

[145] Howard, *Venice and the East*, 67–70; Thomas Dale, 'Pictorial Narratives of the Holy Land and the Myth of Venice in the Atrium of San Marco', in *The Atrium of San Marco in Venice: The Genesis and Medieval Reality of the Genesis Mosaics*, ed. Martin Buchsel, Herbert L. Kessler and Rebecca Muller (Berlin, 2014), 247–69.

[146] Dale, 'Pictorial Narratives', 251.

constituted more than 1,400 *jam* stations, serviced by 44,293 horses and other pack animals.[147] Given the burden of its upkeep, the system was already crumbling by the early fourteenth century.[148] Yet, the *jam* still facilitated travel during the lifetime of Caterina Vilioni, and the post-road duty survived in Tibet and Mongolia as late as the mid-twentieth century.[149] The postal tablets authorised the requisition of fresh horses, escorts, as well as room and board. Although the serial numbers suggest that the Yuan government issued such travel *paizas* by the thousands, only four are extant.[150] These exemplars are thus invaluable testimonies of the material legacy of this once extensive post-road network. In an analogous vein, Caterina's gravestone, erected in Yangzhou some 8,700 kilometres away from Venice, underscores the existence of global trade and social networks that bridged vast distances already in the medieval period. Although the precise paths through which her family reached Yangzhou cannot be charted, the fact that this voyage took place matters. Thus, Caterina's tomb, similarly to a *paiza*, acts as another tangible token of mobility.

Furthermore, Caterina's Latin tombstone is inscribed with a foreign script, much like surviving *paizas*. Since passports were used to assist travel and border-crossing, they were often labelled in multiple languages. The tablets made in the Yuan all included 'Phags-pa, developed from Tibetan-Indic letters, which Khubilai Khan proclaimed as the official script of the Mongol empire in 1269.[151] On the Ulaanbaator *paiza*, 'Phags-pa was paired with Chinese, Arabic-Persian and Uighur.[152] The record, however, is set by another round Yuan *paiza*, recovered from Ke'er'qin Youyi Zhongqi in Inner Mongolia.[153] This is labelled with no less than five different scripts: 'Phags-pa Mongolian, Uighur Mongolian, Tibetan, Arabic-Persian and Chinese.

In 1962, a round Yuan *paiza* was unearthed in Yangzhou.[154] The metal tablet, which permitted its user to travel at night, was engraved in Chinese on one side, while bearing a double inscription in 'Phags-pa (left) and Arabic-Persian (right) on the reverse. The Chinese text reveals that it was issued by the military and regional administrative office of the Pacification Commission and Chief Military Command.[155] This dates the *paiza* to a brief interval, since the office

---

[147] Peter Olbricht, *Das Postwesen in China unter der Mongolenherrschaft im 13. und 14. Jahrhundert* (Wiesbaden, 1954); Hosung Shim, 'The Postal Roads of the Great Khans in Central Asia under the Mongol-Yuan Empire', *Journal of Song-Yuan Studies*, 44 (2014), 405–69.

[148] Hodong Kim, 'Mongol Imperial Institutions', in *The Cambridge History of the Mongol Empire*, ed. Michal Biran and Hodong Kim (Cambridge, 2023), I, 399–442, at 436.

[149] Atwood, 'Mongol Messenger', n. p.

[150] Dang, 'The Paizi', 42.

[151] Christopher P. Atwood, 'The Empire of the Great Khan. The Yuan Ulus, 1260–1368', in *The Cambridge History of the Mongol Empire*, ed. Michal Biran and Hodong Kim (Cambridge, 2023), I, 107–80, at 115–16.

[152] Dang, 'The Paizi', 34.

[153] *Ibid.*, 36.

[154] Cai Meibiao, 'Yuandi yuanpi liangzhong zhi kaoshi', in *Yuan shi lun ji*, (Beijing, 1984), 698–710; De Rachewiltz, 'Two Recently Published P'ai-tzu', 415; Dang, 'The Paizi', 36.

[155] Meibiao, 'Yuandi yuanpi', 708.

was established in 1355 and the wall in which the tablet was discovered was erected in 1357.[156]

The Yangzhou *paiza*, made in the decade following the death of Caterina Vilioni in 1342, was incorporated in the same section of the base of the western city wall by the now-demolished South Gate as Caterina's tombstone.[157] A number of Islamic tombstones inscribed in Arabic were already excavated in the surroundings of the South Gate during the 1920s.[158] The fact that many of these slabs were relatively recently carved, including Caterina's only a few years earlier, suggests that there was an effort to uproot foreigners' tombstones and eliminate them from plain sight in the city. Moreover, while lithic spolia have been often reused in wall constructions in the period, it is telling that a metal *paiza* was also thrown into the same ditch, through which it stored various mismatched objects inscribed with foreign scripts. That the mid-fourteenth-century residents of Yangzhou decided to get rid of these objects together underscores the relevance of considering the *paizas* and Caterina's 'otherworldly passport' in tandem. Yet it is also worth remarking that these objects, which were meant to facilitate the crossing of boundaries – whether for night travel on the road or the voyage between this life and the next – were both subsumed into the city walls by the South Gate of Yangzhou to form part of a threshold themselves.

Conclusions

The primary objective of this study was to examine the crossing of boundaries, not only through the geographical, social, linguistic and religious distance between trecento Italy and the Yuan realm, but also through the immaterial transition from this life to the next which the funerary marker literally set in stone. The notarial documentation of mercantile activities, the written memoirs of friars and missionaries and the surviving diplomatic correspondence have allowed historians to chart the movement of men across great distances and widely different societies between Europe and Asia. The narrative that emerges from these sources is one of dynamic and powerful voyagers, who embarked on dangerous trips fuelled by the pursuit of spiritual wealth or material riches. This, however, is only an incomplete account, from which women, children and families have so far been nearly entirely exempt. Shifting the attention from the living to the dead, however, can cast light on these previously marginalised segments of society. Caterina Vilioni's gravestone attests not simply to the presence of a European Christian woman in premodern China, but a close examination of its inscription and imagery revealed a great deal about her complex identity with ties both to the local cosmopolitan setting in Yangzhou and also to her ancestral homeland in Venice.

---

[156] Cai Meibiao, 'Dui Keyou Zhongqi yexun pai A'labo zimu wenzi dushi de yijian', *Minzu Yuwen*, 3 (1995), 124–43, at 130.

[157] *Ibid.*; De Rachewiltz, 'Two Recently Published P'ai-tzu', 414.

[158] Mukai, 'Muslim Diaspora', 236; Nu'er, 'Yangzhou yisilanjiao beiwen xinzheng', *Haijiaoshi yanjiu*, 5 (1983), 105–9.

In exploring the intertwined visual language and the multicultural geopolitical context of Caterina's tombstone, a key goal was to shed light on the dynamic processes behind how cultural and religious barriers were negotiated in premodern Eurasia. This article recontextualised Caterina Vilioni and her gravestone through three focal points. Firstly, it investigated the origins of the Vilioni family and explored the magnitude of Sino-Italian mercantile interactions. While there have been uncertainties regarding the Vilioni, the surviving evidence suggests that the family stems from Venice. Despite trade along the Silk Roads still being primarily modelled on indirect exchange conducted through chains of middlemen, the case study of the Vilioni suggests the possibility of direct trade between China and Italy either by land or by sea, coordinated by extensive family enterprises. Furthermore, the expensive chess and backgammon set listed in Pietro Vilioni's will from Tabriz shows that merchants also travelled with more personal objects. The hagiographical narrative of Caterina's gravestone strengthens this interpretation by drawing attention to the likely transmission of small-scale devotional artefacts between Italy and China, such as illuminated manuscripts and ivory diptychs. Secondly, instead of attempting to locate the inspiration for certain features of the imagery of the tombstone in either Buddhist or Christian art, this article suggested that the visual language intentionally communicated cultural ambiguity. The form of the gravestone, the fluidity of the narrative and the specific visual features of the composition were not a random amalgamation of the cosmopolitan context of the commission. Instead, by recognising that the cultural and religious context of the tomb was purposefully left ambiguous, we can better comprehend why this multivalent imagery was especially suitable to project the polymorphic identity of Caterina Vilioni as a 'stranger', as well as a settled immigrant in Yangzhou. This offers an opportunity to move beyond the more traditional models of investigating the mere intelligibility of objects stemming from cross-cultural heritage, and to push the investigation towards in-depth questions of the role of artistic patronage in presenting the complicated identity of uprooted Europeans as strangers in the Mongol empire. A western traveller, an Islamic merchant and a native resident from Yangzhou would have each perceived some details as familiar and some as distinctly out of place, regardless of whether they were able to chart the source of origin for the latter. Through displacement, mobility thus functions as an added value on its own in the slab's imagery, and a useful interpretative vector. Finally, by comparing it to Mongol *paiza*, this article has proposed that Caterina's tombstone functioned as an 'otherworldly passport', which invoked spiritual protection and promised safe passage between two realms. This enquiry highlighted how the visual programme of the tomb evoked two locales: Sinai as a key *locus sanctus* of western Christianity in the era, and Alexandria, which was important for the Vilionis' homeland, Venice, for both commercial and symbolic reasons. As the example of the Polo family shows, the *paiza* were prized possessions and were even recorded in their owners' last wills. Instead of being melted down for their precious metal, the *paizas* were kept as souvenirs, being not only tangible mementos of their owner's time spent in the Mongol empire, but also badges of identity and personal standing. Made from stone, another extremely resilient material, and in a way echoing strikingly similar messages, Caterina Vilioni's tombstone ultimately offers invaluable tangible evidence that helps us to shed more light on the creation and promotion of the identity of a European Christian woman in the Yuan realm, even when the written sources are silent.

Acknowledgements. I would like to thank Deborah Howard and Craig Clunas for reading drafts of this article. I am also grateful to the editor Jan Machielsen and the two anonymous reviewers for their helpful suggestions.

Cite this article: Ilko K (2024). Yangzhou, 1342: Caterina Vilioni's Passport to the Afterlife. *Transactions of the Royal Historical Society* **2**, 3–38. https://doi.org/10.1017/S0080440124000136

Transactions of the RHS (2024), **2**, 39–61
doi:10.1017/S0080440124000069

ARTICLE

Migrant Voices in Multilingual London, 1560–1600

John Gallagher

University of Leeds, Leeds, UK
Email: j.gallagher1@leeds.ac.uk

(Received 28 March 2024; revised 7 June 2024; accepted 10 June 2024;
first published online 18 September 2024)

Abstract

Early modern London was multilingual, and early modern urban life was shaped by linguistic diversity. This article draws on the multilingual archives of Elizabethan London's 'stranger churches' – Protestant congregations which catered to the needs of French-, Dutch- and Italian-speaking migrants (among others) – to explore how linguistic diversity shaped social relations. These sources offer insights into the everyday multilingualism of the early modern city. They demonstrate London's migrant communities' intense interest in what people said and why, and show how different languages and their speakers interacted on the streets and in the spaces of later sixteenth-century London. By charting how linguistic diversity was part of the lives of ordinary Londoners in this period, including close examination of incidents of multilingual insult, slander, and conflict, this article argues that the civic and religious authorities relied on the stranger churches' abilities to carry out surveillance of speech in languages other than English, and that urban social relations and urban spaces were shaped by multilingualism. It ends by arguing that linguistic diversity played an essential but understudied role in the social history of early modern cities.

Keywords: multilingualism; migration; London; strangers; orality; insult; scandal; polyglossia; translation; urban history

Introduction

In London, in October 1571, Alixe le Roy told a story about an argument with her daughter-in-law, Philipine Seneschal. Alixe recounted how, in the middle of the street and in the middle of the day, Philipine had called her a murderer and a thief. Philipine believed that Alixe had had her son imprisoned, and so she took her revenge by telling her mother-in-law that she would shame her, crying out in the street that she should hang. Lots of their neighbours had heard the argument, among them a Flemish woman named Franchoise Sero and an

Englishwoman called Alice Jones ('Aelles Joanes' in the source's spelling). Both women agreed that they remembered the argument well – they had heard Philipine cry 'hang, hang', along with the other insults, and they said that the quarrel had gone on for a long time. They also recalled that the insults thrown by Philipine at her mother-in-law were delivered in a mixture of French and English.[1] This was a multilingual argument in a multilingual city.

Alixe le Roy and Philipine Seneschal were both members of London's community of 'strangers', one of the terms by which migrants to early modern England were known.[2] Both Protestants, it is likely that they were among the many French-speakers who had come to England to flee the violence and religious persecution of the French Wars of Religion, which rumbled on between 1562 and 1598. In the same period, London – and England – became home to significant numbers of Dutch- and Flemish-speaking Protestants who fled the havoc and persecution of the Eighty Years War in the Low Countries, as well as smaller numbers of Italian, Spanish and other Protestant migrants who feared the threat of the inquisitions in their home countries.[3] These strangers arrived in a city which had long been multilingual.[4] In London, the different varieties of English spoken by migrants from other parts of the realm mingled with the languages of other migrant groups, from Irish and Welsh to the languages of indigenous Americans and Africans, as the world beyond Europe made its presence more felt in England.[5] This was a city which ran on talk, where an only partially literate population understood that words had the power to make or break reputations and relationships.[6] The Elizabethan period represents a migration moment in London's history, a time when a significant number of migrants were arriving in a relatively short period of time. And it is a moment for

---

[1] Anne M. Oakley, *Actes du Consistoire de l'Eglise Française de Threadneedle Street, Londres*, ii: *1571-1577* (1969): this account of Alixe and Philipine's case draws on pages 24–5, 27, 29–30. In this article, I have generally chosen to use the spellings used in the sources rather than attempting to standardise them.

[2] I use 'stranger' and the more modern term 'migrant' interchangeably in this article, in part because these are broader terms which make no assumptions about whether an individual is (for instance) a refugee, exile, a more temporary visitor or an 'economic migrant'. A superb guide to early modern English vocabulary around migration is Nandini Das, João Vicente Melo, Haig Z. Smith and Lauren Working (eds.), *Keywords of Identity, Race, and Human Mobility in Early Modern England* (Amsterdam, 2021).

[3] Key works on these migrations include Andrew Pettegree, *Foreign Protestant Communities in Sixteenth-Century London* (Oxford, 1986); Laura Hunt Yungblut, *Strangers settled here amongst us: Policies, Perceptions and the Presence of Aliens in Elizabethan England* (New York, 1996); Nigel Goose and Lien Luu (eds.), *Immigrants in Tudor and Early Stuart England* (Eastbourne, 2005); Ole Peter Grell, *Dutch Calvinists in Early Stuart London: The Dutch Church at Austin Friars 1603-1642* (Leiden, 1989); Robin D. Gwynn, *Huguenot Heritage: The History and Contribution of the Huguenots in Britain* (1985).

[4] Ardis Butterfield, *The Familiar Enemy: Chaucer, Language, and Nation in the Hundred Years War* (Oxford, 2009), 201–233; Jonathan Hsy, *Trading Tongues: Merchants, Multilingualism, and Medieval Literature* (Columbus, OH, 2013), 1–26.

[5] Laura Wright, 'Speaking and Listening in Early Modern London', in *The City and the Senses: Urban Culture since 1500*, ed. Jill Steward and Alexander Cowan (Abingdon, 2007), 61–4; Coll Thrush, *Indigenous London: Native Travelers at the Heart of Empire* (New Haven, 2016); Imtiaz Habib, *Black Lives in the English Archives, 1500-1677: Imprints of the Invisible* (New York, 2008).

[6] Laura Gowing, *Domestic Dangers: Women, Words and Sex in Early Modern London* (Oxford, 1998).

which we have substantial multilingual archival evidence – rich records in French, in Dutch, and in Italian, as well as in English – made by members of these stranger communities and which attest not just to their presence and their activities in the city, but to their voices and words.

The importance of the spoken word to these strangers and the communities in which they lived should not be underestimated. Because some members of the stranger churches were extraordinarily well educated and had significant cultural impact, it is easy to lose sight of something highlighted by the first minister of the French church in 1561, when he wrote that 'this church is small, and consists for the most part of illiterate people'.[7] That many members of the congregations were deeply religious does not mean that they were confidently literate – many were reliant on sermons and oral catechising to learn the principles of their faith. These were largely communities of artisans, not scholars, even though those who kept their records, represented the community to the English, or made their literary or intellectual mark on English society were often highly literate and multilingual.[8] Literacy was not a precondition for being multilingual: early modern people could be confident speakers of multiple languages without being able to read a word in any of them. The stranger churches' records allow us to listen in on speech and oral culture, and to think about the meanings and practices of multilingualism for a wide social range of people, many of whom were either partly or not at all literate. The 'speechscape' of early modern London was multilingual, and people's experiences of the city were shaped by the languages they used and heard, by words they understood and words they did not.[9]

This article uses the consistory records of London's French, Dutch and Italian churches in the latter half of the sixteenth century to show how social relations in early modern London were shaped by the city's multilingualism. Whereas the rich scholarship on orality in early modern England has generally focused on speech in English, I make the case here that London's oral culture was multilingual, and that attending to the city's diversity of languages and how they interacted offers new perspectives on community, conflict and urban space.[10] By charting sixteenth-century London's everyday multilingualism, this article first argues that language shaped ideas of community and belonging in the Elizabethan city. It then makes the case that the civic

---

[7] 'ceste eglise est petite, & consiste la plus part de gens non lettrez': Nicolas des Gallars, *Forme de police ecclésiastique, instituée à Londres en l'Eglise des François* (n.p., 1561), B3r.

[8] The essential account of Dutch in early modern England is Christopher Joby, *The Dutch Language in Britain (1550–1702): A Social History of the Use of Dutch in Early Modern Britain* (Leiden, 2015). See also A. D. M. van de Haar, 'The Linguistic Coping Strategies of Three Netherlanders in England: Jan van der Noot, Lucas d'Heere, and Johannes Radermacher', *Early Modern Low Countries*, 5 (2021), 192–215.

[9] On 'speechscapes' in the early modern city, see John Gallagher, *Learning Languages in Early Modern England* (Oxford, 2019), 171–2; *idem*, 'Language-Learning, Orality, and Multilingualism in Early Modern Anglophone Narratives of Mediterranean Captivity', *Renaissance Studies*, 33 (2019), 647.

[10] The most comprehensive work on English oralities in this period remains Adam Fox, *Oral and Literate Culture in England 1500–1700* (Oxford, 2000); see also Adam Fox and Daniel Woolf (eds.), *The Spoken Word: Oral Culture in Britain 1500–1850* (Manchester, 2002).

and religious authorities relied on the stranger churches' abilities to carry out surveillance of speech in languages other than English, and that the city's spaces were shaped by the languages its people spoke. It ends by arguing that multilingualism's role in shaping early modern urban life demands historians' closer attention, not only in London but in cities throughout the early modern world. The early modern city was not just made up of buildings and people – it was shaped by words and voices which themselves created urban spaces and urban society.

Language and belonging

Alixe and Philipine were both members of London's French church, located on Threadneedle Street in the east of the city. Edward VI had given permission for the foundation of a church for strangers in 1550, and the period after Elizabeth I came to the throne in 1558 saw the emergence of three distinct stranger churches in London: the French church in the chapel of St Anthony on Threadneedle Street, the Dutch church at Austin Friars and the Italian church whose congregation worshipped in Mercers' Hall on Cheapside. These communities followed the more austere Calvinist strand of Protestantism, rather than the faith and practices of the church of England, and they catered to the city's growing numbers of strangers, made up of those fleeing persecution, those who had been resident in London since earlier in the century, and those who came to England primarily to practise their trade.[11] The stranger churches were, at least to some degree, communities bounded by language. Their services were held and their records kept in the main language of each church, though Latin remained as a language of study and communication: some Latin was used interchangeably with Dutch in the records of the Dutch church in the early 1560s and remained a medium of written and oral communication between the different stranger churches and with the English religious authorities.[12] When the three stranger churches met in a body known as the 'coetus', the language they used for their records was French.[13] The stranger churches played host to Latin language lessons as well as theology classes and sermons in the language, counted language teachers among their members and hosted multilingual performances, as in November 1560, when the ministers and elders of the French and Dutch churches met at Austin Friars to hear a sentence of excommunication pronounced in Dutch and probably in French, followed by the Bishop of London's exhortation in English from the pulpit.[14]

[11] Pettegree, Foreign Protestant Communities; Lien Bich Luu, Immigrants and the Industries of London, 1500–1700 (Abingdon, 2005); Steve Rappaport, Worlds Within Worlds: Structures of Life in Sixteenth-Century London (Cambridge, 1989), 104–5.

[12] A. A. van Schelven (ed.), Kerkeraads-Protocollen der Nederduitsche Vluchtelingen-Kerk te Londen 1560–1568 (Amsterdam, 1921); Joby, Dutch Language in Britain, 93.

[13] The language of coetus records is French from at least 1575 onwards, but may first have been Latin: O. Boersma and A. J. Jelsma, Unity in Multiformity: The Minutes of the Coetus of London, 1575 and the Consistory Minutes of the Italian Church of London, 1570–91 (1997), 19.

[14] Elsie Johnston (ed.), Actes du Consistoire de l'Eglise Française de Threadneedle Street, Londres, i: 1560–1565 (1937), 16.

But questions of language remained contentious, particularly when it came to baptism and marriage. In 1573, the deacons of the Dutch church had ruled that it was improper for English people with no knowledge of Dutch to act as godparents for children baptised in the church, while a colloquy of England's French churches in 1587 warned 'those of the French language who do not understand English at all' not to serve as godparents to an English child, and not to ask English people who did not understand French to serve as godparents to their own children.[15] When the Flemish goldsmith Martin van de Zande asked the Italian church, of which he was a member, if he might present his son to be baptised in the Dutch church, since the godparents did not understand Italian, his request was approved.[16] Similar requests occur around weddings: there are a number of requests to the Dutch church consistory like that made by Olivier Brassen, who asked for permission to be married in an English church 'since his bride was an Englishwoman and understood no Dutch'.[17] An agreement drawn up in French and Dutch in 1581 stated that the French church would take in any new arrivals who spoke 'the French or Walloon language', while the Dutch church would welcome those 'of the High Dutch [meaning German], Low Dutch, or Flemish language'.[18] These communities organised and defined themselves on broad linguistic lines, accepting speakers of a variety of different but related languages in a way that suggests that the ability to communicate with each other was the essential principle at work. These cases also show that social and romantic relationships between strangers and the English were relatively normal, even if the English did not speak the strangers' languages, which suggests that the new arrivals were often quick to forge new relationships in the language of their host nation.

So these were communities in which language and belonging were linked, but they still remained linguistically diverse – even to refer to the Dutch or French Churches as Dutch- or French-speaking, for instance, elides the diversity of languages and varieties spoken by their members. Many individuals would have been partially or entirely bilingual in Dutch and French, while the varieties of each language spoken by different members with different backgrounds would have been noticeable (and indeed are, in some cases, in the churches' archives).[19] At one point the French church auditioned a new Flemish preacher, only to turn him away because 'He doesn't have the proper

[15] A. J. Jelsma and O. Boersma (eds.), *Acta van het Consistorie van de Nederlandse Gemeente te Londen 1569-1585* ('s-Gravenhage, 1993), 313; Adrian Charles Chamier (ed.), *Les Actes des Colloques des Eglises Françaises et des Synodes des Eglises Etrangères refugiées en Angleterre 1581-1654* (Lymington, 1890), 12. On the dispute over godparents which especially divided the Dutch church, see Silke Muylaert, *Shaping the Stranger Churches: Migrants in England and the Troubles in the Netherlands, 1547-1585* (Leiden, 2021), 65-7; Pettegree, *Foreign Protestant Communities*, 243-7.

[16] Boersma and Jelsma, *Unity in Multiformity*, 146.

[17] 'dewijle zijn bruut een Ynghelsche was ende gheen Duytsch en verstondt': Jelsma and Boersma, *Acta*, 64.

[18] 'du Language francoise, ou Wallon'/'van fransche ofte walsche spraeke'; 'de Langage allemande, bas alleman ou flamen'/'vande hooghduytsche, Nederduytsche, ofte vlaemsche Sprake': London Metropolitan Archives, CLC/180/MS07410, 12-13.

[19] Joby, *Dutch Language in Britain*, 14-16 and *passim*; *idem*, 'French in Early Modern Norwich', *Journal of French Language Studies*, 27 (2017), 431-51.

tongue for French at all.'[20] That he spoke French well enough to deliver a sermon in it was immaterial when it was not the right kind of French. In 1572, the Genovese merchant and elder of the Italian church Antonio Giustiniani explained to the consistory of the French church how the Italian congregation contained a number of Spanish people who understood their language; by 1598, when the Italian church could not find an Italian-speaking minister to serve them, their members were advised to join either the Dutch or the French church, depending on which language was more familiar to them.[21] While each stranger church was linguistically diverse, the ideal of a shared language shaped them as communities. In making this argument, I differ from Charles Littleton, who argues that in London's sixteenth-century French church, 'the consistory was in fact not concerned with creating a Francophone national or linguistic identity among its members', but that '[i]t was above all concerned with defining the boundaries of a supranational godly community of the elect'. Littleton argues that '[t]he commonality of all these members [of the French church] was not ethnicity or even a common first language, but their Protestantism and devotion to its cause throughout Europe'. While Littleton is correct to emphasise the importance of theology and ecclesiastical discipline in the creation of community, this reading of the churches' approach to language and belonging shows that these were multilingual communities in which the idea of a common language nonetheless served practical and symbolic purposes.[22]

The stranger churches were not insulated from English. They had English members and were frequented by English-speakers who were curious about their ways of worshipping or simply seeking to burnish their language skills.[23] The consistories regularly questioned English-speakers, and we can assume that in at least some of these cases, English-language testimony has been silently translated into the language of their records. The scribes who kept their records often transcribed English place names and terms phonetically, so that we find the Dutch recording an incident in 'een eylhuyss' in 'Holeway' (an alehouse in Holloway) and the French noting events in 'ungne aele houys in Temstrytt' (an alehouse in Thames Street).[24] The accounts of the Dutch church in the early seventeenth century show the language changing to English where they need an entry to be read and signed by an English craftsman, while some bills that were presented to the church for payment were then annotated in Dutch.[25] The archives often contain English where the words themselves matter, especially in situations of insult or conflict, such as when Bernard Lure and Guillaum Nourry complained that Gabriel Heymon's wife had called their wives 'pocking houre'. When Pieter de Bert reported having heard Englishmen

---

[20] 'Il na point la lange propre pour le francois': Johnston, *Actes 1560-1565*, 69.

[21] Oakley, *Actes 1571-1577*, 91; Boersma and Jelsma, *Unity in Multiformity*, 110. On London's Spanish Protestant community, see Paul J. Hauben, 'A Spanish Calvinist church in Elizabethan London, 1559-65', *Church History*, 34 (1965), 50-6.

[22] Charles Littleton, 'Ecclesiastical Discipline in the French Church of London and the Creation of Community, 1560-1600', *Archiv für Reformationsgeschichte*, 92 (2001), 232-63.

[23] John Gallagher, *Learning Languages in Early Modern England* (Oxford, 2019), 3.

[24] Jelsma and Boersma, *Acta*, 667; Oakley, *Actes 1571-1577*, 155.

[25] London Metropolitan Archives, CLC/180/MS07402/07, item 22.

mocking a very drunk Jan the bookseller as 'Droncken Vlaminck', we are reminded that an English-speaker would not necessarily need to know Dutch to understand some terms of abuse.[26] When a dispute arose between some weavers who were members of the Dutch church and the Weavers' Company, the representatives sent by the consistory to discuss the problem reported back that their admonitions had been met with abuse: the act book of the consistory recorded that the weavers had said to them 'Goe your wayes knefs [knaves]'.[27]

If, for recently arrived migrants, a shared language could be an indicator of belonging to a stranger church, rejection of that shared language could indicate separation from the community. English was sometimes used in the consistory by strangers who wanted to signal their distance from or reject the authority of the stranger churches. In 1560, a schoolteacher named Gilles Berail said angrily that he did not wish to be subjected to the authority of the French church, since he already paid tax in his English parish, 'and that he understands English as well as French'.[28] When Denis de Restingam was questioned about why he had not attended the Lord's Supper for two years, he said that he had left the church after accusing the consistory of misusing funds that had been collected for the poor. De Restingam's questioners noted that he had said this to them and others, among other accusations, in English.[29] In 1572, Ollivier le Neveu was called in to be admonished for his words against certain women, and got into a heated exchange with the minister. Le Neveu wanted to speak, and tried to interrupt the minister, who told him to wait, to which le Neveu responded 'I don't know if I will wait, since you speak so evilly.' The minister told him to step outside for a moment, at which point le Neveu 'rising suddenly and leaving said, "god boye"'. With those parting words in English, he left and refused to return in spite of the minister's urging.[30] As time went on, English had other troubling implications for belonging: in 1580, one former member of the Dutch congregation wrote to their minister to say that he had lived in England so long that he had nearly lost his Dutch entirely.[31] In the seventeenth century, as the stranger churches' congregations dwindled and were increasingly made up of children and

---

[26] Oakley, *Actes 1571-1577*, 22; Jelsma and Boersma, *Acta*, 212, 217. My assumption is that the insult was delivered in English as 'drunken Fleming', but it would have been mutually intelligible to speakers of either English or Dutch.

[27] Jelsma and Boersma, *Acta*, 213. On tensions relating to stranger weavers, see Luu, *Immigrants and the industries of London*, 204–7; on strangers and citizenship, see Rappaport, *Worlds Within Worlds*, 54–60.

[28] 'et quil entend aussy bien lenglois que le francois': Johnston, *Actes 1560-1565*, 20.

[29] The consistory noted that this had taken place 'when the search [la queste] was taking place in St Martin's, they being part of the search among others', suggesting that the French Church representatives were accompanying English officials in their work. Johnston, *Actes 1560-1565*, 102; Littleton, 'Ecclesiastical Discipline', 257.

[30] 'Luy voulant parler et interrompre le propos. Le ministre luy dit attendes un peu et laisses oy achever. Luy respondit je ne scay si jattendray car vous parles trop sinistrement. Le ministre luy en dit sortes donc un peu dehors, luy se levant subitement et sortant dit, god boye. Le ministre luy dit ne vous en alles pas du tout, mais il narresta point': Oakley, *Actes 1571-1577*, 74.

[31] Jan Hendrick Hessels (ed.), *Epistulae et Tractatus Ecclesiae cum Reformationis tum Ecclesiae Londino-Batavae Historiam Illustrantes: Ecclesiae Londino-Batavae Archivum*, II.2 (Cambridge, 1889), 659.

grandchildren of first-generation migrants, their linguistic role shifted to one of defence and preservation of their shared language in the face of English.[32]

Policing strangers' speech

The ruling body of each stranger church was called the consistory, and the role of this all-male body was to oversee the government of the church and the behaviour of its members. Each church elected elders and deacons, each responsible for one of twelve *quartiers* or *wijken* – meaning districts – of the city.[33] In his 1561 text on the organisation of London's French church, the minister Nicolas des Gallars wrote that it was important that the elders should come from different parts of the city, 'in order to have eyes everywhere'.[34] In the French church, new elders swore an oath promising that:

> I will keep an eye on all those who are members of the church, and espe-
> cially on those who are committed unto my charge ... I will prevent scan-
> dals, procure the peace and unity of the whole church in general, and of
> everyone in particular ... I promise to keep and maintain ... the honour and
> profit of this Kingdom.

They further swore to inform the Bishop of London of anyone who might seek to trouble the peace and unity of England.[35] Like London's livery companies, the stranger churches took a role in policing their members' speech, working to keep their disputes out of the city's courts and to maintain harmony among their congregations and between strangers and their neighbours.[36] This fits with the pattern outlined by Raingard Esser, who argues that urban authorities and the leaderships of England's stranger churches practised 'shared authority' which devolved some of the responsibility for the control of crime and illicit activity onto stranger communities' leaders.[37] Consistory records are complex

---

[32] Grell, *Dutch Calvinists in Early Stuart London*, 8; Joby, *Dutch Language in Britain*, 97–8, 127.

[33] On the London stranger church consistories and social discipline, see Pettegree, *Foreign Protestant Communities*, 182–214; Susan Broomhall, 'Authority in the French Church in Sixteenth-Century London', in *Authority, Gender and Emotions in Late Medieval and Early Modern England*, ed. Susan Broomhall (2015), 131–50; Littleton, 'Ecclesiastical Discipline'. On consistory records, see Andrew Spicer, 'The Consistory Records of Reformed Congregations and the Exile Churches', *Proceedings of the Huguenot Society*, 28 (2007), 640–63.

[34] 'àfin d'avoir l'oeil par tout': des Gallars, *Forme de police*, B4r.

[35] '[J']auray l'oeil sur tous ceux qui sont du troupeau de ceste Eglise: & principallement de ceux qui me seront commis & baillez en charge ... [J'] empecheray les scandales, procureray la paix & union de toute l'Eglise en general, & d'un chacun en particulier ... Tiercement je promets de garder & maintenir en tant qu'en moy sera, l'honneur & le profit de ce Royaume': des Gallars, *Forme de police*, c6v–c7v.

[36] Jennifer Bishop, 'Speech and Sociability: The Regulation of Language in the Livery Companies of Early Modern London', in *Cities and Solidarities: Urban Communities in Pre-Modern Europe*, ed. Justin Colson and Arie van Steensel (2017), 208–24.

[37] Raingard Esser, '"They obey all magistrates and all good lawes ... and we thinke our cittie happie to enjoy them": Migrants and Urban Stability in Early Modern English Towns', *Urban History*, 34 (2007), 64–75.

sources: created by a disciplinary body, they record conflict more reliably than peaceful coexistence, and represent the perspectives of elders whose status in the community – as well as their level of education – was likely to be higher than that of the average member.[38] But at the same time, they offer rare opportunities to eavesdrop not just on the spoken word in these communities, but also on the voices of members across the spectrums of social status and literacy.

The stranger-church consistories sought to uphold their oaths through the rigorous policing of their members' speech. When the French church admonished Martin Fontaine's wife for her tendency to swear, she admitted that she had insulted one of her accusers but that beyond sometimes saying 'by my faith' she was not guilty of any swearing.[39] Admonition was one of the means of disciplining members available to the consistories; they could also demand that an offender do penance either before the consistory or before the whole congregation, depending on the nature of their crime, or bar them from participation in the eucharist. As part of a long investigation into the conduct of the silk-worker Gasparo de'Gatti, the Italian consistory found that 'the said Gasparo argues almost every day with his wife and with others of his household and, what is worse, ordinarily does nothing but blaspheme'.[40] The policing of women's speech by the consistories is evident throughout their records, and their concerns over women's tongues seem sometimes equal to their condemnation of men's more serious crimes, as in the case of Pierre Fouré, who was admonished for beating his wife while drunk; in the same breath, the consistory admonished his wife 'for not knowing how to contain her tongue against her husband'.[41]

In order to police the speech of their congregations rigorously, the consistories needed to have ears in many places. When the Dutch elders took an interest in the parentage of Sandryne Srijcken's child, they gathered evidence 'from the mouth of a woman who came from overseas' and 'from the mouth of an Englishman', while also taking the testimony of a woman who had been present during Sandryne's labour, who had joined the midwife in urging her to say the name of the child's father.[42] They sought oral information of this kind because it was key to understanding ungodly and scandalous behaviour among members of their congregations. But at the same time, the consistories sought to control and quell rumours which spread within and beyond their communities. In early modern societies, rumour was thought of as an almost irrepressible force – it was characterised as 'running' between speakers and hearers, and its spread was cause for concern among authorities throughout

---

[38] Judith Pollmann, 'Off the Record: Problems in the Quantification of Calvinist Church Discipline', *Sixteenth Century Journal*, 33 (2002), 423–38.

[39] Johnston, *Actes 1560-1565*, 30–1.

[40] 'detto Gaspari quasi ogni dì è in contentione con la moglie et con altri di casa e, che è peggio, ordinariamente non fa che biasfemar': Jelsma and Boersma, *Unity in Multiformity*, 183.

[41] 'de ne savoir contenir sa langue vers son mary': Oakley, *Actes 1571-1577*, 20.

[42] 'uuten mont van eenen vrauwe die van overzee was ghecommen'; 'uut den mont van eenen Ynghelschen man': Jelsma and Boersma, *Acta*, 398. On scandal, see Littleton, 'Ecclesiastical Discipline', 245–7.

early modern Europe.[43] Rumours could bring scandal on the congregation, so the consistories commonly asked members to account for what was being said about them, as when Tanneken de la Noy answered the consistory's queries by admitting 'that evil rumours had followed her, which were untrue, and that she was ready to answer for herself against her accusers, if they would appear'. In de la Noy's case, the accusation was that she had become involved with a young man during her husband's absence from London, and that they had been caught together by the local constables.[44] While the interest in rumour is something we see elsewhere in early modern Europe, it was especially important in these mobile communities of migrants, many of whom had been uprooted from their former lives and found themselves in England. The consistories expended significant effort in trying to find out if they were being told the truth about people's pasts, regularly investigating whether those who claimed never to have been married were telling the truth, or if they had spouses and families beyond the seas.[45] Strangers were pursued by rumours and stories and the economy of reputation and honour stretched beyond London's walls and England's borders.

Consistories were careful to monitor illicit speech in part because they were targeted by it. Their records are rich in moments when the members of the stranger churches attacked their elders and deacons – comparing them to the Spanish inquisition,[46] accusing them of treating congregants worse than 'heathens and Turks',[47] and signalling their displeasure at the consistory's decisions by yelling 'Pope, Pope', in order to accuse them of papistical tyranny.[48] Some strangers were aggressive in their denunciation of the churches and their refusal to live under their rule, like Barbara Michiels, who told the deacons 'I don't want to come to the church or to the consistory, since there is no justice for the poor there',[49] or the woman named Lijsken who said 'I'd rather live with a devil than with people like those from the church.'[50] They were especially concerned with incidents where grumblings against the consistory came to the ears of those outside the community, such as when Maerten

[43] Jeanice Brooks, 'Gossiping to Music in Sixteenth-Century France', *Renaissance Studies*, 30 (2016), 17–18.

[44] 'datter quade geruchtten achter haer gaen dewelke onwarachtich sijn, ende sij berreyt was haer te verantworden teghen haere beclaghers, so ie tevoorschijne quamen': Jelsma and Boersma, *Acta*, 288.

[45] Jesse Spohnholz, 'Instability and Insecurity: Dutch Women Refugees in Germany and England, 1550–1560', in *Exile and Religous Identity, 1500-1800*, ed. Jesse Spohnholz and Gary K. Waite (Abingdon, 2015), 111–25; Broomhall, 'Authority in the French Church'.

[46] Hans Stel told the Dutch consistory that 'Het gaet hier tewercke ghelijck mette Spaensche inquisitie': Jelsma and Boersma, *Acta*, 114.

[47] Loys Thiery complained to the Dutch consistory 'dat men dus tusschen heydenen ende Turcken niet en handelde': Jelsma and Boersma, *Acta*, 119.

[48] These were the words of Guillaume Cocq against the Dutch consistory: Jelsma and Boersma, *Acta*, 175.

[49] 'Ic en wil daeromme in de kercke ofte in de consistorie niet commen, want aldaer gheen recht voor den aermen en was': Jelsma and Boersma, *Acta*, 387.

[50] 'Ic hadde liever metten duvel te woonen dan met zulck volck van de kercke': Jelsma and Boersma, *Acta*, 389.

van Dale accused the Dutch minister of preaching false teachings 'not only among the Dutch but also among the English nation'.[51] The French church hauled Nicolas Wilpin before the consistory on multiple occasions because he 'will not stop spreading scandalous words against the consistory throughout the city'.[52] We get a sense of how these words might have slipped between the different communities in the account given to the Dutch consistory of Pieter Noppe's saying that the elders and deacons of the church were 'drunkards, whoremasters, and usurers'; Noppe's words were spoken in the crowded Three Horses in Mile End Green.[53]

The oath taken by the elders of the French church revealed a concern with scandal which is threaded through stranger church consistory records. In August 1571, the French consistory admonished a hatmaker named Piere de la Mare, also nicknamed Le Brave, accusing him of haunting taverns, and citing an incident in which he put a knife in a pot and sought to make others drink from it. De la Mare's drunken misbehaviour was bad enough, but the consistory was especially concerned because this was a cause for scandal among those who were not members of the church, and who said among themselves 'behold the people of the church, behold the Reformed people'.[54] The consistories of the stranger churches were painfully aware that their members' presence in England and their rights to worship in a way that differed from the English church were both conditional. Even before the congregations came under significant direct pressure from Archbishop Laud in the 1630s, they were frequently reminded by the English authorities of the precarity of their position and of the religious liberty they enjoyed.[55] As such, the stranger church consistories viewed with particular concern any scandals which threatened to draw the eye of the English community and the English authorities. In November 1569, the Dutch consistory admonished Hendrick Cnoop for his drunkenness and 'unchristian rudeness', which had redounded 'to the great scandal of the congregation and the English nation'.[56] The consistories needed to restrain their members from engaging in the disputes of the English church, as when Willem Fogghe informed the Dutch consistory in the summer of 1571 that there were many members of the same church 'who speak evilly and scandalously about the square cap which the English ministers wear', words which risked dragging an already precarious community into the ongoing controversy over ministers' garments, which was a source of much rancour among

---

[51] 'niet alleen bij de Duitsche maer ooc bij de Inghelsche natie': Jelsma and Boersma, *Acta*, 249.

[52] 'ne cesse de semer par tout la ville parolles scandaleux contre le Consistoire': Johnston, *Actes 1560–1565*, 29.

[53] 'drunckards, hoererers ende woeckeraers': Jelsma and Boersma, *Acta*, 654.

[54] 'Dont les scandal en sont suruenu aux aultres qui ne sont de leglise en dissant voilla les gens de leglise voila les gens Reformez': Johnston, *Actes 1560–1565*, 52.

[55] Grell, *Dutch Calvinists in Early Stuart London*, 224–48.

[56] 'Verscheen Hendrick Cnoop. Wiert hem vertoocht hoe dat hij hier tevooren eens vermaendt was gheweest bij der consistorie van zeker dronckenscap ende onchristelicke insolentien bij hem begaen ende nu nieuwelinghe wederomme ververscht, ter grooter scandale van de ghemeinte ende de Ynghelsche natie': Jelsma and Boersma, *Acta*, 16.

English Protestants.[57] Even more concerning were those moments when internal church disputes spilled over into the wider anglophone community, something which happened more than once amid disputes in the Dutch church about the minister Gottfridus Wingius (Godfried van Winghen). One member of the church, Jacob Caert, described Wingius as 'a false heretic' while drunk in the shop of Loys le Seigneur. When members of the consistory went to Caert's house to admonish him, he had more insults to share, saying that 'those from the consistory are all monks'. The consistory noted that these words were all said in English.[58]

Strangers and neighbours

In the autumn of 1579, the stonemason Vincent de Coninck – known to his English neighbours as Vincent King – was living with his wife Lisken in the parish of St Leonard in Aldersgate ward, just a few minutes' walk from St Paul's Cathedral.[59] The pair knew another couple from the Low Countries, Hans and Peryne Montenaken, who lived across the city in Aldgate Ward.[60] By this point, the relationship between the four had evidently become strained, since Vincent had warned Hans not to show his face at Vincent's shop because Lisken was angry with him, but Hans ignored the warning and came anyway. Once at the shop, Hans whistled and used slanderous words, including calling Lisken a whore. His wife, Peryne, added her own insults to the mix, calling Lisken and Vincent 'a false whore and a false thief'.[61] The couple had apparently come to challenge Lisken and Vincent about what they had been saying behind their backs. Vincent and Lisken gave as good as they got, and at some point they switched the language of their comebacks to English:

---

[57] 'die qualick ende schandaleuselick spreken van de viercante bonnette die de Enghelsche ministers draghen': Jelsma and Boersma, *Acta*, 216.

[58] 'Loys le Seigneur zeght leden es ontrent twee jaeren, jij in zijne wyncle hoorde eenen Jacob Caert spreken dese ofte ghelijcke woorden, dat Godfridus Wingius een valsch ketter was ... Ende als hij hem zeyde dat men hetzelve der consistorie zoude te kennen gheven, andwoorde daerup: Dat men mij daer ontbiede, ic zal noch vele meer zegghen, want het al munneken waren die van de consistorie zijn. 'tZelve gheschiede al tusschem heml. in Ynghelsche taele': Jelsma and Boersma, *Acta*, 370-1.

[59] In a 1571 Return of Aliens were listed as living in St Leonard's Parish in Foster Lane 'Vincent Kinge, dennyzein, and stonecutter, bornne in Andwarpe, and Elizabeth his wyfe, have byn in Englande v yeares, and cam for thencrease of there lyvinge, and are of the Douche churche': R. E. G. Kirk and Ernest F. Kirk (eds.), *Returns of Aliens dwelling in the City and Suburbs of London from the Reign of Henry VIII to that of James I, part II, 1571-1597* (Aberdeen, 1902), 49. In 1576, 'Vincent Kinge' was listed as a stranger living in the same place, while in 1582-3, 'Elizabeth King, wedowe, late wief of Vincent King, stonne cutter' was noted as a denizen, still living in Aldersgate ward: *ibid.*, 183, 284.

[60] Hans Montenaken is probably 'John Montenakers of Lucklande Marchaunte', listed in the return for Aldgate ward in 1583; Peryne shows up in the parish of St Katherine Coleman (in the same ward) as 'Perina Montenaken' in 1585: Kirk and Kirk, *Returns 1571-1597*, 319, 382.

[61] 'een valsche hoere ende een valsch dief': Jelsma and Boersma, *Acta*, 528. This paragraph reconstructs the argument from the testimony given by all four participants across a number of consistory sessions in September and October 1579: Jelsma and Boersma, *Acta*, 528-9, 532.

Lisken cried out in English that Peryne Montenaken and her husband were 'people who wanted papistry to be brought back in here'.[62] Peryne told the consistory that Vincent and his wife had shouted loudly, again in English, 'Look what kind of people they are, such people are not worthy to be tolerated here.'[63] Vincent's wife insulted Hans with a variety of insults, calling him a knave, a thief, and saying that it would be better he were hanged at Tyburn. As the argument escalated, it drew an audience – not only the English gentleman who was present in the shop when it kicked off, but also people in the street outside who had stopped to listen and gawk.

If we reconstruct this four-way argument from the consistory records, the picture that emerges from the different participants' testimonies is of a set of decisions. Hans and Peryne came to Vincent's shop as a semi-public space where they could challenge him and his wife; they would have known that others might be present, and that an argument could be audible outside in the street. Lisken and Vincent's choice of English for their retorts, and the kind of accusations they made – that Hans and Peryne were actually Catholics who wanted to overturn the English religious settlement, that they did not deserve the toleration shown to Protestant refugees, that Hans should be punished at London's famous execution site – seem like a deliberate performance to their (at least partly) English audience, using the English language and playing on typically English prejudices. Paul Griffiths notes the power of insults which referenced places and instruments of punishment in early modern England.[64] They cemented this impression when, after Peryne and Hans refused to leave, they called the constable to have them arrested. Vincent and Lisken implicated English customers, passers-by and representatives of the city authorities in a multilingual argument between strangers. They demonstrated a common feature of these records: evidence that strangers, regardless of their levels of literacy or education, had a sophisticated understanding of how insult, slander and reputation worked, and could switch between languages to make their use of insult and accusation as effective as possible, often in ways that demonstrate a real knowledge of how space, sound, and the distinction between the public and the private worked in the early modern city.[65]

These encounters between speakers of different languages were unavoidable in the context of London's housing and the circumstances in which many strangers lived. Bishopsgate, a ward which housed a high proportion of the city's strangers, was described by the antiquarian John Stow in his *Survey of London* as featuring many houses which were 'of late time too

---

[62] 'Vyncents wijf daertegen riep uut in Engels, seggende onder anderen, dese waren luyden die wilden dat de papisterie wederom hierin gebrocht werde': Jelsma and Boersma, *Acta*, 529.

[63] 'Ende Vincent ende sijn wijf in Engels luyde uutriepen: Syet wat volck dat dit is, sulck volck en is niet waert hier gedoocht te sijn': Jelsma and Boersma, *Acta*, 529–30.

[64] Paul Griffiths, 'Punishing Words: Insults and Injuries, 1525–1700', in *The Extraordinary and the Everyday in Early Modern England: Essays in Celebration of the Work of Bernard Capp*, ed. Angela McShane and Garthine Walker (Basingstoke, 2010), 66–85.

[65] On honour, reputation and insult in early modern London, see Gowing, *Domestic Dangers*; Eleanor Hubbard, *City Women: Money, Sex and the Social Order in Early Modern London* (Oxford, 2012).

much pesterd with people (a great cause of infection)'.[66] In 1593, a doggerel poem which came to be known as the 'Dutch church libel' was pasted against the wall of the Dutch church at Austin Friars. This anonymous screed drew on a variety of well-worn anti-immigrant stereotypes, accusing the strangers of taking work from English labourers, faking their religious beliefs while being secretly in the service of the Spanish enemy, and manipulating the English markets and currency to the detriment of English subjects. Among the accusations levelled by the libel's author was one which touched on this question of overcrowding: the author wrote that 'In Chambers, twenty in one house will lurke', and that the stranger presence in the city's accommodations was the cause of 'Raysing of rents, was never knowne before', while 'our pore soules [i.e. the English], are cleane thrust out of dore'.[67] The Returns of Aliens which documented the city's stranger population attest to households and buildings where speakers of different languages lived in close quarters. Laura Gowing has written about how '[t]he tensions engendered by London's combination of high mobility and crowded living' could find an outlet in insult, often sexual in nature.[68] In areas with higher numbers of stranger inhabitants, and those where overcrowding of this kind was commonly complained of, such as some of the city's eastern wards, the multilingual speechscape would have been especially audible. In this context of cheek-by-jowl living, of porous walls and shared staircases, strangers' words and languages were audible beyond the boundaries of the household, meaning that neighbours and passers-by were commonly implicated in conversations and arguments.

Noise and insults troubled the boundary between the public and the private. In March 1572, the Dutch consistory called in Gheeraert Arthus to address the rumours that were swirling around his relationship with his wife and his maid – they claimed that the 'great strife and disagreement' between them was 'not private but public'. Arthus claimed that since their arguments had taken place in the couple's home, they were private, but a queue of neighbours was ready to testify to the words and the violence that they had been able to overhear.[69] Dieric Schaep, Arthus's neighbour, said that their English neighbours had heard it too, and that they had said among themselves 'that is an honest man who is beating his wife'.[70] 'Honest' is not a Dutch word (more

---

[66] Charles Lethbridge Kingsford (ed.), *A Survey of London by John Stow reprinted from the text of 1603*, i (Oxford, 1908), 165; Rappaport, *Worlds Within Worlds*, 65–7.

[67] Arthur Freeman, 'Marlowe, Kyd, and the Dutch Church Libel', *English Literary Renaissance*, 3 (1973), 50; Lien Bich Luu, '"Taking the bread out of our mouths": Xenophobia in Early Modern London', *Immigrants and Minorities*, 19 (2000), 1–22.

[68] Gowing, *Domestic Dangers*, 22. See also Lena Cowen Orlin, *Locating Privacy in Tudor London* (Oxford, 2007), 152–92.

[69] Arthus was questioned 'dewijle daer een openbaer gheruchte es gheweest datter grooten twist ende oneenicheyt zij gheweest tusschen henleer, 'twelcke niet privaet maer publycq zoude zijn.' He claimed it was not public but private, 'te weten binnen den huuse; ende daer en conde niet ghehoort zijn dan eenen schreeu'. Jelsma and Boersma, *Acta*, 262. Compare Tessa de Boer, Ramona Negrón, Jessica den Oudsten, '"Good evening, you hag": Verbalizing Unhappy Marriages in Eighteenth-Century Amsterdam', in *Ordinary Oralities: Everyday Voices in History*, ed. Josephine Hoegaerts and Janice Schroeder (Berlin, 2023), 31–47.

[70] 'Dat es een honest man die zijn wijf slaet': Jelsma and Boersma, *Acta*, 264.

common in the consistory records is 'eerlick', or 'eerlijk' in modern Dutch), so there is a sense here of Schaep or the consistory scribe specifically echoing an English vocabulary of moral judgement, even though the strange statement attributed to the English neighbours is hard to parse: is it sarcastic, disapproving, or something else?[71] Rumours about what was going on in the Arthus household seem to have gone back and forth between the Dutch- and English-speaking communities: Gabriel Bart's wife told the consistory that she had heard rumours of what had happened from the English, and had then gone to ask Gheeraert Arthus's wife if what she had heard was true, while Dieric Schaep's wife testified that Arthus's wife had told the English of her plight herself. The consistory even recorded the response of the English neighbours in a note: 'And the English said they had never thought that Geeraert would have been such a man.'[72] Susan Amussen writes that in early modern England, '[t]he acceptance and expectation that neighbours would watch events in a family, and intervene if necessary, made domestic violence a public issue'.[73] The case of Gheeraert Arthus, his wife and their neighbours shows how dealing with domestic violence could require the negotiation of linguistic boundaries as well as spatial ones.

Strangers' neighbours were more than just witnesses to incidents of insult, argument and violence. The English and other non-members of the churches could be called to the consistories as witnesses, and when a dispute was settled by the consistory, it was common for them to insist that those who had witnessed it be informed of the outcome. Loys Creton and his wife Dyna were said to have 'scandalised' their neighbours by their arguments and their 'bad way of living'; the French consistory insisted that they be reconciled in the presence of their neighbours from the church, 'present Jehan du Molin, Spanish, and the other neighbours from the Barbican'.[74] In October 1570, the Dutch consistory ordered one member to explain to his English neighbours that he had been incorrect when he had accused another member of being a thief.[75] A public dispute between Michel du Crocq and Jacques Boulenger was brought to reconciliation by the French consistory, with the pair 'promising to make their reconciliation apparent to the English their neighbours', some of whom had had stones thrown at them by Michel in the course of

---

[71] Alexandra Shepard, 'Honesty, Worth and Gender in Early Modern England, 1540–1640', in *Identity and Agency in England, 1500–1800*, ed. Henry French and Jonathan Barry (Basingstoke, 2004), 87–105. On neighbours and neighbourliness, see Hubbard, *City Women*, 148–88; Griffiths, *Lost Londons*, 268–76; Ian Archer, *The Pursuit of Stability: Social Relations in Elizabethan London* (Cambridge, 1991), 74–82; Tim Reinke-Williams, *Women, Work and Sociability in Early Modern London* (Palgrave, 2014), 127–35.

[72] 'Ende de Inghelschen zeyden, ze en dochten noyt dat Geeraert sulcs en man zoude gheweest hebben': Jelsma and Boersma, *Acta*, 268.

[73] Susan Dwyer Amussen, '"Being stirred to much unquietness": Violence and Domestic Violence in Early Modern England', *Journal of Women's History*, 6 (1994), 70–89.

[74] 'tous les voisins quy sont de leglise qui ont este Scandalizes de leurs debats et de leur mauuais vie'; 'present Jehan du molin espagnol et les autres voisins de barbacaine': Johnston, *Actes 1560–1565*, 88.

[75] 'Franchois Simoens beloofde te verclaren voor zeker Yngelschen, zijn ghebeuren dat hij Baillys met quaeder cause dief gheheeten hadde': Jelsma and Boersma, *Acta*, 139.

the argument.[76] The stranger consistories took seriously the work of explaining, understanding and reconciling disputes which crossed the boundaries of language and community. This work was a kind of translation: it required the decisions of the consistory to be communicated to members of the multilingual and multinational communities in which their neighbours lived.

The bad words and misbehaviour of strangers could come to the attention of the English authorities as well as the consistories of the stranger churches. London's constables, who policed sexual morality alongside other misdemeanours, were frequent sources of information passed to the consistories.[77] When the shoemaker Hans Willems was rumoured to be the father of an illegitimate child, the story came to the Dutch church via a chain of hearsay which began with Adriaenthen Seneschael, who told a constable in the Minories named Laurence Thomas, who told the elders Mattheus Lull and Hans Gast, who brought the information to the consistory.[78] In 1571, just a few days apart, two members of the French church separately got themselves put in the stocks (one in Aldgate, the other in Whitechapel) for their drunken words to the watch.[79] The consistories engaged with figures ranging from the archdeacon of St Paul's to aldermen, justices of the peace and 'een meester van Bruytwel' ('a master of Bridewell').[80] Sometimes strangers helped the English authorities with their enquiries, as when members of the of Dutch church were ordered to act as translators in an investigation into supposed Anabaptists by the Bishop of London.[81] These encounters show two things: firstly, that many strangers had the linguistic knowledge and flexibility to communicate effectively in the linguistically diverse city, whether that was to help the authorities with their enquiries or to get their own back on their neighbours. And secondly, it shows that London's civil and ecclesiastical authorities had to work multilingually too, finding ways to surveil and manage the speech of the stranger communities. The authorities' ability to hear what was being said in the city – from disorderly words to heresy – relied on multilingual surveillance, translation and communication by members of the stranger communities. The consistories were important mediators here, translating between the strangers and those who ruled over them, especially when migrant voices came to the attention of the city's own systems of surveillance and punishment. The situation of London's migrant communities was not a simple one of inclusion or exclusion, but demanded a complex array of listening, surveilling and

---

[76] 'La remonstrance faicte furent reconciliez euz promettant de faire apparoir leur reconciliation aux Anglois leurs voisins': Oakley, *Actes 1571-1577*, 201–2.

[77] On constables, beadles, informers and London's policing apparatus, see Griffiths, *Lost Londons*, 291–331 (and 296 on the expectation that stranger householders would serve as constables); Archer, *Pursuit of Stability*, 215–56.

[78] Jelsma and Boersma, *Acta*, 517.

[79] Oakley, *Actes 1571-1577*, 13, 14. Paul Griffiths notes that in 1563 '[a] merchant's servant got 'a dossyn good lashes with a rodde' for not owning up to being a Frenchman and telling Aldgate's deputy to 'serche also his tayle and to kysse it' when he made house-to-house searches in 1563': Griffiths, *Lost Londons*, 322.

[80] Jelsma and Boersma, *Acta*, 680.

[81] Hessels, *Epistulae et Tractatus*, ii.2, 704.

translating, which required stranger communities, stranger churches, and the urban and ecclesiastical authorities to listen and speak one to another.

Space and speech

Strangers' voices were heard all over the city. Clement Wouters's wife was heard complaining of her husband's drunkenness and violence in a Westminster street.[82] Claerkin Corbeels was seen assaulting and speaking threateningly to a woman on London Bridge.[83] There was gossip being spread about the troublemaker Jacob Caert at Leadenhall market.[84] Jehan Bocquet's crimes crossed the city – he got into a brawl with an Englishman at a tavern in Bishopsgate; later, he would be heard uttering 'villainous statements and insults mixed with swearing and blasphemies' in Southwark.[85] Public spaces, where people gathered to trade, share news and information, or just hang around, were ideal spots for a row or an accusation. The consistories heard from the widow Verslote how Passchier Fleurken had called her a 'perjurious whore' in the Guildhall, and how a group of Dutch women had traded insults outside the door of the French church.[86] When Melken van Asch made statements against Peter Tryon in Mercers' Hall (where the Italian church was located, too), the Dutch church was so concerned about the controversy it had caused among the English and among strangers that it made the participants go and explain themselves to all the witnesses.[87]

Language shaped urban space. You did not have to be multilingual or even literate to hear London's other languages when passing through its streets. Some spaces were characterised by their linguistic diversity, becoming sites where informal and oral translation helped news, gossip and slander spread through the urban speechscape. And space shaped language, too: the meaning and the force of words could change depending on the place where they were uttered. Londoners were experts in the fine art of making a scene, and there were few better places for a multilingual showdown than London's Royal Exchange. Finished in 1568, the Exchange was a site of international and multilingual trade and information brokerage. Visiting in 1598, the German traveller Paul Hentzner remarked on 'the stateliness of the building', 'the quantities of merchandise' and 'the assemblage of different nations'.[88] In John Eliot's

---

[82] Jelsma and Boersma, *Acta*, 199.

[83] *Ibid.*, 424.

[84] *Ibid.*, 379.

[85] 'villains propos et injures mesles de juremens et blasphemens': Oakley, *Actes 1571–1577*, 23, 142.

[86] The widow Verslote told the consistory 'dat Fluerken huer in Guylhall angheseit heeft, dat se eene meyneedighe hoere was met meer andere injurieuse woorden, waerof zou kennesse ghenomen heeft' – that mention of other 'injurious words' which were heard but not recorded by the consistory is intriguing, and suggests that some terms may have been considered too offensive to write down: Jelsma and Boersma, *Acta*, 145. On the Dutch dispute outside the French church, see Jelsma and Boersma *Acta*, 725–6.

[87] Jelsma and Boersma, *Acta*, 422–5, 428.

[88] Quoted in Ann Saunders, 'The Building of the Exchange', in *The Royal Exchange*, ed. Ann Saunders (1997), 45.

Ortho-Epia Gallica, a semi-satirical French conversation manual published in London in 1593, one character suggests a walk 'To the Exchange, to heare the newes out of France'. Later, a character says 'I will be below in the Change, either walking among the Italians, or troking with the French, or pratling amongst our English, or carroussing with the Flemings at the Cardinals hat', and the text contains the multilingual greetings of the Exchange's international traders, including an Italian's 'Buon Giorno e buon anno Signori' and a Castilian's 'Buenos dias ayan vuestras merçedes'.[89] The playwright Thomas Dekker wrote that in the Exchange 'They talk in severall Languages, And (like the murmuring fall of Waters) in the Hum of severall businesses: insomuch that the place seems Babell, (a Confusion of Tongues.).'[90]

This Babel was a place where strangers came to trade, to share information, to gossip and to socialise. It provided an audience for arrests, arguments and accusations that ranged from debt to sexual assault. The Exchange was witness to political and religious argument between and beyond the members of the stranger churches. It was a site where their collective reputation could easily be damaged by wayward words or actions, as when the Dutch church became frustrated with the news that a number of their members were meeting at a silversmith's by the Exchange, where they formed a 'college of drunkards' and caused trouble.[91] The Exchange was meant to be a male-dominated space, but women made their voices heard there.[92] In 1579, the Dutch consistory heard a complaint from an Englishman named Matthew Field, who had had a Dutchman named Jan Pauwels imprisoned in the King's Bench prison due to an outstanding debt. Field reported that Pauwels's wife had come to find him at the Exchange, where she had followed him to the shop of a man named Jeffrey Ducket, all the time loudly accusing him of unjustly imprisoning her husband.[93]

While the Exchange was the cause of frequent frustration for the elders and deacons of the stranger churches, it was also a rich resource for their own investigations. In 1581, the Italian church sent two members of the consistory to the Exchange to gather information about the life and behaviour of the silk-worker Gasparo de'Gatti. De'Gatti was reported to have told listeners at the Exchange that the Italian minister was 'a mercenary idiot

---

[89] John Eliot, *Ortho-Epia Gallica. Eliots Fruits for the French* (1593), 25-6.

[90] Quoted in Julia Gasper, 'The Literary Legend of Sir Thomas Gresham', in Saunders, *Royal Exchange*, 101.

[91] 'een zeker collegie van dronckaerts tot eenen silversmit bij de bursse': Jelsma and Boersma, *Acta*, 263. On Anglo-Dutch encounters at the Exchange, see Marjorie Rubright, *Doppelgänger Dilemmas: Anglo-Dutch Relations in Early Modern English Literature and Culture* (Philadelphia, 2014), 162-88.

[92] Jean E. Howard, *Theater of a City: The Places of London Comedy, 1598-1642* (Philadelphia, 2009), 32. See also Laura Gowing, '"The freedom of the streets": Women and Social Space, 1560-1640', in *Londinopolis: Essays in the Cultural and Social History of Early Modern London*, ed. Paul Griffiths and Mark S. R. Jenner (Manchester, 2000), 143-4. On the complex relationship between gender, space and defamation, see Fiona Williamson, 'Space and the City: Gender Identities in Seventeenth-Century Norwich', *Cultural and Social History*, 9 (2012), 169-85. For a recent historiographical perspective, see Danielle van den Heuvel, 'Gender in the Streets of the Premodern City', *Journal of Urban History*, 45 (2019), 693-710.

[93] Jelsma and Boersma, *Acta*, 496.

and a rogue'.[94] Digging into witness testimony, the Italians learnt that Gasparo's insults against the minister had been spoken in the presence of Hans Montenaken, whom we last met insulting Vincent and Lisken de Coninck in Vincent's shop, and were reported by Francisco Marquina, an Italian school-teacher and member of the Dutch church who moonlighted as a translator and court interpreter in cases involving participants who did not speak English. Marquina went on to tell the consistory that he had heard Gasparo say that brothels were good and necessary in a republic, and that the authorities should allow them.[95] Gasparo was a repeat offender, and was investigated on another occasion for having dealt with a problem with his cauldron by seeking the help of a woman in Rochester who may or may not have been a witch. This had sparked a debate among the Italians at the Exchange over whether this was Christian behaviour or not, and the consistory carefully compiled the testimony of all those who had participated in the conversation.

One case handled by the Dutch consistory gives a sense of the verbal and linguistic strategies that strangers used in this most public – and multilingual – of London's spaces. In August 1579, the Dutch consistory first heard a rumour of a dispute which had occurred between Lowys Thiery and Paschier van der Mote: Lowys had apparently had Paschier arrested without going through the consistory first, and there had been public insults and fights between the two men. A version of the story can be pieced together from the two men's statements to the consistory and from the accounts given by witnesses. Paschier, it seems, had approached Lowys on the Exchange and accused Lowys of having tried to have him arrested. As they argued, one of Lowys's creditors had appeared, and in his hearing Paschier had called Lowys a number of insulting names, including 'knave and bankrupt knave, with many other evil words'.[96] Now, this is already interesting from a linguistic point of view. The consistory recorded Paschier's words as 'knaif ende banckeroet knaif', but 'knaif' is a word that does not exist in early modern Dutch, suggesting that this is an attempt to note without quite translating the exact English term that Paschier had used. 'Knave' was an actionable term in English, and Paschier – like the scribe who kept the record of the argument – knew the power that he wielded when he used it.[97] So we already have the sense of a conversation that is happening on the border between languages, and then we hear that turning to Lowys's creditor, Paschier said that Lowys was a

---

[94] 'che altre volte in bolsa il detto Gasparo haveva detto che il nostro ministro era un mercenario idiota e forfante et altre iniurie': Boersma and Jelsma, *Unity in Multiformity*, 183.

[95] *Ibid.* Marquina appears as 'Francis Maquin' and 'Francois Macquin' as an interpreter or 'inter-rogator' in a 1592 separation case between Anne Clemens and Gervase Le Page: London Metropolitan Archives, DL/C 214, p. 258. I am grateful to Laura Gowing for sharing multilingual cases like this one with me. What language Gasparo was speaking, to be witnessed by both Francis and Hans (who was from Liège), is unclear.

[96] 'knaif ende banckeroet knaif, met vele andere quaede woorden': Jelsma and Boersma, *Acta*, 526.

[97] Gowing, *Domestic Dangers*, 62–7. Dutch does have 'knecht', though as the act books suggest this did not carry the same pejorative power. A closer Dutch equivalent (and one which appears regularly as a term of insult in the consistory records) is 'schelm', which can be translated as 'rogue' or 'knave'.

bankrupt, and said – at this point Lowys was clear that these words were in English – 'Don't you owe me thirty pounds?'[98] When it came time for Paschier to give his side of the story, he would agree on these key details – that he had said that Lowys owed him money, and that Lowys had responded by saying 'You lie like a knave [een boef], and similar insults in Dutch and English.'[99] When Lowys tried to walk away to another part of the Exchange, Paschier followed him, continuing to insult him. Lowys went home and began an action against Paschier, whom he caused to be arrested.

The use of English, which both Lowys and Paschier attested to in their statements to the consistory, seems to have been intentional on the part of both parties. They knew they had an audience: Jan Godschalk, Claude Dotigny, Jan Selot and Rafael van den Put would all attest to having witnessed the arguments and to have heard some of the words exchanged, as well as the physicality – Lowys attempting to walk away, Paschier pulling him by his coat – and they could situate it in the Exchange, too, with van den Put and others testifying that this had happened under the gallery at the noon Exchange.[100] The switch to English for the exchange of insults meant that their dispute would be comprehensible – and the scandal attached to the terms they used, of bankruptcy and moral degeneracy – would be understood by Lowys's creditor, with likely financial consequences for Lowys, as well as the wider anglophone public gathered at the Exchange at its busiest time of day. Scholars of migrations past and present have considered questions of assimilation, charting how (and how far) migrant communities integrate into their host societies over time. What we see in these moments of multilingual insult and reputation management in early modern London is a number of different kinds of knowledge at work – knowledge of which languages to use, and how to use them, knowledge of the social dynamics of a multilingual public space, and an understanding of how honour, credit and reputation worked in the multilingual city. We also glimpse how strangers made spaces multilingual – how their voices and languages became part of the urban speechscape, to be heard and interpreted by Londoners in all their diversity.

Conclusion: towards a history of the multilingual city

Early modern London was multilingual. In fact, it was much more multilingual than this article has been able to show. Not far from where Philipine Seneschal and her mother-in-law insulted each other in French and English, two men named Manteo and Wanchese were teaching their Algonquian language to Thomas Hariot.[101] London's migrants spoke Welsh and Scots and Portuguese

---

[98] 'Item dat hi seyde tegen den crediteur: Betrowt ghi desen banckeroetier, hi is mijselve £30 stx. schuldich. Item segge (in Engels): Bistu mij niet £30 schuldich': Jelsma and Boersma, *Acta*, 526.

[99] 'Ghi lieght als een boef, ende diergeliken scheltwoorden in Duyts ende Engels': *ibid.*, 527. 'Boef' can mean 'boy', though it could be used insultingly in a manner equivalent to the English 'knave' – see the usages in *De Geïntegreerde Taalbank* v2.0 (2018), https://gtb.ivdnt.org/iWDB/search?actie= article&wdb=WNT&id=M009616&lemma=boef&domein=0&conc=true.

[100] Jelsma and Boersma, *Acta*, 547–8, 551.

[101] Coll Thrush, *Indigenous London: Native Travelers at the Heart of Empire* (New Haven, 2016), 33–6.

as well as French and Dutch.[102] One commentator described the city as England's 'third universitie', where you could learn Chaldean, Syriac and Arabic, as well as Polish, Persian and Russian, among 'divers other Languages fit for Embassadors and Orators, and Agents for Marchants, and for Travaylors, and necessarie for all Commerce or Negotiation whatsoever'.[103] The stranger churches' records testify to the presence in London of Turks and Swedes, Spaniards, Germans and Greeks. The voices of the city's small but growing African population no doubt brought new languages to London's streets, even if we lack the detailed and linguistically rich archives of their experiences which we are lucky to have for other groups of strangers.[104]

But that London was multilingual should not come as a surprise. What I really want to argue is that London was multilingual for everyone who lived there. It did not matter if you did not socialise with merchants, ambassadors and translators; it did not matter if you were illiterate; it did not matter if you only spoke English: London was multilingual for everyone. Languages other than English could be heard on the streets and in the public spaces of the city, through the walls of homes and the doors of shops. And native Londoners, if we can use that crude term, experienced and engaged with other languages and with the information they carried in ways that were active, not passive.[105] When the bookseller Thomas Harris stopped his French neighbour Jehan de Savoye in the street, it was because he wanted to know what had been said in the noisy French-language row he had overheard.[106] It was not necessary to speak or understand another language to be part of this multilingual urban culture: your rowing neighbours might switch languages to ensure the cause of the trouble was made clear, or the offender might show up on your doorstep in the presence of an elder of their church to explain and apologise. In a fast-flowing argument in a language you did not understand, you might pick up a recognisable word or two – like 'knave' or 'honest' or 'Tyburn' – which gave some sense of what was going on, or draw your own conclusions by observing gesture, body language or physical violence. Translation was a part of everyday life, from the interpersonal to the institutional level.

---

[102] Emrys Jones, 'From Medieval to Renaissance City', in *The Welsh in London 1500-2000*, ed. Emrys Jones (Cardiff, 2001), 37–41. Among the Italian community, Girolama, the widow of Agostino Boas, had a Welsh servant named Maria Jones, while the silk-worker Gasparo de'Gatti had a young Welsh woman ('del paese de Veles') serving him as an apprentice: Boersma and Jelsma, *Unity in Multiformity*, 160, 193–4. For Scots in the consistory records, see Jelsma and Boersma, *Acta*, 729–30 and Oakley, *Actes 1571-1577*, 195–7, 199. Edgar Samuel, 'London's Portuguese Jewish Community, 1540–1753', in *From Strangers to Citizens: the integration of Immigrant Communities in Britain, Ireland and colonial America, 1550-1750*, ed. Randolph Vigne and Charles Littleton (Brighton, 2001), 239–40.

[103] George Buck, *The Third Universitie of England* (1615), 983.

[104] Habib, *Black Lives in the English Archives*.

[105] The complexities of language and identity which emerged especially in the second and third generations of these migrant communities are reflected in the account of John Anderton, who fled prosecution for theft in 1603, and was described as speaking 'like a stranger but an Englishman borne': Griffiths, *Lost Londons*, 255. See also Jacob Selwood, '"English-born reputed strangers": Birth and Descent in Seventeenth-Century London', *Journal of British Studies*, 44 (2005), 728–53.

[106] Johnston, *Actes 1560-1565*, 26.

Because so much of what we know of multilingualism in early modern Europe focuses on the multilingualism of elites, it is easy to fall into the trap of believing that early modern multilingualism was an elite phenomenon. From educational travel to literary translation, we have a well-documented and thoroughly studied understanding of how those who were wealthy and literate lived, thought, read and wrote multilingually. Accounts of elite multilingualism tend to privilege the textual, too. The records of London's stranger churches remind us that multilingualism was not – and is not – an elite experience. Nor was it one which is captured in accounts of linguistic diversity which focus on the literate and the literary. The multilingualism of the early modern city was everyday, and it was oral. Our understanding of linguistic diversity in the early modern world – and specifically of its implications – is still at a relatively early stage, especially when it comes to linguistic diversity as it was experienced and practised beyond elites. In a study of multilingualism in the early modern Mediterranean, Eric Dursteler has argued that:

> [as] the heirs of linguistic nationalism, it is difficult for us to conceive of a context in which multilingualism was the norm, where there were no efforts to impose linguistic homogeneity, and in which language was a marker of identity but not to the exclusion of other elements. The early modern world was a linguistically richer and more complex age than our own, and this was accepted and even celebrated as the norm, rather than being perceived as disorientating.[107]

This is true – even somewhere like England, often thought of too simply as effectively monoglot. Histories of early modern migration have too often treated language as an afterthought where they discuss it at all, leaving a range of questions to be asked about how the experience of communicating across linguistic barriers shaped migrant mobilities and the polyglot communities in which they settled.

And London was not unique – far from it. A hundred miles north-east, in the second city of sixteenth-century England, Norwich's stranger population was much bigger as a proportion of the city's inhabitants than London's, and it has been described as working as a functionally trilingual city.[108] Around the early modern world, urban life was shaped by linguistic diversity. In Venice, a panic spurred by multilingual migrants led to a crackdown on blasphemy and illicit speech.[109] In Granada, the relationship between Arabic and Spanish shaped the post-conquest city.[110] In Algiers and other cities of the early modern Mediterranean, a pidgin language emerged which facilitated

---

[107] Eric Dursteler, 'Speaking in Tongues: Language and Communication in the Early Modern Mediterranean', *Past and Present*, 217 (2012), 77.

[108] Peter Trudgill, *Investigations in Sociohistorical Linguistics: Stories of Colonisation and Contact* (Cambridge, 2010), 49.

[109] Elizabeth Horodowich, 'Civic Identity and the Control of Blasphemy in Sixteenth-Century Venice', *Past and Present*, 181 (2003), 3–33.

[110] Claire Gilbert, 'A Grammar of Conquest: The Spanish and Arabic Reorganization of Granada after 1492', *Past and Present*, 239 (2018), 3–40.

conversations between Christians and Muslims.[111] In Lima, notaries pondered how to establish new systems of trust and legality in the context of the interaction between Spanish and the indigenous languages of America.[112] A city like Manila was a place where Tagalog, Chinese and Spanish were spoken alongside each other, and its urban archives were the result of inescapable processes of translation.[113] Many more examples could be adduced from a variety of global contexts to show that linguistic diversity was a key component of urban life in the early modern world. Early modern cities like London were places which shaped 'standard' or 'correct' language but were themselves profoundly multilingual. Cities were engines of language change and standardisation, but at street level they were places where languages shaped social relations, and where urban authorities had to learn how to listen to multilingual speech.[114]

Histories of migration and of the city have long recognised the importance of diversity and difference in early modern cities, but need to look much more closely at the role of language and multilingualism in these often crowded and noisy environments.[115] We need a global, comparative conversation which will explore how cities made modern languages and how linguistic diversity shaped a city at a crucial moment in its history. Even where cities' archives are often monolingual, as London's are, we need to listen for the multilingual voices which shaped them. In the latter decades of the sixteenth century, the languages of London's strangers were an audible and important part of the urban speechscape, shaping a multilingual oral culture which had to be navigated by strangers and Londoners alike. How they lived and communicated in a multilingual city has implications for our understandings of assimilation and honour, of community and coexistence, of neighbourhood and order, of xenophobia and identity. To listen more closely to linguistic diversity may be to rethink what we know of the social history of the early modern city.

Acknowledgements. This article is based on a Royal Historical Society lecture delivered at University College London in September 2023. I am grateful to Emma Griffin, then President of the RHS, for the invitation, and to Jan Machielsen and the anonymous reviewer at Transactions for their comments on the piece. Thanks, too, to audiences at Newcastle, St Andrews, and KU Leuven, who heard versions of this material, and especially to Laura Gowing, Mark Williams, Raf van Rooy, and Violet Soen.

Competing interests. The author declares none.

---

[111] Jocelyne Dakhlia, *Lingua franca: histoire d'une langue métisse en Méditerranée* (Paris, 2008).

[112] Kathryn Burns, 'Notaries, Truth, and Consequences', *American Historical Review*, 110 (2005), 350–79.

[113] Jonathan Gebhardt, 'Microhistory and Microcosm: Chinese Migrants, Spanish Empire, and Globalization in Early Modern Manila', *Journal of Medieval and Early Modern Studies*, 47 (2017), 167–92.

[114] Christopher Joby has argued for greater consideration to be given to London's (and Norwich's) role in shaping Dutch: Christopher Joby, 'The Role of London and Other English Cities in the Development of Early Modern Dutch Language and Literature', *Dutch Crossing*, 38 (2014), 4–19.

[115] Jacob Selwood, *Diversity and Difference in Early Modern London* (Farnham, 2010).

Cite this article: Gallagher J (2024). Migrant Voices in Multilingual London, 1560–1600. *Transactions of the Royal Historical Society* 2, 39–61. https://doi.org/10.1017/S0080440124000069

Transactions of the RHS (2024), 2, 63–80
doi:10.1017/S0080440124000100

ARTICLE

Guwantu: The Yongzheng Emperor's (r. 1723–1735) 'Illustrated Inventory of Ancient Playthings' (1729) and Imperial Collecting in Eighteenth Century China

Phillip Grimberg

Centre for East Asian Studies, Heidelberg University, Heidelberg, Germany
Email: grimberg@grimberg.eu

(Received 11 October 2023; revised 12 June 2024; accepted 12 June 2024;
first published online 10 October 2024)

Abstract

This article provides a conceptual framework that fills a critical gap at the intersection of Chinese art and cultural history. It focuses on the Yongzheng emperor's 'Illustrated Inventory of Ancient Playthings' (*Guwantu*) and its significance within the context of the collecting and courtly elite culture of the High Qing. Through a comprehensive examination of scroll B/C.8–V&A of the *Guwantu* itself, as well as the relevant source material, this study elucidates the dynamics that shaped the connections between artist, collector and object in the context of the scroll. Furthermore, this contribution throws light on the multiple entangled relationships that underpinned imperial collecting practices of the period, ultimately offering new insights into the socio-cultural milieu of collectors and connoisseurs in early eighteenth-century China.

Keywords: China; court; collecting; Yongzheng; inventory; Victoria and Albert Museum

When on the third day of the sixth month of the fourth year of the Yongzheng 雍正 reign (24 June 1726) the emperor sent twenty-one objects from his art collections to the painting workshops at the Palace Board of Works of the Imperial Household Department (Neiwufu zaobanchu 內務府造辦處) for his head painter of the Oil Painting Studio (Youhuafang 油畫房), Italian Jesuit Giuseppe Castiglione (1688–1766), to produce a series of preliminary sketches of still lives (bogu 博古, lit. 'abundance of ancient [objects] '), he was to embark on the largest documenting project of the imperial art collections in over

600 years.[1] The set of monumental handscrolls that resulted from these drafts, possibly twenty-four in total and each over 20 metres long, with the unassuming title of 'Illustrated Inventory of Ancient Playthings' (Guwantu 古玩圖) and probably painted between 1727 and 1730, are a unique visual representation of the emperor's private art collections and of early eighteenth-century Qing courtly collecting in general.

When Aisin Gioro Yinzhen 愛新覺羅胤禛 (1678–1735) ascended the dragon throne in 1723 and became the Yongzheng emperor of the Manchu Qing dynasty (1644–1911), however, imperial patronage of the arts, antiquarian studies and collecting in China already looked back at a centuries-old tradition. Ruling in challenging times, the Yongzheng emperor consolidated his power by eliminating corruption, infighting and court factions that threatened his reign and questioned its legitimacy.[2] The emperor's 'Great Matter', his quest for legitimacy, became one of the driving forces of much of his cultural politics during his twelve-year reign. Collecting and antiquarian studies of ancient relics that bore the biographical weight of a bygone era of ideal and virtuous rulers were regarded as potent means to obtain this goal and to assert the emperor's prerogative of cultural hegemony.[3]

When the Manchu, a Tungusic people from the north-east, invaded the capital Beijing and seized power in 1644 by toppling the ruling Ming dynasty (1368–1644), they did not have an established rule of succession, and the emperor was free to choose an heir from any of his surviving sons. Therefore, after the death of an emperor power struggles were rather common. Before Prince Yinzhen became emperor, his older brother was named heir to his father's throne. Due to his erratic behaviour, however, the Kangxi 康熙 emperor (r. 1662–1722) demoted his errant eldest son from the rank of crown prince but failed to name a new heir before he died. After his father's death Prince Yinzhen declared himself emperor, basing his claims on his late father's last will and testament, which named 'the fourth son' as his heir and successor.[4] Yet quickly rumours spread that the new emperor had tampered with his father's testament and therefore was illegitimate and even may have murdered his predecessor. Yongzheng was eager to suppress these allegations and refuted them publicly by publishing the 'Record of Great Righteousness to Dispel Confusion' (Dayi juemi lu 大義覺密綠,) in which he tried to clear his name from all rumours by bowing to the late

---

[1] First Historical Archives of China (Zhongguo diyi lishi dang'an guan 中國第一歷史檔案館) and the Museum of the Chinese University of Hong Kong (Xianggang zhongwen daxue wenwu guan 香港中文大學文物館) (eds.), Archives of the Workshops of the Qing Imperial Household Department (Qinggong neiwufu zaobanchu dang'an 清宮內務府造辦處檔案) (Beijing, 2005), 268f.

[2] Madeleine Zelin, 'The Yung-cheng Reign', in The Cambridge History of China, IX, ed. Willard J. Peterson (Cambridge, 2002), 183–229; Huang Pei, Autocracy at Work: A Study of the Yung-cheng Period, 1723– 1735 (Bloomington, 1974).

[3] Lothar Ledderose, 'Some Observations on the Imperial Art Collection in China', Transactions of the Oriental Ceramic Society, 43 (1978), 33–46.

[4] Museum of the Institute of History and Philology/Academia Sinica, Last Testament of the Emperor Kangxi https://museum.sinica.edu.tw/en/collection/17/item/125/ (accessed 3 May 2024).

emperor's wish to name him as his heir.[5] This publication – an unprecedented example of public self-justification by a Chinese emperor – did not achieve its aim of eliminating any trace of doubt concerning his right to rule nor did it shut down any debates about his legitimacy. Rather, the question of legitimacy remained his Achilles' heel throughout the remainder of his reign, and in contemporary and later sources he was portrayed as a dark and gloomy figure, overshadowed by both his imposing father and his ambitious son, the future Qianlong 乾隆 emperor (r. 1736–96).[6]

Far more successful than using his coercive political powers as an absolute monarch, one way of asserting legitimacy was by patronage of the arts. The ruler as scholar – as a culturally refined 'Gentleman' (junzi 君子) who masters the Chinese classical literary and Confucian canon as well as history and the arts, calligraphy, poetry and painting in particular – is a very old trope in the Chinese tradition that goes back to the times of Confucius.[7] During the eleventh and twelfth centuries, a mastery of old relics and antiquarian objects was added to the list of refined pursuits of a Chinese gentleman. Antiquarianism (chin. jinshixue 金石學, lit. the 'study of [inscriptions on] metal and stone') and antiquarian collecting together with the publication of catalogues (of which a large number survives until this day) flourished during the second half of the Northern Song dynasty (960–1127).[8] Antiquarians of the period for the first time in Chinese history applied a (proto-)scientific approach to the study of ancient objects – predominantly bronze vessels of various types that were used as ritual implements from the sixteenth to the second century BCE and, to a lesser degree, other objects from later periods – as supplementary historical sources that were unspoiled by the manipulations and the errors ubiquitously found in manuscripts and other textual records of the time that, in the mind of contemporary scholars, had warped historical research for centuries. After the downfall of the dynasty in 1127 antiquarianism as a scholarly discipline disappeared for more than 500 years from Chinese intellectual discourse. It was only since the second half of the seventeenth century, when so called 'evidential scholarship' (kaozhengxue 考證學) challenged the predominantly textual approaches to the study of Chinese history, that objects and material evidence of past events came to play a prominent role in the study of history once again.[9] One of the main objectives of the early

[5] Jonathan D. Spence, *Treason by the Book* (New York, 2001).

[6] Pamela Kyle Crossley, *A Translucent Mirror: History of Identity in Qing Imperial Ideology* (Berkeley and Los Angeles, 1999).

[7] Ruyu Hung, 'Self-Cultivation through Art: Chinese Calligraphy and the Body', *Educational Philosophy and Theory*, 53 (2021), 1–5.

[8] Patricia Buckley-Ebrey, 'The Politics of Imperial Collecting in the Northern Song Period', in *Windows on the Chinese World: Reflections by Five Historians*, ed. Clara Wing-chung Ho (Lanham, 2009), 29–44; see also on the topic of collecting and antiquarianism during the Song period, Yunchiahn C. Sena, *Bronze and Stone: The Cult of Antiquity in Song Dynasty China* (Seattle, 2019) as well as Hsu Ya-hwei, 'Antiquaries and Politics: Antiquarian Culture of the Northern Song, 960–1127', in *World Antiquarianism: Comparative Perspectives*, ed. Alain Schnapp (Los Angeles, 2013), 230–48.

[9] Phillip Grimberg, 'Archaeology and Antiquarianism in China', in *Encyclopedia of Global Archaeology*, ed. Claire Smith (Cham, 2019), 1–9.

kaozheng-movement of the Ming–Qing-transition period (*c.* 1650–1700) was to restore the original content of the Confucian classics as a means of initiating political and technical reform, as these works were seen as sources of moral and practical guidance. As a side-effect, this 'paradigm shift from philosophy to philology',[10] a shift from abstraction to practical scholarship, greatly benefited palaeography and philology, and hence antiquarian studies and collecting more generally.[11] While the *kaozheng* school of thought reached its zenith only during the Qianlong- and Jiaqing-reigns (1796–1820) of the Qing dynasty, earlier proponents of the movement such as Gu Yanwu 顧炎武 (1613–83) or Yan Ruoqu 閻若璩 (1636–1704) paved the way for a change in the methodology of scholarship in China, including inductive approaches to knowledge acquisition and the requirement for results to be supported by facts.[12]

Departing from the work of McCausland, Falkenhausen, Dematté and others, this article will argue that during the intellectual and scientific reorientation of the period the highest strata of society also devoted themselves with growing interest to the collection and documentation of antique objects. Among them was the Yongzheng emperor. Alongside famous collector and antiquarian emperor Huizong 徽宗 (r. 1101–25) of the Northern Song[13] and his own art-savvy son, the Yongzheng emperor was one of the most prolific and knowledgeable collectors of art and antiquarian objects of the Early and High Qing.[14] In keeping with the spirit of the time, he commissioned the *Guwantu* as a pictorial record of the emperor's art collections, which reflects his keen interest in systematising his collections as well as in their historical and material value as tangible evidence of the past.

Guwantu: 'Illustrated Inventory of Ancient Playthings'

The *Guwantu* were commissioned by the Yongzheng emperor to document visually a portion of his private collections of antiques, curios, and other, more contemporary objects. Originally painted as a set of up to twenty-four scrolls, this study focuses on scroll B/C.8–V&A, one of only two surviving examples of the *Guwantu* painted in 1729, which is kept in the Victoria and Albert Museum in London (Inv. No. E.59-1911). The other scroll dating from 1728 is currently in the possession of the British Museum, London, as part of the Percival David Foundation for Chinese Art (Inv. No. PDF, X.01). and has already been discussed in some detail by Shane McCausland.[15]

---

[10] Benjamin Elman, *From Philosophy to Philology: Intellectual and Social Aspects of Change in Late Imperial China* (Cambridge, 1984).

[11] Michael Quirin, 'Scholarship, Value, Method, and Hermeneutics in Kaozheng: Some Reflections on Cui Shu (1740–1816) and the Confucian Classics', *History and Theory*, 35 (1996), 34–53.

[12] On Cho Ng, Edward Wang, *Mirroring the Past: The Writing and Use of History in Imperial China* (Honolulu, 2005), 229–31.

[13] Patricia Buckley-Ebrey, *Accumulating Culture: The Collections of Emperor Huizong* (Seattle, 2008).

[14] Regina Krahl, 'The Yongzheng Emperor: Art Collector and Patron', in *The Three Emperors 1662-1795*, ed. Evelyn Rawski and Jessica Rawson (2005), 240–69.

[15] Shane McCausland, 'The Emperor's Old Toys: Rethinking the Yongzheng (1723–35) Scroll of Antiquities in the Percival David Foundation', *Transactions of the Oriental Ceramic Society*, 66 (2002), 65–75.

Figure 1. *Guwantu* (detail) (© Victoria and Albert Museum, London).

Scroll B/C.8–V&A presents itself as a mounted hand scroll with dimensions of 64 cm × 2648 cm and depicts a total of 262 objects including the same number of racks, stands, mounts or suspensions framing and re-contextualising the objects within the collection, plus an additional fifteen cabinets and cupboards for storage (Figure 1).[16]

The painting was executed in ink and colour on paper in a Euro-Chinese hybrid style of painting.[17] The outer wrapper of the scroll is made of green silk brocade with patterns of chrysanthemums, dragons and phoenixes, common motives in imperial imagery. On a slip of paper, we find the date and title of the scroll given as 'Illustrated Inventory of Ancient Playthings, seventh year of Yongzheng, series xia, scroll eight' (Guwantu Yongzheng qi nian xia juan ba 古玩圖雍正七年下卷八) in regular script. The seventh year of the reign of the Yongzheng emperor corresponds with the year 1729 in the Gregorian calendar, and 'xia' (下) refers to possibly a third set from a series of three sets in total.[18]

---

[16] See on the concept of 'framing' Anna Grasskamp, *Objects in Frames: Displaying Foreign Collectibles in Early Modern China and Europe* (Berlin, 2019).

[17] McCausland, 'The Emperor's Old Toys', 65.

[18] Xia 下, literally means 'below', 'down'. Its opposite, shang 上, means 'top', 'first', etc. So, series Xia might refer to the second of two sets, but it might also refer to the third of three sets, if we infer that a series zhong 中, 'middle', 'centre', might well have existed too. Therefore, to designate the scroll in question as scroll No. 8 as indicated by the title of either series B, which corresponds to 中 or series C, which corresponds to 下, seems appropriate. Thus, the total number of originally existing scrolls can be estimated at up to twenty-four and the number of depicted objects at up to 6,000. This calculation results as follows: assuming that the designation 下 on the title of the scroll owned by the Victoria and Albert Museum is to be taken as the third series of a larger set, and that at least eight individual specimens are to be assigned to each series, this totals twenty-four. Assuming further that there was an equal number of objects on each of the scrolls and taking the two surviving specimens as a basis (250 and 262 objects respectively), this results in a total number of about 6,000 objects.

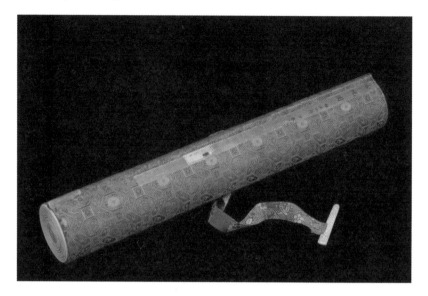

Figure 2. *Guwantu* (detail) (© Victoria and Albert Museum, London).

Moreover, the scroll features an ivory clasp and a strap of white and purple brocade with floral and cloud patterns. Two wooden rolling pins at the beginning and at the end of the scroll are decorated with roll ends of green dyed ivory with dragon motifs. The frontispiece is made of white paper and white silk brocade with phoenix and cloud patterns. In the two surviving copies, neither a preface or a table of contents, nor colophons or dedications have been preserved. These are likely to have been found in the lost first individual scrolls of the respective sets (Figure 2).

Organisation of the scroll

Scroll B/C.8–V&A contains a total of 262 objects, including 137 jades, 96 ceramics and porcelains, 20 bronzes, three objects made of stone, two of burlwood, one of enamel and three of undetermined material ranging in age from the Shang to the early Qing dynasty. Moreover, there are eight cabinets depicted at the end of the scroll, painted black with gold trim and tops in red lacquer with drawers with green-blue jade knobs and further storage compartments individually shaped and designed. Another seven cabinets are found in the centre of the scroll, of which four are tall, slender cabinets with doors in the lower third and white-finished, precisely fitting recesses for the respective objects in the upper part as well four lower shelves with matching compartments. All of these storage cabinets were custom-made from the 'wood workshop' (muzuo 木作) of the *Zaobanchu* (Figures 3 and 4).[19]

---

[19] Lo Hui-chi, 'Political Advancement and Religious Transcendence: The Yongzheng Emperor's (1678-1735) Deployment of Portraiture' (Ph.D. thesis, Stanford University, 2009), 126; see also Shu Lin, 'An Examination of the Aesthetic Sensibilities of the Yongzheng Emperor in Light of the Archives of the Zaobanchu', *Palace Museum Journal*, 6 (2004), 90–119.

Figure 3. *Guwantu* (detail) (© Victoria and Albert Museum, London).

Figure 4. *Guwantu* (detail) (© Victoria and Albert Museum, London).

The organisational structure of the scroll suggests that it indeed had once been used as an inventory of some sort. As McCausland has observed for the Percival David scroll in the British Museum, the objects depicted are not arranged according to date, media, provenance or function, but according to their respective places of display within the palace halls.[20] This assumption is further supported by the depiction of the two sets of cabinets in the middle

---

[20] McCausland, 'The Emperor's Old Toys', 72.

and at the end of the scroll, which probably have contained the objects depicted in the preceding portion of the scroll, helping curators and custodians to find objects that the emperor wished to appreciate.

Manufacture of the scroll

As Lo Hui-chi has aptly demonstrated in her 2009 dissertation, the *Archives of the Workshops of the Qing Imperial Household Department* (Qinggong neiwufu zaobanchu dang'an 清宮內務府造辦處檔案) of the Yongzheng reign, jointly published by the First Historical Archives of China (Zhongguo diyi lishi dang'an guan 中國第一歷史檔案館) and the Museum of the Chinese University of Hong Kong (Xianggang zhongwen daxue wenwu guan 香港中文大學文物館) in 2005, represent the most extensive and reliable source on the history of the *Guwantu*, offering valuable insights into the emperor's commissions and requests to court artists and artisans and his personal involvement in the production of art at his court.[21]

The 'Imperial Workshops' (*Zaobanchu* 造辦處) exercised oversight over several offices and departments, including the 'Painting Academy Office' (*Huayuanchu* 畫院處) and the 'Hall of Fulfilled Wishes' (*Ruyiguan* 如意館), which were both in charge of court painting.[22] Both offices were divided between the Forbidden City and the Yuanming Yuan summer palace in the northern vicinity of the capital and featured smaller, often specialised 'workshops for the production of paintings' (huazuo 畫作).[23]

Giuseppe Castiglione who had come to China in 1714 and already worked as a court painter under the emperor's father, had become head of the 'Oil Painting Studio', which, together with a studio specialising in Chinese landscape painting led by Tang Dai 唐岱 (1673–1755), were the main producers of paintings for the personal use of the emperor.[24] On the emperor's request, the workshops collaborated on various projects. Besides Castiglione and Tang Dai, several other artists of their studios were involved in the production of paintings for the emperor, including Banda Lisha 班達里沙, Yong Tai 永泰, Ge Shu 葛署, Wang Jie 王玠 and Wang Youxue 王幼學.[25]

The *Archives* show that the Yongzheng emperor commissioned the painting workshops of Castiglione and Tang Dai to produce sketches from objects – or, rather, object portraits – he had sent them early in his reign: between 1723 and 1727 the *Archives* record several of these requests.[26] The *Archives*, however, do not mention the *Guwantu* or their commission. Yet, from the available data we can infer that the *Guwantu* project must have begun sometime in 1727, the year of the emperor's last recorded commission of a set of object portraits that may

---

[21] Lo Hui-chi, 'Political Advancement and Religious Transcendence', especially 60, 107, 137, 140.

[22] Marco Musillo, 'Bridging Europe and China: The Professional Life of Giuseppe Castiglione (1688–1766)' (Ph.D. thesis, University of East Anglia, 2006), 35.

[23] *Archives* 5, 420.

[24] *Archives* 1, 185; see also Yang Xin, 'Court Painting in the Yongzheng and Qianlong Periods of the Qing Dynasty, with Reference to the Collection of the Palace Museum, Peking', in *The Elegant Brush*, ed. Ju-hsi Chou and Claudia Brown (Phoenix, 1985), 343–57.

[25] *Archives* 1, 164; 2, 645.

[26] *Archives* 1, 564, 566, 575.

have served as a draft for the emperor before he commissioned the *Guwantu*, and was finished sometime in or before 1730, when he requested painters versed in the 'western style' (xifang shi 西方式) to paint some more 'ancient implements' (guqi 古器) and produce an album for his use.[27] In his order he made it clear that Castiglione should not be involved.[28] The reason for this might have been that Castiglione himself was still involved in putting the finishing touches to the *Guwantu*, so that for this follow-up project, other trusted painters of his studio would have sufficed.

A production period of three years seems ambitious for a handful of painters to paint thousands of objects to the satisfaction of an imperial connoisseur. However, the existence of two scrolls from two different series dating from 1728 and 1729 (the V&A and BM scrolls) suggests that this assumption may well be plausible, and thus allows the set to be dated between 1727 and 1730.

Provenance

After the *Guwantu* project was finished in 1729/30, the sizable convolute of scrolls would have probably been stored on the premises of Yuanming Yuan, the emperor's preferred residence since relocating there in 1725, and the place where he kept the bulk of his private art collections.[29] Yuanming Yuan, Yongzheng's private refuge and originally a gift from his father, was to remain the main residence of successive Chinese emperors until during the reign of the Xianfeng 咸豐 emperor (1851–61) the palace was looted and ransacked by Anglo-French troops during the Second Opium War (1856–60) in October 1860. Millions of objects were either stolen or sold and found their way into collections of European aristocrats and treasure hunters, or they were destroyed on the spot and shared the fate of the palace, which was burned to the ground in 1860 and whose remains were looted and burnt down again in 1900 during the so-called Boxer Rebellion.[30]

The Victoria and Albert Museum, which acquired the 1729 scroll in 1911, describes it in its records as a 'painted Chinese scroll, a pictorial inventory made in 1729 of the art treasures in the Si Ling tombs (looted during the Boxer Rebellion). The scroll contains colour drawings of 262 individual objects of bronze, jade, steatite, pottery, etc., including 15 images of lacquer and inlaid cabinets. (13ft.16 × 25″)'.[31] Furthermore, the Museum's inventory gives the inventory number (E.59–1911) and the date of accession (13 January 1911), as well as the name of the seller, Captain J. S. Rivett-Carnac, and the price of £262 10s. paid for the scroll. The artist is given as a 'local artist', and 'watercolours' are mentioned as the medium (Figure 5).

---

[27] *Archives* 4, 552.

[28] *Ibid.*

[29] Phillip Grimberg, 'Trauma, Memory, and the Nation: The Ruinscapes of Yuanming Yuan and their Afterlife in Modern China', in *Thinking Through Ruins*, ed. Konstantin Klein, Enass Khansa and Barbara Winckler (Berlin, 2021), 239–56.

[30] Geremie Barmé, 'The Garden of Perfect Brightness: A Life in Ruins', in *East Asian History*, 11 (1996), 111–58.

[31] Victoria and Albert Museum, *Records of the Victoria and Albert Museum* (1911).

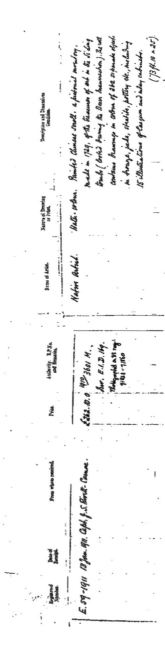

Figure 5. *Records of the V&A* (© Victoria and Albert Museum).

After the purchase of the scroll from Rivett-Carnac, an Indian army captain who was detached to a German army contingent of the Allied Forces during the Boxer Rebellion and a member of the family of the Rivett-Carnac baronets, descendant of James Rivett-Carnac (1774–1846), first Baronet and chairman of the East India Company from 1827 to 1838[32], in January 1911, the records of the V&A identified the scroll as an inventory 'of the art treasures in the Si Ling tombs (looted during the Boxer Rebellion)'. This attribution of the scroll as an inventory of the tomb treasures of the 'Si Ling', which may be identified as the 'Qing Xiling' 清西陵, the Western Tombs of the Qing imperial family in today's Hebei province where the Yongzheng emperor was interred in 1735, seems reasonable enough – even though it is not an inventory of the tomb, but rather an inventory of the art collections that the emperor possessed during his lifetime. Some of the latest research on the provenance of the scroll suggests that the *Guwantu* were kept within the emperor's burial complex Tailing 泰陵 until it was partly looted during the Boxer Uprising of 1900–1 from where they came into the possession of Rivet-Carnac and finally into that of the V&A.[33] McCausland, in his paper on the Percival David scroll, however, identified the toponym 'Si Ling' not as a contemporary transcription of the Chinese 'Xiling', but as a transcription of 'Siling' 思陵, the name of the tomb of the Chongzhen 崇禎 emperor (1628–44), the last of the Ming emperors, whose tomb remains unopened until this day. This assumption, therefore, seems rather implausible.[34]

The title

The title of the scroll, *Guwantu* (古玩圖), translated here as 'Illustrated Inventory of Ancient Playthings', allows for several translations: 'Chart of Old Toys', 'Images of Antique Knick-knacks', 'Scroll of Antiquities', etc., all of which would be a possible approximation of the Chinese title that echoes a tradition of portraying antique objects and collectibles, namely *gu wan*, which dates back to the Song dynasty. However, a more detailed analysis of the title and its components will bring to light some aspects that would otherwise remain hidden in a purely inline translation of the title.

The first character of the Chinese original – 古 (gu) – means 'ancient', 'old', 'antiquity', etc. The *Shuowen Jiezi* (說文解字, lit. 'Discussing Writing and Explaining Characters'), a palaeographic and etymological dictionary compiled by the Han-dynasty (220 BCE–206) scholar Xu Shen 許慎 (c. 58–148) explains the character as '[meaning] old. It derives from [the characters] ten and mouth. [It refers to] understanding the words of the elders' (gu ye. Cong shi kou shi qianyanzhe ye 故也從十口識前言者也).[35] The Dictionary describes the meaning of 古 rather unsatisfactorily with it having the same meaning as *gu* 故, so

[32] C. H. Philips and D. Philips, 'Alphabetical List of Directors of the East India Company from 1758 to 1858', *Journal of the Royal Asiatic Society*, 73 (1941), 325–33.

[33] Ricarda Brosch, 'Plündern in Pekings Peripherie: Die Westlichen Kaisergräber der Qing', *Ostasiatische Zeitschrift*, 46 (2023), 20–35.

[34] McCausland, 'The Emperor's Old Toys', 65 n. 1.

[35] Xu Shen, *Shuowen Jiezi* (Beijing, 1989), 375.

that here too we must look at the etymology. Unfortunately, the *Shuowen Jiezi* in a circular argument refers back to the character 古 and its meaning as 'old' as the etymological origin of 故, so that here we can only follow the explanation that the character 古 originally denoted the wise words of the forefathers, which becomes clearer when analysing its components. The lower part of the character – 口 (kou) – denotes the opening of the mouth, and hence, words uttered from it, often found in Chinese compound characters as the character's radical pointing to acts of speaking, calling, shouting, etc. The upper part of the character gu – 十 (shi) – denotes the number ten, though originally this character meant the point where east and west, north and south meet, namely the centre of the world, and hence in keeping with Chinese traditional worldviews, a point of perfection. Therefore, the interpretation of the character as 'words of the elders' (qianyanzhe ye前言者也) or words of wisdom/perfection seems plausible.

The second character of the title – 玩 (wan) – can be translated as 'toy', 'sth. used for amusement', 'curio', 'to keep sth. for entertainment', etc. The *Shuowen Jiezi* explains it as meaning 'to play with. It derives from [the character for] Jade' (nong ye cong yu 弄也從玉).[36] In his 1815 edition *Shuowen Jiezi zhu* (說文解字注) scholar Duan Yucai 段玉裁 (1735–1815) corrects the etymology of the character *wan* as deriving from the character *wang* 王 (meaning 'king'), rather than from the character for 'jade'.[37] Yet, the meaning of 'toy', 'sth. for amusement' remains the same.

The third character – 圖 (tu) – means 'diagram', 'picture', 'drawing', 'chart' or 'map'. The *Shuowen Jiezi* explains it as 'deriving from [the characters for] enclosure and granary' (cong kou cong bi 從囗從啚).[38] The inner character 啚 (bi) of the compound character 圖 means a granary or storage for rice or grain. The idea of an enclosed granary later came to mean a map, plan or diagram of where the granaries where located. In the course of further language development from ancient to classical, later to middle Chinese and finally to modern (since the fifteenth century) and contemporary Chinese, the character 圖 has lost the reference to storage and stockpiling and simply carries the meaning of 'map', 'picture', 'chart', etc.

Following the preceding explanations, the characters in the title of the scroll warrant some further interpretation: 古 (gu) carries the weight (and the plight) of the (alleged) harmonious perfection of antiquity, where the elders, namely sage rulers and revered philosophers, uttered words of wisdom and moral clarity, therefore becoming an aesthetic category in this context rather than a simple means of temporal classification. This becomes even clearer when we consider the infatuation of Chinese scholars, officials and rulers with the term throughout centuries of Chinese history: the various *fugu* (复古, i.e. 'returning to antiquity') movements within Chinese intellectual history, the Old Text/New Text controversy about the Confucian Classics, the elite's interest in antiquarian studies since the late eleventh century, and

---

[36] Xu Shen, *Shuowen*, 42.
[37] Duan Yucai, *Shuowen Jiezi zhu* (Beijing, 1990), 5.
[38] Xu Shen, *Shuowen*, 650.

the prominent role of (ancient) history and historiography in (pre-)modern Chinese thought in general are but some examples of the significance of the concept of 古 (gu) even to this day. In the context of the *Guwantu*, 古 (gu) transcends its original meaning of 'old' and turns into an expression of an aesthetic assessment of and a value judgement about the objects so designated. They are not just 'old', but sacred by their association with antiquity.

The character 玩 (wan), on the other hand, seems odd and out of place in the context of the scroll, especially regarding the gravitas of the term 古 (gu) as outlined above. Looking at the content of the *Guwantu* even in the most superficial and hasty manner, one can only conclude that the objects depicted are by no means toys, playthings or knickknacks, but products of the highest craftsmanship and of select artistic quality and historical significance. Instead, the term 玩 (wan) may be read as a subtle hint to historical precedents telling a cautious tale about emperors overindulging in the finer things in life and, while enjoying their precious objects and magnificent collections, neglecting politics and the heavenly mandate and losing throne and empire as a consequence. This rather dramatic interpretation of the unassuming term 玩 (wan) is supported by the repeated exhortations of officials to their rulers in the centuries after the fall of the Northern Song dynasty in 1127 to take as a warning the example of Emperor Huizong (r. 1101–25), who eventually neglected government business to devote himself to art and his personal interests and lost both throne and empire to conquering nomads from the north who forced China under foreign rule for centuries.[39]

Finally, the character 圖 (tu) may appear as a straightforward concept, denoting a picture, a drawing, a chart, an illustration, or, plainly, the scroll itself. Yet, its significance transcends the realm of mere visual representation. It quite comfortably lends itself to the interpretation of a comprehensive map – a cartographic guide to the microcosm of Chinese cultural and historical production as represented by the depicted objects in the scroll. As a map, 圖 (tu) unravels the multifaceted layers of Chinese history and creativity. It traces the evolution of Chinese cultural production throughout four millennia of Chinese history and offers insights into the societal shifts, technological advances and philosophical currents that have shaped the Chinese cultural landscape.

Now, looking at the title as a whole, the *Guwantu* appear to be an illustrated cultural map of the empire, connecting the emperor to the revered past through the depicted objects while at the same time cautioning him against frivolity and excessive indulgence. Acknowledging the educative capacities of art so familiar from the Chinese tradition, the antiquarian collecting and display of ancient objects as material evidence of the past was seen as a means of fostering moral refinement and disseminating knowledge that was in danger of being lost, thereby promoting learning and virtuousness, which were among the guiding principles in becoming a Confucian gentleman and a just and

---

[39] Patricia Buckley-Ebrey, *Emperor Huizong* (Cambridge, MA, 2014), 507–8, cites Zhang Juzheng's 張居正 (1525–82) *Dijian tushuo* (帝鑑図説, 'The Emperor's Mirror, an Illustrated Discussion', 1572) as one of many sources from post-Song/Late Imperial China that picked up this narrative.

benevolent ruler. The *Guwantu*, therefore, functioned as a means 'to record and classify China's cultural patrimony in Manchu dynastic time and space',[40] expressing a political programme of cultural hegemony that props up the Yongzheng emperor's claim to power grounded in the Chinese past and represented through his collections of 'ancient playthings'.

Style

The *Guwantu* were painted in a hybrid style of Chinese and European techniques that was to become one of the hallmarks of Chinese court painting during much of the eighteenth century.[41] Shane McCausland has observed that the scroll in the Percival David Collection

> is, in effect, a hybrid form of representation, one that incorporates the Manchu predilection for polychrome; Chinese techniques of observation and rendering, favouring line and outline, which both structure and evoke the qualities of the subject as well as referring to the process of creation through brush strokes; and selected European techniques, shading and perspective, which define surface, dimensionality, and position in space, but conceal the creative process.[42]

This is certainly also true for the V&A scroll. One further aspect closely related to the stylistic hybridity of the *Guwantu*, however, is that in the depiction of the objects we can detect an exceptionally high degree of representational accuracy, which allowed for the correct identification of any given object within the collection and even enables us today to match and identify objects from the scroll dispersed in different museums and collections worldwide. The insistence on accuracy in depicting and identifying a single object by the crackle of its glaze, the colour gradients in the patina of an ancient ritual bronze, or the texture, grain or pattern of wooden objects or such made of rock is based on the Chinese concept of 'writing life' or 'drawing from life'. This naturalistic style, known as *xiesheng* (寫生) in traditional Chinese art, is a distinctive approach that emphasises the realistic portrayal of the natural world. In this tradition, which developed during the Tang dynasty (618–906) and was deeply influenced by Daoist notions of nature, artists aim to capture the essence and form of their subjects with meticulous attention to detail. This style often involves the study and observation of real-life objects, plants, animals and landscapes, and had a particular influence on the genre of 'flower-and-bird painting' (huaniaohua 花鳥畫).[43] Artists carefully render these elements with precision, striving for accuracy in proportions, textures and colours. One of the fundamental principles of *xiesheng* is the cultivation of a keen sense of observation. Artists spend extensive time studying their subjects, often through direct observation or sketching in outdoor settings. This

---

[40] McCausland, 'The Emperor's Old Toys', 72.

[41] *Ibid.*

[42] *Ibid.*

[43] Liu Jie, *Tangdai huaniaohua yanjiu* (Beijing, 2013).

practice allows them to understand the intricate nuances and subtleties of the natural world, which they then translate onto their canvases or scrolls. The use of traditional Chinese painting materials, such as ink and watercolours as we can see in the scroll, is integral to *xiesheng*. Ink wash techniques, which involve diluting ink to create varying shades and tones, are commonly employed to capture the subtleties of light and shadow. This technique allows artists to achieve a sense of depth and three-dimensionality in their works that brings the true nature of the depicted scenes and objects to life. This devotion to faithful representation coincides with the growing interest of early Qing historians, antiquarians and collectors in 'evidential scholarship' and in the study of ancient objects as historical sources and material residues of the past. Together with European modes of representation and painting techniques that produced individual portraits of each depicted object instead of mere typologies, the *Guwantu* and their hybrid style of painting stand as an example of art production during the Yongzheng reign.

Yongzheng as collector

Following the decline of the Northern Song Dynasty in 1127 until the end of the Ming dynasty, pursuits like antiquarian studies and the collecting of historical artefacts did not hold significant sway in intellectual circles. Nonetheless, a pivotal shift occurred during the Ming–Qing transition, spurred by the philological reform movement of the era. This transformation, from philosophical speculation to the more empirical and evidence-based approach of 'evidential scholarship', rekindled interest in proto-archaeological studies, antiquarianism and collecting. This intellectual reorientation prevailed well into Yongzheng's reign. 'Evidential scholarship' challenged the conventional reliance on textual analyses in the study of Chinese history and instead advocated a heightened emphasis on tangible historical remnants as crucial components of scholarly inquiry.

In this climate, Yongzheng emerged as the first Qing emperor systematically to amass an art collection, taking a personal interest in expanding and enriching its holdings.[44] Deeply influenced by Confucian values and traditions, the emperor underscored the significance of scholarship and the preservation of cultural heritage. His appreciation for the arts was not merely a personal inclination, but an integral element of his vision for a prosperous and harmonious reign.

Upon closer examination of the objects depicted in the *Guwantu* series, it becomes evident that the art collections of Yongzheng were remarkably diverse, encompassing a wide range of artistic mediums and styles. His interests extended to porcelain, ceramics, jade carvings, and various other decorative arts. Particularly noteworthy, however, was his fondness of ancient bronzes, which held profound cultural and historical significance within Chinese tradition.

---

[44] Paola Demattè, 'Emperors and Scholars: Collecting Culture and Late Imperial Antiquarianism', in *Collecting China: The World, China, and a History of Collecting*, ed. Vimalin Rujivacharakul (Newark, NJ, 2011), 165–75 (p. 171).

Bronze casting in China can be traced back over three millennia, establishing it as one of the oldest and most venerated artistic traditions in Chinese culture. During the Shang (approximately 1600–1046 BCE) and Zhou (approximately 1046–256 BCE) dynasties, bronze objects held immense cultural, ritual and symbolic importance. They were employed in various ceremonial contexts and often bore inscriptions of dedicatory texts. The practice of emperors collecting bronzes originated with the Han Dynasty (206 BCE–220 CE) and persisted through subsequent dynasties. Emperors viewed the preservation and acquisition of bronzes not merely as a personal pastime, but as a means to connect with the esteemed heritage of their predecessors, affirming legitimacy and demonstrating a deep respect for tradition.[45]

The Qing dynasty, led by the Manchu ethnic group, was characterized by its cultural amalgamation, blending elements of Manchu, Mongol and Han Chinese traditions. This period was marked by a resurgence of traditional Chinese arts, encompassing painting, calligraphy, ceramics and, notably, bronzes. Yongzheng's fascination with bronzes can be interpreted as part of a general renaissance of traditional Chinese arts during the early Qing dynasty. The collection of bronzes, emblematic of ancient Chinese craftsmanship and artistic excellence, served as a means of re-establishing a connection with the rich cultural legacy of China's past. Yongzheng's collection of bronzes was not merely a personal indulgence, but a manifestation of his authority and an affirmation of the dynasty's rightful inheritance of China's ancient cultural heritage.

Unlike his father, who collected books for educational reasons and to maintain the court's traditional role as a centre of (Confucian) scholarship, and his son, who became a mega-collector for the purpose of demonstrating imperial grandeur and universal power, the Yongzheng emperor was a true connoisseur of art and antiquities who was intensely involved with his collections and took a personal interest in their care and documentation.[46]

Like his ill-fated predecessor Song emperor Huizong, Yongzheng was determined to accumulate a collection of the finest examples of Chinese cultural production from earliest times up until his day. Like Huizong, he not only found aesthetic pleasure in his collections, but shared the distinctive antiquarian and scholarly interest of his contemporaries in objects of the past. Unlike his predecessor, however, the Yongzheng emperor was not only an aesthete who spent a good amount of time and resources on his collections, but a shrewd and perspicacious politician who invested in his collections of 'ancient playthings' as political capital that propped up a distinct political programme of legitimising his and his dynasty's rule over the empire. In this context, the *Guwantu* not only function as an 'illustrated inventory' but represent a form of visual documentation of the collected artefacts, serving as object-related

---

[45] Lothar von Falkenhausen, 'Antiquarianism in East Asia. A Preliminary Overview', in *World Antiquarianism. Comparative Perspectives*, ed. Alain Schnapp (Los Angeles, 2013), 35–66.

[46] Lu Wei 卢葳, 'Painting a Portrait from a Collection: The Yongzheng Emperor's Views on Art as seen in the Guwantu', *Zhongguo shoucang*, 9 (2008), 50–1.

cultural representations and expressions of the collector's 'care' for his objects and his deep attachment to and entanglement with them.[47]

Commensurately, the emperor had his collectibles painted as intricate and naturalistic portraits that account for the individuality and biographical value of each item. As representations of both the empires' historical and cultural production as well as the emperor's cultural prerogative and authority of interpretation over this culture, the objects depicted in the *Guwantu* interact with the viewer as 'agents',[48] forming complex networks of historical and cultural affirmation.[49] These networks in turn mediate the ontological aspects of the objects and emphasise their performative, constructive and constitutive powers in view of their role as material evidence of the past.

Throughout Chinese history, the material aspect of rulership, including the possession and use of sacred or symbolically significant objects reserved exclusively for the ruler, has played a significant role.[50] Thus, as physical embodiments of 'tianxia' (天下, 'all under heaven'), a central aspect of the Chinese concept of world, empire and authority, these objects illustrate the different cultural traditions and practices within the empire through their material, historical, biographical and aesthetic properties. It is, thus, safe to assume that Yongzheng, through his careful selection and possession of a thoroughly curated collection of objects functioning as cultural representatives, saw himself as the supreme scholar and guardian of his empire's culture and history.

The *Guwantu* can therefore be seen as a representation of the Chinese cultural cosmos, an ordered system that closely corresponds to the era name chosen by the emperor, Yongzheng, meaning 'harmonious order'.[51] It is this harmonious order that the emperor, as the 'son of heaven' (tianzi 天子), had to maintain in order to rule over the empire by virtue of the 'heavenly mandate' (tianming 天命) that invested him with the power and legitimacy to rule. Through his symbolic command over the things of the world represented in the *Guwantu* and the associated power of order, as a collector the ruler gains access to the forces of the cosmos. Far from being a mere pastime, the emperor's collections and the *Guwantu* as a means of documentation and communication are symbolic of the preservation of the empire and its historical and cultural foundations that he sought to uphold during his reign.

Conclusion

The *Guwantu* as an illustrated inventory of the art collections of the Yongzheng emperor represent an outstanding example of early Qing-period collection documentation, while at the same time offering an insight into the emperor's collecting practices. Scroll B/C.8–V&A possesses a dual historical significance, originating from imperial possession while also bearing witness to the

---

[47] Ian Hodder, *Entangled: An Archaeology of the Relationships between Humans and Things* (Chichester, 2012).

[48] Alfred Gell, *Art and Agency: An Anthropological Theory* (Oxford, 1998).

[49] Bruno Latour, *Nous n'avons jamais été modernes: essai d'anthropologie symétrique* (Paris, 1991).

[50] Ledderose, 'Some Observations', 34–6.

[51] McCausland, 'The Emperor's Old Toys', 68.

backdrop of colonial violence in nineteenth-century China, rendering it an invaluable historical document.

As an art connoisseur, collector and adherent of the intellectual tenets of the *kaozheng* movement, but also as an astute ruler, the emperor sought to establish interpretative authority over the biographically rich and precious relics of China's past, ultimately seeking to legitimise his contentious reign. The *Guwantu*, functioning as a registry of the cultural essence of the Chinese empire, played a pivotal role in this pursuit.

Their near-total loss has meant that the *Guwantu* have received only limited scholarly attention so far. This article fills an important lacuna and emphasises their cultural and historical importance in the study of Qing imperial collecting and the cultural politics of the Yongzheng era. The *Guwantu* can be seen as the beginning of a systematic collecting endeavour that the Qianlong emperor, Yongzheng's successor, elevated to its zenith, laying the foundation for the current collections housed in the palace museums of Beijing and Taibei.

The 'Illustrated Inventory of Ancient Playthings' and the collecting strategies employed by the Yongzheng emperor wielded significant influence over Qing art policy until the close of the eighteenth century, and they continue to influence state collecting practices in China up to the present day.

Cite this article: Grimberg P (2024). *Guwantu*: The Yongzheng Emperor's (r. 1723–1735) 'Illustrated Inventory of Ancient Playthings' (1729) and Imperial Collecting in Eighteenth Century China. *Transactions of the Royal Historical Society* **2**, 63–80. https://doi.org/10.1017/S0080440124000100

Transactions of the RHS (2024), 2, 81
doi:10.1017/S0080440124000173

ADDENDUM

Guwantu: The Yongzheng Emperor's (r. 1723–1735) 'Illustrated Inventory of Ancient Playthings' (1729) and Imperial Collecting in Eighteenth Century China – ADDENDUM

Phillip Grimberg

doi:10.1017/S0080440124000100, Published by Cambridge University Press 10
October 2024

Financial support. The author discloses the generous support for the research of this work from
the Fritz Thyssen Stiftung [2021-2024].

Reference

Grimberg P (2024). *Guwantu*: The Yongzheng Emperor's (r. 1723–1735) 'Illustrated Inventory of
Ancient Playthings' (1729) and Imperial Collecting in Eighteenth Century China. *Transactions
of the Royal Historical Society* 1–18. https://doi.org/10.1017/S0080440124000100

Transactions of the RHS (2024), 2, 83–109
doi:10.1017/S0080440124000124

ARTICLE

Reading his Way to Royalism? Sir Thomas Myddelton, Side-Changing and Loyalty in England and Wales, 1639–66

Sarah Ward Clavier

University of the West of England, Bristol, UK
Email: sarah9.ward@uwe.ac.uk

(Received 13 June 2024; revised 23 August 2024; accepted 23 August 2024;
first published online 3 October 2024)

Abstract

Civil War allegiance has long been a preoccupation of early modern British historians. They have weighed geographical, religious, political, and pragmatic reasons for British people to choose sides in 1642. A study of the changes of allegiance in the years that followed is just as important. Side-changing reveals the fractures and difficulties that war, regime change, and an uneasy peace created. Most scholarship has examined figures whose ideas and beliefs remained consistent as the world around them changed. This article argues that others changed their minds (and their side) because their ideas fundamentally shifted, through an engagement with oppositional literature, a royalist social environment, and relationships built with royalist agents. Through a case study of the parliamentarian Major-General Sir Thomas Myddelton it examines this process of change. The article takes the study of allegiance into the Interregnum and beyond to the Restoration, tracing the impact of Myddelton's reading, experiences, and actions upon his declared loyalty. To do this, the article proposes a methodology that cuts across historical approaches, using evidence from financial accounts, libraries, and legal cases alongside surviving correspondence and printed pamphlets to build a composite image of a changing mind.

Keywords: side-changing; allegiance; loyalty; early modern; Civil War

Consistent and devoted loyalty was an asset following the British Civil Wars. Until 1660 a poor maimed soldier who could narrate a lengthy period in Parliament's service would be much more likely to receive a valuable pension. After the Restoration the flood of petitions and correspondence addressed to Charles II and his advisers demonstrated the hope that royalists of all stations would be rewarded in a similar way.[1] Loyalty was cited in requests for positions, restoration of lands or money, and promotion to higher office. The rhetoric of loyalty and allegiance was crucial and, for many families, became part of their identity in the decades to come. There are many examples of such consistent loyalty to either the King or to Parliament. Many more, however, employed loyalist rhetoric to conceal a significantly more complex history of allegiance. 'Trimming' or side-changing was not celebrated and was often the subject of individual or collective amnesia.[2] Yet side-changing was extremely widespread from the outbreak of the Civil War until the Restoration as, for example, individuals sought to accommodate the reality of changing political or personal circumstances or reacted to events such as the Regicide of 1649. Andrew Hopper has estimated that as many as 10 per cent of MPs changed allegiance at some point in the period 1642–6, and up to a third of those eligible to sit in the House of Lords.[3] Considering side-changing helps us to understand how many individuals viewed, understood and experienced concepts such as identity, allegiance and loyalty in the seventeenth century, but it also interacts with the influence of geography and ideas.

Sir Thomas Myddelton was one such side-changer. His career as a parliamentarian major-general from June 1643 to June 1645 was followed by a slow process of reassessment and a gradual entanglement with oppositional politics and religion. This culminated in a bold public declaration for the king in Booth's Rebellion in 1659. It is hard to see Myddelton in the same way as Lloyd Bowen depicts John Poyer, another Welsh parliamentarian commander whose public allegiance shifted, or as John Sutton describes William, 5th Baron Paget, as men whose principles remained the same while the world around them changed.[4] It would be tempting to understand Myddelton as such, a political Presbyterian whose Puritan upbringing and natural moderation led him to move away from the Commonwealth following the Regicide.[5] This is an argument commonly made by historians of early modern Europe's other conflicts

---

[1] For the most recent research on this subject see Brodie Waddell and Jason Peacey (eds.), *The Power of Petitioning in Early Modern Britain* (2024).

[2] G. E. Aylmer, 'Collective Mentalities in Mid Seventeenth-Century England: IV. Cross Currents: Neutrals, Trimmers, and Others', *Transactions of the Royal Historical Society*, 39 (1989), 1–22, at 6–7; Andrew Hopper, 'The Self-Fashioning of Gentry Turncoats During the English Civil Wars', *Journal of British Studies*, 49 (2010), 236–57, at 241; Mark Stoyle, *Loyalty and Locality: Popular Allegiance in Devon during the English Civil War* (Exeter, 1994), 112.

[3] Andrew Hopper, *Turncoats and Renegadoes: Changing Sides During the English Civil Wars* (Oxford, 2012), 41, 43.

[4] Lloyd Bowen, *John Poyer, the Civil Wars in Pembrokeshire and the British Revolutions* (Cardiff, 2020); John Sutton, 'Loyalty and a "Good Conscience": The Defection of William, Fifth Baron Paget, June 1642', in *Staffordshire Histories: Essays in Honour of Michael Greenslade*, ed. Philip J. Morgan and A. D. M. Phillips (Keele, 1999), 127–56.

[5] G. R. Thomas, 'Sir Thomas Myddelton II, 1586–1666' (M.A. thesis, University of Wales, 1968), p. 44; Andrew Lacey, *The Cult of King Charles the Martyr* (Woodbridge, 2003), p. 68; Elliot Vernon, 'The Quarrel of the Covenant: The London Presbyterians and the Regicide', in *The Regicides and the Execution of Charles I*, ed. Jason Peacey (Abingdon, 2001), 202–24; Elliot Vernon, *London Presbyterians and the British Revolutions, 1638–64* (Manchester, 2021).

as well, but it does not fit Myddelton's behaviour.[6] He was equally no calculating turncoat whose altered stance brought him safety, position or fortune: in the short term it was rather the opposite. Myddelton's allegiance was changed by a combination of ideas, actions and social environment.

Few scholars have considered Sir Thomas Myddelton at any length. Where they have, it has generally been in relation to his military role in the First Civil War. In that regard, historians traditionally portrayed Sir Thomas as a Presbyterian whose parliamentarian allegiance was the result of Puritan beliefs.[7] More recently research has shied away from such a depiction of his religion, though Lloyd Bowen has argued that Myddelton was a political Presbyterian in the later 1640s.[8] Though by their nature individual, Myddelton's choices can be used to examine characterisations of allegiance more widely, and to explore the influence of issues such as identity, belonging and environment upon the behaviour of the men and women who sought to navigate through the unstable years of the Interregnum. We may conclude, as Ann Hughes did of the parliamentarian Rowland Wilson, that the 'profound effects of war, revolution, and regicide' had a transformative effect on Sir Thomas Myddelton, his experiences during and after the First Civil War turning his mind away from the priorities embedded in him within the expansionist mercantile London society of his youth and his family towards the more conservative and rooted environment of North-East Wales.[9]

As historians' arguments about side-switching have changed, their characterisation of the sides has changed too. In 2007 Jason McElligott argued that historians should move away from 'convenient polarities' of royalist and parliamentarian.[10] McElligott and David Smith commented on the patterns of allegiance, the frequency of side-changing, and ths fact that allegiance may no longer be seen as fixed or unchanging.[11] The first monograph on the topic,

---

[6] Stuart Carroll, '"Nager entre deux eaux": The Princes and the Ambiguities of French Protestantism', *The Sixteenth Century Journal*, 44 (2013), 985–1020; Judith Pollmann, *Religious Choice in the Dutch Republic: The Reformation of Arnoldus Buchelius (1565-1641)* (Manchester, 1999).

[7] A. H. Dodd, *Studies in Stuart Wales* (Cardiff, 1952), 126; A. H. Dodd, 'Wales in the Parliaments of Charles I', *Transactions of the Honourable Society of Cymmrodorion* (1946–7), 70; J. R. Phillips, *Memoirs of the Civil War in Wales and the Marches*, I (1874), 163; David Klausner, 'Family Entertainments among the Salusburys of Llewenni', *Welsh Music History*, 6 (2004), 129–142, at 130; Thomas, 'Sir Thomas Myddelton II', 44.

[8] 'Myddelton, Sir Thomas (1586–1666), of Chirk Castle, Denb.', in *The House of Commons 1640-1660*, ed. Stephen K. Roberts (Woodbridge, 2023), 265; J. Gwynn Williams, 'Myddelton, Sir Thomas (1586–1666), parliamentarian army officer', *Oxford Dictionary of National Biography*, Sept. 2004, Oxford University Press, https://www.oxforddnb.com/view/10.1093/ref:odnb/9780198614128.001. 0001/odnb-9780198614128-e-19686 (accessed 4 June 2024); Lloyd Bowen, 'The Politics of Reconquest: Parliament, the Army and North Wales, 1643–49', in Alex Beeton (ed.), *Parliament and Revolution, 1640-1660* (forthcoming).

[9] Ann Hughes, 'A "Lunatick Revolter from Loyalty": The Death of Rowland Wilson and the English Revolution', *History Workshop Journal*, 61 (2006), 192–204, at 201.

[10] Jason McElligott, *Royalism, Print and Censorship in Revolutionary England* (Woodbridge, 2007), 5, 98.

[11] Jason McElligott and David L. Smith, 'Introduction: Rethinking Royalists and Royalism', in *Royalists and Royalism during the English Civil Wars*, ed. Jason McElligott and David L. Smith (Cambridge, 2007), 11, 15.

Andrew Hopper's *Turncoats and Renegadoes*, argued that more work needs to be done to 'properly contextualise individuals' defections'.[12] The response to Hopper's call has been muted but his work has shifted the historical consensus, complicating arguments beyond loyalty versus defection and factional disputes. Scholars such as Bowen have contended that, as the political and religious environment shifted, it placed individual men and women in changing positions regarding the binary positions of royalist and parliamentarian. In 1645 a Presbyterian MP such as Sir Robert Harley, for example, would be favourably disposed to Parliament in a way that, following the Regicide, he would not necessarily be in 1649.

This article examines the political and religious journey of Sir Thomas Myddelton as a micro-historical case study through which to assess these arguments and to explore the complexities of allegiance in the years 1642 to 1660. It will argue that alongside the binaries of consistent loyalty or an altered adherence caused by an interaction between long-held positions and new circumstances, changing sides could also be a gradual process. Switching sides need not be a Damascene conversion. Sir Thomas emerged with a changed political attitude and religiosity after the fire and ashes of the Civil Wars. His position on these issues changed after the First Civil War, contrary to his own interests and (in the short term) those of his family. His gradually changing stance brought with it the risk of censure, loss of status and sequestration, all of which were realised when he joined with Sir George Booth in 1659.

Sir Thomas Myddelton made two significant decisions in his life. The first was to declare for Parliament in 1642. There are many potential reasons for this, but the influence of Puritan and pro-parliamentarian family and friends in London, a fear of Catholicism, the seizure of his estate and his own hesitation may all have contributed. The second was to support the Restoration of Charles II, a decision which fitted better with his more recent self-fashioned identity as a Welsh patriot and gentleman. This decision was achieved through immersion in local culture and society, tentative engagement with royalist agents, and, critically, through intensive reading of royalist and episcopalian works. This article explores these decisions and their consequences for Myddelton.

At first glance it seems the paucity of sources complicates such a study. Despite being at the forefront of Civil War military action in Wales, Myddelton remains an enigmatic figure.[13] As his only biographer has observed, his personality hardly shines out from his surviving papers.[14] A number of surviving elegies perhaps give the best indication of his character: according to them he was a contemplative, serious man, who loved his family, books and garden, and who was interested in medicine, sport and providing charity for anyone from poor kindred to local women.[15] He valued his books so much that he was to hunt for those

---

[12] Myddelton does not feature as turncoat or renegado. A. Hopper, *Turncoats and Renegadoes: Changing Sides During the English Civil Wars* (Oxford, 2012), 10.

[13] In Welsh 'y milwr gymerodd ran mor flaenllaw yn y Rhyfel Mawr'. J. W. Jones, 'Syr Thomas Myddelton', *Cymru*, 46 (1914), 191–9.

[14] Thomas, 'Sir Thomas Myddelton II', 2.

[15] For example, NLW, Chirk F 7381.

looted in 1659 for the remaining seven years of his life. These impressions are borne out in his financial accounts, book purchases and will. Sir Thomas Myddelton was the second son of the North-East Welsh merchant Sir Thomas Myddelton, born in London in 1586 before his father's rise to prominence as a Puritan merchant, a member of the London elite, Lord Mayor and land-owner. Myddelton's father, who had only bought the estate in 1595, made over Chirk Castle to him upon his first marriage in 1612, and he settled down to the life of a Welsh country gentleman – feasting, feuding, holding local office, making excellent marriages for his children and extending his landholdings. Until 1642, Myddelton's life and career was consistent with the expectations of his class. After the outbreak of the Civil War that pattern was broken: not in terms of his military experience but in the contradictions and complexities of his behaviour. Between 1642 and 1660 Myddelton had taken up arms against the king in a strongly royalist area; had become a major-general with a minimum of military experience; had then aided in roy-alist plots during the mid-1650s and outright rebellion in 1659. He took part in the ejection of Church of England clergymen in 1645–6 and then protested against ejections, financially supporting several ejected clergymen and their families. He employed and associated with radical Protestants such as Colonel John Jones and his steward Watkin Kyffin but petitioned against the implica-tions of radical religious initiatives in 1652.[16]

Sir Thomas Myddelton's religious identity was equally complex. John Gwynfor Jones was typically prescient as to Myddelton's reading habits, noticing that Myddelton 'read the works of staunch Anglicans'. His analysis of Myddelton's religion was less successful. Jones argued that he 'to a degree, had adopted his father's Puritanical leanings' and that save 'for a period in the 1640s Middelton [sic] was an Anglican and had, in the 1630s, come under Laud's Arminian influence'.[17] This is rather muddled, and sets up an arti-ficial dichotomy between Elizabethan Puritanism and pre-Civil War 'Anglicanism'. A. H. Dodd explained the problems with identifying Myddelton as a 'Presbyterian', describing him instead as standing for 'militant Protestantism' within a European context, while much earlier John Phillips proposed that Myddelton was probably 'inclined to Puritanism and opposed to the pretensions which were put forward by the high Episcopalians about this time'.[18]

Myddelton's *History of Parliament* biography comes closest to identifying his contradictions. It notes Myddelton's Puritan religious upbringing and his inter-est in religious reform during the Long Parliament, alongside his conformity to Laud's policies and the allegedly decorative environment of his private chapel at Chirk.[19] It describes Myddelton's interest in advancing reformation and

---

[16] NLW, MS 9064E no. 1987; NLW, MS 9064E, no. 1988.

[17] J. Gwynfor Jones, 'Some Puritan Influences on the Anglican Church in Wales in the Early Seventeenth Century', *Journal of Welsh Religious History*, 2 (2002), 19–50, at 41.

[18] A. H. Dodd, 'Civil War in East Denbighshire', *Transactions of the Denbighshire Historical Society*, 3 (1954), 41–89, at 44.

[19] 'Myddelton, Sir Thomas (1586–1666), of Chirk Castle, Denb.', in *The House of Commons 1640–1660*, ed. Stephen K. Roberts (Woodbridge, 2023), 265.

fostering pious clergy, and his dismay at the 'general defection of the ministry' to the royalist cause.[20] Myddelton's political adversary Edward Vaughan described how in the 1630s, in compliance with Laud's reforms, Sir Thomas 'did repaier an ould ruinous chappell in his owne Castle, erected an Altar: and rayled itt: sett upp an crucifix, and Organs'.[21] Although this evidence comes from a source hostile to Myddelton, it is borne out to some degree by the installation of the organ in 1632 and the liturgical content of the part-books containing choral music that survive and which were commissioned for Myddelton's chapel.[22] A letter of December 1655 hints that his grandchild was baptised with godparents (an illegal act at that time), while his establishment of a choral foundation and commissioning of masques also argues against Puritan tendencies.[23]

The *History of Parliament* biography argues that Myddelton's religiosity constituted 'essentially Elizabethan Protestantism' as evidenced in the extensive preamble to his will of 1666, and it argues that this indicates that his political allegiance stemmed from his hope of advancing the Protestant reformation as he saw it.[24] These explanations may hold true for Myddelton at the beginning of his Civil War career but certainly start to falter after the parliamentarian victory in 1647. This article will argue that Myddelton's religious allegiance itself altered over time, maintaining a strong sense of anti-popery but increasingly aligning with the more assertive form of Anglicanism that would become prevalent in North-East Wales after 1660. The preamble, rather than providing evidence of godly belief, will be combined with Myddelton's reading matter and other evidence from his financial accounts to argue for a rather more conservative faith.

Myddelton gradually forged a new identity after 1647, that of a royalist and an active supporter of the Church of England. This began in the late 1640s, and evidence of his royalist sympathies gradually increased. Alongside acts of increasing political subversion, Myddelton's reading became focused on episcopalian apologetic and pro-episcopal tracts. This proceeded alongside an acculturation with Welsh social and political culture, and a growing sense of self-conscious Welshness. These two aspects of identity could be strongly interlinked – to seventeenth-century Englishmen a Welshman's royalism was indivisible from his passion for genealogy, his language, and his strange and

---

[20] Accusations against Myddelton in 1647 describe his chapel as containing a railed altar, crucifix, and an organ, and his family worship as encompassing kneeling and bowing. Although some of this can be supported in other sources, the bulk of the material is confined to statements provided by Edward Vaughan, with whom Sir Thomas was involved in a lengthy political, familial and legal feud. 'Myddelton, Sir Thomas (1586–1666)'; Bodleian, Tanner 60, fo. 41; NLW, Wynnstay 90/16/35.

[21] NLW, Wynnstay 90/16/35.

[22] John Harper, 'Music in Worship before 1650', in *A History of Welsh Music*, ed. Trevor Herbert, Martin V. Clarke, and Helen Barlow (Cambridge, 2022), 53–77, at 69–70; William Reynolds, 'Middleton's Household Chapel: Church Music on the Welsh Border in the Seventeenth Century', *Welsh Music History* 4 (2000), 114–15.

[23] NLW, Add MS 468E no 2089.

[24] 'Myddelton, Sir Thomas', 273.

different customs.[25] Myddelton's actions, therefore, are in this article placed alongside his book purchases to build a picture of Sir Thomas and his changing convictions during the crucial period from 1647 to 1666.

Broadening the source base

This article also seeks to broaden the source base by which changes of allegiance are identified and analysed. One of the difficulties of discussing early modern decision-making in general, or an altered political allegiance specifically, is that actions are often the only way by which such a change can be detected, whether by joining a rebellion, travelling to Oxford or London or publishing printed materials declaring a new allegiance. Those who have left behind traces of their decision-making process have done so in commonplace books, letters and diaries, or in their own declarations after the fact.[26] This article will draw from a broader base of source material. Sir Thomas Myddelton may not have produced clear narrative declarations of his changing ideas, but the Chirk archive is a rich and varied one. It is possible out of that archive to construct a picture that, in its complexity and variety, reveals Myddelton's journey away from parliamentarianism. This archive includes the significant collection of detailed financial accounts alongside Myddelton's surviving letters in the collections of his extended family. Financial accounts do not, in general, reveal private thought, but they do show the journeys Myddelton made, the people with whom he socialised, his actions to protect and rebuild his family and home, as well as the material purchases he made. The books, objects and services he paid for reveal much about his political and religious identity, providing a subsumed biography of his later life.[27] The archive also comprises book purchases and library catalogues, wills, legal papers, manuscript narratives, material objects and printed papers.[28] Individually, each facet of this evidence would be of limited use but set carefully together with Myddelton's actions, documented in printed pamphlets, state papers and parliamentary sources, it combines to trace his changing allegiance.

Sir Thomas Myddelton's book purchases are an important part of that picture. He did not significantly annotate his books and there is no pattern of marginalia within his library. Yet the library evidence is still extremely

---

[25] Sarah Ward Clavier, *Royalism, Religion, and Revolution: Wales, 1642–1688* (Martlesham, 2021), chs. 2 and 3.

[26] Kevin Sharpe, *Reading Revolutions: The Politics of Reading in Early Modern England* (New Haven, 2000), esp. chs. 3 and 4.

[27] Just as Suzanna Ivanic has shown how probate inventories and a material approach can be used to reveal the complexities of European religious identities. Sarah Ward Clavier, 'Accounting for Lives: Autobiography and Biography in the Accounts of Sir Thomas Myddelton, 1642–1666', *The Seventeenth Century*, 35 (2020), 453–72; Suzanna Ivanic, *Cosmos and Materiality in Early Modern Prague* (Oxford, 2021).

[28] In this the article responds to a recent call for historians to make more use of books and libraries as source material for assessing wider political, cultural and social trends in the history of Wales. Mary Chadwick, Sarah Ward Clavier and Shaun Evans, 'Introduction: Books and Manuscripts in Wales', *Welsh History Review*, 31 (2022), 1–16, at 14–16.

informative. Benedict and Léchot were correct to say that a private library reveals not a sharply defined picture of its owner's personal intellectual orientation but 'his larger intellectual inheritance and the range of texts he might have used to think with, or against'.[29] Even more pertinent is Mandelbrote's argument that the 'presence of intellectually important or unusual texts, or the latest books, or the relatively expensive or most difficult to obtain, may well shed light on an owner's priorities and choices' is especially pertinent in Myddelton's case. These priorities changed over time, reflecting the quandaries that Myddelton faced, and the decisions that he ultimately made.[30] Lisa Jardine, Anthony Grafton and William Sherman's work on the Elizabethan scholar Gabriel Harvey famously reveals a tendency to read and cogitate before taking action: that he 'studied for action'.[31] Barbara Donagan has shown how the godly Colonel Hutchinson applied himself to an extensive course of reading before concluding that it was right to go to war in 1642, while Kevin Sharpe has used William Drake's reading notebooks to show how 'a seemingly unpromising collection of extracts and commonplaces may document the shifting values and politics of a learned and moderate gentleman for whom the world had turned upside down'. Myddelton legitimated his actions in a similar way to Hutchinson. The timing of, and themes within, Myddelton's recorded purchases give a picture of the material he was using to 'think with', and in that sense provide an insight into his decision-making at a crucial point in his life. Combined with evidence of Myddelton's actions during the 1640s and 1650s, they will be used to reveal his gradual process of political realignment.[32] While one may quibble with the interpretation of individual data points, therefore, it is possible to build up a picture of Myddelton's likely reading when placed alongside his actions. It is the use of the body of evidence as a whole that constructs a persuasive analysis.

Our knowledge of Myddelton's library and reading habits is drawn from several sources. Myddelton required his steward and senior servants to keep detailed financial accounts. Many of these have survived.[33] Myddelton ordered

---

[29] Philip Benedict and Pierre-Olivier Léchot, 'The Library of Élie Bouhéreau', in *Marsh's Library: A Mirror on the World*, ed. Muriel McCarthy and Ann Simmons (Dublin, 2009), 165–84, at 183.

[30] Giles Mandelbrote, 'Personal Owners of Books', in *The Cambridge History of Libraries in Britain and Ireland*, II: *1640–1850*, ed. Giles Mandelbrote and K. A. Manley (Cambridge, 2006), 173–89, at 178.

[31] Lisa Jardine and Anthony Grafton, '"Studied for Action": How Gabriel Harvey Read his Livy', *Past and Present*, 129 (1990), 30–78; Anthony Grafton, Nicholas Popper, and William Sherman (eds.), *Gabriel Harvey and the History of Reading* (2024); Barbara Donagan, 'Casuistry and Allegiance in the English Civil War', in *Writing and Political Engagement in Seventeenth-Century England*, ed. Derek Hirst and Richard Strier (Cambridge, 1999), 89–111, at 90; Sharpe, *Reading Revolutions*, 170–1.

[32] Kevin Sharpe and Kirstie M. McClure, 'Introduction: Discovering the Renaissance Reader', in *Reading, Society, and Politics in Early Modern England*, ed. Kevin Sharpe and Steven N. Zwicker (Cambridge, 2003), 1–37, at 18–23.

[33] They were published privately in the early twentieth century in two volumes by his descendant, W. M. Myddelton. It should be noted that the published accounts are actually composites of many different manuscripts in the Chirk collection, currently held at the National Library of Wales (NLW). There are many more subsequent volumes. W. M. Myddelton (ed.), *Chirk Castle Accounts, A.D. 1605–1666* (St Albans, 1908); W. M. Myddelton (ed.), *Chirk Castle Accounts, 1666–1753* (Manchester, 1931).

books from trusted booksellers, bought them himself when in London, bought whole book collections locally, and used employees, friends and kindred to acquire them or borrow them. In most instances the accounts give prices of these books and, in some entries, provenance information about the books and manuscripts that Myddelton acquired. Secondly, there is the library cata-logue of 1704, compiled within the lifetime of Sir Thomas's grandson, Sir Richard Myddelton. It reveals that in 1704 Chirk Castle library comprised at least 1257 volumes, ranging from British and European history to religious controversy, and from gardening to witchcraft.[34] This makes the Myddelton library relatively small for a family of that status in the early eighteenth cen-tury, when average collections numbered around 3,400.[35]

Clearly there are problems with using library catalogues as evidence of alle-giance or opinion. For one, the presence of a book published in the 1640s is not necessarily an indicator that it was purchased in the year of publication or by a particular individual. Furthermore, the contents of the catalogue may not reflect the whole collection – it might exclude more ephemeral works, books may have been lent out, or be situated outside the library itself.[36] By 1704 the library at Chirk Castle was not the same as when Sir Thomas Myddelton II died in 1666. His son (Sir Thomas the first baronet) pre-deceased him in 1663, but had contributed some books to the library.[37] His grandson Thomas ordered some books from London via his brother Richard, while Richard him-self was an avid reader and purchaser of books and pamphlets, particularly on the politico-religious controversies of the day.[38] A comparison of the accounts, the 1704 catalogue and the modern catalogue of Chirk Castle library makes it clear that many of Sir Thomas II's books were not in the library by 1704, or had been replaced by new editions of the same works.

Despite this, through later accounts and bills it is possible to demonstrate that, although later Myddeltons bought some older books when reading about a particular topic, most of their purchasing was of contemporary mater-ial. Of the 289 books in the 1704 catalogue that had a publication date between 1631 and 1666, only seven can be *proven* to be bought by individuals other than Myddelton. Almost all of Myddelton's purchases were contemporary, showing an interest in the latest news and religious polemic. Only two of the identifi-able books purchased by him had a date of publication more than ten years before their purchase. This indicates a strong probability that most of the books or pamphlets published in the period of his life, particularly those on contemporary topics, were bought by or for Sir Thomas. Book-plate evidence from the modern catalogue can confirm this further, meaning that the 1704

---

[34] NLW, Chirk A 29.

[35] David Pearson, 'The English Private Library in the Seventeenth Century', *The Library*, 7th ser., 13 (2012), 379–99, at 381.

[36] David Pearson, 'Patterns of Book Ownership in Late Seventeenth-Century England', *The Library*, 11 (2010), 139–67, at 143; Mandelbrote, 'Personal Owners of Books', 178.

[37] These included sermons by Donne and Taylor, works by Hammond and Bramhall, playbooks and political pamphlets. NLW, Chirk F 10597; Myddelton (ed.), *Chirk Castle Accounts, A.D. 1605–1666*, 151–60.

[38] NLW, Chirk A 29.

catalogue can be used to draw conclusions concerning Sir Thomas's purchases beyond the Chirk Castle accounts.[39]

Another difficulty is that purchase of a book does not necessarily mean that the reader agreed with the standpoint of the author. In the religious and political crises of the seventeenth century people attempted to gain different vantage points on events, and purchased widely, including material by those with whom they did not agree.[40] They also armed themselves with the arguments of those with whom they disagreed so that they could persuade their interlocutors. This fitted within a tradition of using 'pro' and 'contra' arguments. Again, although it is impossible to avoid this problem completely, we can draw some useful conclusions when combining this evidence with that from other, more direct sources. Thirdly, there is Myddelton's correspondence and that of his steward and family. Although this is not plentiful, it does cast a light on the books that Myddelton particularly valued.

Myddelton's allegiance, religion and reading, 1640–6

Perhaps the greater mystery than Myddelton declaring for the king in 1659 was that he ever fought for Parliament at all. Myddelton, like many other gentlemen, peers and MPs, struggled with the way that events progressed in the Long Parliament. Andrew Hopper argued that it was difficult even to define a side-changing MP because 'so many sought to postpone or avoid taking sides'.[41] In January 1641 Myddelton wrote to his nephew of 'a greate faction against the Bishops for to roote them out', warning that he 'shall heere shortly of some straunge affects'. In the same letter he wrote of the trial of Strafford, saying that 'I feare he will fayle to free himselfe'.[42] The trial of Strafford particularly interested him – he collected St John's arguments concerning Strafford's attainder, Strafford's answers to the questions put to him at trial, Pym's declaration of the high treason and Strafford's speech on the scaffold. Myddelton eagerly awaited news of the trial's commencement and relayed its progress to his nephew.[43] These words and actions seem anomalous for a future parliamentarian commander. He left London in July 1641 after being active on several parliamentary committees, an action which has been ascribed by J. Gwynn Williams and Gwyn Thomas to unease at the radical direction in which the Parliament was headed.[44] While it is more plausible that his decision was at least partly caused by his wife's severe illness and his daughter

---

[39] National Trust, National Trust Collections Database, http://www.nationaltrustcollections.org.uk (accessed 4 June 2024).

[40] Elisabeth Leedham-Green and David McKitterick, 'Ownership: Private and Public Libraries', in *The Cambridge History of the Book in Britain, Volume IV: 1557-1695*, ed. John Barnard, D.F. McKenzie and Maureen Bell (Cambridge, 2002), 323–38, at 324; David Pearson, 'The English Private Library in the Seventeenth Century', *The Library*, 13 (2002), 379–99, at 384.

[41] Hopper, *Turncoats*, 42.

[42] NLW, Llewenni 175.

[43] NLW, Chirk A 29; Llewenni 179.

[44] Thomas, 'Sir Thomas Myddelton II', 31; Gwynn Williams, 'Myddelton, Sir Thomas'.

Elizabeth's wedding in December 1641, it is significant that he did not return for a whole six months.[45]

Myddelton's return at the time of the Irish Rebellion might be explained by anti-popery or fear of the Irish Rebellion having an impact on Wales.[46] He sat on the parliamentary committee set up to investigate Catholicism in Wales, which even before the Irish Rebellion was concerned with the question of whether there was a 'welsh armie of papists' ready to take over the principality.[47] He owned several pamphlets on the events of the Irish rebellion, including some published a few years after its outbreak, indicating an ongoing interest in Irish events and the interpretation of them.[48] The North-East Welsh gentry had, in general, a remarkably relaxed attitude to the Catholic threat discussed in Parliament, but Myddelton had not spent his formative years in that environment, growing up in London in a Puritan mercantile household.[49] Furthermore many of his English friends and relatives were pre-occupied with the potential consequences of the rebellion in Ireland. If there were initial qualms, the Irish Rebellion may well have settled them. At the same time, a kinsman of Myddelton's wrote to him asking that he raise the matter of Church government in Parliament: specifically the way that the Church under Laud was 'intermedlinge with lay commissiones & Matters', a course which he saw as a 'vice unreformed'.[50] That Myddelton agreed with this assessment may be inferred from his later attempts to keep control of his own presentation rights and tithes.

It is possible that Myddelton's hesitation ultimately meant that others decided his allegiance. Given that Myddelton kept his parliamentary seat until Pride's Purge of 1648, it seems unlikely that he signed the pro-episcopal and proto-royalist North Welsh petitions to the Parliament in 1641 or the king at York in 1642.[51] He made no other positive signs of royalist leanings. By June 1642 Richard Lloyd of Esclusham was able to write that Myddelton was 'the single exception' to an otherwise uniform royalist allegiance among the gentry of North-East Wales.[52] That said, Myddelton may not even have been decided by June 1642. If his regional adversary Edward Vaughan's accusations of the later

---

[45] Myddelton did receive permission to go home to Chirk on 24 July 1641, but was back in London eight months later – he was one of a small number of MPs to work with the Lords on matters such as the petition of the Merchant Strangers in March 1642. *Journal of the House of Commons: Volume 2, 1640-1643* (1802), 222, 499; Thomas, 'Sir Thomas Myddelton II', 31; NLW, MS 5390D, 49–55.

[46] Thomas, 'Sir Thomas Myddelton II', 32; Dodd, 'Civil War in East Denbighshire', 47.

[47] Wallace Notestein (ed.), *The Journal of Sir Simonds D'Ewes* (New Haven, 1923), 325.

[48] For example, Sir John Temple's *History of the Irish Rebellion* (1646) and *A History of the Late Insurrection in Ireland* (Bristol, 1644). NLW, Chirk A 29.

[49] Ward Clavier, *Royalism, Religion, and Revolution*, 115–26.

[50] NLW, Chirk E 5604.

[51] Sir Simonds D'Ewes provides a number of examples of those who were punished by the Commons for being involved in pro-episcopacy or 'scandalous' petitions, for example Sir Edward Dering and the Kentish petition. Anne Steele Young and Vernon F. Snow (eds.), *Private Journals of the Long Parliament, vol. 2: 7 March to 1 June 1642* (1987), 249; British Library (BL), Harley 1980, fo. 76v; Anon., *The Humble Petition of Many Hundred Thousands, inhabiting within the Thirteen Shires of Wales* (1642).

[52] Dodd, 'Civil War in East Denbighshire', 48.

1640s and early 1650s are given credit, Myddelton either rejected calls by pro-parliamentarian individuals in September 1642 to establish Chirk Castle as a safe base for parliamentarians in a hostile area, or actively gave up the castle to the king and promised to serve him after Edgehill.[53] By December 1642, however, Myddelton's parliamentarian allegiance was well known enough to prompt action by his royalist neighbours. An oath was proffered to Myddelton's tenants, in English and Welsh, that bound them to oppose him and the parliamentarian armies as 'Rebells now in Armes against his Majestie and his Loyall subiects and the peace and Lawes of this kingdome'. Those swearing to this oath promised not to communicate any information to Myddelton or to aid him in any way, as well as fighting for the king. The oath was specifically designed, it seems, to prevent the traditional loyalty of a tenant to his landlord.[54]

Myddelton's official response to the oath, printed in London in 1644, was predictably one of outrage. His arguments against the oath are, perhaps, instructive. The priority given throughout the tract to anti-papist arguments confirms that this was a primary preoccupation in Sir Thomas Myddelton's thinking. Sir Thomas decried the encouragement given to English and Irish papists because of the oath. A second element points towards the personal hurt and offence felt by its protagonist, as the printed tract denied treachery, arguing that Sir Thomas's forces were 'neither Traitorously nor Rebelliously Raised, but have His Majesties Royall Authority for their warrant'. He described the oath itself as 'unjust, deceitfull and impossible to be performed'.[55] On 15 January 1643, shortly after the oath was tendered and Myddelton had responded, Chirk Castle was seized by royalist forces and all plate and wealth sold to fund a new royalist regiment.[56]

By early 1643 Myddelton was committed to raising a parliamentarian army. He was appointed Major-General of the five North Welsh counties on 26 May 1643 and on 7 June 1643 he took the new Protestation and the Oath of Covenant.[57] In February 1643 he and his fellow parliamentarian commanders Sir George Booth and Sir William Brereton were indicted of high treason by a Cheshire Grand Jury 'after the Battell at Edg-Hill'. The indictment described those accused as being 'seduced and moved by the instigation of the Divell, utterly withdrawing the love, true, and due obedience' to the king, and 'with all their power striving the common peace and tranquillity of this Kingdom of England to disturbe' by raising a force at Nantwich on

---

[53] No evidence survives for either of these accusations, though the former fits better with Myddelton's movements and with the easy seizure of the castle than the latter. NLW, Wynnstay 90/16/35.

[54] BL, Add MS 46399A fo. 78; Warwickshire Record Office, CR2017/TP646.

[55] *A declaration published by Sir Thomas Middleton, Knight, Serjeant-Major-Generall, and Vice-Admirall for the sixe counties of North-Wales: setting forth the illegallity and incongruity of a pernicious oath and protestation, imposed upon many peaceable subjects within the said counties.* (1644), 4–5.

[56] Norman Tucker, *Denbighshire Officers in the Civil War* (Wrexham, 1964), 71; Phillips, *Memoirs of the Civil War in Wales*, 164–5; Dodd, 'Civil War in East Denbighshire', 50; Robert Williams (ed.), 'An Account of the Civil War in North Wales', *Archaeologia Cambrensis*, 1 (1846), 33–42, at 34.

[57] Myddelton took the original Protestation on 3 May 1641. *Journal of the House of Commons*, II, 132–3; *Journal of the House of Commons*, III, 105, 119.

20 January 1643.[58] This and the loyalty oath angered and humiliated Myddelton, who was as sensitive as other provincial officers about his reputation in London and further afield. Being described both as a traitor and being indicted in such a way was highly dishonourable.[59] A warrant was issued by the king for his arrest on 16 June, so for all his hesitation Myddelton risked his reputation, liberty, wealth and life in the parliamentarian cause.[60] It seems that the royalist gentry's reaction to Myddelton's hesitation, his fears about support for Catholicism within the royalist party and the seizure of his estate had pushed him into a commitment to Parliament, regardless of how limited his enthusiasm might have been for some of the policies and aims of the Long Parliament.

Once appointed as commander of the parliamentarian forces in North Wales Myddelton prosecuted the war as fully as he was able, leading to criticisms by local clergymen, gentry and chroniclers of his and Brereton's troops' behaviour in Wrexham and Hawarden in 1643 and 1645.[61] Welsh preachers, including the radical Morgan Llwyd, travelled with his forces, 'able to preach in the welch tongue'.[62] To all appearances, therefore, the Myddelton of 1643–5 was a committed parliamentarian and, at the very least, a promoter of radical Protestant religion. His closest associates at that time were Myddelton's steward Watkin Kyffin, and his brother-in-law Colonel Thomas Mytton. Myddelton's war efforts were closely associated with those of the Cheshire-based parliamentarian officer Sir William Brereton, another fact that has led to a more radical reputation than he deserves.[63] Brereton was zealously godly before the First Civil War, sitting on a number of committees on religion in the Long Parliament and calling for the abolition of episcopacy in a 1641 petition. Their association happened largely because Myddelton was often forced to campaign (not to mention recruit and raise finance) outside Wales due to the strength of Welsh royalism until the latter stages of the war.[64]

---

[58] The warrant was signed by Richard Grosvenor and John Werden, one of whom would marry into the Myddelton family and the other who would fight with Sir Thomas in 1659. Anon., *A Horrible and Bloody Plot to Murder Sir Thomas Fairfax, Sir William Brereton, Sir Thomas Middleton, Colonell Moore …* (1646), 12.

[59] Hopper, *Turncoats*, 159–60.

[60] NLW, MS Llanfair-Brynodol 53.

[61] Even contemporary accounts comment on Myddelton's lack of support within the borders of Wales. Chirk A 12; *Journal of the House of Commons*, III: *1643-1644* (1802), 320; BL, Harley MS 2125 fos. 67, 135v; Thomas Carte (ed.), *A Collection of Original Letters and Papers …* (2 vols.; 1739), I, 29–34; D. R. Thomas (ed.), *Y Cwtta Cyfarwydd* (1883), 216; BL, Add MS 33373; Dore, *Letterbooks of Sir William Brereton, I* (1984), 239.

[62] This has been seen as another sign of Myddelton's Puritanism, though it appears it was at least partly the scheme of interested Welsh Puritan MPs who wanted to 'facilitate the difficult worke you haue in hand of reducing that countrey to due obedience'. *Journal of the House of Commons*, III, 565–6; NLW, MS 11439D, fo. 23.

[63] Brereton and Myddelton are frequently mentioned in the same printed letters to parliament, in correspondence, as well as in the Journal of the House of Commons. Their collaboration is further evident from Brereton's letterbooks. R. N. Dore (ed.), *The Letterbooks of Sir William Brereton, I*; R. N. Dore, 'Sir Thomas Myddleton's Attempted Conquest of Powys, 1644-5', *Montgomeryshire Collections*, 57 (1963 for 1961-2), 91–118.

[64] The National Archives (TNA), SP 28/346; NLW, Chirk F 12543.

Despite the accusations of royalist neighbours and Myddelton's association with Brereton, however, Geoffrey Smith has described Sir Thomas Myddelton as a 'lukewarm parliamentarian' who sent information to the royalist spy John Barwick even while he was an active military commander.[65] Between the years 1641 and 1645 Barwick identified Myddelton as a spy or informer: one of those who 'set themselves up for reformers, but had not yet wholly imbib'd all their madness'.[66] Barwick's account is not straightforwardly reliable, and there is no other supporting evidence to substantiate the claim that Myddelton was, from 1642, at least hedging his bets. Myddelton's connections with Barwick and the future Charles II were undeniable from the early 1650s onwards, but limited evidence survives of them before that point aside from Myddelton's connections with the royalist Eversfields of Denn. Smith's argument has much to support it in the very early 1640s. Myddelton does not appear to have been a political or religious zealot and was comparatively late to commit to Parliament's side.[67] Barwick's statement concerning Myddelton's moderation is very plausible. Yet Myddelton did fight determinedly in both England and Wales against friends, kin and neighbours. He may have been reluctant, but this did not result in any quarter being given to the royalist 'enemy', nor criticisms of Parliament other than those relating to funding and recruitment.

Myddelton's reading in the early 1640s supports the picture of him as a moderate. As with any gentleman news enthusiast, he sought out contemporaneous information, and received news by personal letters from a range of sources.[68] At the Restoration Myddelton paid for his collection of the Interregnum acts and proclamations of Parliament to be bound but he also evidently collected the king's declarations from 1640 to 1643.[69] The existence among his papers of two manuscript narratives concerning the conduct of the Civil War itself, one depicting Myddelton's own part in the war in a fairly unflattering way, supports a view of Myddelton processing and considering the conflict in which he had been involved. The second narrative, anonymous but from its content possibly written by Myddelton himself, offers a defence of the author's lack of success in Wales, and begs pardon for his 'weakness'. Arguing that 'all slaves to the gentrie and the gentrie all slaves to the king; and scar[ce] knowe any other God', as well as that 'as for there Religion; they cry God and [the] king; and will nott heere of any other way of salvation', it is a document that decries an emotional choice of allegiance while expressing doubt at the conduct of the war.[70]

---

[65] Geoffrey Smith, *Royalist Agents, Conspirators and Spies: Their Role in the British Civil Wars, 1640-1660* (Farnham, 2011), p. 43; Jason McElligott, 'Barwick, John (1612–1664), Dean of St Paul's', *Oxford Dictionary of National Biography*, Jan. 2004, https://www.oxforddnb.com/view/10.1093/ref:odnb/9780198614128.001.0001/odnb-9780198614128-e-1613 (accessed 4 June 2024).

[66] Peter Barwick, *The Life of the Reverend Dr. John Barwick, D.D* ... (1724), 48–9.

[67] NLW, Wynnstay 90/16/35; Wynnstay 90/16/49; Wynnstay 90/16/54; Wynnstay 90/16/98.

[68] Including Sir Robert Napier and John Edwards. His steward Watkin Kyffin also received printed news and letters of news from friends, which alongside almanacks and 'small books' appear to have circulated at Chirk. NLW, Chirk F 12740; Chirk E 4184.

[69] The Chirk account books are unpaginated. References to particular entries and purchases will be identified by date. NLW, MS 6372E: 21 Apr. 1661; Chirk A 29.

[70] NLW Chirk A 16; NLW, Chirk F 13636.

He bought copies of important speeches or pamphlets relating to events of national importance. He was also concerned with the issue of episcopacy and the prayer book, buying several pamphlets from either side of the religious divide.[71] Myddelton was concerned about the question of the army's role in politics at the end of the First Civil War, and owned tracts by the regicide John Cook and the Presbyterian MP John Corbett.[72] His ownership of two of the Welsh royalist Judge David Jenkins's publications regarding the legality of Parliament trying royalists for treason indicates that he was perhaps wrestling with the legalistic arguments facing the nation towards the end of the Civil War (including the legitimacy of Parliament's very authority). Myddelton owned rebuttals to Jenkins as well, his purchases falling on either side of the argument.[73] In all these issues Myddelton owned material by authors on either side of each debate. These practices are in line with many gentlemen of his period and aided in understanding the positions of both opposing sides (whether to come to a decision or to sharpen one's rhetorical edge in preparation for debate). This was shortly to change as Myddelton's political and religious position shifted.

Changing allegiance? 1647–59

Sir Thomas Myddelton was eager to resign his command following Parliament's Self-Denying Ordinance of 1645, despite attempts by his officers to gain an exemption for him. Forced to choose between sitting as an MP and retaining his command, he chose the former.[74] To some extent this would be unsurprising even for a more ideologically committed parliamentarian – his campaigns had been marred with financial problems, recruitment difficulties and a failure to persuade his Cheshire-based allies to undertake the scale of campaign Myddelton wished for in Wales. After spending July 1645 to June 1646 in London, he returned home to Chirk Castle a couple of months after it was surrendered to his eldest daughter.[75] From that point forward Myddelton situated himself either in Chirk, engaging in repairs to the Castle and socialising with neighbours, or at Parliament in London. From 1648 he was barely present in Westminster.

The earliest accusations of crypto-royalism date from 1647. Edward Vaughan, newly elected MP for Montgomeryshire, accused Myddelton of long-standing equivocation and split loyalties, corruption and financial greed.[76] Although Vaughan's accusations were part of a wider regional factional and

---

[71] These included tracts by Lord Falkland, Edward Symmons and Joseph Caryl. Lord Falkland, *Draught of a Speech: Concerning Episcopacy* (1644); E. Symmons, *Scripture Vindicated from the misinterpretations of Stephen Marshal's Sermon* (Oxford, 1644); Joseph Caryl, *Sermon on James 4:8* (1646); NLW, Chirk A 29.

[72] NLW, Chirk A 29.

[73] William Epstein, 'Judge David Jenkins and the Great Civil War', *The Journal of Legal History*, 3 (1982), 187–221, at 193; NLW, Chirk A 29.

[74] 'Myddelton, Sir Thomas', 271; Dore, *Letterbooks of Sir William Brereton*, I, 335–6.

[75] 'Myddelton, Sir Thomas', 271.

[76] NLW, Wynnstay 90/16/35.

kin-based feud, some of his points are substantiated elsewhere. Myddelton's tendencies to amass lands and money had been commented on by others, and his indecisiveness is well-documented. The evidence compiled by Edward Vaughan against Myddelton also included allegations of poor leadership (at best) and cowardice (at worst), standing at a distance from the fight at Montgomery Castle in 1646, failing to go to the aid of his inferior officers, and ultimately that he 'ranne away and would neuer turne head and faight'.[77] Vaughan's witnesses seem either to be Vaughan kin or associates, and the allegations were not recorded outside these papers, but if credited they could contribute to a picture of a man reluctant to risk his life for a cause to which he was only moderately devoted. Parliamentarian fears about Myddelton's loyalty may not have been roused by Vaughan's accusations – no definite outcome was recorded to the enquiry, and it seems neither man's career was damaged by the dispute – but from 1648 onwards Myddelton was suspected of fraternising with royalist agents and delinquents.[78] While Myddelton's earlier allegiance may have been determined by exigency and circumstance, his move towards a committed form of royalism was gradual, arrived at through an initial flirtation with royalist agents and a slow acculturation both to royalist society and royalist and to episcopalian ideological principles.

The year 1647 was the point at which the level of non-engagement by the traditional gentry rulers of North-East Wales became apparent, and when the religious radicalism of the new North Welsh government was established. Sir Thomas returned to spend the majority of his time at Chirk, and his accounts show an increasing level of engagement with local (royalist) gentry society, either by socialising or by lending money.[79] In relation to North Welsh government, Myddelton and his neighbour Sir John Trevor's stewards found few of sufficient status and willingness to become JPs, and were forced to resort to either recent arrivals or those of a lower social status.[80] When Myddelton returned to Wales from London it would have been apparent that the best of North-East Welsh gentry society refused to acknowledge the legitimacy or authority of the government with which he was involved. These included local families with whom the Myddeltons had socialised before the First Civil War, including the Broughtons and Eytons, both of which were fervent royalists.[81] The only other family that participated consistently in parliamentarian politics were the Trevors of Trevalyn, with whom the Myddeltons had been feuding since before the Civil Wars.[82] Myddelton's disillusionment with Parliament and its forces may have been increased by the loss of his goods, taken perhaps mistakenly from Chirk by parliamentarian troops in 1647 to Holt Castle when Chirk was surrendered by the royalist forces, and pursued for some time after.[83]

[77] Ibid.; Wynnstay 90/16/49; Wynnstay 90/16/54; Wynnstay 90/16/98.

[78] 'Myddelton, Sir Thomas', 272.

[79] Including Sir Evan Lloyd, Sir Richard Grosvenor, Sir John Owen, Sir Roger Mostyn, and John Parry of Cwm, all royalists throughout the Interregnum. NLW, Chirk F 12550.

[80] NLW, Chirk F 6087; Flintshire Record Office, D/G/3275 no. 95.

[81] NLW, MS 5390D, 50–5.

[82] Sir John T. Lloyd (ed.), A Dictionary of Welsh Biography Down to 1940 (1959), 981–3.

[83] NLW, Chirk F 6728.

From 1651 Myddelton's move towards royalism and a more robust form of episcopalianism accelerated. Before 1651 he was still trusted by the Interregnum authorities to provide defence against royalist plots. But since late 1649 Myddelton had been viewed by the royalists as a plausible 'Presbyterian' to turn to their side, a commission being issued to Roger Whitley, the royalist exile and agent, to convert Myddelton to royalism. The warrant offered indemnity against Myddelton's former actions, offering that if the three men identified 'will returne to theire dutye', they would also receive favour, honours, offices and rewards as appropriate.[84] He was contacted again in 1650, most probably by Sir John Owen, and by 1651 rumours circulated widely about his allegiance.[85] The Council of State certainly agreed. It appears that Myddelton and his son were arrested March 1651 alongside many prominent Cheshire royalists and Lord Herbert on suspicion of corresponding with the king and the Scots.[86]

A letter from Charles II to Sir Thomas proves that this suspicion was justified. Writing on 17 August 1651, Charles explained that 'my lord of derby hath acquainted me with your affections' and asked Myddelton to 'declare & stirr for me', sending 'speedy intelligence of the condition of Northwales'.[87] This letter resulted in the arrest of the messenger by Myddelton, possibly a sign that the threat of garrison and financial ruin had had an impact.[88] A garrison was placed in Chirk Castle. It was only removed after Myddelton promised to appear before the Committee when summoned, took the Engagement, and made a payment of a surety of £10,000.[89] Nevertheless, after the earl of Derby's execution in 1651 following his involvement in the Second Civil War, Myddelton provided financial support for Derby's chaplain, Christopher Pashley, and, it appears, allowed him to stay at Chirk Castle.[90] Pashley preached there in 1658.[91] Evidence within Myddelton's accounts suggest that his sympathy was certainly straying far away from the government.

This is substantiated in Sir Thomas Myddelton's social life and connections. Myddelton married his daughters Anne into the royalist Herbert family of Chirbury in 1650, Christian into the Grosvenors of Eaton in Cheshire in 1654,

---

[84] David Underdown, *Royalist Conspiracy in England, 1649-60* (New Haven, 1960), 26; BL, Egerton MS 2542, fos. 14–15.

[85] Owen and Myddelton corresponded in summer 1650, and Myddelton apparently met with and made a payment to Owen at his lodgings in January 1651. NLW, Clenennau MS 653; NLW, Chirk F 12550: 31 Jan. 1651.

[86] This groups Sir Thomas and his son with Lord Herbert of Chirbury and one of the Cholmondeleys, families with whom he was connected by ties of sociability and marriage. *Sixth Report of the Royal Commission on Historical Manuscripts* (1877), 434.

[87] TNA, SP 18/16 fo. 34.

[88] NLW, Chirk E 38; Bulstrode Whitelock, *Memorials of the English Affairs from the Beginning of the Reign of Charles the First to the Happy Restoration of Charles the Second* (1853), 335; Underdown, *Royalist Conspiracy*, 50.

[89] Myddelton evidently complained about the speed with which the garrison was withdrawn, and other 'contempts and abuses' made by the officers garrisoned there. TNA, SP 25/65 fo. 155; SP 25/96 fo. 211; SP 25/96 fo. 183.

[90] NLW, Chirk F 12572: 14 Sept. 1654, 22 Sept. 1655; Chirk F 12551: 2 Jan. 1656, 21 Aug. 1656.

[91] NLW, MS 6372E: 29 Mar. 1658.

and Sarah into the Wynns of Gwydir in 1655. He continued to socialise with royalist stalwarts such as Sir Edward Broughton, Kenrick Eyton and Colonel William Price of Rhiwlas, building ties which would be activated in Booth's Rebellion.[92] Indeed along with Colonel Roger Whitley, Kenrick Eyton was engaged in royalist espionage, travelling between the Continent and Wales.[93] Myddelton's visits to Eyton, as well as Eyton's regular mailings of news publications and gifts of salmon, are surely significant.[94] At the same time, Myddelton's relationship with the royalist Eversfields of Denn became closer. This was a long-established kin relationship (Lady Eversfield was Sir Thomas's sister-in-law), but has additional implications in this period because of the involvement of the Laudian royalist spy and networker Dr John Barwick, who was employed as the Eversfields' chaplain.[95] Myddelton's financial accounts show that he stayed with the Eversfields in 1651 and 1652, and that Lady Eversfield returned the visit in 1655, bringing Barwick with her. Barwick visited on his own in 1656, and communicated with Myddelton subsequently by letter, sending news pamphlets enclosed.[96]

The 1650s, therefore, show Myddelton drawing progressively closer to royalist spies, royalist families and royalist plots. It is surely no coincidence that in 1652 Myddelton's son Charles 'bought 2 books for himself and Joseph Myddelton to learn cipher'.[97] The Protectorate was (probably correctly) afraid of Myddelton's potential involvement in royalist plots, and his social milieu became one that was dominated by royalist supporters. He was contacted by some of the most prominent royalist agents in Wales and the West, to the point that Charles II appears to have been convinced of his loyalty. Sir Thomas Myddelton's actions in this period give the impression, not of an opponent of the Stuarts being reluctantly persuaded to support them for convenience, but of one being gradually acculturated and groomed for royalist support. This is supported in the changed nature of his reading.

Myddelton, like the parliamentarian Colonel Hutchinson, appears to have read extensively when in the process of changing his allegiance, legitimating his actions through his interactions with his books.[98] If conscience was 'central' to the Civil War itself, it was no less important in the Interregnum.[99] Whereas Myddelton's reading in the early to mid-1640s was notably balanced, spanning both sides of a given debate, from 1647 onwards it became more concentrated on royalist and episcopalian texts. From 1651 Myddelton regularly purchased pro-episcopacy and royalist tracts, without the balance of those in favour of

---

[92] NLW, Chirk F 12550: 10 Jun. 1657; Chirk F 12551: 20 Feb. 1655, 25 Nov. 1655; 4 Jul. 1656.

[93] Nadine Akkerman, *Invisible Agents: Women and Espionage in Seventeenth-Century Britain* (Oxford, 2018).

[94] For example, NLW, Chirk F 12551: 4 July 1656, 10 Sept. 1656; 3 Oct. 1656; 26 Oct. 1656; 20 Dec. 1656.

[95] McElligott, 'Barwick, John (1612–1664)'; Chirk E 1208.

[96] Myddelton (ed.), *Chirk Castle Accounts, A.D. 1605–1666*, p. 61; NLW Chirk F 12572: 23 Sept. 1652, 4 Oct. 1652; Chirk F 12551: 20 Oct. 1656, 22 Dec. 1656.

[97] NLW, Chirk F 12572: 4 Oct. 1652.

[98] Donagan, 'Casuistry and Allegiance', 90.

[99] *Ibid.*, 92.

the regime –even though these pro-government texts would have been more widely numerous in the light of government censorship efforts. On its own this is not damning evidence of a move towards a change in allegiance. Yet set alongside Myddelton's actions and the opinion of other commentators (both royalist and parliamentarian) in the same period the evidence is more compelling. Unlike some of his Presbyterian contemporaries, Myddelton's doubts appear to have begun before the Regicide.

Myddelton increasingly purchased texts by royalist writers in a way that indicates that he was trying to locate himself within a royalist spectrum. In the period 1648 to 1658 Myddelton bought many royalist works, including tracts by John Bramhall, Thomas Fuller and Sir Robert Filmer. Within these works there is a notably strong theme relating to the maintenance of order and the prevention of chaos, and a question of where legitimate authority rested. The moderate Bramhall argued that political power was 'conferred by God for the purpose of securing the order, stability, and general well-being of human society'. Monarchy was the divinely ordained form of government.[100] He did not deny the problem of regal tyranny but saw popular or revolutionary tyranny as more dangerous, decrying absolutism in any form.[101] Fuller's attempts to reconcile the warring parties, alongside his hatred of civil war as 'like the heat of a feaver, dangerous and destructive of religion', was no doubt attractive to Myddelton. Fuller's support for a balanced constitution of monarchy and parliament may explain Myddelton's ownership of at least six of Fuller's works.[102]

Myddelton's ownership of Arthur Wilson's *History of Great Britain*, critical of the court as corrupt and tending to impair the judgement of a king, supports a sense of a critical moderate, as does his ownership of Edward Gee's *Plea for Non-Subscribers*, a Presbyterian minister's argument against swearing the Oath of Engagement as it conflicted with the existing Solemn League, which swore to protect the life and person of the king. Gee's work made a distinction between the Rump's (usurped) authority and legitimate authority.[103] The collection also included Sir Henry Vane's *Healing Questions* and James Harrington's *Oceana*, notable republican approaches to the question of government and authority, Thomas Hobbes's *De cive*, Philip Hunton's *Treatise of Monarchy*, Thomas White's *The Grounds of Obedience and Government* and Nathaniel Bacon's *Historical Discourse*.[104]

---

[100] John Sanderson, 'Serpent-Salve, 1643: The Royalism of John Bramhall', *Journal of Ecclesiastical History*, 25 (1974), 1–14, at 3.

[101] *Ibid.*, 6.

[102] W. B. Patterson, 'Fuller, Thomas (1607/8–1661)', *Oxford Dictionary of National Biography*, Sept. 2004, https://www.oxforddnb.com/view/10.1093/ref:odnb/9780198614128.001.0001/odnb-9780198614128-e-10236 (accessed 4 June 2024); Bernard Hamilton, 'An Anglican View of the Crusades: Thomas Fuller's *The Historie of the Holy Warre*, *Studies in Church History*, 49 (2013), 121–31, at 128.

[103] Graham Parry, 'Wilson, Arthur (bap. 1595, d. 1652), historian', *Oxford Dictionary of National Biography*, Sept. 2004, https://www.oxforddnb.com/view/10.1093/ref:odnb/9780198614128.001.0001/odnb-9780198614128-e-29640 (accessed 4 June 2024); Edward Vallance, *Revolutionary England and the National Covenant: State Oaths, Protestantism and the Political Nation* (Woodbridge, 2005), 163–5.

[104] NLW, Chirk A 29.

A second theme within Myddelton's political reading is that of the desire for a peaceful and orderly society. He collected many of Grotius's books, including *De Jure Belli ac Pacis* in 1652, and *Prolegomena* in 1655, as well as those by Filmer, Ussher, and several by Bishop Robert Sanderson – including his 'Lectures on the Obligation of an Oath'.[105] Tracts including the exiled royalist Sir Charles Dallison's *Royalists' Defence* again deal with a sense of lawlessness, of the world being turned upside down, and the absence of settled ways.[106] Myddelton bought books on wars in other parts of Europe, including one on the civil wars of Spain and the Netherlands, Jean-Nicolas de Parival's *The History of this Iron Age* (1656) which examined memorable battles and sieges across Europe, and Thomas Fuller's *The Historie of Holy Warre* (1651).[107] These sat alongside the works of royalist poets and writers such as James Howell.

Myddelton was purchasing these books in a period when his financial accounts show him taking active steps towards open royalism. His public and private acts support the impression of a man troubled by the direction of politics, generally supportive of a monarchy, and anxious about the impact of war and disorder upon the country. This description could clearly be applied to many gentlemen in the Interregnum, especially those who had a lukewarm attachment to either parliamentarianism or royalism, but combined with his flirtation with plotting and his communication with royalist spies it does indicate a thoughtful move from one stance to another. This was combined with an even stronger move towards the purchase of episcopalian texts.

Religiously, too, Myddelton appeared to be moving towards an episcopalian-royalist stance. In contrast to his political allegiance, there is much more evidence in his book collection for this than in his public or private actions. The evidence that does survive of his religious opinions in the later 1640s and 1650s suggests an increased sympathy with episcopalian clergy. From the early 1650s Myddelton supported ejected clergymen. He made financial payments to support them and their families, and paid their sons' tuition at Oxford. The accounts show at least nine clergymen whom Sir Thomas supported in this way, many with royalist connections.[108] Although the former rector of Chirk, Robert Lloyd, had tendered the royalist loyalty oath, he and his whole family received financial and legal support from Myddelton.[109]

---

[105] Myddelton also bought Grotius's *Catechism*, and his *On the Truth of the Christian Religion*, as well as a work described in his accounts as 'Authority', all in 1655. NLW, Chirk F 12572: 3 Aug. 1652; Chirk F 12551: 22 Oct. 1655.

[106] Andrew Lacey, 'The Cult of King Charles the Martyr: The Rise and Fall of a Political Theology, ca. 1640–1859' (Ph.D. thesis, University of Leicester, 1999), 29.

[107] NLW, Chirk F 12551: 15 Mar. 1656; Chirk A 29.

[108] Namely Humphrey Jones of Llangollen, Humphrey Wynn of Oswestry, Christopher Pashley, Mr Rowland Owen 'late minister of Wrexham', Mr Jones of Bettws Abergele, Evan Lloyd of Ysceifiog, Dr Lloyd of Ruthin, Thomas Heilin, and William Evans, 'a poore sequestred minister of south wales'. Myddelton (ed.), *Chirk Castle Accounts, A.D. 1605–1666*, 66–8, 140; NLW, Chirk F 12550: 13 Apr. 1657; Chirk F 12551: 13 Oct. 1655; Chirk F 12552: 9 Dec. 1653, 27 Aug. 1657, 9 Nov. 1657; Chirk F 12572: 14 Sept. 1654; NLW MS 6372E: 1 Apr. 1659.

[109] For example, NLW, Chirk F 12551: 20 Apr. 1656; Chirk F 12572: 8 Apr. 1653; Chirk F 12553: 20 Jul. 1661.

From 1653 Myddelton's private chaplain was Richard Wilson, the deprived clergyman of Holy Trinity Church, Chester. He was a royalist who had ministered during the siege of Chester, for which he was deprived by the parliamentarian authorities.[110] Myddelton sent financial support to Samuel Jones, a scholar at Jesus College from the Chirk area who refused to submit to the parliamentary visitation of 1648, replying on being asked to submit to Parliament that 'As farre forth as you have power from the Kinge I doe submitt', an act of open defiance.[111] Furthermore, Myddelton took the opportunity of a trip to London to have his old Prayer Book re-bound.[112] While we can never know the extent to which Myddelton used his copy, Parliament's ban on the Book of Common Prayer in 1645 made this re-binding a clear political act.

Myddelton's reading in the 1650s focused strongly on theological works – specifically those of Henry Hammond, Jeremy Taylor and John Cosin. His accounts show that he purchased at least fifteen of Hammond's works and seven of Taylor's between 1651 and 1659.[113] He collected works by Thomas Pierce, Robert Sanderson, and theological works by Grotius, Thomas Fuller, John Ferriby, Richard Sherlock, Laurence Womack and William Langley, as well as several anonymous pro-Prayer Book pamphlets.[114] Many of these books were by ejected clergymen acting as chaplains to royalist families. These authors were mostly defenders of episcopalian orthodoxy, and taken together indicate a distinct leaning towards a very different spirituality than Myddelton has previously been credited with. Hammond, Taylor, Bramhall and their colleagues attempted to promote episcopalian ideals, writing on a wide range of subjects and defending their ideas against Presbyterians, radical

---

[110] Wilson was living at Cefn-y-Wern, a Myddelton property near Chirk from 1653. M. A. Everett (ed.), *Calendar, Committee for Compounding: Part 3* (1891), 2122; NLW, Chirk F 12552: 10 Aug. 1657; Chirk F 12572: 21 Apr. 1655; Myddelton (ed.), *Chirk Castle Accounts, A.D. 1605–1666*, 40, 43.

[111] Though Samuel Jones later became a leading dissenter, his stance in 1648 appears to have been royalist. Richards sees this as evidence of Myddelton's magnanimity in supporting a royalist while being a Presbyterian and parliamentarian, but Myddelton paid his exhibition before and after Jones's conversion to radicalism. NLW, Chirk F 12548: 12 May 1648; Chirk F 12549: 18 Apr. 1649, 8 Nov. 1649, 14 Feb. 1650, 28 Nov. 1650; 6 Sept. 1652, 10 Oct. 1652; Chirk F 12550: 18 Apr. 1649, 28 Nov. 1650, 14 Feb. 1651; Montagu Burrows, *The Register of the Visitors of the University of Oxford, from A.D. 1647 to A.D. 1658* (1881); D. R. L. Jones, 'Fame and Obscurity: Samuel Jones of Brynllywarch', *Journal of Welsh Religious History*, 1 (1993), 41–65, at 46–7; Thomas Richards, 'The Puritan Visitation of Jesus College, Oxford, and the Principalship of Dr Michael Roberts (1648–1657)', *Transactions of the Honourable Society of Cymmrodorion* (1924), 1–111.

[112] Myddelton bought a new prayer book in 1663. NLW, Chirk F 12572: 7 Sept. 1652; NLW, Chirk F 5949: 21 Dec. 1663.

[113] It is possible that he owned more – several of the entries in Myddelton's accounts only refer to books being sent to Myddelton by friends, and these are not itemised. Hammond: NLW, Chirk F 5932: 19 Sept. 1661; Chirk F 12572: 6 Jul. 1653, 22 May 1653, 28 Nov. 1654, 1 Feb. 1654/5, 31 Aug. 1655; Chirk F 12551: 22 Oct. 1655, 15 Mar. 1655/6, 22 Dec. 1656; 31 Mar. 1656; Chirk F 12552: 20 Feb. 1656/7; NLW MS 6372E: 4 Jun. 1659. Taylor: Chirk F 12549: 28 Aug. 1650; Chirk F 12551: 22 Oct. 1655; Chirk F 5932: 19 Sept. 1651; Chirk F 12572: 6 Jul. 1653; Chirk F 12552: 3 Aug. 1652, 22 May 1653, 21 Nov. 1657.

[114] E.g. Chirk F 12552: 20 Feb. 1656/7; Chirk F 12551: 15 Mar. 1655/6; 31 Mar. 1656; Chirk F 12572: 1 Feb. 1654/6; Chirk A 29.

Protestants and Roman Catholics.[115] Their defence of the Church of England was one in which Myddelton was, at the very least, extremely interested, and in the 1650s it was these men's books that he collected and 'thought with', almost to the exclusion of anything else.

Aside from Myddelton's collection of the writings of Henry Hammond, which seems more concerned with a liking for a particular writer than a specific issue, Myddelton's theological reading followed several principal themes. These concerned unity and faction; church government; defence of the Prayer Book; and the fight against Catholicism. Sanderson's *Lectures on the Obligation of the Oath* and John Gauden's *Hieraspistes* in different ways derided disunity, mirroring in Myddelton's theological reading the theme of disunity in the secular world. Books by Edward Symmons and Anthony Sparrow explicitly defended episcopalian liturgy against Stephen Marshall and its other detractors, and sat easily alongside the writings of Taylor and Hammond, known for promoting the continuation of these traditions throughout the Interregnum.[116] Myddelton's preoccupation with the defeat of Catholicism was a lifelong one, but apparently something that he sought in the work of Hammond and Taylor as well. The Interregnum led theologians like this to 'shift their focus from public to personal Christianity', encouraging and advising devout episcopalians in person and in print.[117] Myddelton was apparently honing his own faith in this period, and using episcopalian theologians to accomplish that aim.

Sir Thomas Myddelton valued his collection of Hammond's works deeply. After Lambert seized Chirk after Booth's Rebellion in 1659, Myddelton pursued his book collection for years, in particular looking for his copies of Hammond and some expensive 'mappe bookes', expensive folio volumes of maps.[118] For several years thereafter he employed agents to hunt for the books, questioning and suing the soldiers responsible for seizing the books, as well as Lambert, Axtell and Biscoe's chaplains, who were known to have taken some of the volumes.[119] In 1663 Myddelton even employed his former chaplain's wife, Mrs Wilson, to go to an astrologer to find out more about his lost belongings.[120] The direction of Myddelton's reading runs parallel to his actions – it supported ejected clergymen, the importance of the Prayer Book, and the role of bishops in the Church. This provides some insight into Myddelton's decision-making process. It was meditative: he preferred to read and think

---

[115] Mark F. M. Clavier, 'The Role of Custom in Henry Hammond's *Of Schism* and John Bramhall's *A Just Vindication of the Church*', *Anglican and Episcopal History*, 76 (2007), 358–86, at 366.

[116] Chirk A 29.

[117] Neil Lettinga, 'Covenant Theology Turned Upside Down: Henry Hammond and Caroline Anglican Moralism: 1643–1660', *The Sixteenth Century Journal*, 24 (1993), 653–69, at 654.

[118] NLW, Chirk E 9.

[119] NLW, Chirk E 9; Chirk E 10; Chirk E 11; Chirk F 6896; NLW MS 6372E; Chirk F 12553: 4 Aug. 1662; NLW MS 6386E.

[120] Myddelton had family connections with the Napiers, who provided the consultations, and had previously sought advice about a range of issues of importance to him, including whether he would have success in an invasion into Wales in 1644. This demonstrates the level of importance Myddelton ascribed to recovering the books. Myddelton (ed.), *Chirk Castle Accounts, A.D. 1605-1666*, 164; Bodleian, MS Ashmole 184, fos. 2v, 4.

about issues that were important to him, and to gain justification for his actions. That these topics were Myddelton's preferred reading matter at a time when he was acting to support ejected royalist and Episcopalian churchmen and apparently pondering involvement in royalist plots is not a coincidence. It also indicates that Myddelton's change from parliamentarian to royalist was not as a result of 'Presbyterianism'. His opinions changed, rather than providing the basis for consistent actions as the world altered around him. His decision was prompted by a slow acculturation with Welsh royalism, in his local region and with his family connections, as well as by an intellectual consideration of the religious and political elements issues at stake.

Open royalism, 1659–66

In 1659, with a group of Welsh and Cheshire royalists and Presbyterians, Sir Thomas Myddelton finally declared his open allegiance to the royalist cause. As with many whose allegiance changed in the First Civil War itself, Myddelton explained his former allegiance as a mistake, or as the result of deception by other people. His funerary monument makes it clear that he wished to be remembered as a royalist, lamenting:

> that the resources of his family could not / restore to his afflicted Prince the whole of his Power. / After that he had seen (chiefly owing to his labour) / the King restored to his Rule, the Kingdom to its laws, / the Church to its ancient Piety, content with/his measure of Life and Glory. / He laid aside this earthy frame.

This claim of royalism may well have been entirely expedient given the political atmosphere following the Restoration, but in the light of Myddelton's actions in 1659 and subsequently, such an accusation seems unlikely. In the rising that became known as Booth's Rebellion, Myddelton risked his life and estate and went again into military action. Aged seventy-three, he led the royalist troops out of Wrexham, having waved his sword in the air (as Edmund Ludlow described it, 'either through Dotage, being almost fourscore Years of Age, or through the Importunity of others, or the natural Depravity of his own Heart') and declared Charles II King of England, Scotland and Wales.[121] The herald Randle Holme described Myddelton at St Werburgh's church in Chester with his fellow commanders, offering up prayers for King Charles II.[122] It would be tempting to see Myddelton's involvement with the godly Booth as resulting from Presbyterianism, but Booth's evident disapproval of Myddelton's overtly royalist act dispels this impression. One contemporary explanation was that Myddelton was compelled by his men to proclaim the king, but this does not seem to make sense in the light of Myddelton's correspondence with the royalist party.[123] Booth certainly wanted to avoid the

---

[121] Edmund Ludlow, *Memoirs of Edmund Ludlow, Esq.*, II (Vevay, 1698), 687.
[122] BL, Harley MS 2129.
[123] *Calendar of Clarendon State Papers*, IV, 343.

depiction of the rebellion as a royalist uprising, seeking to preserve a Presbyterian–royalist alliance. In print, therefore, the uprising was proclaimed in the cause of a free parliament and the liberty of the people of England, and Myddelton's actions risked that image.[124] In Booth's Rebellion Sir Thomas fought alongside royalists with whom he had built a steadily growing relationship – the Broughtons of Marchwiel, the Grosvenors of Eaton, and the Lloyds of Esclusham.[125] When defeated at Winnington Bridge on 15 August 1659 Myddelton fled to shelter in the royalist community in London. Despite his health being 'impaired by age and the winter' he attempted with his elder son to arrange another uprising in the Marches.[126] In March 1660, Myddelton wrote via Barwick to Hyde requesting the king's pardon for his 'old fault, lest he die before he could benefit from the general pardon'.[127] Myddelton's 'courage and zeal' were commended to the king.[128]

His reaction to the Restoration went unrecorded, except by a payment of five shillings to the bellringers of Chirk 'in token of our joye for the Parliament Resolves to send for the kinge'.[129] His son attended the Coronation, which Myddelton commemorated at home with some music. He paid the harper one shilling for this 'Coronation Day' entertainment.[130] After the Restoration Myddelton's sole reward from the Crown was a valuable cabinet, delivered by Dr John Barwick in November 1661.[131] His eldest son (also Sir Thomas) was awarded a baronetcy, and was on the abortive list of those to be created members of the order of the Royal Oak.[132] A younger son, Charles, was promised by the king (via Lord Anglesey) a position at court because of Myddelton's 'ingageing wth my Lord Delamer for his restitution in the late time of usurpation'.[133] Like many other royalists, however, Myddelton was not granted any lucrative positions, lands or titles.

---

[124] Mary-Ann Everett Green (ed.), Calendar of State Papers Domestic: Interregnum, 1659-60 (1886), 162–3; C. H. Firth (ed.), The Clarke Papers: Selections from the Papers of William Clarke, IV (1901), 38; Anon., An express from the knights and gentlemen now engaged with Sir George Booth (1659); Sir George Booth, A Declaration of Sir George Booth, at the general rendesvouz, on Tuesday last, near the city of Chester (1659); Calendar of Clarendon State Papers, IV, 340.

[125] Green (ed.), CSPD: Interregnum, 170; Mary-Ann Everett Green (ed.), Calendar of State Papers Domestic: Charles II, 1660-1 (1860), 154; Norman Tucker, North Wales in the Civil War (Denbigh, 1958), 160–1.

[126] Myddelton's son Thomas Myddelton, who was declared governor of the castle, surrendered and was arrested, to be given two months' freedom on security. Sir Thomas himself fled before the castle was taken. In November 1659 Sir Thomas considered flight to the continent, abandoning the plan in December of that year due to ill health. In this period Barwick, Colonel Roger Whitley, and Colonel Werden were go-betweens. TNA, SP 18/204 fo. 46; F. J. Routledge (ed.), Calendar of Clarendon State Papers. Vol. IV 1657-1660 (Oxford, 1932), 439, 471, 496, 500–1, 506.

[127] Clarendon State Papers, IV, 598.

[128] Ibid., IV, 612.

[129] NLW MS 6372E: 7 May 1660.

[130] NLW MS 6372E: 27 Apr. 1661.

[131] NLW, Chirk F 12553: 9 Nov. 1661.

[132] Philip Jenkins, 'Wales and the Order of the Royal Oak', National Library of Wales Journal, 24 (1986), 339–51, at 344.

[133] NLW, Chirk F 6897.

Myddelton's reaction to the pro-Church measures of the Cavalier Parliament between 1661 and his death in 1666 is hard to discern. As a moderate he should, in theory, have been opposed to some of the more repressive measures taken against nonconformists. Unlike Sir John Trevor, however, there is no sign of Myddelton using his power to protect nonconformist clergy or relatives. Myddelton's will contains a theologically complex profession of faith, similar to some of the ecclesiastical preambles of this period in restating their commitment to the Church of England and its doctrines, but with a lengthy concentration on the Trinity.[134] A long exposition on the Trinity may be seen as a response to the sectarianism that flourished during the Interregnum. While not noticeably heterodox, it is hardly Elizabethan Calvinist, others have argued, and instead should be viewed as part of Myddelton's theological evolution in the last fifteen years of his life.

He continued to buy 'royalist' books, for example Walton's *Compleat Angler*. He bought tracts by L'Estrange and subscribed to diurnalls and the official government newspaper, *The Gazette*.[135] He began to memorialise and read histories about the British Civil Wars. He led the North-East Welsh protest against regicide appointees or supporters being granted positions in Wales, and gave generously to the voluntary contribution of May 1662.[136] Towards the end of his life, from 1661 to 1666 Myddelton began to show an interest in foreign news and its consequences for trade, and in parallel to this purchased tracts and books on the threat of Jesuitism.[137] In that way his concerns moved full circle, again settling on the dangers of foreign Catholicism and conflict abroad. Myddelton ended his life at Chirk, having steeped himself for the few years before his death in Welsh culture, music and traditions. He supported Welsh carollers, the wassail, the wakes and the local *plygain* service.[138] After the 1650s the Myddeltons seemed to assume much more of a comfortable and settled place in North-East Welsh society, staying with or hosting local families. It is speculation to say that his post-Civil War political decisions and his involvement in Booth's Rebellion had made him more palatable to the local gentry, but it is more than plausible given the circumstances and culture of the local area.

---

[134] The theological implications of this document will form a future article on the topic. TNA, PROB 11/323/456.

[135] Myddelton (ed.), *Chirk Castle Accounts, A.D. 1605-1666*, 96, 128, 155, 160; NLW, Chirk E 52; NLW MS 6372E: 27 Apr. 1661; NLW, Chirk F 12553: 9 Nov. 1661; Chirk F 5949: 15 Nov. 1663, 1 Feb. 1664, 18 Feb. 1664.

[136] NLW, Chirk F 12553: 16 May 1662; NLW MS 9066E, no. 2272; TNA, SP 29/1 fo. 78.

[137] One pamphlet argued for a new conspiracy taking place in Ireland: 'Conspiracy for a new Rebellion in Ireland &c.' (1663). Chirk F 6903; Chirk F 6910; Chirk A 29.

[138] *Plygain* is a Welsh-language church service, using the liturgy of Evening Prayer but dominated by the singing of carols in groups or parties. D. Roy Saer, 'The Christmas Carol-Singing Tradition in the Tanat Valley', *Folk Life* 7 (1969), 15–42; NLW, Chirk F 12553: 27 Jan. 1661/2; NLW MS 6386E: 21 Aug. 1664; Myddelton (ed.), *Chirk Castle Accounts, 1666-1753*, 127, 129.

Conclusion

Gwyn Thomas wrote that 'Sir Thomas does not appear to have any clearly distinguishable political views until he became a Royalist.'[139] This is a harsh but
ultimately fair verdict. Myddelton was hesitant and careful, although once
committed to a decision he followed it through to its conclusion. He began
his time in Wales almost as a stranger in his own land, and there is a sense
that until the 1650s he was an unpopular, if authoritative, figure. His journey
from hesitant parliamentarian to devoted royalist is a story of the self-
conscious creation of identity. He imbibed royalist culture by socialising, reading books and pamphlets, and engaging with royalist and Anglican positions on
key issues. His acceptance within the royalist gentry was testament to this –
indeed the only reference to Myddelton as a side-changer came long after
his death, when his grandson was taunted into a duel by the grandson of Sir
John Trevor because Trevor was heard to have 'call'd his father the sonn of
A Traytor'.[140] Religion certainly was central to his life and thinking, but it
was not the 'Presbyterianism' ascribed to him previously. Myddelton's reading,
his appointments, and his private chapel all indicate a devotion to a much
more traditional and visual form of worship – indeed one much more typical
of North-East Welsh gentry royalists. Sir Thomas Myddelton used reading as
one way to fashion his way to loyalty, and once he achieved that he seems
never to have looked back.

The question of allegiance is one that, for many, was far from answered by
the end of the First Civil War. For some it was a process of change, for others
fluctuation depending on anything from personal circumstances to perceptions
of the strength of royalist groups. Sir Thomas Myddelton's journey shows that
side-changing could be a gradual process. It demonstrates that ideas could play
as significant a part as experiences, and that an accretion of dissenting actions
could contribute eventually towards a public and, in national terms, a risky
change of allegiance. Sir Thomas Myddelton changed side because he had
changed his mind, rather than because circumstances had altered, and with
issues of salvation, power and liberty at play, it is likely that others did too.
That change of mind embedded him in his environment and cemented his self-
fashioned identity. The richness of the Chirk archive, and those of the families
allied to the Myddeltons, makes an examination of this journey possible, but in
an age when news, local and national politics, and theological debate were the
lifeblood of many, it is probable that many others travelled on a similar
trajectory.

Sir Thomas Myddelton was neither a diarist nor an annotator of books. He
did not leave behind narratives explaining his changing ideas and allegiance,
nor did he compile commonplace books. Given that traditional explanations
of allegiance often rely on these sources to reconstruct their subjects' motivations it would, at first glance, appear that historians have solely to rely on
second-hand accounts of Myddelton's actions to understand his move from

---

[139] Thomas, 'Sir Thomas Myddelton II', 2.
[140] NLW, Chirk E 53.

parliamentarianism to royalism. This is not the case. This article has shown that the combination of fragmentary and varied forms of evidence can build a complex picture of changing allegiances. Through a consideration of book purchases and reading, financial accounts, legal evidence, surviving correspondence and material objects a composite image appears of a man changing his mind, thoughtfully and gradually. This is an approach that can be fruitfully applied to others, whether the surviving evidence is material, financial or legal, and the conflict in Britain and Ireland or elsewhere. Such case studies can together help to establish the more nuanced understanding of allegiance called for by Hopper and others and complicate patterns of behaviour in the centre and the localities.

Acknowledgements. I would like to thank the editor and the anonymous reviewers for their helpful and constructive comments, and to Ken Fincham, Katie McKeogh, David Scott, Grant Tapsell who read the article during its evolution. Thanks also to Karen George, Dominic Chennell and the staff at Chirk Castle whose collaboration inspired its revision and submission.

Cite this article: Ward Clavier S (2024). Reading his Way to Royalism? Sir Thomas Myddelton, Side-Changing and Loyalty in England and Wales, 1639–66. *Transactions of the Royal Historical Society* **2**, 83–109. https://doi.org/10.1017/S0080440124000124

Transactions of the RHS (2024), **2**, 111–134
doi:10.1017/S0080440123000270

ARTICLE

The Foods of Love? Food Gifts, Courtship and Emotions in Long Eighteenth-Century England

Sally Holloway

School of Education, Humanities and Languages, Oxford Brookes University, Oxford, UK
Email: sally.holloway@brookes.ac.uk

(Received 30 June 2023; revised 28 September 2023; accepted 9 October 2023;
first published online 20 November 2023)

Abstract

This article rediscovers the importance of food gifts in navigating the process of courtship
in England during the long eighteenth century. Studies of courtship and gift-exchange to
date have demonstrated how courting couples exchanged a wide range of gifts to produce
and intensify feelings of love and advance their relationships toward the altar, from garters
and gloves to ribbons, rings, portrait miniatures and locks of hair. Yet the edible gift has
remained conspicuously absent from this picture. The article reinserts edible tokens into
the historiography of love and marriage, revealing how they operated as an indispensable
and unique part of the 'gift mode' during courtship. It demonstrates how courting couples
exchanged a wide range of foodstuffs from cakes and sweetmeats to game, fowl, fish, exotic
fruits and home-grown produce. In doing so, the article advances the burgeoning field of
emotions and material culture by demonstrating how organic or perishable items could
function as powerful emotional objects, able to nourish the human body, provide a source
of sensual and gustatory pleasure and elicit feelings of joy, delight, love and desire. In turn,
these gifts show courtship made everyday, transacted between couples and their families,
and situated in gardens and squares, shops, theatres and around a family's tea table.

Keywords: Food; food gifts; gift-exchange; courtship; marriage; love; emotions;
materiality; material culture

In November 1756, the Bath apothecary John Lovell became acquainted with Sarah
Harvey and her aunt Mary Smith (née Harvey), of Shaw House in Melksham.[1] John

---

[1] John Lovell was the son of Peter Lovell (1686–1767) of Axbridge, Somerset. Mary Smith
(d. 1758) was Sarah's paternal aunt, the sister of Audley Harvey Esq. of Cole Park in

soon found that his acquaintance with Sarah had developed into 'the highest Esteem', which 'gradually improv'd into real Love'.[2] Aunt Smith discouraged the courtship and quashed his proposals owing to his insufficient fortune. Yet he remained a frequent visitor and family friend, receiving 'an exceeding fine Turkey' that year as a Christmas gift.[3] In return, he sent a keg of sturgeon, a large high-status fish typically eaten for a treat or special occasion, which he had received from a friend in London.[4] He then determinedly continued his pursuit of Sarah, resulting in him being promptly exiled from Shaw.[5] In a show of humility and attempt at rapprochement, he once again turned to gifts of food, sending Aunt Smith a 'Baskett with Two Cakes' in July 1757, followed by some produce from his father's garden. These exchanges provide a useful entry point into studying the cultural meanings of food in eighteenth-century England, as they suggest the much wider significance it held beyond simply eating it. As the anthropologist Mary Douglas writes, 'Food is not feed.' Rather, it is a whole system of communication.[6] In particular, the role and significance of food gifts during the process of courtship represents a whole system of *emotional* communication which is waiting to be decoded by historians.

The very everyday nature of food gifts means that they have often escaped our notice in studies of courtship and matrimony. This is despite the fact, as Sarah Ann Robin notes, that they were 'likely the most common of all amorous gifts', exchanged routinely by couples and their families and not always memorialised in text.[7] By their very nature, gifts of food were transient, perishable and designed to be consumed either *by* or *with* a loved one. Their meaning and intent was therefore very different from quintessential love tokens such as gloves, garters, ribbons, rings and locks of hair which were designed to be kept, and touched, kissed and gazed upon ad infinitum.[8] Food gifts were further unique in comparison with items such as seals and silhouettes as they

---

Malmesbury. Mary and her husband John Smith Esq. (1703–1757) lived at Shaw House, built by John's father, the diarist and wool merchant Thomas Smith (1674–1723). See Edward Bradby, 'The Diary of Thomas Smith of Shaw, 1715–23', *The Wiltshire Archaeological and Natural History Magazine*, 82 (1988), 115–41.

[2] John Lovell to Mary Smith, Bath, 29 Nov. 1756, Wiltshire and Swindon Archives, Chippenham (WSA), 161/102/1.

[3] Lovell to Smith, Bath, 24 Dec. 1756, WSA, 161/102/1.

[4] Sturgeon 'was clearly something special', ranked above salmon and oysters and eaten as a 'treat', Joan Thirsk, *Food in Early Modern England: Phases, Fads, Fashions 1500-1760* (2006), 189. Ilana Krausman Ben-Amos similarly situates sturgeon among foods of the 'landed elite', in *The Culture of Giving: Informal Support and Gift-Exchange in Early Modern England* (Cambridge, 2008), 213.

[5] A poem from John addressed to Sarah's dog Dony in *c.* March 1757 reflected on his exile: 'Go on, 'till wise Experience shews, / What Good from Reformation flows. / But from such Change should'st Thou withdraw, / Thy Lot is Banishment from Shaw; / And in Disgrace to mourn too late, / When nothing shall reverse thy Fate', WSA, 161/102/2.

[6] Mary Douglas, *In the Active Voice* (Abingdon, 1982), 117; Mary Douglas, 'Introduction', in *The Anthropologist's Cookbook*, ed. Jessica Kuper, 2nd edn (London and New York, 2009), 7.

[7] Sarah Ann Robin, 'Posies, Pictures and Promises – Love and the Object: The English in the Seventeenth Century' (PhD thesis, Lancaster University, 2016), 111.

[8] On the sensory rituals surrounding courtship gifts see Sally Holloway, *The Game of Love in Georgian England: Courtship, Emotions and Material Culture* (Oxford, 2019), 69–92.

were 'ontologically real and active' objects able to nourish and materially change the human body.[9] Given the flourishing of food history as an area of inquiry, a reappraisal of the social, emotional and material significance of food gifts in the making of marriage is long overdue.[10] This article contends that food represents a crucial component of what Natalie Zemon Davis has termed the 'gift mode' during courtship – 'an essential relational mode, a repertoire of behaviour, a register with its own rules, language, etiquette, and gestures' – which can shed new light on the mechanics of courtship in everyday life, how intimate relationships were navigated through objects, and how edible items could be harnessed as vehicles for emotional meaning.[11]

The article brings several different historiographies into conversation – chiefly histories of courtship and matrimony, food and food gifts, emotions and material culture, also extending to the senses, embodiment and the natural world. Gifts of food have occasionally featured in histories of courtship, though their appearance has been largely incidental. In her study of Tudor customs, Diana O'Hara found that 14 out of 403 couples involved in matrimonial suits in the Canterbury church courts (3.5 per cent) exchanged animals and foodstuffs as tokens, ranging from pigs, cattle, pigeons and fish, to peas, strawberries, spices and cake.[12] In her examination of the London Consistory Court between 1586 and 1611, Loreen Giese similarly found that wine was deployed as a monetary gift by courting men hoping to 'buy' a woman's love.[13] The main challenge for the church courts was determining when these items were intended as contractual symbols of marriage, and when they represented more everyday gestures of goodwill, highlighting the inherent flexibility and malleability of food as a gift. As David Cressy found in one case brought before the Durham Consistory Court in 1605, a man could take a 'kindly received' bag of apples and a piece of root ginger bitten by both parties as a symbol of betrothal, especially when situated alongside other tokens such as hair, gold coins and a ring, though a woman could just as well contend otherwise.[14] It is clear, however, that gifts of food did hold some import as a token of marriage, even if their implications have yet to be fully realised by historians.

While food gifts have not played a substantive role in histories of courtship, a significant body of work has established how food was used to create bonds of friendship and patronage between neighbours, kin, tenants and landlords, farmers and landowners, masters and servants, monarchs and courtiers.[15]

---

[9] David Goodman, 'Ontology Matters: The Relational Materiality of Nature and Agro-food Studies', *Sociologia Ruralis*, 41 (2001), 182–200, at 183.

[10] For an overview of the growth of the field in the wake of the new cultural history, heavily influenced by the work of structural anthropologists and historical sociologists, see Jeffrey M. Pilcher (ed.), *Oxford Handbook of Food History* (Oxford, 2012), esp. pt I, Food Histories.

[11] Natalie Zemon Davis, *The Gift in Sixteenth-Century France* (2000), 9.

[12] Diana O'Hara, *Courtship and Constraint: Rethinking the Making of Marriage in Tudor England* (Manchester, 2000), 68–70.

[13] Loreen Giese, *Courtships, Marriage Customs, and Shakespeare's Comedies* (New York, 2006), 91.

[14] David Cressy, *Birth, Marriage & Death: Ritual, Religion, and the Life-Cycle in Tudor and Stuart England* (Oxford, 1999), 264.

[15] See for example Margot Finn, 'Men's Things: Masculine Possession in the Consumer Revolution', *Social History*, 25 (2000), 133–55, at 143–4; Freya Gowrley, *Domestic Space in Britain,*

These studies have shown how the importance of food gifts declined to some extent in the first half of the seventeenth century, with the growth of London and greater concentration of elite families in the capital, the expansion of retail and the emergence of new patterns of urban sociability. Nonetheless, as Felicity Heal posits, 'more evidence points to the flexibility of the food gift than to its inexorable decline', as a panoply of 'new gifts of the rare and delicate' came to the fore.[16] This article consequently explores the flexible meanings of a diversifying range of food gifts over the long eighteenth century, which has been pinpointed by historians as a key moment in the transformation and revitalisation of gifting practices.[17] In doing so, the article demonstrates how courtship was a key arena in which food gifts retained their vitality in creating and sustaining emotional bonds.

This research also contributes to the rapidly expanding field of emotions and material culture, extending a scholarship which has focused principally on *made* objects which were created, inscribed and preserved by humans to also encompass the organic, the transitory and the ephemeral.[18] As Joanne Begiato has urged, 'there is critical value in including all types of objects in discussions about emotions in the past', from foods to memories and smells, and even entirely imagined objects, calling on historians to be more expansive in their definitions of materiality.[19] The most recent work on landscape and environments has done just this, probing our emotional relationships with nature, land, animals and – most importantly – foodstuffs.[20] Rachel Winchcombe has emphasised the power of foods in maintaining 'emotional

---

1750–1840: Materiality, Sociability and Emotion (2021), 139–73; Felicity Heal, 'Food Gifts, The Household and the Politics of Exchange in Early Modern England', *Past & Present*, 199 (2008), 41–70; Felicity Heal, *The Power of Gifts: Gift Exchange in Early Modern England* (Oxford, 2014); Amanda E. Herbert, *Female Alliances: Gender, Identity, and Friendship in Early Modern Britain* (New Haven and London, 2014), 52–77; Christopher Kissane, *Food, Religion and Communities in Early Modern Europe* (2018); Ben-Amos, *The Culture of Giving*; Susan Whyman, *Sociability and Power in Late-Stuart England: The Cultural Worlds of the Verneys, 1660–1720* (Oxford, 2002), 23–33.

[16] Heal, 'Food Gifts', 69.

[17] Ben-Amos, *The Culture of Giving*, 378–80.

[18] For an overview of the state of the field see Stephanie Downes, Sally Holloway and Sarah Randles, 'A Feeling for Things, Past and Present', in *Feeling Things: Objects and Emotions through History*, ed. Stephanie Downes, Sally Holloway and Sarah Randles (Oxford, 2018), 8–26.

[19] Joanne Begiato, 'Moving Objects: Emotional Transformation, Tangibility, and Time Travel', in *Feeling Things*, ed. Downes *et al.*, 235–6.

[20] For an introduction to 'human–environment entanglements' see Sasha Handley and John Emrys Morgan, 'Environment, Emotion and Early Modernity', *Environment and History*, 28 (2022), 355–61. On affective relationships with animals see Andrea Gaynor, Susan Broomhall and Andrew Flack, 'Frogs and Feeling Communities: A Study in History of Emotions and Environmental History', *Environment and History*, 28 (2022), 83–104; Ingrid Tague, 'Pets and the Eighteenth-Century British Family', *The History of the Family*, 26 (2021), 186–213; John Emrys Morgan, 'An Emotional Ecology of Pigeons in Early Modern England and America', *Environment and History*, 28 (2022), 435–52. On emotions, nature and heritage see Anke Bernau, 'Hedgerow Poiesis', *Emotions: History, Culture, Society*, 7 (2023), 119–44; Alicia Marchant, 'Romancing the Stone: (E)motion and the Affective History of the Stone of Scone', in *Feeling Things*, ed. Downes *et al.*, 192–208; Alicia Marchant (ed.), *Historicising Heritage and Emotions: The Affective Histories of Blood, Stone and Land* (2019).

health', with items such as chocolate believed to stimulate passions such as joy and cheerfulness whilst banishing those of grief and sadness.[21] Sasha Handley has similarly shown how the milky mixture of sack posset could aid fertility and stimulate health, as well as eliciting affective states from loyalty to a monarch to love for a spouse.[22] Such work is shaped by a burgeoning new and neo-materialist scholarship in which foods possess their own active force and lively vitality as a type of matter. As living organisms and what the political theorist Jane Bennett has termed 'edible matter', foods can be treated as 'actants' which exist alongside and inside human beings – 'conative bodies vying alongside and within an other complex body (a person's "own" body)'.[23] Part of the distinctive nature of food gifts as emotional objects therefore lies in their agentic material properties and ability to *act* upon the human body, nourishing it and stimulating feelings of joy, delight, love and desire.

The article at once examines the nature *of* food as an emotional object, and the navigation of courtship *through* food. As scholars such as Christopher Kissane highlight, food is good to think with, as it provides a useful prism to reflect and refract the guiding principles and beliefs structuring everyday life.[24] In doing so, the article draws upon a wide range of source material including material objects, visual sources such as paintings and prints, and textual sources including pamphlets, medical treatises, ballads, songs, plays, periodicals, novels and trade cards. Particularly important are letters and diaries, which are especially revealing of courting practices among the middling sorts and provincial urban gentry, who set out the emotional and social significance of their gifts at great length in writing. These men were schoolmasters, apothecaries, clergymen, composers, lawyers, Justices of the Peace, businessmen, Members of Parliament and landed gentlemen, whilst the women were primarily gentlemen's daughters. These sources provide the most detailed evidence of gifts proffered by courting men, who sent the greatest number and variety of food gifts, having primary responsibility for instigating and actively pursuing a match.

The article's key questions ask: how were gifts of food used to navigate the process of courtship? What exactly distinguished sweets, meat, fish and fruit as suitable items to present to a lover? How did they vary by class, gender, across the country, over the century and through different stages of courtship? What might smelling, tasting and consuming these items reveal about the role of the senses and the body in courting rituals? And more broadly, how were organic or perishable items such as food used to communicate and materialise emotions in practice? In endeavouring to answer these questions, the article is divided into four sections which each examine particular categories of edible

[21] Rachel Winchcombe, 'Comfort Eating: Food, Drink, and Emotional Health in Early Modern England', *English Historical Review* (2023) [Early View]: https://doi.org/10.1093/ehr/cead065.

[22] Sasha Handley, 'Lusty Sack Possets, Nuptial Affections and the Material Communities of Early Modern Weddings', *Environment and History*, 28 (2022), 375–95.

[23] For an introduction to new materialism and its implications for emotions history see Katie Barclay, 'New Materialism and the New History of Emotions', *Emotions: History, Culture, Society*, 1 (2017), 161–83; Timothy LeCain, *The Matter of History: How Things Create the Past* (Cambridge, 2017), 15; Jane Bennett, *Vibrant Matter: A Political Ecology of Things* (Durham, 2010), 39.

[24] Kissane, *Food, Religion and Communities*, 5–6.

gift: sweet treats and snacks such as cakes, comfits and gingerbread; exclusive or rare tokens such as venison and hothouse fruits; items cultivated in a family garden or estate and shared among the families of courting couples; nutritious items designed to safeguard the health of a beloved. These are arranged broadly to follow the progress of a relationship, from the cakes and wine used as a means of flirtation to the game meats used to demonstrate masculine prowess, and the oysters deployed to show concern for the health of a future spouse.

Flirtation, sweet treats and snacks

The question of how to initiate courtship was a vexed one for many suitors, with gifts of food providing an expedient answer.[25] Many courtships began with sweet treats and snacks such as cakes, nuts, comfits and sweetmeats proffered by men to women who excited their romantic interest. In one ballad, a young damsel recounted:

> How many Sweethearts Courted me
> And always loving kind and free,
> They gave me Cakes and Kisses to[o],
> And often did Loves game renew.[26]

These edible tokens were presented by men during the earliest phases of courting games and wooing, often accompanied by kisses and wine.[27] Their material properties were important in provoking certain passions, with sweet foodstuffs believed to stimulate feelings of joy, delight and mirth.[28] The somatic and sensory delight generated by sweet gifts is evident in ballads, where female protagonists recounted how suitors used 'Custards with Cheese-Cakes and kisses' to enchant and 'betray' their senses. As this extract suggests, these foods were also believed to stimulate desire, as a 'ready right way' to reach 'the fountain of blisses'.[29] Sugar retained its medicinal uses as a nourishing food well into the eighteenth century, praised by medical writers as 'an innocent, nutritious, and healthy substance'. Nonetheless, its principal use by this period was as a preservative and sweetener, with writers highlighting the appeal of its 'sweet and obliging Taste'.[30] These sensory and material

---

[25] For a discussion of how best to commence a courtship see Helen Berry, *Gender, Society and Print Culture in Late-Stuart England: The Cultural World of the Athenian Mercury* (Aldershot, 2003), 170–1.

[26] 'Damsels Complaint FOR THE Loss of her Maidenhead', London, 1690, English Broadside Ballad Archive (EBBA), 22262.

[27] 'Short and Sweet, / Or, the happy and Agreeable Wooing of / Oliver and Dorothy / Wherein is discovered the plain and Easy way to a Marriage Estate, / And how Maidens without difficulty may get Good Husbands', 1685–8, EBBA, 21064.

[28] Winchcombe, 'Comfort Eating', 21; Hannah Newton, 'Inside the Sickchamber in Early Modern England: The Experience of Illness through Six Objects', *English Historical Review*, 136, no. 580 (2021), 530–67, at 539.

[29] 'THE West-Country Wedding. Betwixt Roger the Plowman, and Ellin the Dary-Maid [*sic*]', 1671–1702?, EBBA, 21772.

[30] Frederick Slare, *A Vindication of Sugars Against the Charge of Dr. Willis, Other Physicians, and Common Prejudices. Dedicated to the Ladies* (1715); William Falconer, *Observations on Some of the*

properties made sweet foodstuffs the ideal tokens with which to commence a romantic relationship, to be consumed whilst flirting, talking and walking together in public. The purpose of these edible tokens was not commitment, but the frisson of romance, enjoyment and sensual pleasure.

In her study of Old Regime Lyon, Julie Hardwick has demonstrated how 'walking out' in the emergent public sphere represented 'a new form of hetero-sociability', whereby couples strolled through cities, along rivers and through vegetable gardens and orchards while enjoying snacks such as biscuits and grapes together.[31] The ritual also reflected the rise of 'snacking', which 'increasingly occupied the interstices of structured eating' from the late seventeenth century onward.[32] One particularly detailed early account of 'walking out' whilst snacking is provided in the diary of the Colchester schoolmaster George Lloyd (1642–1718) in the 1670s. During the earlier and less turbulent phase of his on-again, off-again courtship with Mrs Gray, he walked out with her in Spring Gardens in Westminster after dinner, drinking wine and eating cheesecake. The following week, the couple visited St Georges Fields in Lambeth to drink cider and eat cake, staying until 8 p.m.[33] These outings provided a safe public setting in which to develop their intimacy and test their compatibility over food, without entailing any further obligation to marry.

The wealth of new urban spaces for sociability and pleasure which sprang up over the eighteenth century developed and embedded these rituals by encouraging the leisured consumption of food between mealtimes. As one pamphlet reported at mid-century, the 'New Breakfasting-Hutt near *Sadler's-Wells*' was 'crouded with young Fellows and their Sweethearts' drinking tea and coffee, repeating love songs, and whiling away the time until dinner.[34] Prints such as Thomas Rowlandson's *St James's Courtship* and *St Giles's Courtship* drew a direct line between the sensual pleasures of food and drink and the thrill of flirtation and seduction. Whilst the St James's couple delicately imbibe cups of coffee, their St Giles's counterparts carouse over a jug of wine.[35] For some gentlemen, the theatre proved a fitting location to treat women who piqued their romantic interest, amongst theatregoers enjoying wine, ham, cold chops and pasties.[36] When attempting to woo the gentleman's daughter Miss Newsome in York in February 1761, the Beverley gentleman John

---

Articles of Diet and Regimen Usually Recommended to Valetudinarians (1778), 38–43; Jon Stobart, *Sugar & Spice: Grocers and Groceries in Provincial England, 1650–1830* (Oxford, 2016), 29–33.

[31] Julie Hardwick, *Sex in an Old Regime City: Young Workers and Intimacy in France, 1660–1789* (Oxford, 2020), 48.

[32] Sara Pennell, '"Great Quantities of Gooseberry Pye and Baked Clod of Beef": Victualling and Eating Out in Early Modern London', in *Londinopolis: Essays in the Cultural History of Early Modern London*, ed. Paul Griffiths and Mark S. R. Jenner (Manchester, 2000), 228–49, at 237.

[33] Daniel Patterson (ed.), 'The Diary of George Lloyd (1642–1718)', *Royal Historical Society Camden Fifth Series*, vol. 64 (2022), 13 May 1676, 139, and 19 May 1676, 142.

[34] *Low-Life: Or One Half of the World, Knows not how the Other Half Live* (c. 1755), 46; Pennell, '"Great Quantities of Gooseberry Pye"', 239.

[35] Thomas Rowlandson, *St James's Courtship* and *St Giles's Courtship*, Britain, 1799, hand-coloured etchings with aquatint, Metropolitan Museum of Art, New York, 59.533.647–8.

[36] As described in *Sophie in London, 1786: being the Diary of Sophie v. la Roche*, trans. Clare Williams (1933), 9 Sep. 1786, 133.

Courtney (1734–1806) sat behind her for a performance of Richard Steele's sentimental comedy *The Conscious Lovers* and 'treated her' with sweetmeats to indicate his attraction. Disappointingly, the next day 'she held down her head' and deliberately passed him by 'on the other side of the street'. Four years later, Courtney again reached for the sweetmeats whilst walking out in town with a 'vastly pretty sensible agreable' young woman from Newcastle called Miss Kitty Rutter. However, he decided to drop his suit the following month owing to her insufficient fortune and overly numerous family.[37] Nonetheless, the sharing of sweetmeats had provided a momentary source of pleasure and a material means of gauging any potential romantic interest in its earliest stages, without being under any subsequent obligation to pursue it.

Sweet foods from bonbons to jellies, ices and spiced cakes were particularly highly valued for their exoticism and high price, as products of imperialism and Britain's trading empire.[38] They could be purchased from the increasing number of cake and confectionery shops in towns, especially London, where they clustered around high-end shopping districts such as St James's, encouraging customers to sit-in and engage in sociability and fashionable display.[39] In the print in Figure 1, two fashionably dressed women depart a cake shop blowing kisses at a pair of stylish dandies by the counter. They call out, 'much obliged to you gentlemen, adieu!' and 'Bye Bye! Dandies! nice Cakes!' The men subsequently realise that they are unable to pay the exorbitant sum of nine shillings and sixpence spent on treats such as sugar plums, crying out 'D--n me if I have any Brass!!' The offer of sugared delicacies could provide men with a valuable avenue for developing greater familiarity with women by treating them and engaging in flirtation and conversation. Yet in their attempts to attract women of fashion by imitating the refined tastes of the upper classes, the conspicuous consumption of simply named 'Bob' and 'Jim' has clearly extended too far. For men who *did* have the means, such tokens could be packaged in expensive decorative boxes such as crystal, porcelain and silver *bonbonnières* which turned these transient gifts into something more concrete. These offerings combined the tangible and intangible in a single token, making the romantic meanings of edible gifts more explicit through evocative depictions of the altar of love, Cupid, his bow and quiver of arrows, blooming flowers and kissing doves.[40]

---

[37] Susan Neave and David Neave (eds.), *The Diary of a Yorkshire Gentleman: John Courtney of Beverley, 1759–68* (Otley, 2001), 34, 101.

[38] On popular imperialism see Troy Bickham, *Eating the Empire: Food and Society in Eighteenth-Century Britain* (2020); Linda Colley, *Britons: Forging the Nation 1707–1837* (New Haven, 992); Bob Harris, '"American Idols": Empire, War, and the Middling Ranks in Mid-Eighteenth Century Britain', *Past & Present*, 150 (1996), 111–41.

[39] Stobart, *Sugar & Spice*, 132; Ian Mitchell, *Tradition and Innovation in English Retailing, 1700 to 1850: Narratives of Consumption* (Farnham, 2014), 102.

[40] A whole collection of such trinkets is described in a satirical advertisement for stolen goods in *The Tatler*, including a silver gilt box containing cashew and caraway comfits with an enamelled lid depicting Cupid fishing for hearts, no. 245, 31 Oct.–2 Nov. 1710. For extant examples see porcelain *bonbonnière* resembling Cupid playing drums in the shape of a woman's breasts, wearing a ribbon painted 'POUR LES CAVALIERS DE CITHERE', London, *c.* 1759–70, 7.3 cm (H) × 6 cm (W), Victoria and

Figure 1. *Dandies Sans-Sis-Sous*, London, *c.* 1819, plate mark 24.8 × 35 cm, hand-coloured etching, courtesy of the Lewis Walpole Library, Yale University, lwlpr11995.

Nonetheless, one of the merits of edible gifts – like related perishable tokens such as nosegays – was that they did not necessarily require a substantial financial outlay, with the *Dictionary of Love* derisively noting that 'a silly girl' could easily be 'seduced by a dozen of stick-cherries'.[41] Labouring men used cakes, nuts, brandy snaps and gingerbread purchased from local feasts and fairs as a way to break the ice and commence the process of courtship.[42] In Christopher Anstey's novel *Memoirs of the Noted Buckhorse* (1756), the protagonist, a boxer, is thunderstruck with love at first sight, causing him to forget that he is already married. He presents the young lady who has inspired his passion with a pennyworth of gingerbread as a token, which she accepts with a bow. He then invites her to drink a glass of wine at a nearby inn and pledges to marry her as soon as she thinks proper.[43] In Jane Austen's *Emma* (1815), the farmer Robert Martin rides 'three miles round one day' to procure the heroine's protégée Harriet Smith some walnuts after she expresses a taste

---

Albert Museum, London (V&A), 414:270-1885; tortoiseshell and gold *bonbonnière* with micromosaic scene, 7.6 cm (D) × 2.5 cm (H), Rome, *c.* 1800, V&A, LOAN: GILBERT.480:1-2008; porcelain *bonbonnière* in the form of Cupid and a lamb in a blooming field, with French inscription, nineteenth century, V&A, 346-1902.

[41] 'Presents', in *The Dictionary of Love. In Which is Contained, The Explanation of Most of the Terms Used in That Language* (1753), 172.

[42] John Gillis, *For Better, For Worse: British Marriages, 1600 to the Present* (Oxford, 1985), 28–9.

[43] *Memoirs of the Noted Buckhorse. In which, Besides a Minute Account of his past Memorable Exploits, That celebrated Hero is carried into higher Life; Containing some very Extraordinary Events* (1756), I, 118.

for them.[44] Later accounts of the courtships of 'common or working people' similarly described young men using nuts and brandy snaps as 'tidings' at local feasts:

> If a young man prevails upon a young woman to accept of a 'tiding', which means accepting [a] brandy-snap and nuts, the ice is broken, and it is mostly looked upon by young and old as a kind of 'god's penny', for the girl feels laid under some obligation to him; it is a proof that they are making love to each other if not actually engaged.[45]

Much like the use of *bonbonnières* by the affluent gentry, such tokens could be sent alongside, or followed up with, tangible keepsakes such as wooden nutcrackers carved with romantic symbols such as hearts, birds, the date, and initials of the recipient.[46] These snacks and treats provided an efficacious means for men and women to socialise, engage in flirtation, arouse feelings of joy, delight and desire, test their attraction and establish a putative match.

Exclusivity, status and masculinity

Some of the most highly valued food gifts in early modern England were exclusive, distinctive or exotic items which conveyed the status and means of the sender. The lack of more mundane domestic foodstuffs in early modern gift-giving rituals has been highlighted by Felicity Heal, who notes the absence of grain, ale, beer, fruits such as apples and pears, and vegetables more generally. Rather, she writes, gifts had 'to be distinctive, in some measure marked out from the quotidian pattern of household consumption'.[47] In their work on Tudor and Stuart customs, David Cressy and Diana O'Hara both cite examples of individuals using root ginger as a token of marriage. This exotic imported spice was native to Southeast Asia and cultivated in Jamaica and other islands from the late seventeenth century, making it a singularly distinctive token of love. Other such exclusive items included spices such as nutmeg and exotic fruits such as oranges.[48]

One such exclusive gift, in the eighteenth century, was the pineapple. The delicacy was first introduced to England from its sugar colony in Barbados

---

[44] Jane Austen, *Emma*, ed. James Kingsley (Oxford, [1815] 2003), 23.

[45] Joseph Lawson, *Letters to the Young on Progress in Pudsey during the last Sixty Years* (Stanninglen, 1887), 11. For a further example later in the nineteenth century see J. Burnley, *Phases of Bradford Life* (1889), 83. One of the most powerful surviving objects in the Foundling Museum's collections in London is a single hazelnut pierced with a hole, which may well have had some connection to the romance which foreshadowed the mother's pregnancy. See 'Token: Hazelnut, Pierced for a String or Cord': https://foundlingmuseum.org.uk/object/token-hazelnut-pierced-for-a-string-or-cord-eighteenth-century/.

[46] See for example the screw thread boxwood nutcracker carved to resemble a bird sitting atop a cage, England *c.* late seventeenth–early eighteenth century, Pinto Collection, Birmingham Museums, 1965T2096; Edward H. Pinto, *Treen and Other Wooden Bygones: An Encyclopaedia and Social History* (1969), 75; Robin, 'Posies, Pictures and Promises', 126–7, 148.

[47] Heal, 'Food Gifts', 56.

[48] Cressy, *Birth, Marriage & Death*, 264; O'Hara, *Courtship and Constraint*, 68–70, 89–90; Heal, 'Food Gifts', 56.

and cultivated domestically in hothouses from the seventeenth century. A single pineapple took two to three years to grow to size, with each plant yielding only a single prized fruit. The vast amount of labour and infrastructure required made this an extortionately expensive symbol of taste and status. Genteel gardeners accordingly rushed to cultivate home-grown pineapples in pineries on their country estates, with 'anyone who was anyone among the upper echelons of society' growing their own pineapples by the 1770s.[49] As the gardener John Giles wrote in his treatise on the subject, 'every gentleman of taste and fortune' was keen to cultivate this 'polite article of gardening'.[50] This included the Essex MP Colonel Isaac Martin Rebow (1731–1781), who had a hothouse installed in his Kitchen Gardens at Wivenhoe Park in Colchester in the 1760s. Between 1769 and 1771 he sent several home-grown pineapples as gifts to his sweetheart and first cousin Mary Martin (*c.* 1751–1804) and her family. In her letters, Mary praised the 'exceeding good' quality of this 'noble' fruit, which she often received situated alongside other exclusive foodstuffs such as venison, partridge and pheasant.[51] The vogue for pineapples among the aristocracy had largely abated by the 1780s, reflecting the accelerating pace and quixotic fashions of consumer society. After this period, the fruit alone was not sufficient to impress, and came to require greater scale, magnificence and grandeur.[52]

A key part of the pineapple's desirability as a gift was its 'delightful fragrant smell' and the 'excellency, fragrancy, and flavour' of its fruit.[53] One delivery received by Mary Martin in 1769 smelled 'as fine as ever I knew one', and she didn't doubt it would 'prove as good in y Taste'.[54] Another savoured by the Martin family on Christmas Day in 1770 was judged 'y highest Flavor of any we have had this latter season', with a further pineapple the following year considered 'as fine a one as ever I tasted'.[55] The taste of food gifts therefore helped to generate an emotional connection between couples by stimulating feelings of delight and gustatory pleasure. In this way, taste could operate as a type of affective currency, helping us to extend the boundaries of materiality beyond objects themselves to also encompass the various sensory and somatic rituals that they were involved in.[56] In doing so, we position objects in what new materialist scholars have figured as a reciprocal partnership

---

[49] See Francesca Beauman, *The Pineapple: King of Fruits* (2011); Christopher Natali, 'Was *Northanger Abbey*'s General Tilney Worth His Weight in Pineapples?', *Persuasions*, 40, no. 1 (2019): https://jasna.org/publications-2/persuasions-online/volume-40-no-1/natali/.

[50] John Giles, *Ananas: Or, A Treatise on the Pine-Apple. In which the Whole Culture, Management, and Perfecting this Most Excellent Fruit, is Laid Down in a Clear and Explicit Manner* (*c.* 1767), 1.

[51] Rosemary Feesey, *A History of Wivenhoe Park: The House and Grounds* (Colchester, 1963), 17; Mary Martin to Isaac Rebow, 26 Dec. 1770, 28 Aug. 1771 and 1 Oct. 1771, Washington State University Library, Pullman, WA (WSU), cg134_17701226, cg134_17710828, cg134_17711001.

[52] Beauman, *The Pineapple*, 222–8.

[53] Giles, *Ananas*, 33.

[54] Martin to Rebow, 18 Nov. 1769, WSU, cg134_17691118.

[55] Martin to Rebow, 26 Dec. 1770 and 15 Oct. 1771, WSU, cg134_17701226, cg134_17711015.

[56] Begiato, 'Moving Objects', 235–6. On the sensory rituals of gazing at, touching and smelling love tokens also see Holloway, *The Game of Love*, 69–92.

with humans, where they are able to shape us – our bodies, identities, feelings, relationships and decisions – as much as we shape them.[57] The enduring influence of the pineapple in shaping familial relationships is perhaps best illustrated in the case of one suitor who, after tasting the fruit for the first time at the home of his future in-laws in 1757, wrote to praise the profound impression it had made upon him, noting that he would 'retain that Favour' in his memory 'as long as I live'.[58]

Such exotic fruits including pineapples, grapes, nectarines and peaches were commonly gifted within landed gentry families, and served to visiting guests.[59] As Maggie Lane highlights in her work on the culinary world of Jane Austen, Mr Darcy's wealth in *Pride and Prejudice* (1813) is indicated by the 'beautiful pyramids' of hothouse fruits that he serves to visitors. Indeed, it is at this exact point in the novel – visiting Pemberley with her aunt and uncle Mr and Mrs Gardiner – when the heroine Elizabeth Bennet first uses the word 'love' to describe her feelings for Darcy, stimulated by food and the hospitality she has received. The scene takes on even greater significance as it is the only mealtime scene in Austen's novels 'which is described straightforwardly by the narrator as impinging on the heroine's consciousness'.[60] It was this precise social cachet that suitors hoped to channel when selecting hothouse fruits as a romantic gift. In 1773 the Norfolk parson James Woodforde (1740–1803) gifted some peaches to his love interest Betsy White, whom he had been regularly dining and taking tea with.[61] The exorbitant price of these treats is satirised in the print of a fruit shop lounge in Figure 2, where a customer looks glumly ahead at his bill of five shillings for one peach, coupled with eighteen shillings for a bunch of grapes. Exotic fruits could therefore operate as important markers of status, whilst eating and drinking together smoothed the path to matrimony as prized opportunities for conviviality and conversation.

The most exclusive food gift unequivocally associated with landed hierarchy and elite masculinity was venison, classified as the private property of landowners and banned from sale on the open market. As Heal notes, venison was 'the food of lords' in early modern England, and as such was singled out as 'the most determined, and most gift-ascribed of all items of consumption'.[62] This exclusive food gift was popularly sent as a token of courtship by aristocratic men as an indication of their wealth and status; the presence of deer indicated a deer park, and a deer park a country seat and judicious match. During his courtship of Elizabeth Jeffreys, heiress of Brecon Priory in Wales

---

[57] Bennett, *Vibrant Matter*, xvii; LeCain, *The Matter of History*, 8, 15.

[58] Lovell to Harvey, 6 Aug. 1757, WSA, 161/102/2.

[59] See for example the diary of Robert Lee of Binfield, where he sends grapes and peaches to his uncle Henry Alexander, Lord Sterline (1664–1739), and his younger brother William Philipps (c. 1708–1777), *Diaries and Correspondence of Robert Lee of Binfield, 1736–1744*, ed. Harry Leonard (Reading, 2012), 34, 139. On pineapples, peaches and melons as highly prized exotic fruits see Kate Feluś, *The Secret Life of the Georgian Garden: Beautiful Objects & Agreeable Retreats* (London and New York, 2016), 168–71.

[60] Maggie Lane, *Jane Austen and Food* (London and Rio Grande, OH, 1995), 146–7.

[61] John Beresford (ed.), *The Diary of a Country Parson, 1758–1802* (Oxford, 1978), 16 Sep. 1773, 85.

[62] Heal, 'Food Gifts', 57–8, 60; Whyman, *Sociability and Power*, 14–37.

Figure 2. *A Fruit Shop Lounge*, hand-coloured etching, London, 1786, plate mark 24.8 × 33.7 cm, courtesy of the Lewis Walpole Library, Yale University, lwlpr05985.

(c. 1724–1779) between 1745 and 1749, the barrister Charles Pratt (1714–1794) sent a side of venison for Elizabeth to consume with her family, likely procured from his family's country estate, Wilderness, in Kent. Elizabeth praised the meat as being 'prodigiously Fat & fine', with the fattest meat also held to be the most flavoursome.[63] The token was particularly important as a show of status since Jeffreys was a wealthy heiress, whereas her suitor – though high-born and well educated – was a financially straitened third son, initially leading her mother to oppose the match.[64]

The hunting of venison, and shooting of game meats such as partridge and pheasant, could further provide an indication of idealised masculine qualities such as courage, resourcefulness and strength of mind and body. Pamphlets in praise of hunting lauded it as evidence of masculine health and virility, a 'Manly Exercise' in stark contrast to the trifling effeminacy of activities such as masquerades and balls.[65] The gifting of venison could therefore gesture more widely to a man's strong constitution, vigour, and skill in horsemanship,

---

[63] Elizabeth Jeffreys to Charles Pratt, 8 Jul. 1749, Kent History & Library Centre, Maidstone (KHLC), U840/C9/30.

[64] See Peter D. G. Thomas, 'Charles Pratt, first Earl Camden (1714–1794), lawyer and politician' (2004), *Oxford Dictionary of National Biography*, Oxford University Press: https://doi.org/10.1093/ref:odnb/22699.

[65] *An Essay on Hunting. By a Country Squire* (1733), 4–5; Monica Mattfeld, *Becoming Centaur: Eighteenth-Century Masculinity and English Horsemanship* (University Park, PA, 2017), 94–6.

which was an essential attribute for the polite gentleman. For one young gentlewoman, the sight of her suitor astride his horse in the 1750s was 'to see him in his Utmost Perfection', emphasising to friends that he was 'remarkable for Riding vastly well'.[66] Shooting, too, was a test of polite masculinity, and of gentlemanly qualities such as coolness, composure and self-control.[67] It is thus unsurprising that some suitors triumphantly reported their successes to their sweethearts. Edward Leathes (1747–1788) was the third son of a wealthy Essex politician and landowner, and like many younger gentry sons was destined for a career in the Church. Following the end of the game-shooting season in February 1772, he proudly shared his 'prodigious' sporting success with his sweetheart Elizabeth Reading (1748–1815). She dutifully responded that 'your hand must be greatly improv'd', flattering him that ''tis well the Season is over, for you would certainly in a little time have become the dread of the whole Feather'd Tribe'.[68] Gifts of venison and game had a dual purpose for courting men as signifiers of wealth and status, and as material tokens of polite masculinity.

Exclusive food gifts reflected the genteel status and manly attributes of the sender, whilst also bestowing honour upon recipients and their families for being part of these landed networks of power. As was the case in gifting networks more widely, such tokens could be consumed in company or shared onward as a way for recipients to reinforce or elevate their own social status. After Elizabeth Jeffreys and her mother received a side of venison from her suitor Charles Pratt in 1749, they re-gifted the neck to his sister Mrs Anne Gee in Richmond, confirming the increasing interconnectedness of their two families.[69] During the 1770s, the Essex gentlewoman Mary Martin used the food gifts sent by her suitor and first cousin Isaac Rebow to host a number of 'grand' meals for friends and family. She reported her delight at how:

> I cut a very smart Figure (thanks to you) both in my Dinner, & Supper & Luckily had y Venison done just as it shou'd be, which was allow'd by every body to be y finest ever seen, & I really beleive [sic] Cut full an Inch & half Deep of Fat, y Wood Pigeons were likewise very fine, & just in high order.[70]

A further delivery of partridges sent alongside some pineapples was likewise used 'to Cut a Figure with' at dinner, for which Mary was 'infinitely oblig'd' to him.[71] These tokens once again highlight the flexibility of food as a gift,

---

[66] Georgiana Poyntz to Theadora Cowper, c. 1754, British Library, London, Add MS 75691.

[67] Benjamin Luke Thomas Jackson, 'Furnishing Masculinity: Men's Material Culture in Eighteenth-Century England' (PhD thesis, Queen Mary University of London, 2020), 273–329, esp. 284–5.

[68] Elizabeth Reading to Edward Leathes, Woodstock, 1 Mar. 1772, Norfolk Record Office, Norwich (NRO), BOL 2/4/3. On the timetable of the game season see Jackson, 'Furnishing Masculinity', table 5.1, 288.

[69] Jeffreys to Pratt, 8 Jul. 1749, KHLC, U840/C9/30.

[70] Martin to Rebow, 7 Jan. 1772, WSU, cg134_17720107.

[71] Martin to Rebow, 15 Oct. 1771, WSU, cg134_17711015.

which could either be consumed by the giver and recipient (like cakes or wine) or eaten by the recipient with others, standing in for the giver *in absentia* (like pineapples or game). Such tokens are a category apart from typical courting gifts such as jewellery and personal accoutrements due to their imbrication in wider networks of hospitality and commensality, conferring power and privilege upon the individuals who sent, received and consumed them.

Familial care, households and gardens

Whilst exclusive and exotic gifts had their merits, there was also clearly enormous value placed upon the local and home-grown, particularly in an age of commerce and industry. To cultivate fruits and vegetables for friends, family and loved ones suggested a particular type of care, thought and effort invested in the recipient.[72] It also ensured the freshest quality, with senders keen to emphasise how gifts such as cucumbers had been 'taken and cut' that morning.[73] In his great treatise on landscape gardening, Humphry Repton (1752–1818) argued that fruits were 'most delicious when gathered by our own hands'. In contrast was the negligible 'care and trouble, in the package and conveyance' of goods from major commercial markets. There was a vast difference, he argued, 'betwixt the strawberries plucked from the bed, and those brought from a fruit-shop, perhaps, gathered with unwashed hands the day before'.[74] Hence a clear line was drawn between the home-grown, thoughtful and individual, and the generic and commercial, tainted by an unknown number of hands.

Fruits cultivated in a family's own garden or estate represented an offering both *from* and *of* a suitor and their kin. It is striking just how many food gifts originated with a suitor's wider family, before being directed to a woman's aunts, uncles and parents. In passing through these networks, gifts of food worked to bring two families together in advance of matrimony. At the end of 1756, the Bath apothecary John Lovell, with whom this article opened, was banished from Shaw House after refusing to curb his pursuit of Sarah Harvey. In an attempt to get back into the good graces of her aunt Mary Smith, he sent her some melons and Brussels apricots grown in his father's garden. Apricots were commonly grown in gentlemen's orchards during this period, particularly across the south of England, with Brussels apricots the most highly esteemed flavoursome variety. Melons were highly prized; once the preserve of royalty, they were now common amongst the better sorts.[75] Alongside the fruits, John included a note for Aunt Smith explaining that they were:

---

[72] See Sarah Ann Robin's analysis of the lawyer and politician Henry Marten's home-grown strawberries in 'Posies, Pictures and Promises', 111–12, and Freya Gowrley's work on Lady Eleanor Butler and Sarah Ponsonby (the 'Ladies of Llangollen'), who used oranges, cheese, strawberries, geese and figs as gestures of friendship and intimacy, *Domestic Space in Britain*, 158–9.

[73] Edward Peach to Elizabeth Leathes, Sundridge, 10 May 1790, NRO, BOL 2/140/2.

[74] *The Landscape Gardening and Landscape Architecture of the Late Humphry Repton, Esq., Being His Entire Works on these Subjects* (1840), fragment xxix: Concerning the Luxuries of a Garden, 558.

[75] Thirsk, *Food in Early Modern England*, 147, 300–1; Feluś, *Secret Life of the Georgian Garden*, 170.

a Testimony of having imprinted on my Mind a truly grateful Remembrance of all her past Favours to me, and of my continuing to bear the same Respect to her as I ever did, and that I shou'd think myself very happy if indulg'd again in the same Opportunities of shewing it, which I had before my being so unhappily, and, as I hope, quite undeservedly, exil'd from Shaw.

In light of Aunt Smith's dissatisfaction with the Lovell family's genteel credentials, it is notable that these highly valued fruits had been grown by John's father, making them 'doubly valuable' to John as a gesture.[76] Furthermore, these tokens moved through much of the family themselves, passing not just between lovers, but from his father, to John, to Sarah, and subsequently to her aunt. Gifts of food were therefore set apart from quintessential love tokens such as garters or gloves by blurring the line between courtship gifts and general tokens of goodwill. As such, they helped to unite two families anticipating a matrimonial tie, as signs of their hospitality and favour.

As dualistic items situated at the boundary between tokens of goodwill and explicit offerings of courtship, gifts of food could also be sent from women to their suitors. However, as with the proportion of courtship gifts more broadly, women's gifting was less regular and less intense in volume.[77] After the death of her first husband in 1788, Elizabeth Leathes (née Reading) rekindled her friendship with her childhood sweetheart Edward Peach. Edward was now a Justice of the Peace and had maintained his connection with the Reading family through managing the estate of Elizabeth's late grandfather Thomas Reading (1714–1768). Edward lived in the Old Hall in Sundridge, Kent, where he owned many of the local establishments including a public house, the workhouse and a nearby farm.[78] In January 1790, Elizabeth sent him a 'very excellent' turkey, a hen pheasant and a brace of partridges, 'all equally good in their kind', for which she had the 'best thanks' of her 'sincere Friend'.[79] These were seasonal gifts, with turkeys typically gifted and eaten at Christmastime. They were also particular to East Anglia, where turkeys were reared in their thousands and made to walk all the way to London to be slaughtered. Perhaps as a result, turkeys had a reputation for being tough and tasteless birds. Yet rearing and slaughtering them locally made a vast difference to the freshness and quality of the meat, and they were commonly gifted as local specialities by inhabitants of Norfolk.[80] In spring the same year, Edward sent half a dozen

---

[76] Lovell to Harvey, 17 Aug. 1757, WSA, 161/102/2. In his poem addressed to Sarah's dog Dony, written during his exile from Shaw House in March 1757, John gave an impression of the atmosphere at Shaw: 'airs will never do at Shaw, / Where Manners stand the reigning Law. / Nor will thy rough-hair'd, coal-black Hide, / Thy flirting airs, or City Pride / Pert Courtships, or high mounted Ears, / Gain half that Love which Dido shares', WSA, 161/102/2.

[77] As I have argued elsewhere, women also sent different *types* of gift, including pressed flowers and hand-made textiles such as ruffles and waistcoats. See Holloway, *The Game of Love*, 69, 75, 81, 88, 90, 99, 103–4.

[78] Celia Miller, *The Amiable Mrs Peach* (Norwich, 2016), 68, 76–7.

[79] Peach to Leathes, Sevenoaks, 8 Jan. 1790, NRO, BOL 2/140/2/21.

[80] Lane, *Jane Austen and Food*, 63–4; Miller, *The Amiable Mrs Peach*, 16, 19.

pigeons as a comparably local offering, and hoped to send some lamb but 'could not find out the proper conveyance'.[81] The frequent exchange of edible gifts signalled the couple's ongoing warmth and affection toward one another, helping to rekindle and advance their romance after twenty years apart.

Other courting women similarly participated in the economy of food gifts, with the Essex gentlewoman Mary Martin sending several parcels of fish such as turbot, crayfish and flounder to Isaac Rebow in the 1770s. Isaac was her first cousin, again situating these tokens both within the realm of courtship and of familial care and goodwill. As was increasingly the case over the later eighteenth and early nineteenth centuries, Mary sourced her fish from local fishmongers rather than fish ponds ('now-a-days, all is looked for at shops', lamented William Cobbett in his *Rural Rides*).[82] Whilst Elizabeth Leathes opted for the turkeys which were particular to Norfolk, Mary selected the fish which were abundant in Essex due to their proximity to the Channel and the River Colne. When certain fish were in season, she could procure them 'at any time'. If none were available, they could be sent for directly from Billingsgate, though at the risk of inferior quality.[83] One parcel of flounder was intended for his mother, Mary's aunt, in March 1770, after Mary was 'greatly Concern'd' by accounts of her health.[84] Another, she wrote to Isaac, was 'really design'd for you, only I thought it was better to Direct them to Her, for fear of a Rumpus'.[85] A third parcel of fish was sent alongside some stockings that she had made for him, 'with which they will come very well', combining the everyday with a hand-made token more explicitly prefiguring marriage, and the care she invested in him as his future wife.[86] Her offerings of fish were particularly appropriate tokens due to their very indeterminacy as a gift, situated both within the economy of courtship and also within broader networks of exchange between family and friends.

Whilst Mary sourced her turbot and flounder from the local fishmonger, she did nonetheless enjoy popular pastimes such as bobbing for eels.[87] Fishing parties were lively occasions for sociability and conviviality, as in George Morland's sentimental depiction of an angling party in Figure 3. Such excursions could bring together mixed groups of young men and women in close proximity for sustained periods of time, therefore providing an invaluable chance to generate a romantic bond under the watchful eye of parents, friends or chaperones.[88] The Justice of the Peace Robert Lee (né Philipps) (*c.* 1706–1755)

---

[81] Peach to Leathes, Sevenoaks, 27 Apr. and 10 May 1790, NRO, BOL 2/140/2.

[82] *Rural Rides in the Counties of Surrey, Kent, Sussex, Hants, Berks, Oxford, Bucks, Wilts, Somerset, Gloucester, Hereford, Salop, Worcester, Stafford, Leicester, Hertford, Essex, Suffolk, Norfolk, Cambridge, Huntingdon, Nottingham, Lincoln, York, Lancaster, Durham and Northumberland, during the Years 1821 to 1832; with Economical and Political Observations* (1885), ii, 254.

[83] Martin to Rebow, 8 Mar. 1770 and 30 Jun. 1770, WSU, cg134_17700308 and cg134_17700630.

[84] Martin to Rebow, 8 Mar. 1770, WSU, cg134_17700308.

[85] Martin to Rebow, 9 Jul. 1771, WSU, cg134_17710709.

[86] Martin to Rebow, 8 Oct. 1771, WSU, cg134_17711008.

[87] Martin to Rebow, 28 Aug. 1771, WSU, cg134_17710828.

[88] On angling as a sociable activity for young men and women, see Andrea Pappas, '"Each Wise Nymph that Angles for a Heart": The Politics of Courtship in the Boston "Fishing Lady" Pictures',

Figure 3. George Morland, *A Party Angling*, Britain, 1789, 63.5 × 76.2 cm, oil on canvas, Yale Centre for British Art, Paul Mellon Collection, B.2001.2.2, Public Domain CC0 1.0.

inherited his great-uncle's estate in Binfield, Berkshire, in 1736. Although a substantial distance from the coast, the area was well supplied by ponds, which were typically stocked with fish such as carp, perch, pike, tench, roach and trout.[89] In 1738, Lee ventured on a fishing expedition on his friend Mr Terry's pond in nearby Winkfield, in a group that included his love interest Molly Hopson, and her sister. At the end of their excursion, they divided the catch between Robert Lee and his friend Mr Seddon, vicar of Warfield, plus a gift for Molly's father. The token fit very clearly into his wider patterns of exchange, where he routinely exchanged locally caught fish with friends and family. In addition to the present for Molly's father, the excursion provided an indispensable opportunity for the couple to spend time together at close quarters, and converse freely both on the water and during their subsequent walk home.[90]

Winterthur Portfolio, 49 (2015), 1–28, and Feluś, *Secret Life of the Georgian Garden*, 82–90. Also see George Morland's accompanying scene *The Angler's Repast* where the group pause to enjoy a picnic lunch, Yale Centre for British Art, Paul Mellon Collection, B.2001.2.21.

[89] Roger North, *A Discourse of Fish and Fish-Ponds* (1715); Thirsk, *Food in Early Modern England*, 265–70.

[90] *Diary of Robert Lee of Binfield*, 31 May 1738, 128. See pp. 92 and 129 for further gifts of fish.

Gifts of food sent to a woman's family home represented a creative way for courting men to elicit an invitation to dine. Eating and drinking together created valuable time for a suitor to converse with a woman and her family, as in the print *City Courtship* in Figure 4, where a man and his sweetheart talk whilst their families take tea. The gout-ridden father on the right echoes William Hogarth's evocation of a marriage settlement, where the two patriarchs negotiate over terms, though in this instance the young couple incline their heads toward one another and talk happily.[91] While courting the gentleman's daughter Elizabeth Jeffreys in the 1740s, the barrister Charles Pratt sent a pig as a gift to her mother. As a result, Elizabeth's mother instructed her daughter to write to Charles requesting his presence at dinner. Elizabeth accordingly entreated him 'you must come so dont be Engaged'.[92] The gentleman Edward Peach utilised a similar tactic in his courtship of Elizabeth Leathes (née Reading), sending her two fowls and a duck as a gift in the 1780s. He evidently expected that his gifts would obtain him an invitation to dinner, asking that 'if it will not be unpleasant and inconvenient to you I will with the greatest pleasure and satisfaction to myself partake of the Duck with you at three o' Clock or any other hour you most approve of. I shall call upon you some time before dinner.'[93] Following dinner, couples could then spend the evening together walking in

Figure 4. Thomas Rowlandson, *City Courtship*, London, 1785, hand-coloured etching, plate mark 21.4 × 31 cm, courtesy of the Lewis Walpole Library, Yale University, 786.01.01.01.

[91] I am grateful to Stéphane Jettot for alerting me to this comparison. See William Hogarth, *Marriage A-la-Mode*, 'The Settlement', oil on canvas, *c.* 1743, National Gallery, London, NG113.

[92] Jeffreys to Pratt, u.d. (1740s), KHLC, U840/C9/9.

[93] Peach to Leathes, u.d. (1780s), NRO, BOL 2/140/2/1.

the garden or sitting up late talking, enabling them to converse freely and ascertain their compatibility as spouses.[94] As the prospect of matrimony became more certain, such meetings became much more frequent, with couples dining and drinking tea and chocolate on an almost daily basis as settlements were drawn up, the articles of marriage were drafted and signed and a licence procured.[95] The tea table could even provide an apposite location for a proposal, with the composer John Marsh (1752–1828) 'declaring & engaging' himself to Elizabeth Brown 'in a low voice' over drinks – much like the couple in Figure 4 – whilst their companions were 'trotting on'.[96]

Health, diet and nourishment

Food was believed to have either beneficial or detrimental effects for a person's bodily health, impacting on their digestive systems, their nerves and reproductive organs. It also directly affected their teeth in the physical process of biting and chewing it, particularly in an era of poor oral hygiene and only partial access to dentistry, where many had lost all of their teeth by their early forties.[97] Loreen Giese has revealed how some suitors in sixteenth- and seventeenth-century England presented women with silver toothpicks and carved earscoops to establish a contract to marry, indicating some investment in and care for their physical health.[98] Engraved fruitwood or bone applecorers or scoops carved with romantic symbols such as hearts and the recipient's initials remained popular gifts crafted by labouring suitors into the eighteenth century. These represented particularly thoughtful tokens as they enabled a beloved to continue eating raw apples after losing their teeth, through scraping out the soft flesh.[99]

One particular foodstuff defined the later stages of courtship, as a beloved sweetheart looked sure to attain the status of wife: the humble oyster. Oysters

---

[94] Robert Lee notes walking in the garden with Molly Hopson 'before & after dinner', 25 May 1738, *Diary of Robert Lee of Binfield*, 127. Also see the courtship of Captain Henry Smith (1723–1794) and the tailor's daughter Sarah Hurst (1736–1808) where he regularly visited to dine, take tea, and sit up talking, May 1761, in *The Diaries of Sarah Hurst 1759-62*, ed. Susan C. Djabri (Stroud, 2009), 204–5.

[95] Neave and Neave (eds.), *Diary of a Yorkshire Gentleman*, 82, 147.

[96] Brian Robins (ed.), *The John Marsh Journals: The Life and Times of a Gentleman Composer (1752-1828)* (Stuyvesant, NY, 1998), 20 Oct. 1774, 113, 126.

[97] On food, diet and health see Joanne Begiato, *Manliness in Britain, 1760–1900: Bodies, Emotion, and Material Culture* (Manchester, 2020), 68–100, and Winchcombe, 'Comfort Eating'. On the emergence of dentistry as a vocation see Colin Jones, *The Smile Revolution in Eighteenth Century Paris* (Oxford, 2014).

[98] Giese, *Courtships, Marriage Customs*, 134–5.

[99] See Fruitwood apple corer, eighteenth century, Opus Antiques: https://www.opusantiques.co. uk/product-page/an-18th-century-apple-corer-love-token; Sycamore apple corer engraved with a heart and the date, eighteenth century, Wilkinsons Auctioneers, lot 126: https://www. wilkinsons-auctioneers.co.uk/product/126-14; Sheep shank bone apple corer or cheese scoop carved with the initials N. W. A. within a heart, and the date 1748 within a circle, England or Wales: https://www.collinsantiques.co.uk/cgi-bin/item-details.pl?itemID=12220; also described in Margaret Lambert and Enid Marx, *English Popular Art* (1951), 21; Pinto, *Treen and Other Wooden Bygones*, 84, pl. 80.

could be purchased for as little as twelvepence a peck (for around twenty-five), rising to three or four shillings a barrel.[100] The most sought-after and expensive varieties were 'the best green native Colchester', and 'Exceeding fine' Pyefleet oysters from Pyefleet Creek in Essex, with proprietors advertising their services to the 'Nobility, Gentry, Tradesmen and Others'.[101] Echoing the emphasis on the hand-picked over the commercial discussed above, such traders stressed that their oysters were picked 'fresh from the Beds' on fixed days, did *not* pass through Billingsgate, and came in branded barrels to guarantee quality. Usefully for courting couples, they could be shipped across the country from oyster warehouses, which often offered free local delivery, or purchased from street sellers, fairs and markets.[102]

Oysters possessed a twofold power in provoking feelings of lust and desire, with pretty oyster girls objectified for their sexual availability, and oysters themselves (alongside other shellfish such as crabs, crayfish and lobsters) renowned for their aphrodisiac properties.[103] The Colchester schoolmaster George Lloyd may have hoped that the lustful qualities of oysters would help to secure his engagement to his beloved Mrs Gray in 1677. She had already informed him in August that 'all things were at an end' between them, but he 'writt an answer' and opted not to send it, deciding that the subject was better broached in person. He travelled to London to propose in October, purchasing a carnelian ring and barrel of oysters as tokens. The act of sharing the oysters would have provided valuable time to repair their broken relationship, potentially reignite their bond by stirring sexual desire, and show his care and investment in safeguarding her physical health. For a short period, at least, it worked, with Lloyd staying over with her 'all night' the following month.[104]

The highly nutritious and 'strength-restoring' properties of oysters made them a particularly apposite choice for nourishing a future wife.[105] In this sense, as Jane Bennett suggests, the emotional power of food as a type of object

---

[100] See the print *Twelve Pence a Peck Oysters*, The Cries of London, 1688, etching, British Museum, London (BM), L,85.23.

[101] Draft trade card of the fishmonger Sarah Bonwick of 77 Queen Street, Cheapside, London, BM, Heal,63*1.

[102] For the shipping of oysters by the barrel see draft trade card of Clarks Shell Fish Warehouse of Soho Square, Heal, BM, 63*2; Draft trade card of John Rawson, barrelled oyster purveyor of Holborn, BM, Heal,63*12; Draft trade card of T. Howell, fishmonger of Minories, BM, D,2.1223; Draft trade card for Pedley Junior's Oyster & Shell Fish Warehouse, Covent Garden, BM, Heal,63*11; Draft trade card of J. Burt, fishmonger of Islington, *c.* 1820, BM, Banks,63*4.

[103] For oyster girls being propositioned by men see the trial of Elizabeth Mordant for pickpocketing, 16 Oct. 1723, t17231016-54, and the trial of Thomas Cash, Mary White and Margaret Boyl for pickpocketing, 23 Apr. 1718, t17180423-49, Old Bailey Online. For oyster girls in visual culture see the prints *Molly Milton, the Pretty Oyster Woman, c.* 1787, hand-coloured mezzotint, BM, 1935,0522.1.109, and *The Fair Oysterinda*, London, 1736–75, BM, 1872,0703.11. On aphrodisiacs see Jennifer Evans, *Aphrodisiacs, Fertility and Medicine in Early Modern England* (Woodbridge, 2014), 90–108.

[104] 'The Diary of George Lloyd', 22 Oct. 1677, 270.

[105] 'When strength-restoring Oysters are in prime; Or in plain English, it was Winter-Time', George Alexander Stevens, *Distress upon Distress* (1752), 45; Drew Smith, *Oyster: A World History* (Stroud, 2010), 37–9.

arises from how it 'modifies the human matter with which it comes into contact', mutually transforming both the eater and eaten.[106] In October 1790 the gentleman Edward Peach sent a barrel to the widow Elizabeth Leathes to aid her recovery from illness, noting they were 'esteem'd very nutritious' and in 'no ways improper for you at this time'.[107] He asked her to 'give me leave to be your Physician' and in addition to the oysters recommended that she consume a 'Neck of Mutton made into Broth' with 'a Turnip or two'.[108] Mutton ranked highly in tables of the most nourishing foods, with meat broths known for their therapeutic properties. Lighter-coloured vegetables such as parsnips were viewed as lighter and therefore easier to digest, coming highly recommended by medical writers for their nourishing properties.[109] This exchange was only a month before the couple's wedding, which took place on 25 November 1790, and so enabled Edward to begin caring for Elizabeth akin to a spouse.

The Derbyshire cotton-trader Joseph Strutt (1765–1844) took a similar approach during the illness of his sweetheart Isabella Douglas (1769–1802) in the spring of 1791. Her indisposition and the fear of losing her made him realise, he wrote, just how much he loved her. As a result, only her 'compleat restoration to health' could secure his future happiness. Joseph's investment in Isabella's ill health, and the lengths to which he was willing to go in order to ensure her recovery, worked to underscore his devotion as a future husband. To his mind, similarly to Edward Peach, the most nourishing foods available were meat and oysters. The former were considered heating foods which warmed and enlivened the body, shaped by the older humoural model and advocated by medical writers throughout the eighteenth century.[110] Yet a woman's personal tastes were also important, both in the arena of courtship and in discourses on diet and health.[111] Since Isabella did not like meat, Joseph opted to send a routine delivery of oysters by the barrel, writing:

I have not heard lately whether your Oysters came regularly & whether you have enough of them – if they do not, or are not good, & you still prefer them, I desire I may know that I may order you some immediately from London; remember you are no longer to treat me with ceremony on this score.[112]

---

[106] Bennett, *Vibrant Matter*, 40, 51.

[107] Peach to Leathes, Norwich, 8 Oct. 1790, NRO, BOL 2/140/2/35.

[108] Peach to Leathes, 17 Oct. 1790, NRO, BOL 2/140/2/36.

[109] George Cheyne, *An Essay of Health and Long Life*, 2nd edn (1725), 25–6; George Cheyne, *The Natural Method of Curing the Diseases of the Body, and the Disorders of the Mind* (1753), 55; John Hill, *The Old Man's Guide to Health and Longer Life: With Rules for Diet, Exercise, and Physic*, 6th edn (1764), 17, 41–2, 47; David Gentilcore, *Food and Health in Early Modern Europe: Diet, Medicine and Society, 1450–1800* (2016), 40, 129.

[110] Evans, *Aphrodisiacs*, 90–100, 107.

[111] See for example George Thomson, *Orthomethodos Iatro Chimiche, or the Direct Method of Curing Chymically. Wherein is Conteined the Original Matter, and Principal Agent of all Natural Bodies* (1675), 26; William Forster *A Treatise on the Causes of Most Diseases Incident to Human Bodies, and the Cure of Them* (1745), 18.

[112] Joseph Strutt to Isabella Douglas, Derby, 17 Apr. 1791, 18 Mar. 1791 and 8 May 1791, Birmingham City Archives, Birmingham (BCA), MS3101/C/E/4/8/23–5.

The strength of his commitment was evinced by the lengths to which he would go to procure her suitable foodstuffs, despite his distance from the coast meaning that there were often 'none fit to eat'. Through food, he declared his desire to 'sit by ... watch over ... wait upon' Isabella in matrimony. He advised that she 'do anything which will contribute to the ease of your mind, or the strength of your body' – through his food gifts, Joseph endeavoured to do the same.[113]

Conclusion

This article has sought to restore the critical importance of food gifts in navigating the path to matrimony in England during the long eighteenth century. In the absence of any a priori symbolic association with love or romance, the emotional meaning of food gifts was shaped by a number of factors, including their rarity, exoticism, freshness, nutritional properties, where they had been grown, by whom, and *with* whom they were consumed. Personal tastes were also important, and the desire to show knowledge of and attentiveness to a recipient's preferences. These tokens are so significant because they represent an entirely unique category of courtship gift, one hitherto neglected by historians, set apart from the garters, gloves, hair, ribbons and rings which have typically been used to distinguish courting behaviour. Through them, we see courtship made everyday, inextricably bound up in the webs of exchange which bound human beings to one another and to the natural world. This was not food eaten to *live*, but utilised as a powerful material means of communication, a vehicle for status, identity and emotion, and the creation of interpersonal bonds.

If melons, turkeys and fish can all constitute emotional objects, what does this suggest about where the boundaries of affective meaning begin and end? The article has endeavoured to demonstrate why we must extend our definition of materiality beyond man-made or machine-made objects, and beyond extant objects preserved in archives and museums, to also include foodstuffs and other perishable or organic items from the natural world. In doing so, we recognise how more ephemeral or transitory items also had important emotional meanings, which continued long after they ceased to exist in any tangible sense. The foodstuffs exchanged during courtship had the power to stimulate love, lust, joy, sensory delight and gustatory pleasure. They could function as gestures of humility, generosity and friendship, and signal thought, effort and familial care. These affective meanings would have looked noticeably different in other contexts, such as in the tokens exchanged between friends, family members or neighbours, demonstrating the cultural and emotional flexibility of food as a gift.

Food gifts further represent unique tokens of courtship as they could be given with the intention of being *consumed* with a loved one, thereby creating further opportunities for intimacy through walking, talking and dining together. They help to illuminate how courtship could be initiated, and the range of spaces in which it was situated: in public gardens and squares, the grounds and ponds of country estates, at fairs or wakes, in theatres, confectionery shops and around a tea table. Such items underscore the continuing importance of

---

[113] Strutt to Douglas, Derby, 18 Mar. 1791, 17 Apr. 1791 and 5 Jun. 1791, BCA, MS3101/C/E/4/8/23, 24, 26.

families in shepherding along successful courtships, through hosting suitors for tea and chocolate, inviting them to dine and sharing the bounties of their gardens or estates. By paying close attention to such gifts, we can reconstruct a whole intangible system of feeling, and intrinsic part of the gift mode, which gave structure and meaning to the social and emotional process of courtship.

Given the centrality of food and food gifts in navigating the rituals of courtship, it is fitting therefore that food also symbolically and practically marked the change in a couple's status from suitors to spouses. Following their nuptials, couples informed their wider friends and family of their marriage by writing to them and distributing slices of the bride cake – a fruit cake decorated with almond and sugar icing – through the post.[114] One tale published in the periodical *The Connoisseur* accordingly figured the whole process of courtship through cake, in a dream purportedly inspired by a slice of the bride cake sent by a newly married couple. In the dream, courting couples crowded into the Temple of the God of Marriage, which was 'covered with a great number of Cakes of different shapes and appearance'. Some cakes were embellished with 'glittering toys' representing the potential rewards of marriage, including a fine house and a coach and six. In the Temple, couples approached the altar and applied to Cupid to gift them a cake. In one sense, the cakes represented virtuous femininity, with the 'most elegant' cakes with the 'sweetest ingredients' costing the largest sum of money. In another, they embodied marriage itself, with some women reaching the altar only to trade their 'plain' cake for a 'much more glittering' alternative.[115] Through cake, courtship comes full circle, from a suitor's opening gambit to a material signification of matrimony. The edible gift emerges as an unparalleled system of emotional communication, at once a symbol and the very literal food of love.

Acknowledgements. I am immensely grateful to Joanne Begiato and Alysa Levene for reading drafts of this article, and to Lucy Allen, Tul Israngura Na Ayudhya, Benjamin Jackson, Stéphane Jettot and Rachel Winchcombe for generously sharing references and unpublished work. This research was presented to audiences at the History Lunchtime Research Seminar at Oxford Brookes University, the Oxford Graduate Seminar in History, the conference 'Emotion, Embodiment and the Everyday, 1500–1800' at the University of Cambridge, and the Franco-British History Seminar at the Sorbonne University in Paris, all of whom provided helpful feedback and suggestions. I am also indebted to this journal's anonymous reviewers for their thoughtful and constructive feedback.

---

[114] For example, Elizabeth Reading spent £1 2s. 6d. on her wedding cake in 1774, which she distributed alongside letters to her friends and relatives. Miller, *The Amiable Mrs Peach*, 13; Elizabeth Raffald, *The Experienced English Housekeeper, For the Use and Ease of Ladies, Housekeepers, Cooks, &c* (1786), 'To make Almond-Icing for the Bride-Cake', 265. On the cementing of the wedding cake as a central aspect of marriage rituals during the nineteenth century see Jennifer Phegley, *Courtship and Marriage in Victorian England* (Oxford, 2012), 122–3; Simon R. Charsley, *Wedding Cakes and Cultural History* (1992); Lucy Cory Allen, 'Classing Enchantment: Rethinking Social Identities with the Material Culture of Weddings in England, 1836–1914' (PhD thesis, University of Manchester, 2021), 175–219.

[115] *The Connoisseur*, no. 45, 20 Nov. 1755, 214–15.

Cite this article: Holloway S (2024). The Foods of Love? Food Gifts, Courtship and Emotions in Long Eighteenth-Century England. *Transactions of the Royal Historical Society* 2, 111–134. https://doi.org/10.1017/S0080440123000270

Transactions of the RHS (2024), 2, 135–155
doi:10.1017/S008044012400001X

ARTICLE

A Sense of a European Present and its Passing during the Revolutions of 1848

James Morris

Department of History, University College London, London, UK
Email: james.r.morris@ucl.ac.uk

(Received 7 November 2023; revised 2 February 2024; accepted 9 February 2024;
first published online 21 March 2024)

Abstract

This article explores the temporality of revolution in 1848. It argues that what united the various revolutionary movements of that year was a sense of participating in a common European 'present', in which old imperial hierarchies collapsed and every cause and people seemed to exist in the same historical moment. The significance of that sense of the present was visible across the continent, but it was of greatest significance in the revolutionary theatres beyond the core imperial centres, and it was those places that would suffer first when that present passed. Too much 'history' was taking place at once, and as events in different settings followed their own particular courses, minds turned away from a European project. As European unity faltered, it was the representatives of imperial counter-revolution who demonstrated their ability to think strategically on a continent-wide level. They defeated the various movements, which had promised a better European present, and deferred improvements to the future. By doing so, they returned the peoples of the continent to their own particular – rather than common European – 'nows'.

Keywords: Revolution; Europe; Temporality; Politics; 1848; Empire; Nation

Dumitru Brătianu spoke extemporaneously. He did not need notes to capture the spirit of the age in the early days of 1848, that year of European revolutionary upheaval, and so when a friend asked whether he could publish the text of Brătianu's speech in his Bucharest gazette during the summer, Brătianu had to reproduce it from memory. Neither man could recall the precise date of the speech. The newspaper editor was not even present when it was delivered, but he had heard the praise of others who were. Standing before his audience in the meeting rooms of the Society of Romanian Students in Paris at 3 Place de la Sorbonne, the twenty-nine-year-old Brătianu wondered whether 'we can have only memories and aspirations'. There were men, he said, who considered the present to be an 'illusion', who argued that 'we should seek only the future, that we should not occupy ourselves with the present, that mankind has only a past and a future, and that the present does not exist'. Brătianu had one word to describe this attitude: 'sophism'. He could not fathom how those men could say that the present was a fiction, most particularly 'today, when all of mankind is entering into a struggle that was unknown in past times'.[1]

By 1848, the historical significance of 'revolution' was well established. As Timothy Tackett has argued, the men who gathered in Versailles for the Estates General of 1789 did not believe that they were revolutionaries engaged in revolution; it was the course of events that made them so. They did not have a revolutionary 'script' to hand, but their successors in the mid-nineteenth century would.[2] These people knew what revolution meant. After posters appeared on Palermo walls in early January 1848, promising that a revolution would take place on King Ferdinand II's birthday (12 January), the people of the city turned out to see history in the making. The presence of so many bodies in the streets spooked the soldiers sent to maintain order, and when a shot was fired, popular indignation fulfilled the poster's promise: a revolution began. It was not the first to take place in the Kingdom of the Two Sicilies. Several states beyond France could claim a revolutionary heritage before 1848. A revolutionary wave crossed the Mediterranean in the 1820s, affecting Portugal, Spain, the Italian states and Greece, while the Polish and the Belgians would follow another French revolution in 1830, heightening the anxieties of European state officials who worried what might happen if the cause of revolution were allowed to spread unchecked.[3] In the spring of 1848, it carried farther, faster, and many of those who witnessed and participated in this historical moment recognised and understood its importance as a European event.

The revolutionary objectives of 1848 varied between theatres and movements, but all were united by what one of Brătianu's friends would later call the European 'occasion'.[4] Historians have long debated the extent to which events in 1848 could be considered 'European'. Hartmut Pogge von

---

[1] The text of Brătianu's speech was published in *Pruncul Român* on 29 July, 1848. It was reproduced in Ioan C. Brătianu (ed.), *Anul 1848 în Principatele Române: Acte şi Documente publicate cu ajutorul Comitetului pentru Rădicarea Monumentului* (6 vols., Bucharest, 1902–10), I, 61–73.

[2] Timothy Tackett, *Becoming a Revolutionary: The Deputies of the French National Assembly and the Emergence of a Revolutionary Culture (1789–1790)* (Princeton, NJ, 1996); on revolutionary 'scripts', see Keith Michael Baker and Dan Edelstein (eds.), *Scripting Revolution: A Historical Approach to the Comparative Study of Revolutions* (Stanford, CA, 2015).

[3] On the 1820s, see Maurizio Isabella, *Southern Europe in the Age of Revolutions* (Princeton, NJ, 2023); Mark Mazower, *The Greek Revolution: 1821 and the Making of Modern Europe* (2021); for the 1830s, see Clive H. Church, *Europe in 1830: Revolution and Political Change* (1983); on fears of revolution see Beatrice de Graaf, *Fighting Terror after Napoleon: How Europe Became Secure after 1815* (Cambridge, 2020); Beatrice de Graaf et al. (eds.), *Securing Europe after Napoleon: 1815 and the New European Security Culture* (Cambridge, 2019); Adam Zamoyski, *Phantom Terror: The Threat of Revolution and the Repression of Liberty, 1789–1848* (2014).

[4] Nicolae Bălcescu, 'Mersul revoluţiei în istoria românilor', in Nicolae Bălcescu, *Opere*, ed. Gheorghe Zane (4 vols., Bucharest, 1961–86), II, 107–13.

Strandmann questioned whether the description makes sense given that 'only four major countries – France, Germany, the Habsburg empire, and Italy – were directly involved'.[5] Both his insistence on 'major' countries and his use of the term 'country' seem misguided. Neither an Italian nor a German state existed in 1848, while the Habsburg empire stretched across much of the continent, covering territory in today's Austria, Italy, Hungary, Czechia, Slovakia, Slovenia, Poland, Romania, Ukraine, Serbia and Croatia. As Miles Taylor has shown, there were also uprisings in British-controlled territories, such as the Greek Ionian Islands, and the Ottoman and Russian empires were implicated, too, by events in the principalities of Moldavia and Wallachia.[6] This European scope was well captured in the lithographer Franz Werner's 'Political Map of Europe' (Figure 1), which shows a continent overrun with people, many of them armed, on horseback, or waving flags. Perhaps this continental scale was the reason that the revolutions of 1848, like those of 1989, came to be known by the year in which they took place.[7] Their geographical extent was so great that time became the defining factor.

Like Brătianu, many participants and observers believed that Europe was entering a shared revolutionary present, and this belief both influenced events and their historical interpretation. Mike Rapport has suggested that the revolutions of 1848 were European in 'the sense that they were genuinely spontaneous across the continent', while Christopher Clark has described the 'revolutionary spring' as the 'only truly European revolution that there has ever been'.[8] Both of these interpretations have merit, but each one misses something out. Although almost every revolutionary outbreak was 'spontaneous' rather than 'planned' by some secret committee, none occurred in a vacuum. Participants were influenced by events elsewhere. And while Clark's assessment would have appealed to many revolutionary activists, it also obscures something inadvertently captured by von Strandmann's doubt: the sense that European states, nations and territories existed within a civilisational hierarchy, divided between the 'Enlightened' core and those on the peripheries who lagged behind.[9] The German conceptual historian Reinhart Koselleck classified this temporal difference as the *Gleichzeitigkeit des Ungleichzeitigen*, which has variously been translated as the 'simultaneity of

---

[5] Hartmut Pogge von Strandmann, '1848–1849: A European Revolution?', in *The Revolutions in Europe 1848-1849: From Reform to Reaction*, ed. R. J. W. Evans and Hartmut Pogge von Strandmann (Oxford, 2000), 1–8, at 2.

[6] Miles Taylor, 'The 1848 Revolutions and the British Empire', *Past and Present*, 166 (2000), 146–80; on Wallachia, see James Morris, 'Locating the Wallachian Revolution of 1848', *Historical Journal*, 64 (2021), 606–25.

[7] Both these revolutions have been considered 'revolutions of the intellectuals', too. See Lewis Namier, *1848: The Revolution of the Intellectuals* (1946); Ivan Krastev and Stephen Holmes, *The Light that Failed: A Reckoning* (2019), 23.

[8] Mike Rapport, *1848: Year of Revolution* (2009), 410; Christopher Clark, *Revolutionary Spring: Fighting for a New World, 1848-1849* (2023), 1.

[9] See Larry Wolff, *Inventing Eastern Europe: The Map of Civilization on the Mind of the Enlightenment* (Stanford, CA, 1994); Maria Todorova, 'The Trap of Backwardness: Modernity, Temporality, and the Study of Eastern European Nationalism', *Slavic Review*, 64 (2005), 140–64.

Figure 1. Franz Werner, 'Political Map of Europe'.

the nonsimultaneous' or the 'contemporaneity of the noncontemporaneous'.[10] A combination of these two renderings seems most apposite: the 'simultaneity of the noncontemporaneous'. Two events could take place at the same time, or simultaneously, but that did not mean they shared something in common, or were contemporaneous. Before 1848, few in Europe believed that the continent existed or even could exist in the same historical moment. As Stuart Woolf has argued, 'by 1789 the leading role of France in the forward march of civilisation was accepted by educated elites throughout Europe'. Other peoples had to follow suit, which meant that the 'integration' of Europe under Napoleon would be a process driven by one power, and the creation of the post-Napoleonic 'security culture' at Vienna would be similarly driven by the continent's leading powers.[11] This way of thinking was challenged by the outbreak of revolution in 1848.

To engage in revolution in 1848 was to participate in a shared European present. The historian Dan Edelstein has suggested that 'revolutionaries make demands in the present tense', but it was not only the demands of 1848 that were framed in that language.[12] References to the present abounded in

---

[10] See Reinhart Koselleck, *The Practice of Conceptual History: Timing History, Spacing Concepts*, trans. Todd Samuel Presner et al. (Stanford, CA, 2002), 8.

[11] Stuart Woolf, *Napoleon's Integration of Europe* (2002), 8; on the 'security culture', see de Graaf, *Fighting Terror after Napoleon* and de Graaf, *Securing Europe after Napoleon*.

[12] Dan Edelstein, 'Future Perfect: Political and Emotional Economies of Revolutionary Time', in *Power and Time: Temporalities in Conflict and the Making of History*, ed. Dan Edelstein et al. (Chicago, 2020), 357–78, at 357.

discussions of history and politics. The Prussian journalist Fanny Lewald wrote from Cologne in March that 'mankind is accomplishing its most important deeds in the present', and the Russian philosopher Alexander Herzen would later lament his own homeland's fight 'against the present'.[13] Lesser known than Lewald and Herzen, it was Brătianu whose speech best captured the experience of that European present. He asked his friends whether they heard the echoing voices from Switzerland and the Italian peninsula carrying across the Apennines and the Alps and spoke of movements in Styria, Bohemia and Croatia. In Palermo, he told his audience, the 'smell of gunpowder rejuvenates the old, arms the young, and makes men of the women'. For Brătianu, these were not the 'serial revolutions' that Clare Pettitt has described.[14] They did not exist in sequence. His speech toured Europe, and it did so in the present tense, collapsing the incipient revolutions into a single, shared historical moment.[15] Europe, it seemed, had entered a common present.

One of the strengths of 'Europe' as a unifying idea lay in its imprecision. As Mats Andrén has argued, it is only since 1800 that the 'concept of Europe' has taken on a primarily political meaning, signifying vague ideas of 'civilisation'.[16] The inchoate and youthful character of this idea of 'Europe' made it readily appealing to political actors in 1848. Every cause and party could appeal to 'Europe' because 'Europe' had no fixed ideological meaning. It could stand for whatever the speaker desired. In Bucharest, for instance, the Provisional Government called on the landowners who had left the city after the outbreak of revolution to return in order to avoid compromising the revolutionary cause in the 'eyes of Europe'. One of those landowners would himself invoke the same European eyes when denouncing the government's plan to transfer land from the nobility to the peasantry: how would Europe respond when it saw that 'our peaceful and common revolution ... begins its work with the abolition of the right of property and the breakdown of human society'?[17] Such tensions regarding the meaning of Europe both within and between movements would undermine its resonance and hamper the development of a revolutionary coalition.

If the spring of 1848 had promised the synchronisation of Europe through revolution, then by the end of 1849, with the suppression of many of those revolutions, that promise had faltered. Europe's ideological resonance was stretched beyond its breaking point. The idea of a shared revolutionary present could propagate the cause of revolution, but it could not sustain it or promote its success. A second glance at Werner's map reveals a continental cacophony. So much was happening that it was difficult to keep abreast of the news from all the different revolutionary theatres. Revolutionary actors could feel that they were contemporaneous with one another, but thinking and acting on

---

[13] Fanny Lewald, *A Year of Revolutions: Fanny Lewald's Recollections of 1848*, ed. Hanna Ballin Lewis (Providence, RI, 1997), 30; Alexander Herzen, *From the Other Shore and The Russian People and Socialism*, ed. Isaiah Berlin (Oxford, 1979), 14.

[14] See Clare Pettitt, *Serial Revolutions 1848: Writing, Politics, Form* (Oxford, 2022).

[15] *Anul 1848*, I, 68–9.

[16] Mats Andrén, *Thinking Europe: A History of the European Idea since 1800* (Oxford, 2023), 4.

[17] Morris, 'Locating the Wallachian Revolution', 620–1.

the basis of those feelings was difficult. The new technologies of the railway and the telegraph, which Reinhart Koselleck argued linked the revolutionary theatres 'like a system of communicating tubes', were not nearly as commonplace as some historians have suggested.[18] It would only be after 1848 that such lines began to link up the continent. Without rapid communication or a practical 'European' programme, there was little to sustain the idea of the European present. Particular rather than European problems were more pressing, and as the imagined revolutionary coalition fractured, its counter-revolutionary adversaries demonstrated their organisational and diplomatic skills, reasserting Europe's old imperial hierarchies against the revolutionary alternative. The statesmen who followed would turn from the present to the future, enshrining progress as a government objective, and here lay the supposed failure of 1848: to keep European politics in the present.

A European Moment

To mark the beginning of the new year, 1848, the French weekly periodical *L'Illustration* offered some semi-satirical predictions for the months ahead. Before the end of January, a traveller would return to Paris from far-flung lands with incredible stories of the cultures he encountered. February would see a 'savage' quit France for his homeland, where his tales of the 'boeuf gras' of Shrove Tuesday would scarcely be believed. March would bring dances, April the visit of a foreign ambassador to the racetrack at Longchamps, and May a procession of the national guard to the Tuileries Palace. Doctors would instruct their patients to take the waters in June, and in July, the French capital would witness contests on the Seine to commemorate the eighteenth anniversary of the revolution of 1830, which brought Louis-Philippe to the French throne.[19]

But revolutionary celebrations came early to Paris, and they did not honour the past, but rather signalled the beginning of a new present. France was not the first European state to experience revolution in 1848. The people of Sicily rose in opposition to union with Naples in January, more than a month before the Parisians stormed the Tuileries palace on 24 February, and already the news bulletins seemed to augur wider change. *Le Constitutionnel* praised the 'great courage' of the inhabitants of Palermo and the surrounding districts, while the *Bayreuther Zeitung* promised 'very exciting news' from the city. *La Réforme* compared the Sicilian struggle to political movements elsewhere, and in Austrian Kronstadt, the *Gazeta de Transilvania* reported that 'all the Great Powers of Europe' were looking towards Italy; as, it seemed, were the

---

[18] Reinhart Koselleck, 'How European Was the Revolution of 1848/49?', in *1848: A European Revolution? International Ideas and National Memories of 1848*, ed. Axel Körner (Basingstoke, 2000), 209–21, at 212–13; Dominique Kirchner Reill has made a similar observation on the limits of railways and telegraphy in 1848. See Dominique Kirchner Reill, *Nationalists Who Feared the Nation: Adriatic Multi-Nationalism in Habsburg Dalmatia, Trieste, and Venice* (Stanford, CA, 2012), 279 n. 12.

[19] *L'Illustration*, 1 Jan. 1848; for more on *L'Illustration* during 1848, see Alexandra Tranca, 'The Illustrated Press and the Writing of History: The *Recueils* of *L'Illustration* in 1848', *Dix-Neuf: Journal of the Society of Dix-Neuviémistes*, 21 (2017), 280–96.

newspapers. Across the Wallachian border in Bucharest, the *Curierul Românesc* put the Piedmontese King Carlo Alberto's promise of a new constitution on the front page.[20] Even before the outbreak of the revolution in Paris, there was a sense of the impending drama, and the fall of Louis-Philippe only seemed to confirm that the revolution would become general. Caught in the afterglow and exhaustion of his own experience in the Tuileries palace, one of Brătianu's Wallachian friends would write on 24 February that events in the French capital had 'redeemed the liberty of the world'.[21]

Paris in the spring of 1848 felt like not only a French revolutionary centre, but also a European one. When Fanny Lewald first heard the news of the February revolution during a journey from Oldenburg to Bremen, she wrote of her excitement to be travelling to Paris, the 'eternally beating heart of Europe'. On reaching the French capital, she found the character of its streets matched that European descriptor. On 19 March, she encountered a group of 'Germans' parading along the Rue Royale with the red, black and gold flag of their national movement. They mixed cries of 'Vive la République' with ones of 'Take the revolution to Vienna! The Republic to Vienna! The abdication of Prince Metternich!' It was not only Germans who trumpeted this message either. One newspaper vendor whom Lewald encountered had set the German tricolour alongside similar slogans promising that Vienna would be next.[22]

French authorities encouraged the foreign communities of Paris to understand the revolution as a shared one, and those communities embraced this ideal. Delegations queued alongside journeymen carpenters, schoolteachers, and bureaucrats to offer both thanks and congratulations to the new republican government. Many brought the standards of their own national movements. On receiving one from Brătianu and his friends, the city's deputy mayor, Philippe Buchez, made clear that he understood the revolution as part of wider project. He told his audience that 'that which was done in Paris is not only a French work, but a European one'.[23] The historian Lawrence Jennings has disparaged these ceremonies, suggesting that French officials only intended to satisfy their audiences by 'extolling "the pastoral virtues" of the Hungarians or the "example of liberty" which the Norwegians had given to the world'. If they went further, then it was only because the speeches were 'delivered extemporaneously and with an air of excitement', but it was precisely that 'air of excitement' that defined the revolutionary culture of Paris in the spring.[24] It reflected a general sense of the historical significance of the moment and its European horizons.

---

[20] *Le Constitutionnel*, 25 Jan. 1848; *Bayreuther Zeitung*, 26 Jan. 1848; *Gazeta de Transilvania*, 2 Feb. 1848; *Curierul Românesc*, 23 Feb./6 Mar. 1848.

[21] Nicolae Bălcescu to Vasile Alecsandri, 24 Feb. 1848. Reproduced in Bălcescu, *Opere*, IV, 86.

[22] Lewald, *A Year of Revolutions*, 24 and 75.

[23] *Le Constitutionnel*, 22 Mar. 1848; an account of the meeting also appeared in the Austrian *Gazeta de Transilvania*, 26 Apr. 1848. It is worth noting that Buchez's vision of Europe excluded the Muslim peoples of the Ottoman empire, whereas the would-be Wallachian revolutionaries in his audience would later emphasise their loyalty to that empire once they took power in Bucharest. See Morris, 'Locating the Wallachian Revolution'.

[24] Lawrence C. Jennings, *France and Europe in 1848: A Study of French Foreign Affairs in Time of Crisis* (Oxford, 1973), 10–14.

Each new revolutionary outbreak increased excitement and conferred further legitimacy on those that came before. News of the Viennese revolution in March proved as momentous as that of Paris. A group of students in the French capital delivered letters congratulating their Viennese counterparts to every newspaper office in the city, while a pharmacist in Florence wrote in his diary that the 'fall of Metternich and his old system of government caused great rejoicing'.[25] The 'old Europe', announced *Le Constitutionnel*, was 'no longer recognisable'.[26] A new one had taken its place. Even outlets that adopted a cautious or hostile approach to the French February revolution now changed tack. The Romanian-language *Organulu Luminarei*, which was published at Blaj in Austrian Transylvania, had described the Parisian uprising as 'tragic' on 3 March. Its editor expressed his fear that the revolution would have terrible consequences for the peace and civilization of Europe, but his opinion changed two weeks later when the stories of Vienna and Hungary arrived. The 17 March edition carried reports of the 'progress towards liberty' instead.[27] Whereas revolution in one theatre could be divisive and destabilising, perhaps indicating the possibility of another European war, the spread of revolution across the continent suggested something different. As one Milanese revolutionary later recalled, every day the news from elsewhere 'roused minds more and more', heightening the 'fever'.[28]

Peoples across Europe discussed and celebrated foreign revolutionary reports. The seventeen-year-old Petre Orbescu, a pupil at the Radu Voda gymnasium in Bucharest, read all the newspaper accounts of events in Paris and Vienna and discussed them with his friends between lessons.[29] In Rome, Pope Pius IX ordered the great bell of the Capitol to be rung when the first stories from Vienna reached the city on 20 March, and its tolls were echoed by other Roman bells. The fourteen-year-old Clara Jane Shaw, travelling in Italy with her family, wrote in her diary that 'joy was painted on every face and before all the cafés numbers of people were collected to congratulate each other'. None had participated themselves in the Viennese revolution, but they seemed to feel a kind of ownership of events. Later in the afternoon, Shaw encountered an immense crowd returning from the Austrian ambassador's residence, where they had torn the coat of arms from the façade. People hissed as it was dragged through the streets, and women cut pieces of wood to stick in their hats.[30] Such hostility towards the insignia of Austrian power might have reflected opposition to the empire's control over Lombardy and the Veneto in northern Italy, but the celebrations of the Viennese revolution itself indicated a less national motive: a sense that what

---

[25] Diary of J. E. Davies, British Library (BL), Additional Manuscript (Add. MS) 59886, 14; Diary of an English pharmacist in Florence. BL, Add. MS 62907C, 10r.

[26] *Le Constitutionnel*, 20 Mar. 1848.

[27] *Organulu Luminarei*, 3 and 17 Mar. 1848.

[28] Felice Venosta, *Le Cinque Giornate di Milano (Marzo 1848): Memorie Storiche* (Milan, 1864), 44.

[29] Interrogation of Petre Orbescu, Arhivele Naționale ale României (ANIC), Comisia alcătuită pentru cercetarea celor amestecați în fapte revoluționare de la 1848, 601/25/1849.

[30] Diary of Clara Jane Shaw. BL, European Manuscripts (MSS Eur) F197/19, 7v–8r.

had happened in Vienna was momentous and would facilitate similar movements elsewhere.

Revolutionary news became an aspect of quotidian life in Europe in 1848, even beyond the ranks of the revolutionary participants themselves. According to Marie-Claire Hoock-Demarle, the French Revolution of 1789 changed the daily lives of educated women across the continent. Before the outbreak of the revolution, their correspondence consisted almost exclusively of personal stories, but after 1789, they began to comment on politics and world events.[31] The revolutions of 1848 had a similar but more widespread effect. The frequency of stories and the scale of their coverage were unprecedented, imprinting European politics on an array of minds. Clara Jane Shaw's diary entries for 1847 consisted exclusively of descriptions of the Italian foods she tried and the sites of art-historical and archaeological interest that she visited, but with the outbreak of a revolution in Naples during her stay, her descriptions of churches steadily gave way to street scenes and reports from abroad. The same was true for the young Laura Anna Harvey in the Bagni di Lucca, who experienced the revolutions primarily through reports in *Galignani's Messenger*. Like Shaw, her 1847 diary entries described Italian art and architecture, whereas in 1848, she began to record the news from France, Italy, Prussia, Bohemia, and even Moldavia, a place that she was unlikely to have ever visited or perhaps even known of before. She was not the only member of her family to become absorbed in European affairs either. The conversations of her household were consumed with revolutionary goings-on.[32]

News knit the local and the European community together and helped to foster a shared sense of the revolutionary present. In his work on the development of nationalism, Benedict Anderson suggested that the act of reading a newspaper brought national communities together. Each reader, he argued, was 'well aware that the ceremony he performs is being replicated simultaneously by thousands (or millions) of others'.[33] His thesis turned on the practice of reading a newspaper, but the contents of that newspaper were just as important in fostering communities, and in 1848, as Harvey's diary entries indicated, people were reading and encountering stories from across the continent. They often did so in public, too. Vendors barked the contents of their dailies to drum up trade, while copies were read aloud in coffee houses and streets. Gondoliers in Venice spoke of 'nothing but politics', and the 'sole occupation' of the Florentines lay in 'discussing the news of the day'.[34] These oral and aural experiences ensured that illiteracy was no bar to participation in the European revolutionary present. In Bucharest, the British consul observed the

---

[31] Marie-Claire Hoock-Demarle, 'Correspondances féminines au XIXe siècle: De l'écrit ordinaire au réseau', *Clio: Femmes, Genre, Histoire*, 35 (2012), 67–88; Marie-Claire Hoock-Demarle, *L'Europe des lettres: Réseaux épistolaires et construction de l'espace européen* (Paris, 2008).

[32] Diary of Laura Anna Harvey. BL, Add. MS 52503.

[33] Benedict Anderson, *Imagined Communities: Reflections on the Origin and Spread of Nationalism*, rev. edn (2006), 35.

[34] Paul Ginsborg, *Daniele Manin and the Venetian Revolution of 1848-49* (Cambridge, 1979), 81–2; BL, Add. MS 62907c, 12r.

'eagerness for news among the lower classes', who gathered in the street at the end of the workday to hear the newspaper read aloud.[35]

Journalists and newspaper editors promoted the sense of a continental revolutionary mission, collapsing geographical distances into a shared historical moment. Before 1848, many European periodicals had discussed foreign affairs as a means to evade censorship and make political points at home. One Mannheim calendar, for instance, compared the urban poverty of industrial England with the plights of Rhenish vintners, Austrian farmers, and Silesian weavers. By focusing on foreign causes and discussing abstract political principles, such calendars could serve as 'compact political primers', according to James Brophy, without risking official reprisal.[36] This logic was often reversed in 1848, with other revolutionary movements rendered intelligible through a local or national lens. A newspaper printed at Ain in eastern France compared the fall of Metternich with that of Guizot, while an Irish nationalist newspaper explained the complex national politics of the eastern Habsburg empire through reference to its own particular cause: Croatia, it reported, was the 'Ulster' of Hungary.[37] Such analogies gave readers a sense of the connections between the various causes. If Croatia was the 'Ulster' of Hungary, loyal to the Austrian Habsburgs as the Protestant population of Ireland was to the British crown, then the Hungarian cause was evidently similar to the Irish. Such parallels were not only used to link international to domestic struggles either. A piece in the Wallachian *Popolul Suveran* reported that the 'scenes from Sicily' were 'repeated' in Venice.[38] Their particular revolutionary objectives may have differed, but their means were shared, and through those means they became contemporaneous.

Participation in the European revolutionary present was of particular importance to what might commonly be understood as the more marginal political causes. The French revolutionary officials who promised support to other national movements in Paris in March probably experienced a different kind of excitement from that of their audiences. For them, a common European revolutionary movement aggrandised France, which could serve as a beacon. Listeners interpreted the matter differently. For them, contemporaneity was an opportunity rather than an abstract ideal. It seemed to promise success, and this interpretation carried across Europe. When news of the February revolution in Paris first reached Messina in Sicily, it was accompanied by

---

[35] Robert Colquhoun to Stratford Canning, 20 July 1848. The National Archives, Kew (TNA), Foreign Office Papers 78/742, 198r.

[36] See James M. Brophy, *Popular Culture and the Public Sphere in the Rhineland 1800-1850* (Cambridge, 2007), 39–41.

[37] *L'Association Démocratique de Bourg*, 26 Mar. 1848. I am grateful to Carine Renoux for sharing her photographs with me. For more on Bourg, see Carine Renoux, 'Living the French Revolution of 1848: Un document inédit dans un fonds d'archives privées de l'Ain', *French History and Civilization*, 9 (2020), 121–34; on Irish newspaper reports of the Hungarian Revolution, see Zsuzsanna Zarka, 'Images and Perceptions of Hungary and Austria-Hungary in Ireland, 1815–1875' (Ph.D. thesis, Maynooth University, 2012).

[38] *Popolul Suveran*, 6/18 Aug. 1848. Other issues featured stories from France, Denmark, Austria, Transylvania, Britain and Ireland.

claims that France would assist 'all nations' that desired to follow suit and 'become republican'. One unsympathetic eyewitness was shocked by the 'bad effect' this rumour had: it prompted many in the town to 'hope' for such assistance and redoubled their convictions.[39]

In the context of a common European present, successful revolutionary change began to seem possible. Messina's inhabitants were not the only people to draw hope from events in other European theatres. The news from major capitals in particular seemed to augur historic change, and many revolutionaries and would-be revolutionaries embraced the opportunity offered. They did not just celebrate the shared historical moment; they tried to shape it. After living through the February upheaval in Paris, the exiled Polish patriot Adam Czartoryski came to believe that the skies were 'clearing' over Europe, and when he heard the news of revolutions in Vienna and Berlin the following month, he wrote to his nephew that Austria and Prussia were 'changing from enemies into allies and are no longer menacing powers'.[40] Given that the two Great Powers were both beneficiaries of the Polish partitions of the eighteenth century, Czartoryski's letter suggested that he understood the cause of revolution as superseding geopolitics: a shared revolutionary culture was more important than particular state interest.

Czartoryski's hoped-for Polish revolution may not have followed, but his belief in the universalist tendencies of revolution was common. Moravia's Chief Rabbi, Samson Raphael Hirsch, was another adherent. In a circular addressed to the 'respectable Israelite communities' of his congregation, he wrote that 'no special fruit will ripen for us, since we shall find our welfare in the welfare of the whole'.[41] He would not advocate Jewish emancipation as a separate cause because he thought it might sow division and attract resentment, jeopardising his community's collective future. Instead, he encouraged Moravian Jews to embrace universal emancipation as a means to overcome intolerance: their struggle was part of a larger, contemporaneous one that would best be won together.

Throughout the spring of 1848, revolution seemed to offer idealistic Europeans an opportunity to realise their political objectives as part of a common cause. The Dalmatian Niccolò Tommaseo had resisted the cause of revolution in the 1840s, instead arguing that the 'only hope [for change] lay in a process lasting centuries', but he changed his mind when the European 'occasion' came in 1848.[42] If revolution could effect change elsewhere, then it could do so in his chosen home of Venice, too. Europe, it seemed, had entered a new historical moment, and it was one in which Tommaseo, Brătianu, and countless others were determined to participate together. It was this sense of contemporaneity that gave those heady months the feeling of a 'Springtime of

---

[39] Diary of Matthew Drake Babington. BL, Add. MS 38067, 97r.

[40] Czartoryski quoted in Marian Kukiel, *Czartoryski and European Unity, 1770–1861* (Princeton, NJ, 1955), 261–2.

[41] Samson Raphael Hirsch, quoted in Michael Laurence Miller, *Rabbis and Revolution: The Jews of Moravia in the Age of Emancipation* (Stanford, CA, 2011), 190–2.

[42] Quoted in Reill, *Nationalists Who Feared the Nation*, 167.

Peoples', as it became known, but unfortunately for the revolutionaries, their European present scarcely outlived the spring.

Revolutions Plural

If European and particular interests seemed to complement one another during the spring of 1848, then by the end of the year, many had lost interest in the European framework, instead prioritising their particular objectives. The Swiss socialist and doctor Pierre Coullery was among the first to identify this change. In an 1851 speech to mark the third anniversary of the revolution in Neuchâtel, Coullery told his audience that almost all of the peoples of Europe had celebrated solidarity, overthrown tyrants, broken their chains and shown that 'the will of the people is the will of God' during the spring of 1848, but that unity had not endured: 'after victory, each people said I am free, now the others free themselves, too, and so we will not look to their affairs'.[43] This inattention, allied with growing frictions between different revolutionary movements, would diminish the European horizon of events as spring gave way to summer, autumn, and winter.

Conflicts and setbacks within states captured national audiences and diverted attention from the wider revolutionary cause. Axel Körner has argued that it was through commemoration and memory that a European revolution was transformed into a series of national ones, but that process began during rather than after the revolutions.[44] In France, the Parisian street battles of the June Days between the city's workers and its national guard focused minds on local and national affairs at the expense of European. A Belgian diplomatic agent reported to his superiors that the French government was 'too preoccupied with [its] own troubles' to think of aiding other causes, and it was not only the government that prioritised internal over external affairs.[45] International news began to take up less space in the press, too. The *Courrier de Versailles*, for instance, had reported on the 'immense effect' of the February revolution in March, with refrains of 'all the peoples' and accounts from Austria, Italy and elsewhere common, but the number of such stories dwindled from June onwards.[46] Their absence reflected a growing insularity. Having promised to lead a continent-wide revolutionary movement in the early spring, the French had abrogated that responsibility. They did so at the precise moment when those young men who had heard the deputy mayor of Paris proclaim the February revolution a 'European' work launched a revolution of their own in Bucharest, though it would be another two weeks before news of that unhappy coincidence became clear.

---

[43] A copy of Coullery's speech was sent to a member of the Orléanist dynasty in exile in Britain. The letter was refused by the royal family and wound up in the dead letter office instead. It can be found at BL, Add. MS 89177/3/5/15.

[44] Axel Körner, 'The European Dimension in the Ideas of 1848 and the Nationalization of its Memories', in *1848: A European Revolution? International Ideas and National Memories of 1848*, ed. Axel Körner (Basingstoke, 2000), 3–28.

[45] Quoted in Jennings, *France and Europe in 1848*, 168.

[46] *Le Courrier de Versailles*, 4 and 29 Mar. 1848.

The Europe of revolution revealed itself to be a Europe of revolutions plural, and their interests and objectives did not necessarily align. When revolutionaries spoke of 'Europe' in the spring, its meaning seemed to them self-evident. They did not need to identify it on a map or with a specific set of goals. It was a revolutionary rallying cry that could and did carry different meanings for different people. Such differences were lost in the excitement of the revolutionary moment of the spring. If all the peoples of Europe rose as one, then it seemed that all could have their freedom, but the simultaneity of the movements began to have a stifling effect. Schleswig-Holstein, for instance, was prized by both the German and the Danish national movements, and no national boundaries could be drawn that were acceptable to all parties. Similar problems prevailed in Transylvania, too. During the spring, several leading figures in the Romanian-speaking community abandoned long-standing fears of forced assimilation to support the Hungarian programme, but the course of revolution in the eastern Habsburg empire drove the two national communities apart, and this divide hampered efforts to forge an international alliance. The Hungarian Prime Minister, Lajos Batthyány, rejected proposals for a Polish–Hungarian–Romanian confederation, and Wallachian attempts to establish a defensive alliance against Russia faltered. The war in Transylvania, according to the man charged with securing an agreement, was too 'barbarous' for national differences to be set aside, while Hungarian partisans regarded his motives with suspicion.[47] Both Transylvanian populations seemed to fear the other more than the Russians. The revolutionary consensus had faltered; some causes now seemed reactionary to others.[48]

Revolutionary movements were no longer in harmony with one another, but rather in competition, and the losers were those already on the periphery. This struggle first became apparent in the summer. Events in Paris, Vienna and Berlin carried significance because these were the capitals of major European powers. They exerted their own gravitational pulls on the continent, and so they were guaranteed to attract the interest of populations beyond their borders. The same was not true for the smaller, more peripheral territories, and the envoys

---

[47] Nicolae Bălcescu to Ion Ghica, 28 Dec. 1848. Reproduced in Bălcescu, *Opere*, IV, 119; John Paget, 'History of the Revolution in Transylvania', Biblioteca Academiei Române (BAR), Mss Engleze 13, 302–5; see also Keith Hitchins, *The Rumanian National Movement in Transylvania, 1780-1849* (Cambridge, MA, 1969), 185–9; on Kossuth, see Apostol Stan, 'Lajos Kossuth and the Romanians during the 1848 Revolution', *Revue Roumaine d'Histoire*, 33 (1994), 355–74; István Déak, 'Lajos Kossuth's Nationalism and Internationalism', *Austrian History Yearbook*, 12 (1976), 48–52; Gelu Neamț, 'Maghiari alături de revoluția română de la 1848–1849 din Transilvania', *Anuarul Institutului de Istorie George Barit din Cluj-Napoca*, 41 (2002), 97–126; István Déak, 'István Széchenyi, Miklós Wesselényi, Lajos Kossuth and the Problem of Romanian Nationalism', *Austrian History Yearbook*, 12 (1976), 69–78; on dialogue between the two national groups after the revolutions, see Ambrus Miskolczy, 'The Dialogue among Hungarian and Romanian Exiles in 1850–1851', in *Geopolitics in the Danube Region: Hungarian Reconciliation Efforts, 1848-1998*, ed. Ignác Romsics and Béla K. Király (Budapest, 1999), 99–129.

[48] See also the Slovenian attitudes to the 'separatist' Italian and Hungarian revolutionaries, as described in Holly Case, 'Slovene Self-Perception through the Slovene- and German-Language Press: 1848', in *Historični seminar 3: Zbornik predavanj 1998-2000*, ed. Metoda Kokole et al. (Ljubljana, 2000), 37–60.

of the governments that seized power in these theatres had to struggle for popular and governmental attention. One frustrated Wallachian diplomat in Vienna begged a compatriot in Bucharest to establish an office of men charged with corresponding with newspaper editors in Vienna, Frankfurt, Berlin and elsewhere to 'describe every event, no matter how small, and without the slightest delay'. Without such information, the 'newspapers will publish nothing', and if they published nothing, then the Wallachian cause would slip from the political agenda, hampering his efforts to secure financial and material support and leaving the principality exposed to counter-revolutionary threat from Russia.[49] The recipient of this appeal was the same man who later wrote of the European 'occasion' of the Wallachian revolution. His colleague, evidently, saw that 'occasion' as vital to the cause. Its opportunity could not be lost.

But competition for resources proved fierce and availability scarce. France's revolutionary history and the French Provisional Government's vague promises of the spring meant that many looked to Paris for support. One revolutionary agent in the French capital reported that he found himself competing with representatives of Ireland, Denmark and the various Italian states in his search for funds and arms. Both were difficult to acquire. French finances were in a parlous state following the agrarian crisis of 1845–7, and what money the state could raise was needed for domestic programmes rather than to support a European revolutionary project.[50] Weapons were similarly scarce, and those that could be found difficult to transport. The Austrian cabinet, for instance, offered no guarantees of safe passage for goods crossing territory under Hungarian revolutionary control, and the Hungarians were themselves unlikely to facilitate shipments of rifles given they needed weapons, too.[51] This situation worsened as counter-revolutionary governments seized power. In 1849, radicals in the German Rhineland found that France refused to export rifles, while those they bought in Belgium were confiscated by Prussian authorities along the Rhine.[52]

If the spring of 1848 had suggested that all of Europe could exist in the same revolutionary present, then by the end of the summer it seemed that the continent had fallen out of sync and the old imperial and national hierarchies had reasserted themselves. Czartoryski's belief that common revolution overcame particular interest now looked misguided, and the governments of the Great Powers were pursuing policies to mitigate the risk of another European war. Events in the Italian peninsula were of particular concern. Whereas the French foreign minister of the spring, Alphonse de Lamartine, had contemplated military engagement, the government of Louis-Eugène Cavaignac was

---

[49] Alexandru G. Golescu to Nicolae Bălcescu, 25 July/6 Aug. 1848. Reproduced in *Anul 1848*, II, 732–6.

[50] Vasile Malinescu to A. G. Golescu, 8/20 Aug. 1848. Reproduced in *Anul 1848*, III, 287. On the French economic crises of the period, see Ernest Labrousse (ed.), *Aspects de la crise et de la dépression de l'économie française au milieu du XIXe siècle, 1846–1851* (La Roche-sur-Yon, 1956).

[51] A. G. Golescu to the leaders of the Wallachian revolutionary government, Aug. 1848. Biblioteca Națională a României (BNR), Fond Brătianu VI/13, 4–5. Also reproduced in *Anul 1848*, III, 150.

[52] Jonathan Sperber, *Rhineland Radicals: The Democratic Movement and the Revolution of 1848–1849* (Princeton, NJ, 1991), 423.

determined to avoid it. His foreign policy, according to the Hungarian Lajos Mandl, was 'completely absorbed by the Italian question', and that focus would affect French policy elsewhere.[53] The French ambassador to the Ottoman Porte, for instance, could offer little support to Wallachia's revolutionary envoy in Constantinople. His priority was to avoid disagreement with Great Britain in order to maintain the Franco-British alliance in Italian affairs.[54] Revolutionary simultaneity had ceased to be a blessing and become an obstacle to overcome, and that obstacle was greatest and most insuperable on the European margins.

Appeals to 'Europe' faltered as revolutionary unity faltered, and events in one theatre ceased to serve as inspiration in others. Instead, they often became cautionary tales. The Venetian leader Daniele Manin was horrified by the violent struggles of the June Days in Paris, which convinced him of the need to prioritise 'internal order'.[55] His perspective was shared by Laura Anna Harvey in the Bagni di Lucca, who wrote of the 'dreadful atrocities' of the Parisian insurgents, reserving particularly harsh judgement for the deeds of women, one of whom had allegedly 'cut into pieces the bodies of 2 of the garde mobile who had been killed!!'[56] Whether true or not, such stories reflected a growing fear of disorder and violence, which fed antipathy to the wider revolutionary cause and contributed to emerging divisions. In Vienna, revolutionary activists no longer saw the Hungarian cause as compatible with their own, and when the Habsburg empire's peasantry was emancipated in September, it would not be accompanied by Rabbi Hirsch's hoped emancipation of the Jews. As Michael Laurence Miller has put it, their cause had been 'severed from the struggle for universal human rights'.[57] The sense of possibility that had stirred hearts and shaped the action of the spring had faded. The European revolutionary present seemed to have passed; continental unity was no more.

Counterrevolutionary Order

As a revolutionary vision of Europe faltered, a counter-revolutionary alternative rose. Pierre Coullery blamed the 'lack of unity' within the European revolutionary party for reviving the 'hopes of the reaction', but it was not only the inability or unwillingness of revolutionary figures to translate European dreams into a practical programme for the continent that saw the counter-revolutionaries triumph from the summer of 1848 onwards.[58] While the revolutionaries became insular, preoccupied by domestic concerns, their adversaries maintained a continental outlook. Theirs was a conservative,

---

[53] Lajos Mandl to A. G. Golescu, 8/20 Aug. 1848. Reproduced in *Anul 1848*, vi, 26; Jennings, *France and Europe in 1848*, 194–5.

[54] Ion Ghica to the Wallachian Minister of Foreign Affairs, Aug. 1848. Reproduced in *Anul 1848*, iii, 501–4.

[55] Ginsborg, *Daniele Manin*, 267.

[56] BL, Add. MS 52503, 99r.

[57] Miller, *Rabbis and Revolution*, 260; on Vienna, see R. John Rath, *The Viennese Revolution of 1848* (Austin, TX, 1957), 151–3.

[58] BL, Add. MS 89177/3/5/15.

imperial vision shaped and influenced by the European 'security culture' that predominated in the aftermath of the Napoleonic Wars and the Congress of Vienna of 1815.[59] These counter-revolutionary men did not endeavour to restore or recreate the congress framework, but they adopted its continental outlook. Unlike the revolutionaries, who dreamt of Europe, the counter-revolutionaries thought and acted in European terms, defeating the disparate causes one by one.

The revolutionary vision of European politics was rivalled by an imperial per-spective that was predicated on a strict hierarchy of nations and states. Jonathan Sperber has suggested that the 'lack of revolutionary activity' in Russia and the British metropole was as significant if not more so than 'events in the smaller states' in 1848, but it was precisely for those smaller states that the absence of British and Russian revolutions was of greatest consequence.[60] Imperial Britain would suppress a revolutionary uprising in Cephalonia, while Russia would flex its reputation as the 'gendarme of Europe' in favour of the old geopolitical order and the supremacy of the Great Powers.[61] In March, Tsar Nicholas I issued a manifesto describing Russian policy on the revolutionary spring: his armies would not interfere in any revolution that did not pose a direct threat to the sta-bility of his empire. France lay beyond his sphere of influence. The Polish border-lands did not. But it would be a revolution in a territory that was under his 'protection' that led Russia to engage in its fight 'against the present', as Alexander Herzen put it. Following the revolutionary outbreak in Wallachia in June, Nicholas issued a second manifesto, in which he extended his concern for internal stability to the neighbouring Ottoman empire. Neither Wallachia nor Moldavia, which had already been occupied by Russian troops, was a 'recog-nised' state. Both were 'pure and simple provinces forming part of an empire', and they had no right to change government as they pleased. Their political status was determined by treaties between his own empire and the Ottoman, and so it was for those two powers to decide how they should be governed.[62]

Nicholas's July manifesto warned of the consequences of unchecked revolu-tion, and his vision of imperial dismemberment rather echoed some of the

---

[59] See de Graaf, *Fighting Terror after Napoleon*.

[60] Jonathan Sperber, *The European Revolutions, 1848-1851* (Cambridge, 2005), second edition, 260-4. For alternative perspectives on Britain and the revolutions of 1848, see Taylor, 'The 1848 Revolutions and the British Empire'; Margot Finn, *After Chartism: Class and Nation in English Radical Politics* (Cambridge, 1993), 60-105; David Large, 'London in the Year of Revolutions, 1848', in *London in the Age of Reform*, ed. John Stevenson (Oxford, 1977), 177-212; Gregory Claeys, 'Mazzini, Kossuth, and British Radicalism, 1848-1854', *Journal of British Studies*, 28 (1989), 225-61; John Belchem, 'The Waterloo of Peace and Order: The United Kingdom and the Revolutions of 1848', in *Europe in 1848: Revolution and Reform*, ed. Dieter Dowe et al., trans. David Higgins (Oxford, 2000), 242-58.

[61] On British interventions in Cephalonia and the other Ionian islands, see Bruce Knox, 'British Policy and the Ionian Islands, 1847-1864: Nationalism and Imperial Administration', *The English Historical Review*, 99 (1984), 503-29; David Hannell, 'A Case of Bad Publicity: Britain and the Ionian Islands, 1848-51', *European History Quarterly*, 17 (1987), 131-43; Maria Paschalidi, 'Constructing Ionian Identities: The Ionian Islands in British Official Discourses; 1815-1864' (Ph.D. thesis, University College London, 2009).

[62] *Journal de Saint-Pétersbourg*, 19/31 July 1848.

hopes of revolutionary figures during the spring. He charged the Wallachians with plotting the establishment of a new and independent Daco-Romanian Kingdom and suggested that success would inspire the Bulgarians, Roumelians and other peoples of the Ottoman empire to follow suit, leading to the collapse of a polity that Nicholas described as 'more than ever an essential condition for the maintenance of the general peace'.[63] Whether Nicholas feared the collapse of a rival or not, such an outcome must have seemed possible or even probable given the revolutionary diffusion of the spring. One Wallachian poet compared its spread to cholera in his memoirs, and it was precisely that pandemic quality that gave Nicholas's claim merit: Bucharest might be an entry point into the Balkans.[64]

The logic of Nicholas's warning about the spread of revolution was an inversion of the argument made by many nineteenth-century national political activists. According to historian Holly Case, writers often argued that the resolution of one national 'question' would in turn solve others, too. In the 1830s, for instance, Adam Czartoryski argued that answering the 'Polish question' was a precondition for the settlement of the wider European one. By granting Poland its independence, Europe would become more stable.[65] Nicholas flipped this argument in relation to Wallachia: a revolutionary 'answer' to its question would not resolve anything and would instead raise further problems. The best way to address national 'questions', in his view, was to avoid raising them in the first place. Through these means, Europe's imperial order could survive unchallenged.

Great Power cooperation would overcome the loose union of peoples. French desire to avoid conflict with the British empire had already undermined Wallachian interests in Constantinople, and soon Russian imperial pressure would push the Ottoman government to intervene militarily in the principality. This intervention was meant to forestall a Russian occupation, but Russian forces soon followed, opening a channel for the broader imperial counter-revolutionary project. Wallachia may have been considered of marginal revolutionary significance, but its importance to the spread of counter-revolution was evident to the decision-makers in Europe's eastern imperial capitals. Following the Ottoman and Russian military intervention, Austrian troops would cross through the principality as a means to outflank their Hungarian revolutionary adversaries, and in the summer of 1849, Russian troops provisioned in Moldavia and Wallachia would enter Hungarian-controlled Transylvania, too.[66] Revolutionary simultaneity was overcome consecutively.

---

[63] *Ibid.*

[64] C. D. Aricescu, *Memoriile Mele* (Bucharest, 2002), 89.

[65] See Holly Case, *The Age of Questions Or, A First Attempt at an Aggregate History of the Eastern, Social, Woman, American, Jewish, Polish, Bullion, Tuberculosis, and Many Other Questions over the Nineteenth Century, and Beyond* (Princeton, NJ, 2018).

[66] On the Russian interventions, see Barbara Jelavich, 'The Russian Intervention in Wallachia and Transylvania, September 1848 to March 1849', *Rumanian Studies: An International Annual of Humanities and Social Sciences*, 4 (1979), 16–74; Ian W. Roberts, *Nicholas I and the Russian Intervention in Hungary* (1991).

After revolution had inspired revolution in the spring of 1848, it was counter-revolution that fed counter-revolution by the summer of 1849. Clara Jane Shaw's family left Italy for Switzerland in May 1848, and she found herself in Heidelberg in the Duchy of Baden by June 1849. Rather than descriptions of jubilant revolutionary scenes, her diary was now filled with stories about the movements of soldiers and the dangers that those movements entailed. She and her family lived in a 'state of suspense', with Prussian and Austrian forces scarcely two hours from the city: 'we have just perceived clouds of dust on the road to Ladenburg and can distinguish arms glistening in the sun'. The triumph of counter-revolution in Austria and Prussia was spreading to Baden, and the news that Shaw had heard from Rome suggested a similar fate there. She learned from a family friend that some 26,000 people were said to be hiding in Saint Peter's Basilica, awaiting the entry of another counter-revolutionary army, this one dominated by the French forces of Louis-Napoléon Bonaparte, whose triumph in the December 1848 presidential election had confirmed the defeat of a certain French revolutionary ideal.[67] In July 1849, as his soldiers toppled the short-lived Roman Republic, it was clear that France was now exporting counter-revolution.[68] The revolutionary present was in the past.

A Europe of orders was reasserting itself against a Europe of revolutions. When the Prussian King Friedrich Wilhelm IV refused the Frankfurt Parliament's offer of a German crown on 3 April 1849, he did so because he did not consider it in the parliament's power to give. His was not an ultimate refusal of Prussian leadership in a German state, but perhaps a recognition that an age of nations and nation-states was one for the future, not yet the present, and that it could not and would not begin with revolution from below.[69] Many moderate revolutionary figures sympathised with this view, too. The Czech František Palacký, for instance, argued that the continued existence of the Habsburg empire served the interests of the Czechs better than any Czech nation-state could and was also integral to the stability of Europe as a whole.[70] It was this moderate strain of thought that conditioned the political culture of Europe after 1848, supporting the continued dominance of the

---

[67] BL, MSS Eur F197/20, 49–51.

[68] On the Roman Republic, see Harry Hearder, 'The Making of the Roman Republic, 1848–1849', *History*, 60 (1975), 169–84; on the French invasion, see David I. Kertzer, *The Pope Who Would Be King: The Exile of Pius IX and the Emergence of Modern Europe* (Oxford, 2018), 190–206; on the subsequent French occupation of Rome, see Alessandro Capone, 'La protection française des États pontificaux, occupation militaire et souveraineté partagée dans l'Italie du Risorgimento (1849–1870)' (Ph.D. thesis, Sciences Po – Institut d'études politiques de Paris, 2019).

[69] On the revolution in Prussia, see Christopher Clark, *Iron Kingdom: The Rise and Downfall of Prussia 1600-1947* (2006), 468–509; on the workings of the Frankfurt Parliament and its attempts to create a German national state, see Brian E. Vick, *Defining Germany: The 1848 Frankfurt Parliamentarians and National Identity* (Cambridge, MA, 2002).

[70] See Axel Körner, 'National Movements against Nation States: Bohemia and Lombardy between the Habsburg Monarchy, the German Confederation, and Piedmont-Sardinia', in *The 1848 Revolutions and European Political Thought*, ed. Douglas Moggach and Gareth Stedman-Jones (Cambridge, 2018), 345–82.

Figure 2. Ferdinand Schröder, 'A Survey of Europe in August 1849'.

imperial Great Powers and reasserting the old civilisational hierarchies. The people of Europe could not 'exist in the same now'.[71]

As the cacophony of revolution died away, a quieter Europe took its place. The difference between these two visions of the continent is perhaps best illustrated by the differences between Werner's 'Political Map of Europe' of 1848 and Ferdinand Schröder's *Düsseldorfer Montashefte* caricature 'A Survey of Europe in August 1849' (Figure 2). Whereas Werner's continent is overrun with people, Schröder's Europe is dominated by a few large monarchical and presidential figures, who sweep away and banish the smaller revolutionary ones. Schröder's Europe is more geographically limited, too. He confined himself to drawing Britain, France, Prussia and Austria. The Italian peninsula and the lands to the east of Pest are cut from the frame. Europe's imperial core was once again the focus; the rest of Europe was lost to insignificance and consigned to peripherality.

Rooted in the Future

Some four years after the people of Berlin took to the streets to demand a programme of reforms in March 1848, the Prussian conservative Friedrich Julius

---

[71] Ernst Bloch, trans. Mark Ritter, 'Nonsynchronism and the Obligation to its Dialectics', *New German Critique*, 11 (1977), 22–38, at 22.

Stahl gave a talk at the city's university titled 'What is the Revolution?' Revolution, he told his audience, was 'not a single act', but rather a 'continuous condition, a new order of things'. It was, he said, the 'characteristic world-political signature of our age'. Stahl's 'semantic inflation' of revolution, according to Christopher Clark, 'made it easier to conflate the events of 1848 with the workings of history'.[72] It was also an approach that robbed the revolution of its status as an 'event' and transformed it into a process. Such an understanding made sense in the context of what Clark has called elsewhere the 'European revolution in government' of the 1850s, but it marked a departure from the European political culture of the spring of 1848, in which the significance of the present moment was seldom far from minds.[73] As Victor Hugo put it at the Paris Peace Conference of 1849: 'the era of revolutions is closing'.[74]

With the passing of the revolutionary present, a certain idea of Europe faltered, too. It seemed self-evident to many of the actors of 1848 that their movement constituted a 'European' revolution that was meant to reshape European society, but the precise parameters of the 'Europe' of which they spoke were unclear. The only certainty seemed to be that it existed in the present moment, with those whose homelands failed to participate in the European moment fearing being 'left behind' by the 'brotherhood of nations'.[75] The choice to speak of 'brotherhood' between nations, which had its origins in the old French Revolutionary ideal of 'fraternity', emphasised the sense of European peoples being contemporaneous with one another: it placed them on the same generational level. Such an idea was of particular significance to revolutionary activists from the so-called 'smaller' states, who celebrated their participation in a pan-European moment.

Some hint of the European dimension of events endured. In the same speech in which he declared the 'era of revolutions' to be over, Victor Hugo prophesied the creation of a future 'United States of Europe'. He was not the lone believer in such a union, either. Another former revolutionary by the name of Ion Ghica described a 'United States of Europe modelled on the United States of America' as the only means for the continent to 'escape shipwreck'.[76] His invocation of the American system probably reflected his own background in one of the smaller European revolutionary theatres. Under the US Constitution, all states were considered equal. None was more important than any other. They existed on the same plane. But neither

---

[72] Friedrich Julius Stahl, 'What is the Revolution?' [1852] in *From Vörmarz to Prussian Dominance, 1815-1866*, ed. Jonathan Sperber [https://ghdi.ghi-dc.org/pdf/eng/4_P_O_Stahl_What%20is%20the%20Revolution.pdf accessed 26 Apr. 2023]; Christopher Clark, *Time and Power: Visions of History in German Politics, from the Thirty Years' War to the Third Reich* (Princeton, NJ, 2019), 138-9.

[73] Christopher Clark, 'After 1848: The European Revolution in Government', *Transactions of the Royal Historical Society*, 22 (2012), 171-197.

[74] Victor Hugo, *Discours d'ouverture prononcé au Congrès de la Paix le 21 août 1849* (Paris, 1849), 5.

[75] Reill, *Nationalists Who Feared the Nation*, 156.

[76] On Hugo's speech, see Maurice Agulhon, 'Victor Hugo et l'Europe: Les États-Unis d'Europe', in *Penser les frontières de l'Europe du XIXe au XXIe siècle*, ed. Gilles Pécout (Paris, 2004), 39-51; Ion Ghica to Constantin A. Rosetti, 12/24 Mar. 1850. Reproduced in Ion Ghica, *Opere*, ed. Ion Roman (6 vols., Bucharest, 1967-88), VI, 149-55.

Hugo nor Ghica considered a United States of Europe to be a realistic short-term possibility. Its realisation could only come in the future. Europe no longer seemed a matter for the political present.

Technological progress rather than a radical revolutionary contemporaneity would bring parts of the continent together after 1848. It was telling, perhaps, that Hugo's vision of the new, post-revolutionary Europe was one rooted in the future, in which 'amelioration' replaced 'revolution': 'thanks to the railways, Europe will soon be no bigger than France was in the Middle Ages'.[77] The unfurling of telegraph lines would have a similar effect to the railways, but such development would be uneven. Progress would not move at a common European velocity.[78] In one way, the historian G. M. Trevelyan was right to suggest that history had reached a 'turning point' and 'failed to turn' in 1848.[79] The old imperial hierarchies still dominated politics. When Christopher Clark identified the developments of the 1850s as a 'European revolution in government', he diverged from the particular national and imperial frameworks that had predominated, but this older interpretative framework itself reflected the breakdown of the European present of the spring of 1848. Like the revolutionaries who had seized power during that brief historical moment, the technocrats of the 1850s looked abroad, too. But unlike the revolutionaries, they did so to study and learn from other approaches rather than to share in a broader political project. Their own polity's future was the priority, not a common European present.

Acknowledgements. I would like to thank the journal's anonymous reviewers for reading and offering helpful comments on the draft of this article as well as my colleagues and mentors Holly Case, Tom Pye, Andrew Seaton, Lauren Lauret, Florence Sutcliffe-Braithwaite, Jack Saunders and Michael Collins.

Funding statement. Some of the research for this article was conducted while studying on a Pigott Doctoral Studentship at the University of Cambridge, and the writing of this article was completed while supported by a Leverhulme Early Career Fellowship at University College London.

---

[77] Hugo, *Discours*, 3.

[78] On the expansion of the railways and telegraphy and their impact on experiences of distance and time, see Wolfgang Schivelbusch, *The Railway Journey: The Industrialization of Time and Space in the Nineteenth Century* (Oakland, CA, 1977); Albert Schram, *Railways and the Formation of the Italian State in the Nineteenth Century* (Cambridge, 1997); Roland Wenzlhuemer, *Connecting the Nineteenth-Century World: The Telegraph and Globalization* (Cambridge, 2013); Jean-Michel Johnston, *Networks of Modernity: Germany in the Age of the Telegraph, 1830–1880* (Oxford, 2021).

[79] G. M. Trevelyan, 'From Waterloo to Marne', *Quarterly Review*, 229 (1918), 73–90, at 79.

Cite this article: Morris J (2024). A Sense of a European Present and its Passing during the Revolutions of 1848. *Transactions of the Royal Historical Society* **2**, 135–155. https://doi.org/10.1017/S008044012400001X

Transactions of the RHS (2024), 2, 157–180
doi:10.1017/S0080440123000300

ARTICLE

Resisting Biographical Illusions: Pandurang Khankhoje, Indian Revolutionaries and the Anxiety to be Remembered

Jesús F. Cháirez-Garza

School of Arts Languages and Cultures, University of Manchester, Manchester, UK
Email: jesus.chairez-garza@manchester.ac.uk

(Received 6 July 2023; revised 10 December 2023; accepted 12 December 2023;
first published online 26 January 2024)

Abstract

Recently, there has been a growing discussion concerning the way historians should approach the study of Indian revolutionaries both within and outside the subcontinent. Described as 'the revolutionary turn', this area of research has not only explored the porosity and ambiguity in defining individuals as revolutionaries but has also questioned the way such revolutionaries sought to write themselves into history as a political act. Continuing this line of interrogation, this article examines the retrospective political claims of heroic revolutionary belonging by analysing the autobiographical notes left by Pandurang Khankhoje, a peripatetic Indian who left his country pursuing dreams of revolution. While in the last decade Khankhoje has become an iconic character in writing histories about global solidarities and anti-colonial resistance, this article asks to what extent can historians believe self-described revolutionary narratives. As this article shows, these narratives privilege what Pierre Bourdieu has called 'biographical illusion', the organisation of life as a history that unfolds coherently and chronologically from beginning to end. Political or ideological differences and inconsistencies are flattened in the name of global ideologies or solidarities. As an attempt to disrupt these narratives, this article will focus on the silences, absences and 'unreliability' of the experiences and sources used to understand the work and lives of Indian revolutionaries abroad, such as Khankhoje, Lala Har Dayal and M. N. Roy. This article argues that the story of revolutionaries reveals important details about how they understood the racial, political and gender structures of different societies in the early twentieth century.

Keywords: Ghadar; Khankhoje; Biographical Illusion; Indian revolutionaries; Har Dayal; Racial Hierarchies

The relationship historians have with the study of Indian revolutionaries is highly complex. On the one hand, since the Indian independence movement is commonly associated with Gandhian values and non-violence, revolutionaries have often been seen as figures awkwardly inhabiting the margins of history, legality and the nation. On the other hand, much of the evidence available to historians about the lives of revolutionaries is embedded in a political bipolarity in which individuals are presented either as dangerous terrorists in colonial sources or as immaculate freedom fighters in nationalist and autobiographical writings. Under such circumstances, historians are presented with the difficult task of deciding how to deal with sporadic archival 'sightings' of revolutionaries often tainted by a colonial, nationalist or even a self-reflective gaze. In recent years, scholars associated with what is often referred to as the 'revolutionary turn' have embraced the challenges of this topic to present revolutionaries as complex figures that are central to understanding the transition of India from a colony to an independent country.[1]

In conversation with the works of this revolutionary turn, this article explores the difficulties and possibilities of writing the history of Indian revolutionaries travelling around the world before the independence of India in 1947. It does so by analysing the autobiographical notes and archives left by Pandurang Sadashiv Khankhoje (1884–1967), a wandering nationalist who left his country of birth pursuing dreams of revolution.[2] As a young man, in 1906, Khankhoje travelled to Japan searching for military education. From 1907 to 1914, he lived on the Pacific Coast of the United States, where he studied agriculture and became involved with the Ghadar Party,[3] a movement attempting to bring down British colonialism in India from abroad. This led Khankhoje to the Middle East, where he would be linked to German forces fighting against Britain (1914–19). Later, he left a trace in Germany and Russia (1921) and arrived in Mexico in 1924, where he would stay for almost thirty years. It is hard to know whether Khankhoje's dream became a reality. Still, his life is a fine example of the complicated situations Indian revolutionaries experienced at this time and their anxieties about being remembered as freedom fighters in their own country.

Khankhoje's political and geographical trajectory mirrors the trail of better-known Indians associated with transnational colonial resistance, such as M. N. Roy, Har Dayal or Heramba Lal Gupta. At different stages of their

---

[1] For instance, K. Maclean, *A Revolutionary History of Interwar India: Violence, Image, Voice and Text* (London, 2015); K. Maclean and J. D. Elam, 'Reading Revolutionaries: Texts, Acts, and Afterlives of Political Action in Late Colonial South Asia', *Postcolonial Studies*, 16 (2013), 113–23; D. Ghosh, *Gentlemanly Terrorists: Political Violence and the Colonial State in India, 1919-1947* (Cambridge, 2019); O. B. Laursen, *Anarchy or Chaos: M. P. T. Acharya and the Indian Struggle for Freedom* (2023); C. Moffat, *India's Revolutionary Inheritance: Politics and the Promise of Bhagat Singh* (Cambridge, 2019).

[2] S. Sawhney, *I Shall Never Ask for Pardon: A Memoir of Pandurang Khankhoje* (New Delhi, 2008); G. Soto Laveaga, 'Largo dislocare: Connecting Microhistories to Remap and Recenter Histories of Science', *History and Technology*, 34 (2018), 21–30.

[3] For Ghadar see M. Ramnath, *Haj to Utopia: How the Ghadar Movement Charted Global Radicalism and Attempted to Overthrow the British Empire* (Berkeley, 2011); E. Brown, *Har Dayal: Hindu Revolutionary and Rationalist* (Tucson, 1975).

lives, these men were linked to prominent political movements and ideologies brewing in India or elsewhere, such as nationalism, the Ghadar Party and cosmopolitan versions of anarchism or communism.[4] In the same way, most of them spent time in Japan, the United States, Europe and, a few of them, Mexico. While many writings about these revolutionaries have focused on the potential of global south connections or anti-colonial solidarities, these works typically do not analyse how the experience of these young revolutionaries was constituted or constructed.[5] As Joan Scott has warned in a different context, historians often use the memoirs left by these revolutionaries as 'evidence of experience' validating the existence of a global anti-colonial movement without questioning how larger discursive notions of nationalism, race, caste and masculinity, among other things, transformed these men.[6] Political or ideological differences and inconsistencies are flattened in the name of global ideologies or solidarities.[7] As an attempt to disrupt these narratives, this article will focus on the silences, absences and 'unreliability' of the experiences and sources used to understand the work and lives of Indian revolutionaries abroad.

This article argues that the story of revolutionaries in exile, such as Khankhoje, reveals how they understood the racial, political and gender structures in which they moved and not necessarily the history of global anti-colonial struggles. As Benjamin Zachariah and Gajendra Singh have shown, if not taken at face value, the documents recollecting the experiences of Khankhoje and others (Ghadaraties, Indian nationalists, socialists) uncover some of the precarious conditions of Indians living abroad, their desire to insert themselves in the history of Indian independence, their encounter with racial hierarchies, and the divisions and instability of fragile political movements.[8] The main primary sources informing this research are a series of autobiographical articles by Khankhoje for the Marathi newspaper *Kesari*. These are kept in Dr Horst Krüger's estate at ZMO Library, Berlin.[9] Virtually unexplored, these memoirs display the anxiety of former 'freedom fighters' to construct triumphal narratives tying their lives to the history of the nation.

---

[4] M. Ramnath, 'Two Revolutions: The Ghadar Movement and India's Radical Diaspora, 1913–1918', *Radical History Review*, 92 (2005), 18–27; A. Raza, *Revolutionary Pasts: Communist Internationalism in Colonial India* (Cambridge, 2020), 1–25.

[5] A. Burton, *The Trouble with Empire: Challenges to Modern British Imperialism* (Oxford, 2015). 190–7; H. K. Puri, *Ghadar Movement: A Short History* (Delhi, 2011).

[6] J.W. Scott, 'The Evidence of Experience', *Critical Inquiry*, 17 (1991), 773–97.

[7] M. Ramnath, *Decolonizing Anarchism: An Antiauthoritarian History of India's Liberation Struggle* (Oakland, 2011).

[8] G. Singh, 'Jodh Singh, the Ghadar Movement and the Anti-colonial Deviant in the Anglo-American Imagination', *Past and Present*, 245 (2019), 187–219; B. Zachariah, 'A Long, Strange Trip: The Lives in Exile of Har Dayal', *South Asian History and Culture*, 4 (2013), 574–92.

[9] I thank Ole Birk Laursen for directing me to these files. P. S. Khankhoje, 'The Story of my Revolutionary Work', Berlin, Zentrum Moderner Orient [ZMO], Krüger Papers [KP], Box 14, File 78, No. 2. I used a digitised version of these files, the columns were translated to English by Khankhoje and J. G. Karandikar. For clarity, I provide the page number of the PDF document and not of the hard copy.

This article has four main sections. It starts by underscoring the importance of breaking what Pierre Bourdieu called 'biographical illusions' in the life stories of Indian revolutionaries.[10] These are coherent 'hero' life journeys culminating in the accomplishment of a predetermined goal. The second section analyses Khankhoje's days as a young nationalist in India and how he imagined his ancestry to cast himself as destined to save the nation. Although he has been branded as a socialist, in his early days Khankhoje was attracted to a type of nationalism, close to the extreme right, that was hostile to non-Hindu minorities. Third, Khankhoje's time as part of a small network of Indian students in the United States is examined. This period in his life has often been used to link Khankhoje to anarcho-syndicalism and to place him as a political leader of Indian anti-colonial resistance abroad. Nonetheless, if read against the grain, the sources relevant to these years reveal long periods of idleness and multiple divisions along caste, religious and racial lines within Indian circles in the United States. The fourth section deals with Khankhoje's recollection of his time in the Middle East. While there is no concrete evidence of the extent of his military involvement during these years apart from a few documents housed in the German Foreign Office,[11] Khankhoje wrote extensively about this episode to record the sacrifice he had made in the name of the nation. While the incursion of Indian revolutionaries in the Middle East has been labelled insignificant,[12] Khankhoje used these events to present himself as a fearless adventurer and servant of his nation. He was anxious to be remembered as a freedom fighter above anything else. To conclude, rather than retelling the usual narrative of Khankhoje's time in Mexico, I offer some general remarks about the challenges of writing history posed by characters like him who inhabit liminal spaces where rumours, legends and historical events meet. The writings of Indian revolutionaries, such as Khankhoje, hold vital historical information to understand the society they inhabited. To access it, historians must resist the temptation of romanticising the life of revolutionaries and look to the larger socio-political context navigated by these individuals. To highlight the need to revise such testimonies and to break the linearity of biographical illusions, this article begins by examining a peculiar episode in the life of Khankhoje during his time in Mexico where his character as a historical narrator is questioned.

Khankoje, Tláloc and biographical illusions

In the autumn of 1930, several small newspapers in Canada and the United States reported that a 'Hindu savant' had discovered an 'archaeological gem' in Coatlinchán, Texcoco, a town near Mexico City. The artefact was a giant

---

[10] P. Bourdieu, 'The Biographical Illusion', in *Biography in Theory: Key Texts with Commentaries*, ed. W. Hemecker and E. Saunders (Berlin, 2017), 210–16.

[11] The Indian National Society to The German Foreign Office, 3 Oct. 1916, RZ 201/021104–067, Politisches Archiv des Auswärtigen Amts, Berlin Germany (PAAA).

[12] Singh, 'Jodh Singh'; S. Kuwajima, *The Mutiny in Singapore: War, Anti-War and the War for India's Independence* (New Delhi, 2006); S. Singh, 'Ghadar Conspiracy' (2015), in *1914-1918-online. International Encyclopedia of the First World War*, ed. by U. Daniel et al.

monolith, 32.5 feet high and 17 feet 10 inches feet thick, representing either an ancient Aztec water goddess, Chalchiuhtlicue, or the god of rain, Tláloc. The notes claimed the discovery was made by Professor Pandurang Khankhoje, a horticulturist who attracted national attention by revealing a perennial bean that was able to bear 'as many as 100 pods', and who had adopted archaeology as a 'side line' activity.[13] *The Brainerd Daily Dispatch* included a picture of Khankhoje before the giant stone, which appears fully unearthed at the bottom of a hill. The reports underscored the importance of the finding as 'no mention of this idol is to be found in any existing books on Mexican archaeology', and even the National Museum of Mexico considered retrieving the enormous idol to house it as part of its collections.[14]

With an archaeological breakthrough of this magnitude, one would expect to find Khankhoje's name in plenty of archaeological volumes in Mexico or elsewhere, but this is not the case. This absence is not related to the historical value of 'La Piedra de los Tecomates', another name for the piece in question. The existence of this object was well documented from the late nineteenth century.[15] Indeed, the provenance of this monolith was the cause of a bitter debate between Alfredo Chavero and Leopoldo Batres, two of the founders of Mexican archaeology, who could not agree about the identity of the idol, whether it was a representation of Tláloc or Chalchiuhtlicue.[16] In 1903, the journal of the Sociedad Científica Antonio Alzate (an association to which Khankhoje would join as a member in the 1920s), also discussed where and how the stone could be visited and acknowledged that locals functioned as guides to arrive at the location of this Aztec monument. Similarly, a few years later, 'La Piedra' found its way to the pages of the *Annales du Musée Guimet* in Paris.[17] In other words, this archaeological item was well known worldwide by the 1930s when Khankhoje claimed to have discovered it. In 1964, the monolith was extracted from Coatlinchán, despite the protests of the local community, and moved to the front of the Museo Nacional de Antropología where it is today. The name of Khankhoje was not to be associated with 'La Piedra' for decades until a recent biography written by his daughter revived the old tale. It is hard to say if Khankhoje was fooled into believing he made an archaeological discovery or whether he attempted to gain fame by claiming to have made such an important discovery. Yet, including this story in Khankhoje's biography indicates that he continued to retell this anecdote to other people, at least those close to him.

---

[13] 'Ancient Idol in Mexico is Found on Hill', *Victoria Daily Times*, 11 Sept. 1930, 20; 'Finds Mexican Idol', *The Pathfinder*, 15 Nov. 1930, 18; 'Hindu Discovers Mexican Idol', *The Brainerd Daily Dispatch*, 7 Oct. 1930, 3.

[14] 'Ancient Idol in Mexico is Found on Hill', *Victoria Daily Times*, 11 Sept. 1930, 20.

[15] E. Noguera, 'El monolito de Coatlichan', *Anales de Antropología*, 1 (1964), 131–41.

[16] L. Lejeal, 'Review Alfredo Chavero: El Monolito de Coatlinchan', *Journal de la Société de Americanistes de Paris*, 2 (1905), 295–6.

[17] E. T. Hamy, 'Croyances et pratiques religieuses des premiers mexicains, le culte des dieux Tlaloques', *Annales du Musée Guimet: Bibliothèque de Vulgarisation, Conférences faites au Musée Guimet*, 25 (1907), 43–80, at 66.

An episode like this would usually amount to an irrelevant funny story in the life of a historical character. However, the case of Khankhoje raises crucial questions about his reliability as a narrator as his memoirs, like those of other Indian revolutionaries, are full of such extraordinary accounts. According to Khankhoje's autobiographical notes, at the time this news was published he had already been involved in what the British colonial government classified as 'terrorist organisations' and revolutionary activities all over the world for over thirty years.[18] He remembered leaving India as a young man and organising revolutionary cells throughout the West Coast of the United States. He also recalled travelling incognito across Europe and Asia to fight in Persia shoulder to shoulder with Wilhem Wassmuss, the 'German Lawrence'.[19] Khankhoje claimed to be imprisoned by British forces but escaped by hiding with nomadic tribes in the Middle East while pretending to be a dervish. Khankhoje then travelled incognito through Europe. He lived in Berlin and Moscow and even met Lenin.[20] Khankhoje asserted that all these endeavours were done with extreme secrecy as he was constantly under surveillance by British spies worldwide. But if Khankhoje's memoirs are credible, and British imperial forces wanted him throughout the globe, why would he publicly announce his whereabouts to newspapers?

Khankhoje's archaeological anecdote illustrates the unreliability of certain historical characters who may distort life events to shape how they want to be remembered or perceived by others. This is particularly important as today the figure of Pandurang Khankhoje has become an exemplary character to write histories about global solidarities including anti-colonial resistance, global networks of revolution, international communism, anarchism, and even the birth of the green revolution.[21] As this article shows, these narratives privilege what Pierre Bourdieu has called 'the biographical illusion', the organisation of life as a history that unfolds coherently and chronologically from beginning to end. In these biographical illusions, the subject and the object of the narrative have a well-defined origin and motivation (a *raison d'être*) that is followed to the end/culmination of the 'life history'.[22] The subject is given an identity (a revolutionary, nationalist, businessman, etc.), and all events are organised and connected to fulfil such identity. Anecdotes such as Khankhoje's archaeological findings represent a problem for historians, and they are often excluded from historical narratives to preserve the cogency of the story.

---

[18] S. Kapila, *Violent Fraternity: Indian Political Thought in the Global Age* (Princeton, 2021), 53–87.

[19] C. Sykes, *Wassmuss: The German Lawrence* (New York, 1936).

[20] Kapila, *Violent Fraternity*, 53.

[21] Soto Laveaga, 'Largo dislocare'; D. Kent-Carrasco, 'De Chapingo a Sonora: Pandurang Khankhoje en México y el tránsito del agrarismo a la agroindustria', *Historia Mexicana*, 70 (2020), 375–421; A. Ortiz Wallner, 'South–South Exchange Networks and the Circulation of Knowledge in 1920s Mexico', in *Handbook of the Historiography of Latin American Studies on the Life Sciences and Medicine*, ed. A. Barahona (2022), 339–53; T. K. Lindner, *A City against Empire: Transnational Anti-Imperialism in Mexico City, 1920-30* (Liverpool, 2023), 139–46.

[22] Bourdieu, 'The Biographical Illusion', 210–16.

In the case of Khankhoje, his life has been imagined as that of an infallible revolutionary and agricultural scientist fighting for the oppressed throughout the globe. The works of Ortiz Wallner, Lindner and Kent-Carrasco illustrate these points well. For instance, Ortíz Wallner, in her work on Khankhoje's time in Mexico, describes the latter as 'agronomist and revolutionary [...] an anti-colonial activist, trade unionist, avant-garde geneticist, as well as an agrarian pedagogue'.[23] She attributes to Khankhoje the authorship of eighteen books (although the bibliographical information is omitted) and places him as a 'key figure' in developing Mexico's project of modernisation of agriculture through his involvement in the National School of Agriculture at Chapingo.[24] Similarly, Lindner conceives Khankhoje's work in Mexico as 'exemplary of an agrarian version of anti-imperialism and of Indian-Mexican cooperation'.[25] In Lindner's account, Khankhoje emerges as a left-wing activist and agricultural geneticist, inspired by the Mexican revolutionary Emiliano Zapata, who was so committed to the cause of agriculture that he even 'taught peasants free of charge'.[26] The problem with the work of Lindner and Ortiz Wallner is that they present a romanticised vision of Khankhoje's activities in Mexico. This is partly due to their wish to write the histories of Global South exchanges, and because their main source of information is the research made by Savitri Sawnhney, Khankhoje's daughter, who broadly views Khankhoje as a revolutionary. Thus, apparent tensions in the narratives about Khankhoje's life are avoided, such as his interest in what might be described today as the Hindu right; his conflicting political allegiances to disparate causes in Japan, the United States, Germany and Russia; or exaggerated accounts of historical events or his interventions in agricultural science and archaeological findings. Even practical questions are evaded such as which language Khankhoje taught the peasants. As noted by Gilberto Aboites Manrique, while Khankhoje was recognised as someone navigating the Mexican agricultural field between 1925 and 1940, he did not 'hizo escuela' [create a school/legacy] due to language and scientific limitations.[27] Emilio Alanís Patiño, one of Khankhoje's students at Chapingo, who would become a leading figure in statistical studies in Mexico, remembered the itinerant Indian as a 'good man' who 'did not know Spanish ... or genetics'.[28] Instead of presenting a romantic image of Khankhoje, this article engages with his limitations to shed light on unexplored areas of his trajectory.

For his part, Kent-Carrasco offers a more nuanced picture of Khankhoje in which the latter is linked to socialist agricultural endeavours and, importantly, to the development of capitalist agricultural companies in Mexico. Filled with rich historical details, Kent-Carrasco's work neatly traces Khankhoje's movements in Mexico for over two decades. Yet, a few tensions in his analysis of

---

[23] Ortiz Wallner, 'South–South Exchange', 345.

[24] *Ibid.*, 339–48.

[25] Lindner, *A City against Empire*, 143.

[26] *Ibid.*

[27] G. Aboites Manrique, *Una mirada diferente de la Revolución Verde: ciencia nación y compromiso social* (México, 2002), 86.

[28] *Ibid.*

Khankhoje seem to return to the appeal of reproducing 'biographical illusions'. For instance, Khankhoje's constant change of jobs, in India and Mexico, is read by Kent-Carrasco as part of Khankhoje's activism rather than inadequacy to fulfil specific posts, a change in the circumstances of the political circle supporting the Indian, or the short-lived nature of state-sponsored agricultural projects that fail to produce tangible results. Similarly, Kent-Carrasco, following Soto-Lavega, tends to overplay Khankhoje's involvement in the origins of the green revolution, claiming that an exchange of seeds between Mexico and India, brokered by the Rockefeller Foundation, was the result of Khankhoje's 'visionary scientific work in Mexico that was now returning to India in the shape of hybrid wheat seeds'.[29] The problem with this narrative is that Khankhoje was not involved in developing these seeds or in the scientific trade between India and Mexico.[30] His research at the time did not relate to wheat but to maize. Even when Khankhoje returned to India, he was excluded from national and international agricultural projects in the subcontinent, leaving him frustrated.[31] It is hard to know whether this exclusion had political reasons or was related to Khankhoje's ability as a scientist. However, the distortions in Khankhoje's life events may be explained due to the desire of most historians, myself included, to tell fully coherent stories with a larger historical meaning.

Attempting not to fall into the temptation of reproducing these biographical illusions, this article looks at often omitted episodes in Khankhoje's life that reveal a great deal of the social and political context he inhabited as a peripatetic Indian travelling around the world at the beginning of the twentieth century. Khankhoje will not be examined as an isolated figure but as one of several Indians who left the subcontinent and followed a similar political path. The point is not to expose Khankhoje as an unreliable narrator (after all, everyone is the hero of their own story), but to understand what else the sources he left behind are saying and how his exaggerated version of events reflects a desire to be remembered as an Indian freedom fighter. To show this, this piece reads Khankhoje's memoirs against the grain. Rather than focusing on his achievements, the following sections focus on Khankhoje's brushes with revolutionary activities and emergent concepts such as nationalism, race and masculinity.

From India to California

This section explores the way Khankhoje experienced nationalism and the reasons that awoke in him a spirit of revolution. As Elam and Maclean have noted, many of the so-called revolutionaries often embraced a dissimilar and sometimes contradictory mixture of nationalism, religion, anarchism,

---

[29] Kent-Carrasco, 'De Chapingo a Sonora', 410.

[30] N. Cullaher, *The Hungry World: America's Cold War Battle against Poverty in Asia* (Cambridge, MA, 2013).

[31] Interview with G. V. Ketkar in *Dictionary of National Biography*, vol. 2, ed. S. P. Sen (Calcutta, 1973), 333.

communism and socialism. As it will be shown, Khankhoje was no different. His understanding of nationalism at this stage, and even when he wrote his memoirs, was centred on the religious oppression of Hindus. He did not have a clear political vision of what independent India should look like, nor was he committed to a socialist or communist cause. Khankhoje's nationalism was inspired by Hindu historical figures and deities, it had an upper-caste outlook, and it frequently excluded other Indian minorities from its vision. Khankhoje's recollections about his background clarify things in this respect.

Pandurang Sadashiv Khankhoje was born sometime in the winter of 1884 in Wardha, India.[32] He came from a relatively well-off Brahmin family that valued education. Khankhoje's father was a petition writer for the colonial government, which may explain his son's fluency in English and social and economic mobility. After completing his primary education, Khankhoje moved to Nagpur to study at Neil City High School. It was during this period that he began to think critically about colonialism. Like many other revolutionaries and nationalists, including Surendranath Banerjea, Tilak and Gandhi, Khankhoje claimed to have been influenced by the figures of Mazzini and Garibaldi and their fight to establish a republic.[33] While none of the written works of the Italian nationalists is mentioned in his memoirs, Khankhoje argued that it was from them that he learned to look 'upon the role of Kings and Emperors as inferior to a republic'.[34] Yet, more than a commitment to republicanism, Khankhoje's gesture to Mazzini and Garibaldi reflected the growth of nationalism or anti-colonialism in the subcontinent, mainly Hindu nationalism.

The importance of religious nationalism over establishing a republic can be appreciated by looking at Khankhoje's reverence for Indian (and Hindu) historical figures such as Rani Lakshmibai of Jhansi, Maharana Pratap and Shivaji Maharaj.[35] These leaders came from a royal and upper--caste family and are usually remembered for defending their religion and fighting 'foreign invaders', usually the British or the Mughals, and not for attempting to establish a republic of equals. Perhaps evidencing how biographical illusions are constructed, Khankhoje linked his lineage to these royals and their defence of Hinduism by claiming his surname was given to one of his ancestors 'who successfully searched and found out one Muslim "Khan" who was secretly converting Gond aboriginals near Nagpur. The Bhonsla rulers of Nagpur had ordered the search (Khoj) of the Muslim (Khan).'[36] In other words, in his recollections, Khankhoje's mission to defend India was set even before his birth. Notably, the nationalism that Khankhoje was attracted to as a young

---

[32] A. Joshi, 'Ban on Prof. Khankhoje', *The Mahratta*, 17 July 1927.

[33] C. A. Bayly, 'Liberalism at Large: Mazzini and Nineteenth-Century Indian Thought', in *Giuseppe Mazzini and the Globalization of Democratic Nationalism*, ed. C. A. Bayly and E. F. Biagini (Oxford, 2008), 355–74.

[34] Khankhoje, ZMO, KP, Box 14, File 78, No. 2, 13 (pdf).

[35] H. Singh, *The Rani of Jhansi: Gender, History and Fable in India* (Cambridge, 2014); R. Sharma, *Maharana Pratap* (Lahore, 1932[?]); J. W. Laine, *Shivaji: Hindu King in Islamic India* (Oxford, 2003).

[36] Interview with G. V. Ketkar, *Dictionary of National Biography*, vol. 2, 333.

man was not particularly inclusive, as the sources of inspiration were strongly associated with Hinduism.

Khankhoje's understanding of nationalism was strongly influenced by the nationalist intellectual Bal Gangadhar Tilak.[37] It was focused on the defence of Hindu religious celebrations, and it was quite popular in Western and Central India when Khankhoje was growing up. Indeed, Khankhoje remembered that one of his first revolutionary activities was associated with the Ganapati festival, the celebration of Lord Ganesh, which became a point of political contention around the intervention of the colonial government in religious matters.[38] His involvement in the Ganapati campaign came through the Bandhav Samaj, a secret society that Khankhoje compared to other associations carrying out revolutionary activities in India, such as Yugantar or Anushilan Samiti.[39] Even though there is no reliable information about the Bandhav Samaj apart from his testimony, Khankhoje placed himself as one of its founders and claimed that the group drew inspiration from Sanskrit epics. The group's main objective was to 'drive the British out of India by war' even if they had to sacrifice their lives. The members of the Samaj lived by the principle of the Bhagavad Gita: 'If you are killed in war you will go to heaven. If you survive, you will rule the earth.'[40] According to Khankhoje, the group consisted mostly of students preaching nationalism and revolution to lower-caste people. When the Ganapati movement emerged, Khankhoje recollected, the Bandhav Samaj attended town gatherings to 'preach that Ganapati meant God of Independence and his worship meant the love of the country'.[41] In other words, to a great extent, Khankhoje associated Hinduism with nationalism and anti-colonialism.

Despite the explicit Hindu character of the Ganapati campaign, Khankhoje claimed that the Bandhav Samaj continuously attempted to recruit Muslims to their ranks. However, he confessed in his biographical notes that regardless of the best efforts of the Samaj, they 'could not induce their [Muslims] minds to love their country'.[42] Even if Muslims were convinced to join the Bandhav Samaj, Khankhoje added, they received different treatment in the organisation. For instance, in one of his anecdotes about this period, Khankhoje explained how after convincing two young Muslim men to join the Samaj, these had to be 'thoroughly tested for their patriotism'.[43] Similarly, the Samaj had to change the admission ceremony welcoming these new members as Muslims were not admitted 'in the sacrificial Vedic rites'.[44] Surprisingly, Khankhoje

[37] P. V. Rao, *Foundation of Tilak's Nationalism: Discrimination, Education and Hindutva* (New Delhi, 2010); S. Seth, 'The Critique of Renunciation: Bal Gangadhar Tilak's Hindu Nationalism', *Postcolonial Studies*, 9 (2006), 137–50; S. Wolpert, *Tilak and Gokhale, Reform and Revolution in the Making of Modern India* (Los Angeles, 1962).

[38] S. Tejani, *Indian Secularism: A Social and Intellectual History 1890–1950* (Bloomington, 2008), 27–74.

[39] Khankhoje, ZMO, KP, Box 14, File 78, No. 2, 41 (pdf).

[40] Khankhoje, ZMO, KP, Box 14, File 78, No. 2, 40 (pdf); *Bhagavad-Gita*, chapter 2, verse 37.

[41] Khankhoje, ZMO, KP, Box 14, File 78, No. 2, 49 (pdf).

[42] *Ibid.*, 55–56 (pdf).

[43] *Ibid.*, 50 (pdf).

[44] *Ibid.*

did not see the association's devotion to Hindu icons or how Muslims were treated as the reason behind the Samaj's failure to recruit members from such a community. Instead, he attributed this to the success of the 'English authorities', who 'sow the seeds of dissension between the Hindus and the Muslims'.[45] In short, even though he wrote his memoirs as an older man, Khankhoje did not seem to be aware that the brand of nationalism he endorsed was sectarian. It excluded Muslims and other minorities by default. More importantly, his narrative of events reproduced the division between Hindus and Muslims that the colonial government used to justify communal policies between these groups.

At the turn of the twentieth century, India went through critical political events that inspired many young nationalists, including Khankhoje, to rebel against the British Empire. In particular, the emergence of the *swadeshi* movement against economic exploitation, the British partition of Bengal in 1905 and the Japanese victory in the Russo-Japanese became landmarks in the stories of Indian revolutionaries abroad embracing the colonial narrative about insurrection brewing across the subcontinent instead of denying it.[46] Khankhoje's version of this period follows the pattern described above, even though his revolutionary activities were limited to lecturing about nationalism and giving political speeches in public. Eventually, these actions created problems for Khankhoje as the local police began to take notice of his activism. After several interventions from his father to keep Khankhoje out of jail, the latter was presented with a marriage proposal.[47] Khankhoje's family was convinced that marriage would encourage the young revolutionary to settle down, but he refused the proposal, arguing that his only interest was to achieve India's independence.[48]

The point about marriage requires an explanation as it became a common trope in the biographies of Indian freedom fighters and opens up exciting points of analysis that have often been neglected. As Kama Maclean has shown in the case of Bhagat Singh, refusing marriage could be interpreted not only as a commitment of young revolutionaries to the cause of independence but also as an acknowledgement that by fighting imperialism, death could arrive unexpectedly.[49] This justification aligns itself with other popular kinds of renunciation in Indian tradition associated with masculine religious figures, such as sanyasis, who gave up family life in the quest for enlightenment, but also with modern examples of Indian revolutionaries who refused to marry or hid their relationship with women from the public such as Har Dayal and M. N. Roy.[50]

---

[45] *Ibid.*, 55 (pdf).

[46] R. P. Dua, *The Impact of the Russo-Japanese War on Indian Politics* (Delhi, 1966); Philip Towle, 'The Russo-Japanese War and the Defence of India', *Military Affairs*, 44 (1980), 111–17; Alexander Nordlund, 'A War of Others: British War Correspondents, Orientalist Discourse, and the Russo-Japanese War, 1904–1905', *War in History*, 22 (2015), 28–46.

[47] Khankhoje, ZMO, KP, Box 14, File 78, No. 2, 120 (pdf).

[48] *Ibid.*

[49] K. Maclean, 'The Portrait's Journey: The Image, Social Communication and Martyr-Making in Colonial India', *The Journal of Asian Studies*, 70 (2011), 1051–1082, at 1064.

[50] In the case of Roy, his first wife, Evelyn Trent, is not even mentioned in his autobiography.

To return to Khankhoje, while his refusal to get married may be read as a sign of his commitment to the nationalist cause, his behaviour after this episode shows that he still did not have a clear action plan to engage in revolutionary activities. In a brief period, Khankhoje toyed with different ideas about his future that his family found so erratic that he was sent to a doctor to assess his mental state. Some of Khankhoje's self-confessed schemes and plans at this stage included living with indigenous communities to raise 'an army of aboriginal Bhils and Gonds' to rebel against the British;[51] joining a national circus to learn how to ride horses and shoot firearms;[52] and travelling to Africa to work as a 'coolie' on the Mombasa railway.[53] None of these activities amounted to anything until an opportunity to travel to Japan emerged. According to Savitri Sawhney, Khankhoje's decision to travel to Japan came after meeting Tilak and G. S. Khaparde,[54] who encouraged the young revolutionary to seek military training abroad.[55]

Khankhoje left Bombay for Japan in February 1906 without papers. His hopes of establishing the foundations of pan-Asian solidarity against European powers died soon after his arrival. Khankhoje found this country harder to navigate than he initially thought. He could not find military training and realised that the Indian community in Japan was divided along class and caste lines. Khankhoje, who had no money and was struggling to earn a living, recalled how after the catastrophic San Francisco earthquake of 1906, news arrived in Japan announcing employment was available even to unskilled and inexperienced workers like himself. This encouraged him to follow his 'long-cherished dream of going to America'.[56] California needed a cheap workforce after the earthquake destroyed over 80 per cent of the city. Labour was also needed for agriculture, lumbering and the construction of railways. Japanese, Chinese and Punjabi workers were allowed to enter the United States, although a rise in anti-Asian discrimination would follow.[57] In other words, economic hardship and financial opportunity were also factors in Khankhoje's decision to leave Japan, not only revolutionary plans. Khankhoje's time in the United States would formally begin two of the most important elements in his life: his connection to the Ghadar Party and his

---

[51] Khankhoje, ZMO, KP, Box 14, File 78, No. 2, 45 (pdf).

[52] *Ibid.*, 122 (pdf).

[53] *Ibid.*, 124 (pdf).

[54] S. Sawhney, *I Shall Never*, 38–9. Tilak is often seen as the sponsor of other young nationalists including Vinayak Savarkar. See S. Kamra, 'Law and Radical Rhetoric in British India: The 1897 Trial of Bal Gangadhar Tilak', *South Asia: Journal of South Asian Studies*, 39 (2016), 546–59.

[55] Khankhoje box, 38(doc) (pdf) 74. For the importance of Japan as a revolutionary place see R. P. Dua, *The Impact of the Russo-Japanese War on Indian Politics* (Delhi, 1966); P. Towle, 'The Russo-Japanese War and the Defence of India', *Military Affairs*, 44 (1980), 111–17; A. Nordlund, 'A War of Others: British War Correspondents, Orientalist Discourse, and the Russo-Japanese War, 1904–1905', *War in History*, 22 (2015), 28–46; C. Stolte and H. Fischer-Tiné, 'Imagining Asia in India: Nationalism and Internationalism, ca. 1905–1940', *Comparative Studies of Society and History*, 54 (2012), 65–92.

[56] Khankhoje, ZMO, KP, Box 14, File 78, No. 2, 18 (pdf).

[57] J. M. Jensen, *Passage from India: Asian Indian Immigrants in North America* (New Haven, 1988).

education in agriculture. It would also open Khankhoje to new experiences in an unknown racial hierarchy.

California dreaming: Khankhoje in the United States

The story of Khankhoje's time in the United States is ambiguous. On the one hand, he left a clear record of his educational activities during his time there.[58] On the other, as Kama Maclean has suggested, the stories of Indian revolutionaries abroad, such as Khankhoje, are full of gaps that are to remain part of a collective history without guarantees.[59] If focused on the growth of revolution, the gaps in his story are difficult to assess. Historians have used Khankhoje's time in the United States to establish links between him and different political groups including revolutionaries from the Partido Liberal Mexicano, the Ghadar Party, and the Industrial Workers of the World (known as Wobblies). However, Khankhoje's name is surprisingly absent from many of the official documents reporting the activities of Indians in the United States. Even the records of the infamous 'Hindu Conspiracy Trial' listing almost sixty Indians involved with the Ghadar Party do not mention Khankhoje.[60] This is rather strange for someone who claimed to be the leader of the 'action (armed) group' of the Ghadar Party.[61] The few documents we have registering Khankhoje's revolutionary activities are biased either by the view of colonial authorities aiming to convict Indians abroad or by a romantic, and often exaggerated, vision of the fight against imperialism. To some extent, the story of Indian revolutionaries abroad is full of speculation about their activities that cannot be denied or confirmed. For instance, the willingness of young Indians to attend foreign universities has often been explained as preparation for a future revolutionary battle. Degrees in engineering or agriculture have usually been associated with an interest in learning how to build weapons or manufacture explosives. The implicit message is that revolutionary activities never ceased and that the Ghadar Party was born from such events. However, this perspective reflects the anxieties of imminent danger put forward by the colonial government. By ignoring important periods of calm and idleness and linking unrelated events, colonial intelligence agents justified their hypervigilance against Indians abroad. In contrast, the autobiographical notes left by Indian revolutionaries suggest that a significant portion of their time in the United States was spent working and attending classes and not planning an insurrection. So rather than repeating the history of Ghadar as a political movement, the sources and documents left by these freedom

---

[58] Diplomas and Certificates of P. S. Khankhoje, New Delhi, Nehru Memorial Museum and Library (NMML), P. S. Khankhoje Papers.

[59] K. Maclean, 'The History of a Legend: Accounting for Popular Histories of Revolutionary Nationalism in India', *Modern Asian Studies*, 46 (2012), 1540–71.

[60] List of defendants in the 1917 Hindu-German Conspiracy Trial, South Asian American Digital Archive (SAADA), https://www.saada.org/item/20120722–795.

[61] I. Singh, *The Gadar Heroics: The Forgotten Saga of Overseas Indians Who Staked Their Lives to Free India from the British* (New Delhi, 2013), 166.

fighters will be used to understand essential elements of the racial and caste structures in which they were immersed.

Looking at this period from a caste and racial perspective shows that the small community of Indians on the West Coast of the United States was divided in terms of caste, religion, region, and class. Upper-caste Indian students, many of them Bengalis, saw themselves as the ethical and intellectual leaders of the revolution and did not think of Indian agricultural workers, usually Punjabis, on equal terms. Regarding the question of race, young Indian nationalists found themselves towards the bottom of a complex hierarchical structure dominated by an emerging category of whiteness.[62] Contrary to accounts highlighting global solidarities, in several instances Indian revolutionaries abroad did not attempt to establish camaraderie campaigns with other oppressed groups and were determined to demonstrate their ancestral Aryan status.[63] Rather than rejecting hierarchical structures of race and caste, often produced by colonial understandings of the world, Indian revolutionaries embraced them and adjusted them for their purposes. Once again, Khankhoje's version of events provides a window to observe this.

Khankhoje arrived in San Francisco in 1907. This journey was not uncommon. Khankhoje recalled finding a pre-established network of students waiting for him in the United States.[64] In 1911, Indian students in America published articles advising interested people about what steps should be followed for those interested in studying on the Pacific Coast. The advice was vast and included tips such as how many bars of soap travellers should pack and how much money one should carry to pass through border control.[65] Prospective students were also instructed to declare to immigration officers that they would receive financial backing from home and that they did not believe in polygamy.[66] Upon his arrival, Khankhoje contacted students and nationalists who had arrived before him, such as Surendra Mohan Bose, Adharchandra Laskar, Khagen Das, and Girindra ('Girin') Mukerjee. This group was responsible for easing Khankhoje into life in San Francisco and 'Birkley'.[67] Through such networks, Khankhoje engaged in a series of odd jobs, including cleaning at a hospital and working in agricultural fields, and would later enrol in full-time education.[68] Interestingly, for Khankhoje and others like him, revolutionary activities took a secondary status at this stage. The priority was to study and survive.

Getting a job for a person of colour in California was more complex than Khankhoje thought. Employment as office clerks was closed to young Indians, and most were pushed to perform manual labour, pushing the limits

---

[62] S. Sohi, *Echoes of Mutiny: Race, Surveillance and Indian Anticolonialism in North America* (Oxford, 2014), 5.

[63] See, for instance, P. Singh, *Ethnological Epitome of the Hindustanees of the Pacific Coast* (Stockton, 1936), 2.

[64] S. Das, 'Information for Indian Students Intending to Come to the Pacific Coast of the United States', *Modern Review*, 10 (1911), 602–12.

[65] *Ibid.*, 604.

[66] *Ibid.*

[67] Khankhoje, ZMO, KP, Box 14, File 78, No. 2, 23 (pdf).

[68] Khankhoje, ZMO, KP, Box 14, File 78, No. 2, 25 (pdf). See also Sawhney, *I Shall Never*, ch. 3.

of their understandings of caste and racial hierarchies. Physical labour was entirely new for those from an upper caste. Khankhoje remembered being fired from construction and cleaning jobs for being too small, too slow or not cleaning properly.[69] Eventually, he could keep a 'very low-paid job' at Saint Mary's Hospital in Oakland.[70] Job security changed things for Khankhoje. After three years, he finished high school in the United States, completed a one-year 'Scientific' course at Mount Tamalpais Military Academy,[71] and enrolled in an agriculture programme at the Oregon State Agricultural College.[72] Throughout his years in college, his busy schedule did not change, as Khankhoje's memoirs confirm:

> Provision for my food was made as I was employed in a private boarding house to do the work of a server and to wash utensils. I got two hours' employment of sweeping clean the mechanical workshop of the college. My daily time table was as follows:- 4 a.m. to 6 a.m. cleaning of the workshop; 6 a.m. to 8 a.m. working in the dining hall; 2 p.m. to 6 p.m. attending classes and studies; 6 p.m. to 8 p.m. – washing utensils etc. and doing next day's studies up to midnight. I could do all these activities – though in a hurried manner for my quarters, the college site and the boarding house where I worked were not at great distance from one another.[73]

In other words, revolutionary work was not a constant in Khankhoje's life for roughly seven years. He admits that most of this work 'was being done in vacation days'.[74] But even at this time, communication with India was not accessible and it was hard to keep up to date with political changes occurring elsewhere.

Pausing revolutionary work to undertake low-paid jobs was not an experience exclusive to Khankhoje. Other Indian students and nationalist leaders wrote about having hard times supporting themselves while in the United States and even denied their involvement in revolutionary activities altogether. Writing for *The Modern Review*, Sarangadhar Das noted that the conditions for 'self-supported' Indian students were not 'rosy' and were fraught with complications, particularly for the upper-caste 'Hindu youth who has never known the struggles of life'.[75] These obstacles, however, were not to stop him from achieving his goals as a 'real man always faces the dangers, the hardships, the loneliness of being away from home and all that'.[76] Sarangadhar Das also commented that the time taken by school and work

---

[69] Khankhoje, ZMO, KP, Box 14, File 78, No. 2, 25 (pdf).

[70] *Ibid.*

[71] Diploma Mount Tamalpais Military Academy. NMML, P. S. Khankhoje Papers, Subject File 1, 31. Khankhoje claims he studied at the military academy while working in the canteen for a year. Yet, a standard programme at the academy lasted four years.

[72] S. Das, 'Why Must We Emigrate to the United States of America', *Modern Review*, 10 (1911), 69–80, at 73.

[73] Khankhoje, ZMO, KP, Box 14, File 78, No. 2, 127 (pdf).

[74] *Ibid.*, 130 (pdf).

[75] Das, 'Information for Indian Students', 610.

[76] *Ibid.*

occluded any possibility of being involved in politics. Sarangadhar Das stated that Indians in the United States were 'too busy with our studies and hard struggle for a living, to be able to handle politics. As I have said before, we don't know anything of the "revolutionary".'[77] Even Har Dayal, who became a catalyst for the Ghadar movement, noted in 1911 that it was typical for Indians attending school on the Pacific Coast to withdraw from any nationalist activism as 'students who work four or five hours every day as house-assistants or labourers and attend the university lectures for 8 hours or more have no surplus energy for other activities'.[78] The rest of the Indians in the United States were 'too much engrossed in the struggle for life to have much time for real patriotic work'.[79] In sum, Indian revolutionaries abroad had to juggle their patriotic aspirations with survival. Their periods of activity and inactivity oscillated between the resources and the time they had available.

Oddly, these student-revolutionaries also used their writings to separate themselves from other minorities in the United States, African Americans in particular, and from the Sikh labourers who composed the majority of Indians on the Pacific Coast at this time. Indian students dissociated themselves from African Americans to avoid discrimination. As noted by Sarangadhar Das, even though prejudice against students was rare within college campuses, 'a section of the general public who are totally ignorant of our social life and our modes of living [...] take us for Negroes at the first sight'.[80] This was a problem not only due to racist segregation laws and practices but also because 'Negro men and women are passing for Hindu Yogis, Yoginis and Mahatmas and making money by fooling the Americans.'[81] That is, Indian students were aware of the racial hierarchies in the United States and how their lives could be affected if they, or their religion, were associated with African Americans. Something similar can be observed in the relationship between these students and Punjabi labourers on the West Coast.

The division between Indian students and labourers might be explained by differences in caste or social status between the two groups and the racial discrimination against Asians prevalent in the United States at this time. First, even though they recognised that they had to engage in manual labour to survive, young revolutionaries like Khankhoje still considered themselves above Sikh agriculturalists in the Indian social hierarchy. These student-nationalists believed it was their duty to teach Sikh labourers about nationalism. But this was to be done carefully as not all Sikhs were open to revolutionary politics or upper-caste students. Khankhoje learned about this problem by observing the work of Girindra Mukerjee as an interpreter among the Indian agricultural workers in California. According to Khankhoje, despite Mukerjee published several newspaper articles in the United States to create a positive attitude towards the Indian workers, 'the Punjabi labourers were uneducated and

---

[77] Das, 'Why Must We Emigrate', 74.

[78] H. Dayal, 'India in America', *Modern Review*, 10 (1911), 1–11, at 3.

[79] *Ibid.*

[80] Das, 'Why Must We Emigrate', 78.

[81] *Ibid.*, 79.

suspicious. They even harboured some misunderstanding against [Mukerjee]. It was then that I realised how all possible care must be taken while working among ignorant people'.[82] Indeed, it was not uncommon for revolutionaries and Indian students to refer to the lack of education of Punjabi workers as a way to highlight their leadership and reaffirm their caste superiority.

Har Dayal, who would become the leader of Ghadar, wrote about Sikh labourers in similar terms. After highlighting that Sikhs were sought after by farmers and fruit growers due to their responsibility, ability and 'low-cost', Dayal claimed that the presence of this group in the United States was not welcomed by everyone. According to Dayal, the labourers were 'simple oriental peasants and cannot adapt themselves to the ways and manners of a highly developed and complex social system which makes enormous demands on the self-restraint, and the good sense of every individual'.[83] Har Dayal claimed that the lack of education among the Sikhs made them vulnerable to the influence of 'unscrupulous persons who trade on their credulity and simplicity'.[84] Yet, since their arrival in America, Har Dayal perceived a political awakening among the Sikhs. The group began to develop a 'keen sense of patriotism which manifests itself in deeds of kindly service to their fellow-countrymen here'.[85] In short, the lack of education among the Sikhs was used as an excuse by self-proclaimed revolutionaries to place themselves as the leaders of the Indian political organisations in the United States.

The second reason young revolutionaries wanted to distance themselves from the Sikh labourers concerned the racial tensions and anti-Asiatic sentiment growing in California in the early twentieth century. The Pacific Coast saw a rise of racially discriminatory practices against 'Asiatic' labourers, particularly against Chinese and Japanese immigrants. Acts of violence were committed by white workers against Asian immigrants to 'protect' the United States against the so-called 'yellow peril'. Sikhs immigrants were also the victims of organised violence by white supremacy organisations such as the Asiatic Exclusion League. Within Khankhoje's circle, students and nationalists were aware of this problem and highlighted their caste and education through their writings to dissociate themselves from the Sikhs. In particular, 'self-supporting students' wanted to clarify that they did not represent an economic threat to white workers. Girindra Mukerjee explained that white workers feared that the Sikhs would displace them because the latter accepted lower wages. This situation had threatened to 'bring on another racial and international complication' as the image of Sikhs was being damaged publicly and legally. Mukerjee noted that 'the public mind seemed to be in such a disordered state that the better class of the Hindus here blushed for shame for their fellow man. The law courts declared the Hindus as "undesirable", not fit to become citizens of the State.'[86] While they might have felt some sympathy for their co-nationals, Indian students on the West Coast certainly did not see themselves as part of the Sikh labourers.

---

[82] Khankhoje, ZMO, KP, Box 14, File 78, No. 2, 23 (pdf).
[83] Dayal, 'India in America', 4.
[84] *Ibid.*
[85] *Ibid.*
[86] G. Mukerji, 'The Hindu in America', *Overland Monthly*, 6 (1908), 305–6.

The relationship between Sikh labourers and Indian students changed somewhat when Har Dayal assumed the leadership of the Ghadar Party. After stints in Lahore, Oxford, London and Martinique, Har Dayal arrived in San Francisco in 1911. Once in California, he became a Professor of Indian Philosophy at Stanford and became an organiser of Indian revolutionaries and workers due to his charisma and his fluency in Punjabi and Urdu. While Har Dayal espoused many different ideologies throughout his life, he was mainly interested in anarchism during his time in the United States. Har Dayal toured the West Coast looking to bring together different Indian associations of workers and students into a single political organisation. According to Khankhoje, he joined Har Dayal on some tours and became one of the main leaders of Indian students abroad. Shortly after this, Khankhoje published journals and propaganda to stir up anti-British sentiment in the United States.[87] Through such efforts, shortly thereafter, the Ghadar Party was created (1913).

In 1914, Ghadar and Khankhoje's political situation leaped forward due to the arrest of Har Dayal and the start of the First World War. In March 1914, Har Dayal was arrested on charges of illegal immigration and accusations of anarchism. His arrest by US authorities became a palpable warning of imperial power across borders and an indication that America was not a safe haven for Indian revolutionaries. On its part, the beginning of the First World War presented itself as an opportunity to find international support for Ghadar. Despite the alleged influence of anarchism and socialism over Ghadarites, Indian revolutionaries found support from imperial Germany. After the release of Har Dayal on bail, members of the party met several times with German agents who, keen to fuel conflict in the colonial territories of their British enemy, agreed to support Ghadar with money and guns. At this time, Khankhoje decided to abandon his PhD in agricultural studies in Minnesota and soon found himself on the way to Europe to plan an offensive against the British army in the Middle East.[88]

Khankhoje's time in the United States was not marked by an ongoing search for global solidarity against imperialism or revolution as his memoirs would make readers believe. Instead, there were periods full of idleness, poverty and racial discrimination where there was little else to do than try to survive. Khankhoje's reminiscences, however, provide important information about the experience of young Indian men in a new social hierarchical structure where they had to adapt fast to changing circumstances.

League of legends

After his time in the United States, Khankhoje's trace becomes hard to follow. We know that his time in the Middle East lasted roughly from 1914 to 1919.

---

[87] One of these journals was the *Bulletin of the Hindusthan Association of U.S.A.* published in August 1913. Khankhoje is listed as a founding member of the journal. See Bulletin of the Hindusthan Association of U.S.A., South Asian American Digital Archive (SAADA): https://www.saada.org/item/20110930-387.

[88] Laursen, *Anarchy or Chaos*, 51–86.

According to his memoirs, Khankhoje wanted to raise an army and enter India through Baluchistan, along with Wilhelm Wassmuss, the 'German Lawrence'.[89] This offensive was intended to weaken the British efforts in the region and loosen the colonial grip on South Asia. The campaign was unsuccessful. As noted by Sunit Singh and Gajendra Singh, the activities associated with Ghadar were ineffective and were often limited to distributing pamphlets among Indian troops in the British army.[90] Khankhoje and his group could not coordinate their efforts simultaneously with other Ghadarites in different parts of the world.[91] They also realised that changing the allegiances of Indian soldiers loyal to the British army was more complicated than they thought it would be. Similarly, when Germany's luck in the war began to run dry, support towards Indian revolutionaries fell quickly off the list of German priorities.

Before moving on, I want to address the difficulty of assessing this period both in Khankhoje's life and that of other Ghadarites. Different works covering the history of Ghadar often focus on the revolutionary activities of the party. Much attention is given to the activism and political mobilisation of this group around the world.[92] This type of narrative, consciously or unconsciously, has created an image of Ghadarites as heroes and even martyrs in the popular domain. The Ghadarite is then portrayed as a fearless soldier willing to pay the ultimate price for India's independence. The problem with such a vision is that it romanticises the harshness, cruelty and precariousness of life in exile to favour a narrative of sacrifice and selflessness owed to the nation. The life of the revolutionary was full of uncertainties and precarity that took its toll. At different points in their life, people like Har Dayal, Chattopadhyaya, M. N. Roy and Khankhoje were doing everything in their power to go back to India regardless of the British presence in the country.[93] They even denied the importance of their incursions in the Middle East. M. N. Roy, whose biographical illusions should also be questioned, for instance, referred to the Ghadar incursion of the Middle East as the 'The tragic story of the Indian Dupes of German intrigue'.[94] Har Dayal dismissed the affair by belittling its relevance and noting how some revolutionaries were more

[89] Sykes, *Wassmuss*.

[90] Singh, 'Jodh Singh', 191.

[91] Giles T. Brown, 'The Hindu Conspiracy, 1914–1917', *Pacific Historical Review*, 17 (1948), 299–310; Karl Hoover, 'The Hindu Conspiracy in California, 1913–1918', *German Studies Review*, 8 (1985), 245–61.

[92] A. C. Bose, *Indian Revolutionaries Abroad, 1905–1922: In the Background of International Developments* (Patna, 1971); S. Bose and K. Manjapra (eds.), *Cosmopolitan Thought Zones: South Asia and the Global Circulation of Ideas* (Basingstoke, 2010); H. Fischer-Tiné, '"Indian Nationalism and the World Forces": Transnational and Diasporic Dimensions of the Indian Freedom Movement on the Eve of the First World War', *Journal of Global History*, 2 (2007), 325–44; H. C. Aspengren, 'Indian Revolutionaries Abroad: Revisiting their Silent Moments', *Journal of Colonialism and Colonial History*, 15 (2014).

[93] See for instance Zachariah, 'A Long, Strange Trip', 574–92; I. Huacuja Alonso, 'M. N. Roy and the Mexican Revolution: How a Militant Indian Nationalist Became an International Communist', *South Asia: Journal of South Asian Studies*, 40 (2017), 517–30; N. K. Barooah, *Chatto: The Life and Times of an Indian Anti-Imperialist in Europe* (New Delhi, 2004); Laursen, *Anarchy or Chaos*.

[94] M. N. Roy, *M. N. Roy's Memoirs* (Bombay, 1964), 90.

interested in gaining fame than in independence: 'There were all kinds of people in the association, sincere but misguided patriots, unprincipled adventurers, self-indulgent parasites, scheming notoriety hunters [...] The number was never very large. Some pamphlets were written, and some foolish intrigues were set on foot.'[95] There are different reasons for the absence of this side of the story but here I only discuss two. First, as noted by Shruti Kapila, while the history of Khankhoje and Ghadar has been presented as a global affair, it remains a profoundly nationalist story which culminates with the goal of independence.[96] The doubts and fears of the revolutionaries are erased from such a perspective. Hagiographical renderings often portray the revolutionary as a coherent whole, as an adventurer and as an individual determined to fight for India whatever the cost with a definite set of ideals. But as noted above, this was hardly true as these revolutionaries did not have a specific action plan or a guiding ideology for Indian liberation. They were ready to associate with German imperialists, Russian spies and anarcho-syndicalists as long as it would help them to survive.

The second reason for the absence of vulnerable episodes in the journey of revolutionaries has to do with the recollections of their own lives. These remembrances, or autobiographical illusions, are shaped by nationalist and male-dominated visions of history in which any type of weakness is minimised. In contrast, many inconsequential events are glorified as great acts of sacrifice. Some of these problems can be seen in Khankhoje's life story. Here, I do not attempt to take away value from Khankhoje's efforts to achieve India's independence. Rather, I want to show the anxieties of Indian revolutionaries to be remembered as larger-than-life heroes in order to leave a mark on the construction of the nation.

One of the only writings left by Khankhoje regarding his crusade against the British appeared on 26 January 1961 in the Punjabi periodical *The Frontier Mail*. The events described are beyond reality, but the article's tone falls in line with the hero's image in an inevitable fight for independence. Even the piece's title, 'An Episode During My Freedom Struggle', is evidence of this. The blurb offered in the article is also romanticised and describes Khankhoje as 'one of those revolutionaries who sacrificed their all in the cause of country's independence'.[97] According to Khankhoje, these events occurred sometime in 1916. While some sources in the German archives do place Khankhoje in the Middle East at this time, the story of his arrest is not described and is placed under the label of 'Rumours'.[98] Along with Wilhelm Wassmuss and others, Khankhoje travelled across Persia fighting the British, then under the leadership of General Sir Percy Sykes. Near Baft, the group was attacked by British troops. Khankhoje was wounded and captured after his horse was

---

[95] H. Dayal, *Forty-Four Months in Germany and Turkey* (London, 1920), 68–69.

[96] Kapila, *Violent Fraternity*, 59.

[97] See P. S. Khankhoje, 'An Episode During my Freedom Struggle', 26 Jan. 1961, *The Frontier Mail*, New Delhi, NMML, P. S. Khankhoje Papers, Subject File 14, 52, Miscellaneous Notes, Published Articles of P. S. Khankhoje.

[98] The Indian National Society to The German Foreign Office, 3 Oct. 1916, RZ 201/021104–077, PAAA.

shot. The British took more prisoners and began to march towards their headquarters in Bandar Abbas. Khankhoje considered escaping but was deterred by 'heavy chains' and 'strict vigilance of guards'. Once his leg was better, Khankhoje came up with a plan.

> I pretended to be suffering from acute dysentery and during three days, I was allowed to take constant trips to the bushes without chains, but I always returned faithfully to my chains. On one of such trips to the bushes I found an opportune time to run away, I did escape. Soon enough, there was gunfire and bullets were fired at me. I was however already climbing a high mountain and was protected by the absolute darkness of the night. I made good my escape. After a while, the soldiers got tired of shooting in the dark.[99]

Khankhoje hid in a cave. Soon, he was alone in a territory 'inhabited by nomadic wild tribes' where 'life was not worth much'.[100]

Here, Khankhoje offers us one of the only instances in which he touches on the theme of vulnerability in the life of revolutionaries. After his escape, he became 'ill with a real dysentery'. Alone, in pain and without food or water, Khankhoje felt 'so sick, so abandoned, so weak and so unhappy' that he thought about ending his life. In desperation, he found a precipice and jumped. However, the fall did not kill Khankhoje, but only worsened his suffering. Subsequently, Khankhoje was found by two riflemen of a local tribe. They took him to their camp after realising that Khankhoje had been fighting the British. The tribe treated Khankhoje as one of their own and even asked him to marry one of the women there. He kindly declined as he had to follow his calling: 'I begged them to let me go and follow my destiny which, incidentally, was going to provide me with many more adventures and dangers during my quest for the freedom of my country.'[101]

Khankhoje left the tribe and headed to Nehriz. Whenever he encountered people on the road or in villages, Khankhoje pretended to be a dervish, a Sufi Muslim ascetic. On one such occasion, another tribe approached Khankhoje. They asked about his destination while the latter bowed and prayed profusely. While talking to the tribe, a map of Persia in Roman characters fell from Khankhoje's trousers. The tribe enquired in an aggressive manner looking for an explanation. Khankhoje said he was going to the holy city of Kerbala, near Bagdad. His reply was enough. The tribe fed and welcomed Khankhoje. He talked to them and even predicted that the 'chief's wife, who was pregnant, would give birth to a son'. Rapidly, Khankhoje realised that making such a claim was a mistake as '[w]ith these ignorant and nomadic people, a daughter is seldom welcomed and is considered a disgrace'. If he were wrong, the chief would not be happy. When the child's birth was closer, Khankhoje escaped to the mountains but quickly lost his way. He returned to the main road and

---

[99] Khankhoje, NMML, P. S. Khankhoje Papers, Subject File 14, 52, Miscellaneous Notes.
[100] *Ibid.*
[101] *Ibid.*

realised that the men of the tribe were waiting for him. Khankhoje remembered this event as 'a lucky strike':

> These men had been sent by their chief who wanted to see me and wanted me to participate in the festivities organised in honour of the birth of his son. This time, without reluctance, I accompanied them and enjoyed a few days without fear and with all the respect due to a good fortune teller.[102]

This is where Khankhoje's anecdote, 'one of the adventurous episodes in which [his] life abounds', ends.

If these stories seem too good to be true it is because they are probably exaggerated versions of events or anecdotes that Khankhoje, or someone close to him, may have heard or experienced. As noted by John-Paul A. Ghobrial, the accounts of travellers about their personal experiences in places that hold a particular image in the mind of the public (whether this is the Middle East, China or India) often reflect the popular imagination of such places.[103] Thus, in such narratives, a place like India may appear as a spiritual or 'exotic' land where sadhus and fakirs are everywhere. While the Middle East might be portrayed as a place full of Sheiks, nomadic tribes and looming danger. This is true in Khankhoje's story. For instance, Wilhelm Wassmuss, Khankhoje's German companion, was famous for his improbable escape stories. In fact, one of Wassmuss's anecdotes closely resembles Khankhoje's escape from British custody. In Wassmuss's version, however, it wasn't he who was sick but his horse. After he was captured, the guards allowed Wassmuss to check on his horse quite often as he was a high-ranking officer. One early morning, when the guards were sleeping, Wassmuss asked again to see his horse. The guards accepted but did not bother to escort Wassmuss. The latter made good his opportunity and galloped away.[104] The similarities in the anecdotes are too great to be a coincidence. However, this does not mean that Wassmuss's version trumps Khankhoje's. Rather, the similarities in the anecdotes say more about society's expectations of the heroic experiences that people involved in war or revolution should have.

The last element to address in Khankhoje's life as a Ghadarite is the vulnerability of being a revolutionary. While part of this article's argument is that the lives of revolutionaries are often romanticised and doubt and crises of confidence are underplayed, Khankhoje's words about suicide seem more like a literary tool than an actual narrative of events. Khankhoje used his suicide attempt as a point of inflexion in the story. In line with biographical illusions, failing to kill himself was not just luck but destiny. He emerged from this experience as a committed revolutionary who even rejected marriage to continue facing 'adventures and dangers' for his country's freedom.

---

[102] Ibid.

[103] J. A. Ghobrial, 'The Secret Life of Elias of Babylon and the Uses of Global Microhistory', Past and Present, 222 (2014), 51–93.

[104] H. RamHormozi, Averting an Iranian Geopolitical Crisis: A Tale of Power Play for Dominance between Colonial Powers, Tribal and Government Actors in the Pre and Post World War I Era (Victoria, BC, 2016), 240.

Khankhoje's time in Persia came to an end around 1919. From then on until 1924, Khankhoje's whereabouts and activities are again hard to pin down. He travelled with a letter of introduction from the Amber of Ghashgai from Fars, Persia. The letter appointed 'Professor P. Hadjiaga Khankhoje' as a representative of the Amber in America. It allowed him to negotiate with 'capitalists, corporations or companies interested in Asphalt and Oil-springs'. In the same way, the letter requested 'all the Persian Ambassadors, Representatives or Consuls to give Professor P. Hadjiaga Khankhoje every kind of official assistance in order to facilitate this journey through different countries'.[105] While Khankhoje did not return to the United States, sources show that he lived in Russia, France and Germany. During his time in Europe, Khankhoje met other influential Indian revolutionaries such as Virendranath Chattopadhyaya (Chatto), Bhikaiji Cama, Heramba Lal Gupta and M. N. Roy. Khankhoje settled in Berlin due to his involvement with the German efforts in the Middle East. However, he abandoned this place after a friend warned him that the British colonial authorities were closing in on him. Khankhoje travelled to hide in Mexico in 1924.

Conclusion

Khankhoje's time in Mexico has been retold many times. Suffice to say that when he arrived in Mexico, he hit the ground running. He became part of a strong political and cultural network that eased him into finding a job as a faculty member of the National Agricultural School at Chapingo. He moved among the most famous artists in the country, including Diego Rivera, Frida Kahlo, Tina Modotti and Edward Weston among others. Many job opportunities were offered to Khankhoje throughout his time in Mexico. He bounced from one job to the next, particularly during his first ten years in the country, until he settled in the private sector. The government sponsored him to study genetics in Europe and at some point he began introducing himself as Dr Khankhoje, although there is no record of him completing his PhD. When Khankhoje finally returned to India after the end of colonial rule, he expected to be welcomed as a hero, but this did not happen. After he died in 1967, Khankhoje's name was almost forgotten until Savitri Sawhney brought it back to life through a biography published in 2008. The fame that Khankhoje seemed to have been chasing at different stages of his life finally arrived.

Indeed, Khankhoje's time in Mexico has become one of the main elements of his biographical illusion that continues to grow to this day. In September 2022, a bust of Khankhoje was unveiled at the Universidad Autonóma de Chapingo.[106] Numerous newspapers and magazines in India have used his time there to label him as a 'revered hero of Mexico' who led an 'agricultural

---

[105] Papers Concerning Refusal by the Consul at Mexico to Grant Passport to Dr. Khankhoje to Return to India, Letter of Introduction from The Amber of Ghashghai, Fars Persia, 3 Nov. 1921, New Delhi, NMML, P. S. Khankhoje Papers, Subject File 3, 17.

[106] https://timesofindia.indiatimes.com/india/birla-unveils-bust-of-indian-agricultural-scientist-at-mexico-university/articleshow/93959255.cms.

revolution' in Latin America.[107] However, as this article has shown, Khankhoje's version of events is not entirely reliable and depicts an anxiety about being remembered as a man of great deeds. Even Khankhoje's intervention in Mexican agriculture is hard to assess as he only left a few articles describing his experiments with different plants such as soy, maize and lemon. In the same way, his role in directing free schools of agriculture is equally obscure as there are only a couple of documents recording his work there. While Khankhoje has usually been presented as a man of the people, his time in Mexico was also marked by his interaction with an influential network of intellectuals and politicians that only emerges if the biographical illusions in his memoirs are disrupted. Resisting these illusions, however, does mean disqualifying Khankhoje as a historical narrator. Rather, it suggests that perhaps historical subjects do not choose how they are remembered. Despite the exaggerations found in his recollection of events, Khankhoje's memoirs also hold important information about different political episodes that transformed our understanding of the twentieth century, including the emergence of right-wing nationalism in India; the way Asian migration changed race relations in the United States; the anxiety of Indian exiles to insert themselves in the history of Indian independence; and the way cosmopolitan elites influenced national politics across the world.

For historians, a character like Khankhoje and the archival trail he left behind represents a complex challenge. If taken at face value, Khankhoje's narrative invites itself to fill gaps within exciting new fields relating to global, revolutionary and decolonial turns. But as this article has shown, many of those gaps can only be filled if certain stories in Khankhoje's memoirs are excluded. Rather than 'getting the story right' or demystifying Khankhoje's life, this article has explored what else these autobiographical sources can tell us about the way revolutionaries wanted to be remembered.

---

[107] https://www.peepultree.world/livehistoryindia/story/people/dr-pandurang-khankhoje-the-ironic-revolutionary.

Cite this article: Cháirez-Garza JF (2024). Resisting Biographical Illusions: Pandurang Khankhoje, Indian Revolutionaries and the Anxiety to be Remembered. *Transactions of the Royal Historical Society* 2, 157–180. https://doi.org/10.1017/S0080440123000300

Transactions of the RHS (2024), 2, 181–205
doi:10.1017/S008044012300021X

ARTICLE

Waiting to Die? Old Age in the Late Imperial Russian Village

Sarah Badcock

Department of History, University of Nottingham, Nottingham, UK
Email: Sarah.badcock@nottingham.ac.uk

(Received 7 July 2023; accepted 15 August 2023; first published online 18 September 2023)

Abstract

What was daily life like for old people in Russian villages at the turn of the twentieth century? Elderly people feature as an integral part of Russian rural family life in literary and in scholarly accounts, and are predominantly framed as able, skilled, omniscient community members. This article suggests that constructions of old age that see the elderly retaining physical prowess and community leadership overlook the lived realities of ageing. As elderly people lost physical and mental capacity, they slipped out of view in the Russian village, desexed, unseen and unremarked. The experience of the frail elderly allows us to explore the values accorded individuals within rural communities, and the extent to which families, communities and legal structures could and did intervene in the private sphere.

Keywords: Russian history; history of ageing; peasant studies; nineteenth century; rural life

Introduction

> 'Oh, Ivan Petrovich, the time has passed when there was strength and health. How was it then? You work, you eat, you rest, and then you begin again anew; but now it's not like that: every little bit of you hurts ... God forbid you live to see such days, it is better to die while your legs are still working!'
> (Conversation between two old men reported by the teacher Vasilii Ivanovich Ivanov in Novgorod province, 1898–9)[1]

---

[1] D. A. Baranov et al. (eds.), *Russkie krest'iane. Zhizn', byt, nravy. Materialy 'Etnograficheskago biuro' Kniaza V.N. Tenisheva* (14 vols., St Petersburg, 2005–11), VII.1. 85.

This reported fragment of conversation, in which the speaker bemoaned the pains of old age, resonates across time and space. This article seeks to contribute to our understandings of old age in historical context through its focus on the experiences of and perceptions about older people in late Imperial Russian villages. Elderly people feature as an integral part of Russian rural family life in literary and in scholarly accounts, and are predominantly framed as able, skilled, omniscient community members.[2] The idea that the most powerful actors in village communal life and politics were old men (*stariki*) is enduring, but these constructions of old age that see the elderly retaining physical prowess and community leadership overlook the lived realities of ageing.[3] As elderly people lost physical and mental capacity, they slipped out of view in the Russian village, desexed, unseen and unremarked. The experience of the frail elderly allows us to explore the values accorded individuals within rural communities, and the extent to which families, communities and legal structures could and did intervene in the private sphere.

A rich scholarship on the experience of older people in different chronological and spatial contexts has established that there was no universal respect for old people at any time, even though respect for elders was a universal aspect of religious thought and folkloric myths. Attitudes towards old age were consistently ambivalent, incorporating respect for wisdom and maturity alongside pity and even revulsion at the illustration of inexorable time.[4] While the history of childhood in Russia has generated a significant body of work, and old age in Soviet Russia is an emerging field, old people are largely absent in the scholarship on rural spaces in Imperial Russia.[5] The last, debilitated stages of old age have been neglected in the broader scholarship

---

[2] See for example Lev Tolstoy's account of an elderly peasant mowing, in *Anna Karenina*, pt 3, ch. 5. Tolstoy insisted on the dignity and importance of old age and was preoccupied with both the ageing process and with death. See Stephen Lovell, 'Finitude at the Fin de Siècle: Il'ia Mechnikov and Lev Tolstoy on Death and Life', *The Russian Review*, 63 (2004), 296–316, esp. 297, 303.

[3] Boris Mironov, 'The Russian Peasant Commune after the Reforms of the 1860s', *Slavic Review*, 44 (1985), 447.

[4] Pat Thane, 'Old Age in European Cultures: A Significant Presence from Antiquity to the Present', *The American Historical Review*, 125 (2020), 385–95, at 387; Thijs Porck, *Old Age in Early Medieval England: A Cultural History* (Woodbridge, 2019), pp. 6–7.

[5] See Elizabeth White, *A Modern History of Russian Childhood: From the Late Imperial Period to the Collapse of the Soviet Union* (2020) for a survey treatment of Russian childhood. Recent works on Soviet ageing include Alissa Klots and Maria Romashova, 'Young Minds – Young Bodies: The Emotional and the Physical in the Late Soviet Discourse on Aging', *The Soviet and Post-Soviet Review*, 48, no. 2 (2021), 189–210; Susan Grant and Isaac McKean Scarborough (eds.), *Geriatrics and Ageing in the Soviet Union* (2023). Scholarship on old age in the Russian Empire includes Adele Lindenmeyr, 'Work, Charity, and the Elderly in Late-Nineteenth-Century Russia', in *Old Age in Preindustrial Society*, ed. Peter N. Stearns (New York, 1982), 232–48; Aleksandr A. Panchenko, 'Obraz starosti v Russkoi krest'ianskoi kul'ture', *Otechestvennyi zapiski*, 3 (2005); Z. Z. Mukhina, *Russkaia krest'ianka v poreformennyi period: vtoraia polovina XIX – nachalo XX veka* (St Petersburg, 2018), 389–401, 441–73. A recent and excellent synthetic study of family and household in Russia has no indexed references to old age or elderly people, but fifty-one references to children: Barbara Alpern Engel, *Marriage, Household and Home in Modern Russia: From Peter the Great to Vladimir Putin* (New York, 2021).

as well.[6] This article considers a group who face a series of intersecting marginalisations in historical discourse, as lower-class, rural, elderly people. This article does not aspire to offer a model of 'typical' old age in pre-modern societies, or indeed in Imperial Russia. Old people were not a uniform category: their experiences were gradated by gender, by wealth and privilege, by race and ethnicity and cultural norms, and by the individual circumstances of their lives. Old people are represented, and represent themselves, in multiple ways, both as individuals and as a group.[7] This article recognises that experiences of old age were diverse, and that old age was both a process and a destination.

This article is based around fourteen published volumes of material collected by Prince Tenishev's ethnographic bureau between 1898 and 1901, including survey responses from 167 correspondents in thirteen provinces of central Russia.[8] Tenishev commissioned responses to a detailed questionnaire about rural life among ethnically Russian peasants of Orthodox faith from local correspondents in Russia's central and northern regions.[9] The material in this article reflects the social and cultural spaces of the Slavic, Orthodox, ethnically Russian rural dwellers of the Russian Empire, who made up a minority of the Empire's richly diverse rural population.[10] While the questions posed in Tenishev's survey anticipated and shaped correspondents' responses, this article's focus on old age to some extent confounds Tenishev's scripts, given that old age, unlike say popular justice, or violence, was not intended as a focus.[11] Correspondents' accounts are certainly partial, constructed and flawed, but they nevertheless offer us glimpses into otherwise inaccessible spaces of private homes and family practice.[12]

This paper asks a series of intersecting research questions. The first section tackles the challenge of how to define old age, and at what stage old age begins. The second section explores societal constructions and hierarchies around ageing people in their 'third age'; that is, those older people who are still physically active and engaged in the community's economic, social and

---

[6] Susannah Ottaway, 'Medicine and Old Age', in *The Oxford Handbook of the History of Medicine*, ed. Mark Jackson (Oxford, 2012), 338, 349.

[7] Pat Thane, *Old Age in English History: Past Experiences, Present Issues* (Oxford, 2000), 271.

[8] These thirteen provinces were Kaluga, Kostroma, Kursk, Moscow, Nizhnii Novgorod, Novgorod, Olonets, Pskov, St Petersburg, Tver, Tula, Vologda and Yaroslavl. Baranov *et al.* (eds.), *Russkie krest'iane*, I, 6–7.

[9] For the published questionnaire, see V. N. Tenishev, *Programma etnograficheskikh svedenii o krest'ianakh tsentral'noi Rossii* (Smolensk, 1898). For a discussion of the challenges around its publication, see L. S. Zhuravleva, 'K Istorii Publikatsii "Programma" V. N. Tenisheva', *Sovetskaia Etnografiia*, 1 (1979), 122–3.

[10] Of the population of the Russian Empire, 44 per cent were categorised as 'Russian' (by virtue of language use), and 69 per cent professed practice of Eastern Orthodox religious faith. Data drawn from *Pervaia obshchaia perepis' naseleniia Rossiiskoi Imperii 1897g. v. 89 tomakh* (St Petersburg, 1897).

[11] Dmitry Baranov, 'V. N. Tenishev's "Peasant" Programme: Ideology and Practice', *Forum for Anthropology and Culture*, 3 (2007), 193–205, esp. 195, 197, 200.

[12] For further discussion of the challenges of ethnography as a historical source, see Sarah Badcock, 'Time out from the Daily Grind: Peasant Rest in Late Imperial Rural Russia', *Slavonic and East European Review*, 100 (2022), 674–704, at 680–1.

cultural life.[13] This looks at respect and power for older people in the community, and the moral, cultural and working roles taken on by older people in the community. The final section looks at the so called fourth age, or the 'oldest old', a term coined to describe the combination of chronology and chronic illness that betokens the terminal phase of people's lives.[14] This section starts by discussing attempts by older people to exercise agency in preparing for their 'fourth age'. It then goes on to look at the care afforded the oldest old, in the community, and in the family.

When does old age begin?

Peasant men and women in our area begin to grow old noticeably around the age of sixty, but continue to work, lighter peasant work, until disease puts them to bed, and death puts them in the ground. The death of peasants and peasant women in our area is around seventy: but diseases cause death earlier, and there are old people who live to eighty years, and in rare cases till eighty-five or ninety.
(Savva Yakovlevich Derunov, peasant from Yaroslavl province)[15]

There was no universally accepted demarcation for the beginning of old age: while chronological age offers a relatively fixed defining point, old age is often societally recognised and defined by fitness to work, by appearance and by debility.[16] Old age is a 'state of becoming' rather than an achieved identity, and is directly connected to senescence, the biological process of physical deterioration through ageing.[17] Historians have adapted a range of models to define old age.[18] The two definitions that emerge as most useful for this article are 'chronological age', whereby individuals are categorised as old when they have lived for a certain number of years, and 'functional age', when an individual is considered old when they are no longer able to perform specific work-based tasks.[19] Chronological age provides a useful starting point but does not

---

[13] Paul Higgs and Chris Gilleard, 'Fourth Ageism: Real and Imaginary Old Age', *Societies*, 11 (2021), 12; Peter Laslett, 'The Emergence of the Third Age', *Ageing and Society*, 7 (1987), 133–60.

[14] Higgs and Gilleard, 'Fourth Ageism'.

[15] Baranov *et al.* (eds.), *Russkie krest'iane*, II.1, 548.

[16] Sophie Newman *et al.*, 'Growing Old in the Industrial Age: Aging, Health, and Social Identity in Elderly Women (Eighteenth–Nineteenth Centuries A.D.)', *Bioarchaeology International*, May 2023. https://doi.org/10.5744/bi.2023.0003.

[17] Rebecca L. Gowland, 'That "Tattered coat upon a stick": The Ageing Body: Evidence for Elder Marginalisation and Abuse in Roman Britain', in *Care in the Past : Archaeological and Interdisciplinary Perspectives*, ed. Lindsay Powell, William Southwell-Wright and Rebecca Gowland (Havertown, 2016), 72.

[18] Thane, *Old Age in English History*, 24. Bourdelais points to the chronological age of sixty as a starting point for old age in French contexts: Patrice Bourdelais, 'Demographic Aging: A Notion to Revisit', *The History of the Family*, 4 (1999), 31–50.

[19] Paul Johnson, 'Historical Readings of Old Age and Ageing', in *Old Age from Antiquity to Post-Modernity*, ed. Pat Thane (1998), 4; for medieval use of functional age, see 'Afterword', in *Aging and the Aged in Medieval Europe: Selected Papers from the Annual Conference of the Centre for Medieval Studies*, Papers in Mediaeval Studies, 11 (Toronto, 1990), 204–5.

adequately encapsulate working parameters and experiences of old age. The highly elastic construction of 'functional age' – that is, if you were unable to work, you were 'already old' – is the dominant framing of old age in our material.[20] This elasticity is reflected in the Tenishev correspondents' responses to the question of when old age begins, which produced a broad range of answers, and which unfailingly offered a gendered distinction: women were likely to become unfit for work younger, but to live longer.

Very low life expectancy levels obscure the lived demographics of late Imperial Russia, as they did in multiple other historical contexts.[21] High infant mortality drastically lowered average life expectancy figures, and these figures can give an erroneous impression that old people were a rarity in late Imperial rural life. In 1897, the average life expectancy in Russia was a little under thirty for men, and around thirty-two for women. If we look at the data of life expectancy for a forty-year-old person, life expectancy shot up to around sixty-seven for men and women.[22] These figures reflect the very high chance of death in infancy and early childhood; 250 out of every 1,000 babies did not survive their first year, a rate significantly higher than in other European countries.[23] The 1897 census indicated that elderly people made up around 7 per cent of the population, and that there was no significant disparity between men and women, which correlated with data from Western European countries.[24]

The most commonly cited age for the onset of old age in the Tenishev survey was around sixty-five to seventy, though different correspondents offered widely digressing start points for decrepitude, from forty-five to seventyplus.[25] This figure corresponded with broader European trends, which saw old age as beginning in the seventh decade of life.[26] Some accounts of health and ageing in the villages pointed to high levels of vivacity and competence, and retention of working faculty, into advanced years. A. Mirets-Imshinetskii from Tver province recounted that old men and women in his parish were strong and adroit into advanced old age. 'Even elders in their seventies work perfectly vigorously in the field.'[27] The nobleman Aleksei Alekseevich Fomin reported that decrepitude did not usually affect the older people in his experience of Yaroslavl province, and that only one ninety-year-old in the whole village was not able to work. In most cases, old men and women continued to work 'until they died', even in their seventies and eighties.[28]

---

[20] Baranov *et al.* (eds.), *Russkie krest'iane*, ɪɪ.1, 344.

[21] Thane, 'Old Age in European Cultures', 386. For a discussion of the question in early medieval England, see Porck, *Old Age in Early Medieval England*, 4.

[22] N. E. Pashintseva, E. V. Voronina and L. A. Kazachenko (eds.), *Naselenie Rossii za sto let (1897-1997). Statisticheskii sbornik* (Moscow, 1998), 166–70.

[23] Timur Natkhov and Natalia Vasilenok, 'Ethnic-specific Infant Care Practices and Infant Mortality in Late Imperial Russia', *Economic History Review*, 76 (2022), 783–806.

[24] Lindenmeyr, 'Work, Charity, and the Elderly', 233.

[25] Baranov *et al.* (eds.), *Russkie krest'iane*, ɪ, 416.

[26] Thane, 'Old Age in European Cultures', 394.

[27] Baranov *et al.* (eds.), *Russkie krest'iane*, ɪ, 409

[28] *Ibid.*, ɪɪ.2, 261.

Migrant workers were more likely to die prematurely, and those that returned permanently to village life after a stint of urban life were more likely to have damaged health, and to age prematurely. This reflected the ways in which the timing of physical decline is connected to cultural, social and economic contexts.[29] Barbara Engel's study of out-migration in Kostroma province attributed this premature ageing to poor living and working conditions.[30] A number of Tenishev's correspondents corroborate Engel's analysis.[31] The experience of reduced longevity and reduced quality of life in migrant factory workers is reported in other global industrialising contexts.[32] The reduced longevity and more rapid descent to frailty experienced by factory workers reinforces the overall point that chronological age does not adequately encapsulate the shape and space of ageing.

The place of older people (culture, power, work)

In social histories of the late Imperial Russian village, older men and women have been placed at the head of their households and their communities, in what are widely recognised to be patriarchal power structures. The scholarship has tended to emphasise gender as the primary organising factor in village power relationships, followed by generation.[33] Gender and seniority, along with wealth and status, defined individuals' positions in their family and in their community. Men dominated power structures, and senior women had power and authority over younger women within their household.[34] For women, status was associated with wealth and with bearing and rearing children.[35] Elder men and women, the *bol'shak* and *bol'shuka*, had massive authority in the household and directed daily economic and social life in the home.[36] The senior man and woman (*khoziain* and *khoziaka*) were fully empowered heads of the family, though the senior woman was subservient to men in her household.[37] In communities with high levels of male out-migration, older women participated in the management and

---

[29] Rebecca Gowland, 'Growing Old: Biographies of Disability and Care in Later Life', in *New Developments in the Bioarchaeology of Care*, ed. Lorna Tilley and Alecia A. Schrenk (Cham, 2017), 237–51, at 240.

[30] Engel, *Between the Fields*, 52–3.

[31] See for example Baranov *et al.* (eds.), *Russkie krest'iane*, III, 421, 563.

[32] Martin Gorsky, Bernard Harris, and Andrew Hinde, 'Age, Sickness, and Longevity in the Late Nineteenth and the Early Twentieth Centuries: Evidence from the Hampshire Friendly Society', *Social Science History*, 30 (2006), 571–600; Kovalenko Ruslan *et al.*, 'Occupational Safety and Health of Factory Workers in European Countries in the Nineteenth Century: Historical and Legal Analysis', *Labor History*, 61 (2020), 388–400.

[33] For an excellent discussion of the challenges of defining generations, see Stephen Lovell (ed.), *Generations in Twentieth-Century Europe* (Basingstoke, 2007), 1–18.

[34] Christine D. Worobec, *Peasant Russia: Family and Community in the Post Emancipation Period* (Princeton, 1991); Corinne Gaudin, *Ruling Peasants: Village and State in Late Imperial Russia* (DeKalb, 2007); David Ransel (ed.), *The Family in Imperial Russia: New Lines of Historical Research* (Urbana, 1976).

[35] Engel, *Between the Fields*, 15–16.

[36] Worobec, *Peasant Russia*, 175–207; A. Balov, 'Ocherki Poshekhon'ia', *Etnograficheskoe Obozrenie*, 40–1 (1899), 193–224, at 217.

[37] Baranov *et al.* (eds.), *Russkie krest'iane*, III, 443.

administration of the village.[38] These generational power structures are compelling, and they point to the visibility and power of older people in their 'third age'; that is, older people who retained high levels of physical and mental capacity.

Moral arbiters and placeholders of the past

On religious holidays, the young stroll and the old pray.
(Stefan Fedorovich Klimentov, soldier, Yaroslavl province)[39]

Old people were seen by their community as arbiters of religious practice and religious leaders.[40] Multiple accounts present the old as the most active members of the community in religious practice. They read and listened to religious books, aloud and for their own pleasure, in Church Slavonic and in Russian.[41] They were more likely to pray, and when they prayed they tended to do so in a more committed way, prostrating their bodies to the ground.[42] They were more likely to fast and to abstain from meat, more likely to attend church and to go on pilgrimages to holy places.[43] Fasting for Lent was reported as being on the wane in general by the early twentieth century, and several accounts noted that 'only a few old people' continue to fast.[44] The old were most likely to lead requests for special prayers, and to practise and reinforce religious practice.[45] In Il'insk village in Yaroslavl province, the custom of putting out a baked star for dinner on the eve of the resurrection of Christ was only preserved among those families with old people – the star was then eaten by the whole family.[46] This custom indicates the ways in which the old family member could not just preserve a relic of 'old' practice, but put it into action so that the whole family engaged with it.

Old people were represented by Tenishev's correspondents and by the community themselves as placeholders of the past. Old people remembered a different kind of life, of serfdom and longer military service.[47] The old were often

---

[38] Engel, *Between the Fields*, 54.

[39] Baranov *et al.* (eds.), *Russkie krest'iane*, II.2, 404.

[40] Greg Freeze, 'A Pious Folk? Religious Observance in Vladimir Diocese, 1900–1914', *Jahrbucher für Geschichte Osteuropas*, 52 (2004), 323–40; Vera Shevzov, *Russian Orthodoxy on the Eve of Revolution* (New York, 2004). In his excellent treatment of popular piety, Chulos does not refer to generational shifts within Orthodox religious practice; Chris J. Chulos, *Converging Worlds: Religion and Community in Peasant Russia 1861–1917* (DeKalb, 2003).

[41] Baranov *et al.* (eds.), *Russkie krest'iane*, I, 68.

[42] *Ibid.*, VII.4, 273; III, 513 – on praying and prostrating.

[43] *Ibid.*, v.4, 101–2 – on church attendance and pilgrimages by the old; I, 295 – on abstaining from meat and fasting; III, 424, 271 – church attendance; II.1, 591 – on abstention from meat.

[44] *Ibid.*, II.1, 2, 232; II.2, 71, 314 – old observing Lent.

[45] *Ibid.*, I, 443 – old leading requests for special prayers.

[46] *Ibid.*, II, 248.

[47] For example, *ibid.*, v.2, 262 – on old discussing serfdom; VII.4, 258 – on old people reminiscing. On nostalgia, see Hannah Skoda, 'Nostalgia and (Pre-)modernity', *History and Theory*, 62 (2023), 251–71.

held up as the source and repository of past knowledge.[48] E. E. Grigor'ev, a teacher from Kaluga province, reported that the elderly regarded comets as a sign from God of forthcoming calamity: war, harvest failure, hunger, pestilence. They recall that 'There was a comet in 1812, in the Hungarian March, in the Sevastopol war and in Turkey.'[49] Rumours and knowledge of Russian history often come from the old. Alexander II, for example, was remembered as the Tsar-Liberator; 'God grant him, father, the Kingdom of Heaven: the great benefactor defended the peasants from the nobles and received a cruel death.'[50] Several accounts referred to old people as repositories of the 'old songs' and suggested that young people neither knew nor cared about old songs.[51]

This placeholder role combined nostalgia and knowledge of the past, manifested in storytelling and anecdote, with moral waymarking, highlighting aspects of change in everyday life. This moral role could highlight anxieties about modern life, with its technology, urban intersections and growth of literacy, secularism and individualism. It also intersected with constructions of the elderly as repositories of superstition.[52] Some correspondents presented the old unambiguously as fixed defenders of 'old ways'.[53] This could be in the economy, in agriculture, in gender norms or in cultural practice. One flashpoint was in elderly people's responses to technology. The assumption in these narratives is that old people were a brake on progress. Aleksandr Nikolaevich Golubtsov, a deacon from Vologda province, reported old people saying:

'Before the end of time man will be a cunning demon: in every house snakes will hiss – these are our samovars – and there will be a fiery chariot on all roads – this is a car – and truthfully, there will no horse drawn carts – so it goes; and already, the end of the century is coming.'[54]

When the railway first came to one district, it attracted great attention: 'All the local residents, including the old people, ran three and a half versts to the station, in order to watch the steam engine, but within a month they began to lose interest ... now you only hear from the peasants about the machine, "there it goes, like a horse! What a stupid whistle it has!"'[55] In another account, young people called the railway 'chugunky' (cast iron). Several of the old, especially the old men, called the steam train 'ognennoi kolesnitsei' (fiery chariot).[56] In Kaluga province where the old rarely saw, or had never seen, the railway,

---

[48] Stephen Lovell, 'Biography, History, and Finitude: Understanding the Life Span in Early Nineteenth-Century Russia', *Slavonic and East European Review*, 82 (2004), 246–67, esp. 255.

[49] Baranov *et al.* (eds.), *Russkie krest'iane*, III, 488.

[50] *Ibid.*, V.4, 175.

[51] *Ibid.*, VII.2, 562. See also Badcock, *Time out from the Daily Grind*, 701.

[52] S. Dixon, 'Superstition in Imperial Russia', *Past & Present*, 109 (2008), 207–28.

[53] Baranov *et al.* (eds.), *Russkie krest'iane*, VII.4, 11.

[54] *Ibid.*, V.2, 26.

[55] *Ibid.*, II.2, 321.

[56] *Ibid.*, II.2, 318.

they talked doubtfully about the steam train and described it as 'the devil's horse'.[57] The language used here indicates religiously founded apocalyptic fears of the modernisation process.[58]

The teacher E. E. Grigor'ev, writing about Kaluga province, suggested that violence towards children and women was perpetuated by the attitudes of the old, but that the younger generation disowned such attitudes.[59] In referring to one another, old spouses didn't use their given names, but instead adopted 'grandfather', 'grandmother' or 'my old one' (*maia starukha/moi starik*). Younger married people mocked the old people for their ways and called one another by name in Zhizdrinsk district of Kaluga province.[60] The peasant, poet and journalist Savva Yakovlevich Derunov, from Yaroslavl province, argued that old people were challenged, and ultimately defeated, by the forces of youth and modernity. In his account, the old in the village were a flesh-and-blood embodiment of 'old' ways, superstition, ignorance and passivity. Derunov discussed attitudes towards literacy, knowledge, alcohol, tobacco and religion, and concluded:

> The younger generation bring to to life greater enterprise, agility and activity and homes neatness and better nutrition than was the case with the old … in all aspects of everyday life … Old and new trends in rural life collide, but the victory is always with the new.[61]

This negative construction of old people as always resisting change was not universal. Multiple accounts pointed to enthusiasm among the old for schooling, and pride in those children who could read.[62] Literacy rates among the old were much lower than for the younger generation, and those who could read were often not fluent enough to read aloud.[63] The old tended to prefer sacred and spiritual books, and some were hostile to secular literature. One correspondent recounted the response of an old peasant to him in relation to reading secular books:

> '*Oi, shchoi-to ty, batiushka!* [*Come off it, father!*] Reading devilish books to us? Lord save us and every christened person!'[64]

---

[57] *Ibid.*, III, 518.

[58] For discussion of peasant attitudes towards disruptive modernisation and associations with apocalyptic thought, see Lynne Viola, 'The Peasant Nightmare: Visions of Apocalypse in the Soviet Countryside', *Journal of Modern History*, 62 (1990), 747–70. See also John R. Hall, *Apocalypse: From Antiquity to the Empire of Modernity* (Oxford, 2009), ch. 5.

[59] Baranov *et al.* (eds.), *Russkie krest'iane*, III, 549; VII.2, 278.

[60] *Ibid.*, III, 88. Alexander D. Nakhimovsky, *The Language of Russian Peasants in the Twentieth Century: A Linguistic Analysis and Oral History* (Lanham, 2020), 10–11, discusses the importance of the Tenishev collection as a resource for direct peasant speech.

[61] Baranov *et al.* (eds.), *Russkie krest'iane*, II.1, 587.

[62] See Sarah Badcock and Felix Cowan, 'Lower-Class Reading in Late Imperial Russia', *The Russian Review*, 83, no. 4 (2023), 1–19.

[63] Baranov *et al.* (eds.), *Russkie krest'iane*, V.4, 167.

[64] *Ibid.*, V.1, 195.

The old reproaching younger generations for the decline of their morality is a persistent theme in our accounts.[65] It also resonates with age-old concerns about moral decay. These notions of moral decay often tied into ideas about cultural and economic decline, and not infrequently hinged on the notion that the youth were 'spoiled', most often in reference to food, drink and tobacco.[66] The priest Aleksandr Rozhdestvenskii argued that old people believed that general prosperity in the community was declining, and that this could be blamed upon the 'spoiled' nature of the current generation. One old man is reported as saying, 'now if there isn't white bread on the table, then the holiday is considered poor, but in our time we were treated to some sort of chaff, and that was all right' ('da i ladno').[67]

The drinking of tea was ubiquitous across Russia in the nineteenth century.[68] In some correspondents' reports, 'nobody says anything about tea – not even the old refuse it'.[69] But there are other accounts where old people regarded tea as corrupting and bad for health. One eighty-year-old man in Novgorod province believed that tooth problems were the result of pampering.

'Earlier', he said, 'we never heard of any kinds of tooth illnesses; the people were stronger. And stronger from what? Less pampering. This tea, that we've read about, wasn't even heard of fifty years ago. In our whole village (Korotovo, seventy people) there was only one samovar, at Ionov's, but now every last homeless fellow sups tea, rinsing his teeth and his belly. Little boys and girls who don't even understand how to wipe their noses are already asking for tea. And you see teeth get painful.'[70]

Old people were most likely to retain hostile attitudes towards tobacco use in general, and smoking in particular.[71] One correspondent noted that 'In the old days, all peasants avoided smoking and even disdained tobacco, calling it a filthy and accursed herb. Now (old people) still disdain it ...'[72] Old were the only ones reported as still chewing tobacco, and this habit was on the wane even among the old – smoking was becoming ubiquitous as delivery of tobacco among rural men.[73] One old man, when asked why he added crushed pine needles to the makhorka tobacco that he smoked in a pipe, answered with a grin

---

[65] See for example ibid., vi, 244.

[66] For a discussion of enduring elite anxieties about the corrupting influences of tea, for example, see Audra Jo Yoder, 'Tea Time in Romanov Russia: A Cultural History, 1616–1917' (Ph.D. thesis, University of North Carolina at Chapel Hill, 2016), ch. 6.

[67] Baranov et al. (eds.), Russkie krest'iane, v.1, 66.

[68] Alison K. Smith, Recipes for Russia: Food and Nationhood under the Tsars (DeKalb, 2008), 95; Morinaga Takako, 'Tea Drinking Culture in Russia', Journal of International Economic Studies, 32 (2018), 57–74.

[69] Baranov et al. (eds.), Russkie krest'iane, ii.1, 490.

[70] Ibid., vii.2, 413.

[71] Ibid., i, 459. See also ibid., vi, 157. For a discussion of attitudes towards smoking, see Tricia Starks, Smoking under the Tsars: A History of Tobacco in Imperial Russia (Ithaca, 2018), 162–200.

[72] Baranov et al. (eds.), Russkie krest'iane, v.2, 301.

[73] Ibid., ii.2, 344 – reference to chewing tobacco only among old men; ibid., iii, 75.

and a cackle, 'It's not too harmful, and the smell is nicer, and you look, it's more fun.'[74]

Attitudes varied of course, between individuals and between regions. We can see this in reports of old people's attitudes towards dance. In Cherepovets district of Novgorod province, the teacher Antipov suggested that the old praised skilled dancers; one old man said 'Look how the son of a bitch dances, look how he moves his feet!'[75] Aleksei Fomin noted that old people in the district were approving about 'walking songs', relatively quiet dances like quadrilles:

> 'If they walk quietly, do not stomp, do not kick up, then let them walk. God is with them,' the old men say. 'There is no sin there.' The Russian squatting dance, however, was considered by all older people to be a great sin: 'Dancing', they say, 'is great devilry. Those who dance, it is all one, as if spinning, will be hanged upside down in the next world, because here in this world he spins to please the devil.'[76]

The construction of old people as moral arbiters is of course deeply problematic and relative. This survey of the roles taken by older people in village culture indicates the individualism of older people's contributions. They could be framed as repositories of past knowledge and as moral guardians of village communities, but there were also examples of older people embracing change.

A useful life? Work and responsibilities for the old

In rural economies, work was integral to everyday life. Those who could, worked. This need to be socially and economically productive and useful was reinforced by tax responsibilities, which were defined by the number of souls per area of land, without any exclusions for the old and others not physically able.[77] This requirement to pay tax was not rescinded 'even if they have only a crust of land, or only a market garden'.[78] While collective responsibility for taxation was abolished in most of European Russia in 1903, in practice village elders continued to bear responsibility for the allocation of taxation, and tended to follow existing practice.[79]

Older people were critical workers within rural communities. Their experience in agriculture and specific industries meant that they could contribute beyond their individual strength to the success of the household and the community. For women, their status and experience within the household enabled

---

[74] *Ibid.*, v.2, 16.

[75] *Ibid.*, vii.2, 533.

[76] *Ibid.*, ii.2, 319; see also *ibid.*, iii, 520.

[77] *Ibid.*, i, 220.

[78] *Ibid.*, i, 302.

[79] Yanni Kotsonis, *States of Obligation: Taxes and Citizenship in the Russian Empire and Early Soviet Republic* (Toronto, 2014), ch. 9, provides a thorough analysis of this problem. See also Gaudin, *Ruling Peasants*, 39.

them to take on running households even as they disavowed the most physically demanding work. The teacher Liubov Il'inichna Solov'eva noted that in Oboiansk district, Kursk province, while women usually withdrew from fieldwork from the age of about fifty, they then took on critical and leading roles in the household, running the house, heating the stove, looking after the children and so on.[80] There were skills that only the old exercised – in one village, people were no longer wearing woven shoes (*lapti*), and only the old wove them anymore.[81] Aleksandr Rozhdestvenskii noted that in Rozhdestvensk district, Vologda province, older women spun *krasna*, a long canvas cloth, which required high levels of skill and dexterity, and which skilled women completed into old age.[82] Beekeeping was mentioned as an occupation practised exclusively by old people.[83] In one village, an old man who wasn't fit for fieldwork exercised his skill as a tar maker when it was required.[84] Washing the dead was a task reserved exclusively for old people, with men washing men's corpses, and women washing women's corpses. They were paid for these services, and only orderly, decent folk were chosen for the task.[85]

Anther core area of respect and responsibility for old people in village life was as healers, traditional midwives and practitioners of magic. Traditional midwives (*povitukhi*) were almost invariably older peasant women.[86] Their role was to care for the mother in labour and to provide more generic support for the family unit after the birth, cooking, cleaning, fetching water and fuel. Traditional healers, a category that encompassed 'wise people' (*znakhar/znakarkha*), midwives, bloodletters and bonesetters, were usually older people, and a significant number were women. They commanded respect 'because of their age and experience' and were consulted on a bewildering array of household and community issues, from personal health to fortune telling, from finding things that were lost to doctoring cows.[87] Witchcraft and sorcery were also skill sets usually ascribed to older people – elderly and widowed women were prominent in cases of witchcraft. One Tula folktale recalled that a witch was 'a woman as old as old can be'.[88] These roles as healers and arbiters of the spiritual world were a distinctive and important contribution to community life

---

[80] Baranov *et al.* (eds.), *Russkie krest'iane*, VI, 30. Another rich account of the importance of the old woman's role in the home in *ibid.*, I, 448.

[81] *Ibid.*, v.1, 65.

[82] *Ibid.*, VI, 30.

[83] *Ibid.*, I, 456.; beekeeping carried out by middle-aged and old in *ibid.*, III, 73; *ibid.*, v.3, 325.

[84] *Ibid.*, v.3, 582.

[85] *Ibid.*, I, 441; II.1, 606; v.1, 113. On death practices in the village, see Chulos, *Converging Worlds*, 38–40.

[86] Samuel C. Ramer, 'Childbirth and Culture: Midwifery in the Nineteenth Century Russian Countryside', in *The Family in Imperial Russia: New Lines of Historical Research*, ed. David L. Ransel (Chicago, 1976), 218–35, esp. 229.

[87] Samuel C. Ramer, 'Traditional Healers and Peasant Culture in Russia, 1861–1917', in *Peasant Economy, Culture and Politics of European Russia 1860–1921*, ed. E. Kingston-Mann, T. Mixter and Jeffrey Burds (Princeton, 1991), 207–32, esp. 210, 222–3.

[88] Christine D. Worobec, 'Witchcraft Beliefs and Practices in Prerevolutionary Russian and Ukrainian Villages', *The Russian Review*, 54 (1995), 165–87, esp. 168, 173, 177.

and demonstrate that old people had core spheres of influence in the community's spiritual, economic and collective lives.

For older people whose physical or mental strength was failing, work entailed taking on roles that required lower levels of strength, skill and dexterity. Market gardening, that is, production for the household on home plots, and maybe for sale locally, was work for 'the weak of strength'; that is, the old and children.[89] When the 'able' working hands were all mobilised at harvest time, the elderly 'rushed around the garden' with the children, picking and preparing berries.[90] A correspondent from Kostroma province, K. E Rashchin, reported that people who were not fit for physical labour could be hired as herdsmen (*pastukhi*), including able old people, teenagers and sometimes 'idiots' (*durachki*) of both sexes. The very word *pastukh* could be used as an insult.[91]

The roles that the old might take on varied according to the shape of the local economy. In Griazovetsk district, Vologda province, the old practised spinning in summer and winter.[92] In Lapshante, a village in Kostroma province, a few old men did nothing but fish all year round.[93] In Novoladozhsk district of St Petersburg province, old women were responsible for weaving fishing nets from best linen.[94] In Poshekon'e district of Yaroslavl province, where there was a bark industry, the old, along with other 'weak' family members (children and women), were sent out to strip bark from willow bushes and shrubs. These materials were supplied to local factories.[95] For those areas with high levels of seasonal and urban out-migration, old people were often 'left behind' in the village, and were responsible both for fieldwork and for the maintenance of the household.[96] The very old, along with young children, were the only community members not to go out on seasonal work at Lent in the community of Soligalichsk district, Kostroma province.[97] These areas with high out-migration patterns were full of old people who had spent their working lives in the city. These folk were described as 'unwitting villagers'.[98]

Many of Tenishev's correspondents remarked on the relationship between productive work and access to food. An anecdote from Vasillii Antipovich Antipov, a teacher from Novgorod province, offers a useful illustration:

> In Korotov village there's an eighty-year-old man, Grigory. He works on a par at every task with his son and grandson: he ploughs, and mows, and hammers in the forge. Once the priest met Gregory mowing in the field,

---

[89] Baranov *et al.* (eds.), *Russkie krest'iane*, II.1, 2, 305.

[90] *Ibid.*, VII.1, 430.

[91] *Ibid.*, I, 383.

[92] *Ibid.*, V.2, 14.

[93] *Ibid.*, I, 69; see also *ibid.*, V.3, 325.

[94] *Ibid.*, VI, 344.

[95] *Ibid.*, II.1, 2, 177.

[96] Engel, *Between the Fields.*

[97] Baranov *et al.* (eds.), *Russkie krest'iane*, I, 307; see also *ibid.*, III, 476 and II.2, 250.

[98] *Ibid.*, VI, 70.

and said to him: 'You've done your time, Gregory, it's time to give it up.' Grigory answered, 'well father, as I keep up with scything in the row, so I do not lag behind at the table.'[99]

Grigory's case hinted that if he wanted to eat well, he needed to work well. Does a human still have value if they can no longer contribute economically to the household or the community? This difficult question did not have straightforward answers in the late Imperial Russian context. The distribution and division of food was one of the most often reported spaces of intergenerational tension within households and offers insight into the sharp end of the relationships between life, worth and living. There was a consensus in the Tenishev reports that old people should eat less than working family members.[100] Household tensions were most heightened in times of dearth, and food could provoke heated quarrels.[101] These quarrels were often spaces in which old people were explicitly targeted. Aleksei Grigorevich Vasil'ev reported from Novgorod province that it was rare for a mealtime to pass without bickering, and that the old were often targeted by their children for eating too much or too quickly. In one family, the son berated his old parents every mealtime: 'You've scooped all the beef out of the soup! Now I'm eating empty soup! You eat, you don't work, and you're the first to eat!'[102]

This overview of work patterns for older people confirms their economic and cultural significance within village life. It also emphasises that worth and value within the family and the community was to some extent conditional on capacity to contribute to economic life.

The fourth age: waiting to die?

At the Dvuchasovs' country house, their old Nyanya was readying herself for death; she had been doing this for ten years ... in a corner behind a dresser, she would sit or lie on her trunk and carry on with her dying till spring.

Come spring, she'd pick a dry, sunny day, stretch a rope between a pair of trees in the birch grove, and air her burial clothes: a long-yellowed linen shirt, a pair of embroidered slippers, a pale blue belt – embroidered with a prayer for the repose of the dead – and a small cypress wood cross.[103]

Nyanya's theatrical preparations reflected a broader peasant tradition of old age as a period where one awaits death.[104] The care of old people at the end of their lives allows us to explore and to test the final frontiers of attitudes towards older people. People ailed and died primarily in village domestic

---

[99] Ibid., vii.2, 283.

[100] For example, ibid., ii.2, 129–30; ii.1, 600; ii.2, 371.

[101] Ibid., iii, 323; vii.4, 20.

[102] Ibid., vii.2, 562.

[103] 'Soul in Bond', in Teffi, Other Worlds: Peasants, Pilgrims, Spirits, Saints, ed. Robert Chandler, trans. Elizabeth Chandler, Sara Jolly and Nicolas Slater (2021), 13.

[104] Panchenko, 'Obraz starosti'.

spaces, cared for by their relatives and neighbours. Contemporary elites looked at inadequate care for old people as one of the indicators of modern decay, along with the development of an urban working class, the evolution of mass literacy, and autonomous cultural practices.[105] Russia's elite society regarded the stability of the family as critical to the stability of the state. Care for the frail elderly was one of the litmus tests of society's functionality and viability.[106] This final section starts by exploring the ways in which older people sought to plan and prepare for their final years, through manipulation of their wills and familial relations. We then go on to look at the mechanisms in place to provide care and support for the frail elderly at community level. The final part reflects on the lived experience of frail elderly people within their family homes. Frailty and infirmity are used in contemporary medical discourse to refer to the physical decline of advanced old age. The term frailty captures the 'residuum and repository of feared old age', and it is this aspect of life which is the focus of this final section.[107]

Property rights and adoption

The inheritance and distribution of property was a tangible means for old people to negotiate their status and care within the family or community. Expectations that they would be cared for in extreme old age and buried respectfully were tied into their decisions and capacity to disburse property. Tensions within households are most often visible to us as historians when they were brought to the district (*volost*) court for legal resolution.[108] This happened most often around questions of the family property's separation and redistribution (*razdel*).[109] The legal status of inheritance and family property disputes was extremely complex. District courts had jurisdiction in civil disputes between all non-privileged country dwellers about any property acquired under emancipation, or any other property up to the value of 500 roubles. At district level, judges were expected to consider local customs or customary law, which was a reference to patterns of behaviour regarded as 'normal' or 'right' or 'obligatory' in the familiar situations of daily life. They were to evaluate these local customs alongside written legal code, usual referring to the civil laws (*zakony grazhdanskie*) in part 1, volume 1 of the Full Digest of Laws (*svod zakonov*) that dated back to 1832.[110] What local custom might constitute was of course subject to rigorous contention. The testimony of old

[105] William G. Wagner, 'Family Law, the Rule of Law, and Liberalism in Late Imperial Russia', *Jahrbücher für Geschichte Osteuropas*, 43 (1995), 519–35, esp. 533–4.

[106] *Ibid.*, 533–4.

[107] Chris Gilleard and Paul Higgs, 'Frailty, Disability and Old Age: A Re-appraisal', *Health*, 15 (2011), 475–90, at 484.

[108] The landmark work on this topic was Jane Burbank, *Russian Peasants Go to Court: Legal Culture in the Countryside, 1905-1917* (Bloomington, 2004).

[109] Baranov *et al.* (eds.), *Russkie krest'iane*, v.3, 328. For scholarship on *razdel*, see Cathy A. Frierson, 'Razdel: The Peasant Family Divided', *The Russian Review*, 46 (1987), 35–51.

[110] Gareth Popkins, 'Code versus Custom? Norms and Tactics in Peasant Volost Court Appeals, 1889–1917', *The Russian Review*, 59 (2000), 408–24, esp. 409–11.

people was permissible as proof of what local custom constituted, an example of respect for the elderly as arbiters of the past.[111]

Property rights and authority are usually presented as tied explicitly to seniority and to gender hierarchies – the older male has authority and legal possession of properties. In practice, this was not always the case. Older people could be marginalised or even entirely disempowered if their capacity to work, or their mental faculties, deteriorated. The old could resort to the district court if they were being neglected in the household, or even starved, though one correspondent noted that they were usually very reluctant to do so, because of the ire this could provoke within the household.[112] We can see some of the complexities of this with the Petrov family in Yaroslavl province. Fedot Petrov, the patriarch, was sixty years old but no longer able to work. His married son Pavel was forty years old and had been working for the household for twenty years. Fedot applied to divide the property, intending to give significant parts of it to his married daughters. Pavel appealed against this in the district court, and the court found in his favour – the father, Fedot, could not divide the property which Pavel lived and worked in, but the son, Pavel, had to feed and care for Fedot till his death. The correspondent reports that this outcome was agreeable to both parties, and that they went on to live 'in love and agreement'.[113]

Several accounts reinforced the notion that the elder man retained power and control over household division and inheritance. Family property's separation and redistribution (*razdel*) was usually hindered by the elder, whose authority was great in most families, and who often refused *razdel* while they lived; 'after I die you can do what you like, but while I'm alive, don't you dare'.[114] Nikolai Kolosov, a teacher from Kostroma province, noted that no matter how old and decrepit the father was, he held full authority over the property as long as he was of sound mind, and the property could not be divided without his consent.[115] Sergei Aleksandrovich Dilaktorskii, a nobleman and veterinary surgeon from Vologda province, noted that if the property was divided before the elders' deaths, but they were not to live with their children, then formal provision was made that the children were to provide specific foodstuffs, firewood and money to the old parents.[116] The prevailing opinion in one village was that while grandfather was alive, he was master of the house, even if the son had in practice been running the household for years. Despite this, the correspondent went on to note that in practice there might be adjustments to distribution of property without grandfather's permission. In Kalyagin village, a peasant cut off one of his sons, who had married against his will, even though the grandfather did not approve:

---

[111] *Ibid.*, 419.
[112] *Ibid.*, v.4, 180.
[113] *Ibid.*, ii.1, 344.
[114] *Ibid.*, ii.1, 345–7.
[115] *Ibid.*, i, 332.
[116] *Ibid.*, v.2, 604.

'Of course, according to the rule, it would be impossible to go against the old man,' the father said about this incident, 'because he will not go from the stove to the community gathering (*skhod*) in his old age, well, and you do as you yourself want.'[117]

The use of wills for the control of inheritance became increasingly normalised by the turn of the twentieth century. Peasants were permitted by law to draw up testaments using simplified procedures, though local customs defined adjudication of these processes.[118] Nikolai Falalevich Preobrazhenskii noted that in Vologda province the old often drew up written wills, primarily to ensure that the child or relative who cared for them in their old age be proportionately rewarded: 'After all, he fed and watered me till I died,' thinks the old person, 'and he will bury and remember me.'[119] In the case of a wealthy old couple from Novgorod province, the elder son separated from the household, taking a third of the property, and leaving the old couple to live with the younger son in the larger property. The younger son neglected his parents, and this caught the attention of the elder son and his wife. They surreptitiously moved the parents to live with them, and the old man drew up a new will whereby the elder son inherited a greater share on the old man's death.[120]

Childless older people deployed a range of strategies to secure support for their fourth age. Property and other forms of wealth could be used by old people as leverage to secure care. If an old couple had no son, then they might 'adopt' their son-in-law or brother-in-law, and allow him to inherit their property, with the condition that they would be cared for until their death and buried 'honestly' in accordance with Christian rites.[121] If they had no daughter, then they might adopt an unrelated person to take on this role. This form of old person 'adoption', referred to in Chupovets district of Novgorod province as 'feeding', was approved by the commune (*obshchina*), and was overseen by the district board.[122] The adoption was not formally registered, but the adopted son (*primak*) was regarded as heir. Another version of this was that an old person would be taken into another family, either a relative or someone unrelated. The old person would be cared for until death, and their immovable property would be inherited by the carers.[123] The practice of 'adoption' is well known and documented, but accounts usually stress the practice's function in avoiding dispersal of family property. By thinking about the process from the perspective of vulnerable older people, we can see less the welfare role of the peasant household, and more the ways in which elderly people mobilised to try

---

[117] *Ibid.*, ii.2, 319.

[118] Gareth Popkins, 'Russian Peasant Wills in the Decisions of the Ruling Senate, 1861–1906', *Journal of Legal History*, 20, no. 2 (1999), 1–23, esp. 2, 13, 18.

[119] Baranov *et al.* (eds.), *Russkie krest'iane*, v.2, 707.

[120] *Ibid.*, vii.2, 302.

[121] *Ibid.*, v.2, 439.

[122] *Ibid.*, iii, 384–5. See also *ibid.* vii.3, 96.

[123] *Ibid.*, vii.3, 249.

to protect themselves in advanced old age.[124] We can also see that these arrangements, which were often sanctioned by the community, functioned as mechanisms to reduce the perceived burden of caring for the elderly. The community's expectation was that an adopted son would need to care for the parents in old age.[125] One case explicitly suggested that a son who agreed to take in or support elderly parents had the right to a greater share of their property.[126] An 1885 resolution in Beloomut stipulated that a woman without other forms of support could only sell her property on the condition that the buyer committed to pall any taxes and dues that she owed, and to support the woman in her old age.[127]

One source suggested that disputes within families were usually handled without recourse to external authorities, or that in worst-case scenario, the village assembly or the village court of elders would intercede.[128] Several accounts, however, refer to disputes over inheritance and care for elderly relatives turning up regularly both in the *volost* courts and in the higher courts of appeal (from 1891). In Ryazan region in 1910, an absentee peasant-worker appealed the *volost* court's approval of his ailing mother's right to one-third of the deceased father's property. The communal assembly was engaged on behalf of the old woman and sent a representative to speak on her behalf. The appeal court ruled against her because she was 'incapable of running the household, and could not therefore request a division'.[129]

Care in the community

Most elderly people lived out their days in their homes and were to some extent cared for by family and community. The prevalence of kinship relationships as the main source of caregiving in later life is enduring across time and place.[130] In late Imperial Russia, the village commune was responsible for providing aid and support to the aged, decrepit and disabled. In practice, this responsibility was unevenly and patchily met, and relied primarily on individual community members' acts of charity.[131] Formalised healthcare had been virtually non-existent in Russian villages before the establishment of zemstvo, a form of representative local government, in 1864. The zemstvo made healthcare their biggest area of expenditure, and increased access to doctors and medical assistants (*feld'shers*) exponentially by the turn of the century. Despite this, medical

---

[124] Worobec's excellent treatment of the process articulates the welfare role but does not draw out older people's agency and need to self-protect so much. Worobec, *Peasant Russia*, 57–62.

[125] Popkins, 'Code versus Custom', 414–15.

[126] Gaudin, *Ruling Peasants*, 123.

[127] *Ibid.*, 140.

[128] Cathy A. Frierson, '"I must always answer to the law …" Rules and Responses in the Reformed Volost' Court', *Slavonic and East European Review*, 75 (1997), 308–34, esp. 329–30.

[129] Gaudin, *Ruling Peasants*, 127.

[130] Gowland, 'Growing Old', 238.

[131] Mironov, 'The Russian Peasant Commune', 454; Adele Lindenmeyr, *Poverty Is Not a Vice: Charity, Society and the State in Late Imperial Russia* (Princeton, 1996), 51.

expertise and support in most rural areas was rudimentary or entirely lacking.[132] Hospices did not exist in this context. Hospitals were few and far between and were regarded by older people and the community with fear and suspicion.[133] One correspondent reported that hospitals were seen by villagers as places to die.[134] The medicalisation of ageing that was reaching the Russian Empire by the early twentieth century had not reached rural lower-class spaces.[135]

It was a core expectation in rural communities that children should feed and care for their parents in old age. Household units (*dvor*) were expected to care for their members when they were no longer able to work.[136] The responsibility to care for one's parents was deeply held in the community and applied to families where children had moved out and set up their own households, as well as where the family all lived together.[137] As one correspondent noted, 'Without the blessing of father and mother, there will be no luck or happiness in anything.'[138] This emphasis on parental care left childless old people at a particular disadvantage.[139] Russia at the turn of the century did not have any public welfare organisation, and had no pension provision for older people. Pensions for poor elderly people were established in multiple other states in the early twentieth century: Germany in 1889, Denmark in 1891, New Zealand in 1898, Australia and Britain in 1908.[140] Welfare provisions in Russia, such as they were, stemmed primarily from family and community interventions. While urban spaces saw the development of very limited provision of welfare in the form of almshouses, there was no such provision for most rural spaces.[141] This differed from some other parts of Europe, where state-sponsored welfare organisations offered some degree of safety-net welfare for impoverished old people.[142]

Filial duty enabled the community to function effectively, and where children failed to care for their elderly parents, or if the elderly had no one to care for them, the onus for care moved towards the community at large.

---

[132] Steven Nafziger, 'Did Ivan's Vote Matter? The Political Economy of Local Democracy in Tsarist Russia', *European Review of Economic History*, 15 (2011), 393–441, esp. 397–400. Samuel C. Ramer, 'The Zemstvo and Public Health' in *The Zemstvo in Russia: An Experiment in Local Self-Government*, ed. Terence Emmons and Wayne S. Vucinich (Cambridge, 1982), 279–314; see esp. table 8.1, showing coverage of zemstvo doctors and medical assistants.

[133] F. A. Brokgauz and E. A. Efron, *Entsiklopedicheskii slovar Brokgauza i Efrona*, vol. IV (St Petersburg, 1891), 325–7. Lindenmeyr, 'Work, Charity, and the Elderly', 237ff., discusses almshouses, and notes peasant resistance to institutionalised support.

[134] Baranov et al. (eds.), *Russkie krest'iane*, IV, 178, 183.

[135] Lovell, 'Finitude at the Fin de Siècle', 298.

[136] Engel, *Between the Fields*, 42.

[137] Baranov et al. (eds.), *Russkie krest'iane*, IV, 124.

[138] *Ibid.*, IV, 116.

[139] For a broader framing of the problem of old age for childless people, see Christian Deindl and Martina Brandt, 'Support Networks of Childless Older People: Informal and Formal Support in Europe', *Ageing & Society*, 37 (2017), 1543–67.

[140] Thane, 'Old Age in European Cultures', 390–2.

[141] Lindenmeyr, *Poverty Is Not a Vice*.

[142] On the English case, see Thane, *Old Age in English History*, 192–3.

Care for the vulnerable was part of the rural community's remit, but these obligations should not be romanticised. A zemstvo survey of Moscow province in 1911 found that only 22 per cent of the 137 communes surveyed provided named support to the elderly and infirm. This did not necessarily indicate dedicated support for vulnerable elderly people. Of these, half of the communes had passed a resolution that rotated the obligation to feed and care for the vulnerable elderly around the community.[143] There were sometimes conflicts between authorities and the community over the provision of communal welfare.[144] In practice, community care for frail elderly was patchy, and might constitute no more than the provision of alms to beggars.

The community could intervene on multiple levels in cases where children failed to care for their old parents. The peasant Stepan Fedotovich Stavoverov noted that in some cases in Vologda province, daughters-in-law mistreated their old parents–in-law, and that in these cases, fellow villagers were condemnatory but did not intervene, 'except for close relatives of the sick and decrepit, who could take them for a while, under the guise of an invitation to visit, and give them proper rest and care for a while'.[145] In another case, a wealthier peasant divided his property, but was neglected and treated disrespectfully by his younger son, whom he and his wife had moved in with. The old man complained with tears in his eyes to the correspondent, Aleksandr Grigorevich Vasil'ev, that he was being oppressed, but that nothing could be done, since the division was made legally and formalised. 'I thought they would understand my kindness, take care of me and the old woman in our old age, but this is what happened!'[146]

There were cases where children wilfully neglected their old parents. In Zimnichka village, Kaluga province, the priest's daughter V. E. Zorina recalled the tale of Agaf'ia Zhukova, who told her that neither her husband, Pavel Zhukov, a landless peasant from Khimok village, nor his brother, Akim Zhukov, would care for their own father, who was paralysed. The father took his case to the district court, and the court instructed the brothers to share responsibility for their father. The old man rotated a week at a time between the two households. Agaf'ia found out that Akim was not giving his father enough to eat and was not keeping him clean, so she secretly visited him to bring extra food and to change his linen.[147] This case is revealing in multiple respects: the court intervened on behalf of the neglected father, and the daughter-in-law displayed care and compassion in attending to the father-in-law's needs even against the wishes of her husband.

E. N. Kuznetsov, a student from Kostroma province, noted that the village *skhod* could intervene if it was felt that a child was not caring for his father, either 'not feeding him, or pulling his beard.' If the *skhod*'s intervention was not effective, then the district court sentenced the son to fifteen lashes with

---

[143] Gaudin, *Ruling Peasants*, 141.

[144] Ibid., 177.

[145] Baranov *et al.* (eds.), *Russkie krest'iane*, v.2, 273.

[146] Ibid., vii.2, 546.

[147] Ibid., iii, 55.

the birch and ordered that he must feed his father until the father died.[148] Sergei Vladimirovich Korvin-Krukovskii, from Nizhegorod province, reported cases where parents appealed to the local district court with complaints about neglect from their children. In these cases, the district court could assign a cash maintenance sum, which it determined based on the relative wealth of the children.[149]

Support in old age presented specific challenges for those old people without children.[150] In Shava village, Makar'evsk district, Nizhnii Novgorod province, they were referred to as 'orphans', and they 'live somewhere at the end of the village in uncomfortable places'.[151] In Ulomsk region of Cherepovetsk district, Vologda province, landless old men and women were given a small garden plot with which to sustain themselves.[152] The nobleman and historian Aleksandr Evgrafovich Mertsalov reported that in Kadnikovsk district of Vologda province, old people without relatives were rootless and uncared for.[153] The teacher Aleksandr Grigorevich Vasil'ev suggested that in Cherepovets district of Novgorod province, the whole community cared for those sick and old people who had no family of their own, taking turns in lighting the stove, bringing food and cleaning them up. If they didn't have their own hut, unsupported old people were allocated housing in a church cell and taken care of there.[154] His was the only account to articulate support for old people so confidently.

The account of Mikhei Fedorovich Kholin, from Nizhnii Novgorod province, reinforced the idea that the community provided structured support to childless old people. Kholin noted that almost everywhere in the local villages one could find some rootless and landless old men and women who live 'by the mercy of Christ', either supported by well-off households or who lived in 'cells' provided by the church. These church-supported paupers didn't beg round the village, but received alms, usually money, from worshippers in the church who could leave donations on a small shelf arranged on the jamb of the window.[155] Finally, the childless old person could sell their land, and use the proceeds to support themselves.[156]

The complete absence of state support and intervention for old people in rural spaces ensured that the spectacle of old people begging around the houses within their own community, or walking between villages to receive support, was entrenched in late Imperial rural society. Beggars were rarely refused in rural spaces, which had a strongly developed culture of providing crusts for the

---

[148] *Ibid.*, I, 76.

[149] *Ibid.*, IV, 116. See also *ibid.*, IV, 118.

[150] See Deindl and Brandt, 'Support Networks of Childless Older People'; Kersti Lust, 'Aging without Children in Nineteenth and Early Twentieth Century Rural Estonia', *Journal of Family History*, 47 (2022), 172–92.

[151] Baranov *et al.* (eds.), *Russkie krest'iane*, IV, 337.

[152] *Ibid.*, VII.2, 30.

[153] *Ibid.*, V.2, 712.

[154] *Ibid.*, VII.2, 543.

[155] *Ibid.*, IV, 170.

[156] *Ibid.*, III, 365.

needy, even from households that were themselves poor.[157] Various accounts reported that the elderly made up a significant number of village beggars, and that they came either on their own behalf, or they were sent out to beg by their impoverished families. Korvin-Krukovskii reported that most beggars were old people without property or relatives to support them, and who were totally incapable of work as a result of decrepitude or illness, and lived exclusively on alms.[158] This strategic use of the elderly by needy families indicates that the old were seen by the community as particularly deserving of charity.

Care in the home

One universal in remarks was that the sick and decrepit were housebound, and this meant that in periods of busy fieldwork, but especially in the summer, the sick were left at home. Care was generally better for the housebound sick in the winter, with neighbours 'considering it their duty' to pop round.[159] Some correspondents suggested that neighbours and other old people took care of the sick and the young children in homes where the other folk were out in the fields, and that in general 'old folks and especially children, are not left to starve'. In this account, visiting the sick was considered 'a good thing', and neighbours popped by with food and drinks for the invalid.[160] Other accounts, however, describe terrible neglect for the decrepit, and assert that they were left with no support, and often died alone.

> For the sick here, in general, care is very bad, and is sometimes altogether out of sight; in the summertime, for example, in work time, a ladle of water is left near the patient and they are left alone for the whole day … decrepit old people are left especially often … Here in the village, a decrepit old woman, unable to move, lay alone in the hut for days, in the end, she died alone; when the family returned from work, they found her already dead.[161]

We can observe a range of attitudes towards sick and dying old people, with a spectrum of care from unfettered kindness and solicitude all the way through to life-shortening abuse.[162] The rationale for quality of care varied from philosophical ('they've had their time') to practical ('no time when the fieldwork is busy') to economic (no time or resources to support non-productive family member). The balance of accounts veers towards philosophically and practically based neglect of sick old people. The seminary student Vasilii Arkad'evich Shesterikov argued that the miserable condition in which the decrepit old lived in Vologda

---

[157] Lindenmeyr, 'Work, Charity, and the Elderly', 242–3.

[158] Baranov, *Russkie krest'iane*, IV, 169. See also *ibid.*, v.3, 123; VII.3, 360, 363, 365; VI, 378; VII.1, 297; VII.2, 404.

[159] *Ibid.*, VII.4, 285.

[160] *Ibid.*, II.1, 604. On old as carers, see also *ibid.*, IV, 183.

[161] *Ibid.*, II.2, 389. See also *ibid.*, v.2, 97, 381–2.

[162] *Ibid.*, II.1, 604; for positive account of cared-for old people, *ibid.*, VII.2, 424.

province meant that their desire for death and sense of hopelessness was 'natural'. 'Unfit for work, old and sick, they sincerely ask God for death.'[163]

The nobleman Sergei Vladimirovich Korvin-Krukovskii presented a more nuanced view, recounting that in Nizhnii Novgorod province, within the family setting, reproaches to old people and poor quality of care came about when the family experienced extreme need and poverty, either because of failed harvests or because of accident. Such desperate situations meant that those not capable of work because of decrepitude faced reproaches about their long lives, and articulation of the desire that they would die. He stressed, however, that these views never developed into actions that might shorten the old person's life as this 'would be, in the opinion of a peasant, a grave sin and a grave crime tantamount to murder'.[164]

Other accounts suggested that those old people who were no longer fit to work were treated in ways that necessarily shortened their lives through moral suffering and neglect. The ethnographer Balov suggested that in some households other family members, including children, spoke about the old person in their earshot, though not to their faces, in extremely harsh and derogatory terms, 'If only God would come for him, then our hands would be untied,' and so on. The correspondent went on to suggest that in some households the harsh treatment of the old went beyond cruel words, and into active neglect.[165] These grim depictions of life for the old are supported in multiple other accounts. One telling insight is the account of the topics of conversation among old people when they met for a chat. As well as the state of their health, they discussed the amount of work that they were expected to do in the household, and whether they did this of their own volition or under duress, and they talked about whether they were treated with respect by the other householders, and if they were treated as a burden.[166]

Many correspondents told tales of misery and humiliation for the very old. An old woman in Gridino village, Novgorod province, had two sons. She was sent to live with one of them when the property was divided. She was treated cruelly by her son and his wife, and left lying on the stove for days, sometimes without food. The other son refused to intervene, claiming it was not his responsibility. Neighbours dropped food in for the old woman, and the son was reproached by everyone in the village for his actions, but there were no further interventions.[167] Multiple correspondents offered accounts of households berating the sick elderly for continuing to live.[168] Some correspondents suggested that care for sick elderly people was rude and poor, but that this was because of a lack of time and resources, not a lack of sentimental care.[169] One recounted the attitudes of a peasant woman he knew, Eugenia, who complained bitterly about her ailing mother-in-law, and the demands placed on her by the sick woman; 'she tied me hand and foot'. When the old woman

---

[163] *Ibid.*, v.1, 605.

[164] *Ibid.*, iv, 215.

[165] *Ibid.*, ii.2, 102.

[166] *Ibid.*, vii.1, 85.

[167] *Ibid.*, vii.1, 275. See also *ibid.*, v.3, 508; ii.2, 389; iii, 289.

[168] *Ibid.*, iv, 194; vii.2, 283, 424; vii.3, 375.

[169] *Ibid.*, vii.2, 283.

died, though, Eugenia expressed remorse for her own harsh words and said 'I feel sorry for the old woman: we lived together for thirty years.'[170]

These accounts offer us some snapshots of life behind closed doors for the frail elderly, and they indicate that many frail elderly people lived out their fourth age in environments where love and nurture were not very evident.

Conclusions

This article has sought to explore the experience of elderly people in Russian villages at the turn of the twentieth century. Wherever possible, the perspective of the elderly people themselves has been privileged. The ethnographic sources that this study draws from offer some insights into these experiences. They also, however, reinforce the fundamental challenge of accessing and respecting the perspectives of older people themselves. Most of what we know and hear of older people is reported about them, not by them. This article has tried to tackle this challenge head-on by trying to use older people's own accounts and stories wherever possible. The picture that emerges from this study both reinforces the importance and value of older people to community and family life, while simultaneously highlighting the poor treatment and sorry prospects for the 'oldest old', as frailty and ill health reduce or remove individuals' working capacity.

The first section asks when old age begins. It acknowledges the primacy of functional age over chronological age – that is, that perceptions of a person's age were connected most closely with their capacity to work, and not their birth year. The second section reinforces the importance of 'third age' active older people in family and community life. Older people played important cultural, social and economic roles, as storytellers and repositories of the past, and as moral arbiters. Older people were the most active and consistent in their practice of Russian Orthodox faith. Their working hands were necessary and valued parts of village life, whether they were deployed in roles that only they had the skills to perform, or in the jobs for the weak that they fulfilled alongside children. The third section explores the area of old age that has been most neglected in the scholarship so far, the so-called 'fourth age', that is, the period of old age characterised as decline towards the 'terminal phase' of life. By considering the use of wills, and of formal and informal adoption of heirs who would be required to take on caring obligations, we can see the ways in which older people exercised agency in planning their own futures. The picture of community care is mixed. There are some examples of specific welfare measures taken by communities to care for frail old people. The ubiquity of old people begging in many accounts indicates that care in the community was patchy and partial at best and relied heavily on individual charity and individual requests for assistance. The final part, looking at the quality of care offered to frail elderly people in their homes, indicates that end-of-life experiences were often lonely and uncomfortable. There were a suite of explanations offered for this end-of-days care. While individual circumstances

---

[170] *Ibid.*, III, 526.

differed, the overarching sense was of a philosophical lack of solicitude towards the frail elderly.

It is undoubtedly the case that old women, and especially widows, were in a more precarious position within the community than old men. This article has not however explored gendered differences in old age, which reflects a lack of gendered difference in the ways in which the sources discussed older people. This absence of gender differentiation for the frail elderly reinforced a sense that frail elderly people were desexed and to some extent denied individuality and agency. This exploration of the experience of old age suggests that we need to adjust and realign our understandings of seniority and power in late Imperial Russian villages. For those old people who became incapable of work, their status and value within the community and within the family collapsed. While elder men had power over their families and access to formal village power structures, this study has shown that their authority and power was eroded by frailty and old age. Hierarchies of ableness, or capacity to work, superseded generational hierarchies.

Acknowledgements. The author wishes to thank Simon Dixon, Geoffrey Hosking, Jonathan Kwan and Aaron Retish for their help with the manuscript.

Author biography. Sarah Badcock is Professor of Modern History at the University of Nottingham. She is the author of multiple books and articles on various aspects of late Imperial and revolutionary Russian history. Her most recent book was A Prison without Walls? Eastern Siberian Exile in the Last Years of Tsarism (Oxford University Press, 2016).

Cite this article: Badcock S (2024). Waiting to Die? Old Age in the Late Imperial Russian Village. *Transactions of the Royal Historical Society* **2**, 181–205. https://doi.org/10.1017/S008044012300021X

Transactions of the RHS (2024), **2**, 207–232
doi:10.1017/S0080440124000148

ARTICLE

The India League and the *Condition of India*: Agnotological Imperialism, Colonial State Violence and the Making of Anticolonial Knowledge 1930–4

Abhimanyu Arni

St. Edmund Hall, University of Oxford, Oxford, UK
Email: Abhimanyu.Arni@seh.ox.ac.uk

(Received 8 February 2024; revised 20 July 2024; accepted 22 July 2024;
first published online 1 October 2024)

Abstract

This article explores the 1932 visit to India of a delegation of Labour party figures associated with the India League, a prominent anticolonial organisation based in London, charged with investigating the colonial state violence unleashed by 'Ordinance Rule'. It also examines efforts taken by the Government of India, India Office and Indian Political Intelligence to suppress their findings, through which it explores a dialectic between anticolonial knowledge-making and agnotological imperialism, which often took the form of the latter 'exceptioning' examples produced by the former of excessive colonial state violence. It offers the conclusion that the contradictions between liberal imperialism and the rule of colonial difference and repression in the age of mass nationalism in India and mass democracy in Britain meant that liberal imperialism in India increasingly flowed, paradoxically, from illiberalism in Britain.

Keywords: anticolonialism; agnotology; liberal imperialism; colonial violence; India League

> There she was, incomprehensible, firing into a continent.
> Joseph Conrad describing a French warship off the coast of Africa,
> *Heart of Darkness*[1]

> I had had to think out my problems in the utter silence that is imposed on
> every Englishman in the East.
> George Orwell, *Shooting an Elephant*[2]

---

[1] Joseph Conrad, *Heart of Darkness*, ed. Owen Knowles and Allan H. Simmons (Cambridge, 2016), 14.
[2] George Orwell, 'Shooting an Elephant', in *Essays*, ed. John Carey (2002), 237.

Introduction

In 1932 the India League, by then developing into one of the most prominent anticolonial organisations in interwar Britain,[3] sponsored a delegation of four Labour Party members (including the well-known Ellen Wilkinson) to India. Ther hope, in line with the long-term strategy of the India League, was that the delegation's findings would help fight public ignorance of 'Un-British'[4] methods of rule in the subcontinent and thereby generate public support in Britain for India's claim to political freedom.[5] The delegation travelled extensively and interviewed villagers, Congress Party volunteers and leaders, policemen, colonial officials and even the Viceroy. Despite the efforts of the government to limit who they met and what they saw, the delegation left with an impression of an oppressive and exploitative imperialism that maintained inhuman labour conditions and feudal land tenure through brutal state violence in the prisons and especially on the street.

Their dissenting version became the basis of a book, the *Condition of India*,[6] parliamentary questions, articles in the British (left-wing) press, and speeches at India League and Labour Party Conferences. Despite the strenuous and unconstitutional efforts of the India Office to repress it's findings in Britain, the delegation's visit and subsequent publications have been described by historians as a 'coup' for the India League, as having a dramatic impact on Labour party thinking and a still-relevant indictment of Britain's colonial record.[7] So far, the *Condition of India* has only been the focus of one study, a section of an article that addresses it from the perspective of the history of the book and it has therefore never been placed in conversation with major imperial and colonial historiographical debates.[8]

This article investigates the production of the *Condition of India* as an example of anticolonial knowledge-making on the subject of empire, with a particular focus on colonial violence. It also investigates the strategies that the India Office and Government of India used to repress and counter the

---

[3] Note on Vengali Krishnan Krishna Menon [n.d.] British Library/India Office Records [hereafter BL/IOR]/L/P&J/12/323.

[4] Nehru Memorial Museum and Library, New Delhi [hereafter NMML]/Annie Besant Papers (Microfilm) [hereafter ABP]/Part II/14c-D-19, *Home Rule for India League: Pamphlet No. 1: What India Wants* (n.d., probably 1916).

[5] *Ibid.*

[6] See The India League (in this case, Leonard Matters, V. K. Krishna Menon, Bertrand Russell (foreword), Ellen Wilkinson and Monica Whately), *The Condition of India: Being the Report of the Delegation sent by the India League, in 1932* (1934) [hereafter IL, *COI*].

[7] See, respectively, Nicholas Owens, *The British Left and India: Metropolitan Anti-Imperialism 1885–1942* (Oxford, 2007), 208; Stephen Howe, *Anticolonialism in British Politics: The Left and the End of Empire 1918–1964* (Oxford, 1993), 129; and Rozina Visram, *Asians in Britain: 400 Years of History* (2002), 329.

[8] See Jack Bowman, 'The Early Political Thought and Publishing Career of V. K. Krishna Menon, 1928–1938', *The Historical Journal*, 66 (2023), 641–65. There have only been a few comprehensive studies of interwar British anticolonialism, see Partha Sarathi Gupta, *Imperialism and the British Labour Movement 1914–1964* (Cambridge, 1975); Howe, *Anticolonialism in British Politics*; Priyamvada Gopal, *Insurgent Empire: Anticolonial resistance and British Dissent* (2020); and Owens, *The British Left and India*.

League's findings in order to examine British imperialism as a project of conscious and active ignorance-making, or agnotology. The principal argument in this case is that when the two epistemic projects of anticolonial knowledge and imperial ignorance-making compete it is not around the facticity of event or phenomenon, but rather its *generalisability*. A case of excessive and exemplary colonial violence was, for the anticolonialist, an exemplification of imperialism, whereas to the empire, it was a regrettable and necessary exception to an imperialism that was liberal, civilised and civilising.

A secondary, methodological, argument is that anticolonial knowledge-making projects are useful historical resources for supporting decolonial histories of empire, especially on topics where colonial archives might be silent, such as colonial violence. A central section of this article therefore surveys the *Condition of India*'s investigation of colonial violence as lawless, exemplary and profoundly 'Un-British'. This helps us uncover the ways in which the 'rule of colonial difference',[9] to borrow from Partha Chatterjee, produced a state of exception that in turn enabled brutal state violence. Even as liberal imperialism made universalist claims to civilise, the enduring difference between the European and the colonial subject permitted methods of colonial rule that would be inappropriate at home. This was an uncivilised violence that therefore had to be denied even as it was committed. The India League's anticolonial witnessing therefore forced the colonial state into clear and contorted denials of its own violence and, as a result, is powerfully revealing of liberal imperialism's dependence on both exemplary violence and its disavowal. This article first explores the twinned themes of anticolonial knowledge and imperial ignorance-making before applying them to the India League's visit to India, the (obscured) nature of colonial violence they found there, and the repression of the League's findings that followed its return to Britain. This repression forms a final argument: that the authoritarian empire in India increasingly depended on the limits of liberalism in Britain, including the weakness of individual MPs in Parliament, the power of the secret state and the deference shown by the press to government and empire.

Anticolonial knowledge

Colonial knowledge-making is one of the principal themes in imperial history-writing and powerfully influences postcolonialism. It lexically implies a largely unexamined opposite: anticolonial knowledge-making. This is also suggested by the founding 'duty of the [India] League to spread among the people of the United Kingdom the knowledge which will convince them that they are ... bound to co-operate with India in the establishment of Home Rule'. This anticolonial knowledge was to be of the illiberal 'un-British methods'[10] used by the colonial government in India. I do not intend to offer a *general theorisation*

---

[9] Partha Chatterjee, *The Nation and its Fragments: Colonial and Postcolonial Histories* (New Delhi, 1994), 10, 19.

[10] 'Home Rule for India League: 'Pamphlet No. 1: What India Wants' (n.d., probably 1916), NMML/ABP/Part II/14c-D-19(5).

of anticolonial knowledge-making but to sketch some ways in which the key insights into colonial knowledge-making (which has been extensively studied[11]) can be used to explicate its mirrored other and in doing so, demonstrate the potential for both the empirical richness and theoretical possibility of anticolonial knowledge-making as a form of resistance to imperialism.

Colonial and anticolonial knowledge-making are both linked to political programmes, be it the discursive justifying or undermining of empire. Both claim the right to represent based on methodology or authoritative status (who *really* knows India? Statistic-wielding colonial officials or the Indians themselves?). In the colonial case, the ethnographic state produced knowledge that informed governmental modalities and often distorted colonial societies as a result. Anticolonial knowledge *might* produce a dissenting valorisation of 'native' society and culture as a political resource, but it also produced an inverted ethnography of empire: its peculiarities, personnel and methods. The *Condition of India*, for example, includes investigations into colonial prisons instead of cadastral surveys, dissects colonial law rather than 'native' customs and instead of an ethnography of the castes and tribes of India, studies one particular collectivity: the colonial police and its habits of violence.[12]

Unlike the ethnographic *Raj*, the India League had no recourse to the authority or power of the state and therefore transmitted its anticolonial knowledge through a network of transnational activist solidarity. The India League's core leadership and membership mixed sympathetic Britons with diasporic Indians but its network substantially exceeded this, allowing it to draw on Congress for information and rediffuse it through its British allies in the Independent Labour Party, Trades Union movement, Communist Party, left-wing press and the Labour Party, including many MPs. By the end of the war the League's public meetings were drawing thousands and it had branches all over Britain. At various times it could also count on the membership or support of many Britons and others who were prominent in public or political life: newspapermen such as Kingsley Martin at the *New Statesman*, public intellectuals such as Bertrand Russell and Harold Laski, as well as Labour politicians such as Aneurin Bevan and Sir Stafford Cripps. It was also supported by the African American antiracist and popular musician Paul Robeson, the celebrated actress Sybil Thorndike and the 'Red Earl' of Huntingdon, an artistic disciple of Diego Rivera and Frida Kahlo.[13]

---

[11] The literature is vast, but landmark studies include Bernard S. Cohn and (ed.), *Colonialism and its Forms of Knowledge: The British in India* (Princeton, NJ, 2022); Nicholas Dirks, *Castes of Mind: Colonialism and the Making of Modern India* (Princeton, NJ, 2011); Peter Van Der Veer and Carol Breckenridge (eds.), *Orientalism and the Postcolonial Predicament* (Philadelphia, PA, 1993) and most explosively, Edward Said, *Orientalism* (2003).

[12] IL, *COI*, passim.

[13] NMML/Krishna Menon Papers[hereafter KMP]/191, Minutes of the Meeting of the Secretariat, India League, 6 Jan. 1943; NMML/KMP/188, Secretary's Report to the Council of the India League, 17 Jan. 1932; NMML/KMP/177, 'Memorandum on India League Reception for Nehru at Kingsway Hall', 27 Jun. 1938, BL/IOR/L/P&J/12/293.

Imperial agnotology

When the dissemination of anticolonial knowledge directly threatened the colonial state, it naturally moved to repress it. While this usually took place in the colony where censorship would be crudely determinant, in the case of the India League it took place in liberal Britain where ignorance-production was more subtle but also more critical. This was because Gandhian civil disobedience in India had prompted a contradictory rise in both repressive state violence *and* the claims of liberal imperialism as the justification for empire in the face of his challenge.[14] In her study of the interwar covert empire in the Middle East, Priya Satia finds the term 'agnotology' to be a 'useful means of describing the strategy behind official secrecy about empire in an age of mass democracy'.[15] Coined by Robert Proctor, agnotology is the study of deliberately or socially produced doubt and ignorance that reveals the 'historicity and artifactuality of non-knowing'.[16] It can be distinguished from false belief by its *deliberate* production, which evokes Charles Mill's notion of a racialised ignorance that does not passively retreat in the face of enlightenment, but 'fights back'.[17] Based on this, 'an agnotological approach seeks to dissect the ignorance production methods and tactics of messengers of disinformation',[18] which might include censorship but also propaganda, especially that which *manufactures doubt*. Crucially, agnotological studies investigate the power and interests served by the production of ignorance: Paul Gilroy calls for 'a new corrective disciplinary perspective that interprets the power that arises from the command of *not knowing*'.[19]

The importance of agnotology to British power in India can be demonstrated by its institutionalisation into specialist and global bureaucracies of censorship and propaganda. The Government of India devoted considerable resources to censorship and press control and enjoyed a cosy relationship with Reuters which prevented embarrassing stories or criticisms from reaching Britain.[20] It also had recourse to the Delhi Intelligence Bureau and the Information Officers of both the Government of India and the India Office in London, which also housed Indian Political Intelligence (IPI). Founded in 1909 and funded by Indian taxes, IPI mostly spied on Indians outside India. Surveillance served

---

[14] Karuna Mantena, *Alibis of Empire: Henry Maine and the Ends of Liberal Imperialism* (Princeton, NJ, 2010), 11.

[15] Priya Satia, 'Inter-War Agnotology: Empire, Democracy and the Production of Ignorance', in *Brave New World: Imperial and Democratic Nation-Building in Britain between the Wars*, ed. Laura Beers and Thomas Geraint (2011), 218.

[16] Robert N. Proctor, 'Postscript on the Coining of the Term "Agnotology"', in *Agnotology: the Making and Unmaking of Ignorance*, ed. Robert Proctor and Londa Schiebinger (Stanford, CA, 2008), 27.

[17] See Charles Mills, *Black Rights/White Wrongs: The Critique of Racial Liberalism* (Oxford, 2017).

[18] Tom Slater, 'Agnotology', in *Keywords in Radical Geography: Antipode at 50*, ed. Antipode Editorial Collective (Hoboken, NJ, 2019), 21.

[19] Paul Gilroy, 'The Crises of Multiculturalism?' Paper presented to the 'Challenging the Parallel Lives Myth: Race, Sociology, Statistics and Politics' Conference Proceeding, London School of Economics (5.2009).

[20] Chandrika Kaul, *Reporting the Raj: The British Press and India c. 1880–1922* (Manchester, 2003), 46.

agnotology as IPI dossiers were supplied to imperial, American and European police services to justify the arrest, deportation or conscription of anticolonial Indians, to subject them to forced labour, to swing judicial cases against them,[21] and, as is demonstrated below, to bolster imperialist claims made by the press and right-wing political groups in Britain in order to discredit and silence Indian activists and their British allies. IPI also, notably, provided funding and information to the British Library of Information in New York, which worked to counter politically active Indians in the United States, a reminder that the imperial agnotological network exceeded empire itself.[22] Even if accounts of colonial violence reached Britain, there was a well-established journalistic practice in Britain of seeking 'balance' between these and official views. This culture of deference gave official self-justification a powerful role in determining what was 'objectively true' about empire and automatically ascribing to anticolonial claims the label of 'one sided', thus preserving a biased balance that protected empire from its critics. The India League was aware of this: at a meeting held in 1930 an India League speaker denounced the 'censorship of news by the proprietors of the "Yellow Press"' who were engaged in 'the shielding of British interests in India'.[23]

The India League, the dual policy and the agnotological empire

While the League was kept informed by private correspondence much of this was lost to postal censors and therefore, overall, the League felt that the 'information we get from India is very scanty'.[24] It was particularly hard to get information on colonial violence: Both Satia and Mills agree that one the most comprehensive projects of historical ignorance-making has been about the excessive nature of colonial violence.[25] In 1932 the League hoped to correct this by holding an exhibition on colonial violence to be held in the House of Commons which included a sample *lathi*, the iron-bound wooden truncheon that was universally used by the police in India, often to attack *satyagrahis*, the volunteers in Gandhi's non-violent civil disobedience campaign. This exhibition was based on the fear of the Secretary of the India League, V. K. Krishna Menon, that 'most people [in Britain] think a *lathi* is a light piece of bamboo which cannot even hurt the skin'.[26] Peter Freeman, a former chairman of the India League, had visited India and brought one back to show at public meetings. Menon believed 'the most effective part of his argument was the *lathi* which he showed to his audience and banged on the table.

---

[21] IPI to W. Croft and D. Monteath, 21 Nov. 1946, BL/IOR/L/PJ/12/662. See BL/IOR/L/P&J/12/489, IPI to Silver, 1 Feb. 1943; BL/IOR/L/PJ/12/455, IPI to Silver, 9 Jan. 1943; BL/IOR/L/P&J/12/645, IPI to Silver, 1 Feb. 1943; BL/IOR/L/PJ/12/455, BL/IOR//L/PJ/12/325–341, BL/IOR/L/P&J/12/1295.

[22] See BL/IOR/L/P&J/12/781.

[23] 'Extract from New Scotland Yard Report' [hereafter ENSYR] 25 Jun. 1930, BL/IOR/L/P&J/12/356.

[24] Menon to M. M. Malaviya, 23 Apr. 1932, NMML/KMP/567.

[25] Priya Satia, 'Inter-War Agnotology' and Charles Mills, 'Global White Ignorance', in *Routledge Book of Ignorance Studies*, ed. Matthias Gross and Linsey McGoey (New York, 2015), 218, 222.

[26] Menon to M. M. Malaviya, 23 Apr. 1932, NMML/KMP/567.

People were horrorstruck. We have therefore decided to plan an exhibition ... showing the weapons and methods used in the maintenance of law and order in India.'[27] The exhibition would also include photographs of police atrocities and of injured persons, 'originals or copies of orders of a particularly iniquitous nature', as well as evidence of 'government attacks on the Red Cross' and 'places of worship, including Moslem mosques' as well as 'attacks on children and boys'.[28]

The India League enjoyed the cooperation of several Labour MPs who used parliamentary questions and speeches to spread its anticolonial knowledge. For example, Menon managed to have David Grenfell MP read out an 'eleven hundred word cable' that accused the British government of presenting a picture of India that was 'incorrect and misleading' because the reality was 'brutal revolting repression' with 'volunteers beaten half dead then left on road stripped of all clothes ... persons beaten even after their becoming senseless ... even small boys whipped'.[29] The telegram had been provided to the India League by a Congress leader, Mohan Madan Malaviya, which was a small miracle given the activity of the censors.[30] The speech alarmed the India Office but the problem remained that even if the League managed, despite all the odds, to lay such information before the House of Commons it could be easily dismissed by the Secretary of State citing the authority of government information.[31] Menon conveyed an example of this to Malaviya, noting how an 'MP who has come back from India tells the same tale of repression ... but of course Lord Lothian [Under-Secretary of State for India] can "correct" all this if he is so inclined'. The problem was that India League-affiliated MPs might not have even visited India, making their account appear less credible than the seemingly authoritative one provided by ministers or retired colonial officers now sitting on the Conservative backbenches. To overcome this disadvantage that anticolonial knowledge-making had in competing with the agnotological empire, the League found 'that what is wanted is that there should be someone who can stand up in the Chamber itself and challenge the Secretary of State on personal knowledge. We are therefore considering the idea of proposing a deputation consisting of at least one MP.'[32]

The original idea for a delegation came, however, from Madeleine Slade, the spiritual devotee of Gandhi whom the Mahatma had renamed Mira Behn. She also believed that the official and press version being presented in Britain bore no resemblance to the horrors of colonial state violence that she was seeing in India.[33] At this point it is crucial to note that the violence that she was witnessing was *deliberately* created as one wing of the 'Dual Policy'. As the Home

---

[27] Menon to M. M. Malaviya, 2 Apr. 1932, NMML/KMP/567.

[28] 'Copy of a Strictly Confidential Memorandum, No. 1196/C from Madras Special Branch', 21 Apr. 1932, BL/IOR/L/P&J/12/448.

[29] House of Commons Debate [Hereafter: HC Deb], vol. 263 col. 1209, 20 Mar. 1939, *Hansard*.

[30] Menon to M. M. Malaviya, 6 Mar. 1932, NMML/KMP/567 and Govind Malaviya to Menon, 6 Jan. 1932, NMML/KMP/567.

[31] Menon to M. M Malaviya, 18 Mar. 1932, NMML/KMP/567.

[32] Menon to M. M. Malaviya, 9 Apr. 1932, NMML/KMP/567.

[33] Mira Behn to Tom Williams, 7, 8 and 9 Jan. 1932, NMML/KMP/566.

Member of the Government of India, Harry Haig, put it to the Prime Minister, the reaching of 'practical conclusions about the constitution [was] ...the constructive side of the "dual policy"...side by side with this we must maintain the other wing of this dual policy, we must defeat the menace of civil disobedience'. This was achieved by promulgating a series of ordinances which Haig admitted amounted to 'a species of martial law administered by civil officers'.[34]

The other 'wing' of the Dual Policy was also the latest episode in India's process of constitutional reform. After the 1857 revolution compelled the Crown to take power from the East India Company, successive Acts had involved some few Indians in advisory councils while ultimately preserving the absolute power of the Viceroy and Governors. In 1909 and again in 1919 Liberal Secretaries of State increased Indian representation in assemblies of limited power, accompanied by an emerging system of 'dyarchy' where the pleasanter portfolios (sanitation, education, public work) might be transferred to Indian ministers while the commanding heights of finance and security (along with considerable reserve powers of veto and promulgation) remained vested in British officials.

The 1919 reforms had included the provision for a decennial review, which was brought forward by the Conservatives to keep it out of the hands of Labour[35] and took the form of the all-British Simon Commission. This was boycotted in India and produced some very limited proposals which the new Labour Prime Minister, James Ramsay MacDonald, refused to be bound. He instead summoned a series of Round Table Conferences to discuss progress towards dominion status in which he intended to include the all-important power of 'responsibility at the centre'.[36] Congress had boycotted the first Conference, only been allowed to send a single delegate (Gandhi) to the second, and was banned during the third, reducing it to a farce. Meanwhile, Labour weakness and the formation of the National Government meant that Conservatives were increasingly able to dominate proceedings. Amidst a dangerous diehard revolt led by Winston Churchill, Sir Samuel Hoare, the Conservative Secretary of State for India, oversaw the production of the 1935 Government of India Act. This was drafted by a Joint Parliamentary Committee, which contained no Indians at all and limited 'responsibility' to the provinces, made no mention of the promised 'dominion status' and ensured that the next step, an all-India Federation, would be conditional on the voluntary involvement of the reliably loyalist Indian princes. Federation never actually happened and elections to the reformed assemblies were only called in 1937, producing a Congress landslide. Two years later (justified by war) the Act's major concessions were annulled at a stroke.

The other wing of the Dual Policy was Haig's 'civil martial law', enacted through a series of repressive Ordinances that would violently defeat civil

---

[34] Haig to Innes, 18 Jan. 1932 National Archives of India, Home(Political) Series [hereafter NAI/Home(Pol)].

[35] Lord Birkenhead to Lord Reading, 10 Dec. 1925, BL/IOR/L/PO/6/22.

[36] James Ramsay MacDonald, Diary Entry 23 Nov. 1931, cited in David Marquand, *James Ramsay MacDonald* (1977), 708.

disobedience and entice moderates and even Congress off the streets and into the elected institutions provided by the 'new constitution' being drafted in London.[37] In a sense, this was nothing new: the 1919 reforms had been accompanied by the Rowlatt Act which sought to normalise repressive wartime regulations and 'defend the process of constitutional reforms from those who might threaten it'.[38] These 'black acts', as Congress called them, were bitterly opposed and repealed (among other repressive measures) in 1922 without ever actually being implemented. While emergency acts had been used in 1857 and were held in reserve ever after, the Dual Policy implemented 'the first ever comprehensive Emergency Powers Ordinance the British ever issued'[39] under the Crown, in peacetime and on an all-India basis. The press was crushed, Congress proscribed, and its methods criminalised. Local officials were given draconian powers to arbitrarily detain or internally exile Indians, deprive them of property and harshly restrict their lives. The ability of the courts to review these acts was heavily curtailed, effectively indemnifying the colonial state from its spiralling excesses.[40] Civil martial law appears to have exercised as tight a control over Indian life as military rule would have, save only that the police did not formally hand over the responsibility of maintaining order to the army, lest that produce the fatal scandal of another Amritsar. Between that extreme and the deficiencies of the ordinary court-and-prison system (which was liable to become deliberately clogged by *satyagrahis*) civil martial law finessed a new form of extrajudicial state violence: the mass use of the '*lathi*-charge': a public attack on protestors by baton-wielding police, designed to injure, terrify and deter but not kill Indian protestors. By avoiding the scandal of countable dead bodies, the colonial state could mask the intrinsic violence of the Dual Policy, although airpower and firepower were still used against certain social groups.[41]

Thus, the two wings of the Dual Policy concretised the contradiction between the self-image of liberal imperialism and the violent reality of colonial rule, making agnotology increasingly important in squaring the circle, especially in Britain. Inadvertently, it also provided opportunities for anticolonial knowledge-making: The India League had already appealed to the Labour party not to participate in the 'constitutional process' because that implied that the party was 'consenting to the method of trying to affect a "constitutional settlement" with the bayonet and the *lathi* in full play at the same time'.[42] In late June the India League held a meeting on the Dual Policy at the House of Commons which drew 'a very large number of Members of Parliament', who were addressed by Harold Laski, and the Labour leader,

---

[37] Haig to Mieville 13 Apr. 1932, cited in D. A. Low, '"Civil Martial Law": The Government of India and the Civil Disobedience Movements, 1930–1934', in *Congress and the Raj: Facets of the Indian Struggle 1914-1947*, ed. D. A. Low (New Delhi, 2004), 178.

[38] Durbah Ghosh, *Gentlemanly Terrorists: Political Violence and the Colonial State in India* (Cambridge, 2017), 32-3.

[39] Low, 'Civil Martial Law', 174.

[40] See NAI/Home(Pol) F13–14 ii (1932).

[41] Taylor C. Sherman, *State Violence and Punishment in India* (Abingdon, 2010), 77.

[42] Menon to George Lansbury, 26 Jan. 1932, NMML/KMP/419.

George Lansbury. Lansbury argued that the government's aim was to 'crush the Congress Party' through a 'policy of continued repression' alongside a 'settlement of constitutional issues without consultation or negotiation'. Laski dismissed the constitutional wing of the Dual Policy as unrepresentative and argued that Britain governed India 'nakedly by the sword' under the 'ancient philosophy' that racially separated Indians and sanctioned violence against them under the assumption that 'the Indian mind only understands the strong hand'. In countering Hoare's assertion that the Ordinances would be lawful, proportionate and necessary, in that they 'will operate when the situation demands', Laski invoked the ghosts of the Amritsar massacre: 'From reading in great detail the history of the Punjab under martial law in 1919 I know how such powers can be abused.'[43]

Making the delegation

In the eyes of the India League, therefore, the delegation was created to expose the hollowness of a 'Dual Policy' that showcased 'civilised' liberal imperialism at the Round Table Conferences in London by producing anticolonial knowledge of the hidden violence of colonial rule in India. Before it could be formed, however, funds had to be secured and the League was, as ever, broke. When the wealthy Malaviya family was asked for support from India, the response was that 'people are not unwilling to contribute' and that 'many would give us thousands' but the 'ordinances are being so ... vindictively enforced that anyone who contributes anything does not part with that amount alone but actually authorizes thereby the authorities to confiscate ... all that he may possess'.[44] An appeal for funds went out in Britain in June 1932, signed by Laski, Bertrand Russell and others,[45] but by July the League had failed to raise any substantial funds in Britain and so the Malaviyas[46] and the industrialist Birla family took the risk of furnishing funds from India.[47] In accordance with the long-standing strategy largely to 'appear British' the India League had a preference for the delegation to consist of sitting Labour MPs or peers as they were the most suited to refuting the claims made by the Secretary of State and would be well placed to 'make a breach in public opinion'.[48] Owing to an emergency recall of Parliament no sitting MP was available and so the League settled on Menon himself, Ellen Wilkinson, Monica Whately and the left-wing journalist, Leonard Matters. Monica Whately was then Vice-President of the Labour candidates' association and Menon described her as a 'member of the British governing classes ... a very effective speaker and one of the foremost women in the militant suffragette struggle'.[49] It was Wilkinson, however, who represented the real coup for the delegation with Menon noting that she 'has the *entrée* into the press here and

---

[43] 'Memorandum: Meeting Held at the House of Commons', 28 Jun. 1932, NMM/KMP/187.

[44] Govind Malaviya to Menon, 9 May 1932, NMML/KMP/567.

[45] Indian Political Intelligence [hereafter IPI] to Nott-Bower, 12 Jul. 1932, BL/IOR/L/P&J/12/448.

[46] M. M. Malaviya to India League (Cable), 3 Jul. 1932, NMML/KMP/567.

[47] Unsigned (probably Menon or J. F. Horrabin) to Malaviya, 9 Jul. 1932, NMML/KMP/567.

[48] Menon to M. M. Malaviya, 23 Apr. 1932, NMML/KMP/567.

[49] Menon to M. M. Malaviya, 9 Jul. 1932, NMML/KMP/567.

in America. Personally, I think she is worth any three or four other people whom we might send.'[50] Both the India Office and the Government of India feared the public and parliamentary reaction to the delegation's report, which was presumed to be hostile,[51] particularly in left-wing circles as they aware of the delegation's prominence within the Labour party.[52] The India Office therefore wrote to the Government of India, outlining the agnotological strategy of preserving the 'biased balance': giving the delegation 'an opportunity of acquiring correct information and being animated by a broad official perspective'.[53]

Violence and agnotology in the colonial state of exception

Examining the evidence the League collected in India permits a unique opportunity to investigate the nature of colonial violence by bringing it into conversation with critical theorisations of the lawless and exemplary state violence generated by the rule of colonial difference. Equally, the very act of anticolonial witnessing forced the empire into an active position of denial, laying bare its dependence on both exemplary violence and its simultaneous disavowal, achieved through the strategy of agnotological exceptioning: making an exception out of every demonstrable case of violence. As the India League delegation travelled through 12,000 miles of British India, visiting every province bar one, the Government of India was forced to admit the failure of their initial agnotological strategy of maintaining the 'official perspective'. The Madras Presidency even admitted that the delegation 'lived in an atmosphere of civil disobedience throughout their stay' and that 'the delegation were everywhere confronted with stories of police excesses'.[54] The delegation rejected the widespread claim that 'the police are conducting themselves with great restraint, that the measures are necessary to maintain law and order ... and that only minimum force required is used'.[55] They drew on the authority of 'medical certificates' which gave 'particulars of injuries of head, chest and limbs, of death resulting from police beatings, samples of which we have in our possession, [which] belie this "minimum force" argument'. They found 'that in several places hospitals which received government aid would not render medical assistance to the victims of police excesses'.[56]

The delegation found the colonial state of emergency in India to represent not the suspension of law, but rather its intensification into something they called 'lawless law'.[57] This anticipates Caroline Elkins's critical idea of 'legalised lawlessness'[58] or even what Nasser Hussain calls

---

[50] *Ibid.*

[51] William Peel to Maurice Hallet, 14 Aug. 1932, NAI/Home (Pol): 40/XII/1932.

[52] William Peel to Maurice Hallet, 5 Aug. 1932, NAI/Home (Pol): 40/XII/1932.

[53] 'Confidential Note' in Hallet to Stewart, 4 Jul. 1932, NAI/Home (Pol): 40/XII/1932.

[54] 'Copy of a note on the activities of the India League Delegation in the Madras Presidency' in Hallett to Clauson, 10 Aug. 1932, BL/IOR/L/P&J/12/448.

[55] IL, *COI*, 163.

[56] *Ibid.*, 210.

[57] *Ibid.*, 49.

[58] Caroline Elkins, *Legacy of Violence: A History of the British Empire* (2022), 140.

'hyperlegality':[59] the position where a flurry of laws, ordinances, immunisations, tacit permissions and legalised exceptions culminates, as Deana Heath argues, in the legalised 'power to undertake whatever exceptional means are deemed necessary'.[60] In the absence of a global language of human rights, the delegation lamented how this produced the 'unlawful and according to British ideas, thoroughly unjustified way in which police are allowed to take the law into their own hands'[61] because they were not 'answerable before a court of law' as 'the Indian government indemnifies its police and officials in advance'.[62] The result was that un-British 'rule appears more arbitrary than even a martial law regime when police, military and district civil officers may shoot people dead or order firing and no inquiry is held after the incident'.[63] This matches the colonial 'man on the spot' to Judith Butler's description of 'petty sovereigns':[64] the dispersal of sovereign power over life and death into innumerable administrative figures which reduces those who are subordinated to them to what she calls a 'precarious life'. The delegation recorded numerous examples of the precarious life produced by the British in India. In Hashanabad 'the police opened fire, killing two and wounding many others. Three of the wounded died in hospital later'.[65] In Mamlatdar a female protestor recounted how, even though they 'made no resistance and were not violent ... they were struck from behind by the police as they were marched off'.[66] The delegation saw a 'procession soon surrounded by police constables. British sergeants then "charged" the Congress volunteers, which is the name apparently given to the merciless beating with *lathis* that we witnessed.'[67] Thus, the delegation witnessed the transformation of Indians by the British into a version of Agamben's *homo sacer*: a paradoxical creature so encased in colonial law as to be completely outside it.[68]

The India League found colonial violence to be brutally performative. In Bochestan, the delegation witnessed a procession which 'consisted mainly of women' being subject to 'the most savage beating ... Policemen swung their five-foot *lathis* with both hands and delivered blows on the heads and shoulders. It was a ruthless *performance* [my emphasis], savage in the fury with which the police delivered the blows.'[69] A local magistrate offered as a reason for the violence the need that 'others must be shown that they can't do this sort of thing'.[70] This was not confined to a single incident: the general argument was that the use of *lathis* was legitimate as a 'deterrence against the continuance of picketing'. To the delegation this was unacceptable as 'the use

---

[59] Nasser Hussain, 'Hyperlegality', *New Criminal Law Review*, 10 (2007), 514–31.

[60] Deana Heath, *Colonial Terror: Torture and State Violence in Colonial India*, (Oxford, 2021), 55.

[61] IL, *COI*, 168.

[62] *Ibid.*, 168.

[63] *Ibid.*, 191.

[64] See Judith Butler, *Precarious Life: The Powers of Mourning and Violence* (2004).

[65] IL, *COI*, 188.

[66] *Ibid.*, 197.

[67] *Ibid.*, 182.

[68] Giorgio Agamben, *State of Exception* (Chicago, 2005).

[69] IL, *COI*, 170.

[70] *Ibid.*, 197.

of force as a "deterrent" ... is contrary to all accepted notions of administering law'.[71] Michel Foucault and Norbert Elias have argued that such performative spectacles of state violence were replaced over the nineteenth century by an instrumentalised violence that was minimised to what was needed to maintain the 'disciplined society'[72] with this becoming an increasingly important component of the legitimation of the state and its claims upon its citizens.[73] Liberal empires, on the other hand, justified themselves with the claim that they were holding down a natural propensity to internecine violence among their savage subjects. As John McGuire points out, however, in the case of Australia, public executions (a form of performative violence) were phased out in the nineteenth century, but an exception was made as they were *brought back* for the execution of native Australians, especially those accused of murdering a European and sometimes in front of a native audience that had been transported specially to witness the spectacle. This was because they were held to have a tutelary or deterrent effect on racially essentialised (and often criminalised) native populations.[74] Colonial state violence was therefore excessive[75] and exceeded that of other state formations, partly due to paranoia and a failure to establish legitimacy[76] but mostly because of Laski' 'ancient philosophy', of the strong hand, which Kim Wagner has described as 'the ... logic of [colonial] difference insisting that brute force was the only language natives understand'.[77] After General Dyer killed hundreds of unarmed Indian civilians in Amritsar in 1919, his defence provided the most infamous crystallisation of this logic: 'I fired and continued to fire until the crowd dispersed, and I consider this the least amount of firing which could produce the necessary moral and widespread effect.'[78]

Giorgio Agamben has famously used the term 'state of exception'[79] to theorise the coexistence of liberal democracy with instances of state repression and illiberal violence in the camp and elsewhere, which might appear to map

---

[71] *Ibid.*, 168.

[72] Nobert Elias, *The Civilising Process: State Formation and Civilisation* (Oxford, 1982), 238, and Michael Foucault, *Discipline and Punish: The Birth of the Prison*, ed. Alan Sheridan (1991).

[73] Partha Chatterjee, *The Nation and its Fragments: Colonial and Postcolonial Histories* (Princeton, NJ, 2022), 17.

[74] See John McGuire, 'Judicial Violence and the "Civilising process": Race and the Transition from Public to Private Executions in Colonial Australia', *Australian Historical Studies*, 29 (1998), 187–209.

[75] See Caroline Elkins, *Legacy of Violence: A History of the British Empire* (New York, 2022).

[76] Violence was cheaper than manufacturing consent through an expensive state apparatus, see Dierk Walter, *Colonial Violence: European Empires and their Use of Force* (2017), a consent that in any case was impossible to generate. See Ranajit Guha's now-classic study, *Dominance without Hegemony: History and Power in Colonial India* (Cambridge, MA, 1997).

[77] Kim Wagner, 'Savage Warfare: Violence and the Rule of Colonial Difference in Early British Counterinsurgency', *History Workshop Journal*, 85 (2018), 231. See also Rudrangshu Mukherjee, '"Satan Let Loose Upon the Earth": The Kanpur Massacres in India in the Revolt of 1857', *Past and Present*, 128 (1990), 92–116.

[78] *Report on the Committee ... to investigate the Disturbances in the Punjab etc.* (HMSO. Cmd. 681. 1920), 1088.

[79] Agamben, *State of Exception.*

neatly on to wings of the Dual Policy. Stephen Morton has argued, however, that one of the limits of Agamben's theory is how it 'fails to consider ... how colonial sovereignty was experienced as a permanent state of emergency from the standpoint of the colonised'.[80] Achille Mbembe has described the European colony as 'the location par excellence where the controls and guarantees of judicial order can be suspended – the zone where the violence of the state of exception is deemed to operate in the service of "civilization."'[81] It is thanks to Mbembe, therefore, that we can understand how the 'constitutional wing' of the Dual Policy provided the cover of legitimate, reforming liberal governance that justified the violence repression of 'illegitimate' civil disobedience. Colonial violence, in turn, could be presented as a necessary state of exception to the latter, permitting it to pose as the norm of empire.

The question remains whether the Dual Policy was itself a state of exception to actual colonial rule, or an intensification of normal practices. My view is that it is concentric: a state of exception within the state of exception that was colonial rule itself. To contemporaries, as Morton suggests, it would have depended on the vantage point. For the colonised it was business as usual, if more brutal, but to the coloniser the violence of the Dual policy was *necessarily* an exception to their benevolent, civilising, liberal imperial rule. Amritsar, again, provides a good example of this: after the massacre produced extensive outrage, Winston Churchill attempted to contain it by arguing that it was 'an extraordinary event, a monstrous event, an event which stands in singular and sinister isolation'.[82] Purnima Bose calls this the 'rogue-colonial individualism' argument where a 'specific person is scapegoated ... through the censure of the most egregious offenders of colonial brutality such as General Dyer, the authoritarian nature of colonial rule is obscured by the trappings of ... democracy'.[83] Such agnotological disavowal through exceptioning leaves the practice of performative colonial state violence largely intact: Nasser Hussain notes how the Hunter Commission (convened to investigate the Amritsar massacre) found the 'object of performative violence' to be 'everywhere disavowed' and yet 'foundational'.[84] Against this denial, not to mention the long-standing tendency of imperial historiography to remain silent on the issue of colonial violence,[85] the Amritsar massacre has now attracted a

[80] Stephen Morton, 'Reading Kenya's Colonial State of Emergency after Agamben', in *Agamben and Colonialism*, ed. Simone Bignall and Marcelo Svirsky (Edinburgh, 2012), 112.

[81] Achille Mbembe, *Necropolitics* (Durham, NC, 2003), 23.

[82] HC Deb, vol. 131, col. 1825, 8 Jul. 1920, *Hansard*.

[83] Purnima Bose, *Organizing Empire: Individualism, Collective Agency, and India* (Chapel Hill, NC, 2003), 31.

[84] Nasser Hussain, *The Jurisprudence of Emergency: Colonialism and the Rule of Law* (Ann Arbor, MI, 2003), 131.

[85] Richard Drayton, 'Where Does the World Historian Write From? Objectivity, Moral Conscience and the Past and Present of Imperialism', *Journal of Contemporary History*, 46 (2011), 671–85. The silence is now shattered. See e.g. Jordanna Bailkin, 'The Boot and the Spleen: When Was Murder Possible in British India?', *Comparative Studies in Society and History*, 48 (2006), 462–93; Caroline Elkins, *A History of the British Empire* (New York, 2022); Deana Heathe, *Colonial Terror: Torture and State Violence in Colonial India* (Oxford, 2021); Elizabeth Kolsky, *Colonial Justice in British*

productive density of scholarship pointing to the ways in which Amritsar was *not* the exception to the modalities of British colonial state violence in India,[86] as was pretended at the time – and which the *Condition of India* reveals to be a deliberate agnotological strategy.

Anticolonial witnessing reveals the paradox of colonial state violence: that, according to its own terms, in order to successfully uphold colonialism it must be exemplary while remaining an exception, making it reliant on agnotological excepting. The India League, like the Hunter Commission, found violence and its disavowal to be foundational to British rule in India. The *Condition of India* includes a quote by Dewan Bahadur H. Sarda, a retired judge and member of the Legislative Assembly who had moved away from a position of collaboration with the Government of India to one of opposition: 'I fail to find out under what law a man who sits on the side of the road can be assaulted with a *lathi* or fired at. Arrest and imprison him. There is now nothing but the rule of *lathis* in the land.'[87] The problem for a colonial state whose governmentality has been reduced to the performative violence of the *lathi raj* was, as Taylor Sherman puts it, that 'by using punishments for essentially spectacular purposes, governments in India helped transform penal practice into political spectacle' which could backfire as 'these acts of violence became battlegrounds for representation'.[88] The India League, like Congress, was fighting on this discursive battleground but also perceived the agnotological strategy of its enemy, the colonial state. This was 'a conspiracy of silence and wilful ignorance on the part of officials'[89] demonstrated by the 'instructions given [by the Government of India] ... that we were not to see beatings; that we were not allowed to see beatings. But we did see *lathi* beating – when boys were beaten into unconsciousness. We had those boys carried into our bungalow; we tended them'.[90] The delegation soon noticed that police behaviour changed when they knew the delegation was there: they were only able to witness the Bochestan violence by arriving 'before daybreak' so that the 'police did not know we were in the place; we were well hidden by the parapet wall'. In Calicut, the delegation witnessed the police 'raining a show of *lathi* blows on the volunteers'; however, after the police noticed the members of the delegation 'we saw no more beating'.[91]

The contradictions produced by the reliance of the colonial state on both exemplary violence and its disavowal could produce bizarre unrealities. In

---

India (Cambridge, 2010); John Newsinger, *The Blood Never Dried: A People's History of the British Empire* (2006).

[86] See e.g. Helen Fine, *Imperial Crime and Punishment: The Massacre at Jallianwala Bagh and British Judgment, 1919-1920* (Honolulu, 1977) and Kim Wagner, *Amritsar 1919: An Empire of Fear and the Making of a Massacre* (New Haven, NJ, 2019).

[87] IL, *COI*, 177.

[88] Sherman, *State Violence*, 6–7.

[89] 'Report on the private meeting arranged to welcome the India League Delegation', 26 Nov. 1932, BL/IOR/L/I/1/50.

[90] Monica Whately, 'What We Saw in India', *New Clarion*, 14 Jan. 1933.

[91] IL, *COI*, 170.

Mardan, in the militarised North-West Frontier Province, the delegation witnessed a meeting being violently broken by up police who were

> belabouring them violently with their full-sized *lathis* and hitting men with rifle butts. A number were savagely beaten with the *lathis* swung against their head and bodies. An old man ... had his turban snatched, his hands tied up with it and his subjected to a rain of *lathi* blows ... We noticed that the pounding on the chest has removed thick layers of skin and tissue ... It was a *display* [my emphasis] of wanton and savage force on people who had done no harm, committed no offence or violence, and were not assembled for any unlawful purpose.[92]

This continued, in Ellen Wilkinson's words, until 'suddenly an Indian in mufti arrived on a bicycle. There was a sharp order. The police formed into twoes [sic] and marched away ... I couldn't understand why.'[93] Despite what they had seen, 'the authorities denied for some little time, even the next day, that there were any police in the area at all'.[94] An official later complained to the delegation that 'I do not think you have treated us fairly. If you had told us where you were going, we should have given the strictest instructions that no beating was to take place while you were there' while another admitted that 'As soon as we knew you were there, word was sent to withdraw the police.'[95] The Police Superintendent was most concerned about the delegation not writing to the papers in Britain about it.[96]

The broader official view, communicated to London, was that 'it is a matter for gratification that worse did not occur' and the colonial police were to be forgiven because

> the task of maintaining law and order in a vast subcontinent containing 350 million people, the vast majority of which are ignorant and illiterate is one of extreme difficulty...it must, in view of the inadequacy of the police force, and the strain and provocation to which its members have so long been exposed inevitably from *time to time be punctuated by unfortunate incidents* [my emphasis].[97]

This was a clear demonstration of agnotological exceptioning and how it was tightly braided with the 'ancient philosophy' of the strong hand. The 'unfortunate incidents' were the exception made necessary by native deficiency – the ignorance and illiteracy of Indians (after more than a hundred years of British rule) and not colonialism itself. Other evasive strategies were used,

---

[92] *Ibid.*, 417.
[93] Ellen Wilkinson, 'India League Delegation's Visit to India: Miss Wilkinson's trenchant reply to Sir S. Hoare', *The Tribune*, 28 Dec. 1932.
[94] IL, *COI*, 425.
[95] *The Tribune*, 28 Dec. 1932, and IL, *COI*, 425.
[96] IL, *COI*, 425.
[97] 'Report on the India League delegation' (n.d., probably Nov. 1932), BL/IOR/L/I/1/50.

including the blaming of the victims: 'if any member of the assembly was roughly handled, he had only himself to blame for disobeying police orders'.[98]

The delegation also found, to their surprise, that *they* were 'in the position of being held responsible for the police having run amok'. They also felt that 'generally the answer to everything is "this is the Frontier."'[99] Officials justified their actions to each other by arguing that the 'necessity for prompt action when crowds of Pathans become unruly requires no emphasis'.[100] Elizabeth Kolsky shows how the Frontier and the Pathans who lived there were particular victims of the colonial practice of establishing durable states of exception where colonial punishment was made, not by the universal criteria of juridically demonstrable 'guilt' or 'innocence' but by the rule of colonial difference: racialised fantasies of the essential savagery or fanaticism of certain social collectives. In these cases, different legal orders (exceptions) enabled a greater degree of colonial state violence underpinned by a reduced accountability, which was held to be necessary because of the alleged propensity to violence of the *colonised*.[101] Thus, the necessity for excessive, exemplary violence in the Mardan case is derived not just from the nature of colonialism, nor even the particular policing methods of the ordinances and the frontier, but is split between a contingent (and false) claim of unruliness and the enduring rule of colonial difference. By being beaten in the street the process of arrest, trial and punishment is compressed into a single gesture, where exemplary punishment is rendered necessary by the invariant fact of a Pathan being a Pathan. To the coloniser, this was a necessary exception produced by this fact, but from the victim's perspective, the colonial state of exception is permanent because it is generated by an identity that he can neither escape nor change.

Officials struggled, however, to make this argument to the delegation who had, after all, seen the violence happen unprovoked. Instead, officials offered the implausible explanation that 'the police, whom we saw, were probably not police but Red Shirts [members of the *Khudai Khidmatgar*, a Congress-allied anticolonial movement composed principally of Pathans] dressed in police uniform!' The claim was that they had beaten themselves in order to 'to stage an atrocity'.[102] This mirrored an earlier argument made to the delegation by a Circle Inspector in Siddapur, which held that police violence against women was exaggerated, as shown by a case of where 'one women had beaten all her arrested companions in order to make out that the police beat women'.[103] The delegation predicted that the patently ridiculous Mardan 'police ballet' would die 'a natural death',[104] but it was debated in the provincial legislative

---

[98] 'Copy of a Demi-Official No. 1720 15.1.1932' from Government of North West Frontier Province to the Secretary to the Government of India, Home Department, 15 Nov. 1932, BL/IOR/L/P&J/12/448.

[99] IL, *COI*, 424.

[100] I. M. Stephens, 'Note on the India League Delegation', n.d. BL/IOR/L/I/1/50.

[101] Elizabeth Kolsky, 'The Colonial Rule of Law and the Legal Regime of Exception: Frontier "Fanaticism" and State Violence in British India', *The American Historical Review*, 120 (2015), 1218–46.

[102] *The Tribune*, 28. Dec. 1932.

[103] IL, *COI*, 197.

[104] *The Tribune*, 28 Dec. 1932.

assembly and endorsed by senior officials at the India Office in London[105] and eventually the Secretary of State for India.[106] Thus, under critical pressure, a fantasy was generated by the interaction of the two converging wings of colonial exceptioning. The first was the generation of exemplary colonial violence by concentric states of exception (colonial rule, the ordinances, the frontier, the Pathan) that telescope away from the vision of liberal imperialism performed by the constitutional process in Britain, and which arises from the rule of colonial difference premised on racially essentialised native deficiencies. The second was the disavowal of colonial violence by the permanent insistence that it is always the necessary *exception* to an illusory civilised norm, and this makes the 'Pathan who beats himself' an obligatory hallucination when these claims break down under the pressure of anticolonial witnessing and a useful example of the deep integration of agnotology into the core biopolitics of the late British empire.

The agnotological empire strikes back

Upon its return to Britain, the members of the delegation declared that 'the Round Table Conference is an attempt to delude England'.[107] The agnotological bureaucracies of the British empire now swung into action to preserve that delusion. The India Office was aware that what they were spreading was ignorance because they acknowledged the truth of what the India League recorded, thus fulfilling the key criteria of agnotology: the *deliberate* spreading of ignorance. An official conceded privately that the delegation's account in Mardan, for example, 'had to be taken as truthful, despite diverging from the account of the local police'.[108] In a letter to a concerned Major Graham Pole (oddly, a former India League member), the private secretary to the Secretary of State for India accused Monica Whately's account of prison conditions as being 'imaginative' while his private handwritten note admitted that 'there is no reason to suppose that such facts as are stated by Miss Whately … are not substantially correct'.[109] More broadly, there were admissions from the highest levels of the Government of India that the delegation did see systemic police brutality.[110]

Officials held that since 'it is unlikely that individual allegations will always or often be able to be met with flat and effective replies, the chief desideratum is to discredit the members of the delegation and their claims to reliability'.[111] Since they were mostly British and had the 'strong position of eye-witnesses' the strategy was to argue that their tour was 'conducted' by Congress. There were, however, 'heated denials by the Congress press that the Congress has

---

[105] Hallet to Peel, 14 Nov. 1932, BL/IOR/L/P&J/12/448.

[106] *The Tribune*, 28 Dec. 1932.

[107] 'Private Report of India League Conference held 26.11.1932', 27 Nov. 1932, BL/IOR/L/I/1/50.

[108] Matt Perry, *'Red Ellen' Wilkinson: Her Ideas, Movements and World* (Manchester, 2014), 232.

[109] WD Croft to Graham Pole, 6 Feb. 1933, BL/IOR/ L/P&J/12/449.

[110] 'India League "Labour Delegation" to India' (Secret Minute Paper), 16 Oct. 1932, BL/IOR/L/P&J/12/448.

[111] *Ibid.*

nothing to do with these visitors'[112] and a Congress bulletin had proclaimed its 'creed, that India must and will free herself by her own unaided efforts' and therefore to 'rely on the help of British socialists' was 'criminal stupidity'.[113] A different bulletin noted, however, that there were British people who were not satisfied with official sources, including the Labour party which might 'harbour some useful doubts'.[114] Chakravarty Rajagopalachari, the leader of the Madras Presidency Congress party, helped organise the southern leg of the delegation's tour in the hope that its members would be able to 'fight the intoxicated [Conservative] majority in the House'.[115] The banned All-India Congress Committee instructed provincial committees to show the delegation 'confiscated buildings, looted houses, and other marks of police atrocities'. Care was to be taken to 'avoid all exaggerations' and to 'bring only thoroughly reliable witnesses before it'.[116] A provincial committee believed that 'it would be effective if Congress activities such as processions, picketing, etc. dispersed by *lathis* could be arranged during their stay and witnessed by them'.[117] Papers seized from the Congress socialist Jayaprakash Narayan showed that he was involved in 'preparing the ground' for the delegation, a sign of the 'lively interest displayed by Congress in the delegation's activities'.[118]

This is unsurprising: Amritsar had 'hastened the process of Gandhi's alienation from the British *Raj*'.[119] While Gandhi promoted his own non-violent politics for its intrinsic spiritual value, when international news recorded examples of violent police attacks on his followers the British could be profoundly discomfited. Congress knew this and often contested official explanations of police violence,[120] while 'literally thousands of accounts of police violence were produced, not only in newspapers, but in vernacular poetry and proscribed pamphlets'.[121] The delegation, therefore, was only successful thanks to the initial funding and cooperation of Congress members in the joint project of demonstrating the violence of empire. This was a double-edged sword, however: Congress would not have pursued this strategy if it was not guaranteed to lead to a violent police response (moral responsibility therefore lies with the colonial state) and the campaign did provide the India League with an accurate impression of colonial police violence. The British government, however, was now able to argue that Congress was responsible for the violence as it had

---

[112] 'Extract from weekly report of the Director, Intelligence Bureau, Home Department, Government of India' [hereafter DIB/EWR] 24 Aug. 1932, BL/IOR/L/P&J/12/448.

[113] Maurice Hallet, 'Note on the India League Delegation', 11 Oct. 1932, NAI/Home (Pol) 40/XII/1932.

[114] 'The Congress Bulletin', 13 Aug. 1932, NAI/Home (Pol) 40/XII/1932.

[115] P.A. Kelly to C.B.S. Clea, 18 Jul. 1932, NAI/Home (Pol) 40/XII/1932.

[116] DIB/EWR 25.8.32 BL/IOR/L/P&J/12/448.

[117] 'Memorandum on the India League Delegation', n.d., BL/IOR/L/1/I/50 and DIB/EWR, 8 Sept. 1932 BL/IOR/L/P&J/12/448.

[118] DIB/EWR 8.9.1932, BL/IOR/L/P&J/12/448.

[119] BR Nanda *Gandhi and his Critics* (Oxford, 1994), 34.

[120] Vinay Lal, 'Committees of Inquiry and Discourses of "Law and Order" in Twentieth-Century British India' (Ph.D. thesis, University of Chicago, 1991).

[121] Sherman, *State Violence*, 63.

'made strenuous endeavours to organise lawless demonstrations and acts of defiance to authority calculated to bring the populace into conflict with the police'.[122] On the basis of these arguments, the India Office drew up a memorandum containing 'reserve ammunition'[123] to refute India League claims and answer questions in Parliament by putting out 'suitable material based on the information we have supplied to show the extent to which the members of the delegation from the outset of their tour have allowed themselves to be runand influenced by Congress'.[124]

While in India, a member of the delegation had complained to an audience that:

> If any of us stand up in Parliament to speak on India, some Major or Captain or some such person who has just returned from India snubs us down by asking what we know of India. To this the die-hards will cheer, we have to sit-down quietly ... Where is democracy even in England?[125]

Upon their return, they realised their visit had failed to rectify the biased balance that privileged the official version. From the Treasury benches Hoare accused the delegation of 'not being disposed to credit accurate information when it was supplied to them' by officials as they preferred to take 'impressions from Congress workers who are known to have received for the purpose careful instructions from their headquarters as to staging for their benefit Congress demonstrations which would involve clashes with the police'. A Conservative MP even raised the alarm about 'a series of public meetings to disseminate this inaccurate information ... with the support of the right hon. Gentleman the Leader of the Opposition and other prominent Members of the Opposition Front Bench'. A Labour MP (who was also an active India League member) asked in response whether 'any information obtained other than through official Government sources is necessarily inaccurate?' Hoare ignored him and harped on how 'the India League received a substantial donation from a prominent Indian Congress leader about the time that the mission was being arranged'. He also appealed to Conservative MPs to explain 'the real state of affairs to the country'[126] and claimed that 'we have had a large body of evidence taken from Congress sources showing that, from the very start, Congress made its business to stage-manage the kind of picture which they wished the delegation to see'.[127] Hoare was citing an intercepted 'letter from Congress headquarters', which he refused to lay upon the table of the House. Lansbury appealed to the chair to intervene against a violation of

[122] I. M. Stephens, 'Note on the India League Delegation', n.d., BL/IOR/L/1/I/50.

[123] MacGregor to Stephens, 29 Dec. 1932, BL/IOR/L/1/I/50.

[124] I. M. Stephens to H. Macgregor, 24 Oct. 1932, BL/IOR/L/I/1/50 and A. H. Ahmed to Bamford, 5 Oct. 1932, NAI/Home(Pol) 50/XII/1932.

[125] DIB/EWR 6.8.1932, BL/IOR/L/P&J/12/448.

[126] HC Deb, vol. 272, col. 455, 28 Nov. 1932, Hansard.

[127] HC Deb, vol. 273, col. 1259, 22 Dec. 1932, Hansard.

parliamentary procedure, but the Speaker ruled against him and the debate was ended.

Thus, the agnotological empire maps onto a formal weakness of British parliamentary democracy. This was even more pronounced in the pretend democracy of British India. In response to questions in the Legislative Assembly of the North-West Frontier Province, an official member said that an inquiry was made (by the accused police officer himself) and no violence took place, even though privately the Government of the North-West Frontier had admitted that the incident 'must be accepted as true'.[128] The text of the inquiry was confidential and could therefore not be tabled. An Indian Member then asked whether the Pathans 'appeared in Police uniform and that they themselves used *lathis* against their own brethren'. The Honourable Mr. C. H. Gidney felt 'unable to answer his question'. The President of the Legislative Assembly then accused the Indian member of entering into 'arguments', which was against 'procedure, Standing Order and Parliamentary Rule'.[129] The agnotological empire imposed itself in India in other, more direct ways. Directly after the incident in Mardan, the town had 'been blockaded and people had been beaten and forbidden to leave their homes. They were told they were not to go see the "Committee" [the delegation]. People had been chased, their hands tied with their turbans, and beaten.'[130]

Soon after the India League's return to Britain, the British branch of the European Association of India wrote to the India Office demanding that something be done 'to stop dissemination by the India League of scurrilous lies about India'.[131] They were assured that, while there was nothing to be done 'to prevent the distribution of such bulletins in this country [Britain] ... everything possible is being done to dry up the source of supply'.[132] To this end, one S. Venkatapahtaiya, a lawyer from Bangalore, was arrested 'for furthering the activities of the Carnatic Congress party' by bringing 'Leonard Matters, A European, to show him the manner in which the Congress activities were carried out',[133] while a barrister, Bisheswar Prasad Sinha, was arrested for supplying information to the League in London. IPI concluded that 'The efforts of the authorities to intercept it [material from India to the League] must be proving very successful, to judge by the complaints of both the India League and its ally the Friends of India Society "that it is exceedingly difficult to obtain direct news from India"'.[134]

By December the India Office could assure the Government of India that 'with regard to the India League delegation, the whole affair has gone flop

---

[128] Government of the North West Frontier Province to the Secretary to the Government of India, Home Department, 15 Nov. 1932, BL/IOR/L/P&J/12/448.

[129] 'Proceedings of the North West Frontier Province Legislative Assembly, Questions and Answers Session', 9 Mar. 1933, BL/IOR/L/I/1/50.

[130] IL, *COI*, 418.

[131] H.B Holmes to H. MacGregor, 15 Feb. 1933, BL/IOR/L/I/1/50.

[132] IPI to MacGregor, 18 Feb. 1933, BL/IOR/L/I/1/50.

[133] IPI to Peel, 6 Jan. 1933, BL/IOR/L/P&J/12/449.

[134] IPI to Clauson, 18 Feb. 1933, BL/IOR/L/I/1/50.

in the British daily press ... But meanwhile I am afraid that in some quarters perspective has been lost and we have got into touch with certain political organisations to arrange counter propaganda.'[135] A secret report on the India League, based on surveillance and the intercepted letters of former Labour MPs (though care was taken to disguise this), was shared with Conservative Central Office and the Anti-Socialist Union,[136] which overlapped with the British Union of Fascists and had a committee member connected to Joachim von Ribbentrop.[137] The India Office also sought to drive a wedge between Wilkinson and Labour on the one hand, and the delegation on the other.[138]

In its British campaign against the *Condition of India*, the India Office adopted a clear strategy of agnotological exceptioning, or in its own words of 'ignoring the general and investigating the particular'.[139] To take an example, the India Office managed to obtain an advance proof copy of the *Condition of India* from E. W. Davis, the Secretary of the Newspaper Association. The India Office told Davis that 'this is a publication which no responsible Englishman should be associated' with and that:

> the government would deplore the publication of such a book at any time and especially at a time when conditions in India have greatly improved, and English statesmen are employed in the task of securing the constitutional advance of India on the most reasonable line ... Abroad the book must do incalculable harm by suggesting an absolutely false picture of British rule ... Its method is the translation to England of the Indian Congress use of exaggeration, misrepresentation and *the suggestion of the exceptional as representing the general* [my emphasis].[140]

These views were conveyed to J. S. King, who represented the publisher Jonathan Cape,[141] along with threats of 'probable libel action'.[142] The India Office was able to report to India with glee 'our endeavours to keep the book out of the hands of reputable publishers. In this we succeeded, but the control of publishers other than reputable is beyond us.'[143] Despite the India Office's best efforts and the near-bankruptcy of the obscure publisher the League eventually secured, dozens of copies of the *Condition of India* were

---

[135] H. MacGregor to I. M. Stephens, 1 Dec. 1932, BL/IOR/L/I/1/50.

[136] 'H.A.R' to M. Seton and 'Rab' Butler, 29 Nov. 1932, BL/IOR/L/I/1/50.

[137] Richard Griffiths, *Fellow Travellers on the Right: British Enthusiasts for Nazi Germany 1933-9* (Oxford, 1983), 225.

[138] 'H.A.R.' to MacGregor, 26 Nov. 1932, BL/IOR/L/I/1/50.

[139] W. D. Croft to Graham Pole, 6 Feb. 1933, BL/IOR/ L/P&J/12/449.

[140] H. MacGregor to E. W. Davies, Secretary of the Newspaper Society, 18 Aug. 1933, BL/IOR/ L/ P&J/12/449.

[141] E. W. Davies, General Secretary, Newspaper Society to Hugh MacGregor, 19 Oct. 1933, BL/IOR/ L/P&J/12/449.

[142] MacGregor to Peel, 18 Oct. 1932, BL/IOR/ L/P&J/12/449.

[143] Macgregor to I. M. Stephens, 2 May 1934, BL/IOR/ L/P&J/12/449.

ordered,[144] including from the Labour Party Research Department, the No More War group, Foyles, Essex Hall bookshop, the Socialist Bookshop, W. H. Smith, the National Christian Council of India, the 'Diwan bookshop of Jerusalem and others'.[145] Some 200 copies were dispatched to the United States, attracting the attention of the editor of the New York-based magazine *Asia*, who was interested in Bertrand Russell (who had written the preface) writing for them. The India Office told the British Library of Information in New York that the book was 'altogether a poisonous publication'[146] and requested that crucial node of British imperialist propaganda to prepare the usual 'counterblasts'.[147] There was real official fear over the book's 'considerable sale in India' and that it was therefore 'clearly liable to proscription under Section 99-A of the Criminal procedure code'.[148] The Government of India noted that there might be objections 'on grounds of European liberalism [to] the proscription of the India League Delegation's Report' but held that this was a 'theoretical rather than a practical objection, under Indian conditions'[149] and so the book was prohibited under the Sea Customs Act.[150]

While the India Office could not ban the book in Britain, the British press was more than delighted to discredit the India League, defer to officialdom and protect the biased balance. After the India Office wrote to the Foreign Editor of the *Daily Mail*, urging him to 'recognise that the India League is merely a tool used by the Gandhi Crowd',[151] the chummy reply was that the proscription of *The Condition of India* in India was 'the best thing that could happen to that pestiferous lot'.[152] The India Office had always been planning for the *Times* and 'one or two of the more liberal-minded papers' to receive from the Delhi Intelligence Bureau messages 'commenting on the visit and impressing the fact that most unfortunately the sources of information tapped by the delegation were very untrustworthy'.[153] Their success in delaying the publication of the *Condition of India* changed the strategy, however, and they began to prefer it if the press ignored the book, but apparently the editor of *The Times* 'did not wish the opportunity of criticising the tactics of the delegation to slip by'.[154] *The Times* review argued that it 'serves to emphasize the diverse views that might be taken of the Indian problem. No doubt a delegation of the India Defence League [an organisation that had helped organise the Tory revolt against the 1935 Act] could proceed to India and produce a report exactly

---

[144] Jonathan Griffin to Menon, 5 Feb. 1935, NMML/KMP/241.

[145] See NMML/KMP/241.

[146] MacGregor to Fletcher, 24 Aug. 1934, BL/IOR/L/I/1/50.

[147] IPI to Johnston, 21 Sept. 1934, BL/IOR/L/P&J/12/449.

[148] Home Department to Secretary of State for India, 25 Mar. 1934, BL/IOR/P&J/12/449.

[149] Director, Public Information, Home Department, Government of India to Desmond Young, 11 Apr. 1934, BL/IOR/L/I/1/50.

[150] 'Index to Statements of Prohibitions etc. prohibited from entering under Section 19 of the Indian Sea Customs', 10 Sept. 1932, BL/IOR/L/P&J/12/23.

[151] H. MacGregor to Douglas Crawford, 31 Mar. 1934, BL/IOR/L/I/1/50.

[152] Douglas Crawford to H. MacGregor, 2 Apr. 1934, BL/IOR/L/I/1/50.

[153] 'India Office Information Office Secret Minute Paper', 16 Oct. 1932, BL/IOR/L/I/1/50.

[154] A. H. Joyce to I. M. Stephens, 12 Mar. 1934, BL/IOR/L/I/1/50.

contrary to this.' It was also impossible to produce definitive information about the British empire in India, because any facts could *always* be the exception; in such a vast country it was easy to 'secure material that will support a given view; it does not necessarily follow that the view is of the people as a whole'. *The Times* also preserved the rule of colonial difference and recycled the racist official argument (producing an echo of the Pathan who must be beaten for being a Pathan) when it reminded its readership that 'in dealing with police methods some cognizance must be taken of the psychology of Oriental peoples'. None of this, however, amounted to evidence that the government was 'coercing nationalism' because this was being legitimately expressed at the Round Table Conferences in London where the real obstacle was Gandhi's refusal to recognise the 'realities inherent in the constitutionalist controversy'.[155] The *Manchester Guardian* admitted that 'things have been done under the Ordinances which Britain might well wish to forget and of them this catalogue is a formidable indictment'. Moreover, 'many of the cases of oppression and police terrorism can be amply checked from other sources'. Despite the value of its 'amassing of evidence' the problem was that the *Condition of India* had some 'frequently prejudiced generalisations'.[156] In this further echoing of the official argument being presented as journalistic comment, we find the most illogical agnotological exceptioning: that the verifiable evidence catalogued by the delegation was still somehow the exception to the civilised nature of the British empire.

The India Office duly noted the preservation of the biased balance: 'The English press had not fully lost its perspective and patriotism and the English public has not lost its sanity.'[157] It might have succeeded in controlling the press narrative and damaging the publication prospects of the *Condition of India* but they were not all powerful: the delegation received considerable coverage in India[158] and its members authored a few articles in the British left-wing press.[159] These had a small circulation and there is no evidence that the delegation had a demonstrable impact on public opinion outside the political left, however. There, the real triumph came at the Labour Party Conference of 1933. In a Conference that was much exercised by the horrors of dictatorship and fascism Monica Whately stated that 'In India to-day, under the British flag, there is a form of dictatorship that is comparable to the dictatorship of Hitler at the present time.' She compared Indian prisons to German concentration camps and argued that 'the Labour Party, as a great working-class movement, had great work to do with regard to Italy and Germany, but more directly for India, because it came under our own Government'. The Conference passed a composite resolution moved by India League leader Reginald Sorensen that pledged the party to a 'policy of self-

[155] *The Times*, 10 Mar. 1934.

[156] *The Manchester Guardian*, 17 Apr. 1934.

[157] MacGregor to Stephens, 18 Feb. 1933, BL/IOR/L/1/1/50.

[158] BL/IOR/L/1/I/50 has extracts from the Indian press.

[159] Monica Whately, 'What We Saw in India', *New Clarion*, 14 Jan. 1933 and Ellen Wilkinson, 'India League Delegation's Visit to India: Miss Wilkinson's Trenchant Reply to Sir S. Hoare', *The Tribune*, 28 Dec. 1932.

determination and self-government for India'.[160] While the immediate impact of the book eventually petered out, the theme of colonial violence did not. At a 1941 India League meeting, a British speaker held that while 'Amritsar was now a symbol representing a decisive step in the Independence movement' what was 'of more importance today were the "little Amritsars" which were constantly occurring'. The other speakers at the meeting confirmed that Dyer 'was merely one of others, that he was the natural product of the imperialist system, and that his mentality was not a strange phenomenon'.[161] Denunciation of colonial violence continued at increasingly large public meetings,[162] the Trades Union Congress,[163] and especially the 1944 Labour Party Conference where Trades Union leaders allied to the India League denounced the violence of British rule and successfully passed a resolution calling for immediate and unconditional Indian independence.[164]

Conclusion

The objectives of the delegation show how the League remained committed to those two assumptions first outlined by Annie Besant: that British rule in India was un-British and that this was obscured from view in Britain. In pursuing the resulting strategy of anticolonial knowledge-making about empire, the India League competed with imperial agnotology that operated in Britain as much as in India, and part of the competition was not over fact or phenomenon but whether that fact or phenomenon was an exception to the general character of liberal imperialism. The *Condition of India* episode, and the ways in which it illuminates the operation of secrecy and surveillance in Britain in defence of empire, is also a demonstration of how the colonial state of exception could rebound into the metropole in complex ways that depended upon, revealed and constituted limits to British liberalism. This included the limits on the power of MPs in questioning the government and the existence of IPI, the principal organ of a secret imperial state, given free rein to overstep liberal boundaries of constitutionality by intercepting the correspondence of Labour party members and so helping the India Office to tip the scales of parliamentary debates and collaborate with the illiberal right wing and an ostensibly independent press. This provides a concrete example of Aimé Cesaire's instinct that there were 'boomerang effects'[165] of imperialism, even within robustly liberal Britain. Thus, while the false promise of British imperialism was to make India more 'civilised' like Britain, when challenged by the India League with the opposite truth of colonialism, the organs of the imperial state made Britain, in certain small ways, more like the *Raj*.

---

[160] Labour Party, *Report of Annual Conference* (1933).

[161] IPI to Silver, 17 Apr. 1941, BL/IOR/L/P&J/618.

[162] See e.g. Report by India-Burma Association on the India League Demonstration at the London Coliseum, 13 Jan. 1943, BL/IOR/L/I/723.

[163] Trades Union Congress, *Report of the Proceedings of the 75th Annual Trades Union Congress 6th–10th September 1943* (1943).

[164] Labour Party, *Record of Annual Conference* (1944).

[165] Aime Cesaire, *Discourse on Colonialism* (New York, 2000), 3. 6

The *Condition of India* provides valuable support for Caroline Elkins, Deana Heath, Kim Wagner, Taylor Sherman and other historians who argue for the frequency and intensity of British colonial violence.[166] Equally, the evasions the delegation witnessed, and the repression of its findings, reveal the increasingly important role of agnotology in shielding this colonial violence and allowing it to continue, thus preserving liberal imperialism from collapsing into its own contradictions. The book also speaks to our contemporary politics of memory, something the India Office feared. In 1932 an official noted that:

> the repercussions of this egregious publication have, so far, been few, in that it is not according to the spirit of the times, but the wheel of events might turn to circumstances more favourable and it is from the point of view of the future rather than the present that I am inclined to regard the publication with some concern.[167]

The official concession that the *Condition of India* contained anticolonial knowledge that was true but somehow un-knowable at the time, but might become intelligible in the future, invites those of us who live in that very future to ask whether Amritsar, ordinances, police firing, aerial policing and *lathi* charges are remembered by the British people as examples of, or exceptions to, the history of their empire. If the latter, does that mean, despite the overthrow of empire, that imperial agnotology has triumphed over anticolonialism as post-imperial forgetting? If we are properly to decolonise our memory of empire, therefore, we need to be attentive to both the lessons of anticolonial knowledge-making and the lingering effects of agnotological imperialism.

---

[166] Elkins, *Legacy of Violence*; Heath, *Colonial Terror*; Wagner, *Amritsar 1919*; Sherman, *State Violence*.
[167] MacGregor to Stephens, 2 May 1934, BL/IOR/L/1/I/50.

Cite this article: Arni A (2024). The India League and the *Condition of India*: Agnotological Imperialism, Colonial State Violence and the Making of Anticolonial Knowledge 1930–4. *Transactions of the Royal Historical Society* 2, 207–232. https://doi.org/10.1017/S0080440124000148

Transactions of the RHS (2024), **2**, 233–265
doi:10.1017/S008044012400015X

ARTICLE

'Luxuries of the mind': Contextualising Art Photography, Eroticism and History of Medicine in the Social *tableaux vivants* of Lejaren à Hiller's *Sutures in Ancient Surgery* (1920s–1940s)

J. T. H. Connor

Faculty of Medicine, Memorial University of Newfoundland, Canada
Email: jconnor@mun.ca

(Received 23 November 2023; revised 17 July 2024; accepted 18 July 2024; first published online 23 September 2024)

Abstract

In 1927 Lejaren à Hiller (1880–1969) produced a series of black and white art photographs entitled *Sutures in Ancient Surgery* evoking scenes from the distant past of surgery and medicine. Commissioned and distributed in North America by Davis & Geck, Inc. to promote sales of its surgical sutures (stitches), several depictions were erotic owing to the centrality and poses of nude female models. The first series appeared as ads in professional technical journals, then as packets assembled in paper portfolios distributed to doctors who were primarily men. The creation of Hiller's *oeuvre* in different forms over almost a century – journal advertisement, portfolio, book, exhibit, magazine features and textbook illustration – highlights his enduring broad appeal, although his work has since been subject to criticism because of its perceived sexism. At its root, *Sutures* was an advertising medium that connected a seller to a potential buyer. The content and presentation of the project also connected medicine present with medicine past, which also may have helped physicians to connect with the then blossoming field of medical history. The appeal *Sutures* may have had for a past male medical culture would not resonate with the more gender-inclusive and less overtly sexist medical profession of today, which also prompts discussion of the associations across art, obscenity, medicine and society. My reassessment of Hiller's work based on analysis of his artwork, contemporary interviews, published critiques, Hiller's own writings and DG company records extends previous analyses as it is more comprehensive in scope and also considers more fully works by Hiller antecedent to *Sutures* that probably greatly influenced it, such as photopoetry books, other advertising projects and his silent movie films.

Keywords: Lejaren à Hiller; medical history; art photographs; eroticism; advertising

In 1927 the Davis & Geck (hereafter DG) medical supplies company retained the renowned photographic illustrator Lejaren à Hiller (1880–1969) to produce images evoking scenes from the distant past of surgery and medicine. A series of art photographs entitled *Sutures in Ancient Surgery* (hereafter *Sutures*) was produced and distributed to physicians in North America. This commission to promote sales of its surgical sutures resulted in several series of black and white photographs, many of which were erotic owing to the centrality and poses of nude female models. Images first appeared as ads in professional technical journals, then as packets assembled in paper portfolios that simulated leather with the company name along with the title *Sutures* in raised gilt script lettering. As will be noted here thousands of these images may have also hung on the walls of doctors' offices. Each image was printed on quality stock with a protective tissue cover sheet obscuring the 13.5 cm by 16.5 cm image beneath. The portfolios were distributed to doctors (who were then overwhelmingly male) by 'detail men' (company sales representatives who were then also primarily male).[1] Collections of these images also circulated at a later date collated into a bound quarto-sized (26.0 cm by 21.0 cm) book with the title of *Surgery through the Ages: A Pictorial Chronicle*. In this form, sixty-eight of Hiller's images were presented, along with accompanying text describing the historical scene presented.[2] Individual selections of Hiller's images also appeared as spreads in pictorial magazines such as *Life* and *Playboy*, and in curated art exhibitions over the decades, including in 2006 at the National Gallery of Canada.[3] More recently, Hiller's non-erotic artwork resurfaced in 2019 as an accompanying illustration in a specialised surgical textbook.[4]

As will be discussed, the creation of Hiller's *oeuvre* in different forms – journal advertisement, portfolio, book, exhibit, magazine features and textbook illustration – over almost a century highlights his enduring broad appeal. Although the primary viewers for Hiller's *Sutures* series were medical professionals, his images have attracted different audiences that have responded to *Sutures* in numerous ways, especially to Hiller's staged photographs involving nude women models. Important, too, are the distinct formats in which his work appeared with respect to diverse venues/viewers, and they invite brief explanation, for each required a different production/reproduction process. The original images printed in journal ads and those that would later be

---

[1] G. R. Cain, 'The Detail Man: What the Pharmaceutical Industry Expects of Him', *Bulletin of the New York Academy of Medicine*, 38 (1962), 126–34; Jeremy A. Greene, 'Attention to "Details": Etiquette and the Pharmaceutical Salesman in Postwar America', *Social Studies of Science*, 34 (2004), 271–92; and J. W. Freeman and B. Kaatz, 'The Physician and the Pharmaceutical Detail Man: An Ethical Analysis', *Journal of Medical Humanities and Bioethics*, 8 (1987), 34–9.

[2] Lejaren à Hiller, *Surgery Through the Ages: A Pictorial Chronicle* (New York: Hastings House, 1944). Hiller is usually ascribed authorship of the book, but he was assisted by Leon Banov, Jr and Paul Benton; an introduction to the work was written by the renowned physician and popular medical writer/radio broadcaster cum historian, Iago Galdston.

[3] Lori Pauli (ed.), *Acting the Part: Photography as Theatre* (2006), 123, fig. 118.

[4] Daniel B. Jones and Steven Schwaitzberg (eds.), *Operative Endoscopic and Minimally Invasive Surgery* (Boca Raton, FL, 2019), 567–8.

published in book form were halftones. The halftone process enables mass production of photographic images with good graphic quality; the resultant reproduction is made up of numerous dots of varying sizes to permit shades and different tonal effects. The process of photogravure used for images contained in the *Sutures* portfolio results in superior quality but more expensive and difficult to produce reproductions. During this process, a metal plate with the original photographic image etched on to it is inked and used to print directly on to paper. The final format in which Hiller's works appeared was that of enlarged silver photographic prints, which in comparison to the two other process described are the highest-quality reproductions; Hiller's images used in art exhibits were produced in this manner.[5] This article argues that the eroticism of Hiller's photographs that I have selected ought to be fully contextualised and with a more nuanced understanding of them within the histories of art, consumerism and medicine when they were originally crafted and published. My reassessment of Hiller's work is based on analysis of his artwork; contemporary interviews; published critiques; Hiller's own writings; and DG company records extends previous analyses as it is more comprehensive in scope and also considers more fully works by Hiller antecedent to *Sutures* that probably greatly influenced it, such as photopoetry books, other advertising projects and his silent movie films. It also more fully takes into account Hiller's use of *tableaux vivants* (living pictures). This recognised art technique harks back to the Victorian era of theatre and photography, while presaging the films by painter Peter Greenaway (e.g. *The Draughtsman's Contract*, 1982; *Drowning by Numbers*, 1988), which consisted in part of a series of highly structured, staged and strikingly memorable tableaux presented sequentially that ran as a movie, while without accompanying dialogue.[6] Finally, I interpret major contributions of his *oeuvres* within several identifiable fine arts traditions, but especially Expressionist dance, and also Expressionist films and movie stills of that era – most notably Fritz Lang's *Metropolis* (1927).[7] In so doing, the presentist question of female nudity and its male exploitation, which has exercised both his detractors and his apologists, may not dissolve per se, but becomes more fully contextualised. It is not my intention to rehabilitate Hiller; rather, I wish to present an appreciative perspective for a new generation of viewers of his work as it relates to history of medicine and to the human body. Also, Hiller's ads in the *Sutures* series, despite their historical content, were modern like the product they promoted, along with the medicine itself, which was then becoming a pillar of modernity.

---

[5] See https://photogravure.com/story-of-photogravure/. Interestingly, the copper metal plates that were originally used to produce photogravures of Hiller's *Sutures* images have also attracted the attention of collectors; see https://www.liveauctioneers.com/en-gb/item/116475053_lejaren-a-hiller-sutures-in-surgery-archive-1927-32.

[6] Leon Steinmetz and Peter Greenaway, *The World of Peter Greenway* (North Clarendon, VT, 1995); David Pascoe, *Peter Greenaway: Museums and Moving Images* (1997).

[7] Michel Minden and Holger Bachmann, *Fritz Lang's Metropolis: Cinematic Visions of Technology and Fear* (Rochester, NY, 2002).

Sutures in Ancient Surgery: differing historical perspectives

Duffin and Li in their medical historical study of the highly successful *Great Moments* ad campaign mounted by the pharmaceutical company Parke, Davis in the 1950s and 1960s addressed Hiller's *Sutures* in passing, dismissing this work as 'dated-looking, elaborated posed photographs ... that now seem to have been selected to provide medico-historical pretext for depicting the female breast' with such depicting 'nude or seminude young women, most in the bloom of health despite being victims of bubonic plague or dissection'.[8] But such an assessment is normative and restrictive. First, *Sutures* preceded by several decades the *Great Moments* ad campaign; indeed, it probably inspired it. Secondly, these historians charge Hiller with 'flagrant transgressions of verisimilitude' in his depictions, but the same could be said of the wooden and contrived, painted imagined images of the Parke, Davis series. And if the former can be charged with being sexist by today's standards, the latter has been deemed to exhibit medical violence towards women and to be racist.[9] That said, Hiller might be deemed racist too. In the tableaux of the Aztec empire and 'South American natives', both of which are dated 1936, we are told that the Aztecs observed good wound hygiene, used human hair to suture and could splint fractures effectively. The accompanying image shows three men in ceremonial costumes with elaborately plumed headdresses who, presumably, were physicians tending to a male patient. Sitting beside the patient is a woman in a skirt who is also wearing a wide necklace that partially conceals her breasts (Figure 1). The latter tableau has three men dressed in loin cloths, along with two women wearing only grass skirts tied around their waists. One of the women is the patient and is lying on the ground; a hut made from palm leaves is in the background. This indeterminate group of 'South American natives' was known for its use of a species of ant with 'tenaculum-like jaws' that aided in wound closure. 'A row of these ants heads and lo! – they have Nature's challenge to the modern skin clip' the copy read (Figure 2). Perhaps the main issue with these tableaux is less that of their portrayal of women's bodies, as their overall (mis)representation or stereotyping of 'other' ethnic cultures or civilisations. For ill or not, Hiller's portrayals of 'natives' and/or non-whites was not inconsistent with pictorial

---

[8] Jacalyn Duffin and Alison Li, 'Great Moments: Parke, Davis and Company and the Creation of Medical Art', *Isis*, 86 (1995), 1–29, at p. 4; Jonathan Metzl and Joel Howell, 'Making History: Lessons from the *Great Moments* Series of Pharmaceutical Advertisements', *Academic Medicine*, 79 (2004), 1027–32.

[9] One image in *Great Moments* depicts an enslaved black woman kneeling on a table while being viewed by Dr J. Marion Sims, a surgeon who operated on women to perfect his gynaecological surgical techniques. Sims and his practices using 'volunteer' slaves have been debated; see Kathleen Pierce, 'Instrumentalized Images: The Trouble with Representation, Truth, and Affective Power in Histories of American Gynecology', *Synapsis* (11 November 2023), https://medicalhealthhumanities.com/2023/01/11/instrumentalized-images-the-trouble-with-representation-truth-and-affective-power-in-histories-of-american-gynecology/; http://www.nytimes.com/2003/10/28/health/scholars-argue-over-legacy-of-surgeon-who-was-lionized-then-vilified.html; https://www.nytimes.com/2017/08/18/nyregion/j-marion-sims-statue-removal.html. Sims's statue has been relocated; see http://www..nyc.gov/site/monuments/index.page.

In the great Aztec Empire established on the plateaus
of Mexico, the physicians played an important role
though their practice contained some mysticism. The
Spanish conquerors wrote of the high standards of
surgery, and the excellent wound hygiene. Sutures
were made from human hair and effective methods of
splinting fractures were developed.

COPYRIGHT 1935 DAVIS & GECK INC.

Figure 1. This 1936 tableau by Hiller was explained by noting that Aztec physicians were important in the empire, but 'their practice contained some mysticism'.

representations of the day, as the pages of *National Geographic* magazine illustrated with respect to indigenous peoples across the globe.[10]

[10] Jessamyn Neuhaus 'Colonizing the Coffee Table: *National Geographic* Magazine and Erasure of Difference in the Representation of Women', *American Periodicals*, 7 (1997), 1–26; Robert Wheelersburg, '*National Geographic* Magazine and the Eskimo Stereotype: A Photographic

Figure 2. This Hiller tableau of 1936 portrayed an indeterminate group of 'South American natives' that was known to use a species of ant with 'tenaculum-like jaws' to aid in wound closure.

Analysis, 1949–1990', *Polar Geography*, 40 (2017), 35–58; and Tamar Y. Rothenberg, *Presenting America's World: Strategies of Innocence in* National Geographic Magazine, 1888–1945 (Milton Park, 2007). *National Geographic* also confronted the matter of racism with special issue for April 2018: see Susan Goldberg, 'To Rise Above Racism of the Past, We Must Acknowledge It', *National Geographic* (April 2018), 4–6, and https://www.nationalgeographic.com/magazine/2018/04/from-the-editor-race-racism-history/.

Thirdly, referring to *Sutures* as 'dated-looking' wholly misses the point. Rather, as I shall explain, the images are emblematic of their period yet have also had lasting popular appeal. In comparison, the style of the *Great Moments* series has been derisively dismissed as the artwork did 'not always carry entire conviction; the women look undeviatingly 20th Century Fox [sic] whether they be Babylonian, Greco-Roman or lunatic' – a reference to the garish Hollywood historical film epics of the early 1960s.[11] Finally, that women appearing to be in the 'bloom of health' were cast in the role of cadavers for dissection situates Hiller within a long-standing art/anatomical tradition. Eighteenth-century life-size wax figurines of women that could be displayed and disassembled (disembowelled) for instruction were beautiful in form and seductive in appearance.[12] While disturbing, this concatenation of contexts shows that the *oeuvre* of Hiller had its artistic antecedents.

More probative is Bert Hansen's discussion of *Sutures*, medical history and art photography.[13] Overall, Hansen is appreciative of Hiller's *Sutures* series by contextualising it within the histories of art and medicine. Along with a nod to changing advertising techniques, Hansen ensures that his readers and any viewers of Hiller's works understand and appreciate them. A recurring theme of his discussion is the issue of female nudity in *Sutures*. 'As I have learned from conversations with colleagues',' Hansen writes, 'many of us in the field today find their images slightly creepy, whether for excess female nudity and simulated violence or because photography did not exist in the eras they would seem to record.'[14] Indeed, Hansen revealed that one of his anonymous journal peer reviewers 'suggested that I consider labelling these surgical photographs "doctor porn."' Although not concurring with that evaluation, Hansen conceded that 'Hiller's images surely resonated with the unquestioned superiority of male surgeons over their female patients, and the visual possession of their bodies, whether in staged photographs or in the actual examining rooms and lecture halls.'[15] Yet Hansen concludes rightly that Hiller's nude figures 'were neither needless nor inappropriate, nor were they present simply because he liked it that way. They were no idiosyncratic whim, but an explicit sign that the photographs he was creating were not documents or illustrations; they were works of art.'[16]

---

[11] Eric Gaskell, 'Review of *Great Moments in Medicine and Pharmacy: A History of Medicine and Pharmacy in Pictures*', *Medical History*, 11 (1967), 320.

[12] Joanna Ebenstein, in *The Anatomical Venus: Wax, God, Death, and the Ecstatic* (Thames and Hudson, 2015), http://morbidanatomy.blogspot.ca/; Anna Maerker, 'Anatomy and Public Enlightenment: The Florentine Museo La Specola', in Samuel J. M. M. Alberti and Elizabet Hallam (eds.), *Medical Museums: Past, Present, Future* (2013), 88–101; and Thomas Schnalke, *Diseases in Wax: The History of the Medical Moulage*, trans. Kathy Spatchek (Chicago, 1995).

[13] Bert Hansen, 'Medical History's Moment in Art Photography (1920–1950): How Lejaren à Hiller and Valentino Sarra Created a Fashion for Scenes of Early Surgery', *Journal of the History of Medicine and Allied Sciences*, 72 (2017), 381–421.

[14] *Ibid.*, 382.

[15] *Ibid.*, 410.

[16] *Ibid.*, 409–10.

Drawing from Hiller's archive preserved in Rochester's Visual Studies Workshop (VSW), Doug Manchee demonstrates how well-trained, innovative, talented and exacting Hiller was an artist, designer and photographer. And, owing to its extensive and lavish use of illustrations that includes photographs of Hiller's finished work, candid and staged shots of him actually at work, and previously unpublished reproductions of his preliminary planning artwork, the book is also valuable as a primary historical source. Regarding the elaborate advertising commission for DG sutures, Manchee concludes that it 'remains a pioneering advertising campaign. That it ran for nearly twenty-five years attests to its effectiveness as a selling tool for the client. And its over-the-top theatricality in combination with remarkable production values established its importance in the history of American photographic illustration.'[17] Such a positive evaluation of Hiller's contributions serves as a springboard for my analysis.

Manchee's remarks on the use of nude female models is apposite. He is aware that some of Hiller's *Sutures* series have raised controversy, quoting scholars of advertising, business and photography history as saying, respectively, that the *Sutures* series was 'merely an exercise in sexual titillation', consisting of 'semi-pornographic images masquerading as art', and how Hiller was 'best known for his humorous and slightly erotic ad campaign, now considered sexist'. For Manchee it is 'irrefutable' that Hiller 'cast young and attractive members (of both sexes) to model' in the series, but such an advertising tactic dated back to the nineteenth century. Moreover, such critical comments 'weaken' when the whole series of almost ninety images is considered. In Manchee's estimation only about fifteen of the series depict women unclothed (in varying degrees); of these by his undefined standards, 'perhaps half could be seen as having erotic overtones'.[18] If Hiller was 'guilty of anything, it may have been of naiveté', for he had sketched nudes from his early student days and perhaps failed to appreciate the difference in viewers' reactions to a drawn figure from a photographic one. In any case, in Manchee's opinion, 'by the time a serious dialogue began regarding the portrayal of women in advertising imagery, Hiller had been out of the industry for more than twenty years'. If Hiller himself is to be believed, he was nonchalant about such matters. In an undated interview with a reporter who observed male and female models in various states of undress in his studio, Hiller stated that he employed a matron and that 'we are so used or seeing the human figure in the altogether that we look upon it much as a medical man looks at his patient – entirely impersonally. We are only concerned in line and form'[19] But, as will be discussed, not all those who viewed the product of Hiller's 'line and form' did so 'as a medical man ... entirely impersonally'.' Indeed, the juxtaposition of the concepts of medical men, patients and female nudes was and remains problematical.

---

[17] Doug Manchee, *Sutures and Spirits: The Photographic Legacy of Lejaren à Hiller* (Rochester, NY, 2018), 54.

[18] *Ibid.*, 53.

[19] *Ibid.*, 54.

The artist and his medium: Lejaren à Hiller (1880–1969)

John Arthur Hiller, born in Milwaukee, Wisconsin in 1880, planned to be an artist when from the age of 15 so he began art and printing apprenticeships in his home town where he assisted in the design and production of various advertising and promotional printed material. In 1900 he studied at the School of the Chicago Art Institute, where he trained in classical fine arts and commercial art. Hiller's extracurricular activities centred on theatrical stage design and lighting techniques for school productions; he also acquired skills in photography: shooting personal portraits, groups and artist's models, many of which he was able to sell. Art Institute personnel also encouraged an understanding of photography as an art form, while they also sponsored exhibitions featuring notable photographers such as Alfred Stieglitz. As Doug Manchee concludes, upon completion of Hiller's training in 1904 he was already 'experimenting' with techniques and effects that would become his future hallmarks, such as the use of soft-focus lenses and hand-painting on photographic prints. For the next three years Hiller worked as peripatetic commercial artist and photographer across the United States and elsewhere, but in 1907 he settled permanently in New York City. In this period John A. Hiller underwent frenchification (he had travelled in Europe and spent considerable time sketching in the bohemian sections and nightclubs of Paris) and officially styled himself as Lejaren à Hiller, presumably based on his family nickname of Jaren. Initially, Hiller freelanced as a commercial illustrator and produced drawings that appeared as magazine covers in *Cosmopolitan* and *Harper's Bazaar*. Around 1913 he adopted photography as his preferred medium and secured a contract to illustrate a short story in a magazine. These illustrations were highly original in both style and construction, for Hiller superimposed a staged studio photograph of a man and a woman who portrayed characters in the story on another photograph of an outdoors street scene that also pertained to the magazine storyline. The resultant composite image was further enhanced by a chiaroscuro effect to make it dark, moody and dramatic.[20] The process of combination printing as it was called had been devised in the nineteenth century by two photographers in England, although Hiller's use of the process created a novel and original genre of commercial illustration, which was immediately appreciated by readers and publishers alike.[21] Hiller then quickly became successful as a photographic artist-illustrator.

Interviews conducted by the *New York Times* in 1918, based mainly on the words of his then business partner and fellow artist-illustrator, Henry Guy Fangel (1875–1945), relayed how the 'idea of illustrating fiction with

---

[20] On Hiller's biographical details, see Manchee, *Sutures and Spirits*, *passim*; Elspeth H. Brown, 'Rationalizing Consumption: Lejaren à Hiller and the Origins of American Advertising Photography, 1913–1924', *Enterprise and Society*, 1 (2000), 715–38, see esp. 725–7; also Brown, *The Corporate Eye: Photography and the Rationalization of American Corporate Culture, 1884–1929* (Baltimore, 2005).

[21] David L. Jacobs, 'Rejlander, Oscar Gustav', in *Encyclopedia of Nineteenth-Century Photograph*, ed. John Hannavy, ii (New York, 2008), 1187–8; and David Coleman, 'Robinson, Henry Peach', in *Encyclopedia of Nineteenth-Century Photograph*, ed. Hannavy, ii, 1202–3.

photographs for which models are posed under expert stage management to represent the story's characters ... is attracting the attention of publishers and editors'. Fangel further explained: 'We study the composition of the photograph as an artist would plan the composition of a drawing. We give special and careful attention to lighting, and we work often like stage directors to get the right expression on a model.' The use of models was critical; a card-index of over 3,000 men and women was maintained, which included movie and stage actors, along with many ordinary 'working girls and men'. A scout sought suitable 'original' characters for assignments, for example 'real east side tradesmen, real farmers from the high grass'.[22] Hiller's eccentricity and sense of theatre developed, as did his success. In 1939, he was described as 'dean of American illustrative photographers' and perhaps the highest-paid illustrator in the United States. Hiller's three-storey studio consisted in part of Mayan ruins, igloos, totem poles, pyramids and the occasional camel; his personal New York City house was also part menagerie, part museum. Sharing this lifestyle was Hiller's wife, Anita Plummer, who had modelled for him and was a Ziegfeld Follies dancer, and whom he described as having 'the craziest notions'.[23]

Hiller's commercial innovation: *tableaux vivants* and the pictorialist 'social tableaux'

Hiller had retired by the early 1950s and died in 1969, his work mostly forgotten. But in the mid-1980s his work underwent a revival when the VSW curated an exhibition consisting of about sixty of his works, which it and the Rochester Institute of Technology had rescued and preserved. The exhibition and its catalogue highlighted his career through his novel technical achievements, in particular his trademark style of creating the 'entire photograph' using exotic sets, his directing of human models and his supervision of the photographic production process. All of this work resulted in 'elegantly pre-visualised images'. The exhibit's curator declared that 'anyone with interest in the evolution of photographic illustration in America or in the production of fictive images will appreciate Hiller's seminal and long-term influence on this genre'.[24]

Photography historian and *New York Times* writer/critic Gene Thornton further explicated Hiller's important place in and contribution to commercial photographic illustration. The works of Hiller, 'one of the forgotten masters' of twentieth-century photography, were 'so well known in the magazine-reading public of the 1920's, 30's, and 40's, that they will undoubtedly be remembered by middle-aged and elderly visitors' to the exhibit. Thornton highlighted Hiller's use of *tableaux vivants*, while using dramatic lighting and unusual

---

[22] Anon., 'Using the Camera to Illustrate Fiction: Models Pose for Photographs Showing Scenes in the Story', *New York Times*, 6 Jan. 1918, Section T, 75.

[23] Robert W. Marks, 'Portrait of Hiller: Temperamental as They Come, You Can't Argue with Neither His Eccentricity nor Success', *Coronet*, 5 (1939), 147–57.

[24] *Lejaren à Hiller: A Half Century of Photographic Illustration* (Rochester, NY [1986]); on the VSW, see http://www.vsw.org/about/.

camera angles; he maintained that 'By and large ... Hiller's constructed tableaux are still remarkably convincing even when seen in the large original prints of the exhibition rather than the smaller half-tone reproductions for which they were intended.'[25] Thus far from being 'dated-looking' as Duffin and Li opined, Hiller's tableaux were still clearly considered remarkably current.

The aesthetics of Hiller's work notwithstanding, the use of *tableaux vivants*, as Thornton also identified, was to sell products, for Hiller increasingly moved from illustrating stories in magazines to creating arresting images for advertisers. In this regard, Roland Marchand has coined the term 'social tableaux', which he derived from *tableaux vivants*, the photographic components of ads that began to appear in the 1920s. Typically, they depict a person or group of people in a scenario that produces an emotional response in the viewer, even if any accompanying text or copy is not read. There is a story or feeling imbedded or implied in the photograph that engages the viewer. Visual clichés that evoked family values, comfort, security or social identity were common. Owing to the universality of this emotive advertising approach ever since, its novelty may now not be fully appreciated. In contrast before about 1920, ads were mostly text-based (perhaps with a simple graphic of the product) and were grounded in logic and facts: the appeal to the reader was to be mostly rational rather than emotional.[26]

An important point to underscore in this context is that the employment of *tableaux vivants* was a long-standing tradition in amateur and professional theatre, then photography and other visual arts. Recreation of historic, literary or classical Greek scenes along with great works of art would be staged by actors in costume, who did not move as they posed in their assigned roles; some tableaux were staged with large frames around them and gauze in front to simulate paint varnish. A special form of tableau was the *pose plastique*, which typically consisted of nude women draped in diaphanous veils – erotic but publicly acceptable as the women were stationary and deemed to be artistic.[27] As Lori Pauli makes clear, 'theatricality' should be recognised as a photographic feature as much as it has been in painting and sculpture. With this in mind, the themes of 'actor', 'artist' and 'storyteller' ought to be considered in the interpretation of staged photographs aka *tableaux vivants* or social tableaux.[28] Hiller's novelty very much rested on his imaginative and creative adherence to the importance of these themes, in particular his skills respecting *mise en scène*, or setting the stage – something he had honed from his extensive experience with previous projects in several visual media.

The 'new' advertising with its focus on the use of social tableaux saw the rapid ascendancy of illustrative photographs to sell products. Lejaren à

[25] Gene Thornton, 'When *tableaux vivants* Flowered in the Magazines', *New York Times*, 2 Mar. 1986, H29.

[26] Roland Marchand, *Advertising the American Dream: Making Way for Modernity, 1920–1940* (Berkeley, 1985), ch. 6.

[27] Stephen Petersen, 'Tableaux', in *Encyclopedia of Nineteenth-Century Photograph*, ed. Hannavy, II, 373–5.

[28] Pauli, *Acting the Part, passim*.

Hiller now was poised to exploit this trend commercially, if not drive it. His experience as a magazine illustrator, his use of innovative photographic techniques, and his understanding of how *tableaux vivants* were created and staged, and how the models in them needed to be directed, all played to his advantage. Hiller, as Elspeth Brown notes, was fundamentally pictorialist in style. She further explains how adherents of this early twentieth-century popular movement believed that the camera and photography were artists' tools that could be used to break away from the 'tyranny of fact'. Furthermore, the 'preference for classical tableaux ... pushed the camera image beyond the mechanical recording of social fact to express intimacy, ecstasy, ambiguity, and revelation'. One major outcome of this was the blurring of boundaries and motives: '[T]he line between fiction and advertising, between the material and the nonmaterial worlds, were growing profitably indistinct', again according to Brown.[29] Hiller was cognisant of the changing times and his role in them. Writing in 1920 in *Printer's Ink Monthly*, he expressed what might be tantamount to a manifesto:

> modern advertising, as it is exemplified in the higher class of periodicals, must often possess qualities that appeal to the reader with infinitely more subtlety than a mere statement of such material facts as widths, lengths, weights, colors, and prices ... there are luxuries of the mind which must be hammered out no less than those for the body.[30]

Three other major projects undertaken by Hiller reinforced his skill in the creation and construction of tableaux. In the 1915 photopoetry book *Bypaths in Arcady*, Hiller undertook the accompanying original photographs. In this genre, text and image equally complement and explain each other, but by all accounts, Hiller's illustrations overpowered the verses. One commentary notes that his 'lush photogravures act almost as stills from pantomimic performances and, in their sparing use of costume, are risqué in their representation of partially nude male and female figures'.[31] Next, Hiller ventured into cinema when from 1920 to 1922 he created five silent films, four of which have survived; he was their art director and, on occasion, cameraman. Film archivist and historian D. J. Turner concludes that while the surviving films were 'consciously artistic or "arty"' they were also 'somewhat slow and sentimental'. More importantly, they were 'of a high professional and artistic standard and drew praise for their photographic and plastic qualities', for which Hiller was duly credited.[32] While the fifth film remains lost, a series of about forty black and white and hand-coloured stills have survived, which 'bear elegant witness to Hiller's mastery of decoration and composition as well as his treatment of

---

[29] Brown, 'Rationalizing Consumption', 728–9.

[30] Hiller quoted in Brown, 'Rationalizing Consumption', 729.

[31] https://arts.st-andrews.ac.uk/photopoetry/servlets/displaybook?title=bypaths_in_arcady. Hiller's images in *Bypaths in Arcady* can be viewed at http://www.photogravure.com/collection/searchResults.php?page=151&medium=2&view=medium.

[32] D. J. Turner, 'Lejaren à Hiller and the Cinema', *Film History*, 19 (2007), 302–18, at 313.

the then-popular subject of Orientalism depicted in the film'.[33] Underscoring Hiller's skills, most of these films were structured around a similar narrative that illustrated how a famous painting was created by its artist, allowing Hiller to design and construct numerous historical tableaux in his studio, which would then become scenes in the film. In effect, his 'movies' may best be understood as a series of 'stills' (*tableaux vivants*) connected in a logical sequence (à la Peter Greenaway sixty years on). Understanding this technique helps explain the appeal of his later advertising campaign such as the *Sutures* series.

Hiller's distinctive style permeated *Time Telling Through the Ages*. This book, sponsored by the Ingersoll watch company to celebrate its twenty-fifth anniversary, appeared in 1919. Each chapter described a mode of telling time in a particular era. The accompanying photographs by Hiller consisted of painted backdrops, live models in period costume, miniature models and full-size objects, which he designed and arranged, sometimes with these elements superimposed on each other. Although Hiller was not officially credited on the book's title page, the author's preface noted that the 'photographic compositions are the result of the enthusiasm, the understanding and the art' of Hiller; each image also bore his signature. *Time Telling Through the Ages* was not an advertising commission per se, but it clearly was a promotional package for the Ingersoll company.[34] By the early 1920s, Hiller's repertoire of artistic techniques – set design, properties construction, book illustration, special effects photography, historical interpretation, direction of live models (including nudes) and advertising knowledge – was comprehensive, if not unique in the business. In 1925 he joined Underwood & Underwood of New York City as its corporate vice president.[35] Beginning in the late nineteenth century, this company made its name by making and selling dramatic stereographic photographs of the wonders of the world, along with narrative tales.[36] That the New York City company of Davis & Geck would approach Hiller to undertake a wholly new advertising campaign to promote its line of surgical sutures is logical.

Davis & Geck and its *Sutures in Ancient Surgery* series

Charles T. Davis and Fred A. Geck founded their company in 1909 in New York City, which would become the second largest manufacturer of surgical sutures. The success of the company owed much to its mass production of sterilised, pre-packaged sutures with needles attached, all of which were contained in hermetically sealed glass tubes. Doctors and hospitals found these innovations convenient to use, along with being time- and cost-saving. In 1930 the

---

[33] *Ibid.*, 315. Hiller's attraction to Orientalism is suggestive as this notion often resulted in sets and scenes that were moody, exotic, sensual and steamy.

[34] See https://archive.org/details/timetellingthro00breagoog; Manchee, *Sutures and Spirits*, 23, 27.

[35] Manchee, *Sutures and Spirits*, 8, 29–30.

[36] David Burder, 'Underwood, Bert and Elmer', in *Encyclopedia of Nineteenth-Century Photography*, ed. Hannavy, II, 1417–20.

company was sold to the American Cyanamid Corporation conglomerate.[37] The ads of 1916, when DG patented and began promoting its brand of sutures, imitated the format and fonts of silent move subtitles. They were excessively text-heavy with a detailed description of the science and technology behind the product as an ad from *The Modern Hospital* of April 1916 illustrated (Figure 3). Later ads just prior to the release of the *Sutures* series remained text-based, were fact- and figure-laden, and geared to appeal to a logical not an emotional response from potential buyers. Copy consisted of item catalogue numbers, product description and size, cost and ordering information, and a brief account of manufacturing processes and an explanation of technical terms employed; any illustrations used were limited to line drawings of the actual product and graphs or charts. Ad captions aimed to persuade were direct, informative, and blandly descriptive: 'A wholesale discount of 25% is accorded hospitals and surgeons on any quantity of sutures down to one gross' (Figure 4).[38] Or they might incorporate a simple graphic (Figure 5). The contrast with the planned *Sutures* campaign could not be more striking. Within the style and *mentalité* of advertising of the late 1920s, the marketing strategy of *Sutures*, with its use of *tableaux vivants* and social tableaux, is noteworthy. In its images, Hiller's notion of luxuries of the mind and of the body abounded. Replacing the recitation of dry facts about heat sterilised surgical sutures were new ads which featured one of Hiller's arresting photographic tableaux accompanied by a brief essay caption explaining the scene that also would allude in some way to suturing techniques or ligatures in the era depicted. A stylised logo for 'D&G Sutures' along with the tag line 'THEY ARE HEAT STERILIZED' rounded out the formulaic layout.

Hiller's artistic photographs are central to the *Sutures* series, but they became more meaningful through the accompanying historical vignettes. Hiller may have been artistically gifted, but he was obviously not a medical historian. Who, then, was responsible for the ideas and accompanying text? Robert E. Skinner has identified that the key person was Dr Samuel Clark Harvey, a claim based on information provided to him by Charles T. Riall.[39] Riall, a long-standing DG employee, was involved in the physical production of *Sutures*; he would become head of advertising at DG, then director of company professional relations.[40] Samuel Clark Harvey (1886–1953) was a

---

[37] Subsequent to its purchase by American Cyanamid, DG was subject to several other takeovers and mergers. This brief corporate history is based on finding aids and material related to the company that are held at the University of Connecticut; see http://archives.lib.uconn.edu/islandora/object/20002%3A860124274. I am grateful to archivist Laura Smith for sharing and providing this information.

[38] DG advertisement for 'Surgical Sutures Claustro-Thermal Catgut', in *Modern Hospital* (May 1922), n.p.

[39] Robert E. Skinner, 'Photography, Advertising, and the History of Medicine: Notes on the Medico-historical Art of Lejaren à Hiller', *Watermark*, 6 (1982-3), 11–12. Skinner cites only a personal communication by Riall to him dated 22 November 1982 that although it cannot be confirmed is plausible.

[40] Charles T. Riall, 'The AORN Audiovisual Committee: Thirty-three Years of Perioperative Nursing Education', *AORN Journal*, 58 (1993), 980–8.

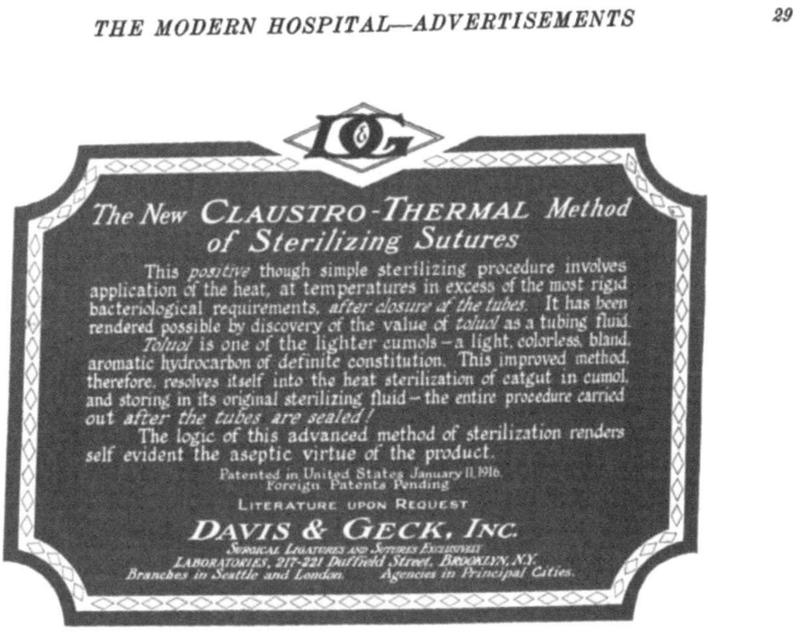

Figure 3. A 1916 ad from *The Modern Hospital* for DG sutures illustrating the initial text-heavy format.

surgeon and a scholar. After graduation from Yale Medical School in 1907, he became a member of its department of surgery in 1919; Harvey also edited the *Yale Journal of Biology and Medicine*. His interest in medical history was long-standing.[41]

Sutures had the financial backing of an established company; Hiller's creativity was indisputable; changed attitudes and styles of advertising bode well for it; and the consultancy of someone highly connected with, and respected in, American surgery who also had a recognised penchant for medical history was an additional bonus. Further boosting the project was the apparent attention to technical detail in production. To highlight his set designs and the use of theatrical properties, Hiller used long lenses on his cameras to

[41] Elizabeth H. Thomson, 'Samuel Clark Harvey – Medical Historian, 1886–1953', *Journal of the History of Medicine and Allied Sciences*, 9 (1954), 1–8; John F. Fulton, 'Samuel Clark Harvey (1886–1953)', *Bulletin of the History of Medicine*, 28 (1954), 275; Max Taffel, 'Samuel Clark Harvey, 1886–1953',*Yale Journal of Biology and Medicine*, 26 (1953), 1–7; and Alfred Blalock, 'Samuel Clark Harvey: A Tribute from a Fellow Surgeon', *Yale Journal of Biology and Medicine*, 23 (1951), 522. See also   http://histmed.org/documents/AAHM1954_NewHavenCT.pdf?_ga=2.201697553.1628473636. 1516386411-1456747550.1516386411   and   http://surgery.yale.edu/education/program/Harvey%20Lecture%207.15_271032_153_4291_v1.pdf.

248   J. T. H. Connor

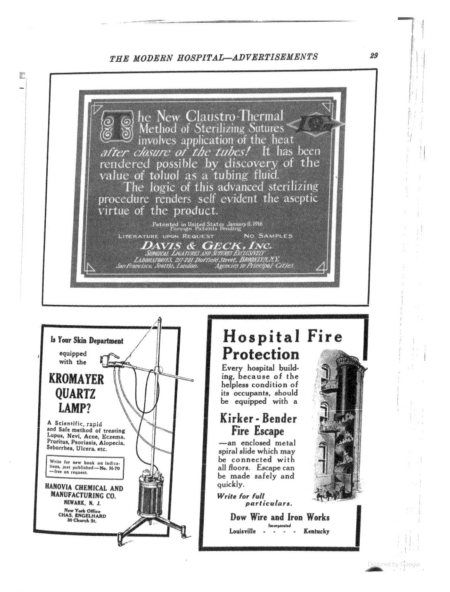

Figure 4. Later ads dating from 1922 remained text-based, were fact- and figure-laden, and geared to appeal to a logical not an emotional response from potential buyers.

make the 'spectator feel that he is actually in the picture and transmits a feeling of sympathy with and for the characters'. Hiller's use of 'simple, dramatic lighting' was also crucial to create the right effect.[42] He apparently eschewed

---

[42] Lejaren 'A [sic] Hiller, 'Surgery through the Ages Shows 2000 Years of Surgery in 20 Years of Pictures', *Popular Photography*, 14 (1944), 22–5, 87, at 22.

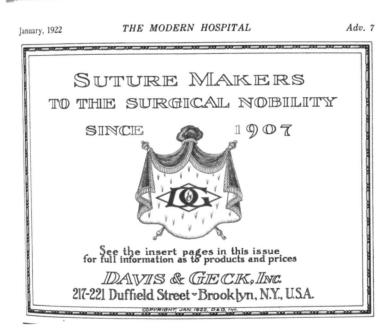

Figure 5. Occasionally a simple graphic might have been used in DG ads as this one from *The Modern Hospital* of 1922 illustrates.

electronic or any other type of flash lighting, which further added to his skill in lighting.[43] Using such flexible fill-in lighting also allowed Hiller to have his medical historical art imitate or gesture to other medical historical art. Most notable was his rendition of Joseph Lister of antiseptic/aseptic surgery fame in which Hiller had the British Victorian surgeon bathed in the light from a period lamp angled towards him. The resultant image resonated with Sir Luke Fildes's Victorian painting of *The Doctor*, reproductions of which were ubiquitous. Charles Riall's recollections are again useful here. In 1997 when he was 83 years old, Riall described the intricate photogravure (and halftone) production process:

> After the photography of the scenes by Hiller he would retouch the negatives to give the proper ambience to the pictures. The finished art then went to Harding [Photo-] Engraving Company in New York who were the numero uno in engraving. The engraving or original then went to Flower [*sic* – F.A. Flowers Company?] who produced half-tone plates for letter press printing. On receipt of the plates at the 'Private Press of Davis & Geck in America' ... Fred Entler who was a superb pressman

---

[43] Manchee, *Sutures and Spirits*, 131.

printed the ads with the art and later the art reproductions we distributed to surgeons. There probably are thousands still on doctors [sic] walls.[44]

Examples of the engraved plates themselves, along with the resultant ads, are available to view online. Both reveal how the format of the *Sutures* ads during the 1930s were wholly in contrast to early company promotions: the image of the staged tableau is central and dominant, with the accompanying historical text underneath it and to left of centre. To the bottom right of the ad still appears the phrase 'D & G Sutures', but now along with the new slogan or tag line of 'THIS ONE THING WE DO'.[45] Other configurations and layout designs were also used, perhaps around 1940.[46]

Riall also compiled an inventory of the almost 100 images that comprised the *Sutures* project. In sum, the scenes depicted and their text constituted an encyclopaedic survey of medical history ranging from prehistoric times, classical Greece and Rome, the Middle Ages, and through to the nineteenth century; nothing is featured from the twentieth century. Typically, great medical men who hailed from eastern and western traditions were portrayed: Albucasis, Avicenna, Celsus, Fallopius, Fabricius, Galen, Harvey, Hunter, Rhazes and Vesalius, for example, all take a bow. And the great moments in medicine associated with these names were explained within their respective fields of anatomy, physiology, pathology and medical practice. Occasionally, ads might address medicine with respect to different cultures in a past era such those of the Aztec empire, Egypt and India. The place of women in *Sutures* will be explored more below, but suffice it to say for the moment that only Dame Trotula (an eleventh-century woman to whom is attributed one of the earliest textbooks on gynaecology) appeared as a central, identified medical character in these advertising tableaux. The Whiggish historiographical bias of *Sutures* towards great, dead (and mostly white) men, and their good deeds, along with a message of the progress of medicine and surgery may not resonate with today's tenets of medical history, but it fully reflected the aims, approach and standards of the period.

Understanding *Sutures* within the academic milieu of history of medicine of the late 1920s and early 1930s, especially in America, allows it to be judged as more than a curiosity, a commercial ad campaign promoting a particular product, or archival ephemera. History of medicine at this time was not an historical field; rather, it was a subfield of medicine: it was supported not by scholars per se, but by practising doctors who were devotees and *amateurs* in the truest sense, and who wrote about the inexorable rise and triumph of scientific medicine. Yale's Dr Harvey as *Sutures'* consultant was a good example. Critical organisational activities in the history of medicine also occurred at this time. In 1925 a small group of physicians formed the American Section of the

---

[44] Letter from Charles T. Riall dated 12 June 1997 contained in DG company archival material, University of Connecticut.

[45] See https://www.liveauctioneers.com/en-gb/item/116475053_lejaren-a-hiller-sutures-in-surgery-archive-1927-32.

[46] Manchee, *Sutures and Spirits*, 48-9.

International Society for the History of Medicine; in 1928 the group reorganised as the independent American Association of the History of Medicine.[47]

The years around the appearance of *Sutures* were a heyday for medical history, seeing the publication of many tomes of encyclopaedic length and style, which were typically authored by physicians.[48] Might these books might have been sources of material for *Sutures*? Their sweeping nature would have allowed Samuel Harvey to select topics for inclusion; certainly the content of both the books and the ad campaign vignettes overlapped. As historian Bert Hansen reasonably believes, Garrison's *Introduction to the History of Medicine* was a regular go-to source.[49] Hiller himself once wrote that it took 'considerable rummaging through old medical and historical books to find out the sort of clothes he [the surgeon subject] wore, his surgical tools, the furnishings of the time, little idiosyncrasies of the, man, how he looked, operating methods of the period, and so on'.[50] More important, however, was the overlapping of the explicit messaging to the medical profession contained in the two media. Medicine around 1930 represented the new, the advanced and the modern as epitomised in a new generation of sophisticated technological hospital complexes and medical schools with both institutions grounded in laboratory science, but along with this came a realisation that it had a history which was cast not just as the *past* but as the *primitive*.[51] In this context it can be more readily understood why the phrase 'ancient surgery' was used in the series title even though it depicted events up to the nineteenth century.

This period around 1930 remains remarkable. Thus an additional reason to appreciate *Sutures* was not only that it contributed to this first wave of medical history by introducing medicine's history to its practitioners, but that it could also symbiotically ride its crest for commercial purposes. The take-home message for doctors viewing these ads, whether they consciously realised it or not, was that *they* were modern, so were DG sutures, along with the whole enterprise of medicine, which was now a pillar of modern civilisation. A concluding passage in Haggard's 1929 study of the history of medicine

---

[47] Genevieve Miller, 'The Missing Seal, or Highlights of the First Century of the American Association for the History of Medicine', *Bulletin of the History of Medicine*, 50 (1976), 93–121; and Jennifer Connor, *Guardians of Medical Knowledge: The Genesis of the Medical Library Association* (Lanham, MD, 2000), 106–7.

[48] Noteworthy were books such as Arturo Castiglioni, *A History of Medicine*, trans. E. B. Krumbhaar (New York, 1941), originally published as *Storia della medicina* (1927); Charles Singer, *A Short History of Medicine Introducing Medical Principles to Students and Non-medical Readers* (Oxford, 1928); Howard Haggard, *Devils, Drugs, and Doctors: The Story of the Science of Healing from Medicine-man to Doctor* (Garden City, NY, 1929); the fourth edition of US Army Surgeon Fielding H. Garrison's classic *An Introduction to the History of Medicine with Medical Chronology, Suggestions for Study and Bibliographic Data* (Philadelphia, 1929); and S. G. Blaxland Stubbs and E. W. Bligh, *Sixty Centuries of Health and Physick: The Progress of Ideas from Primitive Magic to Modern Medicine* (1931).

[49] Hansen, 'Medical History's Moment', 398.

[50] Hiller, 'Surgery through the Ages', 22.

[51] See Charles E. Rosenberg, *The Care of Strangers: The Rise of America's Hospital System* (New York, 1987); Annmarie Adams, *Medicine by Design: The Architect and the Modern Hospital, 1893-1943* (Minneapolis, 2008); and Katherine L. Carroll, *Building Schools, Making Doctors: Architecture and the Modern American Physician* (Pittsburgh, 2022).

underscored that primitivism, progress, civilisation and medicine were interconnected, but he warned that:

> Medicine and civilization advance and regress together. The conditions essential to advance are intellectual courage and a true love for humanity. It is as true today as always in the past that further advance or even the holding of what has already been won depends upon the extent to which intellectual courage and humanity prevail against bigotry and obscurantism.[52]

The notion that progressive times could easily regress to a more primitive era when people are inattentive suggests how the *Sutures* images may be viewed or interpreted as allegories. The use of light and darkness in many of the images invokes a sense of good and evil, as also those that have religious characters or symbolism. Thus in many there are implied binary opposites that are in tension with each other such as, it can be argued, the progressive and the primitive. The typical viewer of *Sutures* – medical doctors – represented the progressive and the scientific, while what was portrayed, even when the scene was a 'great moment in medicine', was the primitive. Hiller's elaborative use of costume and props ensured that the scene was distinctly disconnected from the modern present. Yet his use of real people whom we know little about personally, except that they ranged from 'derelicts, to actors, to high-priced models ... [and] students of a nature dancing school',[53] suggested the constancy of humanity in Hiller's photographic time travels. Here was the new advertising in full gear using emotion, not logic, to connect and appeal. But did this approach sell more sutures? In the absence of annual sales figures this question remains unanswerable. In a way, however, it is irrelevant. Even if the money spent of *Sutures* did not result in a spike in the sales of products, it was not wasted. The *Sutures* campaign was as much about public relations as anything to make clear that DG was corporately friendly to the medical enterprise (regardless of any self-interest); in some ways it may be likened to a Big Pharma company today giving a goodwill unconditional donation to a medical school or hospital, thereby keeping its name and brand prominent throughout the institution without actually selling or promoting any specific product.

Hiller and the female nude

Women figured prominently in many *Sutures* images. Their roles, however, generally were passive and their poses were recumbent and submissive; occasionally, they feigned death. Often, too, Hiller's female models were partially or wholly nude (in comparison there were no fully nude male models) – leading to the already cited criticism by Duffin and Li that these particular vignettes were a 'medico-historical pretext for depicting the female breast'. Perhaps one might merely shrug this off as an example of the adage that sex sells.

---

[52] Haggard, *Devils, Drugs, and Doctors*, 396–7.

[53] Personal communication by Charles T. Riall to Arnold Sovari dated 22 November 1982 quoted in Skinner, 'Photography, Advertising, and the History of Medicine', 12.

Historian of advertising Stewart Ewen has analysed how from the 1920s sex was entering the advertising world more overtly using 'veiled nudes and women in auto-erotic stances'.[54] And in the context of the new advertising, which was emotion-based using visual clichés, perhaps making the selling of sterilised surgical sutures sexy is cause for wonderment. Yet, dismissing Hiller's artwork in this way is to discount it. To address this matter, several of the examples of tableaux featuring women ought to be examined more completely, allowing a discussion of how text and image interact in the ads.

The tableau about dame Trotula (1930) shows a group of four women in medieval costume clustered around a female patient who is clothed but lies on a bed; the 'matron of Salerno' is identifiable through her more elaborate dress. One of Trotula's assistants holds a new-born baby up to the recumbent women for her to view. Complementing the image, the copy notes that Trotula 'became the most famous woman in early medical history' as a result of her contributions to the study of obstetrics and gynaecology through writings such as *Concerning the Cure of the Diseases of Women before, during and after Delivery*. Contained in this treatise, the text highlighted, was the earliest description of perineorrhaphy in which Trotula noted that lacerated tissues due to childbirth could be repaired using silk sutures. These elements were formulaic: a historical tableau containing a visual cliché (a safe birth and motherhood); a medical history reference for context; and a link to a surgical procedure that alludes to sutures.

Contrasting with this ensemble was another of a cluster of women, young and slender in classical Greek costume. In this 1933 tableau, a bucolic setting, a Greek column and scrolls add to the scene's atmosphere. Another distinguishing part of the image is that each of the women has her right breast prominently displayed from under loosely draped robes. Trying to reconcile this tableau with the accompanying medical history copy that relates to obstetrics, gynaecology, diseases of women and the use of ligatures in venesection might reasonably be considered as a bit of a reach! The key, however, is confusion around the 'legendary figure' of Aspasia, which was the title of this ad. On the one hand, inspiration for the image may have derived from the entry on Aspasia by Haggard in his contemporary *Devils, Drugs, and Doctors*, which described her as a courtesan and high-class prostitute who operated an Athenian brothel that was much frequented by the likes of Pericles during the fifth century BCE.[55] On the other hand, physician and early feminist Kate Campbell Hurd-Mead, who wrote on women in the history of medicine, noted the obstetric contributions of Aspasia that were known only through quotations by Aetius (527–566 CE). Hurd-Mead also makes clear that there were probably three Aspasias over time, with the earliest being the Athenian courtesan who was not the later one concerned about women's health matters.[56] This ad is

---

[54] Stuart Ewen, *Captains of Consciousness: Advertising and the Social Roots of the Consumer Culture* (New York, 1976), 179.

[55] Haggard, *Devils, Drugs, and Doctors*, 267.

[56] Kate Campbell Hurd-Mead, *A History of Women in Medicine from the Earliest Times to the Beginning of the Nineteenth Century* (Boston, 1973; reprint of 1938 edn.), 64–6; and Toby Appel, 'Writing Women

thus a historical mash-up based on historical material that would have been available to Hiller at the time. While this may not entirely explain away any notion of the gratuitous display of women's body parts by Hiller, it certainly explicates his rationale. It also addresses an implicit criticism by Hansen of Hiller for including this image.[57]

A final group of six tableaux dating from 1927 to 1935 is particularly noteworthy. All portray activities by European surgeons from around the sixteenth century, and all except one depict a surgical procedure in progress. Further uniting this selection is the presence and roles of women. In all six tableaux, wholly or partially naked women are depicted as the patient or victim of disease; in four, other women are also present as onlookers, who may be assistants or nuns. In all scenes male characters other than the highlighted surgeon are also present, usually assisting by restraining the female patient. Two of the scenes also include men as dying or deceased. Further unifying these tableaux are religious icons and imagery. In 'Jeremias Trautman of Wittenberg' (1929), the surgeon is depicted performing the 'first cesarean section of record' in 1610 with a bishop in attendance. A religious triptych in 'Giovanni Andrea Dalla Croce' (1932) overlooks the struggling naked body of a woman probably undergoing the first hysterectomy (Figure 6). And in 'Ambrose Paré' (1935), a life-sized Christ on a crucifix and two nuns in full religious habit are prominent, along with the sixteenth-century surgeon who kneels at the side of a tangle of the naked dead and dying (Figure 7). In addition to including overt religious symbols, Hiller's artwork in these six tableaux also contains a suggested theme or allusion. Although there are variations, the women portrayed typically have their heads tossed back and tilted with their mouths slightly open; they are in a sensual swoon. And in almost all instances these patients are being subjected to pain inflicted by a sharp bladed instrument.

To my mind, the inferential leap from these scenes to Bernini's *Ecstasy of Saint Teresa* is a short one. In the seventeenth-century religious sculpture, based on the memoir of the Carmelite nun Teresa, a male angel repeatedly thrusts and withdraws his spear into her body with the result that 'the pain was so great, that it made me moan; and yet so surpassing was the sweetness of this excessive pain, that I could not wish to be rid of it. The soul is satisfied now with nothing less than God. The pain is not bodily, but spiritual; though the body has its share in it.'[58] Teresa's words combined the spiritual with the somatic; Bernini's sculpted rendition of eroticised them (but admittedly maybe not all early modernists might agree with this assessment).[59] For Hiller to capture these various sentiments, emotions, responses and moods in his

---

into Medical History in the 1930s: Kate Campbell Hurd-Mead and "Medical Women" of the Past and Present', *Bulletin of the History of Medicine*, 88 (2014), 457–92.

[57] Hansen, 'Medical History's Moment', 396.

[58] *The Life of Saint Teresa of Avila by Herself*, ch. 29; part 17.

[59] See Franco Mormando, 'Did Bernini's *Ecstasy of St Theresa* Cross a Seventeenth-century Line of Decorum?', *Word and Image: A Journal of Verbal/Visual Enquiry*, 39 (2023), 351–83.

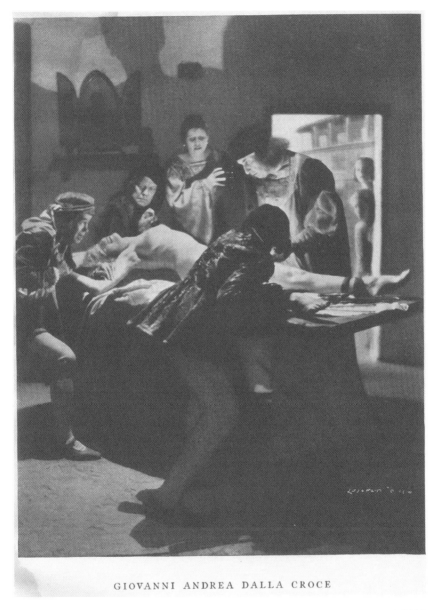

GIOVANNI ANDREA DALLA CROCE

Figure 6. *Tableau vivant* of Giovanni Andrea Dalla Croce performing a hysterectomy in 1610 (1932).

photographic tableaux as a trained artist is totally plausible. His image of the female patient in the ad under the title of 'Felix Würtz' (1935) is particularly apposite in this context. While it may have been a pretext to display her ample bosom in an alluring way, the composition, her facial expression and her clasped hands lying on her lap signifying surrender all channel the

AMBROISE PARÉ (1517-1590)

Figure 7. *Tableau vivant* of Ambrose Paré the sixteenth-century surgeon kneeling at the side of a tangle of the naked dead and dying (1935).

Ecstasy of Saint Teresa (Figure 8). What might Sister Wendy, the world-renowned and popular art historian, who was also a Carmelite nun like Saint Teresa, conclude about Hiller's works? On sexual imagery in art she commented how it can stand for 'life which presses on ... this is what we live in, the chaos, we have to live among death and disaster and the possibility that our

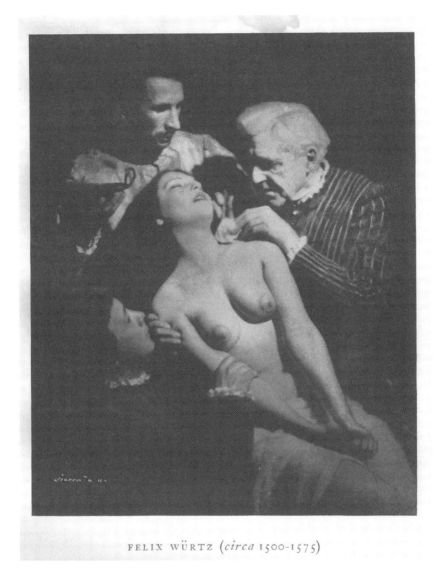

FELIX WÜRTZ (*circa* 1500-1575)

Figure 8. *Tableau vivant* of Felix Würtz which channels the 'Ecstasy of Saint Teresa' (1935).

lives will come to nothing'.[60] Maybe on occasion Hiller overshot the mark, but the fact remains that this advertising commission in his hands and mind ended up perhaps being more than DG originally conceived. At the most fundamental level the *Sutures* project is about pain and suffering; life and death; hope and

---

[60] Quoted from http://www.independent.co.uk/life-style/john-walsh-meets-sister-wendy-beckett-1338165.html.

fear; order and chaos; and bodily decay and restoration – across time and cultures.

These paired opposites also allow us to make sense of Hiller's homage to the sixteenth-century French doctor Etienne Gourmelin, which was already criticised for its gendered nudity at the time (Figure 9). At first glance it is an over-the-top, dramatic scene of plague in Paris in 1581 with several corpses in carts or lying in the street; more corpses being handled by hooded men; and other plague sufferers being treated by, presumably, Gourmelen. In the background is a stylised painted backdrop of period houses that are in obvious disrepair and perhaps abandoned. Adding to the scene's inventive illusion is the healthy appearance of the five lithe, naked and unmarred bodies of women who had apparently died from the plague; bare breasts here visibly outnumber buboes (the dark swellings that are the tell-tale physical signs of bubonic plague – the Black Death). When this photograph, along with a few others of Hiller's, was later reproduced in *Life* magazine in 1939, readers reacted through letters. One reader drew attention to the 'beautiful' nudes, but wondered why only the women were naked. Similarly, another noted sarcastically how 'good old bubonic plague' was discriminatory based on gender as 'male victims died with their boots on but the gals stripped before kicking in'. *Life* also printed Hiller's response to these observations. On the one hand, he invoked an historical explanation by noting that thieves often stripped corpses, while on the hand he responded glibly and rhetorically: 'If you were doing the pictures, which would you undress?'[61]

Focusing on the sexualised nature of this image is understandable and may be unavoidable – and Hiller's flippant remark, for good or ill, reinforces it. Such mockery, by reducing the tableau to its pornographic component, obscures as much as it reveals. The staged scene is much better described as choreographed. Overall, the style is redolent of German Expressionist theatre, dance and film, along with related cultural movements of the 1920s and 1930s. Firstly, what might appear to be a makeshift and cartoonish backdrop was actually a design feature. The distortion and exaggeration of the painted houses was a style characteristic of Expressionism, which sought to favour a sense of inner emotionalism rather than surface realties. Secondly, the dramatic use of lighting to create brooding shadows as well as to foreground detail was another element (again, think film noir). Thirdly, the bodily positions of the naked female victims may be static, but they might better be described as motion that is frozen in time: in particular the woman who is being carried aloft by the hooded men with arms extended is almost flying. Her pose can be likened to Expressionist dance of the era, which challenged traditional dance and ballet by its sweeping and exaggerated movements. This is not surprising as it is known that Hiller recruited students from a nature dancing school as models. As Karl Toepfer explained, performance involving nudity, movement and dance was tagged to an ideal of modernity.[62]

---

[61] Quoted in Manchee, *Sutures and Spirits*, 52.

[62] Karl Toepfer, *Empire of Ecstasy: Nudity and Movement in German Body Culture, 1910–1935* (Berkeley, 1997), 384.

ETIENNE GOURMELEN

Figure 9. *Tableau vivant* of the sixteenth-century French doctor Etienne Gourmelen attending the plague-stricken in Paris (1934).

The notions of modernity and ecstasy have previously been mentioned in connection to Hiller's images, but in the plague tableau they resurface albeit in other cultural and artistic contexts. Finally, the whole tableau, blending as it does techniques that are photographic, cinematographic, theatrical and choreographic, is testament to the power of spectacle of which Hiller was capable. For some viewers specific examples of Hiller's work might be excessive in style, perhaps moving into the realm of *kitsch*. In my view, the closest we get to Hiller crossing that boundary is his depiction of 'Giovanni Andrea Dalla Croce' (1932), already referred to for its religious imagery. In this tableau several men restrain the naked female patient despite the fact that it appears that she is shackled at the ankles to the operating table. Her back is arched, her chest and bare breasts thrust upwards; here surgery perhaps bleeds into violation and torture. Violence against women by men driven by sexual desire and social anxiety regarding modernity was certainly another element of the film, art and literature of German culture at this time. Even here, the motivations fuelling the genre of *lustmord* (mutilation culminating in sex murder) cannot credibly be read into Hiller's work.[63]

That Hiller was influenced by aspects of German Expressionism may be circumstantial, but the notion is helpful in further appreciating his work; similarly, the possible influence of Fritz Lang's *Metropolis*, which had its debut in New York City in 1927. Did the *New York Times*' review of the film which noted that 'its scenes bristle with cinematic imagination, with hordes of men and women and astounding stage settings' or the *New Yorker*'s evaluation that 'the setting, the use of people and their movement, and various bits of action stand out as extraordinary' strike a chord with him as an artist?[64] Possibly, Hiller, who had been an art film maker from which his stills survived and who lived close to the Rialto theatre where *Metropolis* was screened, was similarly moved. As Weimar German 'decadent' culture was dismantled under National Socialism, many artists, including Fritz Lang, settled in America, which influenced art trends. What can be said with certainty is that Hiller's tableaux could, in isolation, easily be mistaken as 'movie stills' taken from films of the era and were influenced by the art of the times. Again, invoking *Metropolis* is important, as stills were derived from the filming while in progress and used to illustrate a magazine-serialised version of the original novel on which the film screenplay was based. Thus such stills were not just promotional images for use in cinemas at the time of showing the film, but in effect were *tableaux vivants* of scenes used ahead of release as illustrations in a magazine to accompany text. Hiller's images used in potential ad campaigns other than *Sutures* bears out the fluid use of such stylistic images. In one, a mob of over a dozen men, women and children display expressions of open hostility, disgruntlement and anger; many are armed with rifles, cudgels and other weapons. One member of the group holds up a placard reading 'Down with Law and Order',' while others are shouting and gesticulating violently, with one woman with arms outstretched upwards.[65]

---

[63] Beth Irwin Lewis, '*Lustmord*: Inside the Windows of the Metropolis', in *Women in the Metropolis: Gender and Modernity in Weimar Culture*, ed. Katrina von Ankum (Berkeley, 1997), 202–32; and Maria Tatar, *Lustmord: Sexual Murder in Weimar Germany* (Princeton, 1995).

[64] Mordaunt Hall, 'A Technical Marvel', *New York Times*, 7 Mar. 1927, available at https://www.nytimes.com/1927/03/07/archives/a-technical-marvel.html and Oliver Claxton, 'The Current Cinema', *The New Yorker*, 12 Mar. 1927, 80–1; see also Herman G. Scheffauerand, 'An Impression of the German Film "Metropolis"', *New York Times*, 6 Mar. 1927, Section X, 7; and Minden and Bachmann, *Fritz Lang's Metropolis*, 37.

[65] This image is reproduced in Manchee, *Sutures and Spirits*, pl. 87, at 145.

By itself, one might readily conclude that this still was from a movie from the late 1920s or 1930s; the composition and message of this particular shot are particularly reminiscent of the workers' revolt and other scenes in *Metropolis*.

But what of the primary audience for these images – did doctors discern the art behind the ads? These practitioners probably never appreciated the subtleties of German Expressionism or visual references to Bernini arguably embedded in *Sutures* as they perused the portfolio of images given to them by a detail man, but something nonetheless resonated with them. Perhaps it was primarily the medical history they contained; or their visual clichés. Recall that in the late 1990s DG employee Charles Riall mused that 'there probably are thousands [of images] still on doctors [sic] walls'. This seems likely to be an overly inflated estimate, but the *Sutures* portfolio currently circulates in rare book circles where it is still considered of interest and value. Perhaps another gauge of their contemporary cultural value is to be found in the fact that the portfolio of images used as the basis of the present study was part of a donation of artefacts on behalf of a deceased doctor who graduated in 1936, which was contemporaneous with the DG ad campaign; that *Sutures* made it as far as the North Atlantic island and then independent country of Newfoundland, was not discarded and was among his prized possessions, also including a group portrait of his medical fraternity brothers, is noteworthy.

Hiller, *Sutures*, female (nude) bodies, art, eroticism and medicine: stitching everything together (as best I can)

At its root, *Sutures* was an advertising medium that connected a seller to a potential buyer. The content and presentation of the project also connected medicine present with medicine past, which also may have helped physicians to connect with the then blossoming field of medical history. The images through their creation and composition connected differing art forms. While *Sutures* can be dated to a specific era, it does possess a distinct look; the criticism of it being 'dated looking' is problematic: the 1939 *Life* magazine feature of Hiller's work noted that 'medical men repeatedly mistake the photographs for fine reproductions of old masterpieces which never existed', suggesting that that they were modern remakes of Renaissance paintings.[66] The resurgence of *tableaux vivants* by avant-garde photographers and artists attests to the endurance of this art form.[67] *Sutures* may be classified in an archival sense as ephemera, yet the portfolio is not ephemeral, for in its entirety it acts as a bridge connecting sensibilities over time. As historians, our role is to interpret and contextualise the past: *Sutures* images, whether selected or all-encompassing, allow an additional insight into the mindset of medicine past.

---

[66] 'Speaking of Pictures ... These are Milestones in the History of Surgery', *Life,* 23 Jan. 1939, 6.
[67] See   http://sites.psu.edu/morethanaselfie/tableau-vivant/;   http://www.ryanschude.com/ Tableaux-Vivants/1; http://www.sarahsmall.com/files/accolades/washingtonpostreview/.

That notion notwithstanding, a similar ad campaign would probably not be mounted by any reputable medical supply company in our current more inclusive and less overtly sexist and gender-exploitative culture. Whatever appeal *Sutures* may have had for a past male medical culture, it would probably not resonate with the medical profession of today in which women are numerically dominant.[68] So was Hiller's use of women gratuitous and meant to titillate? Or were his compositions genuinely contextualised in various artistic traditions? If his work occasionally appeared risqué, was it appropriate for a mostly male medical audience of his era? Bert Hansen also identified these issues in his analysis. As noted, he concluded that Hiller's tableaux ought to be considered as 'works of art' and justifies this position in part by offering a brief history of the long-standing tradition of the posed nude woman in many works of fine art. Yet, perhaps displaying some ambivalence, he also acknowledges that even up to the 1970s the 'open and unembarrassed display of provocative female images within the medical profession' and in textbooks continued.[69] Hansen's reference to thirteen of Hiller's *Sutures* images reproduced in the May 1954 issue of *Playboy* magazine is also suggestive, but he does not comment further so the matter is left hanging.[70] A cursory survey of collectors' websites relating to *Playboy* magazine, however, reveals that the four-page article on Hiller is typically classified as sadomasochism. Moreover, when David Lambkin analysed issues of the first year of *Playboy* (1953-4) to study its rhetorical construction of masculine sexuality, he referred to the Hiller piece. The images of nude female patients attended by clothed male doctors in a 'men's magazine' was 'Smuggling a little pornography into a text under the cover of "art."' Lambkin's assessment was arrived at without historical context, but his reaction to Hiller's works illustrate how they can easily be interpreted less as pastiche and more as pornographic.[71] Such an assessment resonates with one previously quoted when Hansen noted that one of the external reviewers for his article referred to Hiller's work as 'doctor porn'. Just as apposite was the insight offered by an external reader for this essay who seized upon DG employee Charles Riall's assertion that 'there probably are thousands [of images] still on doctors [sic] walls' thereby concluding that Hiller's nudes could be classified as 'pin-up girls'.

To pluck selected images for republication in a magazine such as *Playboy*, for example, and label them as pornography, pin up girls or cheesecake, perhaps

---

[68] Laura Weiss Roberts, 'Women and Academic Medicine, 2020', *Academic Medicine*, 95 (2020), 1459-64. For insights into the recent evolution of women in medicine and changing attitudes to sexism and gendered discrimination, see Earle Waugh, Shelly Ross and Shirley Schipper (eds.), *Female Doctors in Canada: Experience and Culture* (Toronto, 2019) and Margaret A. Campbell, *Why Would a Girl Go into Medicine? Medical Education in the United States: A Guide for Women* (Old Westbury, NY, 1973).

[69] Hansen, 'Medical History's Moment', 410.

[70] *Ibid.*, 385, 411.

[71] David John Lambkin, '*Playboy's* First Year: A Rhetorical Construction of Masculine Sexuality' (1999), *LSU Historical Dissertations and Theses*, 111, https://digitalcommons.lsu.edu/gradschool_disstheses/6997.

does a disservice to his reputation.[72] Yet the fact that that happened is instructive and points to why many people might find the images unsettling. More important than any personal reaction, however, is a much larger discussion of the associations of the female nude image in art, especially photographs, and medicine/doctors/patients.

Ludmilla Jordanova, who embraces multiple fields as feminist, cultural historian and historian of medicine when generally analysing gendered images in art and biomedicine, brings many insights to this discussion. One of her conclusions might have resonated with some of Hiller's thoughts on preferences for unclothed models; she writes that 'Unveiling men makes no sense, possibly because neither mystery nor modesty are male preserves.'[73] This comment is grounded in her larger gendered argument centring on the centuries-old personification of Nature as a veiled beautiful woman that Man seeks/needs to unveil as manifest in numerous works of sculpture and visual art. 'Science and medicine, since they claimed special truth status for themselves', Jordanova explains, 'were drawn both to personification of nature as woman and to the image of unveiling in order to represent their privileged relationship to Truth and to Nature. They thereby become the domains strong enough, as a power nexus, to grapple with the complex forces that nakedness unleashed.'[74] Likewise, art historian Mary Hunter describes how the Paris Académie de Médecine is home to numerous female nude statues 'scattered around' it, including *Nature unveiling herself before Science.*[75]

Such visual tropes when connected to medicine clearly fall within the realm of art and in and of themselves are respectable and in no meaningful sense might they be construed as obscene or pornographic. Hunter continues, however, to note that art when applied to medicine can have its seamier side. Her discussion of the making and display of realistic wax body parts including female genitalia depicting various diseases illustrates how these teaching objects and other medical *objets d'art* when viewed out of their clinical context could easily glide into the erotic, if not the pornographic: 'fantasy, and pleasure' were in tension with the 'rational façade of modern scientific medicine and professional duty'.[76] Similarly, Rebecca Whitely in her analysis of a nineteenth-century text on obstetrics illustrated with coloured plates that were actually movable flaps demonstrated how this work 'intertwined issues of sex, nakedness, pornography, and the nude'.[77] These perspectives

---

[72] For discussion on what such designations and categories mean culturally and historically, see Maria Elena Buszek, *Pin-Up Grrrls: Feminism, Sexuality, Popular Culture* (Durham, NC, 2006) and Joanne Meyerowitz, 'Women, Cheesecake, and Borderline Material: Responses to Girlie Pictures in the Mid-Twentieth Century U.S.', *Journal of Women's History*, 8 (1986), 9–35.

[73] Ludmilla Jordanova, *Sexual Visions: Images of Gender in Science and Medicine Between the Eighteenth and Twentieth Centuries* (Madison, WI, 1989), 110.

[74] *Ibid.*, 94.

[75] Mary Hunter, *The Face of Medicine: Visualising Medical Masculinities in Late-nineteenth Century Paris* (Manchester, 2016), 135.

[76] Hunter, *The Face of Medicine,* 154.

[77] Rebecca Whitely, 'Spratt's Flaps: Midwifery, Creativity, and Sexuality in Early Nineteenth-Century Visual Culture', *British Art Studies*, 19 (2021), https://www.britishartstudies.

help us to understand how selective images of Hiller's work can take on a pictorial life other than what he originally intended or was commissioned to do. But the real lesson is in the medium Hiller chose: photography – not sculpture, wax models or printed text. Recall that Duffin and Li criticised Hiller for the lack of 'verisimilitude' in his images, but I would argue that part of their problem is not so much its *lack* as its *presence* in the form of live human models qua photographs. Similarly, Hansen, as already noted, stated that some people with whom he was in contact invoked the nature of the medium as the basis for criticism 'because photography did not exist in the eras they [the images] would seem to record'. And one of his peer reviewers took exception to 'these surgical *photographs*' (my italics). Even Doug Manchee circled around this issue. In his defence of Hiller's use of naked women, he wondered if Hiller failed to appreciate the differences in an audience's reaction to a drawn nude and a photographed one.

Sander Gilman has demonstrated how erotic or sexual art in various visual media existed before and after the invention of photography, but his discussion of a daguerreotype (an early photographic technique) dating from 1855 depicting a naked male with an erection kissing a naked female while also fondling her breasts and vulva, however, illustrates how this new medium was novel with respect to vicarious sexuality. The image presents 'in the most direct manner ... an early example of the sexualized touch captured in the most "realistic" of media, the photograph, a medium that was endowed in the mid-nineteenth century with the claim of immediacy of verisimilitude'.[78] Despite the theatricality and contrived historicity of Hiller's images, maybe it is the 'immediacy of verisimilitude' that is their key. Art historian Lynda Nead is emphatic and unequivocal about the power of photography in relation to eroticism and pornography with respect to the female nude. She argues how a photograph is an 'unmediated image ... If the object in question is the female body, then the photograph can be seen to afford direct access to that body, and sexual arousal with the minimum interference from the medium itself.'[79] To recast Marshall McLuhan's dictum in this context, the medium certainly is the message. But when both medium and message are medical, the intellectual and social stakes are raised considerably, for notions of sexual arousal vis-à-vis doctors, who supposedly are assumed to be professionally detached from such thoughts and actions when on the job, is cause for social anxiety.

To see 'pin-ups' or an advertising cheesecake calendar on the walls of an all-male locker room or on those of an automotive repair shop might well cause no more than a raised eyebrow for most persons, but today to view similar images in a doctor's office might be a bit of a 'Wow!' moment, especially

---

ac.uk/issues/issue-index/issue-19/spratts-flaps, 3. Public titillation also resulted from viewing medical exhibits in anatomy museums; see J. M. M. Alberti, *Morbid Curiosities: Medical Museums in Nineteenth-Century Britain* (Oxford, 2011), 189–91.

[78] Sander L. Gilman, *Sexuality: An Illustrated History Representing the Sexual in Medicine and Culture from the Middle Ages to the Age of AIDS* (New York, 1989), 245.

[79] Lynda Nead, *The Female Nude: Art, Obscenity and Sexuality* (Routledge, 1992), 97. On the broader topic of viewing female anatomy as social taboo, see James Elkins, *The Object Stares Back: On the Nature of Seeing* (San Diego, 1996), 105–7.

while current viewers would have no knowledge of the original historical milieu and context respecting medicine and modernity. But that is now. What about then? Perhaps the allure and success of Hiller's *Sutures in Ancient Surgery* in its time is an unexpected historical insight into the expectations of professional propriety and demeanour of that era. If indeed there were 'thousands' of Hiller's images on doctors' walls during his time which did not occasion any public outcry, then apparently such photographic renditions, erotic or otherwise, were acceptable. The past may be a foreign country; certainly the medical past is.

Cite this article: Connor JTH (2024). 'Luxuries of the mind': Contextualising Art Photography, Eroticism and History of Medicine in the Social *tableaux vivants* of Lejaren à Hiller's *Sutures in Ancient Surgery* (1920s–1940s). *Transactions of the Royal Historical Society* **2**, 233–265. https://doi.org/10.1017/S008044012400015X

Transactions of the RHS (2024), 2, 267–291
doi:10.1017/S0080440124000057

ARTICLE

Cricket, Literary Culture and In-Groups in Early Twentieth-Century Britain

Ollie Randall

King's College London, London, UK
Email: ollie.randall@kcl.ac.uk

(Received 6 March 2024; revised 24 May 2024; accepted 25 May 2024;
first published online 9 September 2024)

Abstract

This article posits that team sports can provide fresh insights into the place of leisure pursuits in the lives, networks and outlooks of historical literary figures. The social and literary role of the Authors Eleven, a cricket side of London-based writers active between 1899 and 1912, is explored through three case studies. George Ives was a pioneering campaigner for gay rights, who used cricket to bolster his homosexual identity. E. W. Hornung, creator of the famous cricketer-thief Raffles, saw cricket as the ideal training – and analogy – for imperialism. And P. G. Wodehouse, author of the Jeeves and Wooster stories, first made his name writing cricket-filled magazine pieces. All three writers saw their involvement in cricket, particularly the Authors Eleven in-group, as an essential component of their social status. The Authors Eleven thus presents a potent example of embodied sociability, whereby the specific nature of what these individuals were doing together (in this case, playing cricket) has a bearing on their friendships and their intellectual outlooks. As ways of understanding the lives and cultural significance of historical figures, shared physical activity and embodied sociability need to be accorded much more importance than they have been hitherto.

Keywords: Edwardian culture; intellectual history; embodied experience; literary industries; cricket; Arthur Conan Doyle; P. G. Wodehouse

Since 2009, several of Arthur Conan Doyle's appointment diaries have been publicly accessible in the British Library's special collections. Eight volumes from the years 1898 to 1906 survive intact, available for perusal by cultural historians and Sherlock Holmes fans alike.[1] Yet the diaries seem to have

---

[1] British Library (BL), Arthur Conan Doyle Papers, Add MS 88924/5/4–12.

disappointed most readers to date; they have not yet received any attention in print.[2] They are indeed strikingly sparse: Doyle's laconic entries are mostly few and far between. The one major psychological insight provided by the diaries has been neglected.

What researchers have ignored is the diaries' emphatic demonstration of Doyle's great passion for cricket. Although it is widely known that Doyle was a keen cricketer, its place in his life has typically been relegated to the margins: his many biographers only discuss it in passing.[3] But in Doyle's diaries, cricket is the central element, prioritised over everything else. It is the one thing that he unfailingly records in the diaries, revealing that his summers were filled with cricket matches. In 1899, for instance, he played in forty-three fixtures; in 1903, he played in thirty-three.[4] For most of these years, he recorded every match he played in, with his score and the number of wickets he took.[5] In 1901, cricket formed the only entries in the whole diary.[6] At the end of each year, he totted up three sets of sums at the back of each volume: his annual income; his annual list of stories written and the total word-count; and his batting average for that year. These were, it would seem, the three sets of figures by which he lived his life.

The failure of scholars to take Doyle's cricket as seriously as he himself did is emblematic of a wider tendency. When historians study intellectual figures, such as writers, they often treat their subjects' cerebral lives as separate from their leisure pursuits – especially if these individuals' chosen recreations were physical activities, such as sports. Current treatment of intellectuals' hobbies regularly implies that their recreation was inconsequential to the serious business of writing. For instance, J. B. Priestley's interwar football-playing has never been considered as part of his construction of a communitarian ideal of Englishness, and the link between Edmund Blunden's pastoral attitude to cricket-playing and his pastoral poetry and prose remains unexplored.[7] Benjamin Britten's intense love of sports, especially tennis, was a critical and revealing aspect of his psyche, as attested by his intimates; yet his biographers routinely pay it little attention.[8] Leading works of scholarship examining the social backdrop to intellectuals' lives in Britain, such as William Lubenow's

---

[2] The diaries are not even among the 2,110 sources consulted in Brian Pugh's herculean attempt to produce an exhaustive day-by-day chronology of Doyle's life: dozens of Doyle's cricket matches, recorded in the diaries, are therefore overlooked. For instance, Authors XI matches on 1 and 2 July 1902, recorded in BL, Doyle Papers, Add MS 88924/5/7, are missing from the latest edition of Pugh's chronology. Brian W. Pugh, *A Chronology of the Life of Sir Arthur Conan Doyle, May 22nd 1859 to July 7th 1930: Revised 2018 Edition* (2018), 95.

[3] For example, Andrew Lycett, *The Man Who Created Sherlock Holmes: The Life and Times of Arthur Conan Doyle* (2007).

[4] BL, Doyle Papers, Add MS 88924/5/5, 8.

[5] For instance, 22 May 1903: 'Authors V Artists. 28. (Bowled) 1w.' *Ibid.*, Add MS 88924/5/4/8.

[6] *Ibid.*, Add MS 88924/5/4/6.

[7] For instance, Priestley's football interests are scarcely discussed in John Baxendale, *Priestley's England* (Manchester, 2007). In the one full-length biography of Blunden, cricket gets a few pages within an 'Interlude' section: Barry Webb, *Edmund Blunden: A Biography* (1990), 255–64.

[8] See 'Britten at Home: Britten's Sports', part of *Britten 100* (2013), BBC Radio 3, 21 Nov. 2013, https://www.bbc.co.uk/programmes/p02nrygb (accessed 21 May 2024). Biographies that ignore

Only Connect and Stefan Collini's *Absent Minds*, overlook sports, especially team sports.[9] Leslie Stephen's Sunday Tramps, including many late-nineteenth-century luminaries, have their own entry in the *Oxford Dictionary of National Biography*, but yet the group has never been systematically scrutinised.[10] Albert Camus, a keen footballer in his youth, once said, 'What I know most surely about morality and the duty of man I owe to sport' – but the Albert Camus Society dismissively assures us that 'People have read more into these words than, perhaps, Camus would want them to.'[11] Time and again, it is assumed that what intellectuals like Doyle did with their bodies is separate from what they did with their minds. But this is a fallacy: we know from our own experiences that life is lived holistically, and we carry our outlooks from one sphere of our lives to another. Furthermore, it was these shared leisure pursuits which often underpinned intellectuals' friendships with one another, their sharing of ideas and their sense of belonging to the same in-groups. If we fail to take seriously the pleasurable pursuits of historical figures, then our understanding of them will be impoverished.

Some historians have already begun to redress this – for instance, Paul Readman's demonstration of the central place of walking and mountaineering in the life of the polymath politician James Bryce (1838–1922), as well as his work on the role of walking in the imaginative processes of antiquarians and historians.[12] There is now a considerable body of scholarly literature on both climbing and walking.[13] This reflects the fact that these particular activities have been presented by their participants as cerebral undertakings since the nineteenth century – we can think of the writings of William Wordsworth and Edward Whymper, as well as more recent examples such as Robert Macfarlane.[14] However, despite a little work on Oxbridge rowing, modern scholarship has not yet looked at the links between physical exercise and book-focused intellectual activity in the case of most team sports.[15] Perhaps the

---

or skim over Britten's sports include Humphrey Carpenter, *Benjamin Britten: A Biography* (1992), and Neil Powell, *Benjamin Britten: A Life for Music* (2013).

[9] William C Lubenow, *'Only Connect': Learned Societies in Nineteenth-Century Britain* (2015); Stefan Collini, *Absent Minds: Intellectuals in Britain* (2006).

[10] William Whyte, 'Sunday Tramps (act. 1879–1895)', *Oxford Dictionary of National Biography* (ODNB).

[11] 'Albert Camus and Football', https://camus-society.com/2017/11/29/albert-camus-and-football/ (accessed 21 May 2024).

[12] Paul Readman, 'Walking and Environmentalism in the Career of James Bryce: Mountaineer, Scholar, Statesman, 1838–1922', in *Walking Histories, 1800–1914*, ed. Chad Bryant, Arthur Burns, and Paul Readman (2016), 287–318; and Readman, 'Walking, and Knowing the Past: Antiquaries, Pedestrianism and Historical Practice in Modern Britain', *History*, 107 (2021), 51–73.

[13] For instance, Peter H. Hansen, *The Summits of Modern Man: Mountaineering after the Enlightenment* (2013), as well as Bryant, Burns and Readman (eds.), *Walking Histories*.

[14] Edward Whymper, *Scrambles Amongst the Alps in the Years 1860-69* (1871); Robert Macfarlane, *Mountains of the Mind: A History of a Fascination* (2003). For the links between Wordsworth's walking and his literary output, see Anne D. Wallace, *Walking, Literature, and English Culture: The Origins and Uses of Peripatetic in the Nineteenth Century* (Oxford, 1993).

[15] For rowing, see Andrew Warwick, 'Exercising the Student Body: Mathematics and Athleticism in Victorian Cambridge', in *Science Incarnate: Historical Embodiments of Natural Knowledge*, ed.

most surprising omission is cricket, which– as the example of Doyle illustrates – would seem to be a particularly fruitful line of inquiry in this regard. In the first place, it comes with an unusually rich repertoire of symbolic connotations, and it is associated with a resonant value system that was long believed to underpin particular ideals of Englishness. From the 1870s to the 1950s, cricket was the focus of an extraordinary level of fervour throughout England; drawing vast crowds from many sectors of society, it was something of a national obsession.[16] And yet, outside sports history, this is not adequately reflected in the existing scholarship.

The second advantage of putting cricket at the centre of an investigation into intellectual figures is that the subject offers a clear starting point: the writers who congregated around Arthur Conan Doyle to play cricket with him. Between the 1880s and the 1960s, a tight-knit group of London-based writers played cricket together each summer. I call this phenomenon 'literary cricket", taking the term from one of its early participants.[17] Doyle was central to this group until he gave up cricket in 1912. A little has been written about authors who have *written about* cricket; but almost nothing – except for passing remarks and the odd passage about an individual – has been written about authors who *played* cricket, much less played cricket *together*.[18] The closest we come to an exception is Kevin Telfer's cricket-themed biography of J. M. Barrie, *Peter Pan's First XI*, which focuses on Barrie's cricket team.[19] Barrie, along with Doyle, was indeed instrumental in establishing the early literary cricket network. However, Telfer's book was written to entertain and is not an academic study; and it rests on the assumption that only the remarkable Barrie could ever have sustained a literary-themed cricket team. The opposite is the case: the network continued to flourish for sixty years after Barrie retired from literary cricket in 1905.

To participate in a team sport is qualitatively different from being a keen spectator, let alone admiring it in the abstract for its symbolic connotations. Yet time and again, the actual playing of cricket by writers is downplayed or ignored, and cricket's vast literature is explained away as though its authors simply liked the idea of cricket.[20] Although historians of sport generally recognise that the physical experience of participation is highly important, this is not reflected in cricket's current treatment by cultural historians. Anthony Bateman, for instance – who has written some of the best work to date on the socio-cultural role of cricket literature – treats the game so entirely as a textual phenomenon that he seems completely to lose sight of cricket as a

---

Christopher Lawrence and Steven Shapin (Chicago, 1998), 288–326; and M. C. Curthoys and H. S. Jones, 'Oxford Athleticism, 1850–1914: A Reappraisal', *History of Education*, 24 (1995), 305–17.

[16] Derek Birley, *A Social History of English Cricket* (1999).

[17] Philip Trevor, 'Literary Cricket', in *The Lighter Side of Cricket* (1901), 179–92.

[18] For an example of the former, see Anthony Bateman, *Cricket, Literature and Culture: Symbolising the Nation, Destabilising Empire* (2010).

[19] Kevin Telfer, *Peter Pan's First XI* (2010).

[20] For example, this is the implication of anthologies such as *Lord's and Commons: Cricket in Novels and Stories*, ed. John Bright-Holmes (1988).

real-world, tangible activity.[21] Cricket (and indeed other sports) cannot be reduced to a textual construct: and while an emphasis on the recovery and analysis of discourse has dominated the past few decades of cultural history, we must balance this with a re-examination of the material and social realities in which these discourses are contained. Cricket is a carefully governed cultural practice, and literary cricket is best understood as a self-conscious enacting of the rituals that comprise this practice. A literary cricket match was a stage-managed performance, which was important for bonding, for establishing an in-group of writers, and for reinforcing particular aspects of its participants' sense of self. What those aspects were, as we shall see, varied from player to player.

Pierre Bourdieu's theory of social and cultural capital provides a useful theoretical framework. In Bourdieu's terms, social capital depends on one's personal ties to other people, while cultural capital is determined by status markers such as desirable knowledge, skills and rank.[22] Sociologists have built on Bourdieu's ideas, for example in the case of Ronald S. Burt's concept of the 'broker' of social capital.[23] According to this model, a well-connected individual gains even more social capital when they act as a broker by providing a fruitful link between two other members of their network. Effective networks therefore act as a multiplier of social capital. And literary cricket also provided cultural capital, through the status markers attached to cricket and literature – both of which were prestigious forms of English cultural activity, until cricket declined after the 1950s.[24]

The literary cricket network reached its pre-war peak in the years 1899–1912, when it took the form of a team called the Authors Eleven, usually captained by Doyle. The Authors' main opponents were a succession of shorter-lived teams, the Artists, the Actors and the Publishers; and most of their matches were played either at Esher in Surrey, or at Lord's Cricket Ground, 'the home of cricket', in St John's Wood.[25] The team was an important phenomenon in the literary culture of the day.[26] Contemporary observers believed that the cricket of the Authors was important to what they wrote. 'Men of letters have taken to games', observed a journalist in 1903,

and with so much enthusiasm that they cannot help writing about them. The old idea of the author, as a man with bowed shoulders, wrinkled brow, and long, lean, white hands, cramped by much pen-holding, has passed away. In his stead we have such vigorous figures as Sir Conan Doyle and Mr. J. M. Barrie – both of whom played in the cricket match between Authors and the Royal Engineers at Chatham last week … They

---

[21] Bateman, *Cricket, Literature and Culture.*

[22] Pierre Bourdieu, 'The Forms of Capital', in *Handbook of Theory and Research for the Sociology of Education*, ed. John G. Richardson (Westport, CT, 1986), 241–58.

[23] Ronald S. Burt, *Brokerage and Closure: An Introduction to Social Capital* (Oxford, 2005), 7.

[24] Birley, *Social History*, 288–300.

[25] Sources include Albert Kinross, *An Unconventional Cricketer* (1930), 110–14.

[26] For instance, see Alec Waugh, 'Lunching with Plum', in *P.G. Wodehouse: A Centenary Celebration, 1881-1981*, ed. James Heineman and Donald Bensen (Oxford, 1981), 10.

are players of games, men of the open air, keen and vigorous in national sports; and the effect of this life is evident in their books.[27]

There has never before been an academic study of the Authors Eleven – but when we examine the careers of some of its members in light of this cricket team, we see a new aspect to their lives, their works and their context. I want to look at three of the keenest literary cricketers, men who played for the Authors at every opportunity: George Cecil Ives, E. W. Hornung and P. G. Wodehouse. Through these three case studies, we will see the value of cricket to these men and their work. Their sense of personal and in-group identity, and their intellectual output, were closely tied to their enthusiastic involvement in cricket. It is crucial that they played, rather than simply watched or read about, cricket matches. A study of the Authors Eleven can advance ongoing work on the topics of affective relationships; the history of ideas; the history of British literary culture; and the interconnections between historical subjects' minds and bodies.[28] This article will do so by looking at the social connections that Ives, Hornung and Wodehouse made through the team, and the consequences on their lives and careers. It will also explore how their societal attitudes and their writings – including some of their most famous creations – were closely linked to their membership of the team. As such, this article will provide insights into the development and transmission of these three writers' ideas, their sense of their position in Edwardian society, and how this was all tied to the embodied sociability of cricket. In so doing, it can contribute to a substantial broadening of the limits of how we think about intellectual lives.

George Ives: playing cricket, reimagining queer masculinity

As the scholarly literature on masculinities and queer identities continues to grow, the relationship of George Cecil Ives (1867–1950) with literary cricket presents an illuminating example of how individual strategies of identity-building can combine multiple self-conscious roles (poet; sportsman; persecuted homosexual; courageous campaigner) to create a protean sense of self. Ives, the first man to captain a cricket team styled 'the Authors Eleven', was an obscure poet, the illegitimate son of a baronet.[29] A pioneer of sexual understanding, an ardent campaigner for penal reform and a gay man himself, he especially cared about crimes concerning homosexuality. He was deeply passionate about his private campaign (which he termed 'the Cause' and 'the Faith') to work against the social stigmas and legal penalties that then accompanied homosexual practices. He co-founded the British Sexological Society to further scientific investigation into 'inverted' sexual practices, and established a secret club called the Order of Chaeronea, the earliest-known support group

---

[27] 'Athletic Authors', *Londonderry Sentinel*, 11 June 1903, 6.
[28] For existing work expanding the boundaries of these topics, see Lawrence and Shapin (eds.), *Science Incarnate*, and Laura Forster, 'The Paris Commune in London and the Spatial History of Ideas, 1871–1900', *The Historical Journal*, 62 (2019), 1021–44.
[29] Matt Cook, 'Ives, George Cecil', ODNB.

for homosexual British men. Ives kept a diary, writing long, impassioned entries, in which he returned to these themes on almost every page. Ives has occasionally been recognised – principally by Matt Cook – as a figure worthy of serious study for those interested in Edwardian social and sexual attitudes, and the inner lives of those who departed from accepted norms.[30] However, nobody has spent more than a sentence or two on his relationship with cricket, despite the fact that it was an integral part of his lived experience – one which sheds light on the man as a whole, and on his relationship with masculinity at a time of tension around this category.[31]

In 1895, 1896 and 1898, the recently established Authors' Club fielded a cricket team, the Authors Eleven, against the Press Club at Lord's. Ives, already a regular in Barrie's literary team, was its captain.[32] In 1896, Barrie and Doyle both featured.[33] In the lead-up to the 1896 match, Doyle showed his enthusiasm by sending a letter to Ives listing the writers he ought to pick.[34] Doyle won the match for the Authors with 101 not out, an event which Ives excitedly described in his diary as 'somewhat sensational'.[35] Discussing Lord's in his autobiography, Doyle wrote, 'I got a century in the very first match that I played there ... My bat, still encrusted with the classic mud, hangs as a treasured relic in my hall.'[36]

In December 1898, Ives resigned from the Authors' Club. The club secretary, G. H. Thring, who had played in the 1898 match, wrote two letters to Ives urging him to reconsider: 'The Club would specially miss your assistance in the Summer at cricket. Our annual match would not be the same without your captaincy. I hope, therefore, that you will see fit to withdraw your resignation.'[37] Ives's mind, however, was made up. He wrote in his diary that he had 'chucked' the Authors' Club:

> I have never forgiven a conversation I overheard about *the homosexuals* though it did not touch me personally; the language they used, the bloodthirsty cutthroat malice and spite of the creatures: one said that certain people should be taken into a back yard and have their throats cut: I said not one word, but went on reading; the cad, I thought ... I have never spoken to any of them since.[38]

---

[30] Matt Cook, *London and the Culture of Homosexuality, 1885–1914* (Cambridge, 2003); George Ives, *Man Bites Man: The Scrapbook of an Edwardian Eccentric*, ed. Paul Sieveking (1980).

[31] On this tension, see John Tosh, *Manliness and Masculinities in Nineteenth-Century Britain* (2005).

[32] Rayvern Allen, *Peter Pan and Cricket*, 87. Ives's captaincy is proved by two letters from the Authors' Club to George Ives, Harry Ransom Center, the University of Texas at Austin (HRC), British Sexological Society Records (BSSR), 19.13.

[33] 'Authors v. Press', *Evening Mail*, 18 Sept. 1896, 8. Despite writing a book on Barrie's cricket career, Telfer overlooks this match when he erroneously states that Barrie never played at Lord's: Telfer, *Pan's XI*, 31–2.

[34] Doyle to Ives, 30 Aug. 1896, HRC, BSSR, 21.1.

[35] HRC, Ives Papers, Diaries, xxix, 40–1, 18 Sept. 1896.

[36] Arthur Conan Doyle, *Memories and Adventures* (London, 1924), 283.

[37] Authors' Club to George Ives, 16 Dec. 1898, HRC, BSSR, 19.13.

[38] HRC, Ives Papers, Diaries, xxxiii, 106, 8 Dec. 1898.

His enthusiasm for literary cricket was undimmed, however, so presumably none of the players ever made Ives feel unwelcome. The year 1899 saw the emergence of the 'real' Authors Eleven, unconnected to the Authors' Club, and Ives played for this side under Doyle's captaincy until 1911.

Ives's poetry dwells on the struggles of a loving soul to cope with the harshness of existence: he was a man badly in need of an anchor of stability, which cricket seems to have provided for him.[39] His diaries certainly suggest that cricket was essential for his mental health. On 16 September 1895, for instance, he wrote one of his frequent passages idealising suicide, addressing 'Beautiful Death'.[40] His emotional state was fragile after the conviction of his friend Oscar Wilde a few months earlier. Then three days later, on 19 September, Ives's next entry was a much heartier account of the first Authors' Club versus Press Club match the previous day. 'They have put the game in all the big "dailies" and the match was a great success in every way; we hope it will be an annual affair.'[41] Throughout the diary, cricket seemed to put him in a more practical state of mind; his cricket entries did not tend to be accompanied by his usual outpourings of tortured emotion.

Ives played other cricket, but he was highly strung and frequently ill at ease in company; among fellow-writers he clearly felt a sense of belonging and legitimacy, which other teams probably could not offer him.[42] He was not particularly close friends with the other Authors, and perhaps this separation between his inner life and his cricketing life was what enabled cricket to be a refuge for him. Nonetheless, the Authors network still brought him dividends: on 1 and 2 July 1902, he wrote entries from Esher, where he was playing for the Authors; he records a conversation with Doyle, who as Chairman of the Authors' Club tried to persuade him to rejoin.[43] A week later, Ives recorded excitedly, 'I have been asked to play in a first class match!! M.C.C. v. London

---

[39] Ives's poetry is almost unreadable now, but the opening verses of a poem called 'My Soul' are typical:

> On eddies swept along life's stream
> Now here, now there, upon its course
> Helpless as sleeper in a dream
> And rolled along with fearful force.
>
> And yet my little will is mine
> Though I be God's, my very all
> It sees, although it can't confine
> The torrent in its fool-tossed fall ...

George Ives, *Eros' Throne* (1900), 30.

[40] HRC, Ives Papers, Diaries, xxv, 64–5, 16 Sept. 1895.

[41] *Ibid.*, xxv, 70–1, 19 Sept. 1895.

[42] *Ibid.*, xxxix, 107, 23 June 1901: 'Meyrick-Jones made 64 the first day & 135 the next, but I fear he is not an author.' The implication that Meyrick-Jones was an outsider shows that Ives, by contrast, self-identified as an insider.

[43] *Ibid.*, xli, 69, 1 and 2 July 1902.

County; this is really amazing in my old age' – he was thirty-four – 'for I never dreamed to play in a 3 dayer in this world ...'[44] This was to be his only first-class match, and he clearly saw it as a highlight of his life.[45] Doyle was one of his MCC teammates in the match. Considering that Doyle had probably had more opportunity than other MCC players to observe Ives playing, and that the invitation came so soon after their latest weekend in Esher together, it seems likely that Doyle was instrumental in having his fellow Author selected for what Ives considered to be a great honour.

Ives's connection with cricket was closely tied to his adoption of an idealised form of Hellenism – the supposed values of Ancient Greece. Cook notes that according to Ives, the Greeks had prized athletic and intellectual vigour, aesthetic beauty – especially of the male physique – and simple, healthy living, to be identified with the countryside in opposition to the degraded modern city.[46] Ives declared that 'there seem only two great things in the world: Love and Nature', and he believed that the Greeks had got closer to these ultimate values than any other civilisation.[47] Ives's professed 'Hellenic' values were tied not only to his sexuality – an explicit link in his diaries, to the point that he used the word 'Greek' whenever he meant homosexual – but also to the appeal of cricket, especially literary cricket, which embodied them all.

Most telling of all is the entry for the 1898 Authors versus Press match. While batting, he caught a ball on the finger and split it open, not realising the damage until the blood started soaking through his glove and dripping onto his bat.

> They wanted me to go in 'my boy get it bandaged, said the umpire' [sic] but I kept at my post till the end because I am a soldier of the Faith, nor shall *we* mind hurt! *We* with the battles before us, with prison or death (oh may it be the latter, for Death is a dear lover of mine, near whom I had slept so often) in prospect, and the most glorious Cause for which ever poor misguided humanity fought. No, we must be above the terrors of the flesh, for the Faith's sake.[48]

Here, Ives presents us with a striking twist to the discourse that cricket was a test of courage and manly fraternity. He saw it as a chance to hone his spiritual resolve and physical hardiness, precisely because he was a persecuted gay man. The core elements of Ives's approach to cricket – treating it as an invigorating, soul-nourishing form of social occasion; bonding with fellow men with whom he formed an in-group; the prestige to be won from earning cricket honours; and a personal test of manliness and character – were all aspects that his team-mates would have recognised and with which they would have identified. But Ives was interpreting these values in his own idiosyncratic way, reimagining

---

[44] *Ibid.*, XLI, 72, 10 July 1902.
[45] *Ibid.*, XLI, 75–6, 16 and 17 July 1902.
[46] Cook, *London Homosexuality*, 122.
[47] HRC, Ives Papers, Diaries, XXV, 32, 10 Aug. 1895.
[48] *Ibid.*, XXXIII, 56–7, 16 Sept. 1898.

them so that they served his private, defiant homosexuality. By recasting literary cricket on his own terms, Ives was able to queer it and use it to buttress his own turbulent sense of identity.

E. W. Hornung: brokering cricket networks, reconceptualising the English gentleman

In September 1892, a fledgling writer called Ernest William Hornung (1866–1921) played in an early literary cricket side organised by Doyle. It was to have profound consequences for him: also attending that match was Doyle's sister Connie, who married Hornung twelve months later.[49] In the months after playing for Doyle's team, Doyle and Hornung became close friends; and in 1895, Doyle was made godfather to the Hornungs' only child, Arthur Oscar, who was named after him.[50] And while Doyle generally captained the Authors Eleven, Hornung was the team secretary, organising the fixtures. One teammate recorded:

> The most delightful of my London (or near-London) matches were those I played in for the Authors. The late E. W. Hornung, of 'Raffles' fame, arranged them and they were mostly played at Esher. I had seen a paragraph in the paper saying that Hornung was getting up a side of Authors to play against a side of Artists, so I wrote and asked whether he had room for me. I did not know him, but cricket is cricket.[51]

A reporter for *The Boy's Own Annual* in 1904 agreed that 'the team is really got up by E. W. Hornung', and some newspapers even called the side 'E. W. Hornung's XI'.[52] Hornung's scanty surviving correspondence bears this out. A postcard to Ives, in April 1904, reads: 'Esher Matches May 20 & 21. Please let me know that I may count on you for both. *E. W. Hornung*'.[53] In 1907, he wrote a letter to Elliott O'Donnell, a junior member of the network, in which O'Donnell's place in the side is linked to Hornung's willingness to do him a professional favour:

> I had hoped to get hold of your Book before this, or indeed I would have written sooner ... If I can do so with sincerity, I shall be only too glad to bring it (or cause it to be brought) before the notice of some theatrical manager. Could you bring a copy with you when you come to Esher? So far I have a full team for the first day but not for the second; but we may easily want to play twelve a side, either day; & then again it is

---

[49] 'The Literary Cricketers', *Morning Leader*, 7 Sept. 1892.
[50] Peter Rowland, *Raffles and his Creator* (1999), 97–8.
[51] Kinross, *Unconventional Cricketer*, 110.
[52] Thekla Bowser, 'Authors and Artists at Cricket', *Boy's Own Annual 1904*, xxvii. An example of 'E. W. Hornung's XI' may be found in *Cricket: A Weekly Record of the Game*, 25 May 1905, 18.
[53] Hornung to Ives, 18 April 1904, HRC, BSSR, 23.2.

only too likely that one or two will fail me at the last moment, so that I shall be very glad of a reserve man.[54]

(In the event, O'Donnell was to be disappointed: Hornung wrote apologetically a few months later to say that he thought the book's constantly changing scenery and copious bloodshed made it unsuitable for the theatre.)[55]

Hornung is nowhere referred to as the secretary of the Authors team; but this is certainly what he considered himself to be. He wrote a short story in 1912, 'The Power of the Game', about the secretary of a Surrey cricket club, who is responsible for setting up fixtures and assembling teams for them – just as Hornung had done for the Authors.[56] Hornung often included such autobiographical elements in his stories.[57] As his exchange with O'Donnell demonstrates, Hornung was positioned to act as a broker in an important section of the fragmented literary world, providing opportunities for networking and for taking part in culturally prestigious cricket events. The attendant publicity was a major part of the appeal of the Authors Eleven, as we may judge from a titbit of journalistic gossip in 1903: 'The authors played a cricket match at Esher last week, and they are very indignant that only one London paper sent a representative to describe their prowess. So an angry member of the team tells me.'[58] It was Hornung who dictated which writers made the team and therefore got exposure from this (normally) reliable source of public attention. In Bourdieu's terms, having established plenty of cultural and social capital for himself, he was in a position to bestow them upon other writers in turn. This is a striking degree of power for a man who has been very largely overlooked as a historical figure, and whose only biographer, Peter Rowland, believed Hornung scarcely played cricket at all.[59] Indeed, besides two books by Rowland, little has been written about Hornung; and Rowland's two principal claims, that he was gay (and in love with Oscar Wilde) and that he had a hostile relationship with his brother-in-law Doyle, are both undermined by the evidence of his Authors career.[60]

In the preface to a posthumous collection of Hornung stories, including three about cricket, Doyle recorded that Hornung

---

[54] Letter from Hornung to O'Donnell, 24 May 1907. Portsmouth City Council (Portsmouth), ACD1/G/4/7/20.

[55] Letter from Hornung to O'Donnell, 5 Aug. 1907. Portsmouth, ACD1/G/4/7/21.

[56] 'The Power of the Game', first published in *Bristol Times and Mirror*, 6 July 1912, 16.

[57] Malcolm Tozer, 'A Sacred Trinity – Cricket, School, Empire: E. W. Hornung and his Young Guard', in *The Cultural Bond: Sport, Empire, Society*, ed. J. A. Mangan (1992), 13.

[58] 'Our London Letter', *Derby Daily Telegraph*, 28 May 1903, 4.

[59] Rowland, *Raffles*, 157–8.

[60] *Ibid.*, 69–81, 160–2, 251. The diaries of George Ives show that he was keenly aware of suppressed homosexuality among his acquaintances, and as a devotee of Oscar Wilde, he would surely have noticed if Hornung felt similarly; but his diaries are devoid of any hint that Hornung was a potential recruit to Ives's 'Cause'. A rare mention of Hornung in the diaries is entirely neutral, noting a brief batting partnership that they shared at Esher (HRC, George Cecil Ives Papers, Diaries, x, 34, 1 June 1907). As for the fallout with Doyle, Rowland proves that they had their clashes; but his extrapolation that their relationship was constantly and irredeemably strained does not fit with their cheerful joint leadership of the Authors between 1899 and 1907.

was the best read man in cricket lore that I ever met, and would I am sure have excelled in the game himself if he had not been hampered by short sight and a villainous asthma. To see him stand up behind the sticks with his big pebble glasses to a fast bowler was an object lesson in pluck if not in wicket-keeping.[61]

Hornung's major literary contribution, begun in 1898, was the character of Raffles, a successful county cricketer who was secretly a thief. Raffles was perhaps the most famous fictional cricketer of the twentieth century. Andrew Lycett even suggests that Raffles's personality may have been modelled on Ives.[62] The Raffles stories were indebted, in both format and style, to Doyle. In 1891, Doyle had achieved his professional breakthrough with Sherlock Holmes after coming up with the idea of writing short stories in a series, rather than serials of single narratives across several issues. That is, the main characters were constant throughout the series, but each episode could stand alone as a complete story, saving readers the trouble of reading every instalment in order. Doyle claimed to have invented this genre: 'I was a revolutionist, and I think I may fairly claim to the credit of being the inaugurator of a system which has since been worked by others with no little success.'[63] One of the most successful of these others was his brother-in-law, whose Raffles stories became a sensation rivalling that of Holmes himself.[64] The first Raffles story was published by *Cassell's Magazine* in June 1898. Their impact on society was heightened by the moral shock caused by its attractive, yet villainous, antihero, and Hornung found himself 'positively notorious' for the stories' 'breathtaking audacity', breaking Victorian ethical taboos around storytelling.[65] Much of the shock value of the Raffles stories derived from the idea that a first-class cricketer, of all people, could be a crook – this at a time when 'cricket' was shorthand for the entire British value system of honour and integrity.[66]

The stories are narrated by Raffles's sidekick, Bunny, who is in awe of Raffles's brilliance and always a step or two behind his cunning mind; in this respect, they parallel – and cunningly subvert – the Watson–Holmes relationship. Nor is this unconscious or coincidental: the first edition of Raffles stories was dedicated by Hornung 'To A.C.D. This Form of Flattery',[67] and Doyle noted in his memoir that 'I think I may claim that his famous character Raffles was a kind of inversion of Sherlock Holmes, Bunny playing Watson. He admits as much in his kindly dedication.'[68] Hornung had written an earlier story, featuring the death of a well-educated criminal. In 1909 he claimed that Doyle had said to him, 'What a pity you killed that fellow! A public-school

---

[61] Doyle, Preface to E.W. Hornung, *Old Offenders and a few Old Scores* (London, 1923), vi–vii.

[62] Lycett, *Doyle*, 229.

[63] Quoted *ibid.*, 174. The quotation is from *Tit-Bits*, 15 Dec. 1900.

[64] Rowland, *Raffles*, 122, 176.

[65] *Ibid.*, 122.

[66] Nick Rance, 'The Immorally Rich and the Richly Immoral: Raffles and the Plutocracy', in *Twentieth-Century Suspense: The Thriller Comes of Age*, ed. Clive Bloom (1990), 4–5.

[67] Rowland, *Raffles*, 131.

[68] Doyle, *Memories and Adventures*, 259.

villain would be a new figure for a series. Why not revive him?'[69] This, according to Hornung, was the genesis of Raffles. Nor did the chain of cause-and-effect end there: Rowland writes that 'it is, certainly, generally acknowledged by his biographers that the decision to bring Holmes back to the land of the living, in *The Return of Sherlock Holmes* ... was prompted simply and solely by his jealousy of Hornung's success with A. J. Raffles.'[70]

Both of Raffles's epithets – 'the Amateur Cracksman' and 'the Gentleman Thief' – use a play on words to link his elite social rank to his upper-class status in cricket. Cricketers were either unpaid amateurs (also known as gentlemen), who were aestheticised as the game's heroic ideal, or professionals (also known as players), paid cricketers of lower social background and correspondingly of lower status. (The Authors were self-consciously proud of their amateur status.) Raffles demonstrates a suave superiority that comes with being an amateur, not a professional, cricketer; and he applies this to his criminal exploits too. A story in which Raffles is playing country-house cricket while outfoxing lower-class professional criminals, whom he scorns, is called 'Gentlemen and Players'.[71] Cricket's two-tier system is thus used as a metaphor to describe the social divide between the public-school thief and his rival professional burglars. By making Raffles a sportsman – a gentleman with an honour-bound code – as well as a thief, Hornung was both expanding and undermining the category of gentleman; a piece of subversion that had a troubling impact on the traditionally deferential Edwardian reading public.[72] Raffles and the Authors both laid claim to being part of the in-group of cricket's amateur tradition – yet Raffles posed a threat from the inside. Time and again, Raffles uses his social and cultural capital as a member of the English elite to pull off his escapades: the Raffles stories positively revel in the fact that he is able to do what a lower-class man could never get away with.[73] Interestingly, Raffles is a bowler, traditionally an art largely left to the professionals, while the heroic amateurs preferred to focus on batting, where more public glory was to be won.[74] Raffles's preference for bowling is a hint that there is something shady about him: Hornung depicts his bowling as a devious, cunning art, and Raffles openly admits that he uses this skill as a way for him to hone his kleptomaniac wits: another coded social statement.[75]

Cricket, in fact, infused Hornung's whole worldview, and is impossible to disentangle from his moral, political and religious beliefs. The scholarly

---

[69] Quoted in Jeremy Larance, 'The A. J. Raffles Stories Reconsidered: Fall of the Gentleman Ideal', *English Literature in Transition, 1880–1920*, 57 (2014), 101.

[70] Rowland, *Raffles*, 137–8.

[71] Hornung, 'Gentlemen and Players', in *Raffles*, 56–79.

[72] Larance, 'Raffles Reconsidered', 99–125.

[73] For instance, 'Wilful Murder' features a scene in which Bunny, Raffles and a friend of theirs from their club – who has just killed someone in a home invasion – make their getaway from the murder scene. Bunny notes with glee that nobody who saw these three well-bred gentlemen could have suspected a thing, or connected them to the crime. Hornung, *Raffles*, 116.

[74] Richard Holt, 'Cricket and Englishness: The Batsman as Hero', *International Journal of the History of Sport*, 13 (1996), 48–70.

[75] 'If you can bowl a bit your low cunning won't get rusty.' Hornung, 'Gentlemen and Players', in *Raffles*, 56.

literature of empire is of course vast, but to date, only one published essay acknowledges Hornung's value in providing a way of understanding Edwardian muscular Christianity. Malcolm Tozer demonstrates how public schools, cricket and empire were the three themes that obsessed Hornung; but this has not given Hornung the mainstream academic attention, as an emblematic Edwardian imperialist, that Tozer's conclusions suggest he deserves.[76] As Tozer recognises, Hornung was an advocate of muscular Christianity *par excellence* – a believer in Henry Newbolt's famous exhortation in the poem *Vitaï Lampada* to 'Play up! Play up! And play the game!'

The identification of cricket with empire was not automatic, and Bernard Porter has influentially challenged the view that interest in empire was hegemonic throughout British society.[77] Indeed, Ives's poetry shows him to have been an ardent critic of imperialism, calling it 'a Devil's gibe that might is right | And that the weak must go.'[78] But Hornung was more conventional and much more imperialist than his teammate. He enthusiastically subscribed to the then-popular view of cricket as an ideal way for Englishmen – especially schoolboys – to enact society's desired values: it was seen to demonstrate manliness and facilitate male bonding.[79] His last significant work of fiction, *Fathers of Men*, was about the life of a boarding school based on his own, Uppingham.[80] True to the genre, its climactic scene was a cricket match.[81] This book reflected Hornung's real-world pedagogical activities. In the years following the Boer War of 1899–1902, Hornung preached Sunday sermons in schools, very much in Newbolt's vein – sometimes using the metaphor of 'the Game of Life', in which life itself was a cricket match.[82] Often he urged the schoolboys to be willing to die for their country, as some of their predecessors had done in South Africa.[83] Hornung even had Raffles redeem himself in this very way: the gentleman thief died a patriotic death in the Boer War, reeling off cricket analogies in his final gunfight. 'I can't see where that one pitched; it may have been a wide; and it's very nearly the end of the over again.'[84]

On 5 July 1914 – a week after Archduke Franz Ferdinand's assassination – Hornung gave a sermon at Stone House School called 'The Game of Life', in which his three lifelong passions – cricket, empire and religion – were conflated into a single ideal of an English life worth living.

The word 'sportsman', as we use it among ourselves, has come to signify every virtue which is dearest to our hearts. Courage, honesty,

---

[76] Tozer, 'A Sacred Trinity', 11–26.

[77] Bernard Porter, *The Absent-Minded Imperialists: Empire, Society, and Culture in Britain* (Oxford, 2004).

[78] Ives, 'A Song of Empire', in *Eros' Throne*, 35.

[79] Keith A. P. Sandiford, 'England', in *The Imperial Game: Cricket, Culture and Society*, ed. Brian Stoddard and Keith Sandiford (Manchester, 1998), 14–16.

[80] Hornung, *Fathers of Men* (1912).

[81] Tozer, 'A Sacred Trinity', 16.

[82] Shane Chichester (ed.), *E. W. Hornung and his Young Guard, 1914* (Crowthorne, 1941).

[83] *Ibid.*, 15–16.

[84] Hornung, *Raffles*, 216.

unselfishness, chivalry, you can't be a sportsman without all these; and if you *have* all of those, you *must* be a good man. This ideal – this sporting and game-playing ideal – this end and aim and excuse and justification for all the games and sport that they say we think too much about in England – has been finely expressed by one or two of our modern poets ... Who wants an easy victory? Who wants a life of full-pitches to leg? Do you think the Great Scorer is going to give you four runs every time for those? I believe with all my heart and soul that in this splendidly difficult Game of Life it is just the cheap and easy triumphs which will be written in water on the score sheet. And the way we played for our side, in the bad light, on the difficult pitch; the way we backed up and ran the other man's runs; our courage and unselfishness, not our skill or our success ... surely, surely, it is these things above all other that will count, when the innings is over, in the Pavilion of Heaven.[85]

In this and other sermons, Hornung showed how – for him – Christianity, imperialism and cricket were, symbolically, so closely linked as to be almost interchangeable; and they were all tied to a fervent Englishness. For Hornung, ultimately, cricket was subordinate to its greater task, the making of good Englishmen who would die for the empire. And it is essential that we view Hornung's interest in cricket as that of a *performer* – a player in, and an organiser of, matches – rather than as an observer. Hornung was not treating cricket as a convenient analogy that reduced cricket to little more than a text to be read. If we return to Doyle's description of Hornung's cricket as 'an object lesson in pluck', we can recognise that Hornung was physically experiencing the very rhythms of cricket-playing – and enduring the accompanying risk of pain and injury – that he was championing as central to the formation of English gentlemen. He was also serving as the gatekeeper to a prestigious literary coterie that found its form in the Authors Eleven: a broker of social capital. And Hornung's piquant takes on Englishness and gentlemanly values were indeed bolstered by his performing them on the cricket field, before he widely disseminated his attitudes via Raffles and his school sermons. By overlooking Hornung's cricket-playing, Tozer fails to see the form in which Hornung, literally, practised what he preached. A greater understanding of Hornung, his writing, and his use of cricket for a variety of purposes, suggests that he would merit a centre-stage role in studies of Edwardian attitudes towards their social bonds and obligations, as well as towards imperialism and 'manliness'.

For soldiers steeped in Hornung's way of thinking, war sometimes *felt* like cricket – perhaps not often, and not for long, but it helps us recognise that the blurring of cricketing and martial imagery in Hornung's writings was more than just a literary conceit. This is evident in the letters of Hornung's only child Oscar – Doyle's nephew and godson – who fulfilled his father's exhortations with terrible exactness. His high-spirited letters during the First World War showed that he thoroughly subscribed to his father's view

---

[85] Chichester, *Young Guard*, 31–7.

of warfare in the name of England. In early 1915, Hornung wrote a poem called *Lord's Leave*, in which the Western Front is depicted in cricket terms, with the German guns aiming at English 'stumps'.[86] Oscar was working on poetry too: a poem about his prep school, reflecting on the alumni who had fallen in the Boer War – a favourite theme of his father's. The surviving fragments show his filial resolve to 'die as they did, by their schoolboy honour aided'.[87] On 19 June, Oscar wrote to his father that he had been given '*new Hand-bombs – glorious things, just* the size and weight of a *Cricket Ball!*' The previous night, he had led three men on a raid to throw them into the German trench opposite.

> I led off with cricket-ball No. 1 – it was just like 'throwing in' from 'cover' (a fast long hop!) – only this time I had 'some' batsmen to run out and there was a price on those stumps! ... The others then stood up and 'threw in' – the wicket-keep put them down nicely – and we made haste back to the Pavilion! – it *was* a case of 'appealing against the light' – for it was 1.30 A.M. by then and getting uncomfortably light.[88]

This eerily echoes Raffles's last words; and it shows that cricket was not just a tenuous symbolic analogy for war: for participants like Oscar Hornung, the fighting really could remind them of the game they loved. In Oscar's case, this letter is especially poignant: just two weeks later, on 6 July, he was killed. Muscular Christianity had come up against the realities of twentieth-century warfare.

P. G. Wodehouse: building a literary career through playing cricket

P. G. Wodehouse (1881–1975) remains one of the greatest-ever comic writers in the English language. An avid Doyle fan from boyhood, Wodehouse met his hero through the Authors Eleven, debuting in May 1903 at one of the matches organised by Hornung. Within a couple of years, he received invitations to stay at Doyle's house in order to play more cricket together.[89] Wodehouse was always clear that 'I knew him [Doyle] through playing cricket with him.'[90] And he was disarmingly frank about how he used this cricketing connection to advance his own reputation. On 9 August 1912, when Wodehouse was visiting England from his new base in the USA, he wrote to Doyle shortly before they both appeared in an Authors versus Publishers match:

> Dear Comrade Doyle,
>   Will you stand by me in a crisis? A New York lady journalist, a friend of

---

[86] *Ibid.*, 27–8.

[87] E. W. Hornung, *'Trusty and Well Beloved': The Little Record of Arthur Oscar Hornung, Second Lieutenant, 3rd (attached 2nd) Essex Regiment* (privately printed, 1915), 64.

[88] *Ibid.*, 39–40.

[89] N. T. P. Murphy, *A Wodehouse Handbook: The World and Words of P. G. Wodehouse* (2nd edn, 2013 [2006]), 92, 217.

[90] Sophie Ratcliffe (ed.), *P. G. Wodehouse: A Life in Letters* (2011), 517.

mine, is gunning for you. She said 'You know Conan Doyle, don't you?' I said, 'I do. It is my only claim to fame'. She then insisted on my taking her to see you at Crowborough, and mentioned next Sunday, the 11th. Can you stand this invasion? ... (I have traded so much in America on my friendship with you that my reputation will get a severe jolt if you refuse it!)

... I was glad to see you on form with the bat the other day. I hope we shall smash the publishers.

Yours ever

P. G. Wodehouse[91]

This networking aspect must have been a major part of the Authors' appeal for Wodehouse and many of his teammates. As with Ives and Hornung, he would have seen his role in the team in the 1900s as an essential component of his social status. Not only was he now friends with famous and influential writers, but participation in the team gave him a chance to play cricket matches at the prestigious Lord's – against similarly famous and influential actors. For Wodehouse and others, literary cricket meant prestige and valuable contacts – being part of the in-group. This gives a very different picture of the man from the traditional image of a shy, unworldly oddball – an image constructed in later life by Wodehouse himself, and one which has proved difficult to overturn.[92]

But it was not just about networking: the topic of cricket had an overlooked significance to his early career, and this was influenced by the Authors. In 1900, when Wodehouse finished at Dulwich College, his father announced that he could not afford to send him to Oxford or Cambridge as expected, so he had found his son a job at the Hong Kong and Shanghai Bank instead.[93] Determined not to become a banker, Wodehouse began seriously to pursue a sideline in writing.[94] From the time he started at the bank in September 1900, he kept a notebook recording his monthly earnings as a writer.[95] Cricket was the core of his early output, Wodehouse having won a prize for an article called 'Some Aspects of Game-Captaincy' in February 1900; the article was published in the *Public School Magazine* (*PSM*). That September, his second publication, also for *PSM*, was likewise on cricket: 'Wrote a short article on cricket at Malvern. Price 10/6. Paid December 21st.' His October 1900 entry reads: 'Articles on "Football at Dulwich" and "School Cricket of 1900" (Both 10/6) for the "Public School Magazine".' From this foothold on sports topics in *PSM*, Wodehouse gradually established himself as a freelance writer, specialising in school stories and especially in cricket. In September 1901, for instance, he recorded that he had sold 'Cricket at Dulwich' and 'Cricket in Retrospect' to *PSM*. Though boxing, athletics and rugby also featured prominently – likewise

[91] *Ibid.*, 83.
[92] Barry Phelps, *P. G. Wodehouse: Man and Myth* (1992), 17–25.
[93] Robert McCrum, *Wodehouse: A Life* (2004), 37–41.
[94] Murphy, *Wodehouse Handbook*, 65.
[95] Wodehouse notebook 1900–8, BL, Wodehouse Collection, Loan MS 129/1/104.

dependent on Wodehouse's first-hand experiences – Wodehouse wrote in 1901 that for him, 'cricket ranked a long way in front of all other forms of sport'.[96] By 1902, he was publishing a few pieces a month, including a regular column at the *Globe*.[97] In September 1902 he published his first book, *The Pothunters*, whose plot concerned the mysterious burglary of a public-school cricket pavilion.[98] That same month he quit the bank, and began publishing in *Punch*. He later wrote to Owen Seaman, in 1902 the *Punch* Assistant Editor, to say that 'I shall always feel that you gave me the first leg-up'.[99] Seaman was one of the organisers of literary cricket sides, and probably introduced Wodehouse to the Authors.[100]

After debuting for the Authors on 22 May 1903, he played in almost every subsequent pre-war Authors match, even after he had moved to America. On 27 May, *Punch* published a lyric by Wodehouse foretelling the resurrection of Sherlock Holmes.[101] Doyle was indeed working on some new Holmes stories at the time, despite having apparently killed him off in *The Final Problem*. Wodehouse had evidently discovered this at Esher, and promptly used the information to publish a humorous scoop in *Punch*.[102] Just over a month later, an interview of Doyle, conducted by Wodehouse and including cricket references, was published in *V.C. Magazine*.[103] At the time, Wodehouse kept notebooks, titled *Phrases and Notes*, in which he jotted down ideas for stories, dialogue and so on; these notebooks, covering 1902–5, only became publicly accessible when a transcription was published in 2014. In the weeks immediately after his Authors debut, his notebook fills with suggestive cricket-themed entries. One of these unambiguously shows that Wodehouse was imagining ways in which his literary cricket connections could benefit his career:

Mems for 'Punch'

   a) Man who made money by selling literary ideas & titles to authors eg 'Man with the Single Spat' to Conan Doyle. (Might bring this into 'Lodgings in Belgravia')
   b) Advice to Journalists: (Story book) (eg playing v editor in cricket match & bowling to suit him if he'll take article, or offering to run him out).
   c) Song of the Bat.[104]

These jottings pertaining to cricket dominate Wodehouse's notebook for the three months following his Authors debut. Either Wodehouse's appearance

[96] P. G. Wodehouse, *Tales of St. Austin's* (1903), 151.

[97] Wodehouse notebook 1900–8, BL, Wodehouse Collection, Loan MS 129/1/104.

[98] P. G. Wodehouse, *The Pothunters* (1902).

[99] John Adlard, *Owen Seaman: His Life and Work* (1977), 88.

[100] Frankfort Moore, 'More "Old Bangor"', *North Down Herald and County Down Independent*, 20 Oct. 1923, 1.

[101] Telfer, *Pan's XI*, 189; 'Back to His Native Strand', *Punch*, 124 (27 May 1903), 368.

[102] Adlard, *Seaman*, 66–7, 88.

[103] Phelps, *Wodehouse*, 70.

[104] *Phrases and Notes: P. G. Wodehouse's Notebooks, 1902–1905*, ed. N. T. P. Murphy (2014), 39.

for the Authors had directly inspired him to dream about cricket stories; or the two things coincided to a remarkably precise degree. Several jottings relate to a precocious cricketer called 'Young Sammy', who appears to be an embryonic version of his famous character Mike (see below). As such, it was from this fertile period of cricket-related creativity in 1903 that Wodehouse formed one of his most influential literary creations.

A *Punch* article that September showed that the joint themes of cricket and English literature were still in his thoughts: he wrote a mock-proposal for a play about an Ashes cricket match. This included an extract parodying Shakespearean language:

Bowler:	Meseemed I heard a click, and lo! the ball
	Rests safely in the wicket-keeper's hands.
	Umpire, how *was* that?
Hero:	Stay, Sir Umpire, stay,
	Nor give your fell decision ere you've heard me.
	I swear by * * * *
	I touched it not. Two inches clear – and more –
	Inside it did I play; the click you heard
	Was but the grass, or else perchance the strap,
	The leathern strap that girds my snowy pad,
	Which, flapping two and fro beneath the breath
	Of Zephyrus, produced a bat-like sound.[105]

That same September, *Punch* published another comic Wodehouse cricket piece, called 'The Cricketer in Winter'.[106]

Wodehouse's career soon benefitted not just from the inspiration that the Authors provided, but from the contacts he made on the team. In October 1903, Wodehouse started a new school serial in *The Captain* which would be published in 1904 as *The Gold Bat*. This novel, with a cricket reference in its title, starred a rule-breaking schoolboy who was a devotee of Hornung's *Raffles* stories.[107] It was gushingly reviewed by Wodehouse's Authors teammate, E. V. Lucas, in an anonymous *Times Literary Supplement* column: 'No writer of school tales has so much vigour and realistic spirit as Mr. P. G. Wodehouse.'[108] This review was an important milestone for Wodehouse's reputation: schoolboy magazines were not normally a route to literary recognition. In 1906, he published 'A Benefit Match', a cricket story illustrated by George Hillyard Swinstead, another Authors teammate.[109]

---

[105] 'My Cricket Drama', *Punch*, 125 (2 Sept. 1903), 161.
[106] 'The Cricketer in Winter', *Punch*, 125 (30 Sept. 1903), 230.
[107] P. G. Wodehouse, *The Gold Bat* (2nd edn, 1974 [1904]), 23.
[108] Jonathan Wild, *Literature of the 1900s: The Great Edwardian Emporium* (Edinburgh, 2017), 107.
[109] Wodehouse, 'A Benefit Match', *Windsor*, 24 (1906), 330–6.

In all, Wodehouse published seven books of school stories between 1902 and 1909, collected from his magazine serialisations.[110] Six of these were published while he was playing regularly for the Authors. Cricket is a major staple of these books – a fact that has been taken for granted in the little that has been written on them.[111] In *Phrases and Notes*, Wodehouse's 'school story' ideas are almost all about cricket. In Wodehouse's mind, the one meant the other. *Tales of St. Austin's*, published in November 1903, exemplifies this. It consists of twelve short stories (no fewer than nine of which mention cricket or have cricket plots) and four humorous essays, of which cricket is central to three. In an essay entitled 'Now, Talking About Cricket –' Wodehouse insists that cricket is much more than a game, and with cheerful hyperbole he looks forward to the day when it is treated with appropriate reverence and 'becomes a religious ceremony'.[112] In another piece, deploring schools' focus on classical languages rather than sport, Wodehouse humorously laments,

> Our bright-eyed lads are taught insane constructions in Greek and Latin from morning till night, and they come from their holidays, in many cases, without the merest foundation of a batting style. Ask them what a Yorker is, and they will say: 'A man from York' ... When we get schools that teach nothing but games, then will the sun definitely refuse to set on the roast beef of old England. May it be soon.[113]

Tales of St. Austin's illustrates how rich a theme cricket was in Wodehouse's capable hands, and the extent to which it underpinned his major early successes.

Jonathan Wild posits that these stories' vivacity – their slicker, more realistic depiction of public-school life, and their effective deployment of boys' slang for verisimilitude and humour – made them a fundamental contribution to the development of the 'school story' genre. The genre's earnestness and piety since *Tom Brown's Schooldays* had gone stale, and Wodehouse's updates reinvigorated the formula. His refreshing innovations, Wild argues, directly influenced subsequent writers of the genre – especially the hugely prolific Frank Richards, the most important writer of school stories of the twentieth century.[114] In this case, school stories shaped by Wodehouse's modernising style were to be read by millions of boys and girls at a formative age for the next half-century.[115]

---

[110] Wild, *Edwardian Emporium*, 104.

[111] See for instance Tony Ring and Geoffrey Jaggard, *Wodehouse Goes to School* (1997).

[112] Wodehouse, *St. Austin's*, 155.

[113] *Ibid.*, 136–7.

[114] Wild, *Edwardian Emporium*, 104–10.

[115] Kelly Boyd, *Manliness and the Boys' Story Paper in Britain: A Cultural History, 1855–1940* (Basingstoke, 2003), passim.; Eric Midwinter, *His Captain's Hand on his Shoulder Smote: The Incidence and Influence of Cricket in Schoolboy Stories* (2019), 56–62, 106–24. This argument has an intriguing implication. If Wodehouse's school stories were instrumental in shaping the national consciousness along the lines of *Tom Brown's Schooldays*, training the British public to respond to stories in which a boy begins to attend a prestigious, storied boarding school; makes friends, absorbs values of fairness and loyalty, and learns to love the school; finds a wise mentor and/or

In 1907 Wodehouse began a serialisation in *The Captain* starring a schoolboy cricketing prodigy, renamed from 'Young Sammy' to Mike Jackson. *Mike*, about the teenage hero's experiences at two public schools, was first published in book-form in 1909; it was the last and greatest of Wodehouse's school stories, and he later said it was his favourite among his writings.[116] *Mike* was the most important of the dozens of schoolboy stories that were saturating the child-hood imaginations of the age; C. L. R. James, the West Indian nationalist and first-class cricketer, bears this out by singling out *Mike* as one of the formative influences during his Caribbean childhood.[117] Strikingly, *Mike*'s contemporary literary references are exclusively about Wodehouse's fellow-Authors. There is an extended passage in which Mike, having sneaked out of bed in his board-ing house, identifies himself with the roguish Raffles; at another point, the appearance of Mike's new housemaster 'reminded Mike of Smee in *Peter Pan*'.[118] Wodehouse's best lampooning of his teammates is given to Mike's antagonist, Mr Downing: confronted with mysterious rule-breaking, the schoolmaster is upset to discover how much worse a detective he is than Sherlock Holmes, and begins 'to feel a certain resentment against Sir Arthur Conan Doyle'.[119] (The perpetrator turns out to be a former pupil who had returned for a cricket match.) Wodehouse enjoyed sending up his literary hero and teammate. He later wrote, 'It is with the feeling that he would not object that I have sometimes amused myself by throwing custard pies at that great man.'[120] A Wodehouse biographer observes that 'The influence of Doyle, particularly the Holmes stories, permeates the Wodehouse canon'[121] – and certainly his stories contain countless Holmes references.

Mike's second outing as protagonist (or joint-protagonist, with his friend Psmith) was serialised in 1908–9 and published in 1910, under the title *Psmith in the City*.[122] The links to Wodehouse's life are obvious. The book opens with Mike participating in a cricket week hosted by Psmith's father. Wodehouse, especially early in his career, tended to write only about what he knew, and the only cricket weeks which Wodehouse is known to have attended were those hosted by Doyle in 1905 and 1906.[123] Mike, like Wodehouse, is then informed by his father that he will not be going to Oxford or Cambridge, and instead must begin work at the New Asiatic Bank (plainly based on Wodehouse's Hong Kong and Shanghai Bank). The book fea-tures the struggles of Mike and Psmith against the tyranny of the bank, and reaches a climax with Mike finding himself playing cricket at Lord's itself;

---

a mean-spirited antagonist among the teaching staff; and becomes a school hero through his feats for his boarding house in a ball game ... then Wodehouse played a part in creating a culture that was primed to be receptive to Harry Potter.

[116] Hedgcock, 'Introduction', 33; Midwinter, *His Captain's Hand*, 60–2.

[117] Midwinter, *His Captain's Hand*, 56–60; C. L. R. James, *Beyond a Boundary* (1963), 35.

[118] P. G. Wodehouse, *Mike* (2nd edn, 1924 [1909]), 31, 177.

[119] *Ibid.*, 269–70.

[120] Murphy, 'Appendix', in *Phrases and Notes*, 203.

[121] Phelps, *Wodehouse*, 71.

[122] Wodehouse, *Psmith in the City* (1910).

[123] Murphy, *Wodehouse Handbook*, 92; *Sportsman*, 9 Aug. 1905, 2.

something which Wodehouse, thanks to the Authors, had experienced several times. The story ends with Mike – like Wodehouse – triumphantly leaving the bank to pursue his dream: in this case, cricket rather than writing. The stories about Mike are clearly a blend of Wodehouse's fantasies about cricketing brilliance, and his real-life experiences, first at a public school, then at a bank, and finally his cricket exploits with the Authors.

No work to date has explored in such depth the centrality of cricket to Wodehouse's early writing. Murray Hedgcock came closest, in the introduction to a slim collection of Wodehouse's cricket writings.[124] However, Hedgcock's approach is breezy and superficial – he is introducing an anthology, not producing scholarly work – and although he discusses the Authors, he does not speculate on their influence on Wodehouse's cricket writings. Nor did he have access to Wodehouse's *Phrases and Notes*. N. T. P. Murphy, the Wodehouse expert who edited *Phrases and Notes*, refers to Wodehouse's life from 1900 to 1914 as 'the Hidden Years'.[125] Murphy, like other recent writers on Wodehouse, cites Hedgcock on Wodehouse cricket matters, without modifying or building on Hedgcock's account.[126] And yet a reassessment of Wodehouse's literary relationship with cricket opens up interesting historiographical opportunities. For instance, Wodehouse's early career provides striking evidence of cricket's central place in the ideology of the public school.[127] Where Hornung's 'sacred trinity' was school, cricket and empire, Wodehouse's was school, cricket and humour: the two writers have not been compared before, despite their being teammates.

The cricket writings were not the only Wodehouse stories to have been influenced by his involvement in the Authors. Of much larger cultural significance was the Authors' contribution to Wodehouse's greatest creation, Jeeves and Wooster. Wodehouse stated that the indomitable valet Jeeves was named after a cricketer, Percy Jeeves, whom he had seen playing in a county match in around 1912, and who was killed in the First World War.[128] This is well known; but the connection actually goes much deeper. Commenting on this, Murphy has written, 'Arthur Conan Doyle once told Wodehouse that he liked naming his characters after professional cricketers, and a Sherlock Holmes Society member has since informed me that Doyle used this method to name 240 of his 300 characters.'[129] As for the inspiration for Jeeves's personality, Murphy's suggestions include Barrie's real-life butler Thurston; Barrie's fictional character Crichton from *The Admirable Crichton*; and two of Doyle's characters – Ambrose in *Rodney Stone* and Austin in *Poison Belt*.[130] When we consider that Doyle claims *The Admirable Crichton* was itself inspired by a conversation he had had with Barrie, and that Barrie, Doyle and Wodehouse all met one

---

[124] Murray Hedgcock, 'Introduction', in Wodehouse, *Wodehouse at the Wicket* (1997), 25–33.
[125] Murphy, 'Foreword', in *Phrases and Notes*, v.
[126] Murphy, 'Appendix', in *Phrases and Notes*, 202.
[127] Bateman, *Cricket, Literature and Culture*, 31–4; Birley, *Social History*, ix.
[128] Hedgcock, 'Introduction', 38.
[129] Murphy, *Wodehouse Handbook*, 128.
[130] *Ibid.*, 129.

another through literary cricket, Jeeves's credentials as an Authors creation are very strong indeed.[131]

And then there is the fact that the early Jeeves stories use the short-story-series format pioneered by Doyle and borrowed by Hornung. When one sets Jeeves and Wooster alongside Holmes and Watson and – especially – Raffles and Bunny, the parallels are striking. Given Wodehouse's willingness to draw from his Authors teammates and yet treat them with irreverence, Jeeves looks very like a parody of Holmes and Raffles. In all three cases, the plodding narrator exists to bear witness to the brilliant mental feats and deft, bold problem-solving of the heroes. The three narrators provide Holmes, Raffles and Jeeves with an aura of wonder and respect, by emphasising to the reader how much they themselves marvel at their remarkable companions. The joke, of course, is that whereas Watson and Bunny are in awe of someone who is roughly their social equal, Bertie Wooster is in awe of someone who is not merely his social inferior but actually his servant. It is inconceivable that Wodehouse designed the structure of his Jeeves and Wooster stories without thinking of Doyle and Hornung, two of the most high-profile writers during his London writing career, and two of his most valuable contacts. This wealth of circumstantial evidence underlines the case that the Authors Eleven provided crucial context for the creation of the immortal characters Jeeves and Wooster.

Conclusion: New Perspectives on Cultural and Intellectual History

Cricket was central to the worldviews exhibited by Ives, Hornung and Wodehouse. The sport's embodied sociability – the particular nature of the activity that brought these men together – fed into the patterns of their lives and the way they understood themselves, their friendships and their place in society. It is evident that there was a two-way connection between their intellectual work and their cricketing activities. The Authors Eleven helped them get on in the literary world, and influenced their sense of literary mission. Above all, cricket helped all three men negotiate in-groups within Edwardian England's hierarchical, homosocial culture: it provided them with cultural and social capital that smoothed the way for them. Hornung, as a pros-elytiser for empire and for public schools, as well as in his role as the secretary of the Authors, happily exploited cricket's ability to forge such in-groups, working as a broker of social capital. Meanwhile, Ives and Wodehouse – who, at the start of their Authors careers, were outsiders in the literary world – both relished associating themselves with the in-groups that their cricket enthusiasm allowed them to access. All three saw their involvement in cricket as an essential component of their place in the social order. Neither the networking and publicity opportunities of the Authors Eleven, nor the vivid experiential relationship with cricket that was critical to these men's outlooks and aspects of their literary production, would have been achievable had they confined themselves to watching and reading about the

---

[131] Telfer, *Pan's XI*, 167.

game. For them, cricket was no mere repository of symbols: it was an intense physical and social experience.

It is worth stressing that the three men regularly played in the same eleven: between 1903 and 1907, all three were part of the Authors' annual weekend at Esher for five years in a row.[132] Not only does this demonstrate how well they knew each other, it also underlines the fact that their different conceptions of cricket were often in relation to the very same matches. Literary cricket matches were dense with cultural significance, interpreted by participants in varying ways. Yet for all of them, playing literary cricket had an important role in their social networks, their sense of identity and the outlook that shaped their written work.

And this pattern was not confined to these three alone – it was repeated throughout the Authors Eleven. For example, A. A. Milne – who played for the Authors between 1907 and 1909 on the strength of his *Punch* contributions – published his first proper book in 1910, full of humorous vignettes about organising a cricket team of his own. Milne sent a copy of the book to J. M. Barrie, who had retired from literary cricket in 1905; Barrie wrote back enthusiastically, having enjoyed the cricket passages, and symbolically appointed Milne the 'last member' of his defunct team.[133] When Barrie's literary cricket side was resurrected for a one-off match in 1913, Milne played in it.[134] Barrie then championed Milne's fledgling dramaturgical career while the younger man was serving in the First World War, arranging for a one-act Milne play to be performed with two of his own as a triple-bill.[135] Barrie was probably the highest-profile playwright in the country at the time, and Milne's literary career took off from there; a few years later, he created Winnie the Pooh. Barrie's mentorship of Milne was inspired by a shared interest in cricket as well as writing, and was then established on a firm footing through the ritual of a literary cricket match. Milne benefitted professionally from the social opening this gave him, as his cricket captain became a powerful professional asset. Once again, we see how the playing of cricket – and the sense of being teammates with fellow literary cricketers – had an important role in the development of a writing career.

All this has implications far beyond the borders of sports history. In the cases of Ives, Hornung and Wodehouse – not to mention Doyle, Barrie, Milne and others – literary cricket is a valuable analytical perspective that advances our understanding of these men and their intellectual development. We have seen how literary cricket helped Ives shape his self-identity at a critical moment in the history of British queer identity-forming; how Hornung saw cricket as central to his belief system about British gentlemanly behaviour; and how Wodehouse's cricket-playing was intertwined with his early writing career. Yet the Authors Eleven is just one example of the value of cricket as an angle of historical inquiry, and cricket itself is just one example (albeit a

---

[132] 'Authors', https://cricketarchive.com/archive/teams (accessed 27 Feb. 2024).

[133] A. A. Milne, *It's Too Late Now: The Autobiography of a Writer* (1939), 203–4.

[134] Denis Mackail, *The Story of J. M. B. (Sir James Barrie, Bart., O.M.)* (1941), 457.

[135] Milne, *Too Late Now*, 207–8, 223–6.

particularly rich one) of the sports and physical activities which have been essential parts of the lives of so many intellectual figures. Doubtless there is more to uncover here. Other sports teams may or may not be identified which exerted similar influences over other networks of prominent intellectual figures. Either way, the methodology of this study also has a much broader application. It shows how social, personal and lifestyle factors can all provide fresh avenues for investigating cultural and intellectual history. Scholarly focus on texts has come to obscure the material and social contexts in which they were produced. To understand intellectual figures from Doyle to Wodehouse and far beyond, we cannot rely solely on what they wrote: we must also imaginatively reconstruct their wider experiences, including the recreations that occupied so much of their time and energies. It is a mistake to gloss over the ways in which they spent this time, on the basis that their leisure pursuits were simply forms of relaxation. Instead, these same forms of relaxation should be interrogated as integral parts of our subjects' lives and outlooks. Team sports such as cricket make the case particularly clearly, but the point holds true across the whole spectrum of recreational activities, from Britten's tennis to Gladstone's tree-felling.[136] There is plenty of scope to examine these activities anew: scholars who do so will no doubt identify links between people's hobbies and their social and professional networks; and they will surely also find new connections between their subjects' lived experiences and written output.

This article has revealed some of the benefits of reconceptualising sport as a pervasive cultural practice rather than an unserious diversion. It has also demonstrated the value of re-examining the links between individuals' intellectual, social and physical activities. By doing so, we can advance the current effort to update our image of the desk-bound intellectual by expanding our appreciation of how their minds worked. Historical figures' recreations, their social networks and their bodily experiences – all relevant to a cricket match – are vital parts of this more rounded understanding.

Acknowledgements. My thanks to Abi Dalby-Bowler, Tim Deamer, Sarah Limb, Sarah Mansfield and (especially) Paul Readman, as well as my two anonymous referees, for comments and pointers on earlier versions of this article. This work was made possible by funding from the London Arts and Humanities Partnership.

---

[136] Peter Sewter, 'Gladstone as Woodsman', in *William Gladstone: New Studies and Perspectives*, ed. Roland Quinault, Roger Swift and Ruth Clayton Windscheffel (Farnham, 2012), 155–75.

Cite this article: Randall O (2024). Cricket, Literary Culture and In-Groups in Early Twentieth-Century Britain. *Transactions of the Royal Historical Society* 2, 267–291. https://doi.org/10.1017/S0080440124000057

Transactions of the RHS (2024), **2**, 293–316
doi:10.1017/S0080440124000045

ARTICLE

'Providing a Layman's Guide to the Scheme': Museum Computing, Professional Personas and Documentary Labour in the United Kingdom, 1967–1983

James Baker

School of Humanities, University of Southampton, Southampton, UK
Email: j.w.baker@soton.ac.uk

(Received 26 February 2024; revised 22 May 2024; accepted 22 May 2024;
first published online 9 September 2024)

Abstract

Between the 1960s and early-1980s the museum sector in the United Kingdom (UK) was rapidly professionalised and systematised. A crucial moment in this transition was the creation in 1967 of the Information Retrieval Group of the Museums Association (IRGMA), and the subsequent launch of its system for the machine encoding and communication of museum catalogue records. The rise of IRGMA marked an inflection point in museological practice and the normalisation of computerised work within the UK museum profession, a moment when the desire for a 'layman's guide to the scheme' began to give way to new professional personas and forms of documentary labour. This article asks how cultures of museology and professional labour shifted in response to IRGMA. It argues that between the late 1960s and mid-1980s both the implementation of and the debate around computerised cataloguing disrupted the function of UK museums and how museum professionals imagined their labour. And by tracing the emergence of these cultures and their intersections with professional identity and labour practices, this article seeks to tease out the ways museum history can resonate with wider narratives of labour, expertise and technological innovation in contemporary British history.

Keywords: museums; computerisation; professions; twentieth-century Britain; labour

The pilot project to test the communications format, for which OSTI [Office of Scientific and Technical Information] has awarded a grant of £7,000 over two years, was started in October. It is hoping to issue shortly a further IRGMA newsletter outlining progress and providing a layman's guide to the scheme.

Annual Report of the Museums Association, 1971[1]

The modern museum as a space of objects, 'civilised' education and imperial authority is an idea entangled with and bound to enlightenment values,[2] and since its conception those motivated by the ideal of the modern museum have constructed and curated information about the collections under their custodianship. In the early- to mid- twentieth century, the tags, registers, labels and catalogue cards that comprised museum documentation tended to centre the needs of individual collectors, cataloguers and scholar curators, and the labour that produced documentation was often fulfilled by volunteers or clerical assistants. Between the 1960s and early 1980s the museum sector in the United Kingdom (UK) was rapidly professionalised and systematised,[3] and following significant debate,[4] documentation and the projection of 'scientific information' came to be considered among the primary functions of UK museums. This function served institutions and their staff,[5] as well as fulfilling a need for museums to demonstrate accountability for the collections in their care to those local, regional and national authorities that funded their activities.[6] In turn, new sub-professions emerged to administer these new functions. Computerisation was a feature of this period of professionalisation and

---

[1] The National Archives of the UK (TNA), HK 1/14 (Museums Association: Annual Reports), 1971.

[2] Carol Duncan, *Civilizing Rituals: Inside Public Art Museums* (1995).

[3] Helen Wilkinson, '"The Dawning of Professionalism": Constructing the UK Museum Profession in the 1970s and 1980s', *Enquire*, 5 (2012), 49–59.

[4] C. C. Paine, 'Recording Forms', *Museums Journal*, 70 (1970), 28; Jiří Neustupný, 'What is Museology?', *Museums Journal*, 71 (1971), 67–8.

[5] This did not typically include users. And as Kathleen Lawther has observed, when users were considered attention tended to focus on educated users, and therefore did not centre on communities with the greatest stake in collections (Lawther, People-Centred Cataloguing, 2023). Indeed, the dominant frameworks through which objects were curated in the UK in this period maintained that objects contained 'intrinsic' character and that this character was a knowable, objective quality. Daniel Reibel's work on museum documentation suggests that contemporaneous North American practices took a more playful and pragmatic approach to truth, though far from the postmodern tone that began to enter anglophone museology in the early twenty-first century; Daniel B. Reibel, *Registration Methods for Small History Museums: A Guide for Historical Collections* (Nashville, 1978).

[6] D. Andrew Roberts, 'The Changing Role of Information Professionals in Museum', in *Museums in a Digital Age*, ed. Ross Parry (2009), 15. Helen Wilkinson describes museum funding in the UK during this period as a 'mixed economy': national museums received direct funding from government; local museums received funding from county councils, metropolitan authorities, Area Museum Councils (see below), or a combination thereof; and independent museums – often subject oriented – were funded from both public and government bodies, as well as – increasingly – tickets and retail. Mid-1970s changes to local government precipitated a decline in museum funding and a decentring of museums from the heart of civic consciousness; Wilkinson, 'The Dawning of Professionalism'.

systematisation, and a crucial moment was the creation in 1967 of the Information Retrieval Group of the Museums Association (hereafter IRGMA).

IRGMA was one of many special interest groups formed within the Museums Association – the professional body for UK museums and gallery workers – in the mid-1960s. Each of these groups sought to recognise and develop specialist areas of museological practice. As conceived, IRGMA was to provide a forum for those concerned with the quality of collection documentation and interested in unifying documentary theory and practice.[7] By 1970, IRGMA was leading on the design of software, standards and records cards – often collectively described as the 'IRGMA system' – for the machine encoding and communication of museum catalogue records. In 1974 IRMGA became a research project based at the Sedgwick Museum, Cambridge, with funding from the British Library.[8] In 1976 the IRGMA system was launched, and the organisation shifted focus again, this time to supporting the implementation of computerised cataloguing in UK museums. The following year, IRGMA became the Museum Documentation Association (hereafter MDA), formed in recognition of 'the growing awareness of the need for a concerted approach to museum documentation',[9] and with four staff located at the Imperial War Museum branch at Duxford Airfield.[10] In 2008, the MDA became the Collections Trust, a reformed body tasked with supporting a UK museum sector which had by then normalised into professional practice the function of routinely creating, updating and managing collection data through collections databases. Before the launch of the IRGMA system, such databases were rarities.[11] It is simplistic, however, to say that IRGMA caused the museum database to proliferate. While the development and implementation of the IRGMA system was a catalyst for change, one system should not eclipse the profound shift in cultures of museum documentation that took place in UK museums between the mid-1960s and early 1980s.[12] It is then the emergence of these cultures and their intersections with professional identity and labour practices that this article seeks to trace.

The theory and practice of computerised documentation had existed in UK museums before the launch of the IRGMA system. In 1965, Geoffrey Lewis, IRGMA's founding chair, described the obstacles created by a lack of interoperability between existing museum databases. Lewis proposed a 'Museum Communication Format' to facilitate the machine exchange of data, to enable more efficient manipulating and recording of collection information and to form the basis of a national index of collections.[13] The latter idea can be traced

---

[7] J. D. Stewart, 'MDA, MDS and Computerised Archaeology', in *Computer Applications in Archaeology*, ed. Ian Graham and Esmée Webb (1981).

[8] *MDA News*, 1 (1977), 1.

[9] *MDA Information*, 1 (1977), 1.

[10] *MDA News*, 1 (1977), 1.

[11] David Gittins, 'Computer-Based Museum Information Systems', *Museums Journal*, 76 (1976), 115–18.

[12] John M. A. Thompson (ed.), *Manual of Curatorship: A Guide to Museum Practice* (1984).

[13] G. D. Lewis, 'Obtaining Information from Museum Collections and Thoughts on a National Museum Index', *Museums Journal*, 65 (1965), 12–22.

back to the formation of Museums Association in 1889,[14] a desire never realised, stymied by systematic documentation not existing across UK museums. Then and throughout the first half of the twentieth century, the use of formal cataloguing technologies was characterised by the production of bespoke card catalogues, islands of data that were only loosely connected and – with a few pioneering exceptions – prompted few imitators.[15] The launch of the IRGMA system put UK museums on a path towards a national collection, raising hopes that techno-optimist fantasies could be realised. As F. J. Stott, Chair of the MDA Executive Committee and the South-West Area Museum Council, wrote in 1977, 'to realise our full potential to make the contribution we should make to society, there is a need for a national catalogue' and through MDA, Stott continued, 'there is little doubt we shall at long last have a service which will help in a big way to make the Museum Service much more significant throughout the whole of Great Britain'.[16] However what is significant about the IRGMA/MDA moment is not the realisation or otherwise of long-held dreams of information interoperability. Rather it is that this moment of optimism marked an inflection point in the reshaping of museological practice and the normalisation of computerised work within the UK museum profession, a moment when the desire for a 'layman's guide to the scheme' began to give way to new professional personas and forms of documentary labour.

This article asks how the UK museums sector responded to the emergence of computerised cataloguing in the form of IRGMA. To address this question, it traces shifting cultures of museology and professional labour across three parts. First, it examines the formation of IRGMA and the penetration of its work into both the business of the Museums Association and the UK museum profession more widely. Second, it draws out the ways in which a growing number of UK museums sought to integrate computerised cataloguing into their operations. It argues that while some museum professionals resisted the new functions implied by IRGMA, the locus of debate was by the late 1970s centred on who would undertake computerised cataloguing tasks and to what extent this labour would reshape both existing and future museum roles. For some museum professionals, computerisation cataloguing was seen as a moment of temporary rupture. But by contrast, for many UK museum professionals affiliated with the Museum Ethnographers Group, the case of which is explored in the third and final part of the article, developments in computerised cataloguing infrastructure were seen as opportunities to effect change in museological practice, as having provided a vehicle through which to assert the particular significance of both their collections and their museums. The international character of ethnographic collections, and the international

---

[14] Sheila M. Stone, 'Documenting Collections', in *Manual of Curatorship*, ed. Thompson, 127.

[15] Most UK museums lacked the capacity to computerise their documentation. This was especially true for small museums, which also tended to have very little collection documentation, let alone documentation in forms amenable to computerisation; see M. G. Gribble, 'The Economics of Information Retrieval at Buxton Museum', *Museums Journal*, 72 (1972), 21–2, and D. Andrew Roberts, 'Proposals for a Survey of Cataloguing Practice in British Museums', *Museums Journal*, 75 (1975), 78–80.

[16] *MDA Information*, 1 (1977), 31.

networks fostered by ethnographic museums, remind us that the developments were situated within international contexts. Museums Association members represented the UK at the International Council of Museums (ICOM) and the International Committee for Documentation (CIDOC), and they reported back into the UK museums profession through Museums Association reports and conferences. But computerised documentation in the UK was resolutely national in character. Early canonical works that responded to the IRGMA/MDA moment were local in scope and focused on British examples.[17] The MDA did not hold its first international conference until 1987.[18] National dynamics therefore demand attention.

Located within the historiographies of museums, knowledge infrastructures and (information) technologies in twentieth-century Britain, this article argues that during the long 1970s the power to systematise museum documentation and to make knowledge durable was – in part – invested in new forms of what Hannah Turner has in the context of US museums in the mid-twentieth century called 'mindless work'.[19] This was work undertaken by people of all genders whose roles were frequently perceived as akin to those of clerical staff,[20] but whose competencies came to be highly valued and to reshape the professional persona of the UK museum profession. Women occupied many of these roles, and – alongside economic neoliberalism, reconfigurations to the labour force and technological innovation – gender relations were a key context to changing professional values and personas in UK museums. And what these people did had lasting impacts. In particular, their classification decisions, descriptive practices and object documentation remain with us today, whether in whole or in part, entangled with the history and architecture of modern museum information systems.[21] As such then, research into museum documentation practices is part of a multi-disciplinary endeavour to conceive of 'collections as data',[22] to understand the prehistories and social conditions of collection management that produce collections as data and to foreground the knowledge infrastructures – from accession catalogues and filing cabinets to curatorial standards and digitisation regimes – that continue to underpin the preservation, communication and machine processing of collections data.[23]

---

[17] Elizabeth Orna and C. W. Pettitt, *Information Handling in Museums* (1980).

[18] D. Andrew Roberts (ed.), *Collections Management for Museums: Proceedings of an International Conference Held in Cambridge, England, 26–29 September 1987: The First Annual Conference of the Museum Documentation Association* (Cambridge, 1988).

[19] Hannah Turner, *Cataloguing Culture: Legacies of Colonialism in Museum Documentation* (Vancouver, 2020), 26.

[20] TNA, HK 1/20 (Museums Association: Annual Reports), 1977.

[21] Candace S. Greene, 'Material Connections: "The Smithsonian Effect" in Anthropological Cataloguing', *Museum Anthropology*, 39 (2016), 147–62.

[22] Thomas Padilla, Laurie Allen, Hannah Frost, Sarah Potvin, Elizabeth Russey Roke, and Stewart Varner, 'Final Report – Always Already Computational: Collections as Data', 2019, https://doi.org/10.5281/zenodo.3152935.

[23] Tonia Sutherland, 'Archival Amnesty: In Search of Black American Transitional and Restorative Justice', *Journal of Critical Library and Information Studies*, 1 (2017), https://journals.litwinbooks.com/index.php/jclis/issue/view/3; Eun Seo Jo and Timnit Gebru, 'Lessons from

'The world's first': IRGMA in the Museums Association

The Information Retrieval Group of the Museums Association, often referred to by contemporaries as IRGMA, was formed in April 1967. In the late 1960s it became a forum for exploring the possibilities for the machine encoding of museum catalogue records in UK museums and the design features of systems that might reflect the outcome of those explorations. By October 1970, IRGMA had developed standards for encoding collections data that would enable sharing and querying between institutions and was set to embark on a two-year 'pilot project' to test the viability and implementation of those standards.

The 1971 Annual Report of the Museums Association dedicated seven lines to the work of IRGMA, an update nestled alongside reports on a wide variety of Association and sectoral business, from museum education and admission charges to recent publications and the annual Museums Association conference. Framing these reports were substantive updates on major developments in UK museums, an expected government white paper on the museums service – published later in 1971 as 'Future Policy for Museums and Galleries' – and notes on the anticipated impact on museum services of forthcoming reforms to local government.[24] These concerns both dwarfed and intersected with IRGMA's work on collections documentation: for while the technological spirit of IRGMA was absent elsewhere in the 1971 Annual Report, a spirit of professionalisation, specialisation and imminent change was pervasive.[25]

In the early-1970s the hoped for 'layman's guide to the [IRGMA] scheme' began to take shape through workshops, exhibitions and conference sessions delivered by IRGMA members. Museums Association Annual Reports in these years noted that demand for and interest in these sessions was both considerable and diverse: attendees included museum professionals ranging from collection stewards to senior museum officers.[26] Engagement with the sector by IRGMA was both general and specific, including 'meetings of subject panels concerned with the design of "minimum content" recordings forms',[27] and tests of the IRGMA system involving over 100 collection experts from across the UK.[28] Alongside these activities, IRGMA fielded requests for information, assistance and support on appropriate computing infrastructures, data processing and collection-specific implementation. By 1975, IRGMA was a regular and not insubstantial feature of the Museums Association's work and reporting, and after several false dawns the 'IRGMA system' – the contemporary shorthand for a software package, interoperable descriptive standards and record cards – was in January 1976 'formally made available to museums'.[29] Reflecting on

Archives: Strategies for Collecting Sociocultural Data in Machine Learning', *FAT* '20: Proceedings of the 2020 Conference on Fairness, Accountability, and Transparency* (2020), 306–16; Craig Robertson, *The Filing Cabinet: A Vertical History of Information* (Minneapolis, 2021).

[24] The Local Government Act 1972 was implemented in April 1974.

[25] TNA, HK 1/14 (Museums Association: Annual Reports), 1971.

[26] TNA, HK 1/15 – HK 1/18 (Museums Association: Annual Reports), 1972–5.

[27] TNA, HK 1/17 (Museums Association: Annual Reports), 1974.

[28] Roberts, 'Proposals for a Survey of Cataloguing Practice in British Museums' (1975).

[29] TNA, HK 1/19 (Museums Association: Annual Reports), 1976.

their achievements in 1977, the IRGMA Standards Subcommittee wrote with pride that IRGMA had 'developed what are believed to be the world's first national multidisciplinary documentation standards and recording media'.[30]

Throughout this pilot and initial delivery phase, work on the IRGMA Documentation System was complemented by research into museological theory and cataloguing. In 1972, Geoffrey Lewis, Chairman of IRGMA and Director of Merseyside County Museums, provided a justification for this approach at the Museums Association Annual General Meeting, arguing that the entangling of 'theoretical exercises' with work on 'grass-roots problem[s]' was essential to IRGMA's aim to provide 'a common logical standard for museum cataloguing in this country'.[31] In turn, sections dedicated to IRGMA in future editions of the Museums Association Annual Report described the 'experimental re-ordering and retrieval operations' of records for electrostatic instruments, Andrew Roberts's MSc thesis on museum cataloguing practices and Bernard Greaves's survey of UK museum catalogues (funded by the Department of Education and Science).[32] At the February 1972 Museums Association Council Meeting, Lewis restated IRGMA's aims and reaffirmed his belief that 'mechanization for information retrieval and management would become increasingly viable'.[33] Indeed in Museums Association Annual Reports, IRGMA was regularly framed as future oriented, as a promise of and for tomorrow.[34] But the reports also indicate that the museum sector had begun to prepare for tomorrow. By March 1976, just two months after launch, over 140 institutions had ordered copies of the IRGMA cards and three print runs had been insufficient to meet demand – 270,000 cards were sold in a single year.[35] By March 1977, over 170 institutions (roughly 10 per cent per cent of Museums Association member institutions) were using the IRGMA system and jobs in museum documentation were growing in response.[36] Notably, these investments were taking place in the context of economic turbulence, local government retrenchment and severe cuts to museum services.

---

[30] IRGMA Standards Subcommittee, 'Ten Years of IRGMA', *Museums Journal*, 77 (1977), 11.

[31] 'Minutes of 43rd AGM. 14 July 1972', TNA, HK 3/4 (Museums Association: Minutes of 42nd–55th meetings and 32nd meeting of Institutional Representatives), 1971–84.

[32] TNA, HK 1/16 (Museums Association: Annual Reports), 1973; TNA, HK 1/18 (Museums Association: Annual Reports), 1975; TNA, HK 1/19 (Museums Association: Annual Reports), 1976.

[33] Minutes of the meeting of Council 17 Feb 1972, TNA, HK 2/16 (Museums Association: Council agendas, minutes and papers), 1972–4.

[34] TNA, HK 1/17–1/18 (Museums Association: Annual Reports), 1975–6.

[35] Data from IRGMA Standards Subcommittee, 'Ten Years of IRGMA', 14. As both Roberts and Lewis later noted, few museums had computers at this time (Andrew Roberts, *Ideas for Museums: A Biography of Museum Computing* (2013), https://www.youtube.com/watch?v=ZH9lTH3YuLo; Geoffrey Lewis, *Ideas for Museums: A Biography of Museum Computing* (2013), https://www.youtube.com/watch?v=x5odbFSRugo.). However, as the cards could be used in card catalogues without the immediate need for museum input, the IRGMA standard was still of practical application for those museums without computers; TNA, HK 1/20 (Museums Association: Annual Reports), 197.

[36] TNA, HK 1/20 (Museums Association: Annual Reports), 1977. The numbers of cards sold and institutions who bought them varies between sources – for example, *MDA News* reported in October 1977 that 'well over half a million IRGMA/MDA cards have now been purchased by over one hundred United Kingdom museums', *MDA News*, 2 (1977), 1.

Minutes of the IRGMA steering committee, both before and after the launch of their 'system', indicate the challenges associated with an accelerated demand for and rapid uptake of computerised methods for cataloguing collections information. For example, as late as autumn 1975, a few months prior to launch of their system, IRGMA had yet to develop a coordinated approach to computerised cataloguing education with the Museum Studies Department at the University of Leicester, home to the then pre-eminent – and Museums Association accredited – degree programme in museum studies.[37] After launch, matters accelerated. Minutes from early 1976 record a scramble to create an appropriate structure for IRGMA now that it had moved from design and implementation to service delivery and support: financial models were considered, cost estimates were made.[38] Driven by Lewis, an appeal was sent to the Department of Education and Science (DES) to fund a new body, tentatively called the Museums Documentation Advisory Unit, to take on the work of IRGMA outside Museums Association core funding. DES was assumed to be sympathetic to the cause: in 1973 their Wright Report had recommended a minimum standard for museum cataloguing.[39] A sum of £42,000 was requested to launch the new unit, with initial operational costs estimated at £1,000 per annum.[40] DES rejected the appeal, but they included in their rejection letter a note of encouragement and a clarification that 'national museums and the Area Museum Councils were at liberty to allocate funds from their overall budget if they so wished'.[41] By the June 1976, Lewis had approached several national museum directors with the informal proposal to create a unit funded by their museums with a start-up fee of approximately £1,000 per institution. At least two were obliging. By July 1976 sufficient support had been secured for the Museums Association Council to agree to the 'immediate formation of the Museum Documentation Advisory Unit' using a block grant from the Area Museums Councils.[42] In a few short months, the

---

[37] The Department of Museum Studies was formed at University of Leicester in 1966, with its first graduate course running in 1967. The initial syllabus included as compulsory topic on 'principles of classification' (University of Leicester Special Collections (UoLSC), ULA/D4/1/5 (Syllabus for Graduate Certificate Course in Museum Studies), 2 Dec. 1966), and Geoffrey Lewis contributed lectures on 'Information Retrieval' to the visiting lecture series in 1968 and 1969 (UoLSC, ULA/D4/1/5 (Board of Museum Studies), 26 Jan. 1968 and 24 Jan. 1969). The programme's substantive engagement with computerised cataloguing did not take place until Lewis joined the Museum Studies Department in 1978. For disquiet within IRGMA over their lack of engagement with the University of Leicester, see Minutes of the IRGMA Steering Committee 16 Oct. 1975, TNA, HK 2/17 (Museums Association: Council agendas, minutes and papers), 1975–7.

[38] Minutes of the IRGMA Steering Committee 19 Jan. 1976, TNA, HK 2/17 (Museums Association: Council agendas, minutes and papers), 1975–7.

[39] Stone, 'Documenting Collections', 134.

[40] Minutes of the Meeting of Management and Finance Committee 3 March 1976, TNA, HK 2/17 (Museums Association: Council agendas, minutes and papers), 1975–7.

[41] Minutes of the IRGMA Steering Committee 4 June 1976, TNA, HK 2/17 (Museums Association: Council agendas, minutes and papers), 1975–7.

[42] The Area Museum Councils, often referred to as the Area Councils, were regional units funded by central UK government by support the museum sector; Minutes of the Meeting of Council 9 July 1976, TNA, HK 2/17 (Museums Association: Council agendas, minutes and papers), 1975–7.

Information Retrieval Group of the Museums Association was then reimagined as a body separate from the Museums Association, and in 1977 the Museum Documentation Association (MDA) – a new national organisation whose members included twelve national museums[43] – was formed. The MDA quickly became a central node in the UK's museums information ecosystem, tasked not only with assisting museums, training museum professionals, developing good practice in collections documentation and maintaining both the MDA documentation standards and software, but also with promoting museums as sources of rich, significant and nationally important information.[44]

Thereafter, the themes of documentation, cataloguing and computerisation abruptly disappeared from the published bureaucracy and reporting of the Museums Association. Even a 1978 report from the Museums Association Annual Conference themed 'New Trends and Developments on the Museum Service' made no mention of computerisation.[45] That absence was not, however, the experience of museum professionals. The creation of the MDA signalled a clear demand for the kinds of work that IRGMA had introduced, and in turn the MDA took responsibility for dissemination, communication, advocacy, support and training around computerised cataloguing.[46] In 1980 it released GOS, a software package for handling collection catalogues, announced a Software Service to assist GOS users, and launched a Computing Service to support data preparation and processing.[47] Both a newsletter and a new journal accompanied the launch of the MDA, the latter running until 2003. IRGMA was then a catalyst, from which new forms of labour, debate and professional restructure followed.

---

[43] These were the British Museum, British Museum (Natural History), Imperial War Museum, Museum of London, National Army Museum, National Maritime Museum, Royal Air Force Museum, Science Museum, Victoria and Albert Museum, National Museum of Wales, Ulster Museum, and National Museum of Antiquaries of Scotland; *MDA News*, 1 (1977), 2.

[44] *MDA News*, 1 (1977), 2; *MDA Information*, 1 (1977), 1; D. Andrew Roberts, Richard B. Light and Jennifer D. Stewart, 'The Museum Documentation Association', *Museums Journal*, 80 (1980), 81–5. For an example of the MDA as central node in the UK's museums information ecosystem, see the role it would assume in running data storage services for the museum sector: see *MDA News*, 10 (1980), 1–4; Minutes of the Eleventh Annual General Meeting of the Museum Ethnographers Group, Museum Ethnographers Group (MEG), 2 April 1987.

[45] TNA, HK 1/21 (Museums Association: Annual Reports), 1978.

[46] Between the 1960s and the late 1990s workplace computer systems were designed around workplace needs and staff needed training in their use. In turn, there was a flourishing literature on designing documentation and training for workplace computer systems; David K. Farkas, 'Seeking the Future of Computer Documentation', *The Journal of Computer Documentation*, 19 (1995), 24–9; C. A Decker, 'Technical Education Transfer: Perceptions of Employee Computer Technology Self-Efficacy', *Computers in Human Behavior*, 15 (1999), 161–72. By offering training and guidance for museum employees in workplace computer use, MDA operations were in line with contemporary expectations and need. This dynamic was rapidly changed by the proliferation of WIMP-like Graphical User Interfaces whose patterns of use bridged work and home, exemplified by Windows 1995.

[47] *MDA News*, 10 (1980), 1. In late 1981 the MDA expanded staffing of the Software Service in response to demand; *MDA Information*, 5 (1981), 41.

'The revolution has come': implementing the IRGMA system

How then did the implementation of computerised cataloguing catalyse changes in the UK museum sector? Crucially, paper was not simply replaced with digital data – indeed in many cases, museums had no paper catalogues to replace. Instead, the IRGMA/MDA moment produced in the first instance new forms of material documentary practices. To use the Museum Documentation System, museums and their staff purchased 'Record Cards': stiff, matt, A5, cream-coloured card objects priced – initially – at £8.50 per 500 cards that were marked with green-tinged print: sans serif text and horizontal and vertical lines that divided the card into 'elements' and 'headings', new infrastructures of knowing and knowability.[48] A single card was intended to capture everything that needed to be recorded about a single collection item, and against each field on a card information was manually added, by hand or typewriter, intended for keying – at a later stage – into a MDA-compliant computerised catalogue. The categories that were produced by the MDA cards – 'Identification', 'Description', 'Production', 'Association' and so on – and the sub-fields within them, marked space for when, how and by whom object processing took place, broke apart stories of and narratives about objects into formal and formalised categorical genres. In turn, local, situated and historically specific descriptions of objects and their histories, that a hand axe was – for example – 'gifted to the museum in 1951 by one A. H. Bishop', were reconfigured into structured data: the word 'gift' was typed under the heading 'Acquisition Method', or the string 'Bishop, A.H.: 1951' was entered under the heading 'Acquired from : date'. This effect of categorising knowledge into fragmentary units, into snippets of language, was a deliberate outcome of the IRGMA work and the MDA system it produced, for such categorisation facilitated the objective of making museum information communicable and interoperable. In so doing, this work built on and responded to mid-twentieth-century trends in North American cataloguing.[49] But it also responded to domestic priorities, to political narratives that prized efficiency and investments with future-facing agendas, and that anticipated datafied tomorrows. Sheila M. Stone, curator at Verulamium Museum, St Albans, captured this spirit in 1978: 'Museums hold a massive amount of potentially usable data in the form of collections, a potential which is unlikely to be realized unless a museum possesses a policy of comprehensive data recording and efficient information retrieval.'[50]

The implementation of the implementation, the use of MDA cards in UK museums, reveals the ways in which labour reconfigured the MDA system in the making. Some of this reconfiguration happened before the cards were printed and arrived in museums. The final MDA system was not designed to

---

[48] Prices included postage but excluded VAT; for a full price list in 1977, see *MDA News*, 1 (1977), 4. Prices rose to £12 per 500 (excluding postage and VAT) in January 1979; see *MDA Information*, 2 (1978), 74.

[49] Turner, *Cataloguing Culture*.

[50] Sheila M. Stone, 'St Albans Museums Documentation Project', *Museums Journal*, 78 (1978), 117–19.

be universal to all museum collections, but rather offered different cards for different categories of object. Fifteen variants were produced in response to initial community consultation – rising to twenty-three by 1979[51] – and these enabled museum staff to record information particular to archaeological objects, ethnography, fine art, scientific instruments and so on.[52] The inclusion on all MDA cards of a 'Note' field further indicates how the system was reconfigured by its users: contrary to the ambition to enable interoperable communication of collections data, here the system gave way to narrative description, giving museum professionals licence to tell stories about the assumed provenance of objects, about previous – erroneous – documentation, or about the complex reality of objects and their histories.

Once the cards were available to purchase, museums interested in implementing the system had to consider how that implementation might take place. MDA worked closely with UK museums on this and were, even in the early days of the system, apparently relaxed that internal conventions for the use of MDA cards were widespread,[53] this in spite of such conventions potentially impeding the interoperability of the communications format. A report published in 1981 by Manchester Museum – a pioneer in museum computing – offers a window into the labour conditions through which the MDA system was implemented and how those conditions reconfigured the MDA system at a local level. The report describes the work of the Manchester Museum Computer Cataloguing Unit (MMCCU), founded in May 1979 under the supervision of Charles Pettitt. Pettitt was at the time an Assistant Keeper of Zoology, and would in 1983 become the founding chair of the Museums Computer Group. Pettitt had arrived at Manchester Museum in 1975 and had by 1979 significant experience working with computer catalogues and computerised cataloguing.[54] Both a qualified information scientist and an expert on winkles, Pettitt was seconded to the MMCCU's Selected Temporary Employment Programme (known as STEP) to 'monitor and motivate ... and provide essential continuity' for a vehicle designed to provide a workforce for computerised cataloguing.[55]

STEP was funded through the government's Job Creation Programme (JCP), a scheme administered by the Manpower Services Commission (MSC), a body of the Department of Employment formed in 1973. Ostensibly tasked with providing young people with skills and experience, the MSC was also part of a suite of market-oriented reforms to labour and working age benefits: indeed, the success of the JCP – and its successor the Youth Training Scheme – was

---

[51] *MDA News*, 6 (1979), 1.

[52] D. Andrew Roberts, Richard B. Light and Jennifer D. Stewart, 'The Museum Documentation Association', *Museums Journal*, 80 (1980), 82. A sixteenth card was also made to capture details of object conservation activities.

[53] *MDA Information*, 2 (1978), 11.

[54] E. Geoffrey Hancock and Michael V. Hounsome, 'Charles Arthur William "Bill" Pettitt (20 August 1937–26 March 2009): Zoological Curator at Manchester Museum', *Natural Sciences Collections Association News*, 19 (2010), 2–6.

[55] Charles Pettitt, 'The Manchester Museum Computer Cataloguing Unit – a STEP in the Right Direction?', *Museums Journal*, 80 (1980), 188.

used in 1988 to justify the removal of unemployment benefits from school lea-vers under the age of 18.[56] The scheme was a particular boon for arts, culture and heritage organisations, and as Sarah Kenny has shown, JCP labour pro-vided vital funds to community organisations whose radical instincts were at odds with the corporatist goals of the MSC.[57] By the summer of 1977, roughly eighteen months into the scheme, Museums Association members had used the JCP to bring around 400 individuals into the museum sector, over 100 of whom were allocated to cataloguing tasks (the second largest group after labouring tasks). In many cases JCP money was requested to produce MDA-compliant documentation;[58] free labour without which, Helen Wilkinson has argued, many museums would not have been able to index their collections at all.[59]

Writing in the *Museums Journal* in 1978, Frank Atkinson remarked that 'at a time when most museums are experiencing restrictions on their spending, a national grant scheme to museums, on this scale, clearly represents a remark-able windfall'.[60] This was the context in which Manchester Museum made the decision in the autumn of 1978 to apply to the JCP. Once their application was approved, sixteen new posts (rising later to twenty) were created within the MMCCU via STEP.[61] The forty-one individuals recruited into these posts across the first eighteen months of STEP did not have backgrounds in museum studies or the heritage sector. In most cases they had an education in arts and human-ities, with little or no experience in information science, database manage-ment, or workplace computing. This workforce was then ideally suited to testing one of Pettitt's key aims for STEP: the viability or otherwise of using non-specialists as cataloguers.[62] As non-specialists, STEP employees were designated as Assistant Cataloguers, with pay rates pegged below those of other collection-oriented museum staff. Pettitt's aim was for them to create 'working' registers and indexes, information objects explicitly distinct from the 'pretty' catalogues associated with curatorial work.[63] Using information 'culled' from various sources – including 'the object itself, labels, old registers, field notebooks or reference sources'[64] – together with controlled vocabularies and instructions for data entry, the STEP employees completed pre-formatted data input sheets for each collection object with which they were presented. The completed sheets were then passed on to the University of Manchester Regional Computing Centre (UMRCC) – housed since 1972 just 100 metres

[56] Kenny, 'A "Radical Project"'.

[57] *Ibid.*

[58] Frank Atkinson, 'A Report on Job Creation in Museums', *Museums Journal*, 77 (1977), 158–9. In May 1977, MDA reported that '[w]e know of about ten museums that have used these schemes as an aid to documentation'; *MDA Information*, 1 (1977), 12. See also *MDA Information*, 2 (1978), 19.

[59] Wilkinson, '"The Dawning of Professionalism": Constructing the UK Museum Profession in the 1970s and 1980s'.

[60] Atkinson, 'Job Creation in Museums', 158.

[61] Pettitt, 'Manchester Museum Computer Cataloguing Unit', 191.

[62] *Ibid.*, 187.

[63] *Ibid.*, 188.

[64] *Ibid.*

along the Oxford Road from Manchester Museum – for conversion into the punch cards needed for data entry. By late 1980, over 175,000 object records had been created by the STEP employees and their supervisory team.[65]

Notwithstanding the variety and complexity of the collections they worked with, computerised cataloguing undertaken by the STEP employees was repetitive, high-volume labour. To make this labour more tolerable, Manchester Museum allocated resources to creating a working environment suitable for this kind of labour. 'People will not produce their best results', wrote Pettitt, 'if housed in poor conditions'.[66] In turn Pettitt sought to craft working conditions that would enable the STEP employees to produce said 'results'. They shared a workspace that was well lit and appropriately heated. They had space to lay out and to store documents and objects. They had access to training and professional development opportunities. They were encouraged to take regular breaks and had access to a dedicated rest area, to grievance-reporting processes and to supervisory support.[67] The treatment of the STEP employees – as described by Pettitt – was intended to be caring. But it was also constructed in recognition that – done well – data production was labour that demanded attentiveness, that lapses in attention created errors and that errors were contrary to the very enterprise of computerising catalogue data, predicated as it was on enabling an escape from the subjectivities of paper-based methods and on delivering the promise of interoperable information communication.

For all Pettitt's conviction that computerised catalogue data would benefit museums, the collections they looked after and curatorial work, it is significant that the design of STEP and their description of it in operation indicate that for Pettitt this labour was distinct from curatorial labour – a discrete unit that completed particular tasks of a routine nature fit for a general workforce that needed only minimal oversight from established museum professionals. Underpinning this view was the goal-oriented framing of STEP, a belief that its work comprised a project that could be completed, done, moved on from, rather than representing an ongoing function. This perspective chimes with evidence reported to Frank Atkinson in his mid-1970s survey of UK museums and their experiences of the JCP. Atkinson noted that the uses of the scheme that had proven most successful were 'those where something could be done, as a 'one-off' job which otherwise would *not* get done'. Cataloguing – including 'transferring existing records on to the IRGMA format' – was substantial among the 'one-off' jobs UK museums used the JCP to fund,[68] and many other museums, after initial testing of the MDA system, appear to have been waiting on a successful application to the JCP scheme before initiating the computerisation of their records.[69] That is, while the structure of the JCP did contribute to the separation of computerised documentary labour from everyday museum work, those labour conditions were also brought into being by how the UK

---

[65] *Ibid.*, 191.

[66] *Ibid.*, 190.

[67] *Ibid.*

[68] Atkinson, 'Job Creation in Museums', 159.

[69] Sheila Stone, 'MDA User Experience: St. Albans Museums', *MDA Information*, 3 (1979), 51.

museums regarded the nature and scope of computerising documentation. The temporary nature of JCP labour closely aligned with a line of thought in the UK museum sector that computerised documentation was temporarily bounded, a 'one-off' task facilitated by investments in infrastructures like the MDA system, something that did not need to be integrated into the professional persona of museum curators in the UK.

Manchester Museum then used the JCP to achieve a particular goal, to create a workforce that was transient, a workforce built and trained without a future workforce in mind, for an imagined future in which the computer cataloguer would not be needed by their employer or by the museum sector. Manchester Museum was not alone in taking this view. Atkinson's work suggests that it was the prevailing opinion of UK museum leaders in the mid- to late 1970s. However, dissenting voices indicate that the debate was not settled. At Tyne and Wear Museums, another beneficiary of JCP labour for computerised cataloguing, 'cataloguer typist[s]' were hired to underpin the conversion of museum documentation to MDA-compliant data, but curators were involved throughout both pilot and delivery phases in drafting catalogue cards, quality assurance and actively feeding their experiences back into MDA card development committees.[70] At the Hunterian Museum in Glasgow, Euan Mackie and his colleagues used JCP to build a small team capable of transferring records of the museum's Prehistoric, Roman and Ethnographic collections onto MDA cards.[71] Like Manchester Museum, the Hunterian were pioneers in museum computing, and in Mackie had a representative who was highly active in museum documentation. And their JCP staff, like those at Manchester, operated separately from existing Hunterian staff, and undertook labour that was limited to data entry onto MDA cards: the actual transfer of catalogue data onto a computerised system and subsequent production of hard-copy collection indexes was undertaken by the MDA (for a fee). But whereas Manchester Museum used the JCP to create a new form of non-specialist labour, the Hunterian used the JCP to hire specialist cataloguers without experience in computerised cataloguing, this despite few such workers meeting the unemployment criteria of STEP.[72] And in a further contrast to Manchester Museum, this new workforce was empowered to participate in the design, implementation and iteration of that data entry processes. The result was high-quality work, providing the Hunterian 'with a powerful impetus for the future refinement and improvement of [their] artefact classification system'.[73] Based on the Hunterian's experience of implementing the MDA system, Mackie was emphatic that this method of computerisation represented a radical rupture in the recording of museum data: 'the revolution has come', Mackie wrote in 1980, 'and it is no longer possible to ignore the developments or to pretend that the cards "do not suit our collection" or that "our

---

[70] *MDA News*, 4 (1978), 1–2.

[71] Euan W. Mackie, 'Using the MDA Cards in the Hunterian Museum', *Museums* Journal, 80 (1980), 86–9.

[72] *Ibid.*, 86.

[73] *Ibid.*, 89.

old cataloguing system is adequate'".[74] Moreover, by using the JCP to train specialists in the use of the MDA system, Mackie *was* imagining a new professional persona for museum professionals. Of the four cataloguers the Hunterian hired through the JCP in 1977, three – all of whom were women – subsequently found employment in the sector.[75] For Mackie this was evidence that the Museums Association had 'a duty to recommend the MDA cataloguing system as part of standard museum work and to train future members of the profession in it'.[76]

The use of JCP by Manchester Museum, the Hunterian Museum and the wider Museums Association membership underscores the penetration of the MDA system into the UK museum sector – indeed, supported by the MDA, the number of institutions using computerised cataloguing doubled between 1977 and 1981 to over 300.[77] Museum education was slow to catch up with this shifting professional landscape and the transformations to the production of museum documentation that were facilitated by computerisation. When it did, it embodied the turn towards cataloguing fulfilling the civic role of UK museums: 'Collection documentation', stated the University of Leicester's 1986 study guide for Museum Studies students, 'is necessary in order that publicly supported institutions are able to show they are managing their affairs to accepted standards'.[78] Indeed shortly after Geoffrey Lewis joined University of Leicester as Director of Museum Studies in 1978, their MA, MSc and Diploma programmes all integrated knowledge of MDA and – once released – GOS software into the learning outcomes of the programme, and retained those themes throughout the 1980s.[79] Members of the MDA team visited the department to deliver lectures to students and to provide learning materials.[80] And exam questions tested prospective museum curators on approaches to training new staff in how to use the MDA system,[81] recent developments in computerised documentation,[82] and how systems such as MDA might improve collection research.[83] The impact of these initiatives was not immediate. But what they speak to are the competing visions of museum work that emerged in the late 1970s and mid-1980s, the proliferating of views on the significance of computerised cataloguing to the profession. At one extreme, this labour was considered a 'one-off' task that would pass through the sector without

---

[74] *Ibid.*

[75] *Ibid.*, 86.

[76] *Ibid.*, 89.

[77] *MDA Information*, 5 (1981), 34.

[78] UoLSC, Uncat. Dept Mus. Stud Box (Collection Management (Museum Studies Note 2)), 1986.

[79] UoLSC, Uncat. Dept Mus. Stud Box. (Learning Goals in Museum Studies Training), 1980, 1982, 1984 and 1988.

[80] UoLSC, Uncat. Dept Mus. Stud Acc 2019/26 (Susan Kirby's Notes from Study on Museum Studies Degree), 1978–9.

[81] UoLSC, Uncat. Dept Mus. Stud Exam Papers (Midsummer Examinations: 1979 – Museum Studies – Paper 1: General), 1979.

[82] UoLSC, Uncat. Dept Mus. Stud Exam Papers (Midsummer Examinations: 1981 – Museum Studies – Paper 2: General), 1981.

[83] UoLSC, Uncat. Dept Mus. Stud Exam Papers (Midsummer Examinations: 1985 – Museum Studies – Paper 2: General), 1985.

reshaping its workforce; at the other it was considered an essential component of the present and future curatorial profession. To better understand the emergence of these positions, it is useful to turn to the theoretical debates that accompanied the development of the IRGMA system, and – in particular – to examine the engagement of one group of UK museum professionals with the concept of computerised cataloguing: curators at ethnographic museums.

'A stimulus for discussion': IRGMA and the Museum Ethnographers Group

The opportunities to implement computerised cataloguing that were afforded by the Job Creation Programme coincided with a period of considerable debate among UK museum practitioners. Introspective debate was not new for the sector. But while post-war debates were characterised by a focus on the recovery and expansion of the sector, in the 1970s and early 1980s – notwithstanding anxieties over funding cuts and local government restructuring – debate tended to focus on the purpose and function of UK museums: what they did not do but should do, whose interests they served and whose they should serve, and why that was the case.

How did museum documentation fit into this debate? *Museums Journal*, the sectoral journal published quarterly by the Museums Association, offers one way into this question. Between 1967 and 1983 alongside papers reporting on – *inter alia* – the conclusion of major gallery refurbishments, educational outreach, surveys on regional staffing, innovations in conservation techniques and commentaries on the future of public museums, a steady drip of papers was published on documentation projects, computerised cataloguing and the progress and delivery of IRGMA/MDA. These papers were characterised by optimism, the sharing of best practice and a desire to communicate the scope and extent of change. Elsewhere in the UK museum sector, in specialist communities, publications and venues, in museum practices less well represented by a formal publication such as *Museums Journal*, this picture was complemented by rich and vigorous debate emerging over how best to represent museum collections as data. One area of particular focus was around the extent to which the IRGMA system might systematise and constrain documentary practice in ways that were misaligned with the evolving intellectual agendas of particular communities. In turn, subcommittees were formed that enabled custodians of decorative arts, costume, photography, technology and many others to shape the MDA system to their needs.[84] And as we have seen, fifteen variants of the MDA cards were designed in response to this community consultation. Ethnography cards were one such category. As a subfield whose professional coalescence in the UK coincided with the maturation of IRGMA, museum ethnography offers a useful case study of sectoral debates around the implementation of computerised cataloguing and the professional persona of curators in UK museums. Moreover, museum ethnographers had a long tradition of thoughtful engagement around documentary practice. During

---

[84] *MDA Information*, 1 (1977), 60; *MDA News*, 3 (1978), 1–2.

the 1940s, the Pitt Rivers Museum in Oxford – then the UK's foremost ethnographic museum – developed a model for classifying ethnographic collections that systematised the museum's accession records into over 400 file drawers of card indexes.[85] This work, led by Beatrice Blackwood, would form the basis of the museum's computerisation work into the late 1980s. In *The Classification of Artefacts in the Pitt Rivers Museum Oxford*, published in 1970, Blackwood paints a vivid portrait of this labour:

> The laborious work of copying in duplicate on 5″ X 3″ index cards the entries in the Accessions Books (until then the only record of what the Museum possessed), was done by [T.K.] Penniman and his colleagues during the dark days of the Second World War. We could not black-out the Museum, but we could, and did, pick up an Accessions Book, a few packets of index cards and a portable typewriter, and take them to a blacked-out room.[86]

What is captured neither by Blackwood's description of their role in the production of these card indexes, nor by the sense that the work was unremarkable (if having taken place in remarkable times), was the particularity of the classificatory system Blackwood developed: fifty pages of classificatory headings from death and divination to techniques and time indicators, all developed to meet the specific needs not of an individual collector but rather of a particular group of professionals working with ethnographic collections at a particular place and time.[87]

It is fitting then that Blackwood was one of many women curators – roughly half of the total participants – who in 1974 and 1975 attended gatherings of ethnographers from UK museums that culminated in 1976 with the creation of the Museum Ethnographers Group (hereafter MEG). MEG continued the tradition – exemplified by Blackwood – of museum ethnographers taking a keen interest in the task of arranging the collections under their care, and of women playing a key role in how and in what ways that arrangement was implemented. Formed as IRGMA was moving into an implementation phase for its system, MEG initially occupied itself with a core set of priorities that emerged from its members: training in identifying ethnographic collections, qualification and professional recognition, human remains and restitution, publication and outreach, liaison with professional bodies such as the Museums Association (who almost immediately redirected ethnographic queries and matters to MEG),[88] growing their membership, understanding and documenting ethnographic holdings in the UK and communicating those

[85] Minutes of the Eighth Annual General Meeting of the Museum Ethnographers Group, MEG, 6 April 1984.

[86] Beatrice Blackwood, *The Classification of Artefacts in the Pitt Rivers Museum Oxford*, Occasional Papers on Technology 11 (Oxford, 1970), 12.

[87] As Dan Hicks argues, the history of the Pitt Rivers Museum is steeped in white sight, colonial exploitation and racially inscribed museological practice; Dan Hicks, *The Brutish Museums: The Benin Bronzes, Colonial Violence and Cultural Restitution* (2020).

[88] Secretary's Report 1977/78, MEG, 1978.

collections to interested publics. As part of the latter, MEG members recognised that ethnographic collections would benefit from more rigorous cataloguing, and that in the context of the IRGMA project their collections demanded a bespoke solution, a view that was reported in the first *MEG Newsletter*.[89] The following year, Len Pole – then curator at Saffron Walden Museum – described in the *MEG Newsletter* his attempts to design an IRGMA ethnography card. Pole was encouraged to do so by Andrew Roberts, one of the Research Assistants working on IRGMA at the Sedgwick Museum. Pole's aim was to work towards a card format that would be acceptable to most museum ethnographers in the UK and in turn make interoperable the collections information they held and produced. Debate and consensus were, for Pole, central to the process:

> The card produced ... is not intended to be the final version, but merely to act as a stimulus for discussion. It is, particularly, not intended for use until a final version has been worked out and accepted. It is not my intention to coerce others into accepting it. I am, however, of the opinion that some version of a card employing the format worked out by the IRGMA is to be preferred, for use by those museums not already blessed (or encumbered?) with a developed cataloguing procedure, to a card produced independently of it.[90]

In the late 1970s many ethnographic museums in the UK were in this 'blessed' position. Ethnographic collections tended – despite the field's historical engagement with innovative documentary practice – to lack comprehensive documentation. A 1981 survey of 311 museums with ethnographic collections found that 93.9 per cent had nothing published about those collections, 53.7 per cent had neither documentation or archives relating to them and only 53 per cent were able to estimate the extent of the collections.[91] This absence meant that museum ethnographers were well positioned to respond to developments in computerised cataloguing 'without' – as Pole sharply mused – 'the encumbrance of past curators' foresight'.[92]

At a meeting held at the Museum of Mankind in November 1976 to discuss collection documentation, MEG members were joined by Richard Light, representing what would soon be the MDA.[93] Having not worked with ethnographers during the development of IRGMA,[94] Light was keen to learn if their field 'present[ed] any special difficulties'. The prompt revealed a variability of practice among museum ethnographers, and their inexperience with the

---

[89] 'Information Retrieval', *Newsletter (Museum Ethnographers Group)*, 1 (1976), 4.

[90] Len Pole, 'Suggestions for a Future IRGMA Ethnography Object Catalogue Card', *Newsletter (Museum Ethnographers Group)*, 3 (1977), 10.

[91] David Jones, 'The Register of Ethnographic Collections: A Report on Work in Progress', *Newsletter (Museum Ethnographers Group)*, 11 (1981), 58.

[92] Pole, 'Suggestions', 9.

[93] 'M.E.G. Information Retrieval Meeting', *Newsletter (Museum Ethnographers Group)*, 3 (1977), 10–11.

[94] Pole, 'Suggestions', 10.

kind of approach that IRGMA invoked. While some members were already experimenting with computerised cataloguing, others were more hesitant and felt that more foundational cataloguing and classification protocols would need to be worked through before implementation of the IRGMA system could be considered. And while one attendee 'pointed out that despite what ethnographers may like to think, the complexity of ethnographic material is not greater than that of other kinds of museum object',[95] by the autumn of 1977 a MDA Ethnography Committee had been formed to compare existing approaches and to explore the possibility of developing a card specifically for documenting ethnographic material.[96] In January 1978 a draft form of that card was ready for community scrutiny.[97] Second and third drafts appeared in February and June respectively and were again made available for comment.[98] The already generous section that allowed for the input of free text description was expanded.[99] And in October 1978 the results of this work went into print as 'Ethnography/Folk Life' cards,[100] at which point the MDA Ethnography Committee was dissolved and members turned their attentions to enabling the consistent usage of the cards.[101]

Like all MDA cards, the Ethnography/Folk Life Record Card was A5 in size with headings and boxes printed on obverse and reverse. The structure of the card built on the earlier Archaeology card by – unlike most MDA cards – including dedicated space for recording details of field sites and object collection.[102] But the Ethnography/Folk Life card also deviated by, as described in its accompanying guide, placing 'emphasis ... on the object in the context of pre- or non-industrial society'.[103] For example, after the museum number, the first element a cataloguer would be presented with when completing or using an MDA card was the 'Identification' element. This was subdivided into headings for recording simple, alternative and full names for the object and any external identifiers associated with it (e.g. in a published classification scheme). The Archaeology card built on this convention by including a 'Materials/keyword detail' heading in the 'Identification' element, a nod towards the priorities of archaeological curation. But the Ethnography/Folk Life card went further, effectively upending the conventional structure of the 'Identification' element. The 'simple name' heading was retained for

[95] 'M.E.G. Information Retrieval Meeting', 11.

[96] Minutes of the Second Committee Meeting of the Museum Ethnographers Group, MEG, 28 Oct. 1977; 'Museum Documentation Association', *Newsletter (Museum Ethnographers Group)*, 4 (1977), 30.

[97] 'Museum Documentation Association', *Newsletter (Museum Ethnographers Group)*, 5 (1978), 18.

[98] Minutes of the Third Committee Meeting of the Museum Ethnographers Group, MEG, 17 Feb. 1978.

[99] *MDA Information*, 1 (1977), 107.

[100] 'Museum Documentation Association', *Newsletter (Museum Ethnographers Group)*, 6 (1978), 18; Minutes of the Fifth Committee Meeting of the Museum Ethnographers Group, MEG, 6 Oct. 1978.

[101] Minutes of the Fourth Committee Meeting of the Museum Ethnographers Group, MEG, 16 June 1978.

[102] Alignment with the Archaeology card was agreed late into the development of the Ethnography/Folk Life card; *MDA Information*, 2 (1978), 27.

[103] *Ethnography/Folk Life Card Instructions*, Museum Documentation System (Duxford, 1979), 6.

recording 'one readily understood keyword suitable as an index heading', such as 'fan' or 'sword'.[104] The 'full name' heading was retained to provide space for 'one or more series of descriptions which amplify the "simple name"'.[105] And the 'classified identification' heading was retained, with the instructions for its use that drew on ethnographers like Blackwood and the prominence of controlled vocabularies in their approach to documentation.[106] But placed leftmost in the 'Identification' element and therefore foremost in its use were two new headings – 'Continent' and 'area' – intended as spaces to record the geographical origins of the object. These supplemented headings for places of production and object collection elsewhere in the record card, foregrounding locality as the datatype that MEG members saw as the main reason for ethnographic collections needing a bespoke solution within the MDA system, a data type that – in line with contemporaneous ideologies in museum ethnography – emphasised homogenised people over individual creators, ethnographic objects as representative of unchanging place-based cultures rather than dynamic and polysemous human agency.[107]

Initial sales of the Ethnography/Folk Life card were brisk: 23,100 copies were sold in its first year of issue.[108] MEG, then, used a moment of debate around the practice of museum ethnography to leverage the MDA system to serve the needs of ethnographic institutions and their staff. New approaches to classifying and cataloguing ethnographic collections were published and recommended to MEG members.[109] Controlled vocabularies were developed and the case for their implementation established.[110] The relationship between staff turnover and terminological inconsistency was investigated.[111] Museum

---

[104] *Ibid.*, 24.

[105] *Ibid.*, 24–5.

[106] *MDA Information*, 1 (1977), 72–3; *Ethnography/Folk Life Card Instructions*, 24.

[107] Making African Connections Project, 'Making African Connections: Decolonial Futures for Colonial Collections. Initial Findings and Recommendations' (2021), https://doi.org/10.5281/zenodo.4456781.

[108] *MDA Information*, 2 (1978), 65; *MDA Information*, 2 (1978), 75; *MDA Information*, 3 (1979), 48. By comparison the general Museum Object card – consistently the highest selling MDA card – sold 45,000 copies in the same period.

[109] 'Museum Documentation Association', *Newsletter (Museum Ethnographers Group)*, 6 (1978), 18.

[110] 'Gazeteer of Obsolete/Alternative Names of the Pacific Islands', *Newsletter (Museum Ethnographers Group)*, 2 (1976), 9; Len Pole, 'On Good Terms: Vocabulary Control in the Description of Ethnography Collections', *Newsletter (Museum Ethnographers Group)*, 13 (1982); Minutes of the Fourth Annual General Meeting of the Museum Ethnographers Group, MEG, 25 April 1980.

[111] Pole, 'On Good Terms'. Note that this debate fell short of cataloguing practice being considered something other than neutral, and the field had yet to respond reflexively to the coloniality of the collections and their practice – a paper from the Latin Americanist Colin Henfrey 'seemed to stun' MEG members by taking the 'radical viewpoint' that the interpretation of a museum object should foreground its entanglement with colonial exploitation; see Minutes of the Ethnology Seminar of the Museum Ethnographers Group, MEG, March 1975. It appears, however, that there were dissenting progressive voices within MEG, and by the close of the decade the MEG Committee felt confident not to accept policy guidance on restitution prepared by Pole that sought to distance a given museum from bearing responsibility for the possession of illegally displaced collections; see Len Pole 'Notes and Guidelines on the Restitution and Return of Cultural

ethnographers debated implementations of computerised cataloguing and how to enable better interoperability between collection documentation.[112] And while Euan Mackie and his colleagues at the Hunterian were convinced that computerised cataloguing was of benefit to museum ethnographers, the collections under their care and their museums, others needed reassurance that computerisation was not an imposition of order onto complexity, that implementing a system like MDA was intended only to enhance the discoverability of collections,[113] and that the IRGMA process had produced a system that was flexible, that was designed to meet the needs of individual institutions.[114] 'It has never been suggested', wrote Pole in February 1978, 'that a well ordered working Index should be immediately replaced by M.D.A cards'. Rather, Pole continued, the 'immediate value lies in the use of cards for those collections which have not yet been properly Indexed'.[115] Among museum ethnographers in the UK, we see then that histories of bespoke cataloguing practice and prior investments – or otherwise – in documentation intersected with the rise in computerised cataloguing to produce a burst of lively, engaged and productive debate around the nature of their curatorial practice. The implementation and implications of computerised cataloguing was a throughline of MEG business into the mid-1980s,[116] indicating that the shifts in practice that IRGMA embodied mattered to their collective sense of what it meant to be a museum professional.

Conclusion

Between the late 1960s and the mid-1980s both the implementation of and the debate around computerised cataloguing disrupted the function of UK museums and how museum professionals imagined their labour. As we have seen, the period was characterised by the emergence of new forms of professionalisation, systemisation and specialisation. Documentation that served institutional and civic need was part of that emergence and became in this period a core function of UK museums. Through IRGMA, museum documentation benefited from investment, from sustained attention that made it theoretically possible to communicate and cross-search information about museum

Property', *Newsletter (Museum Ethnographers Group)*, 7 (1979), 18–19, and response Minutes of the Sixth Committee Meeting of the Museum Ethnographers Group, MEG, 19 January 1979.

[112] 'M.E.G. Information Retrieval Meeting', *Newsletter (Museum Ethnographers Group)*, 3 (1977), 10–11; Minutes of the Seventh Committee Meeting of the Museum Ethnographers Group, MEG, 16 March 1979; Minutes of the Tenth Committee Meeting of the Museum Ethnographers Group, MEG, 10 Dec. 1979.

[113] 'M.E.G. Information Retrieval Meeting', *Newsletter (Museum Ethnographers Group)*, 3 (1977), 11.

[114] Len Pole, 'Suggestions for a future IRGMA Ethnography Object Catalogue Card', *Newsletter (Museum Ethnographers Group)*, 3 (1977), 9–10.

[115] Len Pole, 'Museum Documentation Association', *Newsletter (Museum Ethnographers Group)*, 5 (1978), 18.

[116] Minutes of the Seventh Annual General Meeting of the Museum Ethnographers Group, MEG, 22 April 1983; Minutes of the Ninth Annual General Meeting of the Museum Ethnographers Group, MEG, 19 April 1985.

collections in ways that were attentive to museological subfields and their curatorial expertise. And through the MDA infrastructure of software, standards and input cards, as well as the opportunities presented by the JCP, many UK museums began to computerise their collections information and expertise for the first time. In turn there was a shift in the work that people did in UK museums, the types of people who did that work and the ascriptions of value afforded to different types of museum labour.

This shift was not uniform. Some museums drew on temporary labour, some did not. In some cases, clear distinctions were drawn between curatorial staff and those who could and – crucially – *should* use computers,[117] spawning new 'clerical', 'typist' and 'trained recorder' roles.[118] In other museums – especially smaller museums[119] – computerised cataloguing became yet another responsibility of museum curators, a new function bolted onto their already time-pressed, jack-of-all-trades professional persona. Museum education was slow to catch up with this shifting professional landscape. Euan Mackie's call in 1980 for the Museums Association to prioritise professional training on the MDA system indicates that both 'mindless' and critical approaches to computerised documentation were not filtering through from educational settings into museum workplaces as fast as some hoped they would. And the silos created by specialisation – signalled by the disappearance of computerised cataloguing from core Museums Association communications after the formation of the MDA – appear not to have helped the likes of Mackie to gain traction for their views within the profession, at least in the short term.

Nevertheless, it is clear that computerisation contributed to a cultural shift in UK museums, and that the emergence of IRGMA and its development as the MDA marked a growing, if uneven, recognition of the importance of good documentation to good museum practice. It is also significant that some museum subfields, such as museum ethnographers, embraced this change as a lens through which to reflect more widely on their curatorial practice – they, like Euan Mackie, Manchester Museum, University of Leicester's Museum Studies Department and the 300 or so UK museums that had by March 1981 invested in IRGMA cards, perhaps saw that there was no going back, and resolved to shape the change that was coming rather than let narratives of technological efficiency happen to them. At the same time the rise of computerised documentation did not mean that the – usually male coded – scholar curator was immediately displaced, either in practice or in the professional imaginary. When Lewis spoke about the potential advantages of IRGMA at the February 1972 Museums Association Council Meeting, they emphasised the benefits of the proposed system in terms of museum budgets at a time of fiscal retrenchment: by mechanising cataloguing labour, cheaper people could be found to do that labour, freeing – by implication – curators

---

[117] David Gittins, 'Computer-Based Museum Information Systems', *Museums Journal*, 76 (1976), 115–18.

[118] Laurel Ball, 'Recording Agricultural Collections', *Museums Journal*, 72 (1972), 55–7.

[119] Stone, 'Documenting Collections', 129.

to do other things.[120] The 'layman's guide to the scheme' was not then imagined by Lewis as a cheat sheet that would transform every curator into a computerised cataloguer and their museums into sites of datafield information exchange. Rather it was a prospectus on an imagined future workforce, of new professional personas and forms of documentary labour that had by the early 1980s not yet fully arrived, but that were beginning to take shape as computerised work was normalised within and fashioned by the UK museum profession.

These shifts did not take place in a vacuum. The history of museums shaped and was shaped by broader currents of contemporary British History. The emergence of computerised cataloguing in museums aligns chronologically with the rise of (white) male-identified dominion over British computing jobs and – once defeminised – the attendant reconfiguration of those jobs as sites of power, expertise and innovation.[121] The uneven approach taken by UK museums to new forms of documentary labour, especially those roles funded by the Job Creation Programme, contributes to our understanding of the ways Britain's governing classes attempted to structure youth training and education during deindustrialisation,[122] as well as broader reappraisals of who made, sustained and benefited from neoliberal politics.[123] The role of the Department of Education and Science in supporting – if not decisively funding – IRGMA/MDA contextualises work on the political drivers of technological change and furthers our understanding of both state and quasi-governmental systems and the levels of technical expertise that drove their development.[124] The assumed training need created by the IRGMA/MDA system underscores the everyday frictions experienced as information technologies entered mid- to late twentieth-century workplaces and civic environments.[125] The decisive role of the UK museum sector in the development of its own cataloguing software, standards and systems offers a localised perspective on the information revolution. In particular, it provides insight into visions of national leadership in technological development that pre-dated assumptions of North American economic hegemony, and a globalised information, what Richard Barbrook and Andy Cameron would later call

---

[120] Minutes of the meeting of Council 17 Feb. 1972, TNA, HK 2/16 (Museums Association: Council agendas, minutes and papers), 1972–4.

[121] Mar Hicks, *Programmed Inequality: How Britain Discarded Women Technologists and Lost its Edge in Computing* (Cambridge, MA, 2017).

[122] Peter Mandler, *The Crisis of the Meritocracy: Britain's Transition to Mass Education since the Second World War* (Oxford, 2020); Sarah Kenny, 'A "Radical Project": Youth Culture, Leisure, and Politics in 1980s Sheffield', *Twentieth Century British History*, 30 (2019), 557–84.

[123] Aled Davies, Ben Jackson and Florence Sutcliffe-Braithwaite (eds.), *The Neoliberal Age? Britain since the 1970s* (2021).

[124] David Edgerton, *The Rise and Fall of the British Nation: A Twentieth-Century History* (2018); Jon Agar, *The Government Machine a Revolutionary History of the Computer* (Cambridge, MA, 2003).

[125] Carmen Flury and Michael Geiss (eds.), *How Computers Entered the Classroom, 1960–2000: Historical Perspectives* (Berlin, 2023); James Baker and David Geiringer, 'Space, Text and Selfhood: Encounters with the Personal Computer in the Mass Observation Project Archive, 1991–2004', *Contemporary British History*, 33 (2018), 293–312; Paul Dourish, *Where the Action Is: The Foundations of Embodied Interaction* (Cambridge, MA, 2001).

'The Californian Ideology': a belief in the emancipatory potential of techno-logical progress unencumbered by regulation, taxation and state intervention that Barbrook and Cameron read as an exploitative fiction concocted by 'hip and rich' – and mostly white – east coast Americans, largely for their own advancement and enrichment.[126] Finally, museum documentation – and the classification, standardisation and intuition dressed up as reason that they embody – are forms of authority that have remarkable durability.[127] Researching the conditions that produced museum documentation in the years after the formation of IRGMA is then vital to understanding the records that remain with us today, because it was those records that would form the basis of museum databases as the sector encountered later and accelerated phases of computerisation. And it is the shadows, legacies and positionalities of those records which not only remain entangled in the information systems of the present but continue to be projected into our shared futures.[128]

Acknowledgements. My thanks to Polly Bence, Nicola Stylianou, Vicky Holmes, Richard Light, Louise Ellis-Barrett, and Verna Acres for helping me to find collections that I could not seem to find. Colleagues in the Department of History at the University of Southampton gave a draft manu-script a hard time at a 'Conversations in Research' session, and the final version is all the better for it. Two anonymous peer reviewers provided thoughtful, constructive and insightful comments. All errors of interpretation, judgement and fact remain my own.

Author biography. James Baker is Director of Digital Humanities at the University of Southampton. He works at the intersection of history, cultural heritage and digital technologies.

---

[126] Richard Barbrook and Andy Cameron, 'The Californian Ideology', *Science as Culture*, 6 (1996), 44–72.

[127] Turner, *Cataloguing Culture*; Ann Laura Stoler, *Duress: Imperial Durabilities in Our Times* (Durham, NC, 2016).

[128] Jacques Derrida, *Archive Fever: A Freudian Impression* (1996).

Cite this article: Baker J (2024). 'Providing a Layman's Guide to the Scheme': Museum Computing, Professional Personas and Documentary Labour in the United Kingdom, 1967–1983. *Transactions of the Royal Historical Society* 2, 293–316. https://doi.org/10.1017/S0080440124000045

Transactions of the RHS (2024), 2, 317–343
doi:10.1017/S0080440123000294

ARTICLE

Rethinking Transnational Activism through Regional Perspectives: Reflections, Literatures and Cases

Thomas Davies[1] , Daniel Laqua[2] , Maria Framke[3] , Anne-Isabelle Richard[4] , Patricia Oliart[5] , Kate Skinner[6] , Pilar Requejo de Lamo[7] , Robert Kramm[8] , Charlotte Alston[2] and Matthew Hurst[9]

[1]Department of International Politics, City, University of London, London, UK, [2]Department of Humanities, Northumbria University, Newcastle upon Tyne, UK, [3]Department of History, University of Erfurt, Erfurt, Germany, [4]Institute for History, Leiden University, Leiden, The Netherlands, [5]School of Modern Languages, Newcastle University, Newcastle, UK, [6]Department of History, Bristol University, Bristol, UK, [7]School of History, University of St Andrews, St Andrews, Scotland, UK, [8]School of History, Ludwig Maximilian University Munich, Munich, Germany and [9]Department of History, University of York, York, UK
Corresponding author: Email: daniel.laqua@northumbria.ac.uk

(Received 9 May 2023; revised 7 November 2023; accepted 17 November 2023;
first published online 8 January 2024)

Abstract

This collectively authored article argues for a regional turn in the historical study of transnational activism. By considering not only pan-regional movements but also examples of borderland contexts, transregional connections and diasporic understandings of 'region', our discussion identifies fresh possibilities for investigating the evolution and functioning of transnational activism. Based on a Royal Historical Society-funded workshop held at and supported by Northumbria University, the article brings together insights from diverse locations and arenas of contestation. The first part considers literatures on three macro-regional settings – South Asia, Western Europe and Latin America – to illustrate the importance of distinctive regional contexts and constructs in shaping transnational activism and its goals. The second part turns to case studies of transnational activism in and beyond Eastern Europe, West Africa, the Caribbean and East Asia. In doing so, it explores very different notions of the regional to identify how transnational activism has both shaped and been shaped by these ideas. Taken together, the two parts highlight the role of regional identities and projects in challenging inequalities and external domination. Our analysis and examples indicate the possibilities of a regionally rooted approach for writing histories of transnational activism.

Keywords: Transnational history; global history; activism; social movements; regions

Transnational activism – the cross-border mobilisation of individuals, groups and movements advocating for social and political change – has become one of the richest areas of historical enquiry. Research on anti-colonial, environmentalist, feminist, humanitarian, pacifist, socialist and many other mobilisations has generated a diverse historical literature, stimulated by developments in the field of global history as well as approaches from sociology and political science.[1] Many of these activist movements portrayed themselves in 'global' terms – both by proclaiming the universality of their cause and by pointing to supporters in different countries and continents. Given the context-specific nature of purportedly 'global' causes and campaigns, it is evident that we cannot take such self-representations at face value.[2] The inherent tensions between global claims and more limited practices underscore the challenges of writing history in genuinely global terms and, as such, raise broader methodological questions.[3]

As Su Lin Lewis has recently argued, the study of transnational activism offers opportunities to decolonise our research perspective, namely by tracing the concepts, connections and campaigns of actors from the Global South.[4] Like Lewis, we are interested in bonds that shift attention away from European and North American thinkers, movements or institutions. At the same time, we propose a different approach to this subject by treating 'region' as a central unit of analysis. As we suggest, an emphasis on regional dimensions allows us to rethink the concepts employed by activists themselves. Many movements linked their endeavours to categories or conditions that they deemed global – be it class for socialists, sex or gender for feminists, or 'race' for Pan-Africanists. Yet while such phenomena were certainly transnational, their manifestation was far from uniform across the globe – and a regional focus acknowledges this variability. Rather than testing the 'global' scope of activists' efforts or discussing local adaptations (which are sometimes described as 'glocal'), our article shows that region mattered in multiple ways. Thus, we are also able to revisit questions of 'scale', which have been a key concern in transnational history.[5]

---

[1] The literature on this subject is vast and it is impossible to list examples from every one of these sub-fields here. For books that explore different cases, see Stefan Berger and Sean Scalmer (eds.), *The Transnational Activist: Transformations and Comparisons from the Anglo-World since the Nineteenth Century* (Cham, 2018); and Daniel Laqua, *Activism across Borders since 1870: Causes, Campaigns and Conflict in and beyond Europe* (2023). For further reflections on transnational activism, see Kiran Klaus Patel and Sonja Levsen, 'The Spatial Contours of Transnational Activism: Conceptual Implications and the Road Forward', *European Review of History*, 29 (2022), 548–61; Fiona Paisley and Pamela Scully, *Writing Transnational History* (2019), 153–88.

[2] Jessica Pliley, Robert Kramm and Harald Fischer-Tiné (eds.), *Global Anti-Vice Activism: Fighting Drinks, Drugs and 'Immorality'* (Cambridge, 2016).

[3] For reflections on these issues, see Sven Beckert and Dominic Sachsenmeier, *Global History, Globally* (2018); and Afro-Asian Networks Research Collective, 'Manifesto: Networks of Decolonization in Asia and Africa', *Radical History Review*, 131 (2018), 176–82.

[4] Su Lin Lewis, 'Decolonising the History of Internationalism: Transnational Activism across the South', *Transactions of the Royal Historical Society* (FirstView access, 18 Oct. 2023), 1–25.

[5] Bernhard Struck, Kate Ferris and Jacques Revel, 'Introduction: Space and Scale in Transnational History', *International History Review*, 33 (2011), 573–84.

Our article originated in a Royal Historical Society workshop held in March 2023.[6] Convened by two historians of transnational movements and international organisations (Thomas Davies and Daniel Laqua), the event featured contributions from scholars with different regional specialisms and with expertise on diverse forms of activism, including humanitarianism (Maria Framke), regional cooperation and decolonisation (Anne-Isabelle Richard), Indigenous rights (Patricia Oliart), Esperanto (Pilar Requejo de Lamo), anti-colonialism (Kate Skinner), the Tolstoyan movement (Charlotte Alston), anarchism (Robert Kramm) and civil society efforts in Hong Kong (Matthew Hurst). Instead of choosing a traditional format of historical writing, we have produced a piece that integrates the voices of ten different scholars. By embracing co-authorship on a scale that is fairly uncommon in our discipline, we take up Lynn Hunt's argument that '[h]istory writing in the global era can only be a collaborative form of inquiry'.[7] There are evident limitations to our approach – most obviously the fact that we are all based at European institutions, even if our research spans five continents.[8] Nonetheless, we hope that our article indicates new possibilities for integrating the work of authors with different scholarly backgrounds.

Compared to other formats, our approach offers distinct rewards. While articles in themed journal issues may address an overarching theme, they tend to be written and read as stand-alone pieces. By contrast, our piece contains sections that have been written, edited and redrafted for thematic coherence and overall consistency, while still offering the breadth that one might otherwise find in larger collections of texts. In adopting an integrated approach, our article also differs from published 'roundtables'. The combination of our perspectives allows us to combine reflections on specific historiographies with examples drawn from primary research. To this end, our article comprises two principal parts. Part A is largely historiographical, with Framke, Richard and Oliart's expertise underpinning a discussion of research on three particular regions – South Asia, Western Europe and Latin America. Through this selection, we illustrate how transnational activism was shaped by particular regional contexts, but also how activists contributed to the understanding of such regions. Part B broadens the perspective both geographically and empirically. Primarily drawing on the work of de Lamo, Alston, Skinner, Kramm and Hurst, it deploys several case studies that nuance our understanding of transnational activism and its modi operandi. These cases elucidate different ways in which a regional focus can be opened up in writing histories of transnational activism.

---

[6] We thank the Royal Historical Society and Northumbria University for funding our workshop. As convenors and lead authors, Davies and Laqua took responsibility for putting together the article and drafted the overarching sections. The order in which co-authors are listed largely reflects the sequence of their most prominent contribution. Individual footnotes further credit their work; however, all sections are based on dialogue and collaboration. In addition to the co-authors, we are grateful for Vikram Visana's comments prior to the drafting of this article.

[7] Lynn Hunt, *Writing History in the Global Era* (New York, 2015), 151.

[8] For important points on collaborative modes of working and ways of involving scholars from the Global South, see Lewis, 'Decolonising the History of Internationalism', 20–4.

Before moving to these main parts, however, it is necessary to clarify the concepts that underpin our analysis. The term 'activism' encompasses a variety of efforts to effect social and political change. These may include voluntary action, social movement campaigns, the formation of non-governmental organisations as well as diverse methods of protest and advocacy. *Transnational* activism is a form of activism in which individuals, groups and movements forge ties across national borders.[9] The term emphasises the cross-border nature of relationships; at the same time, it draws attention to non-state – or even anti-state – actors and organisations. While broad in nature, 'transnational activism' can be distinguished from 'global activism': the latter term emphasises the perspective of activists who stress the universality of their concerns – which, as we have already noted, is potentially misleading.

The other central term for our discussion is 'region'. Regions may be considered as entities that rarely map onto state borders and can be very extensive, potentially stretching across a continent or further. Although regions are often perceived as being geographically conditioned, they are cultural, social and political constructs that manifest in diverse forms. For our enquiry, this aspect is crucial, as activists could imagine themselves as parts of regions in very different ways.[10] The approach taken forward in this article reflects this diversity: Part A focuses on regions that, at least partially, tend to be associated with geographical categorisations, notwithstanding the role of cultural visions and political realities in shaping such understandings. Part B extends the discussion: by considering borderland contexts and diasporas with a regional identification among our case studies, we shed light on features that both 'glocal' and global perspectives on transnational activism tend to obscure.

Why, however, choose such a wide-ranging conception of region? We argue that the ambiguity can be deployed constructively: it offers the opportunity to 'play with scales' when it comes to examining transnational activism.[11] Regions are fluid and, at the same time, distinct from both the national and the global; by thinking about 'region', we can thus explore a much wider array of scales. This is not a purely theoretical matter, as activists worked with different scales to further their cause: they addressed audiences on local, national, global and highly diverse regional levels – alternatively, successively or simultaneously,

---

[9] For a discussion of these concepts, see Laqua, *Activism across Borders*, 3–9. For different manifestations of this phenomenon, see Stefan Berger and Holger Nehring (eds.), *The History of Social Movements in a Global Perspective* (Cham, 2017); and Thomas Davies, *NGOs: A New History of Transnational Civil Society* (2013).

[10] Martin W. Lewis and Kären E. Wigen, *The Myth of Continents: A Critique of Metageography* (Berkeley, 1997); Benedict Anderson, *Imagined Communities: Reflections on the Origin and Spread of Nationalism*, 2nd edn (1991); Benedict Anderson, *Under Three Flags: Anarchism and the Anti-Colonial Imagination* (2005); Anne-Isabelle Richard and Stella Krepp, 'Regional Rights Projects and Decolonization in the Twentieth Century', in *The Cambridge History of Rights*, vol. v: *The Twentieth and Twenty-first Centuries*, ed. Samuel Moyn and Meredith Terretta (Cambridge, forthcoming).

[11] The notion of (and the phrase) 'playing with scales' featured in Struck *et al.*, 'Introduction', 574. It has subsequently constituted an overarching theme in Jan de Vries, 'Playing with Scales: The Global and the Micro, the Macro and the Nano', *Past & Present*, 242, suppl. 14 (2019), 23–36.

depending on the circumstances. Our regional perspective not only provides an alternative to accounts that privilege activism within state boundaries or that take national identities as a given, but draws attention to diverse challenges to state sovereignty, whether by advancing 'regionalisation' or by articulating alternative visions of global order.[12] For instance, many African feminists have used a regional 'African' perspective to highlight that the world order they knew was rooted in inequality, exploitation and injustice. By inserting their own voices and experiences, they have questioned the universal framings often used by Western feminists and, in doing so, have shifted understandings of 'the global'.[13]

In sum, our article considers how transnational connections among activists emerged from diverse regional contexts and reflected regionally rooted ideas, identities and practices – even when they cast their concerns and visions as global. We will demonstrate that regional perspectives can illuminate complex and sometimes overlapping sets of ideas, spaces and identities, including ones that were not always tied to precisely demarcated geographical boundaries. We explore how the concept of transnational activism informs scholarly research on different regions, outline the features of regionally sensitive approaches and show how 'the regional' as a scale of analysis enriches our understanding of the dynamics by which transnational activism functioned.

Part A: Reassessing the literature on transnational activism

Notwithstanding earlier work on its different manifestations, it was from the late 1990s onwards that the concepts of transnational and global activism came to the forefront on scholarly agendas, especially in sociology, political science and international relations (IR). Growing interest in this subject coincided with diverse social and political mobilisations at a time when 'globalisation' became a master-narrative for ongoing developments. By 2005, sociologists Donatella della Porta and Sidney Tarrow described the 'relational mechanisms that are bringing together national actors in transnational coalitions' as generating '[t]he most striking developments of the last decade'.[14] Such alliances manifested in large-scale protests – famously during the World Trade Organization (WTO) meeting in Seattle in 1999 – and in new activist ventures, for example the sessions of the World Social Forum from 2001 onwards. These developments stimulated further research on campaigns for

---

[12] On regionalisation, see for instance Luk Van Langenhove, *Building Regions: The Regionalization of the World Order* (Farnham, 2011). For this concept's application in research on activism, see Jackie Smith, 'Building Bridges or Building Walls? Explaining Regionalization among Transnational Social Movement Organizations', *Mobilization: An International Quarterly*, 10 (2005), 251–69. For a non-Western perspective, see Burleigh Hendrickson, 'March 1968: Practising Transnational Activism from Tunis to Paris', *International Journal of Middle East Studies*, 44 (2012), 755–74.

[13] Balghis Badri and Aili Mari Tripp, 'African Influences on Global Women's Rights: An Overview', in *Women's Activism in Africa: Struggles for Rights and Representation*, ed. Balghis Badri and Aili Mari Tripp (2017), 1–32.

[14] Donatella della Porta and Sidney Tarrow, 'Transnational Protest and Social Activism: An Introduction', in *Transnational Protest and Global Activism*, ed. Donatella della Porta and Sidney Tarrow (Lanham, MD, 2005), 9.

global justice and transnational causes, with the ambition to trace forms of 'globalisation from below'.[15]

Even when contemporary phenomena were their primary concern, social scientists acknowledged the deeper history of their subject. In 1998, Margaret Keck and Kathryn Sikkink drew attention to the workings of 'transnational advocacy networks', with examples ranging back to abolitionist movements.[16] Five years later, Tarrow acknowledged historical antecedents of 'the new transnational activism'.[17] Moreover, he and della Porta noted that 'contentious politics at the turn of the millennium' had elements that 'were familiar from the history of collective action'.[18] Their comments emphasised similarities with the protests against the US-led attack on Iraq (2003), but an awareness of such links was not confined to anti-war activism. For example, in 2004 Peggy Antrobus traced the emergence of a 'global women's movement' but argued this had 'formed out of many movements shaped in local struggles and brought together in the context of global opportunities and challenges'.[19]

The specific historical circumstances that sparked social scientists' growing concern with transnational and global activism are also relevant when bearing in mind historiographical developments in the same period: the early 2000s constituted a peak for arguments for the adoption of transnational or global perspectives in history.[20] Research on histories of transnational activism emerged as one significant line of enquiry, exemplifying transnational history's interest in 'human-made connections'.[21] This literature is certainly alert to potential boundaries and tensions. For instance, some studies have noted the specific national contexts in which some forms of transnational activism unfolded.[22]

---

[15] Donatella della Porta *et al.*, *Globalization from Below: Transnational Activists and Protest Networks* (Minneapolis, 2006). See also Ruth Reitan, *Global Activism* (2007).

[16] Margaret Keck and Kathryn Sikkink, *Activists beyond Borders: Advocacy Networks in International Politics* (Ithaca, 1998).

[17] Sidney Tarrow, *The New Transnational Activism* (Lanham, MD, 2003).

[18] Sidney Tarrow and Donatella della Porta, 'Conclusion: "Globalization", Complex Internationalism, and Transnational Contention', in *Transnational Protest and Global Activism*, ed. della Porta and Tarrow, 228.

[19] Peggy Antrobus, *The Global Women's Movement: Origins, Issues and Strategies* (2004), 1. For other examples from this period, see Myra Marx Ferree and Aili Mari Tripp (eds.), *Global Feminism: Transnational Women's Activism, Organizing, and Human Rights* (New York, 2006); Nancy A. Naples and Manisha Desai (eds.), *Women's Activism and Globalization: Linking Local Struggles and Transnational Politics* (New York, 2002).

[20] For a few examples from this period, see Jürgen Osterhammel, 'Transnationale Gesellschaftsgeschichte: Erweiterung oder Alternative?', *Geschichte und Gesellschaft*, 27 (2001), 464–79; Thomas Bender (ed.), *Rethinking American History in a Global Age* (Berkeley, 2002); Patrick O'Brien, 'Historiographical Traditions and Modern Imperatives for the Restoration of Global History', *Journal of Global History*, 1 (2006), 3–39; Sebastian Conrad, Andreas Eckert and Ulrike Freitag (eds.), *Globalgeschichte: Debatten, Ansätze, Themen* (Frankfurt/Main, 2007); Patricia Clavin, 'Defining Transnationalism', *Contemporary European History*, 14 (2005), 421–39.

[21] On 'human-made connections' and the role of different kinds of 'connectors', see Pierre-Yves Saunier, *Transnational History* (Basingstoke, 2013), 35–6.

[22] David Stenner, *Globalizing Morocco: Transnational Activism and the Postcolonial State* (Stanford, 2019); Daniel Laqua, *The Age of Internationalism and Belgium, 1880–1930: Peace, Progress and Prestige* (Manchester, 2013).

Other work has noted how experiences of gender or 'race' shaped particular forms of cross-border activism.[23] Moreover, various historians have shown how cross-border cooperation was not a prerogative of the Left.[24] To some extent the latter work resonates with contemporary observations: media discourses and studies on the question of a global 'populist' wave since the mid-2010s illustrate that transnational activism can have different ideological underpinnings.[25]

With more than a quarter-century of research on the nature, workings and history of transnational activism, we are in a position to take stock of this literature, building on exercises that have explored the state of global and transnational history more generally.[26] Rather than pursuing the impossible quest of a purportedly 'comprehensive' survey, the following three subsections show how transnational activism can be traced in the literatures on South Asia, Europe and Latin America, drawing especially on the regional expertise of co-authors Maria Framke, Anne-Isabelle Richard and Patricia Oliart. These studies focus on the 'regional' as a scale of analysis. By acknowledging the regional specificities of transnational activism, they also set up the lineaments for the discussion in Part B.

Transnational activism and histories of South Asia[27]

Transnational activism has long featured in the scholarly literature on colonial South Asia – initially without being explicitly named as such. Earlier works

---

[23] Elora Shehabuddin, 'Between Orientalism and Anti-Muslim Racism: Pakistan, the United States, and Women's Transnational Activism in the Early Cold War Interlude', *Meridians*, 20 (2021), 340–69; and the special issue (S20; ed. Celia Donert) on 'Women's Rights and Global Socialism: Gendering Socialist Internationalism during the Cold War', *International Review of Social History*, 67 (2022).

[24] Andrea Mammone, *Transnational Neo-Fascism in France and Italy* (Cambridge, 2015); Madeleine Herren, 'Fascist Internationalism', in *Internationalisms: A Twentieth-Century History*, ed. Glenda Sluga and Patricia Clavin (Cambridge, 2017), 191–212; Arnd Bauerkämper and Grzegorz Rossoliński-Liebe (eds.), *Fascism without Borders: Transnational Connections and Cooperation between Movements and Regimes in Europe from 1918 to 1945* (New York, 2017); Agnieszka Pasieka, 'Introduction to the Special Section: National, European, Transnational: Far-Right Activism in the Twentieth and Twenty-first Centuries', *East European Politics and Societies*, 35 (2022), 863–75.

[25] Such narratives are increasingly prevalent in politics and the media: see e.g. the report by the Tony Blair Institute for Global Change, 'High Tide? Populists in Power around the World, 1990–2020', 7 Feb. 2020, https://www.institute.global/insights/geopolitics-and-security/high-tide-populism-power-1990-2020 (last accessed 13 Apr. 2023); John Harris, '"A Politics of Nostalgia and Score-Settling": How Populism Dominated the 2010s', *The Guardian* (online version), 26 Nov. 2019, https://www.theguardian.com/culture/2019/nov/26/politics-of-nostalgia-score-settling-populism-dominated-2010s-john-harris (last accessed 13 Apr. 2023). For academic perspectives, see Daniel Wajner, 'The Populist Way Out: Why Contemporary Populist Leaders Seek Transnational Legitimation', *British Journal of Politics and International Relations*, 24 (2022), 416–36; Daniel Wajner, 'Global Populism', in *The Palgrave Handbook of Populism*, ed. Michael Oswald (Cham, 2021), 351–67.

[26] Paul Thomas Chamberlin *et al.*, 'On Transnational and International History', *American Historical Review*, 128 (2023), 255–332; Richard Drayton and David Motadel, 'Discussion: The Futures of Global History', *Journal of Global History*, 13 (2018), 1–21.

[27] This section particularly draws on Maria Framke's expertise.

explored examples in the nineteenth and early twentieth centuries (for instance, British women advocating for more rights and better conditions for their Indian 'sisters') or traced the lives of transnational activists (such as Gandhi), yet they did so mostly as part of writing (new) imperial history or the history of the Indian national movement.[28] More recently, there has been growing interest in understanding transnational activism as part of the wider history of colonial South Asia and postcolonial India. Research in this vein has covered women's rights, humanitarianism and various social reform causes.[29] Several historians have examined transnational networks and advocacy campaigns from beyond South Asia, with a growing understanding of South Asian participation in such initiatives.[30] Transnational perspectives can also show how the category of 'caste' – generally construed in 'local' Indian terms – became globalised through its resonance with the activism of other marginalised groups.[31]

If we turn to a specific area, namely the history of humanitarianism, we can see that a regional lens requires us to reassess assumptions that have informed some of the earlier work on transnational activism. The ideas, practices and campaigns to help others in distress have often been understood in universalistic terms, as something featuring commonalities across world regions. Nonetheless, the majority of historical work has focused on humanitarian approaches from Europe and North America, even when it has problematised the way in which 'Western' perspectives were deployed in other regions. Broader surveys have often marginalised the forms of humanitarianism that originated independently of and existed alongside those developed in the 'West'.[32] Recent research on Chinese, Egyptian, South Asian and Southeast Asian aid initiatives in the late nineteenth and first half of the twentieth

---

[28] For some examples from the 1990s, see Antoinette Burton, *Burdens of History: British Feminists, Indian Women, and Imperial Culture, 1865-1915* (Chapel Hill, 1994); Barbara Ramusack, 'Cultural Missionaries, Maternal Imperialists, Feminist Allies: British Women Activists in India, 1865–1945', *Women's Studies International Forum*, 13 (1990), 309–21; Judith Brown, *Gandhi: Prisoner of Hope* (New Haven, 1998).

[29] Rosalind Parr, *Citizens of Everywhere: Indian Women, Nationalism and Cosmopolitanism, 1920-1952* (Cambridge, 2021); Sumita Mukherjee, *Indian Suffragettes: Female Identities and Transnational Networks* (New Delhi, 2018); Zoë Laidlaw, '"Justice to India – Prosperity to England – Freedom to the Slave!" Humanitarian and Moral Reform Campaigns on India, Aborigines and American Slavery', *Journal of the Royal Asiatic Society*, 22 (2012), 299–324; Heather Goodall and Ghosh Devleena, 'Reimagining Asia: Indian and Australian Women Crossing Borders', *Modern Asian Studies*, 53 (2019), 1183–221; Harald Fischer-Tiné, 'Eradicating the "Scourge of Drink" and the "Unpardonable Sin of Illegitimate Sexual Enjoyment": M. K. Gandhi as Anti-Vice Crusader', *Interdisziplinäre Zeitschrift für Südasienforschung*, 2 (2017), 113–30.

[30] Adrian Ruprecht, 'The Great Eastern Crisis (1875–1878) as a Global Humanitarian Moment', *Journal of Global History*, 16 (2021), 159–84; Shehabuddin, 'Between Orientalism and Anti-Muslim Racism'; Elisabeth Armstrong, 'Before Bandung: The Anti-Imperialist Women's Movement in Asia and the Women's International Democratic Federation', *Journal of Women in Culture and Society*, 41 (2016), 305–31.

[31] Suraj Yengde, *Caste: A New History of the World* (forthcoming).

[32] Michael Barnett, *Empire of Humanity: A History of Humanitarianism* (Ithaca, 2011); Silvia Salvatici, *A History of Humanitarianism, 1755–1989: In the Name of Others* (Manchester, 2019).

century shows that the 'Western' periodisation of humanitarianism and related transnational activities cannot be applied easily to other contexts.[33] With regard to the Indian case, the conceptual label 'imperial humanitarianism' – as proposed by Michael Barnett for the period up to 1945[34] – would ignore influential humanitarian practices and ideas driven by nationalist, internationalist or communal actors and agendas.[35]

Researching the ideas, agendas and initiatives of transnational activism in their regional contexts adds nuance to narratives that might otherwise over-emphasise universal concerns. For instance, Indian independence activists who participated in transnational left-wing solidarity networks organised humanitarian work and contributed to humanitarian discourses not only out of a universal concern for helping others. Their activism was also motivated by strong anti-colonial and anti-imperial sentiments. Transnational aid activities were coupled with political campaigns in support of democracy and freedom; they thus enhanced the status of the Indian National Congress on the international stage and bestowed legitimacy upon it. Seen in this way, Indian humanitarianism was closely entwined with visions of, and strategies for, emancipation from colonialism.[36]

While this selection of research perspectives has focused on the early twentieth century, an emerging literature goes one step further by highlighting transregional cooperation during decolonisation. The 'Bandung Moment' of 1955 involved the leaders of newly independent states from Africa and Asia, yet recent work has identified a wider history of South–South activism in this era.[37] In this respect, the transnational links of South Asian activists highlight the significance of transregional connections, a theme we shall explore further in the next two sections.

---

[33] For examples that do not deal specifically with South Asia but exemplify this concern for non-Western humanitarianism, see Mark Frost, 'Humanitarianism and the Overseas Aid Craze in Britain's Colonial Straits Settlements, 1870–1920', *Past & Present*, 236 (2017), 169–205; Alexandra Pfeiff, 'The Red Swastika Society's Humanitarian Work: A Re-interpretation of the Red Cross in China', *New Global Studies*, 10 (2016), 373–92; Shaimaa Esmail El-Neklawy and Esther Möller, 'Between Traditions of Aid and Political Ambitions: Endowments and Humanitarian Associations in Egypt, Late 19th–Mid 20th Century', *Endowment Studies*, 6 (2022), 192–220.

[34] Barnett, *Empire of Humanity*, pt 1.

[35] Eleonor Marcussen, *Acts of Aid: Politics of Relief and Reconstruction in the 1934 Bihar–Nepal Earthquake* (Cambridge 2022); Joanna Simonow, *Ending Famine in India: A Transnational History of Food Aid and Development, c. 1890-1950* (Leiden, 2023); Maria Framke, 'Indian Humanitarianism under Colonial Rule: Imperial Loyalty, National Self-Assertion and Anticolonial Emancipation', in *The Routledge Handbook of the History of Colonialism in South Asia*, ed. Harald Fischer-Tiné and Maria Framke (2021), 486–96.

[36] Maria Framke, '"We Must Send a Gift Worthy of India and the Congress!" War and Political Humanitarianism in Late Colonial South Asia', *Modern Asian Studies*, 51, 1969–98; Joanna Simonow, 'The Great Bengal Famine in Britain: Metropolitan Campaigning for Food Relief and the End of Empire, 1943–44', *Journal of Imperial and Commonwealth History*, 48 (2020), 168–97.

[37] Su Lin Lewis and Carolien Stolte, 'Other Bandungs: Afro-Asian Internationalisms in the Early Cold War', *Journal of World History*, 30 (2019), 1–19, which introduces a themed journal issue featuring various examples on this subject. See also Lewis, 'Decolonising the History of Internationalism'.

Rethinking Europe and Europeanism[38]

For obvious reasons, Europe has featured prominently in the historiography on transnational actors advocating regional cooperation. After acknowledging the literature on this particular form of activism, we turn attention to Europe's relationship with other regions, in a way that contrasts with traditional approaches that extrapolate from the European experience to other parts of the world.

The literature on activism and regional integration in Europe contains four major strands. One prominent strand is biographical, looking at figures that promoted European integration, covering individuals such as Paneuropa founder Richard Coudenhove-Kalergi.[39] A second approach considers European integrationist groups and campaigns within national contexts,[40] while a third perspective traces the development of Europeanist ideas.[41] A fourth strand explores European integration from the perspective of transnational actors, from political parties to technical experts.[42] Somewhat counter-intuitively, the national perspective has often emphasised transnational connections, whereas transnational approaches have tended to highlight national specificities amongst the regional actors working for a common regional goal.[43]

In contrast to these well-established fields, global perspectives on European cooperation and integration are still emerging.[44] A perspective that acknowledges the links between the regional and the global is highly significant. In historiographical terms, it further 'provincialises' Europe by showing how categories that are often seen as intrinsically European have been shaped by wider relationships and flows.[45] Moreover, such an approach draws attention to the way in which transnational actors both within and beyond Europe thought about world regions and their relationships. Traditionally, when the literature on European integration has looked beyond Europe itself, it has focused on the role of the United States.[46] More recently, however, the impact

---

[38] This section particularly draws on Anne-Isabelle Richard's expertise.

[39] See e.g. Anita Ziegenhofer, *Botschafter Europas: Richard Nikolaus Coudenhove-Kalergi und die Paneuropa-Bewegung in den zwanziger und dreißiger Jahren* (Vienna, 2004).

[40] See e.g. Geneviève Duchenne, *Esquisses d'une Europe nouvelle: L'Européisme dans la Belgique de l'entre-deux-guerres (1919-1939)* (Brussels, 2008).

[41] Mark Hewitson and Matthew D'Auria (eds.), *Europe in Crisis: Intellectuals and the European Idea, 1917-1957* (New York, 2015); Patrick Pasture, *Imagining European Unity since 1000 AD* (Basingstoke, 2015).

[42] Wolfram Kaiser, *Christian Democracy and the Origins of European Union* (Cambridge, 2007); Vincent Lagendijk, *Electrifying Europe: The Power of Europe in the Construction of Electricity Networks* (Amsterdam, 2008).

[43] Anne-Isabelle Richard, 'Les boutiquiers idéalistes: Federalism in the Netherlands in the Interwar Period', in *Générations de fédéralistes européens depuis le XIXe siècle: Individus, groupes, espaces et reseaux*, ed. Geneviève Duchenne and Michel Dumoulin (Brussels, 2012), 93–108.

[44] Kiran Klaus Patel, *Project Europe: A History* (Cambridge, 2020).

[45] For this concept, see Dipesh Chakrabarty, *Provincializing Europe: Postcolonial Thought and Historical Difference* (Princeton, 2000).

[46] Geir Lundestad, 'Empire by Invitation? The United States and Western Europe, 1945-1952', *Journal of Peace Research*, 23 (1986), 263–77.

of colonial relations has become a significant research area.[47] Ties between Europe and Africa have attracted particular interest in this context.[48] Further emphasis on these connections is necessary, given that Western European integration was taking shape in the 1950s and 1960s – at a point when this region was transitioning from its formerly dominant (colonial) position.

Crucially, we can see the importance of such a relational approach even in earlier forms of Europeanist activism. The Paneuropa movement emerged in the early 1920s, at a point when ideas about Europe were entwined with a profound sense of crisis – not only because of the devastation caused by the Great War, but also because of challenges to Europe's global role. This period saw many questions about the nature of Europe, its relationship with other regions and its rapport with supposedly global institutions, notably the League of Nations.[49] Coudenhove-Kalergi is one example of a transnational activist who sought to address these questions: his emphasis on European regional integration was informed by a global vision of Europe's position in the world and the assumption that other regions would build their own federations. His visions mirrored the concepts of other activists – for instance his conceptualisation of Europe and Africa as part of the same region, Eurafrica. After the Second World War, these trends were reinforced, and actors from different colonies employed the concept of a Eurafrican region for their own purposes. Senegalese politician Léopold Senghor, for example, used it in discussions on the European Convention on Human Rights to argue for greater rights and self-government in areas then still under French rule.[50]

A transregional approach to European integration must link it to the history of decolonisation. In recent years, research on decolonisation has highlighted alternatives to the nation state, for example federation projects in decolonising or postcolonial regions.[51] Moreover, a vibrant literature on anti-colonialism and anti-imperialism directs attention to the role of transnational actors.[52]

---

[47] Giuliano Garavini, *After Empires: European Integration, Decolonization and the Challenge from the Global South, 1957–1986* (Oxford, 2012); Anne-Isabelle Richard, 'The Limits of Solidarity: Europeanism, Anti-Colonialism and Socialism at the Congress of the Peoples of Europe, Asia and Africa in Puteaux, 1948', *European Review of History*, 21 (2014), 519–37; Véronique Dimier, *The Invention of a European Development Aid Bureaucracy: Recycling Empire* (Basingstoke, 2014).

[48] Marie-Thérèse Bitsch and Gérard Bossuat (eds.), *L'Europe unie et l'Afrique: De l'idée d'Eurafrique à la Convention de Lomé I* (Brussels, 2005); Guia Migani, *La France et l'Afrique sub-saharienne, 1957–1963: Histoire d'une décolonization entre idéaux eurafricains et politique de puissance* (Brussels, 2008); Peo Hansen and Stefan Jonsson, *Eurafrica: The Untold History of European Integration and Colonialism* (2014).

[49] Anne-Isabelle Richard, 'A Global Perspective on European Cooperation and Integration since 1918', in *The Cambridge History of European Union*, vol. 2: *European Integration Inside-out*, ed. Mathieu Segers and Steven van Hecke (Cambridge, 2023), 459–80.

[50] Richard and Krepp, 'Regional Rights Projects'.

[51] Frederick Cooper, *Citizenship between Empire and Nation: Remaking France and French Africa 1945–1960* (Princeton, 2014); Michael Collins, 'Decolonisation and the "Federal Moment"', *Diplomacy & Statecraft*, 24 (2013), 21–40; Gary Wilder, *Freedom Time: Negritude, Decolonization, and the Future of the World* (Durham, NC, 2015); Richard Drayton, 'Federal Utopias and the Realities of Imperial Power', *Comparative Studies of South Asia, Africa, and the Middle East*, 37 (2017), 401–6.

[52] Jonathan Derrick, *Africa's 'Agitators': Militant Anti-Colonialism in Africa and the West, 1918–1939* (2008); Michael Goebel, *Anti-Imperial Metropolis: Interwar Paris and the Seeds of Third World*

By taking the regional and the transregional seriously and by examining other venues besides the colonial, metropolitan or global, we can draw out how anti-colonial actors operated with different scales to bring their causes before the world. Integrating Europe within studies of decolonisation through transnational actors can help us move away from Eurocentric perspectives.

Conceptualising rights from a Latin American perspective[53]

Our third region-specific section shifts attention to Latin America, with one evident link to the preceding discussion: in the early twentieth century, some advocates of European integration viewed Pan-Americanism as a potential model.[54] Such visions were based on selective perceptions: while Pan-Americanism fostered continental cooperation and emphasised respect for national sovereignty, it was also used to justify the United States' political and military interference in Central American and Caribbean nations. These conflicting approaches to hemispheric relations generated vigorous regional debate and transnational political activity that included cultural elites and social movements, establishing anti-imperialism as a central feature of twentieth-century Latin American political life. Historical research has shown how political debates and ideas circulated in cultural journals that, while based in countries such as Peru or Argentina, gathered authors from across the Americas. The protagonists of these debates constituted a plural political and cultural avant-garde, influencing local social and political movements.[55]

For decades, the United States combined direct interventions in Central America and the Caribbean with anti-subversive training to control insurgencies and oppositional movements across Latin America, particularly in the so-called 'military era' (1960s–80s).[56] With their widespread use of torture, assassinations and forced disappearances, dictatorial regimes in Latin America sparked a wave of transnational human rights activism that involved enquiry missions and pressure campaigns. These efforts exemplified the so-called 'boomerang pattern' which, according to Keck and Sikkink, sees activists inveigle foreign governments to apply pressure upon a rights-violating government, either directly or via intergovernmental bodies.[57] As Patrick Kelly has shown, activist interventions made Latin America a central site 'in the construction of global human rights norms since the 1970s'.[58] A regional

---

Nationalism (Cambridge, 2015); Leslie James, *George Padmore and Decolonization from Below* (2015); Ronald Jemal Stephens and Adam Ewing (eds.), *Global Garveyism* (Gainesville, FL, 2019); Carolien Stolte *et al.* (eds.), *The League Against Imperialism: Lives and Afterlives* (Leiden, 2020).

[53] This section is based on Patricia Oliart's expertise.

[54] See e.g. Alfred Hermann Fried, *Pan-Amerika: Entwicklung, Umfang und Bedeutung der panamerikanischen Bewegung* (Berlin, 1910).

[55] Martín Bergel, 'El anti-antinorteamericanismo en América Latina (1898–1930): Apuntes para una historia intelectual', *Nueva sociedad*, 236 (2011), 152–67.

[56] Herbert Klein and Francisco Vidal Luna, *Brazil, 1964-1985: The Military Regimes of Latin America in the Cold War* (New Haven, 2017).

[57] Keck and Sikkink, *Activists beyond Borders*, 12–13.

[58] Patrick William Kelly, *Sovereign Emergencies: Latin America and the Making of Global Human Rights Politics* (Cambridge, 2018).

focus thus offers insights into a decade that many historians associate with the rise of human rights on international agendas.[59] The role of regional developments in the transnational construction of particular causes was also evident in the 1980s, as shown in research on international responses to the civil wars in El Salvador and Nicaragua.[60] In this era, rights-based campaigns operated alongside solidarity-based activism in which anti-imperialist criticisms of US intervention figured prominently.[61]

Some of the literature has seen the growth of transnational solidarity and human rights campaigns in connection with the rise of transnational activism on Indigenous rights in the 1970s and 1980s.[62] Such activism initially focused on tackling violence and threats against Indigenous peoples in remote areas, yet it increasingly moved to support resistance struggles and organisational activities to protect their territories from exploitation. Indigenous rights campaigning had important regional dimensions, both because of Latin America's colonial history and because of the demographic and political prominence of Indigenous peoples in several Latin American countries. Indigenous groups were located in regions that cut across the territory of more than one state, making their situation a transnational one. Accordingly, Indigenous rights groups connected different levels of campaigning: local, regional, national and international.

Given its political relevance, there is an abundant academic literature on transnational activism around Indigenous peoples' rights in the 1990s. Kay Warren and Jean Jackson have highlighted the establishment of regional networks to promote contact, debates and cooperation between Indigenous political actors across Latin America.[63] Such activism has involved tensions around issues of representation, the relationship between leaders and the grassroots, and the implementation of transnational agendas that were not always sensitive to local circumstances.[64] Some research has emphasised how Indigenous activists have influenced international agreements, which subsequently provided a basis to defend rights and resist dispossession both locally and

---

[59] Samuel Moyn, *The Last Utopia: Human Rights in History* (Cambridge, MA, 2014); Jan Eckel, *The Ambivalence of Good: Human Rights in International Politics since the 1940s* (Oxford, 2019); Barbara Keys, *Reclaiming American Virtue: The Human Rights Revolution of the 1970s* (Cambridge, MA, 2014).

[60] Kevin O'Sullivan, 'Civil War in El Salvador and the Origins of Rights-Based Humanitarianism', *Journal of Global History*, 16 (2021), 246–65; Kim Christiaens, 'Between Diplomacy and Solidarity: Western European Support Networks for Sandinista Nicaragua', *European Review of History*, 21 (2014), 617–34.

[61] Jan Hansen, Christian Helm and Frank Reichherzer (eds), *Making Sense of the Americas: How Protest Related to America in the 1980s and Beyond* (Frankfurt/Main, 2015); and the special issue 'Internationalizing Revolution: The Nicaraguan Revolution and the World, 1977–1990', ed. Tanya Harmer and Eline van Ommen, of *The Americas*, 78 (2021).

[62] Jochen Kemner, 'Fourth World Activism in the First World: The Rise and Consolidation of European Solidarity with Indigenous Peoples', *Journal of Modern European History*, 12 (2014), 262–79.

[63] Kay B. Warren and Jean E. Jackson, 'Introduction: Studying Indigenous Activism in Latin America', in *Indigenous Movements, Self-Representation, and the State in Latin America*, ed. Kay B. Warren and Jean E. Jackson (Austin, 2003), 10.

[64] Patricia Oliart, 'Indigenous Women's Organisations and the Political Discourses of Indigenous Rights and Gender Equity in Peru', *Latin American and Caribbean Ethnic Studies*, 3 (2008), 291–308.

internationally. Such issues are important, especially given the extractive activities and ecological impacts that Indigenous populations are faced with – subjects that have generated substantial scholarship in recent years.[65]

The Zapatista uprising in Chiapas in 1994 inspired the formation of new transnational networks, linking opposition to neoliberal policies with the historical demands of Indigenous movements, thus intertwining regional, transnational and global forms of contestation. The Zapatista Army of National Liberation (EZLN) voiced concerns of Indigenous people in a particular region within the Mexican state, but it did so by targeting the launch of the North American Free Trade Agreement (NAFTA). Several scholars have emphasised that this regionally rooted activism was construed in universal terms – the struggle against 'neo-liberal' globalisation.[66]

The case of Indigenous activism in Latin America is but one example of a theme that runs through the literatures that have been discussed thus far: namely how regional identities and networks could be deployed to challenge injustices and rectify inequalities in particular locales. Regional framings enabled activists to develop alternative visions of world affairs. As several of our examples from both South Asia and Latin America have shown, anti-colonialism and anti-imperialism animated diverse forms of regional activism, and regional identities nourished resistance to external domination. Meanwhile, activists in Europe responded and engaged with these developments in different ways, whether by forging alliances based on solidarity or by developing new projects to reposition their own region in the world. Across the historiographies we have considered so far, the need for a fresh perspective on the cross-border bonds of activists is evident. It is this challenge that we take further in Part B, as we turn to cases that map out diverse ways of adopting a regional perspective in writing about transnational activism.

Part B: Rethinking transnational activism through diverse regional experiences

As noted in the introduction, transnational activists and movements have often cast themselves in global terms, promoting aims that were purportedly applicable irrespective of location. This approach was evident in eighteenth-century humanitarianism, with groups such as the ambitiously named

---

[65] Priscilla Claeys and Deborah Delgado Pugley, 'Peasant and Indigenous Transnational Social Movements Engaging with Climate Justice', *Revue canadienne d'études du développement*, 38 (2017), 325–40; Linda Etchart, *Global Governance of the Environment, Indigenous Peoples and the Rights of Nature: Extractive Industries in the Ecuadorian Amazon* (Cham, 2022); Kimberly Theidon, *Legacies of War: Violence, Ecologies, and Kin* (Durham, NC, 2022); Charis Kamphuis, 'The Transnational Mining Justice Movement: Reflecting on Two Decades of Law Reform Activism in the Americas', *Canadian Yearbook of International Law*, 57 (2020), 286–352.

[66] Thomas Olesen, 'Mixing Scales: Neoliberalism and the Transnational Zapatista Solidarity Network', *Humboldt Journal of Social Relations*, 29 (2005), 84–126; Abigail Andrews, 'Constructing Mutuality: The Zapatistas' Transformation of Transnational Activist Power Dynamics', *Latin American Politics and Society*, 52 (2010), 89–120.

Society of Universal Good-will claiming to advance 'the cause of humanity' irrespective of national borders.[67] In practice, the Society of Universal Good-will served as little more than a provider of assistance to destitute Scots in Norwich and London.[68] The 'humane societies' that are often cast among the earliest transnational humanitarian actors drew in both their organisational form and their lifesaving techniques on precursors from beyond Europe,[69] yet the history of transnational humanitarianism has overwhelmingly been presented in terms of purported Western origins.[70]

The universalising language of early European humanitarianism was far from unique to the eighteenth century: it was replicated by later movements, in different contexts and with different political connotations. Into the nineteenth and twentieth centuries, an array of humanitarian, peace, socialist and women's associations were labelled 'international' but, in effect, had memberships that were largely limited to Europeans and North Americans.[71] In some cases, claims to 'universality' involved double standards, especially in the case of supposedly progressive associations imposing the standards of purported 'civilisation' to justify differential treatment of those within and beyond Europe.[72] Contemporary observers from beyond Europe drew attention to this asymmetry, as exemplified by the Indian nationalist and women's rights activist Kamaladevi Chattopadhyay. Having attended the Berlin congress of the International Alliance of Women in 1929, she noted her initial 'shock' as it 'was a misnomer to call it "International"'. As Chattopadhyay pointed out, the meeting 'was composed of national representatives from the East limited only to Egypt and India', while most areas under colonial rule 'were represented by their rulers and not the country's nationals'.[73]

Twentieth-century anti-colonial movements and, ultimately, decolonisation triggered a reconfiguration of causes and organisations. One such example was the Associated Country Women of the World (ACWW), which had begun in 1929 as an organisation of predominantly 'Western' women's conservative rural associations. Over time, the agendas of rural women's groups from the Global South became more prominent in the ACWW's membership and organisation.[74] ACWW's area vice-president for Asia from 1959 to 1965 and its world president from 1965 to 1971 was the Indian women's rights and development activist Aroti Dutt. During and after her tenures, the association initiated

---

[67] Quoted in Amanda Bowie Moniz, '"Labours in the Cause of Humanity in Every Part of the Globe": Transatlantic Philanthropic Collaboration and the Cosmopolitan Ideal, 1760–1815' (PhD thesis, University of Michigan, 2008), 39.

[68] Society of Universal Good-will, *An Account of the Scots Society in Norwich: From Its Rise in 1775, Until it Received the Additional Name of the Society of Universal Good-will, in 1784* (Norwich, 1784).

[69] Thomas Davies, 'Rethinking the Origins of Transnational Humanitarian Organizations: The Curious Case of the International Shipwreck Society', *Global Networks*, 18 (2018), 461–78.

[70] Barnett, *Empire of Humanity*; Salvatici, *A History of Humanitarianism*.

[71] For an overview, see F. S. L. Lyons, *Internationalism in Europe, 1815-1914* (Leiden, 1963).

[72] See, for instance, the critique in Uday S. Mehta, 'Liberal Strategies of Exclusion', *Politics & Society*, 18 (1990), 427–54.

[73] Kamaladevi Chattopadhyay, *Inner Recesses, Outer Spaces: Memoirs* (New Delhi, 1986), 125.

[74] This example draws on Maria Framke's research.

development projects for rural women in South Asia, partly financed by the Freedom from Hunger Campaign, which Dutt advised. That this was possible reflects transregional commonalities across the ACWW's diverse membership, including a certain conception of middle-class benevolence that enabled its work to function across regional contexts.

One major form of inter-regional activism explicitly focused on South–South cooperation, with Afro-Asian solidarity constituting a major example. At the opening of the first Afro-Asian People's Solidarity Summit of 1957, Anwar Sadat described 'the World Mission of the Peoples of Africa and Asia' as being rooted in a shared experience of colonial exploitation.[75] For some activists, such an understanding underpinned conceptions of the 'Third World' as a far-reaching, transregional space for activism. The Third World Network established in Penang in 1984, for instance, described the Third World regional space in terms of the shared experience of multi-sectoral domination by wealthy countries, stressing the overlapping 'economic, cultural and political spheres ... throttling the development of the Third World' as well as the prospects of the Third World as an arena in which 'the struggle for genuine development is a joint struggle of all concerned peoples'.[76]

With the demise of the Soviet bloc, the 'Third World' concept became increasingly perceived as obsolete and, moreover, critiqued as a colonial construct, given its origin as a projection of the European 'third estate' concept to the world as a whole.[77] Some activists defined their agenda instead as relating to the Global South. For instance, Focus on the Global South, founded by Kamal Malhotra and Walden Bello in 1995, aimed to make 'the concept of the Global South as a political entity both tangible and practical', supporting grassroots movements and transnational networks as well as promoting alternatives to neoliberal economic globalisation.[78] However, as Cindy Ewing has noted, while the 'Global South' concept may help us trace 'historical self-understandings of a distinct identity among postcolonial peoples that united them across geographic space as a global community', it is limiting in that it reproduces 'the bureaucratic language of the Brandt Report and Cold War developmentalism'.[79]

These contrasting experiences highlight the tensions between different regional contexts and conceptions of transnational activism, including attempts to forge transregional alliances. In recent years, such questions have attracted significant scholarly interest.[80] While the following sections discuss forms of activism that cut across national borders and, in some cases,

---

[75] *The First Afro-Asian People's Solidarity Conference, 26 December 1957 to January 1, 1958*, 2nd edn (Cairo, 1958), 7–12.

[76] Third World Network, *Third World: Development or Crisis? Declaration and Conclusions of the Third World Conference, Penang, 9–14 Nov. 1984* (Penang, 1984), 5 and 12.

[77] Alfred Sauvy, 'Trois mondes, une planète', *L'Observateur*, 118 (14 Aug. 1952), 14.

[78] Focus on the Global South, 'Who We Are', https://focusweb.org/who-we-are/ (last accessed 4 Apr. 2023).

[79] Cindy Ewing, 'Troubling the Global South in Global History', *American Historical Review*, 128 (2023), 274.

[80] On transregional activism, see Carolien Stolte and Su Lin Lewis (eds.), *The Lives of Cold War Afro-Asianism* (Leiden, 2022).

transcended narrowly conceived regions, several case studies focus on smaller units or episodes to highlight the potential of micro-historical approaches.[81] Taken together, these cases reveal multiple forms of regionally sensitive research. We do not aim for an exhaustive overview but instead offer a selection of promising directions for further scholarship on the histories of transnational activism, with each case study reflecting how our contributors are taking regional perspectives forward.

The first pair of cases – based on research by, respectively, Pilar Requejo de Lamo and Charlotte Alston – considers two purportedly universal causes, Esperanto and Tolstoyism, which in practice reflected their regional roots in nineteenth-century Eastern Europe, before being applied and adapted in other regional contexts. We then shift to micro-histories, via two very different cases of transnational activism rooted in contrasting African contexts. Drawing on Kate Skinner's research, the discussion of Holiday Komedja's activism in the Ghana–Togo borderland highlights both the opportunities and constraints of a regional borderland context and the importance of previously overlooked source materials for a regionally rooted analysis of transnational activism. The subsequent study of early Rastafarianism, based on Robert Kramm's work, elucidates the importance of uprootedness in transnational activism with regard to the African diaspora and its interactions with the global-scale asymmetries that imperialism had embedded. By considering, respectively, an African regional borderland and 'Africa' as constructed among diasporic communities, these two cases highlight distinctive regional features that have tended to be overlooked. The final case study turns attention to yet another aspect of regional contexts: the overlaps between regional and interregional features and their implications for some forms of transnational activism. Grounded in Matthew Hurst's research on Hong Kong, the analysis of campaigns for the rights of local boat dwellers illustrates how multiple regional contexts shaped the dynamics of transnational activism.

Reinterpreting the international through the regional: the cases of Esperanto and Tolstoyism[82]

On the surface, both Esperanto and Tolstoyism seem to constitute phenomena that transcend not only a national but also a regional focus – and this has been reflected in treatments of their historical evolution that emphasise their international characteristics.[83] Here, on the other hand, our comparative analysis of regional features highlights aspects that an emphasis on their international agendas has tended to obscure.

---

[81] The potential of such approaches has been highlighted in John-Paul Ghobrial (ed.), *Global History and Microhistory*, which is a themed issue of *Past & Present*, 242, suppl. 14 (2019).

[82] The analysis of Esperanto is based on Pilar Requejo de Lamo's research, including her doctoral thesis 'Between Internationalism and Nationalism: The Esperanto Movement in the Iberian Peninsula in the Early Twentieth Century' (PhD thesis, University of St Andrews, 2023). The comments on Tolstoyism draw on Charlotte Alston's research.

[83] Roberto Garvía, *Esperanto and Its Rivals: The Struggle for an International Language* (Philadelphia, 2015); Charlotte Alston, *Tolstoy and His Disciples: The History of a Radical International Movement* (2014).

As an international auxiliary language, Esperanto was a globally oriented phenomenon aiming to promote intercultural communication. When Ludwik Zamenhof introduced his constructed language in 1887, he produced a versatile tool for a transnational network of individuals who supported the idea of an official international language. Moreover, Esperantujo, the abstract place where Esperanto is spoken, written and practised, relied on multiple journals, books and other forms of correspondence, and not merely on international congresses.[84] Tolstoyism also emerged as an international movement in the 1880s and 1890s. Inspired by the later writings of Leo Tolstoy, it was a pacifist form of Christian anarchism, built on the rejection of all forms of organisation and coercion, and promoting the principle of individuals following their own conscience. Tolstoyans put their independence of thought into action, happily critiquing key elements of Tolstoy's work.[85] Indeed, while most followers of Tolstoy accepted the label 'Tolstoyan' as a shorthand for their common beliefs, they rejected the idea of a movement.[86]

Despite their respective focus on the universal and the individual, both Esperanto and Tolstoyism were shaped by their regional environments. Esperanto emerged from an Eastern European context: created by the Polish medic Zamenhof, it was launched in the city of Białystok, then under Russian rule. Zamenhof was exposed to the daily challenges for a multilingual and multi-ethnic community. In this case, a problem that was particularly acute in a specific region led to a solution that resonated with a multitude of individuals, creating a global phenomenon.[87] Tolstoyism also originated in the context of the Russian empire, with the Moscow Vegetarian Society as a regular meeting place for Tolstoyans, the publishing house Posrednik ('The Intermediary') as a centre for its communications, and Tolstoyan communities extending to non-Russian parts of the empire.[88] Moreover, Russian Tolstoyans were active in the wider international 'movement', both through their publication activities and through émigrés' involvement in Tolstoyan communities elsewhere.

Esperanto's regional roots encompassed not only its founder's background and the limited Eurocentric linguistic basis of the constructed language: they also informed the way in which the concerns of Esperantists were located between the local and global. Many of its supporters saw Esperantism as a less threatening alternative to the international use of particular national

[84] Guilherme Fians, *Esperanto Revolutionaries and Geeks: Language Politics, Digital Media and the Making of an International Community* (Cham, 2021).

[85] E. V. Agarin, 'L. N. Tolstoi i Tolstovstvo v kritike posledovatelei', *Sums'kii istoriko-archivnii zhurnal*, 23 (2014), 18–29.

[86] Vladimir Chertkov, 'If Tolstoy Were Tsar', *Brotherhood*, 5 (Oct. 1897), 63; Lodewijk van Mierop, 'Geen Tolstoyaan maar Christien', *Vrede*, 2 (15 May 1899), 109.

[87] Walter Żelazny, *Ludwik Zamenhof: Life and Work. Reminiscences*, trans. Katarzyna Orzechowska (Białystok, 2020); Jouko Lindstedt, 'Esperanto – an East European Contact Language?', in *Die Europäizität der Slawia oder die Slawizität Europas: Ein Beitrag der kultur- und sprachrelativistischen Linguistik*, ed. Christian Voss and Alicja Nagórko (Munich, 2009), 125–34.

[88] Ronald D. LeBlanc, *Vegetarianism in Russia: The Tolstoy(an) Legacy* (Pittsburgh, PA, 2001); Robert Otto, *Publishing for the People: The Firm Posrednik 1885-1905* (New York, 1988), 135.

languages.[89] Esperanto offered stateless nations a voice in the international arena, without having to rely on existing languages that would leave them disadvantaged vis-à-vis native speakers. Esperanto also enabled them to spread the word about their cultural particularities, whilst eschewing the pervasive influence of the languages spoken by major powers. In 1909, the Irish Esperantist Patrick Parker urged the '[c]hildren of the small nations' to 'establish through Esperanto a global network for the defense and preservation of our endangered languages'.[90] Along such lines, Esperanto helped create both regional and transregional networks. For example, in Spain, Catalan Esperantists supported the construction of an Esperanto community in which mother tongues took preference over citizenship, giving stateless nations an international voice. At the same time, they supported plans for an Iberian Confederation, built upon a peninsula composed of regions and advanced through the use of Esperanto.[91] Seen from this angle, an ostensibly global movement could be a vehicle for different kinds of regional agendas – both sub-state (Catalan) and transnational (Iberian) – while advancing notions of a transregional community of people from smaller nations. Moreover, regional features also mattered in terms of the causes that were being promoted through the medium of Esperanto, with spiritism being especially significant in parts of South America.[92]

For Tolstoyans, contrasting regional contexts affected the ways in which the movement grew transnationally. The Tolstoyan movement is most often remembered for inspiring 'back to the land' settlements in places as diverse as Sochi on the Black Sea, Maldon in Essex, Blaricum in the Netherlands and Georgia in the American South.[93] In China, in the wake of the May Fourth Movement (1919), Tolstoy's case inspired intellectuals who appreciated his determination to put his ideals into practice and to reach out to the peasant masses.[94] In South Africa, Gandhi drew on Tolstoy's ideas in the context of the satyagraha campaign of the 1910s.[95]

In almost all the regional contexts in which Tolstoy's vision found a receptive audience, activists debated how ideas that had been generated within the agriculturally based economy of Eastern Europe could be applied to very different economic, social and political contexts. In Britain, Switzerland and

---

[89] In the case of Portugal, Esperanto journals often spoke of the 'pretentious use' of foreign languages, which had contributed to the debasement of the Portuguese language: 'O uso preteneioso das línguas estrangeiras', *Portugal-Esperanto*, no. 4 (Apr. 1926), 58.

[90] Patrick Parker, 'La gepatraj lingvoj kai Esperanto', *Tutmonda Espero*, no. 17 (May 1909), 69–71.

[91] 'Memoria del Primer Congreso de Esperantistas Ibéricos celebrado en Valencia bajo la presidencia honoraria de S. M. el Rey D. Alfonso XIII, del 17 al 20 de mayo de 1923', *La Suno Hispana*, no. 81 (Feb. 1924), 17–25.

[92] David Pardue, 'Spiritism and Esperanto in Brazil', *Esperantologio*, 2 (2001), 11–27.

[93] Boris Mazurin, 'The Life and Labour Commune', in *Memoirs of Peasant Tolstoyans in Soviet Russia*, ed. William Edgerton (Bloomington, 1993), 40; George Gibson to Tolstoy, 21 Apr. 1898, GMT, BL216/78.

[94] Shakhar Rahav, 'Scale of Change: The Small Group in Chinese Politics, 1919–1921', *Asian Studies Review*, 43 (2019), 677–8.

[95] Surendra Bhana, 'The Tolstoy Farm: Gandhi's Experiment in "Cooperative Commonwealth"', *South African Historical Journal*, 7 (1975), 88–100.

the Netherlands, publishing houses set up by home-grown Tolstoyans or by Russian émigrés therefore operated heterogeneous publishing policies, drawing also on local texts, including Dutch vegetarian manuals and British tracts on cooperation.[96] British socialists described the attempt to apply Tolstoy's ideas in industrial Britain as a parody – with one critic stating that what was needed was 'not more potatoes, or more shoes, but a fraternal organization in which the potatoes and the shoes, and everything else, shall be abundantly available for all the workers'.[97] Different political contexts also impacted the experience and status of individuals within the movement: this was clearly the case with conscientious objectors who took the ultimate stand by refusing military service. Tolstoyans in countries without conscription struggled to come up with a similar sacrifice. Seen in this way, Tolstoyism constituted a movement with universal claims but exhibited discernible regional features that shaped its different interpretations and manifestations.

As this comparison has elucidated, both Esperanto and Tolstoyan ideas inspired transnational activism, but with prominent regional features, even beyond the environment from which they emerged. In the case of Tolstoyism, regional differences shaped contrasting practices seeking to implement Tolstoyan ideals, while Esperanists used the constructed language to pursue diverse regional causes, including those operating in borderlands such as Catalonia. It is another borderland context that our next case study turns to, as we shift attention to contrasting experiences of transnational activism in distinctive African regional contexts.

Holiday Komedja and print activism in a West African borderland[98]

With our next two case studies, our attention shifts to individual activists while, at the same time, elucidating diverse regional aspects of African transnational activism. The first case study focuses on Holiday Komedja's print activism in West Africa in order to highlight two specific aspects: the importance of borderland regional contexts and the significance of source materials that can no longer be understood exclusively in narrow ethnonationalist terms.

Komedja was a shoemaker who operated in the borderland between British and French Togoland. He therefore came from a region in which 'borderlands' were shaped and interpreted in the context of formal colonisation. Colonial borders were often seen and described as a means of dividing people who

---

[96] Antonella Salomoni, 'Emigranty-tolstovtsy mezhdu khristianstvom i anarkhizmom (1898–1905 gg.)', in *Russkaia emigratsiia do 1917 goda – laboritoriia liberal'noi i revoliutsionnoi mysli*, ed. Iu. Sherrer and B. Anan'ich (St Petersburg, 1997), 112–27.

[97] John Bruce Wallace, 'Coming out of the Old Order', *Brotherhood* (new series), 4 (Nov. 1896), 79–80.

[98] This example is the subject of Kate Skinner's research, including her book on *The Fruits of Freedom in British Togoland: Literacy, Politics and Nationalism, 1914-2014* (Cambridge, 2015) and her collaborative work with Wilson Yayoh in *Writing the New Nation in a West African Borderland: Ablɔɖe Safui (The Key to Freedom) by Holiday Komedja*, ed. Kate Skinner and Wilson Yayoh (Oxford, 2019).

considered themselves related. In this sense, borders were an affront as well as a nuisance, and African activists frequently mobilised with the aim of shifting or eliminating a border. But borderlands were also multilingual zones, sites of new economic projects (especially in the form of licit and illicit cross-border trade), and foci for international attention. African activists interpreted borders, and imbued them with meanings, by devising different – sometimes competing – solutions to the problems that they posed. Such activists organised not only within particular locales, but across borders and in multiple languages, targeting the international bodies (first the League of Nations Permanent Mandates Commission and then the United Nations Trusteeship Council) that were supposed to oversee the administration of British and French Togoland, following the conquest and division of the former German colony of Togo during the First World War. As our discussion of Komedja will show, borderlands contexts provided logistical challenges for activists, but also opportunities to exploit colonial rivalries in the advancement of their political objectives.

In 1959, Komedja established the newspaper *Ablɔɖe Safui* (The Key to Freedom), which he published in Eʋe, a language that was used on both sides of the colonial border.[99] Like other Eʋe-speaking activists, Komedja can be considered within a transnational context: activist networks extended across the British–French Togoland divide and – after independence – across the border between the republics of Ghana and Togo; political pamphlets and newspapers circulated around the entire Eʋe-speaking region; and activists crossed borders for rallies, meetings, and to escape various forms of oppression.[100] Komedja and others were also transnational in their frame of reference and their repertoire of political claims. The Eʋe-speaking activists who sought the reunification and joint independence of British and French Togoland were ultimately disappointed by the international institutions where they pitched their claims. They were outmanoeuvred at the United Nations by the British government and by Gold Coast nationalists who – for different reasons – wanted British Togoland to be integrated into the Gold Coast / Ghana. But in the meantime, Eʋe-speaking activists listened to the radio, followed world affairs, and generated texts to debate differing visions of sovereignty and solidarity.

Ablɔɖe Safui traced the drama of anti-colonial mobilisation, independence negotiations and the rapid shift, post-independence, to authoritarian single-party government. Such publications are essential for understanding transnational activism from a contextually rooted perspective. Komedja was an artisan shoemaker who could not afford to travel outside of West Africa. He did not live in a city that served as a hub of transnational anti-colonialism. But his frame of reference was wide-ranging. He compared the situation of the two Togolands to that of post-war Germany, divided between East and West, and subject to the overbearing influence of global and regional powers. He

---

[99] For further details and Komedja's writing, see *Writing the New Nation*, ed. Skinner and Yayoh.

[100] See, for example, Kate Skinner, 'Brothers in the Bush: Exile, Refuge, and Citizenship on the Ghana–Togo Border, 1958–1966', in *Africans in Exile: Mobility, Law, and Identity*, ed. Nathan Riley Carpenter and Benjamin Lawrance (Indianapolis, 2018).

even approached the West German embassy in Lomé for support for his news-paper. Through *Abloɖe Safui*, Komedja delivered damning critiques of Kwame Nkrumah. Highlighting Nkrumah's use of preventive detention to control dis-sent, and the growing number of Ghanaians who were seeking refuge across the border in the Republic of Togo, Komedja questioned Nkrumah's version of Pan-Africanism.[101] He also reflected deeply upon the meaning of the term 'politics', ideals of national unity, and the role of conscience and self-discipline in salvaging an honourable form of postcolonial citizenship as governing par-ties and presidents became increasingly authoritarian.

Sources such as *Abloɖe Safui* challenge the presumed association between African-language texts and narrow, exclusivist forms of ethnonationalism. African-language texts could convene readerships that were not straightfor-wardly defined by ethnicity: they invited readers to see themselves in compari-son and connection with others elsewhere in the world, and debated a wide range of national and transnational political projects. This is increasingly recognised in specialist scholarship on African print cultures.[102] But such texts can also counter over-reliance upon English-language sources for histor-ies of transnational activism, and they need to be integrated into a wider range of historiographical fields. In this case, we can see that a regionally rooted perspective requires consideration of source materials that have not only pre-viously been marginalised but that also challenge conventional assumptions with respect to the goals advanced by transnational activists.

Leonard Percival Howell, Rastafarianism and African 'uprooting'[103]

A very different African regional context is evident in the case of the early Rastafari movement and its relation to the uprooted African diaspora which, as this section will highlight, shaped both the transnational life story of its founder and the vision of Africa that the movement put forward. Here, we see the importance of constructions of 'Africa' among diaspora communities as an illustration of the significance of regional imaginations in transnational activism.

As elucidated in a rich literature, the 'First Rasta' Leonard Percival Howell led a life that was transnational from an early age.[104] At the age of twelve,

---

[101] See also Kate Skinner, 'A Different Kind of Union: An Assassination, Diplomatic Recognition, and Competing Visions of African Unity in Ghana–Togo Relations (1953–63)', in *Visions of African Unity: New Perspectives on the History of Pan-Africanism and African Unification Projects*, ed. Mateo Grilli and Frank Gerits (Basingstoke, 2021).

[102] Derek Peterson, Emma Hunter and Stephanie Newell (eds.), *African Print Cultures: Newspapers and Their Publics in the Twentieth Century* (Ann Arbor, 2016).

[103] This example is based on Robert Kramm's project on 'Radical Utopian Communities: A Global History from the Margins, 1900–1950', which is funded via a Freigeist Fellowship from the Volkswagen Foundation.

[104] Hélène Lee, *The First Rasta: Leonard Howell and the Rise of Rastafarianism* (Chicago, 2003); Robert Hill, 'Leonard P. Howell and Millennial Visions in Early Rastafari', *Jamaica Journal*, 16 (1983), 24–39; Mark Naison, 'Historical Notes on Blacks and American Communism: The Harlem Experience', *Science and Society*, 42 (1978), 324–43; James Robertson, '"That Vagabond George Stewart of

he journeyed from colonial Jamaica to Panama, where he witnessed the building of the Panama Canal and the exploitation and racist hierarchies on its construction site. He served as a cook in the US Army Transportation Service, which brought him from the Caribbean to Europe, Asia and the United States. Discharged in 1923, Howell made his way to New York, running a tea room in Harlem, which was a hotbed of Black radical political activism. Convicted for sedition in 1931, Howell was deported a year later to Jamaica, where he preached the return of the messiah in the form of the Ethiopian emperor Haile Selassie I. In 1940, Howell established the Pinnacle Commune, which became a haven for the Rastafarian community. Pinnacle survived on self-sustaining agriculture and became the island's largest ganja supplier, which gave the colonial police pretexts for repeatedly raiding the commune and ultimately destroying it in 1954. After years of trial, Howell spent the rest of his life under house arrest, and what remains of Pinnacle attracts Rastafarians globally and allows remembrance of Howell as a spiritual leader, founding father and key actor in the early Rastafarian movement.

Besides its transnationality, Howell's life story illustrates the border- and boundary-crossing regional within the global – as well as the global within the regional – in the early Rastafarian movement. Rastafari inherently involves transnational activism, as Rastafarian peoples, activities and ideas were (and still are) closely entwined with the history of slavery, migration and African diasporas, and with a constant struggle against the constraints of empire, capitalism and the colonial divide – in Rastafarian terms summed up as 'Babylon'. Pioneering scholarship on Rastafari has shown this, but research in this field is dominated by approaches from anthropology, cultural studies, musicology, religious studies and the social sciences, which have shaped perceptions of Rastafari as primarily a cultural, social and religious phenomenon.[105] As Monique Bedasse contends, however, it was not popular culture and cultural representations alone, but also repatriation to the African homeland that constituted Rastafari from within the movement and its international growth.[106] Moreover, repatriation is intrinsically linked with the Rastafarian concept of 'trodding', which means 'to move within, between, and beyond the boundaries of any particular nation-state', including Jamaica, Africa and the Western world.[107] In the Rastafarians' case, trodding specifically recognises how they 'understood Africa to be the root of diaspora. But rather than a root waiting to be merely framed, claimed, or rejected, it talks back to diaspora and helps to shape it.' Moreover, 'trodding diaspora insists that we map the

---

England": Leonard Howell's Seditious Sermons, 1933–1941', in *Leonard Percival Howell and the Genesis of Rastafari*, ed. Clinton A. Hutton *et al.* (Mona, 2015), 69–106; Daive A. Dunkley, 'The Suppression of Leonard Howell in Late Colonial Jamaica, 1932–1954', *New West Indian Guide*, 87 (2013), 62–93.

[105] See, among many others: Barry Chevannes, *Rastafari: Roots and Ideology* (New York, 1994); Chris Potash, *Reggae, Rasta, Revolution: Jamaican Music from Ska to Dub* (New York, 1997); Noel Erskine, *From Garvey to Marley: Rastafari Theology* (Gainesville, FL, 2007).

[106] Monique A. Bedasse, *Jah Kingdom: Rastafarians, Tanzania, and Pan-Africanism in the Age of Decolonization* (Chapel Hill, 2017), 2.

[107] *Ibid.*, 3.

distance between an imagined Africa and the physical journey to discover complex African realities'.[108]

Acknowledging 'roots' as a pivotal signifier in Rastafarian practice and discourse, one may bring this term into conversation with its apparent oppositional gerund 'uprooting'. First, by considering the difference between 'root' and 'uprooting', we can underscore the omnipresent Rastafarian struggle, and the entailing contradictions between their forceful and traumatic displacement from Africa to the Caribbean plantation system and their longing and claims for repatriation. Second, uprooting encompasses the mobility – the physical 'trodding' – already inherent in the early Rastafarian movement, of which Howell's journeying is a striking example. Third, and related to the Rastafarian lifestyle, such as the insistence on natural and divine living, 'root' indicates Rastafari's radicalism that reverberates with Marx's famous quote: 'To be radical is to grasp the root of the matter. But, for man, the root is man himself.'[109] Hence, the term 'uprooting' conveys a form of empowerment that strengthens the notion of early Rastafari not only as a matter of culture and religion, but also as a transnational political movement against racism and colonialism. In that sense, the terminology of 'uprooting' connects with the Rastafarian vocabulary that consciously resists the Babylonian system, and simultaneously highlights the individual and communal divinity – that is, being upright, righteous and truthful – in one's action. Ultimately, uprooting signals the possibility of change through transnational activism: imagining and overcoming racism and colonialism in global capitalism, drawing in this case on constructions of African roots in the diaspora community. Imaginations of regional rootedness and uprooting constitute a fascinating direction for further enquiry.

Rethinking the dynamics of transnational activism: the case of the Yaumatei boat dwellers[110]

Our final example concerns a very different effort to overcome the challenges of a regional context shaped by cross-border relations and impaired by colonial impositions. The case study focuses on activism in 1970s–80s Hong Kong; it thus deals with a context in which proximity to mainland China as well as British colonial rule provided overlapping regional contexts for a local campaign that deployed transnational means. Ever since the Communists took China in 1949, the Hong Kong colonial government's every decision was attenuated by concern for Beijing's possible reaction. To prevent political expression within the colony, which could have troubled Sino-British

---

[108] *Ibid.*

[109] Karl Marx, 'Zur Kritik der Hegelschen Rechtsphilosophie', in Karl Marx and Friedrich Engels, *Werke*, I (East Berlin, 1976), 385.

[110] This section is based on Matthew Hurst's ongoing doctoral research at the University of York, which investigates the role of Hong Kong civil society actors and pressure groups during the 1980s–90s Sino-British negotiations and transfer of Hong Kong from British colonial rule to Beijing's administration. Hurst's research is supported by the Arts and Humanities Research Council (grant number AH/R012733/1) through the White Rose College of the Arts & Humanities.

relations, the authorities enacted oppressive censorship laws and local surveillance, and delayed self-rule indefinitely.[111] Thus, tensions within the immediate geographical region influenced the shape of acceptable activism within Hong Kong. As our analysis of the Yaumatei boat dwellers case illustrates, activists consequently had to navigate regional politics and, looking beyond the boundaries of the colony and region for support, sought to broaden the appeal of essentially local concerns by reframing their plight in the language of supposedly universal values.

In 1972, plans for a road extension project triggered efforts to rehouse more than 600 families who had been living on boats in the Yaumatei typhoon shelter.[112] Over 100 households, however, became embroiled in a row over their accommodation. In May 1978, a social worker from a community rights group, the Society for Collective Organization, began helping the boat dwellers to formalise, organise and expand their movement. In January 1979, seventy-six boat dwellers and their supporters boarded buses with a petition that they intended to hand to the governor unannounced.[113] They were swiftly arrested under the Public Order Ordinance, a law that stipulated restrictions on public gatherings and which had been introduced following Communist-inspired riots, echoing the influence of the region upon the local. The arrests proved a turning point, propelling rather than containing criticism of the colonial government.

The movement expanded in two dimensions: activists began looking outside the confines of the colony to avoid the constraints of the region and, discursively, they sought support by adopting the language of class struggle and universal human rights. Activists forged connections beyond the immediate region, such as in Britain and the wider Commonwealth. A declassified colonial government report comments that Hong Kong-based groups frequently brought such issues 'to the attention of overseas critics of the HK Government'.[114] For instance, British MPs and peers in the House of Lords were lobbied with letters, and supporters from as far as Canada wrote to newspaper editors. The same government report complained of the resources required in preparing 'briefs and explanations ... for use in local or overseas rebuttal'.[115] The dual inside- and outside-pressure approach succeeded in raising the profile of the boat dwellers' case.

The movement also took a discursive turn. Within the colony, academics, journalists, British expatriates and other middle-class locals viewed the incident as illustrative of widespread victimisation of the working class. Seeing themselves as better resourced to defend their positions, in adding their voices

---

[111] Michael Ng, *Political Censorship in British Hong Kong: Freedom of Expression and the Law (1842–1997)* (Cambridge, 2022); Florence Mok, *Covert Colonialism, Governance, Surveillance and Political Culture in British Hong Kong, c. 1966–97* (Manchester, 2023).

[112] Unless otherwise cited, this case study is informed by: Standing Committee on Pressure Groups, 15 May 1979, 'The Role Played by Pressure Groups on Public Issue [*sic*]: The Yaumatei Boat Squatter Affair', The National Archives, London (hereafter: TNA), FCO 40/1264 f13(w).

[113] Po-lin Chan, 'Social Action in Practice: Yaumatei Boat People as a Case Study' (PhD thesis, University of Hong Kong, 1981), 42–52.

[114] Standing Committee on Pressure Groups, 'Role Played by Pressure Groups', 1 and 8.

[115] *Ibid.*

to the movement they not only condemned the treatment of the boat dwellers but also took up an anti-colonial rhetoric aimed at the heart of government itself. Additionally, when turning outside the region, activists reoriented the arrests from a local issue into a human rights issue. For instance, in 1980, an international group submitted a report titled 'Putting Justice and Human Rights in Focus' to the United Nations, arguing that various articles of the International Covenant on Civil and Political Rights had been breached.[116] By using the language of supposed universal values, activists negotiated the highly particular contrivances of the region.

This case highlights the need to refine frameworks for understanding the dynamics of transnational activism such as the 'boomerang pattern' identified by Keck and Sikkink. In this case, the complex regional context constrained the options open to activists but did not prevent them completely. Instead, appreciating the regional context enables a deeper understanding of why this movement evolved as it did. The arrests transformed the Yaumatei case from a local issue into an illustration of suppressive laws, encouraged solidarity between the resource-poor working class and the relatively better-off middle class via shared anti-colonial sentiment, and was reconceived as a human rights issue to facilitate universalisation of the issue. This case study thus exhibits how both practical and discursive choices were heavily dictated by the region. Activists had to bypass one form of imperial authority (the colonial government, whose laws were heavily dictated by regional neighbours) to speak as directly as possible to another (the metropole) or transcend the imperial power system altogether by enlisting allies from beyond the region. The case highlights the need for more fine-grained interpretations of which external actors are the most significant for transnational activism, depending on the particularities of the regional context in which activists are situated.

Conclusion

This article has argued for the importance of 'region' as a category for understanding different forms of transnational political and social activism. Whereas Part A has illustrated how the history of transnational activism can be written from different regional vantage points, Part B has explored the implications of diverse meanings of 'region', both for activists and for writing about transnational activism. As some of our examples have shown, a turn to life stories can help us understand how individuals navigated the overlapping and sometimes conflicting regional contexts of their transnational endeavours – in this respect, we adopted promising perspectives from global history.[117] Moreover, the cases illustrate that a regionally rooted approach involves active engagement with questions of marginalisation, from reappraising marginalised source materials to tracing experiences of 'uprooting'.

---

[116] No author, Aug. 1980, 'Putting Justice and Human Rights in Focus', TNA, FCO 40/1188 f1.

[117] On life stories as a means to understand global histories, see e.g. Amy Stanley, 'Maidservants' Tales: Narrating Domestic and Global History in Eurasia, 1600–1900', *American Historical Review*, 121 (2016), 437–60.

One could push this point even further: namely that the notion of 'uprooting' can extend to regions themselves, which were far from static and shifted shape according to particular historical circumstances. The regional is a scale that at first sight seems clearly defined (as geography, cultural space, climatic realm) but that actually bears an openness, enabling us to explore activists' actions, references, experiences and imaginations of space and scale. Our cases have also highlighted how regionally sensitive approaches require opening up our consideration of regional scales to encompass diverse contexts including borderlands and diasporic communities' identities.

The power dynamics of empire and colonialism were one important contextual aspect. On the one hand, regions were places where imperial domination manifested itself in various ways. On the other hand, regional and transregional cooperation provided means to challenge inequalities and external domination. In some instances, activists evoked regional federations and unions in attempts to promote an alternative world order.[118] We have further seen in the Hong Kong case how the shared context of colonial rule played a role in overcoming class divisions.

Regions have provided important contexts in which activism emerged – and an acknowledgement of this aspect has the benefit of simultaneously challenging both national and global framings. The fact that 'region' could be understood in very different ways is not a problem as such: instead, such ambiguities can help us develop more nuanced understandings of activism which, as we have shown, operated at and across different scales. Our cases have provided a selection of the ways in which regional contexts, conceptualisations and source materials can be opened up in studying the history of transnational activism, and each of these dimensions offers a promising prospective pathway for further investigation.

Author contributions. Thomas Davies and Daniel Laqua are joint first authors of this article.

---

[118] Adom Getachew, *Worldmaking after Empire: The Rise and Fall of Self-Determination* (Princeton, 2019); Frank Gerits, *The Ideological Scramble for Africa: How the Pursuit of Anticolonial Modernity Shaped a Postcolonial Order, 1945–1966* (Ithaca, 2023).

Cite this article: Davies T *et al* (2024). Rethinking Transnational Activism through Regional Perspectives: Reflections, Literatures and Cases. *Transactions of the Royal Historical Society* 2, 317–343. https://doi.org/10.1017/S0080440123000294

Transactions of the RHS (2024), 2, 345–369
doi:10.1017/S0080440123000233

ARTICLE

Decolonising the History of Internationalism: Transnational Activism across the South

Su Lin Lewis

Department of History, University of Bristol, Bristol, UK
Email: sulin.lewis@bristol.ac.uk

(Received 6 July 2023; revised 5 September 2023; accepted 5 September 2023;
first published online 16 October 2023)

Abstract

The history of internationalism has tended to focus on power centres in the Global North – London, Geneva, New York, Paris – and institutions like the League of Nations, United Nations and UNESCO. What happens when we flip our perspective, and view internationalism from the point of view of the decolonising South? What do we get when we shift our focus from world leaders to the internationalism of activists, intellectuals, feminists, poets, artists, rebels and insurgents operating in Asia and Africa? Moreover, how are our methods of researching and debating international history – in universities, archives and conferences in the Global North – structured by economic inequalities, colonial legacies and visa regimes that limit participation by scholars from the South? This paper considers how we might decolonise both the content and the methods of international history, focusing especially on leftist internationalism and South–South connections in Southeast Asia and the wider Global South.

Keywords: Decolonisation; international history; methodology; Global South

The Royal Historical Society's 2018 report on race, equality and inclusion served as a catalyst to highlight racial under-representation in the discipline.[1] It insisted on the importance of globalising and diversifying our teaching curriculum, including challenging Eurocentric perspectives and critically engaging with imperial legacies. Yet if our universities are to be led by research, we must look to decolonising not only the content of our teaching but also our research practices. In this context, to decolonise is not only to

---

[1] Hannah Atkinson et al., Race, Ethnicity, and Equality in UK History: A Report and Resource for Change (2018).

think globally and inclusively, but to be fully attuned to structures of power and inequality that are historically embedded in our disciplines. In this paper, I focus on the field of international history, which has the capacity to globalise and expand our thinking about the mechanisms and mentalities of internationalism but also to replicate the perspectives of international institutions and organisations (and crucially, their archives) in emphasising the centrality of the Global North at the expense of the Global South.[2]

Both global and international history are fields that have grown exceedingly popular with researchers and students alike in the last two decades. They promise a more widely connected and comparative outlook to a discipline that has long been dominated by Western European and American history. But as with any field of history, we must constantly consider the actors on which we focus, the methods we use and the questions are we asking of the field. In this paper, I hope first to highlight ways we might decolonise the content of international history, amplifying recent scholarship that subverts conventional histories of internationalism by focusing on the connections between activists across the Global South. Secondly, I want to highlight new perspectives on international history that might emerge through methodologies of collaborative and participatory research – both with scholars in the academy with research specialities across Asia, Africa and Latin America, and with independent scholars, including activists and curators, from South and Southeast Asia.

Centring the South in the history of internationalism

Internationalism, as Glenda Sluga has reminded us, can involve either the expression of an idea or embody international institutions themselves. Its history has been traced to the Enlightenment cosmopolitanism of Kant and Bentham, to nineteenth-century institutions such as the Concert of Europe or to the internationalism of organisations like the Comintern, whose Moscow-based networks reached out like tentacles to the Global South.[3] In this perspective, internationalism as an idea originates in the North and is diffused to the South. But what does internationalism mean if we root such ideas and institutions in the Global South? What new perspectives do we gain from

---

[2] 'Global South' is an imperfect term that, taken literally, might encompass a wide range of countries in the southern hemisphere with wildly different degrees of economic development. It is both complex and contradictory, denoting what Nina Schneider sees as a metaphorical, political or relational struggle against present-day global inequalities between North and South, one rooted in historical legacies of colonialism and development that benefited the North at the expense of the South. I follow Pamela Gupta, Christopher J. Lee, Marissa J. Moorman and Sandhya Shukla and use it here not only to acknowledge this history of struggle and solidarity, but because of the challenge it poses to 'the geopolitical frameworks of the United States and Europe from a territorial standpoint, underscoring the role alternative regional and global geographies can play in remaking a world order'. See 'Editor's Introduction', *Radical History Review*, 131 (2018), 1–12. See also Nina Schneider, 'Between Promise and Skepticism: The Global South and Our Role as Engaged Intellectuals', *The Global South*, 11, no. 2 (2017), 18–38.

[3] Mark Mazower, *Governing the World: The History of an Idea, 1815 to the Present* (New York, 2012); Glenda Sluga and Patricia Clavin, 'Rethinking the History of Internationalism', in *Internationalisms: A Twentieth-Century History*, ed. Glenda Sluga and Patricia Clavin (Cambridge, 2017), 3–4.

tracing lineages of internationalism as specialists in South and Southeast Asia, the African continent, Latin America or the Caribbean?

The intellectual history of internationalism arose after World War II and focused largely on European interstate relations. As Robbie Shilliam has argued, even as the study of non-Western actors, movements and ideologies shaped the development of the discipline, it has long ignored the role of non-Western *thinkers*.[4] Recently, Patricia Owens and Katharina Rietzler brought scholars together to interrogate the omission of women in the early canon of international intellectual history.[5] The volume focused largely on actors based in Europe and America and *their* interactions with the wider world, pointing to the urgent need for the field to address its own geographical myopia.[6] Yet the volume's interventions – particularly those on African American intellectuals – have nonetheless provided welcome and fundamental tools to enrich and decolonise the intellectual history of internationalism, centring women, globalising the field, posing important questions of who gets counted as an intellectual, and addressing dynamics of gender and race that shape the field.[7] As I hope to show, decolonising the history of internationalism is an inter-sectional project, intimately connected not only to an intellectual history of internationalism which has long neglected women, thinkers of colour and perspectives from the Global South, but a history of decolonisation that has also long focused on the state arena, marginalising women and non-state actors.

International history was long predicated on the study of cooperation between states; the nation was a paramount category of analysis, even as historians recognised the way in which nations morphed and changed. Global history, by contrast, meant overcoming history's traditional focus on the nation state, stressing mobility, interconnection and exchange. Over the past two decades, the global turn has invited a wider re-examination of the history of internationalism. Black internationalism has become a vibrant field of study in itself, uncovering the way in which African Americans, in particular, channelled pan-African and anti-colonial networks abroad.[8] In their wider works,

---

[4] Robbie Shilliam, 'Non-Western Thought and International Relations', in *International Relations and Non-Western Thought: Imperialism, Colonialism, and Investigations of Global Modernity*, ed. Robbie Shilliam (2011), ch. 2.

[5] Patricia Owens and Katharina Rietzler (eds.), *Women's International Thought: A New History* (Cambridge, 2021).

[6] My full review of the volume, and the editors' response to this point, is in *Roundtable Review*, 14-30 (2021), https://issforum.org/to/jrt14-30.

[7] Imaobong D. Umoren, 'Ideas in Action: Eslanda Robeson's International Thought after 1945', in *Women's International Thought: A New History*, ed. Patricia Owens and Katharina Rietzler (Cambridge, 2021), 93–112; Robbie Shilliam, 'Theorizing (with) Amy Ashwood Garvey', *ibid.*, 158–78; Keisha Blain, '"The Dark Skin[ned] People of the Eastern World": Mittie Maude Lena Gordon's Vision of Afro-Asian Solidarity', *ibid.*, 179–97. See the following paragraph for a discussion of the global dimensions of these scholars' wider work.

[8] See for example Brenda Gayle Plummer, *Rising Wind: Black Americans and US Foreign Affairs, 1935–1960* (Chapel Hill, 1996); Marc Gallicchio, *The African American Encounter with Japan and China: Black Internationalism in Asia, 1895-1945* (Chapel Hill, 2000); Carole Elaine Anderson, *Eyes Off the Prize: The United Nations and the African American Struggle for Human Rights, 1944-1955* (Cambridge, 2003); Keisha Blain, *Set the World on Fire: Black Nationalist Women and the Global Struggle for Freedom* (Philadelphia,

Shilliam, Imaobong Umoren and Keisha Blain have examined the entangled, multipolar networks of women and men from both North and South: that of Black Power, Rastafari, Maori and Pasifika activists in Shilliam's case, that of Black Americans, Martinicans and Jamaicans in Umoren's case, and that of pan-Africanists from America, Jamaica and Britain in Blain's case.[9]

Moving away from histories of great men and interstate relations, a good number of scholars have turned their attention to the practice of internationalism in recent years, focusing on the history of liberal international institutions and beyond, including the League of Nations, the United Nations, UNESCO, the Socialist International, as well as humanitarian organisations including Oxfam and Save the Children.[10] Scholars in the past ten years have unravelled the imperial roots of liberal internationalist projects.[11] They have also shown us how institutions like the League and the United Nations served as important anti-colonial platforms for Arab and Asian political organisers, including women.[12] Some have shown us how actors in colonial and post-colonial territories interacted and appealed to such institutions – as

---

2018); Minkah Makalani, *In the Cause of Freedom: Radical Black Internationalism from Harlem to London* (Chapel Hill, 2011); Nicholas Grant, *Winning Our Freedoms Together: African Americans and Apartheid, 1945-1960* (Chapel Hill, 2017); Keisha N. Blain and Tiffany M. Gill (eds.), *To Turn the Whole World Over: Black Women and Internationalism* (Champaign, 2019).

[9] See Robbie Shilliam, *The Black Pacific: Anti-colonial Struggles and Oceanic Connections* (2015); Imaobong Umoren, *Race Women Internationalists: Activist-Intellectuals and Global Freedom Struggles* (Berkeley, 2018); and Blain, *Set the World on Fire*, 133–216.

[10] Sunil Amrith and Glenda Sluga, 'New Histories of the United Nations', *Journal of World History*, 19, no. 3 (2008), 251–74; Michael Barnett, *Empire of Humanity* (Ithaca, 2011); Ana Antic, Johanna Conterio and Dora Vargha, 'Conclusion: Beyond Liberal Internationalism', *Contemporary European History*, 25 (2016), 359–71; Kevin O'Sullivan, *The NGO Moment: The Globalisation of Compassion from Biafra to Live Aid* (Cambridge, 2021); Giusi Russo, *Women, Empires, and Body Politics at the United Nations, 1946-1975* (Lincoln, NE, 2023). For new perspectives on socialist internationalism, see Talbot Imlay, *The Practice of Socialist Internationalism: European Socialists and International Politics, 1914-1960* (Oxford, 2017); James Mark et al., *Socialism Goes Global: The Soviet Union and Eastern Europe in the Age of Decolonization* (Oxford, 2022); Celia Donert and Christine Moll-Murata (eds.), 'Special Issue 30: Women's Rights and Global Socialism', *International Review of Social History*, 67 (2022).

[11] See especially Susan Pedersen, *The Guardians: The League of Nations and the Crisis of Empire* (Oxford, 2015).

[12] Manu Baghavan, *The Peacemakers: India and the Quest for One World* (2013); Nova Robinson, '"Sisters in Asia": The League of Nations and Feminist Anticolonial Internationalism', *Signs: Journal of Women in Culture and Society*, 47 (2022), 987–1012; Nova Robinson, "Arab Internationalism and Gender: Perspectives from the Third Session of the United Nations Commission on the Status of Women, 1949', *International Journal of Middle East Studies*, 49 (2016), 578–83; Cindy Ewing, '"With a Minimum of Bitterness": Decolonization, the Right to Self-Determination, and the Arab-Asian Group', *Journal of Global History*, 17 (2022), 254–71; Elisabeth Leake, 'States, Nations, and Self-Determination: Afghanistan and Decolonization at the United Nations', *Journal of Global History*, 17 (2022), 272–91; Alanna O'Malley and Vineet Thakur, 'Introduction: Shaping a Global Horizon, New Histories of the Global South and the UN', *Humanity: An International Journal of Human Rights, Humanitarianism, and Development*, 13 (2022), 55–65; Emma Kluge, 'A New Agenda for the Global South: West Papua, the United Nations, and the Politics of Decolonization', *ibid.*, 66–85; Stella Krepp, 'Fighting an Illiberal World Order: The Latin American Road to Unctad, 1948-1964', *ibid.*, 86–103; and Miguel Bandeira Jerónimo and

Erez Manela demonstrated in his landmark study of the 1919 Paris Peace Conference, an occasion seized upon by petitioners from Korea, Egypt, India and China to articulate their own nationalist aims.[13]

The locations of anti-colonial interwar internationalism spearheaded by Asians, Africans and, in some cases, Latin Americans have often been traced to urban hubs like London, Paris, Berlin, Brussels, New York, San Francisco and Moscow.[14] As hubs for education, intellectual ferment and migrant crossings, these were important sites for anti-colonial activists to form networks due to the necessity of evading colonial regimes of surveillance.[15] None of us can ignore the importance of these cities, particularly for the revolutionary heroes and political leaders of the Global South. But this might lead us to ask: to what extent do such histories place nationalist elites and leading intellectuals who studied and moved through Europe at the centre of the story of the Global South's internationalism? What does internationalism look like when it emerges *in* and *for* the Global South?[16]

Sujit Sivasundaram has challenged us to rethink the age of revolutions from the point of view of the Indian and Pacific Oceans, and to look at the ways in which indigenous peoples travelled, migrated, adopted new technologies, recalibrated their politics and challenged the crushing force of empires.[17] Toby Green, similarly, has traced the intricate globalism of West African societies, which both inspired and took inspiration from the Haitian Revolution through technology and music, and where itinerant Islamic scholars helped push popular resistance movements to overthrow aristocracies made wealthy

José Pedro Monteiro, '"Colonialism on Trial": International and Transnational Organizations and the "Global South" Challenges to the Portuguese Empire (1949–1962)', *ibid.,* 104–26.

[13] Erez Manela, *The Wilsonian Moment: Self-Determination and the International Origins of Anticolonial Nationalism* (Boston, 2007); Meredith Terretta, '"We Had Been Fooled into Thinking that the UN Watches over the Entire World": Human Rights, UN Trust Territories, and Africa's Decolonization', *Human Rights Quarterly*, 34 (2012), 329.

[14] See for example Leela Gandhi, *Affective Communities: Anticolonial Thought, Fin-de-Siècle Radicalism, and the Politics of Friendship* (Durham, NC, 2007); Harald Fischer-Tiné, 'Indian Nationalism and the "World Forces": Transnational and Diasporic Dimensions of the Indian Freedom Movement on the Eve of the First World War', *Journal of Global History*, 2 (2007), 325–44; Frederik Petersson, 'Hub of the Anti-imperialist Movement: The League Against Imperialism and Berlin, 1927–1933', *Interventions*, 16 (2014), 49–71; Marc Matera, *Black London: The Imperial Metropolis and Decolonization in the Twentieth Century* (Berkeley, 2015); Michael Goebel, *Anti-imperial Metropolis* (Cambridge, 2015); Leslie James, *George Padmore and Decolonization from Below* (2015); Klaas Stutje, *Campaigning in Europe for a Free Indonesia: Indonesian Nationalists and the Worldwide Anticolonial Movement* (Copenhagen, 2019). On a fascinating revolutionary circuit that connects San Francisco/Berkeley from Bengal to London, Paris and Berlin to Istanbul, Kabul and Singapore see Maya Ramnath, *Haj to Utopia: How the Ghadar Movement Charted Global Radicalism and Attempted to Overthrow the British Empire* (Berkeley, 2011).

[15] Daniel Brückenhaus, *Policing Transnational Protest: Liberal Imperialism and the Surveillance of Anticolonialists in Europe, 1905-1945* (Oxford, 2017).

[16] Emma Hunter's illuminating study shows how concepts such as international human rights and democracy were translated and debated in both urban and rural Tanzania. See Emma Hunter, *Political Thought and the Public Sphere in Tanzania* (Cambridge, 2015).

[17] Sujit Sivasundaram, *Waves across the South: A New History of Revolution and Empire* (Chicago, 2021).

through the slave trade.[18] Haiti would go on to serve as an early model of pan-African unity that would inspire a turn-of-the-century movement of African American and African intellectuals.[19] Scholars have recently argued that nineteenth-century Latin America, long neglected in scholarship on 'global history' and the history of international relations, is central to understanding the rise of the nation state and provided lessons in successful multilateralism.[20] By the early twentieth century, another era of revolutionary change, newspaper readers, radio listeners, community organisers and ordinary neighbours throughout Southeast Asia were moved by the great revolutions of the age: the Meiji Restoration, the Philippine Revolution, the Khalifate movement and the birth of the Republic of China.[21] This is not to discount the importance of 1919 for instilling a revolutionary rhetoric of self-determination in the international arena, but it does give us different lineages of the global circulation of revolutionary and internationalist ideas rooted in the Global South.

By beginning with events in the Global South, a different landscape of international engagement emerges, one that accounts for but also moves beyond developments in Europe and North America. Edited volumes and monographs that combine a range of regional perspectives are beginning to chart the multi-centred rise of various kinds of internationalism around the world – from globalist associational cultures to the worldwide rise of radical anti-fascism to underground revolutionary networks across Asia and the Pacific.[22] We might also ask whether older lineages of cosmopolitanism – mentalities on which internationalism depends – dovetailed with the engagement of interwar internationalism by people from, for instance, the coastal regions of East Africa and South and Southeast Asia (more broadly, the Indian Ocean world). These regions were knitted together – and to the world – by networks of trade and communication well before the twentieth century.[23] In Southeast Asia,

---

[18] Toby Green, *Fistful of Shells: West Africa from the Rise of the Slave Trade to the Age of Revolution* (2019).

[19] See Hakim Adi, *Pan-Africanism: A History* (2018); and Leslie M. Alexander, *Fear of a Black Republic* (Champaign, 2022).

[20] See Matthew Brown, 'The Global History of Latin America', *Journal of Global History*, 10 (2015), 378; Tom Long and Carsten-Andreas Shulz, 'Republican Internationalism: The Nineteenth-Century Roots of Latin American Contributions to International Order', *Cambridge Review of International Affairs*, 35 (2022), 639–61. See also Nicola Miller, *Republics of Knowledge* (Princeton, 2020); Mark J. Petersen, *The Southern Cone and the Origins of Pan America, 1888-1933* (Notre Dame, 2022).

[21] See Benedict Anderson, *Under Three Flags: Anarchism and the Anti-colonial Imagination* (2005); Amira Bennison, 'Muslim Internationalism between Empire and Nation-State', in *Religious Internationals in the Modern World*, ed. Abigail Green and Vincent Viane (2012), 163–85; Nicole CuUnjieng-Aboitiz, *Asian Place, Filipino-Nation: A Global Intellectual History of the Philippine Revolution* (New York, 2022).

[22] Andrew Arsan, Su Lin Lewis and Anne-Isabelle Richard, 'The Roots of Global Civil Society and the Interwar Moment', *Journal of Global History*, 7 (2012), 157–65; Kasper Braskén, Nigel Copsey and David J. Featherstone (eds.), *Anti-Fascism in a Global Perspective: Transnational Networks, Exile Communities, and Radical Internationalism* (Oxford, 2020); Tim Harper, *Underground Asia: Global Revolutionaries and the Assault on Empire* (Boston, 2021).

[23] K. N. Chaudhuri, *Trade and Civilisation in the Indian Ocean* (Cambridge, 1985); Abdul Sheriff, *Dhow Cultures of the Indian Ocean: Cosmopolitanism, Commerce and Islam* (2010); Sunil Amrith, *Crossing the Bay of Bengal: The Furies of Nature and the Fortunes of Migrants* (Cambridge, MA, 2015).

long before London boasted of its multiculturalism, colonial port-cities like Penang and Rangoon were dotted with mosques, Buddhist temples, Hindu shrines, churches, and synagogues; these had precedents in pre-colonial cities such as Malacca and Ayutthaya in Siam, which welcomed a range of confessional groups, practising religious tolerance.[24] One did not have to travel to Europe to be an internationalist; the sense of other worlds, other communities was palatable and felt in these microcosms. Whether cosmopolitanism was a vernacular practice or an elitist claim, its presence was a fact of life.[25]

In multilingual Penang of the 1920s (whose population had long included Malays, Indians, Chinese, Japanese, Armenians, Eurasians), when schoolchildren heard of the League of Nations, they jokingly compared the institution to their own multi-ethnic friendship circles.[26] Penang's newspaper correspondents debated the merits of such an institution, and wondered whether Asia deserved its own League, particularly given the failures of that organisation to live up to its promises.[27] Some of these correspondents had gone to mission schools, and many to the Penang Free School, established in 1816 by an English clergyman and Chinese, Tamil, Chulia and Eurasian merchants who agreed to build a school open to pupils of any race, colour and creed. Their educational world was one steeped in liberal traditions, but also one where, in the playground, Chinese, Indian, Malay, Arab and Peranakan vernacular cultures melded, jostled and refracted in kaleidoscopic views of the wider world.[28] One graduate, the renowned epidemiologist Wu Lien-Teh, served as an early adviser to the League of Nations, earned a nomination for the 1935 Nobel Prize and pioneered the use of facemasks, later to prove essential in controlling the COVID-19 epidemic around the world.[29] Penang's multilingual literati practised, and advocated for, the cosmopolitanism that would be heralded by institutions like the UN that espoused world peace, world community and interracial cooperation (see Figure 1). But they were also highly conscious of the contradictions at the heart of the liberal international project.

Discourses of internationalism coursed through Penang's interwar press, including the *Eastern Courier*, a Kuomintang-financed newspaper featuring regular contributions from multi-ethnic Malayan intellectuals. A 1929 article on 'World Brotherhood' pointed to the cleavages between the 'so-called progressive and advanced nations of the world and the so-called backward races

---

[24] Anthony Reid, *Southeast Asia in the Age of Commerce, 1450-1680*, vol. 1: *The Lands Below the Wind* (New Haven, 1988).

[25] Scholarship on the eastern Mediterranean has made us particularly attuned to the dangers of romanticising the cosmopolitanism of these areas, while giving us a more careful reading of its practice and its politics. See Will Hanley, 'Grieving Cosmopolitanism in Middle East Studies', *History Compass*, 6 (2008), 1346–67.

[26] 'The Consequences of a Visit to a Lecture', *Penang Free School Magazine*, Dec. 1921, p. 10.

[27] 'World's Greatest Need: A World League', *Eastern Courier*, 13 Apr. 1929, p. 3.

[28] Su Lin Lewis, *Cities in Motion: Urban Life and Cosmopolitanism in Southeast Asia, 1920-1940* (Cambridge, 2018), 196–201.

[29] Wu Yu-Lin, *Memories of Dr. Wu Lien-Teh: Plague Fighter* (George Town, 2016); Anoushka Bucktowar, Hareesha Bharadwaj and Matan Bone, 'Lest We Forget: Dr Wu Lien-Teh (1879–1960)', *Journal of Medical Biography* (2023), https://doi.org/10.1177/09677720231177679.

Figure 1. Newspaper cuttings from 1930s Penang from the *Eastern Courier* and the *Straits Echo*.

of mankind, for the so-called superior races have always assumed that they are in command of the resources of the world and it is for them to take or give as they see fit'.[30] The idea of 'world brotherhood' relied on friendship and cooperation among equals, and the need for nations to give up 'special privileges, concessions, and territories taken by force'. It relied on young men and women now capable of speaking almost any language 'not excepting Esperanto', who would 'do much to enhance the cordial relations between China and foreign countries, for after all, they are composed of living human beings to whom the appeal of internationalism is as irresistible as it is natural'. It relied, the author argued, on more student exchanges and visits of foreign journalists – all marks of international cooperation in the post-war world. This, however, was an ideal that was far from realisation, particularly given what the author saw as the 'treatment meted out to colored people in the Southern part of the United States'. The ideals of international cooperation advocated throughout the 1920s by America and Northern Europe were betrayed by their imperialism, and the treatment of those on the other side of the global colour line.[31]

---

[30] 'World Brotherhood', *Eastern Courier*, 8 Jun. 1929. The China orientation of the article suggests the author was Straits-Chinese, though the tone is a clear departure from the turn-of-the-century imperial cosmopolitanism of Singapore's Straits-Chinese; on this see Neil Khor 'Imperial Cosmopolitan Malaya: A Study of Realist Fiction in the Straits Chinese Magazine', *Journal of the Malaysian Branch of the Royal Asiatic Society*, 81, no. 1 (2008), 27–47; Tim Harper, 'Globalism and the Pursuit of Authenticity: The Making of a Diasporic Public Sphere in Singapore', *Sojourn: Journal of Social Issues in Southeast Asia*, 12 (1997), 261–92. Rather, it exhibits a strong sense of global social justice characteristic of Penang's multi-ethnic literati by the 1930s; on this see Lewis, *Cities in Motion*.

[31] W. E. B. Du Bois, *The Souls of Black Folk* [1903] (New York, 1982), 54; Marilyn Lake and Henry Reynolds, *Drawing the Global Colour Line: White Men's Countries and the Question of Racial Equality* (Melbourne, 2008).

The view of internationalism from the South relied on the promise of a post-colonial world, in which each nation, each community, deserved its own seat at the table (even if many would disagree on *how* communities should be represented).[32] The League never promised this. It was after the failures of the Paris Peace Conference in 1919 that anti-colonial movements grew increasingly dynamic, militant and resolutely internationalist, campaigning for an end to colonialism everywhere, feeding off each other, creating new (and reviving old) solidarities that lasted well into the post-war era.[33] The League Against Imperialism, which met in Brussels in 1927, drew together leftist internationalists and students, radicals and anti-colonial revolutionaries from across the colonial world.[34] These solidarities overlapped with leftist internationalism, which held that the struggle against colonialism was intimately bound up with the struggle against capitalism – and that both needed to be overthrown for a truly egalitarian world order to emerge. As Tim Harper has detailed so vividly, the suppression of the Indonesian communist movement in 1926, the tightening of surveillance networks followed by waves of exile throughout Asia, and the subsequent slaughtering of communists by Kuomintang officers in Shanghai in 1927, caused irreparable ruptures in what was, briefly, a united movement, and crippled the vibrant, anti-colonial leftist internationalism of the 1920s.[35]

Women's internationalist networks also began to flourish in the interwar era, as Asian women directly challenged the Eurocentrism of Western women's movements. The Pan-Pacific Women's Conference, convened in 1928 in Honolulu, put non-white women from China, Japan, the Pacific Islands and settler colonies into leadership roles.[36] Three years later, Indian women organised an All-Asian Women's Conference in Lahore to create a shared forum in which Asian women could converse among themselves to learn from each other, and distinguish themselves from the so-called 'international' and transnational

---

[32] On claims for self-determination within post-colonial states, see Lydia Walker, 'Decolonization in the 1960s: On Legitimate and Illegitimate Nationalist Claims-Making', *Past & Present*, 242 (2019), 227–64; Emma Kluge, 'A New Agenda for the Global South: West Papua, the United Nations, and the Politics of Decolonization', *Humanity: An International Journal of Human Rights, Humanitarianism, and Development*, 13 (2022), 66–85.

[33] See Michael Adas, 'Contested Hegemony: The Great War and the Afro-Asian Assault on the Civilizing Mission Ideology', *Journal of World History*, 15 (2004), 31–63; Cemil Aydin, *The Politics of Anti-Westernism in Asia: Visions of World Order in Pan-Islamic and Pan-Asianist Thought* (New York, 2007); Ali Raza, Franziska Roy and Benjamin Zachariah (eds.), *The Internationalist Moment: South Asia, Worlds, and World Views 1917–39* (New Delhi, 2014). Some militant anti-colonial movements can of course be traced earlier, amidst the First World War. See Ramnath, *Haj to Utopia*; and Tim Harper, 'Singapore, 1915, and the Birth of the Asian Underground', *Modern Asian Studies*, 47 (2013), 1782–1811.

[34] Michele Louro et al., *The League Against Imperialism* (Leiden, 2020).

[35] Harper, *Underground Asia*.

[36] Fiona Paisley, *Glamour in the Pacific: Cultural Internationalism and Race Politics in the Women's Pan-Pacific* (Honolulu, 2009); Rumi Yasutake, 'The First Wave of International Women's Movements from a Japanese Perspective: Western Outreach and Japanese Women Activists during the Interwar Years', *Women's Studies International Forum*, 32 (2009), 13–20.

networks dominated by European feminists.[37] It aimed for a radical break with European feminism, in full recognition of the distinct and anti-colonial context in which Asian women campaigned. Attendees at the conference included the sisters of the pioneering Indonesian feminist and nationalist Raden Adjeng Kartini, while one of the conference's reception committee, Hansa Mehta, became instrumental in the drafting of the UN Declaration of Human Rights.

The end of World War II is often seen as the beginning of a new world order shaped largely by American and European officials. But a more nuanced perspective suggests more agency by actors in the Global South, and more continuity with its earlier aspirations. Christy Thornton has shown how prevailing accounts of the making of this new institutional order have neglected the role of Latin American officials in the early foundations of the Bretton Woods project.[38] The 1940s saw a range of experiments in federalism that disrupted the teleology of nationhood, some driven by a much-weakened Whitehall and taken up by African and Asian leaders, and some conceived independently.[39] Many of these had long roots: the 1945 Pan-African Congress in Manchester was the fifth in a series of gatherings that began in 1919 as an alternative forum to the Paris Peace Conference.[40] Nehru's vision of a pan-Asian federation paved the way for the 1947 Asian Relations Conference, a legacy of Asia's interwar internationalism.[41] For Asian and African leaders and leaders-in-waiting, the United Nations provided the institutional scaffolding to actualise anti-colonial aspirations already in place, as they began forming new solidarities and conversing about the shape of a post-imperial world both in and out of liberal institutional institutions.[42]

From Japan's insertion of a 'race equality clause' at the dawn of the League of Nations in 1919, Asian, African and Latin American diplomats and technocrats both drove and contested international norms; these ranged from the advocacy of Latin American and Indian women in making the UN Declaration of Human Rights a more inclusive document, to the role of Nehru, Indian migrants in South Africa, and Tibetan and Pakistani refugees

---

[37] *Report of the All-Asian Women's Conference* (Bombay, 1931); Sumita Mukherjee, 'The All-Asian Women's Conference 1931: Indian Women and Their Leadership of a Pan-Asian Feminist Organisation', *Women's History Review*, 26 (2017), 361–81; Shobna Nijhawan, 'International Feminism from an Asian Center: The All-Asian Women's Conference (Lahore, 1931) as a Transnational Feminist Moment', *Journal of Women's History*, 29 (2017), 12–36; on the pan-Asian legacies of the conference see Carolien Stolte, '"The Asiatic Hour": New Perspectives on the Asian Relations Conference, New Delhi, 1947', in *The Non-Aligned Movement and the Cold War*, ed. Natasa Miskovic, Harald Fischer-Tiné and Nada Boskovska (2014), 57–75.

[38] Christy Thornton, *Revolution in Development: Mexico and the Governance of the Global Economy* (Berkeley, 2021).

[39] See Michael Collins, 'Decolonisation and the "Federal Moment"', *Diplomacy & Statecraft*, 24 (2013), 21–40.

[40] See Adi, *Pan-Africanism*; Jake Hodder, 'The Elusive History of the Pan-African Congress, 1919–27', *History Workshop Journal*, 91 (2021), 113–31.

[41] See Stolte, '"The Asiatic Hour"'; Vineet Thakur, 'An Asian Drama: The Asian Relations Conference, 1947', *International History Review*, 41 (2019), 673–95.

[42] See Christopher J. Lee (ed.), *Making a World after Empire: The Bandung Moment and Its Political Afterlives* (Columbus, 2010).

in India in remaking discourses around citizenship and human rights.[43] Although these efforts were not always successful, their campaigns shifted the hegemonic dynamic of these international arenas and forced powerful nations into significant compromises to achieve consensus.[44] Adom Getachew has shown how African and Caribbean leaders used institutions like the United Nations and the World Bank to put the needs of the post-colonial world front and centre of the new world order.[45] These were sites of pragmatic institutional change and coalition-building – and not always successful. As the United Nations saw an exponential increase in membership with the entry of new post-colonial states from Asia and Africa, a Non-Aligned Bloc formed to challenge the supremacy of countries in the Global North, encapsulated by the hierarchies present in the UN's five-member, veto-wielding Security Council. By 1974, the New International Economic Order, a set of proposals to end the dependency of the Global South on the Global North, offered an indicator both of the ambitions of the Non-Aligned movement and the limited capacity of the United Nations to realise them, as well as the collapse of leftist internationalism in the latter half of the cold war.[46]

Yet the United Nations and other multilateral institutions were not the only platforms for actors from the Global South to reimagine the world. The cultivation of a developmental perspective focusing on the needs and imagined futures of the Global South stemmed, too, from alternative forums of South–South cooperation centred in the South. The Non-Aligned movement emerged from connections and conversations – filled with hope and solidarity as well as tension and division – held before, during and after the 1955 Afro-Asian Conference in Bandung, Indonesia, which carries a symbolic meaning lingering well into the twenty-first century.[47] While it has long been seen as the inaugural moment of Third World internationalism – and indeed non-alignment – in the Global South, it has also elided wider and more diverse histories of internationalism, some splintered along these lines. Apart from new leaders – Nehru, Nasser, U Nu and Sukarno – who thrived in new diplomatic arenas such as Bandung's, trade unionists, women, peace activists, religious groups, intellectuals and artists were also part of this moment of post-colonial world-making across the South, meeting at pan-Asian, pan-African, Afro-Asian and

---

[43] On the race equality clause, see Naoko Shimazu, *Japan, Race and Equality: The Racial Equality Proposal of 1919* (2009); Bhagavan, *The Peacemakers*; Mark Mazower, *No Enchanted Palace: The End of Empire and the Ideological Origins of the United Nations* (Princeton, 2009); Ria Kapoor, *Making Refugees in India* (Oxford, 2021).

[44] See Susan Pedersen, 'Getting Out of Iraq – in 1932: The League of Nations and the Road to Normative Statehood', *The American Historical Review*, 115 (2010), 975–1000.

[45] Adom Getachew, *Worldmaking after Empire* (Princeton, 2019); Thornton, *Revolution in Development*.

[46] 'Special Issue: Towards a History of the New International Economic Order', *Humanity*, 6, no. 1 (2005).

[47] See G. H. Jansen, *Afro-Asia and Non-Alignment* (1966); Christopher J. Lee, *Making a World after Empire: The Bandung Moment and Its Political Afterlives* (Athens, GA, 2010); Naoko Shimazu, 'Diplomacy as Theatre: Staging the Bandung Conference of 1955', *Modern Asian Studies*, 48 (2014), 225–52.

Tricontinental conferences across the South.[48] Before and after Bandung, these conferences had already begun assembling people of all ages, beliefs, professions and communities under the banner of diverse internationalisms. Delhi emerged as a hub of the Asian peace movement; Cairo as the site of the Afro-Asian People's Solidarity movement; and Beijing as a bastion of socialist hospitality for leftist internationals worldwide.[49] Afro-Asian women's conferences in Colombo and Cairo centred women in the early history of development, debating issues around women's education, public health and labour, as well as imperial pretensions of foreign aid.[50] Colombo became the headquarters of the Afro-Asian Writers' Bureau (AAWB) from 1958, while Jakarta hosted the Afro-Asian Journalists' Association (AAJA) from 1963 (both organisations split in the wake of Sino-Soviet tensions and political differences among members, one branch relocating to Beijing from 1966, while another branch of the AAWB relocated to Cairo).[51] As with so many of the Afro-Asian projects of this period, both organisations grew from conferences: the AAJA from Bandung, and the AAWB from the Afro-Asian Writers' Conference in Tashkent, which not only served as a bridge between the Soviet Union and the Afro-Asian world, but between Asian and African writers seeking to radically transform the realm of literature into a truly global project.[52]

Conferences, as Stephen Legg and others remind us, served as one of the key locations where internationalism emerged in the post-war world, 'buzzing with life, potential futures, hope, and despair'.[53] In place of London, Geneva and

---

[48] See Vijay Prashad, *The Darker Nations: A People's History of the Third World* (2007); Elisabeth Armstrong, 'Before Bandung: The Anti-imperialist Women's Movement in Asia and the Women's International Democratic Federation', *Signs: Journal of Women in Culture and Society*, 41 (2016), 305–31; Katharine McGregor and Vanessa Hearman, 'Challenging the Lifeline of Imperialism: Reassessing Afro-Asian Solidarity and Related Activism in the Decade 1955–1965', in *Bandung, Global History, and International Law: Critical Pasts and Pending Futures* (Cambridge, 2017); Carolien Stolte, 'Special Issue: Trade Union Networks and the Politics of Expertise in an Age of Afro-Asian Solidarity', *Journal of Social History*, 53 (2019), 331–47; Carolien Stolte and Su Lin Lewis (eds.), *The Lives of Cold War Afro-Asianism* (Leiden, 2022); Wildan Sena Utama, 'Engineering Solidarity: Indonesia, Afro-Asian Networks, and Third World Anti-imperialism 1950s–1960s' (PhD dissertation, University of Bristol, submitted Jun. 2023).

[49] Carolien Stolte, 'The People's Bandung', *Journal of World History*, 30 (2019), 125–56; Reem Abou-El-Fadl, 'Building Egypt's Afro-Asian Hub', *ibid.*, 157–92; Rachel Leow, 'A Missing Peace', *ibid.*, 21–54.

[50] See Su Lin Lewis and Wildan Sena Utama, 'The Politics of Development at Afro-Asian Women's Conferences', in *Socialism, Development, and Internationalism in the Third World: Envisioning Modernity in the Era of Decolonisation*, ed. Su Lin Lewis and Nana Osei-Opare (forthcoming in 2024).

[51] Taomo Zhou, 'Global Reporting from the Third World: The Afro-Asian Journalists' Association, 1963–1974', *Critical Asian Studies*, 51 (2019), 166–97; Duncan M. Yoon, '"Our Forces Have Redoubled": World Literature, Postcolonialism, and the Afro-Asian Writers' Bureau', *Cambridge Journal of Postcolonial Literary Inquiry*, 2 (2015), 233–52.

[52] See in particular Hanna Jansen, 'Soviet "Afro-Asians" in UNESCO: Reorienting World History', *Journal of World History*, 30 (2019), 193–222. On the Tashkent Afro-Asian Writers' Conference see also Rossen Djagalov, *From Internationalism to Postcolonialism: Literature and Cinema between the Second and the Third Worlds* (Montreal, 2020).

[53] Stephen Legg *et al.* (eds.), *Placing Internationalism: International Conferences and the Making of the Modern World* (2022).

New York, the new sites of Third World internationalism emerged in Bandung, Delhi, Beijing, Rangoon, Cairo, Tashkent and Havana.[54] New state-owned airlines, such as Air India and Egyptian Air, ferried Asian and African intellectuals across the Afro-Asian world. Delegates visited the emerging cities of the Global South via short hops along Southern air routes. Some were veterans of these worlds, like W. E. B. Du Bois, who had attended the first Pan-African Conference in London in 1900 at the age of thirty-two; the confiscation of his passport barred him from attending the Bandung conference, but after its reinstatement, he toured Europe and the Soviet Union and attended the Afro-Asian Writers' Conference at the age of ninety. Attendees learned as much about internationalism and its limits from conference exchanges as they did from the action of crossing borders at the pace of a jet airliner, or the new realities of passports, borders and visa restrictions.[55] Both the growing pace of and material restrictions on travel were mirrored in the realm of international communications, as activists both took advantage of the increased pace of communications and challenged the continuing dominance of American and European information networks.[56]

Bandung was thus part of a multi-centred arc of conferences and organisations that formed the sites of South–South cooperation in the 1950s, characterised by various kinds of internationalism splintered in an atmosphere of cold war competition. If Afro-Asianism was one form of collaboration, so were pan-Asianism, pan-Africanism and pan-Arabism – and so was Tricontinentalism, which grew out of these earlier movements, entwining Asia and Africa with Latin America in 1966.[57] Regionalisms were also internationalisms, bringing together people across the new and emerging states of the post-colonial world to meet, often for the very first time. But conferences were only one form of mobilisation in the Global South. The Asian Socialist Conference in Rangoon was not only an event, but an organisation that shared its offices with the Burma Socialist Party, serving as a publishing house with a Ghanaian editor who covered anti-colonial movements across Asia and Africa.[58] The Afro-Asian People's Solidarity Organisation (AAPSO), headquartered in Cairo, constituted a sophisticated organisational structure composed of a permanent secretariat, a council, a finance committee and various national Afro-Asian solidarity organisations.[59]

---

[54] Stolte and Lewis (eds.), *The Lives of Cold War Afro-Asianism*.

[55] Su Lin Lewis, 'Skies That Bind: Air Travel in the Bandung Era', in *Placing Internationalism*, ed. Legg *et al.*, 234–51

[56] See Sarah Nelson, 'A Dream Deferred: UNESCO, American Expertise, and the Eclipse of Radical News Development in the Early Satellite Age', *Radical History Review*, 141 (2021), 30–59.

[57] See Anne Garland Mahler, *From the Tricontinental to Global South: Race, Radicalism, and Transcontinental Solidarity* (Durham, NC, 2018); *The Tricontinental Revolution: Third World Radicalism and the Cold War*, ed. R. Joseph Parrott and Mark Atwood Lawrence (Cambridge, 2022).

[58] On James Markham, the Ghanaian editor of the Anti-Colonial Bureau in Rangoon, see Gerard McCann, 'Where Was the Afro in Afro-Asian Solidarity? Africa's "Bandung Moment" in 1950s Asia', *Journal of World History*, 30 (2019), 89–124.

[59] 'The Afro-Asian Peoples Solidarity Organization from April 1960–April 1961', 15 Jun. 1961, CIA-RDP78-00915R001300050009-3, CREST, 21, https://www.cia.gov/readingroom/docs/CIA-RDP78-00915R001300050007-5.pdf. See also Utama, 'Engineering Solidarity'.

After 1966, AAPSO merged into the Organization of Solidarity with the Peoples of Africa, Asia, and Latin America, publishing its first bulletin shortly thereafter. Militant anti-colonial and intellectual networks brought revolutionaries to Cairo, Algiers, Dar es Salaam and Angola, the new hubs of revolutionary, anti-colonial internationalism across the African continent, throughout the 1960s.[60] London in the 1960s reprised its role as an anti-colonial hub, cultivating overlapping networks of pro-Palestinian, anti-apartheid and anti-war activists, while Beijing and Moscow continued to strengthen their ties across the Afro-Asian world.

While recognising the importance of the UN and other multilateral forums for actors from the Global South, we must also recognise that such institutions were not the only platforms for change: South–South forums provided parallel and often formative arenas of internationalism for transnational actors, including those whose careers intersected with the UN. Civil society actors who moved in and out of UN commissions, projects and events brought with them the networks, knowledge and experiences drawn from such forums. Moreover, as I have shown, South–South forums provided an alternative arena of internationalism, as important as, if not more important than, conventional international forums. They were filled both with activists who appealed to the norms of international solidarity and human rights enshrined at the UN, and others who avoided and distrusted the UN and other humanitarian organisations. All these groups operated transnationally – through peace movements, women's movements, students' movements, labour movements, consumers' associations and environmental movements – while maintaining strong grass-roots networks both within and outside the new urban metropoles of the Global South.

Deeper and participatory histories

Conventional methodologies of international history are insufficient to account for deeper, entangled histories of actors from the Global South both within *and* outside international institutions. Much of the recent history of internationalism has mined the archives of the United Nations and other internationalist and humanitarian institutions, as well as the private papers of internationalist thinkers in the Global North, often kept in publicly accessible archives and libraries. The archives of humanitarian organisations often tell us much about Western 'agents of internationalism', but we must look hard for the interlocutors who made their work possible, and we understand little about their lives.[61] Alanna O'Malley and Vineet Thakur have recently drawn

---

[60] See Meredith Terretta, 'Cameroonian Nationalists Go Global: From Forest Maquis to a PanAfrican Accra', *Journal of African History*, 51 (2010), 189–212; Jeffrey Byrne, *Mecca of Revolution: Algeria, Decolonization, and the Third World Order* (Oxford, 2016); Eric Burton, 'Hubs of Decolonization: African Liberation Movements and "Eastern" Connections in Cairo, Accra, and Dar es Salaam', in *Southern African Liberation Movements and the Global Cold War 'East': Transnational Activism 1960-1990* (Berlin, 2019); George Roberts, *Revolutionary State-Making in Dar es Salaam* (Cambridge, 2021).

[61] See Jessica Reinisch, 'Introduction: Agents of Internationalism', *Contemporary European History*, 25 (2016), 195–205.

attention to the marginalisation of Global South actors in the United Nations, who have long populated the institution while seeking to transform it, 'working through the constraints of power rather than negating it'.[62] These might include not only U Thant, its third secretary general, but also the young diplomats conversing in the halls of the UN's New York headquarters – as well as the Asian, African and Latin American doctors, engineers, technicians, humanitarians and peacekeepers working in its umbrella organisations. The interactions they had were collaborative and constructive as well as contested and hierarchical; it is for this reason that we must approach these relationships without the romanticisation that can often accompany Afro-Asian solidarity and the Global South, but with careful attention to their aims and ambitions, their successes and failures, and their own prejudices.[63] Antoinette Burton's examination of India's relationship with Africa exposes a complex historical relationship imbued with hierarchies of race and gender, one shaped by dynamics of colonial and post-colonial power.[64] As Margot Tudor shows, vocal Iranian anti-colonialists in the UN's General Assembly could display the same sense of racial hierarchy as their Western counterparts in UN peacekeeping missions.[65] Being from the Global South was not in and of itself indicative of anti-colonial or radical politics.[66]

The archives of the United Nations and its associate institutions do tell us about how particular actors from the Global South – often elite or middle-class technocrats – used such forums. They may reveal much about the United Nations as a platform for South–South organising and coalition-building – and also contests and tensions – in the making of the Global South in the international arena. But they often don't tell us about the domestic pressures faced by Asian, African and Latin American actors who employed the UN as a site of contestation and campaigning. They don't tell us of the accusations they might have faced at home – of being elitist, rootless and out-of-touch cosmopolitans. They don't tell us about the tensions between internationalist technocrats and those activists operating transnationally outside liberal international institutions. They don't fully capture the way actors from the Global South had to navigate a thorny labyrinth of interpersonal relationships at the local, national, institutional and international levels, amid persistent racism rooted in deep-seated colonial legacies.[67]

---

[62] O'Malley and Thakur, 'Introduction: Shaping a Global Horizon', 57.

[63] See Schneider, 'Between Promise and Skepticism'; Pamila Gupta *et al.* (eds.), 'Special Issue: The Global South: Histories, Politics, Maps', *Radical History Review*, 131 (2018).

[64] Antoinette Burton, *Africa in the Indian Imagination: Race and the Politics of Postcolonial Citation* (Durham, NC, 2016).

[65] Margot Tudor, *Blue Helmet Bureaucrats: United Nations Peacekeeping and the Reinvention of Colonialism, 1945–1971* (Cambridge, 2023).

[66] I thank Margot Tudor for adding this point.

[67] One only needs to look at the recent comment by a Romanian ambassador, comparing a monkey that interrupted a UN meeting to the African delegation, to see contemporary examples of this: 'Dragos Tigau: Romania Recalls Kenya Ambassador over Racist Monkey Slur', BBC, 10 Jun. 2023, https://www.bbc.com/news/world-africa-65867104.

The Asian Socialist Conference (ASC) – particularly its Indonesian members – provides a complex picture of the interplay between different kinds of internationalism and its legacies for ensuing generations of activists. It also provides a starting point to examine the difficulties in tracing these histories both in and out of international archives, particularly for scholars in the Global South. The organisation served as a home to Asian and African socialist internationalists who operated in multiple internationalist spaces.[68] Many were multilingual, urban cosmopolitans, and worked alongside, and in tension with, socialists active at the grass roots. Some of them knew the UN well: Sutan Sjahrir, the leader of Indonesia's Socialist Party, confidently addressed its Security Council in 1947 at Lake Success over the issue of Indonesian independence, drawing links to other anti-colonial movements elsewhere. The organisation's Burmese head, U Hla Aung, travelled to Central Africa and the Gold Coast before arriving at the UN General Assembly to deliver a fiery speech on the persistence of colonialism on the continent; Wijono, the ASC's secretary general, forged networks of socialists in Malaya as well as in North Vietnam, railing against European socialists at the Stockholm Congress of the Socialist International. Drawing on the networks they forged across the Global South, these representatives campaigned vigorously against continued imperialism and for the need to de-escalate cold war tensions through disarmament and allegiance to UN principles.

One of the junior members of Sjahrir's Socialist Party, Soedjatmoko, was with Sjahrir at the Lake Success meeting; like Sjahrir, he had been at Delhi's Asian Relations Conference, and he even named his daughter Kamala after Nehru's wife. He also attended the ASC (on which he commented extensively in the Indonesian press) and served with the Indonesian delegation at Bandung. He developed a career in internationalism, staying on after Lake Success to become Indonesia's representative to the UN until 1950, and forming working relationships with other Asian and African diplomats and intellectuals in the world of public policy and international development. He witnessed the development of the Non-Aligned movement, while engaging in multiple regional and international forums on history, culture, social justice and equitable development in Southeast Asia and the wider world. He wrote on the primacy of freedom in development almost twenty years before Amartya Sen's Nobel-winning book.[69] He became, in 1982, the rector of the UN's university in Tokyo. That year, he also returned to Delhi – the city where he had attended the 1947 Asian Relations Conference – to give the Nehru Memorial Lecture on 'Non-Alignment and Beyond', expressing the need for regional cooperation and interdependence among developing and underdeveloped nations, and the history of non-alignment as a driving force for global solidarity.[70] For

---

[68] Su Lin Lewis, 'Asian Socialism and the Forgotten Architects of Post-colonial Freedom', *Journal of World History*, 30 (2019), 55–88; Thomas Shillam, 'Socialist Internationalism in South and Southeast Asia, c.1947–1960' (PhD dissertation, University of York, 2021).

[69] Soedjatmoko, *Development and Freedom* (Tokyo, 1980).

[70] Soedjatmoko, 'Non-Alignment and Beyond', in *Jawaharlal Nehru Memorial Lectures*, II (New Delhi, 1998), 1–29.

Soedjatmoko, the early South–South forums and conferences which he attended as a young man were formative platforms to work out developmental priorities and non-aligned pathways for participants across the Global South, even before he arrived in the hallowed halls of the UN.

Working alongside Soejatmoko in the Indonesian Socialist Party was a circle of grass-roots socialists rooted in East Java, in close touch with trade unions and oil workers, led by the veteran activist, journalist and labour mobiliser Djohan Sjahroezah.[71] They too had attended the ASC alongside Sjahrir, with some, like Dayino, staying as Indonesia's representatives.[72] While Soedjatmoko operated in liberal internationalist circles, urging them to understand development priorities from the ground up, Dayino worked at the grassroots level, maintaining close ties with members of the Indonesian Communist Party even as socialists outwardly distanced themselves from its more 'aligned' stance. Despite their differences in strategy, he would remain close to Soedjatmoko until he died.

Their commitment to international activism was carried forth by their children. Soedjatmoko's daughter, Kamala Chandrakirana, studied rural sociology and Southeast Asian studies with Benedict Anderson at Cornell, returned to Indonesia to begin a career with international aid organisations and national organisations and worked with grass-roots institutions in Papua.[73] She later became a prominent leader in both the Indonesian and international women's movement, including at the UN, focusing on human rights and discrimination against women. Dayino's daughter, Ita Fatia Nadia, also became a leading activist, inspired by her parents' activism.[74] She joined the Asian Students Association in the late 1970s and became part of a network of underground student movements throughout Asia that campaigned against the authoritarian regimes led by Ferdinand Marcos in the Philippines, Suharto in Indonesia and Mohammed Mahatir in Malaysia. She was inspired by Gabriela, a powerful umbrella organisation of Filipina women's groups founded in 1984.[75] Ita and Kamala worked together at the Asia-Pacific Women Law and Development (APWLD), a network of feminist organisations that met initially at the 1985 Nairobi Conference, where 12,000 non-governmental organisation (NGO) members including lawyers, activists and academics from the Global South came together to critically review the achievements of the UN Decade for Women. Amid the onset of World Bank and International Monetary Fund structural adjustment policies that negatively impacted women's traditional livelihoods and further centralised state power, resulting in a constriction of democratic space, a network of women lawyers, activists and social scientists

[71] Riadi Ngasiran, *Kesabaran Revolusioner: Djohan Sjahroezah: Pejuang Kemerdekaan Bawah Tanah* (Jakarta, 2015), 243–6; J. D. Legge, *Intellectuals and Nationalism in Indonesia: A Study of the Following Recruited by Sutan Sjahrir in Occupied Jakarta* (Jakarta, 2010), 100.

[72] Ngasiran, *Kesabaran Revolusioner*, 251–2.

[73] Kamala Chandrakirana, interview by author, 4 Jul. 2023.

[74] Ita F. Nadia, interview by author, 27 Sep. 2021.

[75] See Mina Roces, 'Rethinking "the Filipino Woman": A Century of Women's Activism in the Philippines, 1905–2006', in *Women's Movements in Asia*, ed. Mina Roces and Louise Edwards (Abingdon, 2010).

in the APWLD focused on legislating for women's interests and mobilising women in campaigns for women's rights.[76]

It is notable that both Kamala and Ita have been active participants in women's movements in the Global South – particularly as this, along with the activism of their fathers, is part of the lineage that Kamala and Ita come from. Much of what I have described above – the challenge to Eurocentric views of internationalism, the rise of South–South forums, the interplay between organisations from the Global South and those from the Global North, and the UN as a platform for South–South connection – will long be recognised by historians of women's internationalism and transnational organising.[77] Some of the most important histories of the international women's movement from the 1970s onwards have been written by women from the Global South as a mode of documenting their activism and the history of their transnational organisations. These have been sidelined in a history of internationalism that has long prioritised intergovernmental and state archives, and a history of development that has long neglected the role of women.

These include not only the history of the APWLD but the history of Development Alternatives with Women for a New Era (DAWN), another organisation in which both Ita and Kamala have been involved. Like the APWLD, it was formed as part of a series of international conferences around the UN Decade for Women in 1985 as a forum for women from the Global South to share experiences and strategies around alternative development processes. DAWN's secretariat has rotated from Bangalore to Rio de Janeiro to Barbados and Fiji, to Nigeria, the Philippines and Thailand. Economist and activist Devaki Jain's account of the organisation, written as part of a UN intellectual history project, is emblematic of a history of development as viewed from the South, and the role of women's civil society networks in enriching the UN's work.[78] Gita Sen and Caren Grown's book on the organisation was written immediately before the 1985 Nairobi UN women's conference.[79] It called attention to DAWN as a project 'initiated in the Third World' that nonetheless had support from women's movements in more industrialised countries, while also attracting 'the interests of many oppressed and poor women there, who see in

---

[76] Judy Taguiwalo and Trimita Chakma, *APWLD: Herstory 1986-2017* (Chiang Mai, 2019).

[77] See for instance Kumari Jayawardene, *Feminism and Nationalism in the Third World* (1994); Ellen Carol Dubois and Katie Oliviero (eds.), Special Issue on 'Circling the Globe: International Feminism Reconsidered, 1910 to 1975', *Women's Studies International Forum*, 32 (2009); Francisca de Haan, 'Continuing Cold War Paradigms in Western Historiography of Transnational Women's Organisations: The Case of the Women's International Democratic Federation', *Women's History Review*, 19 (2010), 547–73; Francisca de Haan et al., *Women's Activism: Global Perspectives from the 1980s to the Present* (Oxford, 2013); Jocelyn Olcott, *International Women's Year: The Greatest Consciousness-Raising Event in History* (Oxford, 2017); Katherine M. Marino, *Feminism for the Americas: The Making of an International Human Rights Movement* (Chapel Hill, 2019).

[78] Devaki Jain, *Women, Development, and the UN: A Sixty-Year Quest for Equality and Justice* (Bloomington, 2005).

[79] Gita Sen and Caren Grown, *Development, Crisis and Alternative Visions: Third World Women's Perspective* (New York, 1985).

DAWN's analysis and aims an affirmation of their own experiences and visions of a better life'.[80] Sen and Grown challenged the implicit assumption that lay behind many of the UN projects of the Decade, that women simply needed to participate more fully in the development process, and instead pointed to the deeper socio-economic problems within the process of industrialisation that limited women's access to resources and their capacity to fulfil basic needs. How does the history of internationalism and its power relations thus change when we centre women of the Global South, and the organisations they founded to create a collective voice on the international stage?[81]

Apart from these rich organisational histories, the archives of activists in the Global South also exist in the form of personal libraries, such as that of Anwar Fazal, the Penang-based president of the International Consumers' Association, a treasure trove for scholars researching Third World activism. The rich histories of transnational activism come alive through oral history and dialogues with other activists – from the vibrant, dynamic history of leftist internationalism in Asia and Africa in the 1950s and early 1960s, to the struggles of activists to cope with authoritarian regimes propped up by cold war power in the 1960s and 1970s, to a new generation of feminists, environmental activists and consumers' movements emerging with the rise of NGOs in the 1980s, which produced a range of new South–South platforms. To return to the island of Penang, which I mentioned earlier, the interwar internationalism evident in its playgrounds and publications continued well into the latter half of the twentieth century due to the island's long culture of associational life, its outward-facing multi-ethnic identity, its leftist politics and the activism of a few key individuals. As Matthew Hilton has detailed, the Consumers' Association of Penang (CAP), founded in 1969, succeeded in providing a new paradigm of Third World consumer activism, examining the role of producers as well as consumers amidst the onslaught of rapid industrialisation and environmental degradation.[82] Penang would later become the central headquarters of Consumers' International under Fazal, while CAP's long-time president Mohammed Idris would go on to form the Third World Network organisation, which sought to strengthen cooperation across the Global South, particularly around equitable and sustainable development, and represent the interests of the South in international forums. While headquartered in Penang, the organisation is represented in Geneva and has regional secretariats in Accra and Uruguay.

What new perspectives emerge when we listen to the people who lived and practised these South–South internationalisms, or those whose parents and mentors came from previous generations of transnational networking across the Tricontinental world? How do multiple generations of activists from the Global South engage with these wider histories of internationalism? What does collaborative and co-produced research with and between these figures yield?

---

[80] *Ibid.*, 11.

[81] Aurora Levins Morales, 'The Historian as Curandera', in *Women in Culture: An Intersectional Anthology for Gender and Women's Studies*, ed. Bonnie Kime Scott *et al.* (Oxford, 1998), 134–47.

[82] Matthew Hilton, *Prosperity for All: Consumer Activism in an Era of Globalization* (Ithaca, 2009), 75–97.

The methodology behind the Afro-Asian Networks project brought together scholars at the point of archival inquiry.[83] But we recognised that we were scholars based at universities in the Global North, benefiting from institutional and economic inequalities in intellectual practice. As we were all too aware, the work of a global historian has long involved well-funded scholars visiting different archives and discussing ideas at international conferences, often with the ease of travel granted to the bearers of Western passports.[84] What does it mean for the history of internationalism when Asian and African researchers are three or four times more likely to face visa difficulties for short visits, and opt not to attend conferences in the Global North, in the historically dominant power-centres of intellectual production?[85] What does the history of internationalism look like when it is largely scholars from the Global North who are able to visit the archives of international organisations, or participate in international conferences and events where the history of internationalism and South–South cooperation is discussed and debated? Several institutions and scholarly associations have opted, and have advocated, to hold conferences in the Global South for exactly these reasons.[86] Others have learned lessons from online collaboration during the pandemic to circumvent such issues.

Despite Ita and Kamala's living links with a history of Indonesian and Global South internationalism, it is telling that the archives documenting the life and writings of Soedjatmoko and those of Indonesian internationalist women were inaccessible to the very communities who needed to know and publicise their history. Kamala created a digital repository of Soedjatmoko's writings, *Membaca Soedjatmoko*, because she knew that public intellectuals outside academia would not be able to access many of his articles and essays without an institutional affiliation, and wanted to make them more accessible to young Indonesian historians and activists. She used the archive as a platform to inaugurate a series of seminars and conversations with Indonesian civil society about the role of intellectuals in Indonesian development. As a feminist activist, Ita was inspired by a network of women of the Left, both socialist and communist, who had travelled as far as Colombo and Cairo for Afro-Asian

---

[83] Afro-Asian Networks Research Collective, 'Manifesto: Networks of Decolonization in Asia and Africa', *Radical History Review*, 131 (2018), 176–82.

[84] Emily Callaci, 'On Acknowledgments', *The American Historical Review*, 125 (2020), 126–31; Elisabeth Leake, '(In)accessible Stories and the Contingency of History Writing', History Workshop online, 27 May 2022, https://www.historyworkshop.org.uk/museums-archives-heritage/inaccessible-stories-and-the-contingency-of-history-writing.

[85] Connie Nshemereirwe, 'Tear Down Visa Barriers That Block Scholarship', *Nature*, 563:7 (2018), https://doi.org/10.1038/d41586-018-07179-2; Gordon R. McInroy et al., 'International Movement and Science: A Survey of Researchers by the Together Science Can campaign', *RAND Research Reports* (Santa Monica, 2018), https://www.rand.org/pubs/research_reports/RR2690.html.

[86] See for instance 'Africa-Asia: A New Axis of Knowledge', a transnational platform convening scholars, artists, intellectuals and educators from Africa, Asia and Europe which held its 2015 and 2018 conferences in Accra and Dar es Salaam respectively, hosted by the University of Ghana and the University of Dar es Salaam. See Philippe Peycam, 'Towards an Autonomous Academic Africa-Asia Framework', *IIAS Newsletter*, 73 (2016), https://www.iias.asia/the-newsletter/article/africa-asia-framework. See also Insa Nolte, 'The Future of African Studies', *Journal of African Cultural Studies*, 31 (2019), 296–313.

Women's Conferences in 1957 and 1961. But as an independent scholar, she had trouble getting funding to use the International Institute of Social History (IISH) archives in Amsterdam to research the internationalist networks of Indonesian leftist women, some of whom had been interviewed by her husband Hersri Setiawan, a leading member of the AAWB in Colombo.[87]

Troubled by Ita's inability to find funds to research Indonesian leftist women in European archives, I wanted to create a new iteration of the Afro-Asian Networks collaborative project that would bring together a group of scholar-activists from the Global South to engage in collaborative research on global histories of the Left in South and Southeast Asia. As with the initial project, a major component was a week of collaborative research at the IISH in Amsterdam, one of the world's most important archives of leftist internationalism: it holds archives of the Socialist International and International Confederation of Trade Unions, but also important collections of oral histories and documents related to the Indonesian and Malay Left. As it was in World War II, the archive's mission is to preserve the history of oppressed social movements around the world, namely those under threat by the state or not included in national archives.

It is worth commenting that both the Indonesian participants faced visa difficulties and were almost denied entry by the very country that had colonised their homeland for three hundred years, one opting not to come. In the end, there were five of us engaging in one week of collaborative archival research in Amsterdam. They included scholar-activists from South and Southeast Asia keen to participate in dialogues around Afro-Asian and socialist internationalism and use the archives, and who would not normally have access to institutional funds or envision the archive as a possible repository for research. These participants came from Indonesia, Sri Lanka, Malaysia and Singapore, respectively. Some 'lived' these histories, as children of the first generation of socialist intellectuals in their countries. Ita was able to continue her research into Indonesian leftist women and investigate the recently acquired archives of the leftist internationalist Francisca Fangidaaj, who died in exile in the Netherlands. Ita's long history of transnational activism in the region, as a student activist, a feminist and a social campaigner – with Third World Network, with DAWN – made her an invaluable sounding board. Agnes Khoo published a book on oral histories with women involved in the Malayan Communist Party and similarly was involved in various Singaporean activist movements in the 1980s and 1990s; she has taught on development at universities in Ghana and Asia (she was an adjunct lecturer in Seoul at the time, and is now a senior lecturer at Shenzhen Technological University).[88] Fadiah Nadwa Fikri is a PhD candidate at the National University of Singapore, who practised as a human rights lawyer in Malaysia before embarking on a PhD to untangle the primacy of ethnic nationalism in the making of post-colonial Malaya. Sandev Handy is a curator at the Sri Lanka Museum of Modern Art, who co-curated the 2022

[87] On the AAWB, see Yoon, "'Our Forces Have Redoubled'".

[88] See Agnes Khoo, *Life as the River Flows: Women in the Malayan Anti-colonial Struggle (an oral history of women from Thailand, Malaysia, and Singapore)* (Monmouth, 2007).

exhibition 'Encounters', a rotating display featuring art and artefacts that spoke to Sri Lanka's global engagements in the Bandung era, including the AAWB in Colombo.

We were also joined online by Kathleen Ditzig and Carlos Quinon Jr, curators respectively based in Singapore and Manila who had recently collaborated on a digital and travelling exhibition on Afro-Southeast Asian affinities.[89] Along with Sandev, who spoke about 'Encounters', they showed us ways of bringing these histories of internationalism to life through art and artefacts, drawing them into contemporary histories of the image and social media.[90] Ita presented on her work on a mobile museum, a model that she had learned about in Johannesburg's District 6 Museum through her work with DAWN. This was a collaboration between herself and young artists and activists to build awareness of the survivors of the 1965 political genocide against the Left in Indonesia through their private archives – bicycles, dresses, shoes, notebooks and photographs – from their time on Buru Island, the notorious prison camp to which they had been sent. These survivors included Hersri, who had previously been involved in the AAWB, and spoke to the consequences faced by leftist internationalists under the repression of authoritarian regimes propped up by the United States in the midst of a global cold war. Bonnie Triyana, the founder of the Indonesian popular history magazine *Historia* and the lead curator for a stunning new exhibition at the Rijksmuseum, showed us how art objects could bring to life transnational histories of the Indonesian Revolution.

From the outset, the relations within the group were characterised by extraordinary dynamism, and the cooperative spirit with which we approached the archives was enhanced by multiple conversations about resonances and differences across decades and with the present day. (See Figure 2.) Though some of Agnes's previous work had taken a comparative approach, the historical work that Fadiah, Ita and Sandev had been unearthing on the Malay, Indonesian and Sri Lankan Left had previously been centred within national frameworks, and the opportunity to discuss these histories within a broader context yielded a host of exciting new insights and an understanding of the ways in which transnational connections were 'lived'. Fadiah and Ita soon uncovered the channels through which the Malay Left gave support to communist women from Indonesia during the revolutionary period. Ita's husband, Hersri Setiawan, had been a member of the AAWB, which Sandev had been researching for his exhibition, and Ita's Sri Lankan colleagues in the Asian feminist movement had inspired Sandev's own activism.

The questions that this multigenerational group asked of the era of Afro-Asian solidarity were fresh, intimate and profoundly grounded in contemporary histories of activism. They included questions that brought class much more firmly into the picture of Afro-Asian solidarity, examining the stakes of participating in international forums versus grass-roots activism. Coming from various locations, they were attuned to the varying ways in which Afro-Asianism was

---

[89] See Afro-Southeast Asia, http://afrosoutheastasia.com/ (accessed 5 Jun. 2023).

[90] Jessica Hammett *et al.*, 'Art, Collaboration and Multi-sensory Approaches in Public Microhistory: Journey with Absent Friends', *History Workshop Journal*, 89 (2020), 246–69.

Figure 2. Archival collaboration at the IISH.

lived and practised by people from across the social spectrum. Carlos and Kathleen introduced us to Afro-Asian affinities as a field of competing political interests, while Sandev questioned the elite cosmopolitanism of those working at Colombo's AAWB. Fadiah, meanwhile, uncovered documents that spoke to the internationalism of the Malayan Communist Party's Tenth Regiment, a regiment made up mainly of Malay soldiers based in guerrilla bases on the Thai border, and came upon their expressions of solidarity with people fighting against colonialism and imperialism elsewhere in the world. In morning seminars, we engaged in deeper discussions about the nature of the Left: its fractures, divisions and the gulfs that often emerged between leftist internationalists and grass-roots leftist social movements. The ensuing dialogue spoke to the legacies, the fissures, the challenges and the possibilities of connecting histories of activism and internationalism in and across the Global South.[91]

In highlighting the richness of these collaborative modes of research, I also wanted to point to other projects that have taken a similar approach. These include Afro-Asian Futures Past, a collaborative research programme at the American University of Beirut, which brings together multiple institutions across the Global South to investigate transnational intellectual exchanges in the Afro-Asian era. East Africa's Global Lives project held a collaborative archival workshop for UK and East African researchers to trace the biographies of East African individuals. As their recent article contends, life histories give us a richer view of the shifting nature of global connections

---

[91] We continued these conversations at a 2022 workshop on transnational activism at the University of Gadjah Madah in Indonesia and will be publishing a collective dialogue that stemmed from some of these discussions.

and why these mattered – even, and perhaps especially, to those who were never able to travel.[92] The e-workshop recently hosted by the Non-Aligned News Research Partnership brought together scholars from the Global North and South to examine the networks of journalists who sought to transform the economic and cultural imbalances in the flows of global news through the New World Information Order, both through UN Commissions and through autonomous transnational civil society networks across the Global South. Illuminating this global movement were three keynotes by living participants: the Argentinian journalist and activist Roberto Savio of the Inter Press News Service agency; the media sociologist Nabil Dajani, a member of the UNESCO panel on the New World Information Order; and the journalist and scholar Beatriz Bissio, founder of the magazine *Third World Books*.

Individual lives matter, but so do movements, and so do the multiple forums in which internationalism in the Global South came into being. Internationalism has been lived and practised in multiple ways. International governance institutions were, indeed, the most permanent, largely because of the institutional precedent, power and resources behind them that came from the Global North, galvanised by victory and anxious to protect the West's fragile ideological hegemony in 1945. Despite the hierarchies that imbued the organisation, the UN relied for its very existence on its members and interlocutors from the Global South, as well as its engagement with civil society actors who advised the organisation at both the international level and on the ground.

But operating at a no less important level was civil society in the Global South in its own right. For many of these actors, the UN was one platform among many – the village, the national, the regional, the Third Worldist, the developmental – to provide a space for members to confront issues of global inequality. South–South forums, particularly for leftist internationalists, were much more constrained than the UN amid a global cold war, and particularly due to the vast discrepancies in resources available for networking, projects and advocacy. But this is precisely why they need to be recovered and assessed, particularly as new generations of activists in the Global South engage in networks of solidarity against global inequality, environmental degradation and authoritarian regimes.

When discussing her current work with feminists in Sri Lanka and India, Kamala told me: 'Despite the connections from our parents' generation, we have no storyline that connects our work today with that history, with those old and once-powerful links.'[93] These links have been hindered by language barriers, by colonial legacies that created more connections with the metropole and subverted connections across the South, and by the rise of regimes that suppressed leftist activism and distorted its histories. All these have made these connections harder to stitch back together. Ita agrees, and says, 'If I

[92] Ismay Milford, Gerard McCann and Emma Hunter, 'Another World? East Africa, Decolonisation, and the Global History of the Mid-Twentieth Century', *Journal of African Studies*, 62 (2021), 394–410.
[93] Kamala Chandrakirana, interview by author, 18 Feb. 2022.

read through the archive, the internationalist message is so strong – we have lost this vision,' but 'reclaiming the historical interconnections between women from all over the world will allow us to renew the movement'.[94]

If we want to bring these histories to life, and to understand how internationalism was lived, as well as practised, we must engage with life histories, prosopography and organisational histories from multiple geographical and political perspectives.The act of decolonising history – of undoing, challenging and questioning structures of power – must also be an act of democratising history, of globalising history, of stitching back together and forming new regional connections across the South. It must involve making the archives of internationalism more accessible; broadening our view of internationalism; understanding what internationalism looks like from the point of view of activists who speak truth to power; creating opportunities for researchers and activists to meet across borders and recover these histories collaboratively. This can only enrich our collective understanding of internationalism – and in so doing, animate the narratives we tell about its multi-centred histories.

Data Availability Statement. All underlying data are available from sources referenced throughout this paper; this does not include oral history interviews under restricted access, available to bona fide researchers subject to a data access agreement.

Acknowledgements. This paper is based on a talk given to the Royal Historical Society in September 2022. I am very grateful for the invitation from the Royal Historical Society to speak in its lecture series. I am also deeply grateful to Elisabeth Leake and Margot Tudor for their detailed and incisive comments on drafts of this paper.

Financial Support. This research was funded by the Arts and Humanities Research Council's Research Network Scheme (AH/N003020/1) and the Arts and Humanities Research Council's Leadership Fellowship Scheme (AH/V001205/1).

Competing Interest. None.

Ethical Standards. Oral history interviews conducted for this paper have adhered to the University of Bristol Faculty of Arts Ethics Committee guidelines.

Author Biography. Dr Su Lin Lewis is Associate Professor in Modern Global History at Bristol. Her monograph *Cities in Motion: Urban Life and Cosmopolitanism in Southeast Asia 1920–1940* was published by Cambridge University Press in 2016 and won the Urban History Association's Prize for Best Book (2015–16). She was the principal investigator on an AHRC Research Network on 'Afro-Asian Networks in the Early Cold War', a collaborative research project on the transnational movements of political leaders, activists and literati across Asia and Africa in the 1950s and 1960s. She co-edited, with Carolien Stolte, *The Lives of Cold War Afro-Asianism* (Leiden, 2023).

---

[94] Ita F. Nadia, interview by author, 22 Jun. 2023.

Cite this article: Lewis SL (2024). Decolonising the History of Internationalism: Transnational Activism across the South. *Transactions of the Royal Historical Society* **2**, 345–369. https://doi.org/10.1017/S0080440123000233

Transactions of the RHS (2024), **2**, 371–388
doi:10.1017/S0080440123000282

'Slaves' and 'Slave Owners' or 'Enslaved People' and 'Enslavers'?

James Robert Burns

School of History, Politics, and International Relations, University of Leicester, Leicester, UK
Email: jrb49@leicester.ac.uk

(Received 5 June 2023; revised 22 September 2023; accepted 16 October 2023;
first published online 17 November 2023)

Abstract

Studies of slavery increasingly refer to 'enslaved people' rather than 'slaves', and, to a lesser extent, to 'enslavers' rather than 'slave owners'. This trend began with scholarship in the United States on plantation slavery but has spread to other academic publications. Yet 'slave' continues to be widely used, indicating not everyone is aware of the change or agrees with it. Despite this, few historians have justified their terminology. After surveying the extent of the preference for 'enslaved person', I discuss arguments for and against it. Supporters of using 'enslaved person' argue that this term emphasises that a person was forced into slavery – but this emphasis means it is less able to accommodate early medieval cases where people sold themselves into slavery. The accompanying preference for 'enslaver' over 'master' obscures dynamics of ownership and manumission. In addition, 'enslaved people' and 'enslaver' do not necessarily bring us away from the perspective of slaveholders to the perspective of slaves. Nor are they essential for readers to appreciate the humanity of slaves. Overall, historians should use this issue as an opportunity to reflect on the extent to which scholarship of transatlantic slavery should set the terms of debate for slavery studies in general.

Keywords: Slavery; enslavement; slaves; enslaved; early medieval

In the 2022 volume of this journal, of the four articles that mentioned slavery, two referred to 'slaves', while two referred overwhelmingly to variants of 'enslaved people'.[1] The authors of one of the latter articles also used 'enslavers'

---

[1] *Transactions of the Royal Historical Society* [hereafter *TRHS*], 32 (2022). The articles by Catherine Holmes, Stuart M. McManus and Michael T. Tworek refer to 'slaves'. The articles by Alec Ryrie,

as its main term for slave owners.[2] These discrepancies highlight how 'enslaved people' and 'enslavers' have grown in popularity as replacement terms for 'slaves' and 'slave owners' respectively, but have not yet become standard worldwide. This is unsurprising, given that the debate over what terms to use when writing about slavery has taken place rather discreetly, in online forums, with very little published discussion of the theoretical issues at stake. In 2018, Laura Rosanne Adderley, a historian of the nineteenth century, tweeted that, '"Enslaved" solves some problems, but may create others.'[3] Adderley herself still prefers to use 'enslaved people', but her tweet was an acknowledgement from proponents that this term may not always be appropriate. However, several years later, problems with using the term 'enslaved people' remain under-discussed. This is not just a matter of linguistic niceties. At their best, changes in terminology can encourage us to rethink our assumptions and stimulate better historical analysis, as happened with the shift away from using 'feudal' to describe the power structures of medieval Europe. But, unlike 'feudal', where the problems with the term have long been established, an academic debate over the relative merits of 'slave' and 'enslaved person' has barely started. This article is intended, therefore, to develop the discussion, rather than end it.

Historians need to think carefully about what terms we use – including those of us working on societies before AD 1500. There have been forms of slavery across many different periods and places, from medieval Korea to pre-Columbian America.[4] Approaching the debate from my own research interests in early medieval Europe, I find 'enslaved person' and 'enslaver' to be inadequate substitutes for 'slave' and 'slave owner'. I appreciate that other historians, especially those working on different periods to me, may come to different conclusions – but that is precisely why more academic discussion is needed. I hope, indeed, that this article will inspire interesting responses from historians who disagree with me. Once this debate gets going, it should clarify the strengths and weaknesses of using the term 'enslaved person' when writing about slavery in different historical contexts.

Let us start by noting the origins and extent of the preference for 'enslaved people'. Back in 1999, Deborah Gray White stated that, were she to rewrite her book on female slaves on plantations in the American south, she would refer to them as 'enslaved' rather than 'slaves', because, in her view, '"enslaved" says more about black people without unwittingly describing the sum total of who they were'.[5] But it is only more recently that 'enslaved people' has gained widespread momentum. Two important works laid some of the theoretical

---

D. J. B. Trim, Fahad Al-Amoudi, Kate Birch and Simon P. Newman refer overwhelmingly to 'enslaved people'.

[2] Fahad Al-Amoudi, Kate Birch and Simon P. Newman, 'Runaway London: Historical Research, Archival Silences and Creative Voices', *TRHS*, 32 (2022), 223–39.

[3] Laura Rosanne Adderley, @LauraAdderley, X [formerly Twitter], 28 Aug. 2018, https://twitter.com/LauraAdderley/status/1034224696382767104 (accessed 2 Mar. 2023).

[4] See the contributions to *The Cambridge World History of Slavery*, II, *AD 500–AD 1420*, ed. Craig Perry *et al.* (Cambridge, 2020).

[5] Deborah Gray White, *Ar'n't I a Woman?: Female Slaves in the Plantation South* (New York, 1999), 8.

groundwork favourable to this trend: first, a 2003 article by Walter Johnson, which called for historians to speak of 'enslaved humanity' rather than 'slave agency', in order to 'imagine a history of slavery which sees the lives of enslaved people as powerfully conditioned by, though not reducible to, their slavery';[6] second, Joseph Miller's 2012 book, *The Problem of Slavery as History*, which argued that a focus on slavery as an abstract institution obscures the importance of slaving as a dynamic and ongoing process.[7] However, both Johnson and Miller still referred to 'slaves', which suggests that they thought that their respective goals – affirming the personhood of slaves and emphasising that slavery was not a static institution – were achievable without wholesale adoption of the term 'enslaved people'.[8] Indeed, advocates of the term 'enslaved people' more often cite a rubric which Daina Ramey Berry developed for a 2012 encyclopedia on enslaved women in America, alongside P. Gabrielle Foreman's community-sourced style guide on writing about slavery, both of which also recommend referring to 'enslavers' rather than 'masters'.[9] The decision to eschew 'slaves' by the editors of the *New York Times*'s high-profile '1619 Project', on the legacy of slavery in America, has likewise been influential in encouraging academics, heritage institutions and media outlets to follow suit.[10] Works by Thomas A. Foster and Daive A. Dunkley are among academic publications on American plantation slavery which use the term 'enslaved person' except when paraphrasing or quoting from primary sources.[11]

Foreman explicitly states that her style guide is intended as a series of suggestions rather than an orthodoxy to be enforced, given the 'particularities of institutions of slavery in various parts of the Americas, Europe, Africa, and Asia, and also considering how slavery changed over time'.[12] Yet, noticeably since 2019, the preference for 'enslaved person' has grown beyond American scholarship of American slavery. In the United Kingdom, educational resources for the worlds of both the Roman and British Empire (notably BBC Bitesize and the *Cambridge Latin Course*) have started using 'enslaved person' instead of 'slave'.[13] Nonetheless, 'enslaved person' has not percolated everywhere. Only two of the eight research articles in the first 2023 issue of the *Slavery &*

---

[6] Walter Johnson, 'On Agency', *Journal of Social History*, 37 (2003), 115.

[7] Joseph C. Miller, *The Problem of Slavery as History: A Global Approach* (New Haven, 2012), 19, 25–8.

[8] *Ibid.*, 19, 49, 54; Johnson, 'Agency', 115–18; 'slave' was repeatedly used in Walter Johnson, 'Slavery, Reparations, and the Mythic March of Freedom', *Raritan*, 27 (2007), 41–67.

[9] Daina Ramey Berry, 'Introduction', in *Enslaved Women in America: An Encyclopedia*, ed. Daina Ramey Berry and Deleso A. Alford (Santa Barbara, 2012), xx–xxi; P. Gabrielle Foreman *et al.*, 'Writing about Slavery/Teaching about Slavery: This Might Help', community-sourced document, 22 Nov. 2022, https://docs.google.com/document/d/1A4TEdDgYslX-hlKezLodMIM71My3KTN0zxRv 0IQTOQs/mobilebasic (accessed 2 Mar. 2023).

[10] *The 1619 Project: A New Origin Story*, ed. Nikole Hannah-Jones *et al.* (New York, 2021).

[11] Thomas A. Foster, *Rethinking Rufus: Sexual Violations of Enslaved Men* (Athens, GA, 2019); Daive A. Dunkley, *Agency of the Enslaved: Jamaica and the Culture of Freedom in the Atlantic World* (Lanham, MD, 2013).

[12] Foreman *et al.*, 'Slavery'.

[13] BBC Bitesize, 'The Experiences of Enslaved People', 25 Aug. 2021, https://www.bbc.co.uk/bitesize/topics/z2qj6sg/articles/z6cptrd (accessed 2 Mar. 2023); BBC Bitesize, 'What Was Life Like in Ancient Rome?', 15 May 2015, https://www.bbc.co.uk/bitesize/topics/zwmpfg8/articles/

Abolition journal primarily referred to 'enslaved people' rather than 'slaves'.[14] Recent books on aspects of the British Empire by Linda Colley and P. J. Marshall have used the term 'slaves' outside of direct quotation of primary sources.[15] Contributions to a 2023 edited book on the Dutch and Portuguese empires in South America also interchangeably refer to 'slaves' and 'enslaved Africans', though some of the authors appear to prefer the latter term.[16]

'Slave' remains common in both US and non-US academic publications dealing with the ancient world – for example, in books by Franco Luciani, Peter Thonemann and Michael Flexsenhar III.[17] However, other historians, like Roberta Stewart, have started referring to 'enslaved people' instead.[18] A recent book on slavery and sexuality in classical antiquity is illustrative: the editors, Deborah Kamen and C. W. Marshall, avoided using 'slave' in their introduction, as do around half of their fellow chapter authors – but the other half still used it.[19] Perhaps this divide reflects concerns among ancient historians about letting scholarship of early modern slavery (literally) set the terms of debate around slavery in their period, which alerts us to the possibility already that linguistic models inspired by one historical context may not be appropriate for another. Interestingly situated on the spectrum of this debate among classical historians is Kostas Vlassopoulos, whose 2021 book aligns with proponents of 'enslaved persons' in arguing that the term 'slaves' can hide the multiple identities available to the unfree, whereas it nonetheless refers to 'slaves' throughout.[20] Vlassopoulos emphasises that he is not calling for a change in labels, but for historians to avoid thinking about people as merely

---

z2sm6sg (accessed 2 Mar. 2023); Cambridge Schools Classics Project, *Cambridge Latin Course Unit 1*, 5th edn (Cambridge, 2022).

[14] In *Slavery & Abolition*, 44, no. 1 (2023), the articles by Elsa Barraza Mendoza and Lucas Koutsoukos-Chalhoub mainly refer to variants of 'enslaved people', while the articles by Jane Lydon, Isabelle Laskaris, Natalia Sobrevilla Perea, Michael Ehis Odijie, Felicitas Becker *et al.* and Mònica Ginés-Blasi refer repeatedly to 'slaves'.

[15] Linda Colley, *The Gun, the Ship and the Pen: Warfare, Constitutions and the Making of the Modern World* (2021); P. J. Marshall, *Edmund Burke and the British Empire in the West Indies* (Oxford, 2019).

[16] *Pursuing Empire: Brazilians, the Dutch and the Portuguese in Brazil and the South Atlantic, c. 1620–1660*, ed. Cátia Antunes (Boston, MA, 2023). The chapter by Christopher Ebert and Thiago Krause uses 'enslaved Africans' as the standard term.

[17] Franco Luciani, *Slaves of the People: A Political and Social History of Roman Public Slavery* (Stuttgart, 2022); Peter Thonemann, *The Lives of Ancient Villages: Rural Life in Roman Anatolia* (Cambridge, 2022); Michael Flexsenhar III, *Christians in Caesar's Household: The Emperor's Slaves in the Makings of Christianity* (University Park, PA, 2019).

[18] Roberta Stewart, 'Seeing Fotis: Slavery and Metamorphosis in Apuleius' Metamorphoses', *Classical Antiquity*, 42, no. 1 (2023), 195–228.

[19] Deborah Kamen and C. W. Marshall, 'Introduction: Mere Sex Objects?', in *Sexuality and Slavery in Classical Antiquity*, ed. Deborah Kamen and C. W. Marshall (Piraí, 2021), 3–14. In the same book, Emily Wilson, Allison Glazebrook and Katherine P. D. Huemoeller followed the editors in eschewing 'slaves', while Kathy L. Gaca, Kelly L. Wrenhaven, Jason Douglas Porter, Rafal Matuszewski, Sarah Levin-Richardson and William Owens did not. Judging by their frequency of references to 'the enslaved', Ulrike Roth, Anise K. Strong and Matthew J. Perry seem to have preferred that term, but they have not excluded 'slave' outside of primary source quotations altogether.

[20] Kostas Vlassopoulos, *Historicising Ancient Slavery* (Edinburgh, 2021), 111.

and only as slaves. I will return to his work later. For now, I shall proceed with my survey.

Given the ongoing ubiquity of 'slave' in scholarship of other periods, it is unsurprising that prominent recent works in the field of early medieval slavery continue to use 'slave'. Alice Rio, in her 2017 monograph, though she primarily spoke of 'unfree people' and 'unfree status' as a way to acknowledge the overlap between forms of bondage in this period, still used 'slave' to refer to those on the 'most heavily subjected end of the spectrum of unfreedom'.[21] As with the previous volumes in the series, the chapters of the *Cambridge World History of Slavery: Volume 2, AD 500–AD 1420* referred to 'slaves', though some of the contributors more typically – but not exclusively – referred to 'enslaved people'.[22] Chris L. de Wet and all but one of his fellow authors routinely used the term 'slaves' in *Slavery in the Late Antique World* (2022).[23] As do Mary E. Sommar, Roy Flechner and Janel Fontaine, despite all publishing after 2019.[24] There are exceptions. For example, Ben Raffield's work on the Viking age has eschewed references to 'slaves', though this partly reflects his focus on the process of enslavement via raiding, as well as the difficulty in establishing whether captives were enslaved permanently, ransomed, killed or met another fate.[25] But, overall, the difficulties of translating *servus* and the issue of slavery versus serfdom continue to be the greater source of controversy when it comes to writing of 'slaves' in early medieval Europe.[26]

Constrained by lacking an alternative label, medieval historians have also taken care that their use of the word 'slave' does not cause their readers to equate the conditions of unfreedom in the Middle Ages with the racialised chattel and plantation slavery of later periods. It would almost be fortuitous, then, if it were not a partial and probably temporary development, that historians working on American slavery have, by being quicker to change their terms than those of earlier periods, incidentally created linguistic distance between ancient and medieval 'slaves' and early modern 'enslaved Africans'. Indeed, the divergence between forms of slavery may well merit a divergence in terms. Below, I will set out objections to using the term 'enslaved people' that historians of plantation and transatlantic slavery could disregard as irrelevant to their periods. Undoubtedly, these scholars know a lot more about slavery in America than I do. It is not my intention to disregard their expertise, nor the particular significance this issue might have for those whose recent ancestors were enslaved, who may understandably see an emphasis on the

---

[21] Alice Rio, *Slavery after Rome, 500-1100* (Oxford, 2017), 13.

[22] Perry *et al.* (eds.), *AD 500-AD 1420*.

[23] *Slavery in the Late Antique World, 150-700 CE*, ed. Chris L. de Wet, Maijastina Kahlos and Ville Vuolanto (Cambridge, 2022). The exception is Christine Luckritz Marquis.

[24] Mary E. Sommar, *The Slaves of the Churches: A History* (Oxford, 2020); Roy Flechner and Janel Fontaine, 'The Admission of Former Slaves into Churches and Monasteries: Reaching beyond the Sources', *Early Medieval Europe*, 29 (2021), 586–611.

[25] Ben Raffield, 'The Slave Markets of the Viking World: Comparative Perspectives on an "Invisible Archaeology"', *Slavery & Abolition*, 40 (2019), 685.

[26] Samuel S. Sutherland, 'The Study of Slavery in the Early and Central Middle Ages: Old Problems and New Approaches', *History Compass*, 18 (2020), 3.

personhood of enslaved Africans as important in the context of anti-Black racism. But if historians studying different forms of slavery can come to different conclusions about which terms to use, then that gives me even more reason to make my case. By thinking about terms, we can clarify quite how complex and varied slaveholding practices have been.

Despite the limited acceptance of the term 'enslaved people' indicating that not everyone agrees it is a necessary or appropriate substitute for 'slaves', there is relatively little academic literature devoted to either arguing in favour of it or against it. Back in 2006, David Brion Davis criticised the term 'enslaved people' as inelegant and euphemistic, but only in a footnote.[27] Alluding to instances such as this, Berry regretted in 2012 that debates on the terminology of slavery were 'hardly discussed, or equally unfortunate, were left buried and hidden in the footnotes'.[28] Outside of a few honourable exceptions, this continues to be the case.[29] While online forums and conferences have given historians an opportunity to discuss terms with each other, this has mostly not translated into academic publications. Considering that the movement towards 'enslaved people' largely appears to have been driven by individual scholars choosing to adopt the term, rather than journals or publishers, it is surprising that historians have been so unforthcoming about their motives – though perhaps if editors did have set policies, that would spur some into action. The lack of transparent reasoning by historians working on societies beyond the early modern North Atlantic world is especially disappointing, given Foreman's invitation to engage with the historical particularities of slavery. However, some historians – by no means all – have referred to Foreman's style guide, acknowledging their debt to her guidance.[30] That even ancient historians have cited this style guide, with its recommendations inspired by scholarship on transatlantic slavery, is testament to the clarity, cogency and accessibility of Foreman's arguments. But it also highlights the poverty of extended academic analysis of this issue.

Readers of historians who have not elaborated on their preference for 'enslaved people' are forced to infer their motives from what other advocates of the term have stated online, often outside of formal academic forums. Even approached charitably, this process of inference is necessarily fraught. It is very likely that there are arguments for using 'enslaved people' which are not found in the standard reference pieces that largely form the basis of my citations.[31] Indeed, some historians who use 'enslaved people' have not followed Foreman's style guide in other respects, indicating that these historians

---

[27] David Brion Davis, *Inhuman Bondage: The Rise and Fall of Slavery in the New World* (Oxford, 2006), 412–13 n. 13.

[28] Berry, 'Introduction', xx.

[29] Exceptions include Berry, 'Introduction', xx; Stewart, 'Seeing Fotis', 197; Vlassopoulos, *Ancient Slavery*, 111; Nicholas Rinehart, 'The Man That Was a Thing: Reconsidering Human Commodification in Slavery', *Journal of Social History*, 50, no. 1 (2016), 40–1; Gregory O'Malley, *Final Passages: The British Inter-colonial Slave Trade, 1619-1807* (Chapel Hill, 2014), 20–1.

[30] Foreman *et al.*, 'Slavery'; Kamen and Marshall, 'Introduction', 12 n. 1.

[31] I have tried to be comprehensive in surveying justifications for using 'enslaved people', but, given the large numbers of academics publishing on slavery as well as the vastness of social media

have a slightly different approach to the terminology of slavery. Berry and Foreman's advice that slave owners be referred to as 'enslavers' is the most notable and popular of their secondary recommendations – and so will be the subject of much of the ensuing discussion – but even this change has still only partially been adopted by adherents of 'enslaved people'.[32] I therefore encourage academics who believe that I have not recognised all the advantages of using 'enslaved people', or that the proponents I cite do not represent their views, to set out their arguments in response to this article.

I shall nonetheless address a range of reasons for using the terms 'enslaved person' and 'enslaver' by discussing, in turn, the historical, ethical and political issues which the shift towards them raises: how far are these terms historically accurate; how far do they help us to appreciate the humanity and perspective of the unfree, and thereby avoid the harmful implications which advocates argue that 'slave' and 'master' possess; and should historians see any professional advantages in using these upcoming terms in the context of faculty politics? I find that significant problems, arising especially out of the complicated circumstances of early medieval slavery, prevent 'enslaved people' from fulfilling its potential to bring historical and moral clarity to slavery studies. Nonetheless, 'enslaved people' lacks the fundamental flaws of the accompanying preference for 'enslaver', which obscures more than it illuminates. I finish by recommending that historians of all periods engage with this debate more than they have hitherto done.

Historical considerations

The most straightforward argument for referring to 'enslaved people' rather than 'slaves' is that it brings historical clarity. Berry argued that, when discussing 'people of African descent held against their will', '"enslaved" emphasizes the reality that enslavement was an *action* – a verb enacted on individual(s) rather than a noun, "slave," that describes a social position these individuals presumably accepted'.[33] Foreman's style guide puts this argument succinctly: 'People weren't slaves; they were enslaved.'[34] But how far is this applicable to all those who were ever in slavery? The fourth- to fifth-century bishop of Helenopolis in Bithynia, Palladius, wrote about an Egyptian slave who deliberately sold himself into slavery – twice – because he had vowed a life of asceticism and wanted to convert his prospective owners to Christianity.[35] Even if we suspect that most people did not see slavery as an opportunity for piety or that Palladius fabricated these events, there is good evidence that cases of people

---

sites where someone might have posted their opinion, I may have missed some. To those academics, I apologise.

[32] For example, Nikole Hannah-Jones, 'Democracy', in *1619 Project*, ed. Hannah-Jones *et al.*, 7–38, uses 'enslavers'. By contrast, Stewart, 'Seeing Fotis', 197, refers to 'slaveholders' rather than 'masters', even though Foreman's style guide advises against both terms in favour of 'enslavers'.

[33] Berry, 'Introduction', xx–xxi.

[34] Foreman *et al.*, 'Slavery'.

[35] Palladius, 'The Paradise of Palladius: First History', LXVII, in *The Paradise of the Holy Fathers*, I, trans. E. A. Wallis Budge, rev. edn (Putty, NSW, 2009).

voluntarily becoming slaves were unexceptional in the first millennium. Despite the laws against selling yourself as a slave in the Abbasid caliphate, a newly discovered ninth- or tenth-century papyrus shows the author, a prisoner, contemplating doing just that, partly so he could escape his living conditions, but also perhaps as a way to dissolve a relationship with an unhelpful patron.[36] Meanwhile, Alice Rio has drawn attention to the number of early medieval European cases in which people sold themselves into servitude.[37] Moreover, she has shown that self-sales were not necessarily the result of direct coercion or even poverty: the variety of terms and conditions found in legal formulae indicate people of moderate wealth choosing to enter unfree service in exchange for protection or another perceived benefit from their master.[38] In her words, 'People who sold themselves were not always passive victims and could be quite shrewd in bargaining over their freedom.'[39]

Those who want to explicitly mention the personhood of the unfree could practically accommodate these early medieval examples using the term 'self-enslaved people'. Some may see this phrase as a linguistic contortion, while others may believe that it possesses a certain stark elegance. Either way, we are still left with something of a paradox. As noted above, Berry and Foreman suggested that 'enslaved people' should be preferred because it intuitively implies that people did not accept their slave status. Therefore, to apply the label 'enslaved people' to those who sold themselves requires us to negate an implication which is meant to be a key source of that label's strength. Of course, 'enslaved people' is not misleading when people became slaves as a result of conquest or raiding. The particular difficulty for the early medieval historian is that it is rarely obvious from our extant sources where a slave came from. It can therefore be advantageous to use the term 'slave' precisely because it does not specify exactly how a person lost their free status.

If someone is an 'enslaved person', it follows that they had an enslaver. This enslaver could have been a human trafficker, a raider in a war band, a judge, prosecutor or lawmaker who prescribed penal enslavement as punishment for a crime, and/or, as we have seen, the slave him- or herself. But it is actual slave owners that Foreman and Berry have emphasised should be called 'enslavers'.[40] Like 'enslaved person', the label of 'enslaver' reflects a growing perspective that slavery was a dynamic process in which masters continually and violently reasserted the slave status of those they claimed as property – and, indeed, created that status for those born to slaves already under their ownership. Certainly, the response of slaveholders to fugitive slaves in late antiquity brings into focus the need of owners to constantly re-enslave people to maintain their control. The sixth-century bishop Gregory of Tours wrote about how

---

[36] Jelle Bruning, 'Voluntary Enslavement in an Abbasid-Era Papyrus Letter', *Journal of the Royal Asiatic Society*, ser. 3, 33 (2023), 643–59.

[37] Rio, *Slavery*, 11.

[38] Alice Rio, 'High and Low: Ties of Dependence in the Frankish Kingdoms', *TRHS*, 18 (2008), 51–2.

[39] Alice Rio, 'Self-Sale and Voluntary Entry into Unfreedom, 300–1100', *Journal of Social History*, 45 (2012), 676.

[40] Berry, 'Introduction', xx; Foreman *et al.*, 'Slavery'. Kamen and Marshall, 'Introduction', 12 n. 1, refers to 'enslavers' in its endorsement of Foreman's style guide.

a man named Leudast, whose father Leucadius had also been a slave, fled his owners repeatedly, until his owners mutilated his ear, implicitly so Leudast would understand that others would recognise him as a slave whenever he tried to escape.[41] We can interpret the mutilation and recaptures of Leudast as representing only the most extreme and visible end of the recreations of slave status which slaveholders practised on their human property. Gregory of Tours reviled Leudast, and some historians are sceptical of his version of events.[42] Still, it highlights how contemporary slave owners might have acted as enslavers, and so, by extension, how even those born into slavery can be considered 'enslaved people'.

Nevertheless, several important objections remain to making 'enslavers' the standard term for slaveholders. Although slave owners used strategies of enslavement, enslavement is not the only dynamic relevant to slaveholding. 'Enslavers' ignores the opposite direction to enslavement in which slaveholders sometimes acted in relation to their slaves: manumission. It is easy to be cynical about instances of owners freeing slaves, but, as Ilaria L. E. Ramelli and others have shown for parts of the late antique and early medieval world, manumission could be understood as an act of Christian charity pertinent to the salvation of both master and slave; writings about slavery should be able to convey this dynamic.[43] Furthermore, referring to slaveholders as 'enslavers' elides the difference between those who first forced a person into slavery, and the people who subsequently owned slaves as a result of a sale, gift or inheritance. There was plenty of overlap between these groups in both theory and practice, but the distinction between slave owners and enslavers mattered in late antique society. It meant Augustine could justify slavery theologically while condemning slave merchants who kidnapped people to sell them.[44] It meant a bishop like Caesarius of Arles could believe in the virtue of ransoming captives who faced enslavement, while owning slaves himself.[45]

This distinction between slavery and enslavement might have helped early Christian slaveholders assuage their consciences, but it could also have been important to certain slaves themselves. Many enslaved people likely accorded a special violence and significance to the experience of being forcibly

[41] Gregory of Tours, *Historiae*, v, c. 48, ed. Bruno Krusch and Wilhelm Levison, in *Monumenta Germaniae Historica* [hereafter *MGH*], *Scriptores rerum Merovingicarum* [hereafter *SS rer. Merov.*] 1.1 (Hanover, 1951), 257.

[42] Julia Smith, *Europe after Rome: A New Cultural History* (Oxford, 2005), 178.

[43] Ilaria L. E. Ramelli, 'Slavery and Religion in Late Antiquity: Their Relation to Asceticism and Justice in Christianity and Judaism', in *Slavery*, ed. de Wet *et al.*, 45; Rio, *Slavery*, 77; Rio, 'Self-Sale', 668; Lisa Kaaren Bailey, '"Servi Servorum Dei": Serving the Religious in Early Medieval Europe', *Mediaevalia*, 43 (2022), 18.

[44] Augustine, *The City of God against the Pagans*, xix, c. 15, ed. and trans. R. W. Dyson (Cambridge, 1998), 942–4; Augustine, 'Letter 10', in *Saint Augustine. Letters*, vi, trans. Robert B. Eno (Washington, DC, 1989), 76–80; Peter Garnsey, *Ideas of Slavery from Aristotle to Augustine* (Cambridge, 1996), 206–19.

[45] Caesarius of Arles, *Testamentum*, ed. G. Morin, in *Sancti Caesarii opera omnia*, ii, *Opera varia* (Maredsous, 1942), 283–9; William Klingshirn, 'Charity and Power: Caesarius of Arles and the Ransoming of Captives in Sub-Roman Gaul', *Journal of Roman Studies*, 75 (1985), 183–203.

separated from their home communities, trafficked away and sold as property. The *Confessio* of St Patrick, 'the closest thing we have to a slave narrative from antiquity', emphasised how, while born to a free father, he was enslaved as a youth: 'The Lord brought the wrath of his mind upon us and scattered us among many peoples even to the end of the earth.'[46] It is St Patrick's own self-awareness as an enslaved person who had a life before slavery that directs us to be sensitive to the particular role of enslavement as the initial act by which he was severed from his freedom and family. Though slavery encouraged and perpetuated such acts of enslavement institutionally, it should not be conflated with them. Indeed, that there is an ongoing need to distinguish the process of enslaving from the condition of servitude probably explains why some of those historians who have substituted 'the enslaved' for 'slaves' have not substituted 'enslavement' or Miller's preferred term of 'slaving' for 'slavery' – even though 'enslavement' achieves the same purpose as 'the enslaved' in emphasising that people were forced into servitude.[47] So while the term 'enslavement' can be extended to ordinary slaveholding practices, there is value in maintaining its conceptual distance from slavery. This distance cannot be maintained while referring to owners only as 'enslavers', but at least 'enslaved people' can theoretically operate in relation to a range of possible enslavers.

Perhaps recognising the problems which 'enslavers' creates, some adherents of using the term 'enslaved people' have used the terms 'slaveholder' and 'slave owner' while rejecting the term 'master' – even though Foreman's style guide advises against all of these terms.[48] The issues with 'master' as a word which implies domination and superiority are easy to grasp, but are surmountable so long as the reader understands that 'master' equates to contemporary concepts and legal categories, and should not be taken to mean that someone was naturally superior to those that they owned. Still, there are fewer reasons to defend and retain the term 'master' – so long as 'slaveholder' and 'slave owner' are available as acceptable substitutes.

'Enslaver' and 'enslaved person' can be used correctly and valuably to emphasise processes of enslavement, when enacted on free people, captives, fugitives and those born to slave families. But neither can work as historically accurate replacements for 'slaves' and 'slave owners' wholesale. 'Enslaver' is too uncompromising in making enslavement the defining dynamic of slaveholding. While the term 'enslaved people' has more flexibility, early medieval cases of self-sale strongly bring into question one of the supposed key advantages of using it: that is, to emphasise that slaveholders forcibly imposed

---

[46] *Dominus induxit super nos iram animationis suae et dispersit nos in gentibus multis etiam usque ad ultimum terrae*: Patrick, *Confessio*, para. 1, ed. Ludwig Bieler, in *Libri Epistolarum Sancti Patricii Episcopi: Introduction, Text and Commentary* (2 vols., Dublin, 1952), i, 56–7. Translation: Judith Evan Grubbs, 'Sinner, Slave, Bishop, Saint: The Social and Religious Vicissitudes of Saint Patrick', in *Slavery*, ed. de Wet et al., 291. *Ibid.*, 281.

[47] Miller, *Problem of Slavery*, 2; Berry, 'Introduction', xix; Kamen and Marshall, 'Introduction', 12; though for an approach that builds on Miller's recommendation, see James Brewer Stewart and Elizabeth Swanson, 'Introduction', in *Human Bondage and Abolition*, ed. Elizabeth Swanson and James Brewer Stewart (Cambridge, 2018), 1–32.

[48] For example, Stewart, 'Seeing Fotis', 197; Foreman *et al.*, 'Slavery'.

unfree status on other people. By contrast, that 'slaves' and 'slaveholders' do not go into specifics about the origins of a person's unfree status makes it easier for historians to use them when discussing a range of societies.

Ethical considerations

There is more than historical accuracy at stake in this debate. For some historians, using 'enslaved person' and 'enslaver' appears to be an act of justice which better conveys the humanity and perspective of the unfree than 'slave' and 'master'. Kamen and Marshall have argued that 'using terms like "slave" and "master" reinforces the enslaver's viewpoint'.[49] However, I would contend that the term 'enslaver' can do that as well. For certain Roman and early medieval warlords, being thought of as an 'enslaver', and not just a mere 'master', would probably have been a source of pride. In Roman triumphs, victorious generals showed the citizens of Rome that they had defeated and enslaved formerly free barbarian enemies by parading captives in chains before their chariots.[50] The Emperor Augustus boasted in an inscription recording his accomplishments, the *Res Gestae*, that during the war in Sicily he returned 30,000 fugitive slaves to their owners for punishment.[51] Gregory of Tours wrote that a king promised his men that they would get many cattle and slaves if they followed him into battle.[52] Meanwhile, David Wyatt has concluded that, in medieval Scandinavia and the British Isles, 'abduction and enslavement, particularly of women and the young, were ... methods by which rising leaders and their war bands established their status'.[53] Therefore, 'enslaver' can also reflect the attitudes and aspirations of certain slave owners.

It is also far from clear that 'enslaved' and 'enslaver' bring us any closer to the viewpoints of slaves. While historians should heed Vlassopoulos's forceful argument that slaves likely did not understand themselves only as being slaves, Vlassopoulos himself acknowledges that 'most slaves experienced slavery as a direct relationship with their masters'.[54] Indeed, many slaves may well have considered their owners to be their masters, given the control they exercised over their lives. Crucially, this control often went past the point of manumission, even after an owner's death: the seventh-century will of bishop Bertram of Le Mans obliged his freed slaves to annually gather at his tomb and perform tasks for an abbot.[55] Furthermore, relationships which went beyond an owner could actually serve to reinforce a person's self-perception as a slave. Ecclesiastical slaves in late antiquity may have conceived of one such relationship as being with God. Lisa Kaaren Bailey has suggested that the

---

[49] Kamen and Marshall, 'Introduction', 12 n. 1.

[50] Mary Beard, *The Roman Triumph* (Cambridge, MA, 2009), 123.

[51] *Res Gestae Divi Augustae*, 25.1, ed. and trans. Alison E. Cooley (Cambridge, 2009).

[52] Gregory of Tours, *Historiae*, III, c. 11, 108.

[53] Wyatt himself uses 'enslaved people' and 'enslaver': David Wyatt, 'Slavery in Northern Europe (Scandinavia and Iceland)', in *AD 500–AD 1420*, ed. Perry *et al.*, 497.

[54] Vlassopoulos, *Ancient Slavery*, 94.

[55] Rio, *Slavery*, 93.

contemporary belief that pious devotion involved 'slavery to God' could have influenced the self-understanding of slaves at churches and monasteries, to the extent that they accepted their slave status as what God intended for them.[56] At least that brought the consolation that their service would be rewarded in the hereafter. But as Bailey has acknowledged, our reliance on early medieval texts not written by enslaved people limits our ability to know with any certainty what their views were. The only thing that can be safely assumed is that neither all slaves nor all slave owners would have shared a single, straightforward opinion on the nature of slavery. This observation may seem self-evident, but it needs to be stressed. Someone who was enslaved after a lifetime of holding free status may have had a very different understanding of their situation and own identity than someone who, born into bondage, saw freedom not as a lost status, but a goal to be achieved through manumission. Moreover, in certain contexts, it was not just the attitudes of slaves and slaveholders that probably converged, but their practices. Slaves owned other slaves across the medieval period, creating problems for any attempt to use an 'enslaver' and 'enslaved' dichotomy to achieve moral clarity.[57] Ultimately, what is at stake is not the viewpoint of historical enslavers and enslaved people – both are, after all, deceased – but really our own. The rhetorical effect of the labels 'enslaver' and 'enslaved people', which is to always keep the atrocity that slave owners were committing against other human beings in the forefront of the mind of the reader, draws its power from the abhorrence most people have towards slavery today.

Proponents of referring to 'enslaved people' argue that the term 'slave' prevents the reader from achieving this same recognition of the humanity and experience of the unfree. Nikole Hannah-Jones of the '1619 Project' claims that 'The alternative term "enslaved person" accurately conveys the condition without stripping the individual of his or her humanity,' thereby implying that the label 'slave' is dehumanising.[58] Historian Eric Foner disagrees with this assumption. He has stated, 'I do not think that "slave" suggests that this is the essence of a person's being.'[59] But scholarship on ancient and medieval societies supports an awareness that 'slave' was not a neutral descriptor but was part of the construction and legitimisation of the system of slavery. For the classical world, Vlassopoulos argues that when certain authorities labelled people as 'slaves', they were affirming that that categorisation was 'all that

---

[56] Bailey, '"Servi Servorum Dei"', 22–3.

[57] Craig Perry et al., 'Slavery in the Medieval Millennium', in *AD 500–AD 1420*, ed. Perry et al., 20; Alice Rio, 'Freedom and Unfreedom in Early Medieval Francia: The Evidence of the Legal Formulae', *Past & Present*, 193 (2006), 23–4; Noel Lenski, 'Slavery among the Visigoths', in *Slavery*, ed. de Wet et al., 266.

[58] Nikole Hannah-Jones, 'A Note on Terminology', in *1619 Project*, ed. Hannah-Jones et al.; White, *Female Slaves*, 8, and Stewart, 'Seeing Fotis', 197, make similar points.

[59] Eric Foner, quoted by Katy Waldman, in 'Slave or Enslaved Person?', *Slate*, 19 May 2015, https://slate.com/human-interest/2015/05/historians-debate-whether-to-use-the-term-slave-or-enslaved-person.html (accessed 1 Mar. 2023).

mattered' about the lives of those enslaved.[60] For early medieval Europe, Rio has emphasised that unfree status was 'the result of an act of labelling and not ... a static object'.[61] We may ask, though, if the unconsensual imposition of the label 'slave' amid unequal power relations makes it so different from (for example) 'conscript' or 'convict'. Advocates of 'people-first' language in general could fairly respond here that we should refer to 'convicted persons' or 'conscripted persons' as well. Yet when we speak of 'slave owners' or 'enslavers', or 'bishops' or 'kings', we take for granted that they were all human beings, whose lives and identities went beyond these labels, without needing to address them as 'slave-owning people' or 'people who were enslavers' or 'people who were bishops' or 'people who were kings'. We should be capable of extending this same presumption to the less fortunate.

Nevertheless, it is understandable if proponents of the term 'enslaved people' are concerned that the connotations of degradation which 'slave' has long had will get in the way of their audience's sympathy. More so than 'conscript' or 'convict', the term 'slave' has had a strong association with livestock.[62] For example, in the Salic Law of the Franks, slaves were ranked with livestock in clauses dealing with the theft of property.[63] Indeed, there was disquiet in late antiquity against slaveholders categorising people as livestock through calling them 'slaves'; historians today are not the first to have identified that the term 'slave' is problematic. Gregory of Nyssa objected to the boast of masters that they had got slaves on the grounds it implied ownership over other human beings.[64] That the term 'slave' denied someone's humanity, as if they were naturally property or livestock, is the strongest, and oldest, argument against it.

However, 'slave' did not imply that someone was less than human to all early medieval authors.[65] While Gregory of Tours probably owned slaves himself, a combination of his religious beliefs and the enslavement of his own relatives by sixth-century warlords seems to have led him to look with favour on certain slaves.[66] He thought that the life of a slave named Portianus, who became an abbot, illustrated the biblical teaching that God would elevate the poor and servile both in this life and the next.[67] He stated that God had placed Portianus among the angelic choir from which covetous worldly princes were

---

[60] Vlassopoulos, *Ancient Slavery*, 111.

[61] Rio, *Slavery*, 13.

[62] Pierre Bonnassie, 'The Survival and Extinction of the Slave System in the Early Medieval West (Fourth to Eleventh Centuries)', in *From Slavery to Feudalism in South-Western Europe*, trans. Jean Birrell (Cambridge, 1991), 17.

[63] *Pactus legis Salicae*, 47.1, ed. Karl August Eckhardt, in *MGH, Leges nationum Germanicarum* 4.1 (Hanover, 1962), 182.

[64] Gregory of Nyssa, 'Homily 4 on Ecclesiastes', ed. E. Gebhardt, *Gregorii Nysseni Opera* (Leiden, 1967), 5.334–52; Ilaria Ramelli, 'Gregory of Nyssa's Position in Late Antique Debates on Slavery and Poverty, and the Role of Asceticism', *Journal of Late Antiquity*, 5 (2012), 95–100.

[65] Wendy Davies, 'On Servile Status in the Early Middle Ages', in *Serfdom and Slavery: Studies in Legal Bondage*, ed. M. L. Bush (1996), 243.

[66] Gregory of Tours, *Historiae*, III, c. 15, 112–16.

[67] Gregory of Tours, *Liber vitae patrum*, V, in *Libri Miraculorum*, ed. Bruno Krusch, in *MGH, SS rer. Merov.* 1.2 (Hanover, 1885), 227; J. K. Kitchen, 'Gregory of Tours, Hagiography, and the Cult of Saints

excluded. In other words, through talking about Portianus as a slave, Gregory categorised him not just as a soul-endowed being worthy of God's mercy, but as someone who could become more than human. So even a word like 'slave' can have a variety of implications – implications which can change over time. Indeed, most historians who have used the term 'slave' over the past few decades would deny that they were implying that slaves were less than human. Rather, they have labelled people 'slaves' trusting that most of their readers would conclude that it signifies that a person was treated like property, not that the person naturally was property.

Crucially, the embrace of the term 'enslaved people' has followed rather than stimulated the historiographical shift towards emphasising that slaves were historical actors, who had an inherent humanity and agency which slaveholders continually tried to violently suppress.[68] Vlassopoulos and other historians may be right that we can go further still, but, as his own work shows, this need not be tied to wholesale reworking of terminology.[69] An appreciation of this may actually help account for why even some historians who prefer 'enslaved people' still use terms like 'slave-produced' and 'slave trade', even though they incorporate the word 'slave' and so could be seen as linguistic echoes of the attitudes of masters.[70] Indeed, the continued use of these terms, rather than 'produced by enslaved people' and 'trade in enslaved peoples', implies two important logical concessions. First, that concise and familiar expression is a legitimate top priority for historical analysis. Second, that consistently using 'people-first' language is not necessary for a reader to understand the humanity of slaves.

Ultimately, slavery as a subject may be too emotionally charged for any term to be devoid of ethical issues. In a discussion among historians of American slavery on the social media site X (formerly Twitter), Michael J. Simpson tweeted that he received pushback on using 'enslaved' from 'Elder people of color ... [who] felt that use of "enslaved" was whitewashing'.[71] It was to this that Laura Rosanne Adderley replied, 'All words I know to talk about enslaved people of African descent in these Americas prove insufficient, both for the brutality against them, and for their remarkable overcoming ... "Enslaved" solves some problems, but may create others.'[72] Slavery may be

---

in the Sixth Century', in *A Companion to Gregory of Tours*, ed. Alexander Callander Murray (Boston, MA, 2015), 407.

[68] Though each of the following has come under criticism, important historiographical contributions include (but are not limited to) Orlando Patterson, *Slavery and Social Death: A Comparative Study* (Cambridge, MA, 1982); Davis, *Inhuman Bondage*, along with his earlier studies; Miller, *Problem of Slavery*.

[69] Vlassopoulos, *Ancient Slavery*, 111.

[70] For example, in the following articles: Kathryn Gleadle and Ryan Hanley, 'Children against Slavery: Juvenile Agency and the Sugar Boycotts in Britain', *TRHS*, 30 (2020), 97–8; Alec Ryrie and D. J. B. Trim, 'Four Axes of Mission: Conversion and the Purposes of Mission in Protestant History', *TRHS*, 32 (2022), 120.

[71] Michael J. Simpson, @HiddenHistoryRI, X [formerly Twitter], 25 Aug. 2018, https://twitter.com/HiddenHistoryRI/status/1033367315784642560 (accessed 2 Mar. 2023).

[72] Adderley, https://twitter.com/LauraAdderley/status/1034224696382767104.

particularly vulnerable to what linguist Sharon Henderson Taylor and psychologist Steven Pinker have called the 'cycle of euphemism' or 'euphemism treadmill': 'give a concept a new name, and the name becomes colored by the concept; the concept does not become freshened by the name'.[73] It is easy to dispute Pinker's contention that words can be 'unexceptional', and so, by implication, neutral. But if no term can be neutral, is it possible for any term used in reference to slavery to escape our recoil from the horrors of slaveholding practices? As we can see from Simpson's tweet, people have already criticised 'enslaved people' as inadequate even for its original context of slavery in the United States, and I have identified other potential issues with the term. It is unlikely that we will arrive at any labels which are beyond dispute.

The politics of the debate

Of secondary importance to the historical and ethical issues is whether there are any professional gains to be had from using 'enslaved people' over 'slaves'. In the increasingly competitive world of faculty politics, it is understandable if the wish not to appear as an out-of-touch reactionary or be left behind is on the minds of some historians. It remains to be seen whether or not the movement against using 'slave' will mirror the largely successful campaign against referring to the 'Third World', or will start to face substantial pushback, like the movement against using the term 'Anglo-Saxon'.[74] Any historian, especially any medieval historian, who carried on using 'slave' would be alone neither among scholars of their own period nor scholars of slavery generally. But they should be aware that some have implicitly accused users of the term 'slave' of complicity with slavery. Emily Wilson, for example, writes that she uses 'enslaved' 'to avoid complicity with this inherently violent and abusive institution'.[75] Given that people continue to suffer in slavery today, this is a serious accusation. But it seems unlikely that academics can, in practice, help prevent modern slavery by switching to 'enslaved person'. Moreover, proponents of 'enslaved people' for the victims and survivors of the transatlantic slave trade have not demanded that historians of other periods use that term.

---

[73] Steven Pinker, 'The Game of the Name', *New York Times*, 5 Apr. 1995, https://stevenpinker.com/files/pinker/files/1994_04_03_newyorktimes.pdf; Sharon Henderson Taylor, 'Terms for Low Intelligence', *American Speech*, 49 (1974), 202.

[74] On the decline of 'The Third World' in favour of 'The Global South', see Themrise Khan *et al.*, 'How We Classify Countries and People – and Why It Matters', *British Medical Journal Global Health*, 7 (2022); for examples of continuing use of 'Anglo-Saxon' in academic and popular education contexts despite calls to avoid this term, see Howard Williams, 'The Fight for "Anglo-Saxon"', *Aeon*, 29 May 2020, https://aeon.co/essays/why-we-should-keep-the-term-anglo-saxon-in-archaeology (accessed 1 Mar. 2023]; over seventy academics have signed a letter in favour of continued use of 'Anglo-Saxon': John Hines *et al.*, 'The Responsible Use of the Term "Anglo-Saxon"', *A Forum for Multidisciplinary Anglo-Saxon Studies*, 17 Nov. 2019, http://www.fmass.eu/uploads/pdf/responsible_use_of%20the%20term%20_Anglo-Saxon.pdf (accessed 1 Mar. 2023).

[75] Emily Wilson, 'Slaves and Sex in the Odyssey', in *Slavery and Sexuality*, ed. Kamen and Marshall, 36 n. 1.

Foreman acknowledges that the diversity of slavery means that her recommendations should be treated only as suggestions.[76] The comments of Adderley referred only to the specific experience of enslaved Africans in America.[77] Therefore, historians of other periods should not feel obliged to adopt the term 'enslaved people'. Nonetheless, given that 'enslaved person' is increasingly being used in early modern slavery scholarship as well as educational resources even for the classical period, the trajectory is momentarily towards 'enslaved person' becoming the dominant academic term. It could be thought prudent to accept it while there is no consensus among scholars, instead of becoming a late hold-out against this transition when there are reasonable, well-intended arguments for it.

However, in trying not to be disconnected from other academics, there is the potential to become disconnected from the wider public: a *Google Trends* search for April 2022 to April 2023 shows that there were far more online searches for 'slaves' than 'enslaved people'.[78] Moreover, searches for 'enslaved people' were most common – though still much less frequent than searches for 'slaves' – in the United States. This is not a trivial issue at a time when journal editors are concerned with search engine optimisation as they try to ensure articles are seen as widely as possible and have an international reach. At least 'enslaved people' has an advantage over other academic jargon in that it is hardly obscure; there would be little risk of public confusion over whether it refers to slaves. Moreover, academics can hope to shape and inform the general use of terms around slavery through public engagement and social media. Therefore, they should decide how they want to use their influence after consideration of the historical and ethical issues at stake. It would be a self-fulfilling prophecy to use either 'slave' or 'enslaved people' out of deference to their perceived popularity in public or academic spheres.

Conclusion and recommendations

Despite the commendable intentions behind it, 'enslaved person' is not convincing as a universal substitute for 'slave'. While 'enslaved people' emphasises that someone did not choose to be a slave, this very emphasis means it does not fully accommodate those who sold themselves into slavery. The sheer historical diversity of slave experience also precludes 'enslaved people' as well as 'enslaver' from bringing us any closer to the perspective of the unfree. These terms are also not essential to recognise the humanity of slaves, which is an ethical imperative we should demand and expect of ourselves and our audiences regardless of our period of study or which word we prefer. However, while it is primarily early medieval exceptions that should caution historians against making 'enslaved people' the standard term for slavery studies as a discipline, the term 'enslaver' has much more fundamental problems. In

---

[76] Foreman *et al.*, 'Slavery'.

[77] Adderley, https://twitter.com/LauraAdderley/status/1034224696382767104.

[78] 'slaves', 'enslaved people', *Google Trends*, 19 Apr. 2023, https://trends.google.com/trends/explore?q=slaves,enslaved%20people (accessed 19 Apr. 2023).

attempting to bring moral clarity, it loses historical precision, obscuring the historical dynamics of ownership and manumission. Still, proponents of 'enslaver' are on safer ground in highlighting the problems with the term 'master'. 'Slaveholder' or 'slave owner' are better than both terms.

If further scholarship can strengthen the case for referring to 'enslaved people' over 'slaves', historians should be open to using it in most clear-cut cases, while adding clarifying comments when referring to the specific exceptions in which 'enslaved' is misleading. Indeed, a number of historians have chosen to use 'enslaved person' more often than 'slave' without eschewing 'slave' altogether – in effect making 'enslaved person' the default term and 'slave' a synonym occasionally used for linguistic variety.[79] This seems an attractive compromise, for it keeps the emphasis on the personhood of the unfree, while reserving the possibility of using 'slave' for nuanced analysis. Yet any form of mixed use concedes that the term 'slave' can be used in contexts that are not dehumanising – or, at least, not so dehumanising as to matter more than the need for historical accuracy and elegant writing.

Whatever decision we as historians make on this issue, it is important that we are prepared to defend it, because this problem is far from resolved. Many have not acknowledged the existing debate, which indicates that some historians are not aware it is taking place. It has even gone unacknowledged in some edited books, even though the variation in terminology by contributors to the same work is jarring. Going forward, historians should explain their choices of terminology much more directly than most have done previously. Rather than take the use of either 'slave' or 'enslaved' for granted, scholars of different periods need to talk to one another, so that we might better navigate the historical strengths and weaknesses of each term, and how the stakes might vary for slavery in the classical, medieval and modern worlds. Instead of dismissing this dispute over what word to use as irrelevant to the substance of our historical analysis of slavery, we can use it as an opportunity to think carefully about the extent to which scholarship of transatlantic slavery should set the lens of interpretation for slavery studies in general. As the paradigm for slavery, the implications of the transatlantic slave system can both inspire and challenge historians working on other periods. But it also risks clouding the historical variety and complexity of forms which slaveholding practices have taken, especially in the premodern period. After all, I have largely based my arguments on evidence from Europe in the early Middle Ages – perhaps there are corroboratory or indeed counter-examples from other times and places. Future discussion, then, will have the added benefit of illuminating historically contingent aspects in practices and conditions of slavery which are obscured by the common use of one term – whether that be 'slave' or 'enslaved person'.

---

[79] For example, Joshua Rothman, *The Ledger and the Chain: How Domestic Slave Traders Shaped America* (New York, 2021); Christopher Paolella, *Human Trafficking in Medieval Europe: Slavery, Sexual Exploitation and Prostitution* (Amsterdam, 2020); Craig Perry, 'Slavery and Agency in the Middle Ages', in *AD 500–AD 1420*, ed. Perry *et al.*, 240–67.

Acknowledgements. I would like to thank the reviewers and editors for their comments and suggestions, along with Erin Thomas Dailey for his feedback on an initial draft of this article. I am also grateful to the other members of the 'Domestic Slavery and Sexual Exploitation in the Households of Europe, North Africa, and the Near East, from Constantine to c. AD 900 / AH 287' project (https://www.dosseproject.com), including Seth M. Stadel, Tali Artman-Partock, Justin Pigott and Sheida Heydarishovir, for discussing the issue of terminology with me. However, the opinions expressed in this article, and any mistakes, are mine alone.

Author Biography. James Robert Burns is a PhD student researching slavery and the households of sixth-century Gaul, at the University of Leicester. He is a member of the 'Domestic Slavery and Sexual Exploitation in the Households of Europe, North Africa, and the Near East, from Constantine to c. AD 900 / AH 287' project. He is the recipient of the 2021 Garmonsway Award from the University of York for the best average coursework marks in the Medieval Studies MA.

Cite this article: Burns JR (2024). 'Slaves' and 'Slave Owners' or 'Enslaved People' and 'Enslavers'? *Transactions of the Royal Historical Society* 2, 371–388. https://doi.org/10.1017/S0080440123000282

Transactions of the RHS (2024), **2**, 389–400
doi:10.1017/S0080440123000269

Teaching Modern British Political History in a Politically Polarised and 'Post-Truth' Environment

Richard Jobson

Department of Archaeology and History, University of Exeter, Exeter, UK
Email: r.j.jobson@exeter.ac.uk

(First published online 16 October 2023)

Abstract

This article assesses the challenges that university-level teachers of modern British political history currently face in what is often described as a 'post-truth' and polarised political environment. It argues that, whilst these challenges do not always present entirely new pedagogical considerations, the sociocultural and political terrain in Britain today requires careful navigation, particularly in an academic field which addresses recent historical topics that are routinely politicised and contested in contemporary discourse. Although there is a lack of scholarly literature on the topic of teaching modern British political history in a higher education setting, this article draws upon a wide array of educational studies to map out the contours of a successful pedagogical strategy that could facilitate 'deep' learning in the current contextual environment. To this end, it suggests that by utilising modern British political history's interdisciplinary foundations, applying teaching techniques that help students to explore topics from multiple viewpoints, devising new and stimulating interactive tasks, and capitalising on the opportunities afforded by the Internet age, learning can be enhanced and many of the more academically problematic features and characteristics of the current political climate can be counteracted.

Keywords: British; politics; history; teaching; polarisation

Introduction

Academic scholars and commentators have viewed Britain's 2016 vote to leave the European Union as both an outcome and a perpetuator of the nation's recent identity-based political polarisation.[1] In recent years, British society

---

[1] M. Sobolewska and R. Ford, *Brexitland: Identity, Diversity and the Reshaping of British Politics* (Cambridge, 2020), 1–18.

has frequently been portrayed as fractured, divided and locked into incompatible and competing entrenched political understandings of both itself and the wider world.[2] These developments have often been situated within a broader global context that has been characterised by rising levels of populism and heightened political polarisation in established democracies, including in North America and Europe.[3] At the same time and in line with this trajectory, it has been suggested that there has been something akin to a 'post-truth' shift in global politics. Different definitions of this 'post-truth' cultural climate have been advanced by academics, but, broadly speaking, most coalesce around dictionary-style depictions of 'a situation in which people are more likely to accept an argument based on their emotions and beliefs, rather than one based on facts'.[4] This transition from 'facts' to 'beliefs' has been shaped by the rise of a populist-inspired discourse that seeks to devalue and undermine notions of 'expertise' and has led to 'diminishing trust in traditional epistemic systems', including academia.[5] Whilst the historical uniqueness and perceived newness of this 'post-truth' era have been contested, a number of scholars, including Michael Peters, have outlined how the specific dynamics of the Internet age have contributed to the development of a sociocultural environment which generates particularly pronounced issues for educators.[6] In particular, the preponderance of 'fake news' and the development of uncritical algorithmically driven online 'echo chambers' have served to delegitimise objectively provable information and arguments and, via the process of confirmation bias, consolidated pre-existing and binarily located views of politics.[7]

Since modern British political history, by its very nature, tends to focus on politically charged (and, thus, politicised) recent historical events, all of the aforementioned issues are likely to affect the teaching of the subject at universities significantly. Certainly, debates around history and, in particular, the way that the past should be depicted and taught have acquired elevated emotional significance in Britain. Increasingly, in Britain as elsewhere, the country's history has become a battleground on which historical 'culture wars', rooted in the competing visions of the past offered by liberals and conservatives, have been fought, with the type of nuance and balance associated with 'professional expertise' often representing the primary casualty.[8]

---

[2] R. Eatwell and M. Goodwin, *National Populism: The Revolt against Liberal Democracy* (2018), 277–8.

[3] M. Tribukait, 'Students' Prejudice as a Teaching Challenge: How European History Educators Deal with Controversial and Sensitive Issues in a Climate of Political Polarization', *Theory and Research in Social Education*, 49 (2021), 540.

[4] See *Cambridge Advanced Learner's Dictionary* (Cambridge, 2013). Updated version at: https://dictionary.cambridge.org/dictionary/english/post-truth.

[5] C. A. Chinn, S. Barzilai and R. G. Duncan, 'Education for a "Post-Truth" World: New Directions for Research and Practice', *Educational Researcher*, 50 (2021), 57.

[6] M. A. Peters, 'Education in a Post-Truth World', *Educational Philosophy and Theory*, 49 (2017), 565. The novelty of this environment has been contested by T. Bowell, 'Response to the Editorial "Education in a Post-Truth World"', *Educational Philosophy and Theory*, 49 (2017), 582.

[7] Peters, 'Education in a Post-Truth World', 564.

[8] M. Watson, 'Michael Gove's War on Professional Historical Expertise: Conservative Curriculum Reform, Extreme Whig History and the Place of Imperial Heroes in Modern Multicultural Britain', *British Politics*, 15 (2020), 273.

Without a doubt, societal divisions create unique considerations for history teachers.[9] The emotional volatility and conflictual dynamic of a divided society are, perhaps, liable to manifest themselves in the classroom when the historical topics under consideration are inherently 'political' and at the forefront of contemporary debates, such as Britain's relationship with the European Union (EU).[10] This situation might create the potential for the type of combative and disruptive situations that many seminar teachers fear.[11] However, staff working on political topics at British higher education institutions have also noted that the prevailing political climate has sometimes shaped historical and political seminar discussions in less straightforward ways. Paradoxically, students might, simultaneously, feel less inclined to engage in discussions of controversial and contested topics because of a heightened sensitivity and awareness of their emotionally imbued contours.[12]

Education scholars, such as Ruth Neumann, have for a long time made the case for examining 'disciplinary differences in teaching'.[13] Yet there is a dearth of academic literature on the teaching of modern political history, particularly with a British focus, in higher education settings. Moreover, given the significant issues that currently surround the teaching of this discipline in a polarised and 'post-truth' political environment, the lack of recent scholarly attention afforded to this specific discipline is, perhaps, somewhat surprising. This article seeks to address the existing lacuna in the literature and assess some of the mechanisms and techniques that are available to university-level teachers working in this particular academic field and operating within the type of political context that I have outlined. It aims to provide some tentative suggestions regarding the way that teachers can help to facilitate the kind of 'deep' learning of Britain's recent political past that is often advocated in the education literature.[14] It does so by isolating and addressing four distinct, but ultimately interrelated, thematic categories: interdisciplinarity; multiperspectivity; interactivity (with a particular emphasis on simulations); and technology.

Interdisciplinarity

Modern political history is not just the study of the recent political past, nor is it simply a sub-discipline of historical studies. Instead, it combines features and approaches drawn from the disciplines of both history and political science.

---

[9] A. McCully, 'History Teaching, Conflict and the Legacy of the Past', *Education, Citizenship and Social Justice*, 7 (2012), 148.

[10] J. O'Mahony, 'Teaching the EU in Brexit Britain: Responsive Teaching at a Time of Uncertainty and Change', *Journal of Contemporary European Research*, 16 (2020), 47.

[11] P. Race, *The Lecturer's Toolkit: A Practical Guide to Assessment, Learning and Teaching* (2020), 218.

[12] 'How Brexit Changed the Way Politics is Taught', *New Statesman*, 1 Oct. 2019. https://www.newstatesman.com/politics/2019/10/how-brexit-changed-the-way-politics-is-taught.

[13] R. Neumann, 'Disciplinary Differences and University Teaching', *Studies in Higher Education*, 26 (2001), 144.

[14] J. Biggs and C. Tang, *Teaching for Quality Learning at University: What the Student Does* (Maidenhead, 2007), 27.

The idea that academic disciplines retain their own identifiable processes, language, patterns of behaviour and self-reflective understandings of themselves is well established in the academic literature.[15] At the same time, much has been written about the current prevalence of interdisciplinary discourse in higher education. Indeed, Harvey Graff has noted that 'The ubiquitous appearance of the term interdisciplinary in current academic and educational writing might suggest that it is rapidly becoming the dominant form of scholarly work.'[16] Interdisciplinarity can also provide a challenge to existing disciplinary hierarchies and establish new fields and modes of academic enquiry.[17] Yet the interdisciplinary nature of modern political history has been left relatively underexplored. Moreover, whilst there has been some discussion of the way that effective research might combine political-science-style theorising with the kind of rigorous engagement with facts and evidence associated with history, the implications that any points of disciplinary overlap might have for teaching have remained largely neglected.[18]

In many ways, modern British political historians teach from a point of immediate advantage. In seminars and lectures, the way that the past and the present are often closely linked, both thematically and temporally, arguably helps to retain 'students' attention' with greater ease than more distant and less relatable historical subject matter.[19] Also, particularly when it is taught in Britain, the historical material that is under discussion frequently pertains to topics that are both highly contentious and contestable and at the forefront of current debates. Therefore, it is relatively straightforward for academics who are teaching this subject area to convey and generate the type of enthusiasm that is often described as a prerequisite for an effective learning environment.[20] In the classroom, opinions are almost always held, and debate is usually forthcoming. However, as noted earlier in this article, when operating in the current political environment, this can lead to heightened concerns regarding the potential for volatility, conflict and disruption. Here, modern British political historians could learn from political scientists who teach recent historical topics and establish robust ground rules that might 'include attentive listening, no interrupting, "open" questions, letting everyone express him/herself, respect for everyone's opinion etc.'.[21]

In line with Steve Yetiv's analysis of the benefits of an integrated approach to history and international relations research, political historians can

---

[15] A. Booth, 'Rethinking the Scholarly: Developing the Scholarship of Teaching in History', *Arts and Humanities in Higher Education*, 3 (2004), 246.

[16] H. J. Graff, 'The "Problem" of Interdisciplinarity in Theory, Practice, and History', *Social Science History*, 40 (2016), 775.

[17] M. Moran, 'Interdisciplinarity and Political Science', *Politics*, 26, no. 2 (2006), 77–8.

[18] W. Kaiser, 'History Meets Politics: Overcoming Interdisciplinary Volapük in Research on the EU', *Journal of European Public Policy*, 15 (2008), 310.

[19] C. Toplak, J. Pikalo and I. Lukšič, 'Teaching History to Political Science Students: Historiography as Part of Political Process', *Innovations in Education and Teaching International*, 44 (2007), 380.

[20] Race, *The Lecturer's Toolkit*, 15.

[21] Toplak *et al.*, 'Teaching History', 381.

encourage their students to engage with political science concepts and theories in a way that can help them to interpret and scrutinise the nature of change over time in a more rigorous fashion.[22] This type of approach allows for a robust level of academic interaction with recent political developments, up to and including the present day. Perhaps just as significantly, the application and testing of the historical validity of a range of conceptual frameworks enables students to move away from and scrutinise normative judgements in a manner that an untheoretical focus on the historical evidence alone might not facilitate. Direct engagement with the concepts deployed by political scientists, such as the idea of social constructionism, can also encourage meaningful and 'deep' critical analysis of specific historical political events, such as the 1978–9 Winter of Discontent, that have become embedded in contemporary British political discourse.[23]

This type of theoretical interaction with past events can push history students in new directions intellectually and allow them to develop the type of conceptual toolkit that can lead them to challenge their prior-held assumptions about the recent political past in Britain. In turn, history's preoccupation with the study of historiography – that is, the history of history writing – serves to illuminate the way that the past has always been written about in inherently political ways and challenges the idea of politically neutral texts, thereby driving a more critical approach to political discourse and rhetoric in the present.[24] In such a manner, if meaningful interdisciplinary research can be underpinned by the understanding that important questions cannot be answered by recourse to singular disciplinary approaches, so too the points of intersection between history and political science might offer signposts for navigating challenging pedagogical questions in the current polarised political environment in Britain.[25]

Multiperspectivity

Scholars have noted how 'multiperspectivity' has, increasingly, represented something akin to a buzzword in the field of history education studies and that the term itself is typically deployed in reference to 'multiple subjects' views on one particular object; in the case of history education, multiperspectivity typically concerns a historical event or figure'.[26] In the twenty-first century, multiperspectivity's popularity as a topic for academic evaluation has

---

[22] S. Yetiv, 'History, International Relations, and Integrated Approaches: Thinking about Greater Interdisciplinarity', *International Studies Perspectives*, 12 (2011), 94–118.

[23] See C. Hay, 'Narrating Crisis: The Discursive Construction of the "Winter of Discontent"', *Sociology*, 30 (1996), 235–77.

[24] Toplak *et al.*, 'Teaching History', 378.

[25] For the discussion of interdisciplinary research, see E. Pawson and S. Dovers, 'Environmental History and the Challenges of Interdisciplinarity: An Antipodean Perspective', *Environment and History*, 9 (2003), 62.

[26] B. Wansink *et al.*, 'Where Does Teaching Multiperspectivity in History Education Begin and End? An Analysis of the Uses of Temporality', *Theory and Research in Social Education*, 46 (2018), 496–7.

reflected the value attributed to it as a model for successful undergraduate-level teaching and its ability to get students thinking about the past in complex and multifaceted ways.[27] As Alan Booth's recent research has shown, historians believe that, when 'History teaching is at its best', students 'are able to see the world from perspectives that are not their own: to learn to view the past on its own terms; stand in others' shoes'.[28] Yet the contemporary world of political polarisation and 'echo-chamber'-shaped identities that we inhabit, often informed by binarily located views of the past, clearly represents a challenge to the ideal of multiperspectivity.[29] Moreover, for modern history teachers, the proliferation of 'fake news' stories and unsubstantiated emotional arguments regarding the recent past has served to increase the level of responsibility associated with the need to screen, filter and scrutinise problematic views effectively and appropriately. As such, the kind of considerations that have always informed seminar discussions of particularly controversial and emotionally charged historical events are regularly at the forefront of the modern British political history teacher's mind and moral decision-making process.[30]

There has been a significant amount of research into viable pedagogical techniques that can help to facilitate multiperspective-style learning in higher education settings. Academics working on recent 'hot' British political history topics, such as Brexit and the way that the referendum result was shaped by views on immigration, could learn a great deal from the way that university teachers in post-conflict European societies have encouraged seminar discussions that are open and non-judgemental and applied techniques that direct students towards reflecting on their prior-held historical assumptions.[31] Furthermore, when operating in the current 'post-truth' climate, university teachers might want to initiate 'explicit discussions about core intellectual virtues (e.g. open-mindedness and intellectual courage) that are relevant to their planned class activities'.[32] More generally, the educational literature on effective small group teaching contains some useful suggestions for navigating group tensions and dynamics and setting an appropriate 'tone' in seminars that can be helpful when encouraging the core values and skills associated with multiperspectivity.[33] To take one specific example, by practising and teaching the process of 'active listening', tutors can create sensitive and productive learning environments in which students feel comfortable absorbing, expressing and challenging a range of different opinions.[34] Similarly,

---

[27] McCully, 'History Teaching', 152.

[28] A. Booth, 'What Really Matters: A History Education for Human Possibility', in *Teaching History for the Contemporary World: Tensions, Challenges and Classroom Experiences in Higher Education*, ed. A. Nye and J. Clark (2021), 240.

[29] Bowell, 'Response to the Editorial', 582

[30] For these considerations, see Wansink *et al.*, 'Where Does Teaching Multiperspectivity in History Education Begin and End?', 517–18.

[31] Tribukait, 'Students' Prejudice as a Teaching Challenge', 542–3, 564.

[32] Chinn *et al.*, 'Education for a "Post-Truth" World', 58.

[33] D. Mills and P. Alexander, *Small Group Teaching: A Toolkit for Learning* (York, 2013), 16.

[34] S. E. Spataro and J. Bloch, '"Can You Repeat That?" Teaching Active Listening in Management Education', *Journal of Management Education*, 42 (2018), 170–1.

particularly when addressing emotionally demanding material and posing difficult questions, teachers should also consider their body language and non-verbal signals, as an 'open, warm, challenging or sensitive manner may gain more responses of a thoughtful nature'.[35]

Once students feel secure and confident in their understanding of the emotional contours and parameters of a debate, an even more analytically detached and critical approach can be adopted that, amongst other exercises, might include tasks that 'analyze how the [controversial] issue is discussed publicly in the media', with students then being 'asked to identify the emotional forces behind such discussions'.[36] As discussions progress, complex and 'messy' information can be introduced into the debate that cannot be located easily within pre-existing binary narratives.[37] In order to enhance understandings of change over time, students can also be encouraged to isolate and assess the perspectives that have operated at different 'temporal layers' between the past and the present.[38] In much the same manner, the study of historiography can play an important role in developing the type of critical skills associated with multiperspectivity by highlighting the interpretative and contestable nature of historical narratives that lay claim to representing the absolute 'truth' of the past.[39] Above all, students should be supported and equipped to adopt a more critical position with regard to recent political history and develop a more 'empathetic understanding' of perspectives that run counter to their own historical arguments and ideas.[40] In this way, by encouraging students to look at the past sensitively through different lenses, multiperspectivity represents a pedagogical mechanism for destabilising the type of entrenched opinions associated with political polarisation. Yet any effective engagement with new viewpoints is also dependent on the critical evaluation of the evidential basis (or otherwise) on which such interpretations are formed. Therefore, although it might not entirely solve the issue of susceptibility to false or inaccurate sources of information in itself, multiperspectivity can help to contribute to the creation of learning environments in which the disentanglement of fact from fiction is paramount and 'post-truth' historical assumptions can be recognised and addressed.

Interactivity

In the academic discipline of history, the twenty-first century has witnessed a notable shift towards treating undergraduate teaching as seriously and as

---

[35] S. Griffiths, 'Teaching and Learning in Small Groups', in *A Handbook for Teaching and Learning in Higher Education: Enhancing Academic Practice*, ed. H. Fry, S. Ketteridge and S. Marshall (2009), 82.

[36] Tribukait, 'Students' Prejudice as a Teaching Challenge', 546.

[37] Chinn et al., 'Education for a "Post-Truth" World', 58.

[38] Wansink et al., 'Where Does Teaching Multiperspectivity in History Education Begin and End?', 497–8.

[39] C. Hoefferle, 'Teaching Historiography to High School and Undergraduate Students', *OAH Magazine of History*, 21, no. 2 (2007), 40–1.

[40] McCully, 'History Teaching', 153.

rigorously as research.[41] As a result, history scholars in higher education have begun to identify and use innovative and new forms of teaching. The educational literature almost always indicates that seminar activities operate effectively when they have a significant interactive component that enables them to adopt a 'deep approach' to the historical topic that is being covered.[42] Moreover, as the previous section argued, in the current political climate, there is also a pressing need to encourage history students to engage directly with perspectives that are not necessarily their own. With these objectives in mind, it is somewhat surprising that, in contrast to their relative popularity in America, political history simulations have been neglected by higher education history teachers in Britain as both a seminar-based learning vehicle for interactivity and 'deep' learning and a mechanism by which students can be oriented further towards the kinds of values associated with multiperspectivity.[43] Indeed, one of the most significant characteristics of historical simulations – which, broadly speaking, take the form of reconstructive role-play tasks – is the way that they can, potentially, combine both interactive and multiperspectival elements.

Although there is still a distinct lack of research into the use of simulations for teaching political history topics, much of the evidence to date supports the idea that these types of interactive tasks stimulate students intellectually and help them to open their minds to new arguments and perspectives. To this end, William Gorton and Jonathan Havercroft, who are political theorists who utilise historical role-play activities in their own teaching and assessment, have noted that the nature of these simulations means that 'students must forge a hybrid identity of sorts, one that reflects the worldview and interests of their role, but also one that they infuse with their own views'.[44] Additionally, a similar study by Matthew Weidenfeld and Kenneth Fernandez has found that historical simulations, when used to teach political concepts, improve 'student engagement' levels via the production of heightened 'emotional responses' to historical material that enhance cognitive learning processes.[45]

Such results do, of course, need to be caveated by acknowledging the criticisms that have been levelled at simulations by a significant number of teachers, particularly in the academic field of social studies where such activities have been more routinely conducted. Most notably, it has been argued

---

[41] Booth, 'Rethinking the Scholarly', 259.

[42] C. Wekerle, M. Daumiller and I. Kollar, 'Using Digital Technology to Promote Higher Education Learning: The Importance of Different Learning Activities and Their Relations to Learning Outcomes', *Journal of Research on Technology in Education*, 54 (2022), 1; Biggs and Tang, *Teaching for Quality Learning*, 27.

[43] For historical simulations that are popular in the United States, see Barnard College's *Reacting to the Past* website. https://reacting.barnard.edu.

[44] W. Gorton and J. Havercroft, 'Using Historical Simulations to Teach Political Theory', *Journal of Political Science Education*, 8 (2012), 63.

[45] M. C. Weidenfeld and K. E. Fernandez, 'Does Reacting to the Past Increase Student Engagement? An Empirical Evaluation of the Use of Historical Simulations in Teaching Political Theory', *Journal of Political Science Education*, 13 (2017), 57–8.

that students can fail to take simulations seriously and that this can lead to the production of superficial teaching environments.[46] Even studies that have advocated the pedagogical value of interactive role-plays have discovered that 'student time spent reading and preparing for class declined during the simulation'.[47] Nevertheless, most of the challenges associated with historical simulations can be overcome if a well-scaffolded activity is provided that is oriented towards precisely defined learning outcomes that are, in turn, articulated clearly to the students involved.[48] In such a manner, particularly in the current political environment, which is often defined by a degree of narrow-mindedness and ideational inflexibility, the positives appear to outweigh the negatives and the pedagogical benefits of interactive simulations that 'challenge [students] to think critically and develop empathy for people who lived in the past' should not be readily dismissed.[49]

Technology

The coming of the Internet era has presented a number of significant challenges for higher education teachers working on historical topics. History, as an academic discipline, has usually been depicted, sometimes with a substantial degree of merit, as particularly slow to respond to and harness new technological innovations.[50] Alongside this type of implied criticism, there has been, perhaps, a slight tendency to overstate the potential impact of technology on the teaching of history-related subject matter.[51] Yet there is a large amount of research-based evidence that suggests that students can struggle to process the vast quantity of information available to them on the Internet and to assess this material's validity and accuracy in a critical fashion.[52] Indeed, the ever-expanding and voluminous nature of online resources can lead to significant difficulties for history undergraduates who are attempting to conceptualise and operationalise research projects that are based on Internet-related archives and sources.[53]

The pedagogical challenges that new technological developments raise for modern political history educators have gathered further significance with the recent growth of polarised 'post-truth' politics online. A broad scepticism towards the idea of objective political 'truth' has been fuelled by an

---

[46] L. DiCamillo and J. M. Gradwell, 'To Simulate or Not to Simulate? Investigating Myths about Social Studies Simulations', *The Social Studies*, 104, no. 4 (2013), 155–7.

[47] Weidenfeld and Fernandez, 'Does Reacting to the Past Increase Student Engagement?', 58.

[48] DiCamillo and Gradwell, 'To Simulate or Not to Simulate?', 158; Shelda Debowski, *The New Academic: A Strategic Handbook* (Maidenhead, 2012), 49–50.

[49] DiCamillo and Gradwell, 'To Simulate or Not to Simulate?', 158.

[50] A. Crymble, *Technology and the Historian: Transformations in the Digital Age* (Urbana, 2021), 1.

[51] For example, see T. M. Kelly, *Teaching History in the Digital Age* (Ann Arbor, 2013), 127.

[52] D. G. Morais, 'Doing History in the Undergraduate Classroom', *The History Teacher*, 52 (2018), 49–50.

[53] D. Daniel, 'Teaching Students How to Research the Past: Historians and Librarians in the Digital Age', *The History Teacher*, 45 (2012), 265.

information-saturated online cultural milieu.[54] To take one particular case study on a highly contested contemporary political topic, Jane O'Mahony has highlighted how a 'massive expansion in the availability of information and analysis for students ... often representing polarised views of the EU' has created new obstacles for scholars who are teaching the recent history of Britain's relationship with the EU to undergraduates.[55] Similarly, as Tracy Bowell has shown, the increased prominence of social media as an online vehicle for the mass dissemination of information has led to a world in which established forms of expertise, such as academia, are questioned, and a '140 character throwaway remark [on Twitter] can be afforded as much authority on the issue at hand as a carefully researched in-depth article'.[56]

These developments make it ever more pressing for modern British political history scholars to imbue their teaching with the values of critical engagement and methodological scrutiny. Teachers should seek to equip students with the skills that can identify and disentangle any political 'bias' that is contained within online arguments.[57] Furthermore, rather than avoiding the discussion of emotionally charged and potentially divisive arguments, it is often better to 'acknowledge them explicitly and integrate them into our teaching in order to enhance understanding'.[58] This type of direct approach might also be applied successfully in order to address some of the specific issues that currently surround social media content. To this end, given the apparent ever-increasing proclivity of elements within social media to embrace populist 'post-truth' narratives, it is understandable that higher education teachers are now adopting a more cautious approach to the very same websites that were, until fairly recently, more likely to be identified for their 'democratising' pedagogical potential.[59] Yet direct analysis of how and why problematic social media narratives, particularly those that offer either distorted or fabricated views of the recent political past, are formed and sustained, alongside engagement with their lack of evidential legitimacy, can form an important part of the learning process. More generally, as Dominque Daniel has shown, in order to develop and promote the kind of critical skills that facilitate effective web-based learning, historians should seek advice and guidance from other members of higher education staff, such as librarians, who often provide online training and Internet archive-related support that enables 'students [to] become better at using and creating information' and, thus, more critical and discerning consumers of online material.[60]

It is also important to recognise that, alongside the aforementioned challenges, the Internet era has opened up a range of new pedagogical possibilities, many of which could be used successfully to address and nullify some of the

---

[54] Chinn et al., 'Education for a "Post-Truth" World', 51.
[55] O'Mahony, 'Teaching the EU in Brexit Britain', 39.
[56] Bowell, 'Response to the Editorial', 583.
[57] O'Mahony, 'Teaching the EU in Brexit Britain', 39.
[58] Ibid., 46.
[59] A. Blair, 'Democratising the Learning Process: The Use of Twitter in the Teaching of Politics and International Relations', Politics, 33 (2013), 135–45.
[60] Daniel, 'Teaching Students', 262.

effects of 'post-truth' politics and political polarisation. As it stands, historians have only really just started to realise the opportunities afforded by online developments in their teaching practice.[61] The somewhat belated progress that has been made in the depth and quality of online teaching provision has been accelerated by the relatively recent transition to Online Learning Environments as the primary forum for the provision of university-level teaching material.[62] Nonetheless, throughout the twenty-first century, academic enquiries into the pedagogical value of online teaching provision and techniques in the field of historical studies have, typically, reached positive conclusions. Specifically, a considerable body of research has stressed the utility of collaborative and interactive research-based website construction activities for increasing critical engagement with the recent past and providing students with valuable encounters with a diverse array of historical perspectives.[63]

When evaluating one assessed task that required students to build web pages that examined complex historical issues relating to an American university's athletics club, Dominic Morais found that the 'project [forced] students to look at subjects and issues from a number of viewpoints' and that the process helped to generate 'critical thinking' skills, such as 'analyzing evidence, assessing the worth of knowledge claims, and synthesizing complex data'.[64] The existing literature on the use of collaborative wiki-building exercises in higher education points to the similar pedagogical benefits of tasks that are scaffolded effectively, as long as appropriate technological guidance is provided.[65] Wiki construction tasks have also been seen, albeit in research that has been conducted in a pre-university educational environment, to operate particularly successfully when deployed to support historically-oriented teaching because they can provide students with 'the opportunity to practice and demonstrate higher order thinking skills' and, perhaps just as importantly, allow participants to 'engage in rich discourse in a non-intimidating environment'.[66] In other words, when they are supported with appropriate training and guidance, Internet-based research activities can help historians to develop an academically rigorous skill set that is ideally suited to traversing critically through our era of 'post-truth' politics and fostering the kind of tolerant and inclusive discussions that might offer a pathway out of our current fractious political malaise.

---

[61] Wekerle *et al.*, 'Using Digital Technology', 14.

[62] K. Schrum and N. Sleeter, 'Teaching History Online: Challenges and Opportunities', *OAH Magazine of History*, 27, no. 3 (2013), 38.

[63] An early study was N. B. Milman and W. F. Heinecke, 'Innovative Integration of Technology in an Undergraduate History Course', *Theory and Research in Social Education*, 28 (2000), 546–65.

[64] Morais, 'Doing History in the Undergraduate Classroom', 61, 63–4.

[65] J. E. Hughes and R. Narayan, 'Collaboration and Learning with Wikis in Post-Secondary Classrooms', *Journal of Interactive Online Learning*, 8, no. 1 (2009), 63–82; B. Zheng, M. Niiya and M. Warschauer, 'Wikis and Collaborative Learning in Higher Education', *Technology, Pedagogy and Education*, 24 (2015), 357–74.

[66] C. Cabiness, L. Donovan and T. D. Green, 'Integrating Wikis in the Support and Practice of Historical Analysis Skills', *TechTrends*, 57, no. 6 (2013), 46.

Conclusion

This article has argued that, when working in a higher education setting, modern British political history lecturers currently face an identifiable set of dilemmas and tensions that should, necessarily, inform their considerations when they are designing and providing teaching-related content and activities. In terms of their general contours and characteristics, the challenges that this work has highlighted do not necessarily represent entirely novel pedagogical considerations. Regardless of the contemporary context in which they are being discussed, recent political historical events and topics that relate to the country in which the subject is being studied are always likely to excite students and, to a certain degree, represent controversial subject matter. Nevertheless, the growth of 'post-truth' politics and polarised societies, aided by the profligate spread of misleading information and development of online communities that act as mutually reinforcing 'echo chambers', presents additional obstacles to the development of critical and self-reflective teaching and learning environments. In such an environment, lecturers need to display a heightened awareness of the need, simultaneously and, perhaps, somewhat paradoxically, both to embed the values of critical thinking and analytical detachment within their teaching and to 'respect the role of emotion as part of our response to the world and of our lived experiences of it'.[67]

To respond successfully to the challenges of the 'post-truth' age, this article largely concurs with Martin Peters's assessment that university-level teachers 'need an operational strategy to combat "government by lying" and a global society prepared to accept cognitive dissonance and the subordination of truth to Twittered emotional appeals and irrational personal beliefs'.[68] Somewhat tentatively, this work has begun to outline a strategy for modern British political historians that might draw upon the strength of the subject's interdisciplinary foundations; the values of multiperspectivity; interactive exercises such as historical simulations; and the growth of technological opportunities associated with the Internet age. In doing so, it has been informed by the idea that, although the current sociocultural and political challenges faced by higher education teachers are significant, they by no means represent insurmountable barriers to effective teaching.

Author Biography. Dr Richard Jobson is a lecturer in twentieth-century British history.

---

[67] Bowell, 'Response to the Editorial', 584.
[68] Peters, 'Education in a Post-Truth World', 565.

Cite this article: Jobson R (2024). Teaching Modern British Political History in a Politically Polarised and 'Post-Truth' Environment. *Transactions of the Royal Historical Society* **2**, 389–400. https://doi.org/10.1017/S0080440123000269

Transactions of the RHS (2024), **2**, 401–411
doi:10.1017/S0080440123000154

Censoring Our History

Andrew Lownie

Department of Humanities, The University of Buckingham, Buckingham, UK
Email: andrew@andrewlownie.co.uk

(Received 21 April 2023; revised 13 July 2023; accepted 14 July 2023;
first published online 8 November 2023)

Abstract

Andrew Lownie recounts how he became the victim of state surveillance as a result of his successful efforts to secure the release of the personal diaries and letters of Dickie and Edwina Mountbatten – bought by the University of Southampton with public funds to be open to researchers – in what became the largest-ever release of material under Freedom of Information (FOI), 33,000 pages, but which personally cost him over £400,000 in legal fees. Drawing on his own research experiences, he also describes the failure of government departments to deposit records at the National Archives as required by statute, the techniques public authorities use to frustrate FOI requests and suggests how FOI could be improved. All of this curation, he argues, leads to a distortion of the historical record and the censoring of our history.

Keywords: Archives; royal family; Cabinet Office; historians

I have never considered myself as a dangerous radical or enemy of the state, and my background and activities would not suggest it – I have been a Cambridge history fellow, am a member of several smart London clubs and even drive a Volvo. Yet I've been spied on by the state.

The monitoring includes my social media accounts, a flyer for a talk I gave at a private club, details of a lecture at a Cambridge Alumni weekend and a library talk with an internal heading by the Cabinet Office of 'Not just any cook-along this week'. I know this from various Subject Access Requests made to the Cabinet Office and Foreign Office under data protection laws relating to the personal data which they hold on me and which I have applied for over the last few years.

The Cabinet Office eventually admitted that they held so much material on me – they estimated it would take over 656 hours to collect the information –

that my requests needed to be broken down into six-monthly intervals.[1] Their releases showed that my activities were brought to the attention of the permanent secretary, Sir Alex Chisholm, and the 'Cabinet Office COPRA team' (whatever that is); that my speaking engagements, newspaper articles and crowdfunding activities were monitored; and that information was also collected on other parts of my life. This included employment tribunal and linked defamation cases which I had successfully defended and which had nothing to do with my Freedom of Information (FOI) requests or activities as an historian.

My crime? As an historian, to push back against the censoring of our history by government departments and to highlight their failures to adhere to various Public Records Acts and the Freedom of Information Act (FOIA).[2]

My concerns about historical curation go back to researching a biography of Guy Burgess over a decade ago, where I found huge gaps in the record. There was nothing on his time in the Information Research Department, a secret unit set up at the beginning of 1948 to counter Russian propaganda and which he betrayed months after it was set up. Likewise nothing on his time in the News Department, in the private office of Foreign Secretary Ernest Bevin's deputy Hector McNeil nor the British Embassy in Washington between 1950 and 1951 – though there were papers for the period either side of his time in Washington for diplomats doing the same job. In historical parlance this is known as 'dry cleaning' the records.

My suspicions about cover-ups were further confirmed when I began researching a book on Dickie and Edwina Mountbatten, the last viceroy and vicereine of India, in 2016. Their letters and diaries had been extensively quoted in previous books, and a major fundraising campaign had been mounted by Southampton University in 2010 to buy their papers so they could be 'open to all'.[3]

I was therefore surprised to be told by the Southampton University archive that they knew nothing about some of these diaries and letters, part of a £2.8 million purchase of Mountbatten material under the Acceptance in Lieu scheme and with contributions from the Heritage Lottery Fund, Hampshire County Council and other organisations, and withheld other information as they claimed it was exempt from disclosure.

Eventually, after several years, numerous FOI requests, the intervention of the Information Commissioner and the unprecedented[4] threat of contempt proceedings against Southampton University, in 2019 a Decision Notice was issued ordering the release of some of the withheld material and that they

---

[1] Cabinet Office (CO) to Andrew Lownie, 27 Jul. 2022.

[2] Public Records Act 1958 and 1967 and Freedom of Information Act 2000.

[3] https://www.nhmf.org.uk/news/broadlands-archive-hits-fundraising-target-thanks-national-heritage-memorial-fund-grant.

[4] For the first time in its history, the Information Commissioner's Office (ICO) instituted High Court proceedings against a public authority after the University of Southampton ignored the ICO Information Notice – CO/1635/2019. There was no court decision, as the university finally started to comply but only after *The Mountbattens* was published.

should provide the correspondence between Lord and Lady Mountbatten and copies of their respective diaries.[5]

Southampton and the Cabinet Office appealed the decision but then, just before the November 2021 hearing, dumped 99.8 per cent of the material (over 30,000 pages) on the Internet.[6] The material that they had kept closed for a decade, and fought so hard to prevent being made publicly available before my book *The Mountbattens: Their Lives and Loves* was published in 2019,[7] proved to be entirely innocuous.

And Southampton University knew this, because in March 2018, some eighteen months before they appealed the Information Commissioner's Decision Notice, I was told in a conversation by an employee that a review of the material organised by Southampton and the Cabinet Office had concluded there was nothing sensitive in the personal diaries and letters.

The tribunal, however, ruled that the Cabinet Office still had the right to apply FOIA exemptions to the diaries and letters, which meant that just over a hundred redactions – some a single word, others several paragraphs – were applied on the grounds that they were communications with the sovereign, or that they would damage international relations or national security.[8]

Until just before the four-day hearing in November 2021, Southampton had argued they were bound by the mysterious Ministerial Direction controlling the letters and diaries, but they dropped this argument, saying that simply specific FOIA exemptions would be applied.[9] There was no evidence that the diaries and letters had ever been 'closed' – neither the Cabinet Office nor Southampton could cite a specific notice – but an effort was made to argue that by implication they had been caught by the 'undertakings' concerning Dickie's official papers ('strayed records') in agreements in the 1960s and 1980s, though this could not be. The diaries and letters are expressly defined as AIL Chattels in the 2011 Purchase Agreement – not 'Excluded Records', that is, the papers that the Cabinet Office had closed. The 2011 agreement expressly stated that the vendors were free to sell all AIL Chattels and that they are not subject to the Undertakings. Thus, the proviso in the Ministerial Direction couldn't apply in any event to AIL Chattels. On my reading of the Decision, the tribunal did not appear to grapple with this point at all.

The upholding by the tribunal of various requested redactions is also baffling. Some names from the royal household were redacted – even if they were already in the public domain from the *London Gazette* or other books or, indeed, unredacted on other pages of the diaries, both unpublished and published. Other similar roles were not redacted, so there was no consistency in how the FOIA exemptions were applied.

[5] https://ico.org.uk/media/action-weve-taken/decision-notices/2019/2616838/fs50772671.pdf.

[6] https://www.southampton.ac.uk/archives/mountbattendigitisationproject/mountbattendigitisationlordmountbatten.page.

[7] Andrew Lownie, *The Mountbattens: Their Lives and Loves* (2009).

[8] https://informationrights.decisions.tribunals.gov.uk/DBFiles/Decision/i3032/University%20of%20Southampton-EA-2020-0021-(15.03.22).pdf.

[9] Bates Wells to Andrew Lownie, 1 Oct. 2021.

It was also decided that a reference to the leader of Pakistan, Muhammad Ali Jinnah, in Edwina's private diary should be redacted on the grounds that it would be prejudicial to relations with Pakistan, even though the test is that 'The public authority must show that there is some causative link between the potential disclosure and the prejudice and that the prejudice is real, actual or of substance. The harm must relate to the interests protected by the exemption.'[10] It is hard to believe that such a reference in a private diary seventy-six years ago would still damage relations with another country, especially when there is plenty of evidence already in the public domain from books about Edwina, or by family members drawing on their access to the diaries, that Edwina had a low opinion of Jinnah.

This FOIA exemption – section 27 – has a public interest test and Southampton even then had no obligation to apply it but they did so. An FOIA exemption is available to a public authority in respect of any FOI request but it is not bound to plead it; the authority has a discretion – unless providing the information would be unlawful.[11] Southampton were perfectly free to publish the material that allegedly would damage relations with India and Pakistan, but Southampton chose not to do so – in what looks like an academic institution censoring history.

It is quite clear, contrary to the Cabinet Office and Southampton's claims, that the diaries and letters were open when purchased – they would not have satisfied the Acceptance in Lieu scheme otherwise – and that the reasonable course of action would have been to review the collection to see what could be released when it was acquired in 2011 and not only after they had been forced to do so a decade later. This could easily have been done by experts at Southampton. Instead through to the hearing in November 2021 Southampton claimed that all the diaries and letters were so sensitive they had to be closed, that digitisation would take years, the material was illegible and fragile, etc.[12] The fact the material was self-evidently digitised within a few months shows it was possible and not so fragile that it could not be done quickly and easily. If the papers had been bought by an American university, they would have been available to scholars over a decade ago.

Access to the diaries and letters before my book was completed would have made my book richer and more nuanced and, as I was not awarded my costs, it left me personally with a legal bill of over £400,000. No private individual should be financially penalised for seeking access to material which was purchased with taxpayers' money on the basis that it would be open to the public, but that is the position I now found myself in.

Millions of pounds of public monies were spent purchasing the total Broadlands Archive (even though we don't know exactly what was apportioned to the diaries and letters) to make this important collection publicly available. And then, given that Southampton and the Cabinet Office deployed two top

---

[10] The Prejudice Test can be found at https://ico.org.uk/media/for-organisations/documents/1214/the_prejudice_test.pdf.

[11] Under Data Protection Act 2018 and Official Secrets Act 1989.

[12] For example, email from Southampton University to Andrew Lownie, 27 May 2017.

QCs and a plethora of lawyers, probably well over £1 million has been spent suppressing them. However, the Cabinet Office will not say, even after Parliamentary Questions (PQ)[13] and FOI requests, how much public money has been spent on pursuing this needless appeal against the Regulator.

This was only the start of my problems with the culture of secrecy. After I discovered a wartime Federal Bureau of Investigation (FBI) file which claimed Mountbatten was 'a homosexual with a perversion for young boys',[14] I requested other listed files held on him, only to be told they had been destroyed. When I asked when that destruction had taken place, the American authorities candidly admitted, 'After you had asked for them.'[15] Presumably this had been at the request of the British Government, previously unaware that such damaging material existed.

The Irish police, the Garda, accepted that they had car logs for the visitors to Mountbatten's holiday home in Ireland for August 1977, the month two sixteen-year-old boys claimed he had abused them, but they would not release them on the grounds that they were part of the investigation into Mountbatten's murder – which took place two years later.

Even though we now have a twenty-year-rule for deposit of historical records, I found that no files on Mountbatten's 1979 murder had been deposited in archives, either in Ireland or Great Britain. The Garda claimed it was still 'an active investigation', even though the bomb maker had been convicted, served a sentence and was released under the Good Friday Agreement in 1998.[16]

Indeed many of the files relating to Mountbatten's funeral, seen by millions around the world on television, are closed because they apparently reveal sensitive information about the procession route, who sat in which carriage, etc.

For my next book, researching the Duke of Windsor's time in the Bahamas during the Second World War, I discovered that, while the Colonial Office Files in the National Archives were thin on him, there were mirror copies of the files in the Bahamas. These were much more extensive and full of revealing detail – such as the duke posting the commissioner of police to Trinidad on the morning of a murder which the duke wanted covered up.[17]

---

[13] https://questions-statements.parliament.uk/written-questions/detail/2022-03-02/133263.

[14] E. A. Conroy to Director, FBI, 23 Feb. 1944, FBI file 75045.

[15] This was done while researching my book in 2016, on FOIPA Request 1413883. Emails from Information Management Division, US Department of Justice, 16 May 2017, 20 Aug. 2018 and 4 Sep. 2018.

[16] Corporate.Services@garda.ie to Andrew Lownie, 7 Dec. 2022: Previously Chief Superintendent Nyland forwarded you an email dated 3rd November, 2019 stating the following,

> "*I wish to inform you that all such security logs form part of the Garda Investigation file, and for the reasons outlined in email of 7th October, 2019 will not be released*"

> 'It is the policy of An Garda Shiochána not to disclose statements, reports; items of evidence etc. generated during the course of a criminal investigation conducted by An Garda Shiochána and are considered confidential and will not be disclosed to third parties in the absence of a Court Order directing such disclosure. Therefore, all relating records to Earl Mountbatten are withheld from public inspection under the National Archives Act, 1986.'

[17] 30 May 1945, CO 23/785/7, British National Archives.

Last year I requested a 1932 police protection file relating to the Duke of Windsor. Dozens of similar files have been available at the National Archives for twenty years. They contain useful titbits on the then Prince of Wales's movements but nothing remotely secret. The Metropolitan Police refused to release the file on the grounds that it would jeopardise the present safety of the royal family.

That decision was upheld by the Information Commissioner's Office (ICO) so I took the matter to a tribunal. A judge asked if I would supply examples of information from other protection files of the period, but, when I sought to do so, I discovered that the twenty files I had highlighted in my submission, and which had been publicly available for over twenty years, had been withdrawn from the National Archives. They included MEPO 10/35 which reveals Wallis Simpson's affair with a car salesman called Guy Trundle, which has been copied and quoted numerous times by historians and is published in all its juicy detail on the website of the National Archives.[18] Yet historians cannot look at the original file.

No terrorist has mounted an attack after spending hours wading through such files, yet on no evidence whatsoever the file was closed. Incidentally, I was told by the Special Branch weeder that there were dozens of other Special Branch reports on Edward and Wallis but only this representative file had been preserved. The others were not deemed worthy of preservation. Says who?

This case highlights the worrying increase in the 'reclosure' of files that hitherto had been available at the National Archives. My files disappeared almost overnight and it is clear the process is not transparent and does not appear to be subject to any oversight.

The preservation of royal records is a real problem as the division between family and state records is unclear. King Charles has just announced that his mother's diaries, an invaluable historical source, will be vetted by a long-serving footman, a man with no historical training or full understanding of the significance of the diaries.[19] Let us hope that they are at least preserved. It is known that Queen Victoria's daughter burnt many of her mother's diaries and Princess Margaret burnt huge quantities of the Queen Mother's papers. The Royal Archives still give no access whatsoever to files on the reign of Elizabeth II, which include correspondence not just with prime ministers of the UK but premiers and governors general of the Commonwealth realms. They also decide which historians they want to let in or not. Cameras are forbidden and there is no public inventory – rather like a restaurant with no menu.

I am not the only historian who has had problems with royal records. The reputable author Christopher Wilson gave up writing his life of the Duke of Kent's father after being refused access to his papers at Windsor. Barrister and former immigration judge Andrew Rose, the author of *The Prince, the*

---

[18] https://www.nationalarchives.gov.uk/state-secrets/celebrity-scandals/mepo-1035-2/

[19] https://www.dailymail.co.uk/news/article-12230569/Why-Tall-Paul-aide-King-trusts-sort-mothers-private-diaries.html.

Princess and the Perfect Murder: An Untold History, looking to update his book about the Duke of Windsor found that MEPO 38/151 (HRH The Prince of Wales: Protection File: 1924–1935), which he had consulted over a decade ago, was no longer available.

Professor Adrian O'Sullivan researching a book on Charles Bedaux, the millionaire industrialist and close friend of the Duke of Windsor, who committed suicide in odd circumstances while in FBI custody, was originally told by an FBI archivist 'that they had lots of "stuff"' on Bedaux and was encouraged to submit a formal FOI request to them.

> This I did promptly and, several months later during the autumn of 2009, received a reply from the FBI informing me that my FOI application to the FBI for the release of Bedaux records was rejected on the grounds that, 'after a search of the indices to our central records system at FBI Headquarters and all FBI field offices', the Bureau was 'unable to identify responsive main records'.[20]

Dr Alison McClean, a lecturer at the University of the West of England, researching support for both sides in the Spanish Civil War among members of the British aristocracy, has also had trouble, not least at The Royal Archives where she ruefully notes that she was allowed to see only three 'very thin' folders of correspondence relating to Queen Victoria Eugenie of Spain and Princess Beatrice Orleans y Borbon (two British-born first cousins of George V who returned to England after the fall of the Spanish monarchy in 1931).[21]

Recently the campaigning organisation Index on Censorship published a report on censorship of royal records[22] pointing out that almost 500 files at the National Archives were closed including:

- Royal Family flying training 1977–1978. Record opening date 1 January 2066
- Family name of Royal Family members 1952–1960. Record opening date 1 January 2027
- Remains of the Russian Royal Family 1993 Jan.–Dec. 1993. No release date
- Family name of the Royal House 1952. Record opening date 1 January 2053
- Air travel for the Royal Family: Containing information relating to the financial arrangements for and other matters relating to the Royal Family 1936–1952. Record opening date 1 January 2053
- Visits overseas by members of Royal Family 1954. Record opening date 1 January 2055.

---

[20] Adrian O'Sullivan to Andrew Lownie, 5 Jun. 2023.

[21] Alison McClean to Andrew Lownie, 17 May 2023.

[22] https://www.indexoncensorship.org/2022/12/crown-confidential-how-britains-royals-censor-their-records/

Declassified UK recently reported that over 200 files on overseas trips made by King Charles going back to the 1970s remain closed. They include a 1983 visit to Australia which will only be released when Charles is 121 years old.

Historians cannot look at important historical material from almost a century ago yet Prince Harry can spill intimate secrets from a few months ago. As the former MP Norman Baker, author of *And What Do You Do? What the Royal Family Don't Want You to Know* (2019), has said, 'There's no reason for these to be kept secret. The normal excuse given is that it's to uphold the dignity of the crown. But the dignity of the crown is upheld by them not behaving in an undignified manner.'[23]

There are lots of techniques used by public authorities to avoid disclosure. They can kick the can down the road as long as possible, sometimes amounting to over a year. They can keep changing the exemptions deployed as each is addressed and shown not to apply. They can simply not answer requests and hope the requestor gives up. They can play with semantics in carefully phrased replies which are economical with the truth. They can agree to release documents and then do nothing or redact them so heavily as to make them worthless. They can aggregate separate requests and then refuse on grounds of costs of compliance.

Time and time again, authorities hide behind national security or law enforcement or claim not to have material, only to miraculously find it when evidence of its existence is presented. Intriguingly, only the most sensitive documents are ever affected by damp or asbestos. After I recently requested some files on the Lord Lambton political scandal of fifty years ago, I was told by the Metropolitan Police they had 'lost' one of them though it remains in the National Archives catalogue. They have also admitted that they have still not catalogued many of their interwar papers.[24]

A favourite trick by public authorities is to use section 22 (where the information is held by the public authority with a view to its publication, by the authority or any other person, at some future date) but where the material mysteriously never finds its way to the National Archives. A weeder has personally told me that when in doubt reviewing material, they are told to just use an absolute exemption, such as section 23 national security.

That is if the documents have not already been destroyed. A recent FOI request to the Foreign, Commonwealth and Development Office revealed that destruction of their files with no public record is routine:

2013 – 7,066
2014 – 52,352
2015 – 30,634
2016 – 21,886

---

[23] Phil Miller, Declassified UK, 6 Oct. 2022: https://declassifieduk.org/exclusive-hundreds-of-diplomatic-files-on-king-charles-censored/

[24] London Metropolitan Police to Andrew Lownie, 21 Apr. 2022: 'One of the Parts was only identified as missing upon searches being conducted when you submitted the request for access to these files.'

When I asked for details of the files destroyed, I was told by their information rights team: 'We have considered the publication of file destruction list and concluded that this would detract from our release programme.'[25]

My experience with Mountbatten is a good example of public authorities often pleading scant resources when responding to FOI requests, yet deploying costly lawyers to battle invariably under-represented requestors and to try and break them financially. It is clear that the Freedom of Information Act 2000 – both in terms of legislative reach and enforcement power – is simply not fit for purpose and that parliamentary unease at the antics of the Cabinet Office and the weakness of the ICO as a regulator is justified.

There are too many loopholes ('exemptions' which are very broadly drawn), and the government, particularly the Cabinet Office, has become extremely adept at exploiting them. They include, from my own experience:

(i) The licence given to public authorities to entirely change their reasons for refusing to disclose information at almost any stage, however late, in proceedings. This leads to what could be described as the absurd game of 'whack-a-mole' – and of course drives up costs. In my case the Ministerial Direction was used to justify closure for a decade until I questioned its existence.

(ii) The lack of any mechanism to ensure public authorities adhere to deadlines, or even Decision Notices. Because they can ignore these with impunity, researchers are faced with the prospect of incurring costs to bring a delinquent body into line. My lawyers constantly had to chase both Southampton and the Cabinet Office for responses, even though they had statutory time limits, to the extent of bringing contempt proceedings.[26] All this cost me money.

There is scope for some simple reforms such as:

• Statutory deadlines for an authority to respond. There are, for example, no enforceable deadlines for Internal Reviews, which should take no more than forty days. It wouldn't be difficult to tweak FOIA to include unequivocal – and actionable – timetables across the process.
• 'Deemed refusals'. Scotland's FOIA includes this provision, by which the absence of a response within the required timetable is taken as a formal refusal, which can then be appealed by the applicant.
• Sanctions for failures to comply with timetables. Public authorities, routinely flout deadlines – whether statutory or in ICO guidance. The way to discourage this is by an automatic financial penalty, payable to the

---

[25] FOI and DPA Team, Foreign and Commonwealth Office to Andrew Lownie, 22 Jul. 2016.
[26] Contempt proceedings are in Decision Notice 'As a result, under section 54(1) of FOIA, the Commissioner made a certification to the High Court in April 2019 and asked it to deal with the Council as if it had committed a contempt of Court in failing to comply with the Information Notice of 23 January 2019.' See https://ico.org.uk/media/action-weve-taken/decision-notices/2019/2616838/fs50772671.pd.

applicant, for every deadline missed. Train companies, for example, are now required to pay passengers what amounts to a fine for failures to arrive on time: there is no reason why Whitehall should be any different.
• Severely reduced licence for public authorities to 'change horses mid-stream'. If the Cabinet Office pleads section 22 at first FOIA request, it should not be allowed to amend that to a different exemption without the explicit permission of the regulator. And the bar for being allowed to do so should be set extremely high, with accompanying statutory requirements for the disclosure of evidence supporting any such request.

The culture of cronyism needs to go. Either archives are secret or they should be made available to everyone at the same time. Tame journalists are often tipped off about document releases well in advance of the rest of the media and there are a select number of writers who are given privileged and exclusive access to write commercial books.

There needs to be proper, separate oversight. Internal reviews are conducted by the same department and, in my experience, they have all upheld the original decision. There is the Advisory Council on National Records and Archives Committee, but it has little power and its members appointed by the Department for Culture, Media and Sport. It needs to be replaced with a much more robust and independent body and given stronger powers.

The ICO requires more money and staff, it needs to be truly independent of the Cabinet Office (who are the worst abusers of FOIA) and it has to be pre-pared to use its enforcement powers. Indeed, I believe the ICO should be left with just its data protection role and a new regulatory body for information rights set up.

There also needs to be a sea change in attitudes in Whitehall. The weeders need to have a lighter touch and FOI requests need to be dealt with more quickly, while a rather more enlightened attitude must be taken towards FOI exemptions to really protect what is important.

The balance between accountability and transparency on the one hand and protecting national security on the other is a difficult one to strike. Once records are released the genie is out of the bottle, but it is hard to argue that records which in many cases are over sixty years old, and where the officials involved are dead, should not be released. If our history is to be written accurately, we will have to have all the records made available – not just those a government department believes we should have – and historians should not be penalised for seeking to ensure that happens.

Our duty as historians is to try and tell the truth about the past. We cannot do that without the documents being available. This suppression of documents is profoundly undemocratic and reduces trust in the institutions which are meant to serve us. Southampton University and the Cabinet Office's campaign against me was not about safeguarding national security, international relations or data protection but an attempt to make an example of an historian who refused to believe their lies and break me financially. It's a story about the abuse of state power, the failings of the FOI Act, the tribunals and the ICO, the kowtowing of an academic institution to the state, the interference of the royal household in trying to suppress an archive freely sold by one of their chums for in effect £5 million. Let it not also be about the failure of us historians to stand up and challenge this censoring of our history. It is incumbent on us all to highlight these transgressions and, if necessary, challenge FOI decisions with the ICO and in the tribunals.

Author biography. Dr Andrew Lownie FRHistS is the author of biographies of John Buchan, Guy Burgess, the Mountbattens and Edward VIII.

Cite this article: Lownie A (2024). Censoring Our History. *Transactions of the Royal Historical Society* **2**, 401–411. https://doi.org/10.1017/S0080440123000154

Transactions of the RHS (2024), **2**, 413–432
doi:10.1017/S0080440124000021

COMMENT

Naming and Shaming? Telling Bad Bridget® Stories

Elaine Farrell[1] and Leanne McCormick[2]

[1]Queen's University Belfast, Belfast, Northern Ireland and [2]Ulster University, Coleraine, Northern Ireland
Corresponding author: Elaine Farrell; Email: e.farrell@qub.ac.uk

(Received 21 December 2023; revised 29 April 2024; accepted 9 May 2024; first published online 26 September 2024)

Abstract

The Bad Bridget project centres on Irish-born female criminal suspects in North America from 1838 to 1918. Its title derives from the common occurrence of the forename Bridget in nineteenth- and early-twentieth-century Ireland, and its application as a collective name to Irish women in the US. The 'Bad Bridget' title seemed to capture our focus on the individual, as well as the diverse experiences of the girls and women on whom the project is based. While we hesitated about using the title initially, lest 'bad' suggest a shaming of behaviour or individuals, or 'Bridget' a judgement on Irish heritage, we decided that the benefits of the collective name outweighed potential drawbacks. This article expands on the idea that a name can imply shame. It focuses on our use of real forenames and surnames instead of pseudonyms (or other anonymisation alternatives) to identify individual girls and women in our project outputs to date. The article makes the case for the use of real names in this context, exploring in turn our roles and responsibilities as historians, archival and scholarly expectations, our responsibilities towards our subject matter, and our audiences (including the descendants of the Irish girls and women suspected of criminal behaviour).

Keywords: anonymisation; pseudonymisation; genealogy; crime; women

In 2016, four years after the publication of Elaine Farrell's *Infanticide in the Irish Crown Files of Assizes, 1883-1900*, an edited volume of petty sessions witness statements, she was contacted by Will Robinson, a genealogist and historian based in the US. When researching his own family history, Robinson had discovered that his great-grandmother's sister, Jane Quigley, and her father Owen Quigley (Robinson's great-great-grandfather), were named in Farrell's Irish Manuscripts Commission volume. As far as Robinson was aware, nobody from that generation had revealed to their descendants that Jane and Owen had been accused of concealing the birth of Jane's newborn baby in Roscommon in 1896. Having read the transcribed witness statements, Robinson observed that the case offered 'a vivid glimpse of her (and her father's) life as well as the repressive environment of the period'.[1] In naming Jane and Owen Quigley, Farrell's volume filled gaps in this family history. It provided the context for descendants to comprehend the accusation of concealment of birth that Robinson had first encountered in a digitised prison register on a genealogical database.

A year prior to this exchange, in 2015, we were awarded Arts and Humanities Research Council (AHRC) funding for our project, 'Bad Bridget: Criminal and deviant Irish women in North America, 1838–1918' (AH/M008649/1). This research predominantly focuses on the cities of Boston, New York and Toronto, examining the various crimes of which Irish-born girls and women were accused and for which they were institutionalised. To date, the project has resulted in a book, a podcast series, numerous talks, and other written outputs.[2] In 2021, we successfully secured AHRC Follow-on-Funding (AH/V011391/1) and worked with colleagues at National Museums NI to develop a Bad Bridget exhibition at the Ulster American Folk Park in Omagh, County Tyrone.[3] The exhibition opened in 2022 and will remain *in situ* until 2025.

The title of the project and subsequent outputs stem from the common occurrence of the forename Bridget in Ireland in the nineteenth and early twentieth centuries, and its application as a collective name (along with the more derogatory variant 'Biddy') to Irish girls and women in the US. The 'Bad Bridget' title seemed to capture our focus on the individual, as well as to encapsulate the diverse experiences of the many Irish-born girls and women on whom the project is based. It also alludes to perceptions of the Irish abroad, although our aim is to reclaim the name to show the complexities of Irish female migration, rather than to use it in a historically pejorative manner. While we hesitated about using the title initially, lest 'bad' suggest a shaming of behaviour or the individuals themselves, or 'Bridget' a judgement on their Irish heritage, we ultimately decided that the benefits of the collective name outweighed potential drawbacks.

This article expands on the idea that a name could imply shame. It focuses on our use of real forenames and surnames to identify individual girls and

---

[1] Will Robinson to Elaine Farrell, 6 September 2016 (shared with permission).

[2] This includes, Elaine Farrell and Leanne McCormick, *Bad Bridget: Crime, Mayhem and the Lives of Irish Emigrant Women* (Dublin, 2023); Bad Bridget Podcast (2020); articles in *Irish Independent*, 27 January 2023; *Irish Times*, 20 February 2019; *The Conversation*, 13 March 2020; and more than forty public and academic talks across the UK, Ireland and North America.

[3] We worked largely with National Museums NI's Liam Corry, Andrew McDowell and Victoria Millar. The exhibition includes illustrations by Fiona McDonnell, scents developed by Tasha Marks, almost 150 objects, and character totems with listening posts. The exhibition script was written by author Jan Carson. Listening posts include imagined monologues voiced by actresses (Margaret Cronin, Bronagh Donaghey, Isabelle Martin, Carly McCullough, Lucy Rafferty and Maggie Villarini), accompanied by bespoke soundscapes and music developed by Franziska Schroeder and Catriona Gribben.

women in our Bad Bridget project outputs to date. In this article, we reflect on our roles and responsibilities as historians in sharing details of girls' and women's pasts. The first section explores the choices historians make when working with the life stories of individuals in their research. It considers the factors that inform such scholarship generally, as well as the choices we made (and continue to make) in the Bad Bridget project. The second section examines the nature of the sources upon which our research is based, both those housed in archives and those made accessible online, and how this informed decisions on naming. The third section focuses on the issue of consent when researching historic individuals, particularly our roles and responsibilities when dealing with deceased subjects. The final section examines the audience response, and how naming decisions were informed by audience considerations. This section also reflects on potential descendants of the girls and women named in our Bad Bridget outputs, who form part of this audience. This article explains the various reasons why we identified by name in our outputs the historic women and girls we encountered through our Bad Bridget research.

As references to scholarship in this article indicate, other historians are also currently grappling with related ethical and moral questions in their research. This article engages with recent reflections on the use of historical individuals' names in outputs, and how this can inform their visibility or invisibility.[4] Such discussions are predominantly situated in social, medical, crime or family history research in the nineteenth, twentieth and twenty-first centuries, but these issues are not unique to these fields nor time periods. This article also centres on the role of the historian, building on research that explores historians' use of particular case studies and individual stories, their engagement with sources made available for genealogical purposes, and their emotional responses to the individuals they encounter in their research.[5] In doing so, this article encourages reflection on the ways in which we as historians engage with historical subjects and particularly the choices we make in naming or anonymising the individuals we encounter.

---

[4] Recent examples include: Justin Bengry, 'Difficult Stories and Ethical Dilemmas in Family History', History Workshop Podcast (2021), https://soundcloud.com/historyworkshop/difficult-stories-and-ethical-dilemmas-in-family-history (accessed 1 Nov. 2023); Julia Laite, 'The Emmet's Inch: Small History in a Digital Age', *Journal of Social History*, 53 (2020), 963–89; Laura Nys, '"I am F. B.": Historians, Ethics and the Anonymisation of Autobiographical Sources', *Paedagogica Historica*, 58 (2022), 424–38. For discussion on the use of names and self-names in relation to historic transgender individuals, see Leanne Calvert, '"Came to her dressed in mans cloaths": Transgender Histories and Queer Approaches to the Family in Eighteenth-Century Ireland', *History of the Family*, 29 (2024), 112–13.

[5] On historians and emotions, see for example, Katie Barclay, 'The Practice and Ethics of the History of Emotions', in *Sources for the History of Emotions*, ed. Katie Barclay, Sharon Crozier-De Rosa and Peter N. Stearns (2021), ch. 3. For a discussion of empathy in writing, researching and teaching history, see Sara Fox, 'Archival Intimacies: Empathy and Historical Practice in 2023', *Transactions of the Royal Historical Society*, 1 (2023), 241–65. On the selection of sources, see in particular 257–9.

The historian's choice

Historians are regularly confronted with the challenges of distilling vast amounts of primary and secondary source material into textual, aural or other outputs, and are thus required to make decisions on what to include and exclude. Historians often make choices about the added value (or not) of either quoting, citing or referring to certain primary or secondary sources, influenced by multiple personal or practical factors, including their desires to keep the reader or audience engaged, preferences for one source or author above another, word restrictions, or the need to progress or bolster an argument.[6] These decisions inform our writing of history, although we might not always be overly conscious of the factors that influenced these choices, or spend much time in making them.

Because the Bad Bridget project is heavily based on the individual stories of girls and women, we became very conscious of this act of decision-making when selecting case studies for inclusion in our outputs. Over the course of our research, we have encountered thousands of individuals in the historical records of nineteenth- and early-twentieth-century Boston, New York and Toronto. This large sample rendered decision-making difficult on both an emotional and practical level. The Bad Bridget exhibition at the Ulster American Folk Park focuses on the experiences of only six main individuals. Our co-authored monograph, *Bad Bridget: Crime, Mayhem and the Lives of Irish Emigrant Women*, identifies by name just over 200. Most of the girls and women we have encountered in our research, therefore, have not yet been mentioned by name in our outputs. Of those who feature, some were selected because aspects of their life histories were representative in some way, or shared commonalities with other women's stories. Delia Jones, for instance, whose story opens our co-authored monograph, was a typical Irish emigrant in many ways, hailing as she did from the west of Ireland and migrating as a teenager to the east coast of America to her sister who had funded her passage.[7] Other cases were chosen because they were rich in source material: petitions for clemency from Marion Canning's father in Mohill, County Leitrim following her imprisonment for theft in 1891, for instance, provide a fascinating glimpse of the lived realities of an Irish immigrant in New York's sex industry and an insight into transatlantic relationships.[8] Regional focus also shaped decision-making because of our need to highlight experiences in the three North American cities upon which the project is based, as well as to include migrants from different Irish counties. The desire to point to the diversity of crimes, ages and backgrounds of the collective Bad Bridget likewise informed decisions.

We also felt the pressure to preserve in writing or otherwise, however fleetingly, these historic Irish inhabitants about whom little was hitherto known.

---

[6] See also Franca Iacovetta and Wendy Mitchinson, 'Introduction: Social History and Case Files Research', in *On the Case: Explorations in Social History*, ed. Franca Iacovetta and Wendy Mitchinson (1998), 3.

[7] Farrell and McCormick, *Bad Bridget*, 1.

[8] *Ibid.*, 30–3.

McCormick has a particular fondness for the above-mentioned case of Marion Canning, which explains why it has featured prominently in the Bad Bridget podcast, book and exhibition. Katie Barclay has written persuasively about the emotional response to archival research.[9] She explains: 'I do not know how to write the history of the family without some attempt to form a relationship with the subjects whose inner lives I wish to access.'[10] This connection to historic individuals whom we encountered as part of the research adds an emotional aspect to this act of decision-making.

As part of our desire to reveal the complexities of Irish migration to North America through the lens of criminality, we decided, after much deliberation, to identify the girls and women in our records by name where the archives allowed. In doing so, we rejected the alternatives, which were to assign pseudonyms or fictionalised names, or to refer to individuals by their initials. We have several reasons for doing so. Female criminals are often 'othered'.[11] In the nineteenth century, some Irish women who came before North American courts were dehumanised, or described in animalistic terms.[12] In her analysis of anonymisation in historical writing, Laura Nys argues that 'In naming we recognise people as individuals who are part of the human community and acknowledge their identity.'[13] In using real names in our Bad Bridget outputs, we aim to draw attention to the realities of the migratory experience for the millions of Irish-born girls and women who crossed the Atlantic Ocean, through the individual stories of those who ended up on the wrong side of the law in North America. Catherine Griffin, until recently a New York public defender, recognised this effort to acknowledge these real girls and women when she commented that the Bad Bridget project 'returns their humanity'.[14]

In his Proclamation on Irish-American Heritage Month, 2022, US President Joseph Biden observed:

> For centuries, Irish Americans have played a crucial role in helping define the soul of our Nation, and today, nearly 1 in 10 Americans proudly trace their roots back to the Emerald Isle. With hope and faith in their hearts, the first immigrants from Ireland crossed the Atlantic in search of liberty and opportunity. ... The story of Irish Americans has always been one of strength and perseverance through adversity. Many Irish immigrants arrived on America's shores to escape the Great Famine, only to face discrimination, prejudice, and poverty. Despite these hard times, they embraced their new homes in every corner of America ... and helped build and fortify our Nation into what it is today. Irish Americans expanded the American middle class, building ladders of opportunity

---

[9] Katie Barclay, 'Falling in Love with the Dead'. *Rethinking History*, 22 (2018), 460–1.

[10] *Ibid.*, 460.

[11] See Anne-Marie Kilday and David Nash, *Beyond Deviant Damsels: Re-evaluating Female Criminality in the Nineteenth Century* (Oxford, 2023), especially ch. 1.

[12] Farrell and McCormick, *Bad Bridget*, 237–9.

[13] Nys, 'I am F. B.', 433.

[14] Catherine Griffin, as part of 'Bad Bridget: Live Podcast', Cashel Arts Festival, 16 Sept. 2023.

that future generations could climb. They became teachers, firefighters, police officers, labor leaders, farmers, business owners, and more.[15]

The glossy US-published *Irish-America* magazine, which describes itself as 'a celebration of the growing resurgence of Irish heritage among Irish Americans here today', notes its 'emphasis on the enormous achievements of distinguished and diverse Irish and Irish Americans such as superstar and humanitarian Bono, former president of Coca-Cola and chairman of Allen & Company Donald R. Keough, comedian Kathy Griffin, and silver screen legend Maureen O'Hara'.[16] The girls and women who feature in the Bad Bridget project do not easily fit this popular narrative of successful Irish migration to the US. Using pseudonymised names in our outputs would further reinforce this idea that poor or criminal Irish female immigrants to North America should be forgotten, or pushed to the shadows behind the 'successful' identified by name or referred to in these excerpts. In their study of First World War pension files, Jessica Meyer and Alexia Moncrieff observe that individual life histories, including names, can be an act of 'memorialising individuals by making them historically visible'.[17] In naming, we pull from the anonymous mass of immigration to North America some individual Irish-born girls and women and return them to the historical narrative.

Meyer and Moncrieff argue that not to use the stories of particular individuals in scholarship 'may deny visibility to marginalised groups whose histories deserve to be told'.[18] In our view, these Bad Bridget accounts should be told, even though some of the individuals involved committed atrocious acts. In her biography of Norman Douglas, a known pederast, Rachel Hope Cleves argues that the topic of 'adult-child sex' is 'taboo' and 'discomforting' but that the history of sexuality 'cannot avoid an entire range of human behaviour' solely on the basis that 'it arouses feelings of disgust'.[19] Likewise, as Paula Backscheider has noted, 'Biographers do, after all, write the lives of people they consider monsters or repellent human beings.'[20] Even the histories of Irish immigrant women who committed the most violent crimes can offer insights into the complexities of their lived experiences and the wider contexts in which they operated. Antrim-born Sarah Jane Robinson, accused of poisoning several

---

[15] Joseph R. Biden Jr, 'Proclamation on Irish-American Heritage Month, 2022' (28 Feb. 2022), www.whitehouse.gov/briefing-room (accessed 6 Dec. 2023).

[16] See www.irishamerica.com (accessed 6 Dec. 2023).

[17] Jessica Meyer and Alexia Moncrieff, 'Family not to be Informed? The Ethical Use of Historical Medical Documentation', in *Patient Voices in Britain, 1840-1948,* ed. Anne Hanley and Jessica Meyer (2021), 70.

[18] *Ibid.,* 80–1.

[19] Rachel Hope Cleves, *Unspeakable: A Life beyond Sexual Morality* (Chicago, 2020), 6–7. See also Julia Laite, 'The Marginal and the Monstrous: The "Voices" of Prostitutes and Traffickers in Modern History', https://manyheadedmonster.com/2015/07/08/the-marginal-and-the-monstrous-the-voices-of-prostitutes-and-traffickers-in-modern-history/ (accessed 23 Sept. 2023).

[20] Paula Backscheider, *Reflections on Biography* (Oxford, 1999), 39, cited in Jill Lepore, 'Historians Who Love too Much: Reflections on Microhistory and Biography', *Journal of American History,* 88 (2001), 142–3.

members of her family, including her husband, her sister, and her son, offers such an example. She and her sole surviving son maintained her innocence, but she was found guilty of murder in 1888 in Boston and sentenced to death.[21] Her story is revealing of financial strain and family relationships, as well as forensic science advances and attitudes towards female criminality. Following a campaign by the suffragist movement, which criticised the extension of the death penalty to a woman whose gender had had no input in forming the legislation, Robinson's sentence was commuted to life in prison. She died in custody at the age of sixty-eight.[22]

Given our subject matter, we also had practical reasons for using real names. Any alternative would have meant that individuals mentioned in our outputs could have required multiple pseudonyms. Firstly, many Irish inhabitants at this time used variations of their forenames or pet names interchangeably.[23] Secondly, our focus is on immigrants, many of whom adopted new names in North America as a means of assimilation or as part of their new lives abroad. Thirdly, many had criminal convictions and with that, multiple aliases.[24] And fourthly, they were women, who typically changed their surnames on marriage or long-term cohabitation. For example, the aforementioned Delia Jones was registered as Bridget at the time of her birth in County Mayo but went by the variant, Delia. At some point after migration to the US and marriage, she adopted the name Stella Weymouth. But she also had other aliases, including Stella Johnson.[25] Other women who were assigned the forename Bridget at birth changed their names in the US due to the negative associations of the name.[26] It would be challenging, if not impossible from an onomastic perspective, to assign multiple names to girls and women like Delia Jones without losing the specific nuances of their given and chosen names.

Fictionalising only the names of criminal suspects in our outputs (as opposed to witnesses, legal officials and other bystanders) would also require a judgement about the type of behaviour that was criminal. This would not be straightforward, and not solely because we are not legal professionals.

---

[21] *Boston Globe*, 29 June 1888. See also Farrell and McCormick, *Bad Bridget*, 247–9.

[22] *Boston Evening Transcript*, 31 Oct. 1888; *Boston Globe*, 5 Jan. 1906.

[23] For discussion of these practices in early-modern Ireland, see Clodagh Tait, 'Namesakes and Nicknames: Naming Practices in Early Modern Ireland, 1540–1700', *Continuity and Change*, 21 (2006), 313–40.

[24] On the use of aliases by those with criminal pasts, see, for example, Elaine Farrell, *Women, Crime and Punishment in Ireland: Life in the Nineteenth-Century Convict Prison* (Cambridge, 2020), 27–8; Wolfgang Helbich and Walter D. Kamphoefner, 'The Hour of Your Liberation is Getting Closer and Closer ...', *Studia Migracyjne-Przeglad Polonijny,* 35 (2009), 43–58; Richard W. Ireland, 'The Felon and the Angel Copier: Criminal Identity and the Promise of Photography in Victorian England and Wales', in *Policing and War in Europe*, ed. Louis A. Knafla (2002), 53–86 (especially 60); Maria Luddy, *Prostitution and Irish society, 1800–1914* (Cambridge, 2007), 49.

[25] Case file of Stella Weymouth (Delia (Bridget) Jones) (Massachusetts Archives, Massachusetts Reformatory for Women, Inmate case files, HS9.06/series 515, #11095).

[26] Margaret Lynch-Brennan, 'Ubiquitous Bridget: Irish Immigrant Women in Domestic Service in America, 1840–1930', in *Making the Irish American: History and Heritage of the Irish in the United States*, ed. Marion R. Casey and J. J. Lee (New York, 2006), 333.

Legislation has changed so that some of the behaviours that were punished in the nineteenth or early-twentieth centuries are not prosecuted in the same way today. For example, several Irish-born teenagers and young women were prosecuted for the crime of stubbornness or waywardness. Drogheda-born Elizabeth Fingliss was two months short of her twentieth birthday when her father brought her to court on a charge of stubbornness in 1915, because she had run away to New York with a travelling salesman. She was sentenced to two years in prison.[27] And what of the women who were imprisoned for vagrancy? It was, as Saidiya Hartman has observed, 'a status, not a crime'.[28] To change the names of all those arrested or brought before North American courts would thus be to equate poverty with premediated criminal offences such as serial killing.

It is also the case that not all of the Irish-born girls and women suspected of illegal behaviour in North America were guilty. The records are often too fragmentary to distinguish between perpetrators and innocent defendants.[29] It was in a suspect's interests to present herself in a sympathetic manner, and to argue her innocence. One resident in a New York brothel in 1866 (whose name was not given in the original source) was asked why she did not seek employment elsewhere. She explained: 'I have no recommendations to get a place with a family and not clothes enough for a store.' A policeman rejected her statement and those of her associates, saying 'Oh that's all talk ... they wouldn't work for no consideration.'[30] It is difficult from these conflicting views to judge the unnamed woman's situation. Yet it would be unwise to dismiss her claim, and the claims of other women in our research, as untrue. It is similarly impossible to judge the accuracy of verdicts from more than 100 years ago. Just because an individual was tried or has a criminal file with their name on it does not mean that they were guilty of a crime.[31] In the case of an immigrant population, erroneous convictions have the potential to be relatively numerous. In the middle decades of the nineteenth century especially, stereotypes of the Irish as drunken, slovenly or uncivilised persisted.[32] In 1866, for instance, a newspaper report described the inhabitants of one brothel in Five Points, New York as: 'brazen-faced, bloated, debauched young creatures, uncomely, unattractive and uneducated. They are mostly

---

[27] Farrell and McCormick, *Bad Bridget*, 95.

[28] Saidiya Hartman, *Wayward Lives: Beautiful Experiments* (2019), 243.

[29] Adrian Bingham, Lucy Delap, Louise Jackson and Louise Settle, 'Historical Child Sexual Abuse in England and Wales: The Role of Historians', *History of Education*, 45 (2016), 425.

[30] *New York Times*, 21 Jan. 1866.

[31] Stephen Robertson, 'What's Law got to do with it? Legal Records and Sexual Histories', *Journal of the History of Sexuality*, 14 (2005), 62.

[32] See for example, Ciara Breathnach, 'Immigrant Irishwomen and Maternity Services in New York and Boston, 1860–1911', *Medical History*, 66 (2022), 8–10; Deidre Cooper Owens, *Medical Bondage: Race, Gender, and the Origins of American Gynecology* (Athens, GA, 2017), 90; Hidetaka Hirota, *Expelling the Poor: Atlantic Seaboard States and the 19th-Century Origins of American Immigration Policy* (Oxford, 2017), especially chs. 4 and 5; Kevin Kenny, 'Race, Violence, and Anti-Irish Sentiment in the Nineteenth Century', in *Making the Irish American*, ed. Casey and Lee, 364–78.

Irish. I saw but two faces that showed intellect.'[33] In the next brothel, the author observed a single 'intelligent woman in the room ... the rest of them were unmistakably ... from the fatherland of the Fenians, every soul of them, but she looked like an American born'.[34] Margaret Connors was described as a 'weird looking' Irish woman when she appeared in court in Brooklyn in August 1879 accused of being a fortune teller. A servant who testified against her was contrastingly described as a 'pretty and intelligent girl, evidently of American birth'.[35] It is impossible to determine how views or stereotypes of immigrant and non-immigrant populations fed into guilty verdicts against innocent individuals.

The openness of archives

In 1998, Franca Iacovetta and Wendy Mitchinson wrote of historic individuals: 'In uncovering their agency we face a paradox: our legal obligations as researchers to protect the privacy of individuals in the past can lead us to write the marginal into history by writing their names and faces out of it.'[36] Since our research focuses on the period from 1838 to 1918, most of the records upon which the project is based are older than 100 years and are thus open to the public without any legal requirements to change the names of those mentioned. This facilitates the writing of marginal Irish female immigrants into history, alongside their names. It is also highly likely, given the time period, that the girls and women identified over the course of our research are now dead.

For some of the individuals, the records upon which our research is based related to the worst point in their lives: the 'rock bottom' of an alcohol addiction; the horror attached to getting caught for infanticide or abortion and their secret unwanted pregnancy being exposed; the desperate poverty that compelled some women to engage temporarily in the sex industry or to steal to make ends meet. For others, the crime that we first discovered was merely one in a long career of illegal activity. We aimed in our outputs to handle and present each case sensitively, while at the same time doing our job as historians. To that end, we referenced all our primary and secondary sources in our trade book, enabling other scholars to follow our trail through the archives and repositories should they so wish. Many of these references include individuals' names, since that is how they are filed or identifiable in collections. Omission of names is sometimes a condition of using particular archival collections, but since this did not apply in our case, we saw no reason not to reference.[37]

---

[33] *New York Times*, 21 Jan. 1866.

[34] *Ibid.*

[35] *Brooklyn Times Union*, 28 Aug. 1879.

[36] Iacovetta and Mitchinson, 'Introduction', 6.

[37] Some historians have taken the decision for ethical or other reasons to override scholarly and disciplinary conventions by omitting references, or by providing minimal detail that can largely prevent others locating those specific files in the archives. On this subject, see, for example, Sarah-Anne Buckley, *Cruelty Man: Child Welfare, the NSPCC and the State in Ireland, 1889-1956* (Manchester, 2013), xix; David Wright and Renée Saucier, 'Madness in the Archives: Anonymity,

Lack of referencing can also raise issues of accountability.[38] In his discussion of history methodologies, Tom Griffiths writes: 'Footnotes are not defensive displays of pedantry; they are honest expressions of vulnerability, generous signposts to anyone who wants to retrace the path and test the insights, acknowledgements of the collective enterprise that is history.'[39] Referencing also allows other researchers to build on published scholarship through the identification and analysis of additional sources.

While most of our Bad Bridget research was archival, information on many of the girls and women in our study is also accessible through digitised sources.[40] The booming business of family history from the 1970s has resulted in vast amounts of digitised sources becoming available online, or via a library or archive.[41] And this remains ongoing; records are available online now that were accessible only in North American archives when we began the Bad Bridget project. Easily searchable digitised records, often made available by specialist archivists or genealogists, bring significant advantages to historians tracing individuals. Julia Laite has pointed out that her subjects 'walked on and off my stage. Stage left: the start of the police file, court case, or home office correspondence in which I found them. Stage right: the file's end. Digitization means I can chase them off the archive's page.'[42] We chased some of the individuals identified in our Bad Bridget project through digitised institution registers, newspapers, and birth, death and marriage records, which allowed us to supplement criminal records, and to gain some insight of the lives of individuals before and after the crime of which they were suspected. In his discussion of the ethics around queer history, Justin Bengry has similar pointed to the benefits of online family history sources in allowing historians to move beyond mad, bad or sad unidimensional historical figures.[43]

Open access digital archives can make attempts to hide the identities of historical individuals very difficult. As Daniel Grey has argued in the case of defendants and victims in nineteenth-century English and Welsh sexual assault cases, the 'information in newspaper articles (along with published law reports or similar documents) is already in the public domain' and for well-known cases 'anonymity is redundant'.[44] Some of the Irish-born suspects we encountered in our research are likewise already in the public domain.

Ethics, and Mental Health History Research', *Journal of the Canadian Historical Association/Revue de la Société historique du Canada*, 23 (2012), 71–2.

[38] For a discussion in ethnography, see Erica Weiss and Carole McGranahan, 'Rethinking Pseudonyms in Ethnography: An Introduction', Americanethnologist.org (accessed 1 Oct. 2023).

[39] Tom Griffiths, *The Art of Time Travel: Historians and their Craft* (Carlton, Victoria, 2016), 163.

[40] This includes Family Search; Find my Past; Ancestry.com; Newspapers.com; the 1901 and 1911 Irish census; and Irish Civil Records.

[41] Tanya Evans, 'Secrets and Lies: The Radical Potential of Family History', *History Workshop Journal*, 71 (2011), 49.

[42] Laite, 'The Marginal and the Monstrous'. For similar reflections on the potential of the digital turn, see Tom Hulme, 'Queering Family History and the Lives of Irish Men before Gay Liberation', *History of the Family*, 29 (1), 62–83.

[43] Bengry, 'Difficult Stories and Ethical Dilemmas'.

[44] Daniel Grey, '"Monstrous and Indefensible"? Newspaper Accounts of Sexual Assaults on Children in Nineteenth-Century England and Wales', in *Women's Criminality in Europe, 1600–1914*, ed. Manon van der Heijden, Marion Pluskota and Sanne Muurling (Cambridge, 2020), 191 n. 9.

Lizzie Halliday, for example, was the first woman to be sentenced to death in the US by the electric chair. She had her own Wikipedia page before the Bad Bridget project came into being.[45] But just because information is already in the public domain does not mean that it should not be handled sensitively.

The subject's consent

Anonymisation, which includes pseudonymisation or the use of initials or numbers, has come to be expected in certain fields. Historians commonly anonymise twentieth-century victims of sexual assault, or victims or survivors of historic institutional abuse.[46] Clíona Rattigan anonymised defendants in her study of twentieth-century infant murder and concealment of birth, 'given the sensitive nature of such material'.[47] Oral historians too often anonymise participants, particularly in relation to sensitive issues where confidentiality is important. For instance, Laura Kelly assigned pseudonyms to interviewees in her study of contraception in twentieth-century Republic of Ireland, unless they had requested otherwise, and changed the name of partners, relatives or other bystanders who happened to be mentioned in interviews.[48] Good practice guides advise that interviewees should be permitted to view their transcripts post-interview and, depending on the project, to remove any details that they wish.[49] But what happens when the individuals upon whom the research is based are dead? As Jessica Meyer and Alexia Moncrieff note, the deaths of subjects 'leave them unable to provide informed, un-coerced consent' to inclusion in a historical study.[50] These 'historical subjects cannot give consent from beyond the grave'.[51]

---

[45] Lizzie Halliday Wikipedia entry, http://en.wikipedia.org/wiki/Lizzie_Halliday (accessed 23 Oct. 2023).

[46] See, for example, Leanne McCormick, Sean O'Connell, Olivia Dee and John Privilege, *Report into Mother and Baby Homes and Magdalene Laundries in Northern Ireland, 1922–1990* (Belfast, 2021), 12–13; Olivia Dee, 'Navigating Cultures of Silence with Survivors of Northern Irish Mother and Baby Institutions', *Oral History*, 51 (2023), 81–91; Lindsey Earner-Byrne, 'The Rape of Mary M.: A Microhistory of Sexual Violence and Moral Redemption in 1920s Ireland', *Journal of the History of Sexuality*, 24 (2015), 75–98.

[47] Rattigan used initials for individuals mentioned in sources held at the Public Record Office of Northern Ireland, which was an archival requirement because the records were closed, and first names and initials of surnames for defendants tried on the other side of the Irish border whose case files are in the National Archives of Ireland and are open to the public. See Clíona Rattigan, *'What else could I do?' Single Mothers and Infanticide, Ireland 1900–1950* (Dublin, 2012), 28.

[48] Laura Kelly, *Contraception and Modern Ireland: A Social history, c.1922–92* (Cambridge, 2022), 15.

[49] The guidelines devised by the Oral History Network Ireland, for example, note: 'it is good practice to return a copy of the interview to the interviewee for their own use … it might also be required if an interviewee has requested an opportunity to review the content'. See Oral History Network Ireland Practical Guidelines, https://oralhistorynetworkireland.ie/practical-guidelines (accessed 23 Oct. 2023). See also James Rowlands, 'Interviewee Transcript Review as a Tool to Improve Data Quality and Participant Confidence in Sensitive Research', *International Journal of Qualitative Methods*, 20 (2021), 1–11.

[50] Meyer and Moncrieff, 'Family not to be Informed?', 69.

[51] *Ibid.*, 80–1.

Julia Laite has reflected on the issue of visibility with regard to deceased individuals:

> Perhaps we can assume that a person who has published their own writing, especially writing about their life, wants to be remembered, but can we make the same assumption for the legions of the unpublished dead: those who, because they were legally compelled to do so, had their marriage registered or their sea voyage surveilled; those whose criminal records were, as far as they knew, to be kept tucked away in a police station drawer; those whose names were briefly mentioned in newspapers that – they thought – became the next day's kindling? Can we assume that these people, ripped from the dark ever-working chaos of the past and entered onto genealogical and historical databases, want to be there?[52]

None of the girls and women in our study have agreed to be named or included in our research and yet we have done so anyway. We also base our research on sources to which they may not have had access, or sources that were created about them rather than by them.[53] This could be potentially problematic because it obviously shapes our perception of the girls and women in our research, who have not had any say in how they have been presented. For instance, staff at the Massachusetts Reformatory for Women described Irish-born Mary O'Malley, imprisoned in 1914 for nightwalking, as: 'Courteous, [a] splendid helper; has given no trouble in any way.'[54] The official who interviewed her fellow countrywoman Mary Sweeney in Massachusetts in May 1917 was far more critical of the Irish woman in front of her, writing:

> Several times during [the] interview she became excited, raised her voice, and apparently considered the advisability of making a general rumpus but each time decided against it and quieted down. Is a powerful woman. It was evident she wished to make a good impression and to appear very quiet, mild, and much wronged by a charge against her chastity. Several times tried to squeeze out a few tears in speaking of disgrace brought upon family by her alcoholic habit, but insincere and without desire to be temperate.[55]

The records on which our research is based were largely generated when an Irish-born woman encountered a legal authority, implying (erroneously or not) illegal or deviant behaviour. In his study of focused queer histories, Tom

---

[52] Laite, 'The Emmet's Inch', 979.

[53] For discussion of subjects' concerns about what was written about them, see Mark Peel, *Miss Culter and the Case of the Resurrected Horse: Social Work and the Story of Poverty in America, Australia, and Britain* (Chicago & London, 2012), 15–16.

[54] Case file of Mary O'Malley (Massachusetts Archives, Massachusetts Reformatory for Women, Inmate case files, HS9.06/series 515, #10267).

[55] Case file of Mary Sweeney (Massachusetts Archives, Massachusetts Reformatory for Women, Inmate case files, HS9.06/series 515, #10948).

Hulme has likewise reflected on the difficulty of using legal records whereby we 'risk defining queer men solely by their sexual behaviour, not unlike the pathologizing psychiatrists of the past, even if we can claim more compassionate objectives'.[56] He argues that 'the dead cannot decide whether they want to be reborn as a queer hero today'.[57] In the same way, the dead cannot agree to inclusion in a research project entitled Bad Bridget, and all that that name might imply.

Although modern concepts of data protection and consent were not a feature of the nineteenth and early twentieth centuries, the question remains whether the Irish-born girls and women would have wanted their stories and experiences told. Some of the individuals identified in the course of our research sought to conceal their criminal histories from their relatives and friends. 'My poor mother's heart would be broke if she knew', Mary Good said of her sister's work in Boston's sex industry.[58] Their mother was at home in Ireland, evidently unaware of how her daughter was earning a living. According to a prison clerk who documented Catherine Lynch's admission to prison for larceny in Massachusetts in 1900, she 'will not give her peoples names. Does not want to disgrace them.'[59] Lynch and her husband had left Ireland for New York around twenty years earlier.[60] It is not lost on us that we expose such secrets as part of our research.

And this is, of course, a one-way gaze, a one-way exposure of secrets. Laite notes of Lydia Harvey, about whom she has written: 'I can scrutinize her, know very intimate details about her life, and she can never do the same for me, no matter how much of myself I pour into investigating her.'[61] In a way, it can thus feel exploitative to use these cases. In writing or talking about these girls and women, are we also exploiting them, a twenty-first-century echo of the way in which some were exploited in their own lives? We edit their life stories to fit our word count or our arguments, using one individual life history as if it tells all of them. We employ individual stories for entertainment, sometimes utilising our Bad Bridget social media account to showcase some, often humorous, examples. We look for light-hearted cases or stories of defiant women when the heart-breaking cases get too heavy.

As professional historians, we also benefit from this exploitation. Laite also recognises this, observing that historians 'commodify individual lives. We use them to "tell some other kind of tale" in books and articles that feed into our academic appointments, our promotions, and, if we are lucky, our publishing revenue.'[62] But while these issues might be most frequently discussed in relation to modern crime history, in reality they are not unique to the study of criminality nor the modern period. The individuals named in the Bad

---

[56] See Hulme, 'Queering Family History', 63.

[57] *Ibid*, 66.

[58] Farrell and McCormick, *Bad Bridget*, 8.

[59] Entry for Catherine Lynch, 11 May 1900 (Massachusetts Archives, Massachusetts Reformatory Prison for Women, Inmate registers, HS9.06/series 824).

[60] *Ibid*.

[61] Laite, 'The Emmet's Inch', 978.

[62] *Ibid*.

Bridget project are deceased and thus cannot consent to inclusion, but this is not unusual in history practice. Bengry explains: 'As historians we're already using all kinds of records that the people named in them certainly would have wanted nothing more than to see them destroyed.'[63] Political, social, cultural and other historians regularly use sources such as private diaries and journals, family papers, letters and photographs that were never intended for public consumption or dissemination. Likewise, the way historians benefit personally or professionally by writing about the hardship of people in the past is common to many areas of historical research.

The large number of historic individuals in our Bad Bridget project means that it encompasses diverse personalities. While some of the women mentioned earlier expressed shame at their predicaments, others seem to have relished the public platform that they were given in court and enjoyed light-hearted exchanges with those present. 'You here again?' the presiding judge asked Maggie Smith when she appeared before him at Washington Place Police Court in New York in 1876, evidently recognising the Irish woman. She claimed that her drinking was medicinal, insisting, when the judge asked her to sign the abstinence pledge: 'I can't, your Honor, I've got the asthma, and must drink.' When he observed that she was 'a dissolute woman', Smith retorted: 'No, your Honor ... I'm an Irish woman.' 'Well, you're a woman, anyway', the judge surmised, probably in an attempt to conclude the exchange. 'No, I aint ... I'm a girl, twenty-seven years old', Maggie Smith replied, seemingly wanting to have the last word.[64]

Laura Nys has argued that 'anonymising individuals confined in disciplinary institutions perpetuates the idea that contact with such institutions was – and still is – shameful'.[65] It is clear that for reasons of poverty, homelessness, ill-health or otherwise, some Irish women who came before the courts viewed a prison sentence as their desired outcome. When sentenced to twenty-nine days for drunkenness in New York in July 1885, for example, Ann Kelly thanked the judge. She was evidently happy to return to the prison that she had left only a few weeks earlier, and thus 'with a smile on her face she marched back to the pen'.[66] Another Irish-born suspect, Ann Jane Fox, blessed the magistrate who sent her to prison for the same offence in Toronto in 1890.[67] As these courtroom examples indicate, assigning shame to women who were charged or convicted of criminal behaviour through blanket anonymisation would obviously be problematic when they seem to have experienced or expressed no such shame themselves. Given the subject matter of the Bad Bridget project, assigning false names would also reproduce nineteenth- and early twentieth-century notions that shame should be associated with experiences such as pregnancies or births outside marriage,

---

[63] Bengry, 'Difficult Stories and Ethical Dilemmas'.
[64] *New York Times*, 5 June 1876.
[65] Nys, 'I am F. B.', 432.
[66] *Brooklyn Daily Eagle*, 21 July 1885.
[67] *Toronto Globe and Mail*, 7 Jan. 1890.

poverty, or sexual or physical assaults.[68] Not to use real names, therefore, would seem to make us complicit in this shaming.

Some of the women and men in positions of power whom we encountered in our research behaved in ways that might seem inappropriate today, even though their behaviour was not illegal then or now. Charity or child protection workers, for instance, made decisions to fragment families or deliberately to sever parental and sibling bonds. Judges, policemen and other legal authorities likewise made choices to arrest or convict, informed by factors that can seem incomprehensible today. Our evidence also reveals that families too disowned or ignored daughters or sisters in need, which might seem unsympathetic given their circumstances.[69] Concealing the names of some individuals in the past due to concerns about shame or posthumous memory but not the identities of others could thus be seen as inconsistent. It would require us to make judgements about the type of behaviour that might be classified as problematic today, adding to the historian's role an uncomfortable, moralising element.

Anonymisation is also sometimes presented as a means to maintain a dead person's 'dignity'. But the notion that dignity is assigned when we remove individuals' names is not straightforward. Is it not disrespectful to analyse the life of an individual, to take ideas from them, to quote what they said or what someone else said about them, and then not even to credit or acknowledge their input enough to identify them by name?[70] Likewise, assigning a fictious name could be perceived as disrespectful in a historic Irish context where forenames were often passed down through generations. In her discussion of historians' discomfort at using the records of deceased historical subjects, Sarah Fox observes: 'Empathetic approaches to history ... go some way to allay historians' concerns about the ethics of using personal documents.'[71] Maintaining real names for deceased subjects, where the archival records and guidance allow, could thus be interpreted as a facet of an empathetic approach to history practice.

The audience response

The nineteenth-century annual reports of the Association for the Protection of Roman Catholic Children in Boston deliberately excluded the surnames of individuals aided, 'lest the children, when grown up, might be brought to unmerited shame by the revelation of the misconduct of their parents'.[72] It could be

---

[68] Similar concerns have been expressed in relation to queer history. Tom Hulme, for instance, has chosen to use real names in his analysis of men brought to court on charges of so-called 'gross indecency', coupled sometimes with dates of birth and death, address, name of school and names of family members (Tom Hulme, 'Queer Belfast during the First World War: Masculinity and Same-Sex Desire in the Irish City', *Irish Historical Studies*, 45 (2021), 239–61).

[69] See for example, Farrell and McCormick, *Bad Bridget*, 221–3.

[70] Erica Weiss 'Pseudonyms as Anti-Citation', https://americanethnologist.org/online-content/collections/rethinking-pseudonyms-in-ethnography/pseudonyms-as-anti-citation/ (accessed 23 Oct. 2023).

[71] Fox, 'Archival Intimacies', 261.

[72] *Annual report of the Association for the Protection of Roman Catholic Children, in Boston, from Jan. 1, 1865, to Jan. 1, 1866* (Boston, 1866), 5.

argued that 'although the dead feel no shame, their still living descendants can'.[73] These living descendants can constitute in part the audience of historical research. Barry Godfrey, Tim Hitchcock and Robert Shoemaker have explained that they did not anonymise in the Digital Panopticon because the project methodology is record linkage, which by its very nature requires names and biographical details to be available to users. In reference to descendants discovering information about the criminal pasts of relatives, they argue that 'if you engage in historical research, you must be prepared for whatever information you encounter'.[74] The democratisation of historical knowledge through the digitisation of records facilitates such discoveries.[75]

The relatively small pool of forenames used in Ireland at this time, and the commonality of certain surnames, probably prevents some of our audience recognising their own ancestors in our Bad Bridget outputs. For example, of the 6,482 names of Irish girls and women that we extracted from Boston House of Correction registers dating from 1882 to 1915, 1,660 (25.61 per cent) are Marys, 680 are Margarets or Maggies (10.49 per cent) and 633 (9.77 per cent) are Catherines/Katherines (or derivatives such as Kate, Cassie, Kitty, or Katie).[76] This means that at least 45.87 per cent of the forenames extracted from the institution's registers are one of three names. The names Ann/Anne, Annie and Anna were similarly common among the Irish girls and women admitted to the Boston House of Correction between 1882 and 1915, with 702 (10.83 per cent) listed, but some of these might derive from Hannah (of which there are 121), Johanna (of which there are 42) or Rosanna (of which 23 have been taken from the registers).[77] We also see repetition in surnames among Irish-born girls and women in this institution. The surname Murphy occurs 151 times and Kelly/Kelley/O'Kelly 121 times. In many (if not most) cases, a descendant would thus probably need to know some details of their ancestor's migratory history in order to connect them with any degree of confidence to the stories told in Bad Bridget outputs.

The commonality of Irish names at this time hindered our efforts to trace some individuals, but other girls and women proved more visible. As we followed some Irish-born girls and women through civil records or census returns, it was not unusual for us to come across the names of their descendants. We generally shied away from including in our monograph identifiable data on the generations that followed, where they were not involved in the

---

[73] Meyer and Moncrieff, 'Family not to be Informed?', 69.

[74] Barry Godfrey, Tim Hitchcock, and Robert Shoemaker, 'The Ethics of Digital Data on Convict Lives', https://www.digitalpanopticon.org/Ethics_and_Digital_History (accessed 23 Sept. 2023).

[75] Evans, 'Secrets and Lies', 49–73.

[76] These figures include the same women more than once if they were readmitted to the institution. Other names extracted from these Boston House of Correction records, such as Maria, Minnie, Mazie, Madge, Mae and Maud, may derive from Mary or Margaret but are not included in these figures.

[77] Other common names include Ellen (which appeared 318 times, with an additional 23 entries for Helen) and Bridget (316).

crime. We also sometimes excluded information relating to Irish women in the years after their encounters with the law, such as precise details on marriages (including name of spouse in some instances), or place or date of death. Such details, although discoverable through genealogical and other records, were not directly relevant to our research because, in our outputs to date, it has not been our intention to produce full biographies of historic individuals.

It is also problematic to assume that living descendants would be entirely aghast at uncovering information relating to an ancestor who was accused or convicted of a crime. The example that opens this article is a case in point. Genealogical, self-discovery programmes such as the celebrity-focused *Who Do You Think You Are?*, which first aired on BBC in 2004, have popularised having ancestors with unusual pasts.[78] Claire Lynch describes it as 'quite remarkable' that historical documents on *Who Do You Think You Are?*, like 'bigamous marriage certificates, or birth certificates proving illegitimacy, which would once have been destroyed in shame, are now brandished as a treasure, breaking the seal of privacy that would have once prevented the present from intruding on the intimate secrets of the past'.[79] Australia too has seen a growing fascination with convict ancestors, a sharp remove from the 'collective amnesia' of the 1920s and 1930s.[80] In her study of family history in Canada, Britain and Australia, Tanya Evans highlights generational differences, with younger generations wanting to 'share secrets openly to discourage shame' in response to discoveries such as criminality, homosexuality and sexual relationships outside marriage.[81] Our intention is not to expose crimes about which descendants did not already know, but rather to provide a history of Irish girls' and women's lived experiences abroad, through the use of contextualised illustrative individual histories. It is likely, however, that some Bad Bridget ancestors are more palatable than others.

It could be argued that real names would matter less in publications generated specifically for an academic audience than for a non-academic audience. Academics would presumably be reading for the context, analysis and argument rather than the specific histories of individuals. Outputs from the Bad Bridget project to date, however, have been largely public facing and the exhibition, podcast and book have a non-academic audience in mind. Referring to individuals in these outputs by their initials would be confusing (especially due to recurring initials) and their stories could prove difficult to follow, particularly in some of the more complicated cases involving several individuals. Fictional names could also prove problematic. In 2021, anthropologist Carole McGranahan queried the expected use of pseudonyms in anthropological outputs:

[78] Claire Lynch, 'Who Do You Think You Are? Intimate Pasts Made Public'. *Biography*, 34 (2011), 108–18.

[79] *Ibid.*, 115.

[80] Ashley Barnwell, 'Convict Shame to Convict Chic: Intergenerational Memory and Family Histories', *Memory Studies*, 12 (2019), 405.

[81] Tanya Evans, *Family History, Historical Consciousness and Citizenship: A New Social History* (London, 2023), 70.

scholars often presume the reader is another academic trained in similar conventions of method, theory, and ethics. But this is not always the case. Readers of our scholarship are not only other ethnographers. They are also scholars from other disciplines, community members, professionals, journalists, and interested people anywhere in the world. Ethnographers often take for granted the use of pseudonyms; our readers do not. Instead, for some, the use of real names is critical to the ethical production of knowledge. For such readers, pseudonyms disrupt expectations for truth and trust.[82]

It was important for us not to generate such distrust in outputs for our (predominantly non-academic) audience.[83]

Pseudonymisation would also sever the audience connection to a name. Some surnames are particular to or well known in a locality. Forenames too can be specific to certain areas; the name Delia, for example, is markedly evident among immigrants from the western seaboard counties of Clare, Galway and Mayo. The Census of Ireland, 1901, digitised and freely available on the National Archives of Ireland website, indicates that 69.64 per cent of the renumerated Delias were born in counties Clare (1,103), Galway (2,118) and Mayo (1,159).[84] In comparison, the census lists only 73 Delias born in County Dublin (including Dublin city) and 4 born in County Antrim (including Belfast), despite the fact that these two counties boasted the largest populations.[85] In an Irish context, some names also point to parents' religious or political backgrounds. The use of real names allows local or informed audiences to recognise these and other nuances. Assigning new names, which carry their own meanings and histories, could on the other hand cause confusion or erroneous assumptions about an individual's background.

Enabling readers, listeners and museum visitors to connect to historical stories on a personal level facilitates interest and engagement, increasing the relatability of the research and ensuring that the stories are not viewed as fiction. Visitor feedback on the Bad Bridget exhibition at the Ulster American Folk Park in Omagh, County Tyrone, evidences this. One reads:

> Catherine O'Donnell's story broke my heart. As a mother of two & as someone who had a miscarriage, I feel so sad for her trying to make a

---

[82] Carole McGranahan, 'The Truths of Anonymity: Ethnographic Credibility and the Problem with Pseudonyms', https://americanethnologist.org/online-content/collections/rethinking-pseudonyms-in-ethnography/the-truths-of-anonymity-ethnographic-credibility-and-the-problem-with-pseudonyms/ (accessed 1 Oct. 2023).

[83] In the National Museums NI Bad Bridget exhibition, writer Jan Carson wrote imagined monologues based on historical sources relating to six girls and women, which were voiced by actresses. Notices were added to each character totem to make clear that these were fictionalised accounts based on historical evidence.

[84] This includes eleven girls and women named Dellia (seven from Mayo and two from Galway), and one (Delia McCarthy) whose forename was written in the surname column of the census form. See www.census.nationalarchives.ie (accessed 20 Dec. 2023).

[85] *Irish Historical Statistics: Population, 1821-1971*, ed. W. E. Vaughan and A. J. Fitzpatrick (Dublin, 1978), 5–15.

life for herself and her baby only for it to die and then she gets charged with murdering it. It's heartbreaking. It really made me so sad for her.

Another described the exhibition as 'insightful of the experiences of my granny, great-granny & all the other women that endured it'. In the context of Irish women's migration to North America, this engagement has also resulted in audience members or readers making connections to the present, including on topics such as racism in the US, women's experiences or rights at home and abroad, and migration to the island of Ireland.

Conclusion

It would be difficult to produce social history outputs without including individual narratives. It would also be challenging for an academic historian to write history on a sensitive topic or one that involves the hardship or suffering of historic individuals without personally or professionally benefitting from it in some way through workplace promotion or otherwise. Yet avoiding this type of research would leave significant gaps in our understandings of the past, and with the sea of open access archives, avoidance seems redundant. We could lose the context that is vital to understanding these stories and their wider significance.

Nys argues against the use of real names in her research on juvenile reformatories in Belgium between 1890 and 1960 and instead opts for pseudonyms rather than initials to 'convey more humanness'. She asks: 'Would I violate the post-mortem privacy of my research subjects by naming them? I do not believe so. But there is no actual reason to use their real names, either.'[86] We see many reasons to use real names for our research on an earlier time period, for us as historians as well as for the individuals themselves. It enables us to adhere to archival requirements and disciplinary conventions by referencing our sources. It allows us to reclaim the histories of these forgotten Irish women, to complicate the popular narrative of Irish immigration to North America as one of rising up the social ranks from humble beginnings. Avoiding anonymisation and pseudonymisation means that we also avoid reproducing nineteenth- and early-twentieth-century notions of shame, or that we do not read shame into experiences where there was none. In this manner, we regard our use of real names as part of our empathetic and ethical approach to historical practice. The use of real names also enables those in the twenty-first century to connect more easily to the research and to the realities of life in nineteenth- and early twentieth-century Ireland and North America. And perhaps this is particularly important on an island where unwed motherhood was stigmatised until recent decades, sexuality was in some instances repressed, and where, in December 2023, four years after the decriminalisation of abortion in Northern Ireland, Amnesty International UK published a report outlining significant access issues.[87]

---

[86] Nys, 'I am F. B.', 437.

[87] Amnesty International UK, *Legal but not Local: Barriers to Accessing Abortion Services in Northern Ireland* (2023). Grainne Teggart, Northern Ireland Deputy Director of Amnesty International UK

In her study of 'small history', Laite observes:

> If we still want real people to cross the stages of our historical narratives, we must accept that this brings with it all sorts of tricks and problems. I certainly have not overcome these ethical, methodological, and theoretical issues in the history that I am trying to tell. I remain a trafficker in other people's stories.[88]

We have no one-size-fits-all solution to offer either. The choices each historian makes will depend on the nature of the project, the sources and archival requirements, the real or perceived sensitivities of the topic, their personal or professional views of ethical historical practice, and their audiences. For the Bad Bridget project our choices reflected our decisions around these issues.

Acknowledgements. We are grateful to the attendees of the Royal Historical Society lecture at the University of Hertfordshire for responses to our lecture on this subject, and to William Bainbridge, Leanne Calvert and Jennifer Evans for the invitation to present it in October 2023. We are also thankful to Evropi Chatzipanagiotidou, Tom Hulme and the anonymous reviewers for comments on this article.

Financial support. We wish to acknowledge AHRC funding, which facilitated the Bad Bridget research and for which we are most thankful.

---

described the situation: 'Four years on from decriminalisation of abortion in Northern Ireland, access is a right but not a reality for all who need it.' See amnestyinternational.org.uk/press-releases (accessed 20 Dec. 2023).
[88] Laite, 'The Emmet's Inch', 978.

Cite this article: Farrell E, McCormick L (2024). Naming and Shaming? Telling Bad Bridget® Stories. *Transactions of the Royal Historical Society* **2**, 413–432. https://doi.org/10.1017/S0080440124000021

Transactions of the RHS (2024), 2, 433–440
doi:10.1017/S0080440124000070

COMMENT

'Pity the poor independent scholar!': The Lament of a Latecomer Historian

John Sanders

Independent Scholar, Manchester, UK
Corresponding author: John Sanders; Email: mjpdk1@gmail.com

(Received 15 May 2024; revised 3 June 2024; accepted 10 June 2024;
first published online 14 October 2024)

Abstract

This commentary article explores some of the problems encountered by independent scholars seeking to get their work published in peer-reviewed journals and in particular the difficulties they face in accessing online resources. Though often hidden, these issues are nevertheless very real for aspiring historians and those who have returned late to the historical fold. The article acknowledges the efforts of a number of journals to encourage different voices, but highlights how the limitations of current licensing and Open Access arrangements hinders this ambition.

Keywords: independent scholar; online resources; open access; historical journals

The tributes that poured in after the death of Hilary Mantel in 2023 were unanimous in recognising her achievements as a historian as much as a crafter of elegant prose, which according to James Naughtie 'made history sing'. In the *Independent*'s words: 'She understood the nuances of history, power and politics better than many an academic historian.' For Diarmaid MacCulloch, emeritus professor at the University of Oxford, 'she changed the way we think about history' and 'explored the past for herself with a historian's eye and a storyteller's sensibility'.[1] Another esteemed writer of historical fiction, Bernard Cornwell, modestly categorises himself as 'a storyteller' rather than 'a historian'. However, his novels are firmly underpinned by a grasp of the historical detail and nuance of the different eras

---

[1] *Daily Telegraph*, 23 Sept. 2022; https://www.independent.co.uk/arts-entertainment/books/features/hilary-mantel-death-tribute-b2174010.html (accessed 29 May 2023); https://www.historyextra.com/period/21st-century/hilary-mantel-remembered-legacy/ (accessed 29 May 2023).

in which they are set.[2] Tellingly, in neither case, was 'historian' their day-job or the academy their occupational base.

A number of earlier scholars whose work has shaped mainstream historical discourse similarly boasted non-specialist or non-affiliated backgrounds. Before the Robbins expansion of higher education in the early 1960s, such career paths were commonplace. E. P. Thompson was still working as an adult educator at the time he first published *The Making of the English Working Class*. J. F. C. Harrison, eminent historian of Owenism, Chartism and working-class educative endeavours, likewise hailed from an extramural background. Eric Midwinter's early career combined being an inspirational visionary of (local authority) educational practice, a social policy analyst and the author of historical studies of social administration and law and order in early Victorian England. He later became a co-founder of the U3A.[3] Such polymathic trajectories were not uncommon. Countless others went on to pursue valuable careers outside the formal confines of academia, while retaining their enthusiasm for history and their ability to produce thoroughly researched contributions to its canon.

Despite the proliferation of opportunities opened up by the inexorable expansion of higher education, this tradition has persisted in subsequent years. A quick perusal of the potted biographies of contributors to collections of historical essays in fields such as labour history reveal just how many are school teachers, adult educators, civil servants, librarians, trade union officials or activists. As Katrina Navickas noted in 2011, many of the new histories of protest and collective action are predicated on regional or local studies.[4] These continue to flourish under the auspices of local heritage organisations, sustained through the enthusiasms of part-time researchers, who can afford to ignore the methodological controversies and the REF-orientated, paper-producing engines that, in part, drive the political economy of academia.[5]

Such scholars form just part of an army of analogue antiquarians, family history enthusiasts, digital detectorists, 'amateur' historians and re-enactors, who contribute so much to the store of historical knowledge and energy. The role of the non-affiliated specialist is often unrecognised or underrated. Yet, without the skill and enthusiasm of people such as Philippa Langley of the Richard III Society, the former monarch would still be liable for unpaid parking fines in Leicester.[6]

In my own field, it is hard not to be struck by the quality, variety and significance of historical work that has been produced outside the academic

---

[2] https://www.thebookseller.com/author-interviews/bernard-cornwell--im-often-asked-if-i-am-a-historian-and-i-say-no-i-am-a-storyteller-thats-my-job (accessed 29 May 2023).

[3] Jeremy Hardie, *Variety is the Spice of Life: The Worlds of Eric Midwinter* (2023). Midwinter is also a cricket historian and an expert on British comedy.

[4] Katrina Navickas, 'What happened to Class? New Histories of Labour and Collective Action in Britain', *Social History*, 36 (2011), 197.

[5] John P. O'Regan and John Gray, 'The Bureaucratic Distortion of Academic Work: A Transdisciplinary Analysis of the UK Research Excellence Framework in the Age of Neoliberalism', *Language and Intercultural Communication*, 18 (2018), 533–48.

[6] https://www.theguardian.com/uk-news/2013/dec/08/philippa-langley-richard-third-car-park (accessed 29 May 2023).

mainstream. For example, Alan Brooke's *Underground Histories* website provides a wealth of local knowledge and insights into the economic, political and social history of the Huddersfield area. Mark Crail's *Chartist Ancestors* website has similarly become a key reference point for students of Chartism.[7] There are plenty of other producers of historical research, writing and resources, generated beyond the 'ivory towers', whose work deserves to be celebrated.

It is important to acknowledge at this point that I have skin in this particular game. One of the unintended consequences of Covid pandemic and the ensuing lockdown was the opportunity to activate a long-held intention to revisit some of the historical research and writing that I did in the late 1970s and early 1980s, before and during the arrival of children and the need to get a 'proper job'! With some initial encouragement from Keith Laybourn and Matthew Roberts at the Society for the Study of Labour History, this re-engagement has so far borne fruit in the shape of four academic articles published in a variety of journals and an overarching book.[8]

This article reflects on some of the general issues raised by my experience as an independent scholar returning to the academic domain. It is simultaneously a plea for the contribution of non-affiliated researchers to be better recognised and a call for their endeavours to be facilitated by the removal of unnecessary barriers.

These obstacles come in different shapes and sizes. Some are scarcely visible, but they are very real nevertheless. The first are the barriers to accessing sources and resources. Initially these impediments do not appear too onerous or widespread. Public libraries and local authority archives services are welcoming and open to all. A sizeable chunk of the ground floor of Manchester Central Library, for example, is devoted to local studies. It provides access to specialist advice courtesy of the Manchester and Lancashire Family History Society and dedicated computers with free access to all the key family history websites including the coveted 1921 census. The National Archives in Kew proudly proclaims that it 'is now open to everyone'. Anyone can apply for a reader's ticket. The resources of the British Library are similarly available to all.[9]

However, as we approach the realm of higher education things get trickier. The problem is not so much in relation to the stewardship of repositories of

---

[7] https://undergroundhistories.wordpress.com/ (accessed 29 May 2023); https://www.chartistancestors.co.uk/ (accessed 29 May 2023).

[8] John Sanders, 'The Voice of the "Shoeless, Shirtless and Shameless": Community Radicalism in the West Riding, 1829 to 1839', *Northern History*, 58 (2021), 259–81; John Sanders, 'John Douthwaite and "John Powlett": Trades' Unionism and Conflict in Early 1830s Yorkshire', *Labour History Review*, 86 (2022), 8–17; John Sanders, 'Out of Obscurity: Local Leadership and Cultural Wealth in the Radical Communities of the West Riding Textile District, 1825–40', *History Workshop Journal*, 94 (2022), 1–23; John Sanders, 'Turncoats and Traitors, Rogues and Renegades: Reviewing Labour's Lost Leaders in Reform Era Yorkshire', *Social History*, 48 (2023), 426–51; John Sanders, *Workers of Their Own Emancipation: Working-Class Leadership and Organisation in the West Riding Textile District, 1829-1839* (2024).

[9] https://mlfhs.uk/research/getting-help/helpdesk (accessed 29 May 2023); https://www.nationalarchives.gov.uk/ (accessed 29 May 2023); https://www.bl.uk/help/how-to-get-a-reader-pass (accessed 29 May 2023).

precious primary sources. Many university-held special collections are available to all (in person or online) via simple booking procedures, or can be accessed via the purchase of a membership.[10] University stores of traditional secondary sources, literally stacks of books and journals, can also normally be accessed by 'readers', visiting in person and paying an annual membership fee. Such arrangements often include useful, if limited, borrowing rights.

Remote access, in contrast, is more problematic. This issue was particularly highlighted during the pandemic when restrictions applied to walk-in access, and in-person research was impossible. But the pre-existing position has remained fundamentally unchanged post-Covid: universities' ever-expanding store of e-resources (e-books, e-journals, digitalised theses, databases, images and illustrations) is basically not available to the independent scholar. Visitor access to these items is often restricted 'due to licensing restrictions' and requires personal attendance at limited walk-in facilities. The use of these precious resources, increasingly important now that many journals and some books are online only, is generally restricted to current students and staff. Even alumni, whose donations to support current students or future research are regularly solicited, are not included in the privileged recipients of online rights. For example, at the university where I did my PhD four decades ago, I enjoy fairly generous borrowing rights, but am not allowed to access the library's catalogue or digital resources online. Some of the latter are available to 'external readers', but only on-site via two very busy terminals.

Such exclusion perhaps mattered less a couple of generations ago when public libraries were in their pomp and purchased academic texts as well as general interest books. But decades of local government cuts and the undermining of the municipal infrastructure have closed off this route. Many of the secondary sources that underpin any original research are only now available online and in one location: university libraries. However, these have increasingly become sites of e-exclusion. The privatisation of knowledge, like that of public space, is often incremental and obscured behind a shiny new façade. If, as the *Poor Man's Guardian* proclaimed in the 1830s, 'knowledge is power', it is increasingly being hoarded by the already knowledge-rich.[11]

This barrier to scholarly access is hidden in plain sight and is seemingly accepted by all parties, including institutions that rely heavily on public funds and are professedly at the heart of their communities. Indeed, many boast extensive public engagement strategies and have invested heavily in the public domain in the last twenty years, showcasing their museums, art galleries and cultural resources. My own alma mater has not one but two professors of public history and provides an extensive programme of engaging public lectures. Its celebrated origin story, embedded in its logo, links it to the foundation of the local Mechanics' Institute ('Est. 1824') ostensibly created for the very sorts of people – workers, clerks, part-time students – in modern parlance

---

[10] https://forms.library.manchester.ac.uk/public/form/5ca60337f85e57c3bbc9e522 (accessed 29 May 2023); https://www.london.ac.uk/senate-house-library/membership/members-public (accessed 29 May 2023).

[11] https://www.britishnewspaperarchive.co.uk/titles/poor-mans-guardian (accessed 29 May 2023).

lifelong learners, who are effectively now barred by licensing agreements from using its e-resources. The Open University, for which I worked part-time for over thirty years, similarly does not allow former students or staff to access its online library facilities. Jennie Lee would be turning over in her grave.

These institutions are not isolated outliers. Similar restrictions apply throughout the sector. At the same time that most British universities pro-claim their credentials as inclusive institutions with strong commitments to access and widening participation, a key element of their bountiful intellectual store is subject to rationing. As in other elements in our polity, the balance between public good and private gain is out of kilter. The outcomes of aca-demic research funded directly or indirectly out of the public purse and con-ducted mainly by people employed by publicly funded HEIs are appropriated by publishing houses and other content providers and then sold back to the sector's libraries via licensing agreements, to the exclusion of the very people whose taxes have in part funded it. Or am I missing something?

So, in practice, the independent scholar is often forced to beg favours from fellow part-time historians, 'borrow' a login from a sympathetic insider and steal a march by maximising opportunities for 'free' online material. Non-tenured researchers quickly come to appreciate the joys of JSTOR, and to celebrate the authors and their institutions who have paid to allow their schol-arly products to be 'Open Access' (OA). But even here, there is an ironical sting in the tail, since the benefits of OA cannot later be enjoyed fully by 'independents' due the consequent financial burdens. Without access to institutional funding to bear the substantial charges involved, their eventual work is less likely be pub-lished OA, with all the implications that this entails for the visibility of their research and for future job prospects, if they aspire to an academic career.

In general, then, the scholarly existence of non-affiliated historians is always conditional and precarious, and often second-class. They are frequently obliged to proceed (to appropriate Jill Liddington and Jill Norris's phrase) with 'one hand tied behind [them]', without full access to the paraphernalia of academic scaf-folding to support their work.[12] Significantly, the first 'common reason' that the Historical Association's *History* journal's author guidelines cite for rejection of an article is that 'the original research has not been properly related to recent scholarship in the field'.[13] Access to secondary resources, particularly those available only online, increasingly matters in relation to placement. For even when the independent scholar has overcome these access restrictions, their pro-blems are not over. The trials of placement and publication await.

Not all independent researchers wish to 'go the academic route' and seek to publish their work in a peer-reviewed journal. Other avenues are available: whether through local history or heritage organisations, more generalist pub-lications, or self-publishing online or in print. For those who do seek to have their work considered for publication in an academic journal, however, the

---

[12] Jill Liddington and Jill Norris, *One Hand Tied Behind Us: The Rise of the Women's Suffrage Movement* (1978).

[13] https://onlinelibrary.wiley.com/page/journal/1468229x/homepage/forauthors.html (accessed 29 May 2023).

prospect can be daunting. Processes that may seem normal, rational and sensible to insiders can sometimes feel off-putting and occasionally a bit bizarre to newcomers and outsiders.

Before addressing some of the possible problems posed by the current publication practices it is important to acknowledge the many positives. I have nothing but praise for the editors and technical staff of the various journals that I have dealt with as an independent scholar. They have been universally supportive, professional and thorough. Similarly, the double-blind peer-review system worked well. The feedback from referees was consistently thoughtful and insightful, rigorous and fair. Publication would also have not been possible without the support and openness of fellow independent, non-affiliated scholars, who have been, without exception, supportive and generous in sharing their time and knowledge. Getting to the submission stage, however, is far from straightforward.

First of all, find a suitable journal. Not an easy task given the proliferation of specialist titles and academic interest groups during the last decades. It is necessary to understand the different remits and target audiences of the *Labour History Review* as opposed to *Labour History: A Journal of Labour and Social History*; and to appreciate that *Social History* and the *Journal of Social History* are distinct publications. In the end the temptation is to go with what you know or remember from previous flirtations with the academy or to seek the advice of 'friends in the trade'. But what if you are completely new to this process?

Journals' mission statements or 'Author Guidelines' can provide valuable insights, and sometimes unwitting testimony as to their underpinning cultural assumptions. One eminent journal, for example, claims that 'The best contemporary scholarship is represented' in its pages. But how does it know: since it seemingly only encourages contributions from 'early career scholars making a distinguished debut' and 'historians of established reputation'?[14]

In contrast other journals are actively seeking to encourage new voices and wider representation in their contributors. For example, a similarly esteemed publication actively solicits 'submissions from younger scholars and seeks to engage constructively and positively with new authors' and to broaden its range of article formats and subject areas.[15] Another aims to host a 'range of accessible research-driven features written by academic researchers from all stages of career and study, archivists, and practitioners'.[16] Other titles, such as the *History Workshop Journal*, have always had a tradition of history from the bottom up.

Most journals, whatever their origins, now profess open and egalitarian principles. However, their practices, while not deliberately designed to be off-putting or restrictive, are not always totally supportive of such ambitions. This can be illustrated by looking at submission processes: for having found

---

[14] https://www.cambridge.org/core/journals/historical-journal/information/about-this-journal (accessed 29 May 2023).

[15] https://royalhistsoc.org/publications/transactions/ (accessed 29 May 2023).

[16] https://historyjournal.org.uk/about/ (accessed 29 May 2023).

a possible home for a proposed piece, it is then necessary to negotiate the particular (some might even say peculiar) requirements of the selected journal. These might include: word length (which often varies by several thousand words between similar journals), citation styles (footnotes or endnotes), formatting conventions (subheadings or no subheadings, indented paragraphs for all but the opening paragraph of a section) and referencing practices (which of the myriad of possible systems the journal has chosen to use).

The comprehensive style guides that enshrine these minute variations can be invaluable, but they can equally be daunting. Texts that clarify the use of en-dashes rather than hyphens (not forgetting the role of em-dashes), are illuminating, but also serve to emphasise to an academic newcomer that the (written) past is indeed a foreign country. One style guide, for example, advises that roman type should be used:

> for the following abbreviations: cf., ch. (plural chs.), col. (cols.), ed., edn, f. (ff.), fo. (fos.), i.e. (in footnotes and square bracketed text within quotations only; otherwise 'that is' in full), l. (ll.), m. (mm.), MS (MSS), p. (pp.), r. (recto), s.v. (sub voce/verbo), v. (verso/versus); seq. should not be used; 'for example' should always be in full[17]

The level of detail is useful, but simultaneously off-putting.

When I was a part-time Open University tutor over a decade ago I wrote about the proliferation of referencing, 'the pernicious bindweed of academia', and the way that an obsession with the minutiae of referencing systems can potentially be used to frustrate and exclude aspiring students. 'In this reading an excessive emphasis on the scholarly apparatus (particularly as a means of avoiding the accusation of plagiarism) has become a way of preserving mystique and "otherness" – a secret language for the initiated few.' Indeed, 'Far from connecting individual students to the wider academic community it potentially alienates many, particularly those without an HE heritage. It is another thing to get wrong and feel stupid or inadequate about.'[18]

Stylistic conventions and referencing systems potentially play a similar role for aspiring researchers. Some journals recommend citing authors' and editors' surnames in the form in which they appear in the work cited; others prefer a more standardised approach. Some require 'p.' or 'pp.' for page references; others do not. Some accept '*Ibid.*'; others reject it. Some require page references for citations of newspapers; others do not. The list of minor variations is endless. What is sometimes proclaimed as academic rigour can sometimes appear to be a façade behind which to protect the mystery of the trade.

The importance of accuracy, clarity and the checkability of references is not in doubt. But the rationale for some of these minor differences has never been adequately explained. The nuances and variations between different journals

---

[17] https://pastandpresent.org.uk/wp-content/uploads/2019/03/PP-Style-Guide-19_3_19.pdf (accessed 29 May 2023).

[18] John Sanders, 'Horray for Harvard? The Fetish of Footnotes Revisited'. *Widening Participation and Lifelong Learning*, 12 (2010), 48.

(even those in the same stable) bear comparison with the customs tariffs and duties of the Holy Roman Empire. When you cross the border from one journal to another (after the common and salutary experience of rejection) there is always a price to pay in terms of time to reconfigure the submission. It may be good for the soul, but is it really necessary? This is not to argue that scholars should not be meticulous, but the frontier between fastidious and farcical is perhaps too often breached.

We are consistently told that history is for everyone and academic institutions rightly celebrate their star historians and their broader contributions to the public realm. But this beneficence is very much on their terms. Many universities have hundreds of aspiring researchers on their doorstep who are unable to access resources that they, through their taxes, have partly funded.

While care is needed when dealing with collections of precious and delicate records in their stewardship, the same practical constraints do not apply to the vast store of secondary resources and digital material that university libraries hold. This is not to advocate an unregulated free for all. Rather it is suggested that current policies and licensing agreements require a reappraisal and that the balance between public good and private gain needs to be recalibrated. Like the obstacles placed before ramblers seeking to access the countryside nearly a century ago, the barriers faced by aspiring researchers seem unnecessary and fundamentally anti-democratic. The right to roam the country's historical records and secondary sources needs to be reasserted.

Similarly, while not advocating a standard-gauge submission template, some rationalisation and simplification of the plethora of house styles for academic journals would not go amiss. If publications are serious about their aspirations to encourage contributions from a more diverse range of authors, one starting point would be a review of their submission protocols and practices. More generally, publishers are keen to highlight the threats to UK research competitiveness from Open Access initiatives in science,[19] but are seemingly reluctant to acknowledge their privileged position in the chain of knowledge transmission. Equally, there is little recognition that not every potential contributor is going to be university-based or that a more complex scholarly multiverse is emerging though the spread of new technologies and recalibrations of work/life balance.

If not guaranteeing the advent of the next Mantel or Midwinter, a greater appreciation of the contribution and needs of non-affiliated scholars would encourage the emergence of more diverse authorial voices and new lines of research. This in turn would provide an accessible bridge to the mass of people whose enthusiasm and interest – whether listening to podcasts, subscribing to history magazines or researching their family tree – provide the lifeblood of the subject.

---

[19] https://www.publishers.org.uk/economic-impact-of-open-access-policy/ (accessed 3 July 2023).

Cite this article: Sanders J (2024). 'Pity the poor independent scholar!': The Lament of a Latecomer Historian. *Transactions of the Royal Historical Society* **2**, 433–440. https://doi.org/10.1017/S0080440124000070

Transactions of the RHS (2024), **2**, 441–470
doi:10.1017/S0080440124000094

COMMENT

Material and Digital Archives: The Case of Wills

Harry Smith 🆔 and Emily Vine 🆔

Department of Archaeology and History, University of Exeter, Exeter, UK
Corresponding author: Harry Smith; Email: h.j.smith2@exeter.ac.uk

(Received 23 July 2024; revised 24 July 2024; accepted 24 July 2024;
first published online 26 September 2024)

Abstract

The range of digital sources available to historians has expanded at an enormous rate over the last fifty years; this has enabled all kinds of innovative scholarship to flourish. However, this process has also shaped recent historical work in ways that have not been fully discussed or documented. This article considers how we might reconcile the digitisation of archival sources with their materiality, with a particular focus on the probate records of the Prerogative Court of Canterbury (PCC). The article first considers the variety of digital sources available to historians of the United Kingdom, highlighting the particular influence of genealogical companies in shaping what material is available, how it has been digitised and how those sources are accessed. Secondly, we examine the PCC wills' digitisation, what was gained and what was lost in that process, notably important material aspects of the wills. This article does not seek to champion archival research in opposition to digitally based scholarship; instead, we remind historians of the many ways in which the creation of sources shape their potential use, and call on historians to push for improvements in the United Kingdom's digital infrastructure to avoid these problems in future.

Keywords: Archives; Digitisation; Wills; England; Wales

This article explores one of the key questions faced by historical researchers in the twenty-first century – how to reconcile the digitisation of archives with their materiality – through a consideration of the digitisation of one of the largest and most-used archives of English and Welsh historical records: the probate records of the Prerogative Court of Canterbury (PCC). These records, specifically the registered copies of wills made between 1384

(a)

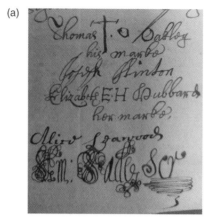

(b)

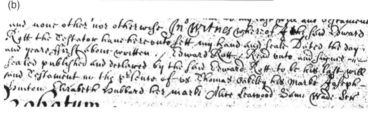

Figure 1. Signatures as they appear in the original will of Edward Rott PROB 10/980 (top) vs in the registered copy PROB 11/317/402 (bottom). (*Sources*: TNA, PROB 10/980; PROB 11/317/402. Photo © Emily Vine.)

and 1858, are used by thousands of historical researchers and genealogists every month, but the overwhelming majority of users access these records though their digital surrogates: the manuscripts are rarely viewed. Indeed, these digital surrogates are several steps removed from the original will drawn up by the scribe or scrivener, signed and sealed by witnesses and the testator, and from the sickbed in which the deceased had made their final wishes known. These digital surrogates reproduce not the original will containing the writing or marks of the scribe, testator or witnesses, but the microfilms of the registered copies subsequently made by the church court clerk.

Some of the issues we will explore in this article become apparent when illustrated by a visual example. Figure 1 compares excerpts from two versions of the will of Edward Rott, a blacksmith of the City of London who died in 1665. It shows the signatures and marks of the witnesses and scribe as they appear in the original will (PROB 10/980, top) and the digital surrogate of the registered copy (PROB 11/317/402, bottom).[1] The original copy contains the signatures and marks of several witnesses who were present when the will was made, including the elaborate autograph of the scrivener, Samuel Wade. The

---

[1] Original will of Edward Rott, The National Archives (TNA), PROB 10/980 and registered copy, TNA, PROB 11/317/402, d.1665.

registered copy was then made when the will was proved after Edward Rott's death. It was written out by a church court clerk, and of course does not replicate the signatures or marks of the witnesses, but neither does it replicate their formatting (the signatures are listed at the bottom of the original will, but appear as part of main text of the copy, separated by commas). The registered copy replicates the content but not the materiality of the original will, and the microfilm or digital surrogate replicates the content but not the materiality of the registered copy. In a climate where researchers increasingly rely on digital surrogates as a proxy for a physical document, as a means of catching a glimpse of the circumstances in which that document was drawn up, we need to be constantly mindful of the complex and centuries-old archival and reproduction histories that have led us to the electronic image on our screen. In the case of Edward Rott, this archival history means we lose any information about literacy and authorship we might have discerned from the individuals' handwriting, as well as evidence pertaining to the stylistic features of early modern wills and the work of the scrivener.

The issues surrounding access and use of wills are faced by all historians who make use of digital sources, so this article begins by surveying existing digitised resources pertaining to British and Irish history. It considers the accessibility of these resources and demonstrates how their temporal coverage largely maps onto the time periods most used by genealogists. It then considers the digitisation and materiality of the PCC's archive of registered will copies and shows how the decision to microfilm the registered copies, but not the original wills, has shaped the types of research that can be conducted. In doing so this article touches upon some important methodological issues facing historical research (broadly defined) including the benefits and limitations of digitisation, the influence of keyword searchable interfaces and the difficulties of replicating the materiality of these sources and their archives. One of its key arguments pertains to the significance of the context of the archive and the problems that arise when digital surrogates remove sources from that context. In concluding it offers some suggestions for best practice for researchers and for the future of digitisation projects.

The current state of digitised material

Over the last fifty years an ever-expanding amount of historical material has been digitised. Others have traced the history of this process, exploring how different institutional, commercial and intellectual factors have shaped what is available and in what format; here, we are concerned with what is available to historians today and how the characteristics of these online sources enable and limit the kind of historical writing that can be produced using them.[2] Our

---

[2] For useful accounts of the British case, see Tim Hitchcock, 'Digitising British History since 1980', *Making History*, Institute of Historical Research, https://archives.history.ac.uk/makinghistory/resources/articles/digitisation_of_history.html (accessed 7 May 2024); Adam Crymble, *Technology and the Historian: Transformations in the Digital Age* (Urbana, IL, 2021), 46–78.

fundamental argument is that, in most cases, users of these sources lack even the most basic information on how the resource was created. The move from the material to the digital is not simply a case of photographing records, or even transcribing them; rather digitisation is the whole process from the selection process, through imaging, storage of images, processing of images whether this involves transcription or not, formatting of resulting data, the creation of metadata and other documentation, and the distribution of the resulting material. Every stage of this process affects the resulting source and impacts how a user can utilise the material. All too often users do not know how the material in a digital collection was selected, what Optical Character Recognition (OCR) software was used, or how the output was checked. These factors and more can have profound effects on the nature of the resource and need to be fully considered by users.[3] Following on from this, we argue that access is not just about having permission to use a given resource; instead, as with non-digital sources, not knowing how and why a digital resource was created will lead the user astray.

Several previous papers have demonstrated how digitisation methods and storage practices can affect what kinds of historical work are possible. For example, Tim Hitchcock noted the problems with poor-quality OCR and obscure search algorithms have created substantial problems in using many digitised texts.[4] Michael Moss and Tim Gollins have drawn attention to the impact of often poorly understood algorithmic and machine processes on what is available digitally, especially when it comes to born-digital content, and urged archivists and historians to avoid a preoccupation with digitising as much as possible and to return to older archival processes of appraisal and reviewing what should and can be kept.[5] Several authors have noted the political aspects of digitisation, highlighting how choices in what material is selected and how it is digitised can create new inequalities and heighten pre-existing ones between the global north and south, and between different kinds of institutions and users.[6] In the British case, much discussion has revolved around the use of digitised newspapers, with many highlighting the opportunities they present, but recent work has shown just how difficult they are to use given the biases baked into them by the digitisation methods used and the

---

[3] OCR is the process by which images of text are converted into machine-readable text.

[4] Tim Hitchcock, 'Confronting the Digital: Or How Academic History Writing Lost the Plot', *Cultural and Social History*, 10 (2013), 9–23.

[5] Michael Moss and Tim J. Gollins, 'Our Digital Legacy: An Archival Perspective', *The Journal of Contemporary Archival Studies*, 4 (2017), article 3. Michael Moss drew particular attention to these issues in the context of state records, see Michael Moss, 'The Hutton Inquiry, the President of Nigeria and What the Butler Hoped to See', *English Historical Review*, 120 (2005), 577–92.

[6] Gerben Zaagsma, 'Digital History and the Politics of Digitization', *Digital Scholarship in the Humanities*, 38 (2023), 830–51; Joseph Nockels, Paul Gooding and Meliss Terras, 'Are Digital Humanities Platforms Facilitating Sufficient Diversity in Research? A Study of the Transkribus Scholarship Programme', *Digital Scholarship in the Humanities* (advance access, 2024); Ian Milligan, *The Transformation of Historical Research in the Digital Age* (Cambridge, 2022), 18–19; Alexandra Ortolja-Baird and Julianne Nyhan, 'Encoding the Haunting of an Object Catalogue: on the Potential of Digital Technologies to Perpetuate or Subvert the Silence and Bias of the Early Modern Archive', *Digital Scholarship in the Humanities*, 37 (2022), 844–67.

particular titles selected.[7] Other sources have recently started to receive similar consideration, notably newsreels, court papers, eighteenth-century and early modern published works.[8] Despite the varied subjects, this literature, in common with our paper, stresses the importance of understanding why and how digital materials are created.

While not disagreeing with these existing arguments, this article seeks to move on from debates over the benefits and drawbacks of digitisation. Instead, in this section, we survey existing digitised primary sources with a view to expanding our understanding of accessibility. Access is not simply a matter of whether or not a source is open to all or subscription based, it is also related to what can be done with that source. If material can be freely accessed by searching a source through a web application but cannot be downloaded in total then only certain kinds of research are possible. Similarly, if a source can only be downloaded in a particular file format, then the data are at least partially closed to those without the resources to process such material.

To examine this issue, we have attempted to identify all currently existing and available digital sources for the history of the United Kingdom and Ireland.[9] This is no simple task given the amount of digitisation which has happened over the last fifty years and it is likely that we have missed some resources and datasets. However, we believe we have covered most key collections and, at least, cover all types of digital resource available to scholars, even if not every example of a given type of source has been identified. Additionally, all sources discussed start their temporal coverage no later than the 1980s; partly to assist us in keeping a handle on the volume of material discussed, but also to ensure that the historical material examined is not overwhelmed by the sheer volume of data and texts produced and available online from the last thirty years. Our focus was on resources which provide historians with access to primary sources, so bibliographies and biographical sources,

[7] Adrian Bingham, 'The Digitization of Newspaper Archives: Opportunities and Challenges for Historians', *Twentieth Century British History*, 21 (2010), 225–31; Gioria Tolfo, Olivia Vane, Kaspar Beelen, Kasra Hosseini, Jon Lawrence, David Beavan and Katherine McDonough, 'Hunting for Treasure: Living with Machines and the British Library Newspaper Collection', in *Digitised Newspapers: A New Eldorado for Historians?*, ed. Estelle Bunout, Maud Ehrmann and Frédéric Clavert (Oldenburg, 2023), 25–46.

[8] Sam Rutherford, 'Researching and Teaching with British Newsreels', *Twentieth Century British History*, 32 (2021), 441–61; Stephen H. Gregg, *Old Books and Digital Publishing: Eighteenth-Century Collections Online* (Cambridge, 2020); Jonathan Blaney and Judith Siefring, 'A Culture of Non-citation: Assessing the Digital Impact of British History Online and the Early English Book Online Text Creation Partnership', *Digital Humanities Quarterly*, 11 (2017), https://digitalhumanities. org/dhq/vol/11/1/000282/000282.html; Sharon Howard, 'Bloody Code: Reflecting on a Decade of the Old Bailey Online and the Digital Futures of Our Criminal Past', *Law, Crime and History*, 5 (2015), 12–24.

[9] There are considerable numbers of sources which should theoretically be available but cannot be accessed because the website hosting them is now defunct. When searching for oral history collections this seems to be a particular problem. This survey was carried out in March and April 2024; since then, more material has become available. For example, between 22 April 2024 and 5 June 2024 Ancestry.co.uk has added 11 new datasets comprising 187,715,831 individual records related to the United Kingdom and Ireland.

such as the *Oxford Dictionary of National Biography* or the *Bibliography of British and Irish History*, were not included.

The resources discussed below were identified through several avenues. Firstly, university library lists of databases were consulted. No university library subscribes to all historical databases, so, secondly, all major commercial providers of historical data were surveyed.[10] This produced a list of 247 historical databases covering a range of aspects of British history. Information on the volume of pages digitised was not available for all these databases, but the 165 cases where we do know the volume of digital material amounted to just over 152 million pages. These sources are broad in topic and type of material available. Many of these resources provide access to digitised newspapers and periodicals. Some are personal archives, although mainly related to important politics figures, such as the papers of the Chamberlain family, or in some cases these are not personal archives but instead state papers organised by person rather than function, such as the Cecil Archives.[11] Others are thematic, collecting various archival and published material around a theme; thus, Adam Matthew has collections such as 'Gender: Identity and Social Change', or 'The Grand Tour'. British Online Archives offers many similar collections, such as 'The Industrial Revolution: Technological Innovation in the Textile Industry, 1672–1929' or 'Slavery, Exploitation and Trade in the West Indies, 1759–1832'. Such collections are somewhat different in nature from the archival or newspaper collections in that they offer a curated selection of material on a given topic rather than attempting to reproduce entire runs of a given publication or the entirety of a personal archive. They are often rather narrower in scope than their titles imply: the grandly titled 'Science and Marxism', for example, actually contains the papers of William Wainwright, the British communist activist and theorist of scientific socialism, an interesting resource but perhaps a smaller topic than its title implies.

Thirdly, there are an increasing number of open access historical resources, some deriving from projects funded by the Research Councils and other bodies, some comprising digitised versions of long-standing analogue primary sources and some arising from university or other libraries digitising their own material, such as the LSE's various digital collections.[12] We have identified 126 of these open resources, along with two others which are partially open: one (Queen Victoria's Journals) is free to UK residents and the other (JSTOR's Ireland Archive Collection) is free to further and higher education institutions.[13] These were identified through several avenues. Some were simply

---

[10] The following vendors were checked, not all of which provide databases fitting the criteria of starting pre-1980 and covering the United Kingdom: ALCS, Adam Matthew, Alexandra Street Press, Bloomsbury, Brepolis, Brill, British Online Archives, Cambridge University Press, Coherent Digital, Eastview, Ebsco, Elsevier, Gale, Heinonline, Irish Newspaper Archives, Iter, JISC, John's Hopkins Press, JSTOR, Liverpool University Press, Macmillan, North Waterloo Academic Press, Oxford University Press, Proquest, Readex, Sabinet, UK Press Online, Wiley, Yale University Press.

[11] Provided by Gale and Proquest respectively.

[12] https://lse-atom.arkivum.net/ (accessed 7 May 2024).

[13] http://www.queenvictoriasjournals.org/home.do and https://subscriptionsmanager.jisc.ac.uk/catalogue/1101 (both accessed 7 May 2024).

resources known to the authors.[14] Others were found using lists of historical resources available online, such as those provided by the Institute of Historical Research or the Bodleian Library.[15] Again, information on the number of pages available was not provided for all these resources, but the seventy-two where these data was available provided over 441 million pages. Nearly 400 million of these pages contained the data provided by three sources: FreeCen, FreeBMD and FreeReg, the volunteer-based, open access versions of the UK censuses, civil registration records and parish registers.[16] These open access resources are extremely varied in topic. Some are produced by the state and typically cover political topics, such as Historic Hansard. Others are the outputs of academic research projects and so cover all manner of areas from the Legacies of British Slavery, to the Pulter Project, to the Survey of Scottish Witchcraft.[17] Finally, others are the outputs of various other organisations such as the membership records of the Inns of Temple.

There is a considerable number of other resources that are available for free but that require registration to access them. The United Kingdom Data Service (UKDS) stores and provides access to a wide range of data on the history of the UK to researchers. There are three types of resources in the UKDS; first, databases in the ReShare repository, which are freely available to anyone. Secondly, safeguarded datasets that can be accessed by anyone but require the user to register with the UKDS. Thirdly, secure access datasets for which the user has to complete a specific request and, in some cases, undertake safe researcher training. In total, the UKDS holds 698 datasets relevant to British history as defined in this article. Of these, 136 are open access, 556 require you to register with the UKDS before downloading and six require more stringent special access licences. We have also included two other datasets which are held elsewhere but similarly require registration in order to access them: the Calum Maclean Project and Around 1968: Activism, Networks, Trajectories.[18] The total size of these databases is hard to judge, but will run to the hundreds of millions of records given the presence of large datasets covering census, civil registration and parish records.[19] Once again the range of historical topics covered by these records is substantial; however, these do tend to be more data heavy. Many are databases derived from historical resources, such as the British Business Census of Entrepreneurs, or the Digest of Welsh Historical Statistics; others are deposits of interviews and

---

[14] Indeed, the authors themselves have contributed to the creation of four of them.

[15] https://www.history.ac.uk/library-digital/collections/online-resources (accessed 25 April 2024); https://www.diigo.com/profile/hfloxford (accessed 25 April 2024).

[16] https://www.freeukgenealogy.org.uk/ (accessed 3 May 2024).

[17] https://www.ucl.ac.uk/lbs/ (accessed 19 April 2024); https://pulterproject.northwestern.edu/ (accessed 19 April 2024); https://witches.hca.ed.ac.uk/home/ (accessed 25 April 2024).

[18] https://www.calum-maclean-project.celtscot.ed.ac.uk/database-access/register-for-access/ and https://around1968.history.ox.ac.uk/ (both accessed 7 May 2024).

[19] The Integrated Census Microdata dataset, for example, is just one resource available from the UKDA but includes 183,470,912 individual records, see Kevin Schürer and Edward Higgs, *Integrated Census Microdata (I-CeM), 1851–1911* [data collection], UK Data Service (2023), SN: 7481, DOI: http://doi.org/10.5255/UKDA-SN-7481-2.

surveys which are now being increasingly used for historical research.[20] These resources, therefore, are similar to the open access ones in their breadth of coverage, but much narrower in the kind of material available, tending to take the form of machine-readable files ready to be processed by statistical software.

The remaining historical sources can be found through various genealogical websites. The expansion of these websites in the last few decades has been one of the main driving forces behind the digitisation of historical material. Of these websites, FamilySearch is mostly free, although you have to register an account to use it.[21] FamilySearch provides access to 231 different databases related to the United Kingdom and Ireland, totalling 876,835,233 records. Other genealogical websites require the user to pay subscription fees, but provide access to vast numbers of historical records. Ancestry has 1,921 datasets covering the United Kingdom and Ireland, containing a remarkable 3,398,576,084 records.[22] FindMyPast has fewer databases, but still provides 1,253 datasets to subscribers, totalling 1,919,888,010 records.[23] Finally, the Genealogist offers a smaller array of records, but has a number of notable differences, notably a set of historical mapping tools, as well as alternative transcriptions of the British censuses. They offer 1,195 datasets. Although it is not easy to discover how many records this dataset covers, it is likely to be in the hundreds of millions. These datasets are all focused on allowing people to trace their ancestors and so tend to have a different focus from many of the sources discussed above, most of which were designed either to provide a complete run of a particular source, whether *The Times* or Newton's personal papers, or were collections created to investigate a given topic, whether that is demographic transition, popular protest in medieval England or the history of the 1641 Irish Rebellion.[24] In contrast the collections on genealogical websites seek to gather as many names as possible; this purpose affects the kind of sources they digitise, the method of digitisation and the format in which the data are stored. Thus, they have a large preponderance of religious and state records, sources related to probate and land ownership, publications which list individuals, such as trade directories and organisation member lists, but relatively few personal archival records, little in the way of political sources and, where they have newspapers or periodicals, the point is not to provide an accurate transcription of such publications, but instead one that is good enough for names to be searched for in their contents. However, given their

---

[20] See 'Roundtable: Historians' Uses of Archived Material from Sociological Research', *Twentieth Century British History*, 33 (2022), 392–459.

[21] https://www.familysearch.org/en/united-kingdom/ (accessed 3 May 2024). Some of their documents can only be accessed through FamilySearch centres, see https://www.familysearch.org/en/centers/about (accessed 10 July 2024).

[22] https://www.ancestry.co.uk/ (accessed 22 April 2024).

[23] https://www.findmypast.co.uk/home (accessed 23 April 2024).

[24] See, respectively, Alice Reid, *Demographic and Socio-economic Data for Registration Sub-Districts of England and Wales, 1851-1911* [data collection] (2020), UK Data Service, SN: 853547, DOI: http://doi.org/10.5255/UKDA-SN-853547; Samuel Cohn, *Popular Protest in Late Medieval English Towns, 1196-1452* [data collection] (2012), UK Data Service, SN: 6979, DOI: http://doi.org/10.5255/UKDA-SN-6979-1; https://1641.tcd.ie/ (accessed 26 April 2024).

resources it is clear that they are happy to digitise all manner of sources and so Ancestry and FindMyPast have several intriguing datasets, which are not primarily of genealogical interest but instead add historical colour or serve to entice users, such as FindMyPast's 'Views of Ireland' database.[25] These points will be discussed below in relation to wills, a key resource for genealogists and academic historians, but those two constituencies have substantially different interests and desires in terms of access, searching, format and, most fundamentally, what is digitised – the whole will or just names and dates.

Taken together these subscription, registration and free historical resources provide scholars with access to billions of historical records. We have identified 5,675 historical databases and other resources that can be accessed online. They include a wide range of different kinds of material: untranscribed images of manuscript material, OCR'd newspapers, partially transcribed indexes to civil registration records, hand-transcribed personal correspondence and databases of millions of census records are just some of the different kinds of material available. In some cases, the original images can be consulted, in others they cannot, but in all cases at least part of the information from the original source is now reproduced in a digital format. We do not seek to ignore the differences between these resources; they have been created in diverse ways, are available in different formats, come with various access conditions and are used in different ways by varied audiences: academics, genealogists, archivists and other members of the public. Figure 2 gives some sense of the variety of material involved in these datasets and how the balance between different types changed over time.[26] However, we group them together here because despite these differences, there are important issues related to all digital resources which affect how any user utilises them. Issues around access, format, metadata and documentation fundamentally link the digital version to the materiality of the original sources and affect how academics and others can reliably use, and interpret others' use of, these digital resources.

Of the resources surveyed, 264 are entirely open source; 795 are free but require the user to register with the service providing them; and the remaining 4,616 are subscription based. These subscription ones are divided between the genealogical websites (4,369 datasets) where the usual method of access is through individual subscriptions and the remaining 247 where access is usually managed through institutional subscriptions.[27] The sheer size of the genealogical resources is such that they dominate the online historical environment

---

[25] Ancestry and FindMyPast's digitisation policies are interestingly discussed in Adam Kriesberg, 'The Future of Access to Public Records? Public-Private Partnerships in US State and Territorial Archives', *Archival Science*, 17 (2017), 5–25; it is not clear to what extent the practices discussed in this article apply to the United Kingdom or whether they are still current.

[26] Only resources with known date coverage have been included; before 1000 there are too few resources to be worth graphing.

[27] Ancestry offers educational institutions access to some of their resources through AncestryClassroom, https://ancestryclassroom.co.uk/k12/k12home (accessed 8 May 2024) and other institutions can subscribe to a program called AncestryLibrary for access to some of the Ancestry holdings. Similarly, FindMyPast offers a library subscription for institutions https://www.findmypast.co.uk/help/articles/360009035958-does-findmypast-offer-group-

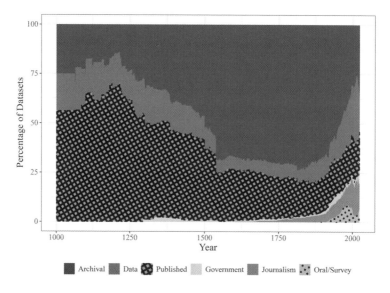

Figure 2. Databases surveyed by category of record, 1000–2024. (*Sources*: see text.)
Note: The categories necessarily cover rather disparate resources. Archival covers all non-published records not found in the other categories; Data contains all resources which provide tabulated or other data derived from sources; Published are all materials which have been published in one way or another including artworks and film, apart from newspapers and periodicals which are contained in Journalism; Oral/Survey includes all oral history archives and all outputs of surveys (whether conducted in person or not). In each year the total number of active databases is counted and the percentage available from each category is calculated. For example, for the year AD 1000 there are 17 active databases: 5 archival, 3 data and 9 published.

to an astonishing extent, providing access to vast amounts of material, but shaping access and coverage in particular ways. This point will be returned to below, but at the most simple level, therefore, access to many digitised historical resources is mediated by an individual's ability to afford personal subscriptions and whether or not they are a member of an body which offers institutional subscriptions. Furthermore, many of the free to access resources that require registration are easier to access with a university affiliation, particularly for the UKDS. Subscriptions are within reach of some, but far from all, and university membership is even more restricted.

We can take this point further. The three categories not only differ in how access is obtained, but also in terms of the material available. Much has been made of how digitised sources are not representative of the totality of the historical record, but instead are selected; particular kinds of sources and particular topics tend to be digitised and others are not.[28] Within digitised material, however, there are patterns in the type of document and time frame covered

---

subscriptions (accessed 8 May 2024). These are generally used by schools and libraries rather than universities.

[28] See references in notes 2–5 above.

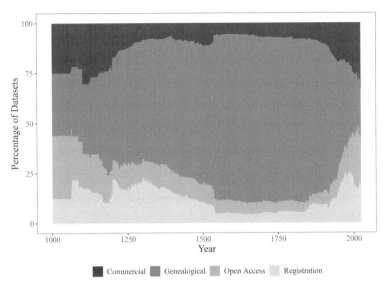

Figure 3. Types of database available by year, 1000–2024. (*Sources*: see text.)
Note: Genealogical covers sources accessible through the four family history websites discussed in the text:
Ancestry, FindMyPast, the Genealogist and FamilySearch; Commercial refers to any source provided by a commercial
body; Open Access and Registration are all products of academics, government, charities or private individuals.

that vary by access. As noted above, open access resources cover a more varied
set of material and topics than those available through subscriptions. This is
unsurprising given that the open sources tend to be the outputs of academic
projects coming from all areas of historical scholarship, whereas subscription
datasets are driven by commercial imperatives, hence focusing on genealogical
sources or material which aligns closely with historical curriculums, and by
how easy a source is to access and digitise. This also fundamentally affects
the time period covered by different kinds of resource and drives much of
the variation in the utility or otherwise of digital material to historians of different periods, as shown in Figure 3, a point of great importance that we will
return to in the next section. This shows that genealogical databases dominate
the available resources for the period 1500 to the late twentieth century, when
between half and three quarters of active databases in any given year are
accessible through the genealogical websites. This is the key period for genealogy in the United Kingdom and Ireland given the nature of the sources most
often used for such work: parish registers, civil registration material and the
census. Before and after that period the other kinds of resource become proportionately more important. Partly this reflects simply not wanting to compete with the genealogical websites, which have far greater resources available
for digitisation, and so other companies and academics focus elsewhere on
materials such as personal letters and archives, newspapers, other manuscript
sources, political papers and so on, which are of less import for genealogists
and so of lower priority for Ancestry, FamilySearch, FindMyPast and the

Genealogist. However, it is also driven by the lack of funds available for digitisation; it is difficult for academics to obtain funding solely for digitising resources, as opposed to digitisation as part of a wider research project, and this means that most large-scale digitisation is left to commercial companies.[29] This is only to consider the origins of these resources, however, not their use. As we will discuss below, sources provided by genealogical companies are often used for scholarship other than family history.

These points about access have been made by others before, in terms of the impact both on users and on archives.[30] However, the question of what history can be written with these digitised historical resources goes beyond a question of open access vs subscription schemes.[31] Not least because the amount of data and other sources available open access is so extensive, as shown above. Furthermore, it is frequently possible to negotiate access to material digitised by companies such as FindMyPast or Ancestry, even if such data often come with certain conditions and perhaps in a format which is designed primarily for genealogical users.[32] Some commercial companies allow users to access the underlying data from their resources through proprietary interfaces. For example, Proquest offer TDM Studio, a platform in which users can undertake various kinds of textual analysis on their digitised collections.[33] Where access to an entire dataset is not available it is also feasible to scrape data from genealogical websites for use in historical study, although there is some uncertainty over whether this is or is not allowed given the terms and conditions of such websites.[34] Alternatively, use is increasingly being made of datasets created

---

[29] Ruth Ahnert, Emma Griffin, Mia Ridge and Giorgia Tolfo, *Collaborative Historical Research in the Age of Big Data: Lessons from an Interdisciplinary Project* (Cambridge, 2023), 23–5.

[30] Barry Godfrey, 'Future Perspectives on Crime History as "Connected History"', *Crime, histoire et sociétés*, 21 (2017), 45–6; David Thomas and Michael Moss, 'The Commercialisation of Archives: The Impact of Online Family History Sites in the UK', in *Do Archives Have Value?*, ed. Michael Moss and David Thomas (2019), 141–66.

[31] The open vs closed issue is surveyed in the context of nineteenth-century sources by Ahnert *et al.*, *Collaborative Historical Research*, 25–32.

[32] For some examples of work where access to such records was granted see Neil Cummins, Morgan Kelly and Cormac Ó Gráda, 'Living Standards and Plague in London, 1560–1665', *Economic History Review*, 69 (2016), 3–34 (Ancestry's parish records); Richard Ward, 'State Authority and Convict Agency in the Paper Panopticon: The Recording of Convict Ages in Nineteenth-Century England and Australia', *Australian Historical Studies*, 52 (2021), 509–32 (Ancestry's Hulks registers and FindMyPast's Prison registers, see also https://www.digitalpanopticon.org/About_The_Project (accessed 9 May 2024)); Fabon Dzogant, Thomas Lansdall-Welfare, FindMyPast Newspaper Team and Nello Cristianini, 'Discovering Periodic Patterns in Historical News', PLoS ONE 11/11 (2016), https://doi.org/10.1371/journal.pone.0165736 (FindMyPast newspapers); Carry van Lieshout, Joe Day, Piero Montebruno and Robert J. Bennett, 'Extraction of data on Entrepreneurs from the 1871 Census to Supplement I-CeM', Working Paper 12, ESRC project ES/M010953, 'Drivers of Entrepreneurship and Small Businesses', https://doi.org/10.17863/CAM.27488 (The Genealogist census data).

[33] https://proquest.libguides.com/tdmstudio/home (accessed 20 March 2024).

[34] Jorge L Contreras, Kyle Schultz, Craig C. Teerlink, Tim Maness, Laurence J Meyer and Lisa A Cannon-Albright, 'Legal Terms of Use and Public Genealogy Websites', *Journal of Law and the Biosciences*, 7 (2020), 1–24; for an example of historical work that uses scraped data which is definitely available for academic use, see Neil Cummins, 'Where is the Middle Class? Evidence from 60

from the outputs of genealogists' work, such as crowd-sourced genealogies which underpin the Familinx database.[35] Such databases combine large numbers of family trees created by genealogists from digital or other sources to produce datasets with millions of linked individuals which are then used for historical studies of migration, fertility, mortality and so on. It is possible, therefore, for historians and others to get access to sources even when they are not explicitly open access; however, this does not settle the issue raised in our introduction concerning the impact of digitisation and access on historical scholarship, because access is not simply a matter of obtaining the source in question. Access is also about the process of digitising a source, the interface used to work with it, and the metadata and documentation provided. All these factors shape what can and cannot be done with a given historical resource. These factors have often not been given sufficient consideration and have had a profound impact on historical scholarship in our digital age. If you have access to a source but have no real understanding of how or why it was created, then research based on that source will probably be flawed, just as it would be if a non-digital source was approached with a similarly uncritical mindset. This section finishes with a brief general consideration of this problem, before returning to the issue in the next section, where we will consider this is more detail in the context of the PCC wills.

The most serious issue with many of these historical resources is the lack of documentation. The sources made available by commercial companies and those from the genealogical providers give little indication of how they were digitised. For example, the sources available on Ancestry that have been transcribed may have been transcribed in a number of different ways. Some are already transcribed datasets which Ancestry has licensed from other organisations, such as many of the UK parish registers; others have been keyed by volunteers through the now-discontinued Ancestry World Archives project. In other cases, there is no information provided on how a source was transcribed.[36] In both cases details on conventions, checking and other aspects of the transcription process are not readily available, meaning that even if you have the entirety of a given dataset you cannot be sure exactly how it was created. This uncertainty limits what can be done; for example, if you wished to study the distribution of surnames in a Welsh parish register you would need to know how Welsh language names were dealt with by the

[35] Joanna Kaplanis, Assaf Gordon, Tal Shore, Omer Weissbrod, Dan Geiger, Mary Wahl, Michael Gershovits, Barak Markus, Mona Sheikh, Melissa Gymrek, Gaurav Bhatia, Daniel G. Macarthur, Alkes L. Price and Yaniv Erlich, 'Quantitative Analysis of Population-Scale Family Trees with Millions of Relatives', *Science*, 360 (2018), 171–5.

[36] The article noting the discontinuation of the Ancestry World Archive project alludes to the use of 'new technologies' for transcription, suggesting they are increasingly using automated transcription. Whether these are Optical Character Recognition or Handwritten Text Recognition algorithms is unclear; the sections about each source also do not record this information, https://support.ancestry.com/s/article/Discontinuing-the-Ancestry-World-Archives-Project?language=en_US (accessed 9 May 2024).

original scribes and by the transcribers; this information is not available on Ancestry for their Welsh parish registers. If you wish to carry out corpus linguistic analysis on the text present in these commercially produced sources, such as the court records, town directories and histories held on ancestry and FindMyPast, it is essential to know whether spellings have been changed, whether to 'correct' them, or to update them to modern spellings; again this information is difficult to obtain for many of these datasets. Finally, genealogical websites often allow users to provide corrections to transcription errors they find while using the website. In many cases these improve the transcription, but because there is no style guide, they sometimes change a name from what is actually written in the source to what the user 'knows' the name to be. For example, PROB 11/319/128 is John Vaughan's will, probated on 18 January 1665. However, this will cannot be found on Ancestry by searching for John Vaughan, or even just Vaughan; instead to find it you need to search for Vaughn, because it has been transcribed as Johes Vaughn by Ancestry. This entry has a user-suggested correction, John Vaughn, but this still has the incorrect surname, despite it clearly being spelled 'Vaughan' in the will itself.[37] Such problems are only increased in cases where the image is unclear. Once again, there is considerable uncertainty about how sources were digitised and, consequently, how scholars should use them and how confident they can be in doing so.

These issues are multiplied when using datasets like Familinx, which ultimately derive from family history sources, many found through these genealogical websites, but which give little to no information about where and why links were created. Such derived databases are, therefore, based on an unknown set of records, which vary, to an unknown extent, in quality and coverage. In terms of quality, both the quality of the original record and the quality of the digitisation can vary. In terms of coverage, this changes by date covered by the link and by the date on which the genealogist created the link, given the expansion and change in records available and methods of searching. In many cases, the creation of these genealogical sources is a black box that fundamentally changes how historians and others can use such material.

This lack of clarity about the methods of digitisation and transcription is not limited to genealogical websites, however. Many commercial historical databases include little or no information on how a given collection was created. Proquest, for example, provides no details on how texts and other sources were digitised. Early English Books Online (EEBO), for instance, has a brief note about transcription being undertaken through the Text Creation Partnership between Proquest and the Universities of Michigan and Oxford, but offers no details on the conventions used, severely impacting how that data can be used. This information can be found on a separate Text Creation Partnership website, but given the absence of such inforamtion from EEBO itself, and the fact that text mining can be carried out on the EEBO corpus through TDM Studio, the potential for misleading analysis is considerable. Other providers give more information, but it is still usually less fulsome than scholars would want. Gale and Adam Matthew, for example, both note where OCR

---

[37] Will of John Vaughan, Gentleman, Montgomeryshire, 18 Jan. 1666, TNA, PROB 11/319/128.

and HTR models have been used to generate transcriptions, but provide no details on how the models were trained, or how the results were checked. Such models are undoubtedly of better quality than they were when Tim Hitchcock warned us about the perils of low-quality transcriptions a decade ago, but the quality of information given to users about the models used has not, leading to a considerable amount of uncertainty even when just searching such datasets, let alone using them to undertake quantitative and statistical analysis.[38] Of the 247 datasets from commercial providers surveyed for this article, 59 gave no information on how the records included were digitised. Of the remaining 188, the only collection which provides a good description of the method used to transcribe the material are the 272 volumes of primary material provided by British History Online, which notes that double rekeying is the usual method of transcription, with closely checked OCR'd material also being added recently. Even they, however, do not provide details on the conventions used, however.[39]

In general, the resources available from the UKDS provide better documentation about how the datasets were created, but even here this is not perfect given that some of the resources have been deposited long after their initial creation as originally analogue databases. For example, see the documentation for a set of transcribed nineteenth- and twentieth-century vaccination registers, which notes just that 'the layout of the spreadsheets is not consistent, and the information contained in them varies. Standard field names have not been used. Some columns are not named. Information is not always placed in the same fields. Standard codes have not been used consistently in all spreadsheets.' This is an artefact of how these records were created; it can be overcome but again it presents a barrier to use and limits what kind of analysis can be reliably undertaken.[40]

Finally, the other open access resources present a mixed picture in terms of details about digitisation. Of the 126 datasets surveyed here, 56 gave no detail on how they were created; the remaining 70 did provide at least some information, but it was often vague or simply notes the kind of transcription performed, whether manual or by OCR or HTR model. Some, however, such as the Prosopography of Anglo-Saxon England, provide excellent documentation on the methods and conventions used in the creation of that particular resource.[41]

As we noted at the start of this section, users of digital historical resources often lack basic information about the material. This is a major problem for using these sources in historical research and for people reading or trying

---

[38] Hitchcock, 'Confronting the Digital'.

[39] https://www.british-history-ac-uk.uoelibrary.idm.oclc.org/about (accessed 18 April 2024).

[40] L. James, C. Fellows, P. Birch. J. Walsh, J. Robinson, S. Green, J. Rider, J. Hack, H. Coleman, N. Cattell, M. Drake, W. Baird, M. Razzell, A. Dix, A. Clark, S. Smith, P. Buckingham, R. Proctor, L. Davies, E. Hall, G. Culshaw, V. Dodgson, T. James and S. Richens, *Decline of Infant Mortality in England and Wales, 1871–1948: A Medical Conundrum; Vaccination Registers, 1871–1913* [data collection] (2001), UK Data Service, SN: 4127, DOI: http://doi.org/10.5255/UKDA-SN-4127-1.

[41] https://pase.ac.uk/about/research-methodology/ (accessed 19 April 2024). Others with notably good documentation include *Old Bailey Online, London Lives, The Digital Panopticon, Addressing Health, The British Business Census of Entrepreneurs, Hearth Tax Digital, Social Bodies*; apologies to others not explicitly mentioned.

to replicate research based on such data. If you do not know how a transcription was produced, how can you rely on any searches made within it? Such searches might claim to have identified all cases of a word or phrase in a given corpus, but if the transcription is faulty or unknown conventions have affected how given words were transcribed, the researcher and reader may only be considering a sample of that population, leading to errors of analysis and interpretation. It is unlikely that such issues will be resolved satisfactorily for existing datasets. Indeed, given the lack of documentation or metadata in some cases, it may be impossible to retrieve any information on how those records were digitised. However, it is possible, going forward, to ensure that such information is supplied with newly digitised resources and, indeed, as the next section will demonstrate, the provision of good documentation and metadata can expand the kind of work that can be accomplished with digital records beyond historians' previous focus on textual and statistical analysis, into the realm of material culture and beyond. Furthermore, we will see how consideration of the material aspects of documents has to be included when digitising documents as these aspects will directly affect the quality of the transcription provided.

The materiality of historical sources

The microfilming and digitisation of PROB 11

Faced with a sea of searchable digitised historical data, it can be easy to forget about the physical manuscripts, printed books and other sources that underpin these databases. This article so far has considered the influence of digitised genealogical records (such as censuses and baptism records) within the landscape of digitised historical resources. It now turns to consider the specific context of digitised wills, and in particular, the registered copies of wills proved before the Prerogative Court of Canterbury (PCC). The digital surrogates of these registered copies of wills are consulted by thousands of researchers each month, for a broad range of historical and genealogical purposes. These registered copies of wills are held at The National Archives (TNA) at Kew, in a series known as PROB 11. Registered wills were copied by church court clerks onto quires of eight leaves, which were bound into large volumes with leather straps or brass bindings. It is important to consider the physical volumes of PROB 11, and the arrangement and referencing system of the wills in each, in order to understand the microfilm and digital surrogates that most researchers make use of. 2263 of these volumes exist: they date from 1384 to 1858 and contain hundreds of thousands of registered copies of wills. Where the original version of the will survives, it appears in a separate series known as PROB 10 – these have largely not been digitised. The decisions made about which series have been digitised (and how they were digitised and through which interfaces they are accessed) have a direct bearing on the type of historical research that can be produced.

The archival history of PROB 11 ensures that there are some inconsistencies with the arrangement and numbering of wills within each volume. The indexes

Figure 4. A photograph of one of the PROB 11 volumes, in this case PROB 11/1040, open at Thomas Arne's will. (*Source:* PROB 11/1040/181. Photo © Emily Vine.)

to these volumes were often compiled before the files were transferred to the Public Record Office, and therefore use a different reference system. These include contemporary manuscript indexes or calendars. Names were recorded as the grant of probate was made, ensuring that each entry could be easily consulted. These records were bound into a volume of the calendar for that year, and now form the series PROB 12. The indexes in PROB 12 use PROB 11 quire references, which mark out each quire of eight leaves. In the PROB 11 volumes themselves, a folio number appears on the recto of each leaf, and quire numbers appear on the first leaf of each quire. These individual volumes, which each contain a few dozen quires, then make up a register for that year which is assigned a name –either the first name in that register, or another 'notable' name that appears in it. For example, the register for 1778 is entitled 'Hay', and is made up of eleven volumes: PROB 11/1038–1048. The first volume, PROB 11/1038, contains Hay Quire Numbers 1–46, the final volume, PROB 11/1048, contains Hay Quire Numbers 474–519. PROB 11/1049, the next volume, is the first volume of the register for 1779, 'Warburton', and contains Warburton Quire Numbers 1–47. The introduction to the PCC will registers on the TNA's website informs researchers: 'It is not possible to tell from the catalogue reference alone which particular register an individual volume belongs to.'[42]

Figure 4 gives an indication of the size and materiality of the PROB 11 volumes. Each volume weighs over 10 kg, and measurements taken of a sample volume give a spine depth of 14 cm, a width of 36 cm and a height of 46 cm.

---

[42] https://discovery.nationalarchives.gov.uk/details/r/C12122 (accessed 22 July 2024).

This example is an eighteenth-century volume, PROB 11/1040, one of the 11 volumes to contain the registered copies of wills proved in 1778. As discussed above, PROB 11/1040 can also be referred to in terms of its quire numbers, in this case 'Hay, Quire Numbers 93–140'. In this photograph, the volume is open on the will of Thomas Arne, proved 16 March 1778, which begins on folio 11. But the catalogue reference of this will is PROB 11/1040/181. As of 2013, the reference numbers of the wills were renumbered in chronological order. Accordingly, the will of Benjamin Jennings, proved on 5 February 1778, appears on folio 186 of PROB 11/1040, but carries the reference PROB 11/1040/1. The wills that have been assigned the numbers between PROB 11/1040/1 and PROB 11/1040/181 appear in a different order in the physical volume PROB 11/1040, but were all proved after Jennings's on 5 February, and before Arne's on 16 March. As with many archives with centuries of administrative history, differing indexing and numbering systems mean that the reference systems on the online catalogues do not represent the order of wills in the physical volumes themselves.

Alongside the physicality and arrangement of the PROB 11 volumes, we also need to consider the different circumstances in which they were microfilmed, and the reasons why. In the 1950s, while the wills were held by the Principal Probate Registry at Somerset House, PROB 11 was microfilmed by the Church of the Latter-Day Saints. These microfilm images contain no folio numbers, as the quire numbers were at this date the only form of internal marking in the volumes. When they were initially microfilmed, these images would only have been available at centres run by the Latter-Day Saints (now 'Family Search' centres). PROB 11 was later microfilmed again once it had been accessioned by the Public Record Office. At this point microfilming was carried out in order to preserve the manuscripts, rather than to make them widely accessible. The decision to initially microfilm PROB 11 (the registered copies of wills) rather than PROB 10 (the original wills) is one that was in itself rooted in the materiality of the manuscripts. The pages of PROB 11 are generally clean, unfolded and fairly uniform, appearing as they do in the standard volumes of bound parchment. The PROB 10 wills are more often folded and appear in bundles, rather than being arranged in bound volumes, making them more difficult to microfilm. The microfilms of PROB 11 were digitised and made available in stages on TNA's website c. 2001–4. In 2013, Ancestry.com also digitised the PROB 11 microfilm.[43] The decision to microfilm and subsequently digitise PROB 11 but not PROB 10 (and to digitise the microfilms, rather than the original manuscripts) continues to have ramifications for research conducted today.

Having sketched out the history of the microfilming and digitisation of PROB 11, it is necessary to reflect on the ways in which researchers access these different versions, and how this shapes the type of research that is possible, or indeed the type of research that users are directed towards. Many

---

[43] Many thanks to Ruth Selman, Early Modern Records Specialist at TNA, for providing a scan of the PROB 11 Introductory Note and for providing further information about its recent archival history.

researchers access the digitised microfilms of PROB 11 through the TNA's 'Discovery' catalogue. They are directed to search for an individual's will by name. Downloading a pdf image of a single will costs, at the time of writing, £3.50 per will. Alternatively, users can create a free account and download up to 100 items (e.g. individual wills) in a 30-day period. While the requirements of many researchers would fall within these restrictions, this still limits large-scale studies. By clicking on the volume reference that the individual will appears in, it is possible to see the references of other wills in the same volume, but it is not possible to browse freely through the digitised scan of an entire volume. Indeed, as has already been established, the numbering system in the catalogue arranges the wills in each volume in chronological order and does not correspond with the order of the wills as they appear in the physical volume. Through this interface individual wills need to be identified, selected and downloaded. Ancestry is also geared around viewing individual wills which are searched for by name. It does however provide the option to browse through whole volumes of the PROB 11 wills. A subscription that allows access to this function costs, at the time of writing, a minimum of £13.99 a month. These records are also available on TheGenealogist.co.uk. At the time of writing, a subscription to The Genealogist which provides access to 'Wills, Probates, and Testaments' costs between £98.95 and £139.95 per year. Both Ancestry and The Genealogist have produced their own indexes to the digitised PROB 11 records. As Jerome de Groot reminds us, sites such as Ancestry are ultimately 'profit-based' businesses; this has a significant bearing on how information is presented and how its websites influence the 'historical imaginary'.[44]

Access to the digital surrogates of PROB 11 is therefore divided and mediated in an uneven manner. PROB 11 is accessible only behind a paywall, or it requires registering for an account and limitations on the number of individual wills that can be downloaded per month. The way in which these interfaces permit the researcher to access these digital surrogates is also uneven: the access granted does not always provide the option to browse through the whole volumes. These interfaces are predicated on the assumption that PROB 11 would be used for certain purposes, primarily genealogical research, or studies which involve searching for named individuals. In the TNA's search interface for PROB 11, users can search by 'First name', 'Last name', 'Occupation', 'Place', 'Date range', or 'Other keywords' – these fields are the metadata that appear in the title of each will. Ancestry's user interface is similar and is orientated around the date and location of an individual's death or another event in their life. The interfaces and presentation of the digital surrogates therefore tend to hamper the type of research that necessitates browsing through volumes of wills or sampling at scale (e.g. studies of long-term patterns of bequests or economic change), that is interested in questions of wills as a source (e.g. the changing nature of preambles, religious language, or notarial practice over time) or ways of accessing the volumes without searching for an individual's name. As Richard Dunley and Jo Pugh have

---

[44] Jerome de Groot, 'Ancestry.com and the Evolving Nature of Historical Information Companies', *The Public Historian*, 42 (2020), 10, 26.

shown, archive catalogues such as TNA Discovery have been increasingly geared towards enabling genealogical research in recent years. Resources have accordingly been directed towards expanding item-level description that enables searching for named individuals.[45] At the same time, the interface has not developed to permit forms of research that look beyond the individual wills of named people, and which would be facilitated by making entire volumes browsable or downloadable.

As noted above, more than ten years ago Tim Hitchcock raised the problems of working from digital surrogates that were 'inaccurate representations of text, hidden behind a poor quality image'.[46] The digital surrogates of PROB 11 that appear on TNA, Ancestry and The Genealogist are digitised versions of the microfilm, and not of the original wills themselves. The versions that researchers have access to are therefore already several steps removed from the original manuscript. Katie Lanning, in a discussion of the digitisation of the Burney Newspaper Collection, which was scanned not from the original papers or the unused master microfilm, but from a used microfilm, asks 'should a popular archive prioritise preservation or access?'[47] For a collection like PROB 11 that contains hundreds of thousands of images, there is the possibility that each stage of microfilming or digitisation introduces human error, such as pages that are overlooked, mislabelled, or that appear in the wrong order. L. W. C. Van Lit cautions us on the use of 'low resolution digital scans of microfilms', which are 'surrogates of surrogates', and notes that a reliance on bad digital images can result in 'bad analyses'.[48] Microfilm copies are often of poor quality and their greyscale or black and white rendering fails to capture some details of the original manuscript, ensuring that low-contrast regions are harder to read. For these reasons, those who frequently transcribe PROB 11 wills have pointed to the difficulty of reading marginalia and inter-lined text on the digitised microfilms.[49] There are also examples of micro-filmed PROB 11 wills which are partially unreadable due to damp or damage to the page, and it is not possible either to read the text or to determine the underlying reason for its unreadability until the original is viewed. 'Bleed through' text from the other side of the parchment also occasionally renders a microfilm unreadable. The digital surrogates would be more readable had they been produced using more recent, high-quality colour digital photography techniques. Text is also frequently obscured by folds or creases on the page which cannot be rectified other than by viewing the original volume. Even without better-quality scans, however, if the record came with metadata on the type and quality of the scan, it would render them easier to use as it would provide some explanation for the problems users experience while

---

[45] Richard Dunley and Jo Pugh, 'Do Archive Catalogues Make History? Exploring Interactions between Historians and Archives', *Twentieth Century British History*, 32 (2021), 591.

[46] Hitchcock, 'Confronting the Digital', 14.

[47] Katie Lanning, 'Scanner Darkly: Unpopularization in the Burney Newspaper Collection' *Archives and Records*, 41 (2020), 222.

[48] L. W. C Van Lit, *Among Digitized Manuscripts. Philology, Codicology, Paleography in a Digital World* (Leiden, 2019), 69–70.

[49] Many thanks to Teresa Goatham for this point.

viewing them and give guidance on where future digitisation efforts should be focused.

There are also factors which render the use of PROB 11 (the registered wills, copied out by a Church court clerk in a uniform legal hand) distinct from PROB 10 (the original wills, written in the hand of a scrivener or perhaps the testator themselves). The introductory note to PROB 11 claims 'there is usually no advantage to be gained from examining the original wills', and indeed the TNA website suggests that 'for most research purposes the registers are easier to use'.[50] This of course precludes a range of avenues of future research, which could for example analyse the original handwriting (as opposed to that of the Church court clerk), which could examine the signatures or marks of witnesses, or which could compare originals with their copies, to cross-check for edits or omissions.

A brief comparison between a sample of original wills in PROB 10 and their counterparts in PROB 11 reveals what can be lost in a focus on the registered copies only. The copies made by Church court clerks were written in one hand (the clerk's), in a uniform secretary or legal hand, without retaining the original formatting and often without retaining the original spelling. This means we can no longer access the distinctions between the hand of the scrivener, or another tasked with writing up a will, and the varied signatures or 'marks' made by the testator or witnesses. This is exemplified by the comparison between the signatures in the original and registered copies of the will of Edward Rott which opened this article.

This also means that we cannot always identify from the registered copies alone wills like that of Benjamin Rogers, who ostensibly wrote out his own will. The writing in this will is hurried and distinct from the formal, considered, style of the scrivener and Rogers's own signature appears to match the hand that wrote the main body of the text. We might attribute this to the rushed and dangerous circumstances in which Rogers found himself – he died in London at the height of the plague, making a will on 30 August 1665 that would be proved three weeks later.[51] The registered copies cannot provide an insight into either the presence of multiple hands or one: all nuance is subsumed by the uniformity of the clerk's hand. Other original wills written during the plague of 1665 provide material insights into the health of the testator.[52] Aspects of this can of course be inferred from information that appears in the registered copies: the short length of time between when a will was written and when it was proved, or the presence of phrases such as 'weake of Bodye' or 'beinge sick in her bed of the sickness whereof she dyed'.[53] But occasionally such phrases are coupled with the testator's markedly

---

[50] Introductory note to PROB 11, with thanks to Ruth Selman; https://discovery. nationalarchives.gov.uk/details/r/C12121 (accessed 10 July 2024).

[51] Will of Benjamin Rogers, made 30 Aug. 1665, proved 26 Sept. 1665, TNA, PROB 10/980.

[52] Many thanks to Judy Lester of Kerrywood Research for sharing her experience of finding 'shaky' handwriting in wills.

[53] Will of William Newarke or Newark, Factor of Saint Michael Bassishaw, City of London, 30 Aug. 1665, TNA, PROB 11/317/382; Will of Jane Rokeby, Widow of Saint Giles without Cripplegate, Middlesex, 8 Sept. 1665, TNA, PROB 11/317/460.

shaky or weak signature, such as the unusually short will of Thomas Roe, who was described as 'being very weake in body'. Roe managed to scrawl his shaky mark when his will was written on 18 September: he died almost immediately, as it was proved two days later.[54] We do not know, of course, precisely how indicative shaky or weak signatures are of the testator's health – they could be comparable with their usual writing. But nonetheless, that avenue of research is precluded if only the registered copies are consulted. There are many reasons why researchers would want to see the original signatures and handwriting of those involved in a will's production, including for studies of literacy, to determine whether a testator or witness had written the rest of a will, or to infer information about the health of the writer.[55] The digitisation of the registered copies, but not the originals, pushes users towards historical research based around people, dates, places and the content of wills, but at the same time ensures researchers are less likely to pursue other questions that wills as a source provoke.

There are other, more material facets that we lose in focusing on the registered copies in PROB 11 rather than the originals in PROB 10. Original wills were written in varying formats: some on expansive pieces of parchment, some on smaller scraps of paper or indeed paper repurposed from other sources, including account books.[56] Some wills amount to a couple of lines that fill half a side, while others stretch to ten, twenty or more pages, with the testator's signature and seal in the bottom right-hand corner of each page. The variety in the format of the original wills, and the fact that they have been tightly folded up in bundles for storage, is of course one reason why microfilming PROB 10 was too complex a task. In some cases, a later codicil on a separate scrap of paper has been stitched or stapled onto the original will. The codicil was often written by a different hand and signed by different witnesses. These varieties of format are lost in the uniform work of the Church court clerk, who in copying out the content of the will into the registered copy books, could not replicate features such as stapled addendums, or the scale or materiality of the paper or parchment used. Where the original wills feature seals in black and red wax, either stamped directly onto the page of the will or attached onto a fold-out of paper, the registered copies can only mark the place of the seal. This practice too is inconsistent, but eighteenth-century wills often represent the seal with 'L.S' or 'Locus Sigilli'. Yet other features of the will, such as the formatting of the text, could have been replicated in the registered copies, but are generally not. We have already seen an example where signatures are incorporated into the main text of the will, rather than retaining their original list formatting. In the unusual will of Margaret Nelham, probably written by Nelham herself onto a repurposed account-book page, money owed to her is listed in a column of the right-hand side of the

---

[54] Will of Thomas Roe, made 18 Sept. 1665, proved 20 Sept. 1665, TNA, PROB 10/980.

[55] Mark Hailwood, 'Rethinking Literacy in Rural England, 1550–1700', *Past & Present*, 260 (2023), 38–70.

[56] One example of this is the will of Margaretta Nelham, TNA PROB 10/979. Our thanks to Laura Sangha for pointing out that the will appears to have been written on account book paper.

(a)

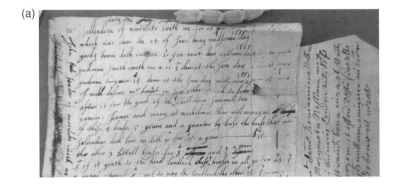

(b)

Figure 5. Original will of Margaretta Nelham (above, PROB 10/979) and its registered copy (below, PROB 11–317–321). (*Sources*: TNA, PROB 10/979; PROB 11/317/321, Photo © Emily Vine.)

page, arranged in the format of pounds-shillings-pence. In the registered copy version, Nelham's itemised list is not retained: instead these amounts appear as run-on sentences, removing this insight into her numeracy. Figure 5 shows both the original copy of Nelham's will (PROB 10/979), with an addendum and probate clause stitched onto the right hand-side of the page, and its registered copy (PROB 11–317–321). The registered copy of Nelham's will, alongside other examples, also demonstrates that church court clerks had an inconsistent approach to retaining original spelling or capitalisation. Here 'mortelake' has been corrected to 'Mortlake', 'goody borne' has been corrected to 'Goody Borne', 'Chilldren' to 'Children'. At the end of the will, the number '4', written numerically in the original, is rendered in the copy as 'fower'. There is also no replication of the writer's (possibly Nelham's) own deletions, scribbles and additions. Very little of the character of the original writings, occasionally produced by the testator themselves, is retained in the registered copies. More concerning still is the possibility that this correction or failure to retain original formatting or spelling has introduced errors or omissions, or has rendered the intentions of the testator inaccurately.

There were practical reasons why PROB 11 and not PROB 10 was originally microfilmed and digitised, and for many research purposes pertaining to names, places, dates and the general content of the wills, the registered copies are sufficient. In other words, the registered copies are useful particularly for forms of genealogical research, and for mass processing of their substantially more regular handwriting, which makes them particularly good candidates for automatic transcription using handwritten text recognition algorithms. But they are not sufficient for other forms of historical research that are predicated on the retention of original spelling, formatting or handwriting, or that are interested in questions of materiality. Digitised collections are of course over-represented in research in comparison to those which are harder to access. The microfilming and subsequent digitisation of PROB 11 has made a valuable archive of English and Welsh history widely accessible, but the decision to digitise it instead of PROB 10, accessible only through a visit to TNA in London itself, has had a direct influence on the forms of research that have been and continue to be produced.

The materiality of PROB 11 and its digital surrogates

There are parallels in how PROB 11 replicates the content but not the materiality of PROB 10, and in how the digital surrogates of PROB 11 replicate the content but not the materiality of the volumes themselves. It is of course not only the readability of the text that can be compromised by digitisation, but also understandings of a manuscript's materiality and archival context. When isolating individual wills from their materiality (bound alongside quires of other wills in leather volumes and arranged into named registers), we isolate them from the complexity and scale of the archive and its history. The materiality of books and manuscripts has long been a point of discussion within wider questions of digitisation and accessibility. As Johanna Green has discussed, manuscript digitisation focuses on 'the page and text, rather than the 3-D codicological object' and is 'not a process of replication but transformation'.[57] Digitisation captures the largely two-dimensional visual features of a book or manuscript, yet even then important visual features can be lost or diminished. The vibrant colours of illustrated manuscripts, or the fainter marks of some marginalia, are not always well replicated in digitisation.[58] Equally, it is often necessary for scholars to get a sense of the size, materiality and weight of a book in order to understand how users would have interacted with it: could it be carried around, placed in a pocket or easily concealed? Some medievalists and codicologists have argued for the importance of being able to view, touch and hold a physical book or manuscript in order to understand fully its usage and reception. Taking this a step further, Ryan Szpiech argued in 2014: 'The manuscript cannot only be seen – it must be touched, smelled, read, received, interpreted in order to be appreciated and understood.'[59] This positioning has drawn more criticism in recent years,

---

[57] Johanna M.E. Green, 'Digital Manuscripts as Sites of Touch: Using Social Media for "Hands-On" Engagement with Medieval Manuscript Materiality', *Archive Journal*, 6 (2018), https://www.archivejournal.net/essays/digital-manuscripts-as-sites-of-touch-using-social-media-for-hands-on-engagement-with-medieval-manuscript-materiality/ (accessed 10 July 2024).

[58] Van Lit, *Among Digitized Manuscripts*, 67.

[59] Ryan Szpiech, 'Cracking the Code: Reflections on Manuscripts in the Age of Digital Books', *Digital Philology: A Journal of Medieval Cultures*, 3 (2014), 90.

including from L. W. C. van Lit who questions how essential haptic or multi-sensual interactions with original books and manuscripts are for understanding them.[60] Equally both Green and Aengus Ward have shown that only the privileged few ever have the chance to touch or hold original books and manuscripts anyway: the general public can only ever interact with them from a distance, or behind glass. In Ward's words, 'if sensory access to the unique object is required for materiality truly to be appreciated ... it cannot be available to those scholars who are unable to access the artifact in person. In this counsel of despair, the previous hierarchy of privilege remains.'[61] This conclusion is drawn from quite a different context to PROB 11, a series that has been continuously consulted by members of the public since the wills were first registered: firstly at Doctors' Commons and subsequently at Somerset House. Yet since PROB 11 was digitised, it has not been possible for members of the public to order up the physical volumes.

This article has already considered the loss of material context that has resulted from the decision to microfilm and digitise PROB 11 rather than PROB 10. It has shown that the registered copy volumes replicate the content of the original wills in a standardised way, without reproducing original formatting, handwriting or materiality. For the purposes of this discussion of the registered copies in PROB 11, the concern is less with the inability to see, touch or smell the physical volumes, but with how digitisation removes the individual wills from the materiality of the volumes and the context of the archive. Unlike, for example, a small pocket bible, very few people would have actually held these volumes at the time in which they were produced, and their size or weight does not have a direct bearing on how they would have been used and consulted. But there are still important material aspects that are lost or complicated by digitisation, and which are worthy of consideration. In losing sense of the physicality of the large, leather-bound parchment volumes, we lose a sense of the scale and physicality of the archive, its expanse and its administrative history. While the digitised version on Ancestry provides the option of viewing pages of some of the volumes as an open book or double-paged spread, they elsewhere appear as isolated pages, cut off from the context of the will preceding or facing (even though wills generally end, and begin, halfway through a page). L. W. C. van Lit has pointed out that the 'cut' of a digitised image – the decision of what is included within the frame of the image and what is excluded, can have an important bearing on how the images are used and understood.[62] When downloading the will of a named individual on TNA Discovery, the final paragraphs of the preceding will often appear on the first page. These paragraphs often appear out of context and do not always contain the name of the preceding individual.

[60] Elaine Treharne, 'Fleshing out the Text: The Transcendent Manuscript in the Digital Age', *Postmedieval: A Journal of Medieval Cultural Studies*, 4 (2013), 274; Van Lit, *Among Digitized Manuscripts*, 61–2.

[61] Aengus Ward, 'Of Digital Surrogates and Immaterial Objects: The (Digital) Future of the Iberian Manuscript in Textual Editing', *Journal of Medieval Iberian Studies*, 14 (2022), 45.

[62] Van Lit, *Among Digitized Manuscripts*, 68.

Inconsistent numbering in the catalogue (where wills are categorised chrono-logically and not in the order they appear in the physical volume) means it is not always easy to locate or identify a preceding will. One of the key complica-tions of the digitisation of PROB 11 is therefore the isolation of individual wills from their archival context (wills that have often been 'pulled up' through keyword-searching), and the 'flattening' of the archive more generally. Katie Lanning, in a study based around the Burney Newspaper Collection, has warned of how microfilming and digitisation decontextualises texts and shifts the 'shape' of the archive. Lanning notes that the British Library had continued to add additional newspapers to the original Burney Collection and that it is now no longer possible to determine where Charles Burney's original collec-tion begins and ends.[63] This has some implications for the way in which the digital surrogates of PROB 11 are accessed. On the TNA website, there is an interface where researchers are directed to search within the catalogue for PROB 11. Yet they can also search for wills, or names of testators, on TNA Discovery, the catalogue which comprises not only the TNA's entire holdings but collections from but other British archives too. There is potential for researchers to be confused about what is and is not PROB 11, or indeed for the boundaries of PROB 11 to be blurred and discarded: for its shape and con-tent to be subsumed within a broader meta-structure of British archives. On Ancestry this is perhaps even more acute: researchers can 'call up' digitised wills from several collections using the same search interface. Entering a name can pull up results from across a number of databases, not only 'England & Wales, Prerogative Court of Canterbury Wills, 1384–1858', but also 'UK, Extracted Probate Records, 1269–1975', 'Irish Records Index, 1500–1920' and 'American Wills and Administrations'.[64] Furthermore, it is not clear, as we saw in the case of Johes/John Vaughn/Vaughan, where the names you are searching came from, or if your search has found every instance or variation. In being presented with isolated results drawn from different source types, databases and archives, aspects of the archival structure and con-text are lost.

Tim Hitchcock, among others, has warned of the complications of keyword searching of a database, which produces results that are isolated or 'deraci-nated' from their archival context. Keyword searching, and the digitisation of seemingly whole archives or series, can also give a false impression of com-pleteness or comprehensiveness. There is a danger that the digitisation of PROB 11, rendered on archival and genealogical websites as 'England & Wales, Prerogative Court of Canterbury Wills, 1384–1858', gives the impression of a complete archive of wills throughout the time period 1384–1858, when the probate process was disrupted for example during the English Civil Wars and Interregnum (there is no extant register for wills proved only at Oxford).[65]

---

[63] Lanning, 'Scanner Darkly', 218–19.

[64] https://www.ancestry.co.uk/search/categories/clp_wills/ (accessed 10 July 2024).

[65] Introductory note to PROB 11, with thanks to Ruth Selman; Van Lit, *Among Digitized Manuscripts*, 54.

Knowledge of the archival context, and the historical context in which documents were produced, remains a prerequisite for using and understanding digital surrogates and searchable databases. Hitchcock cautions that keyword searching 'lets us escape this post-Enlightenment knowledge system, but it also removes the framework of source criticism and classification that we have come to rely upon'. He uses this to argue for more honesty when citing digital sources and for researchers to acknowledge when they have viewed the digital surrogate rather than the original book or manuscript. Researchers 'must be even more honest than is required by the form of a traditional footnote, about how we are searching evidence, and what it is we are searching'.[66] Van Lit has echoed this, arguing 'Being honest about this means that we should refer to the surrogate in our bibliography and we should include a description of the digital materiality of the photos.'[67] The wills in PROB 11 have been widely cited by a broad range of historians or genealogical researchers, the majority of whom will have accessed these records via the digital surrogates only and will not have acknowledged this. For understandable reasons of preservation, TNA discourages researchers from viewing original manuscripts where a surrogate exists 'in digital, microfilm or microfiche formats'. It provides the following exemptions: 'the surrogate is illegible or obscured' or 'viewing the original record provides information not available from the surrogate'.[68] At the time of writing it is not possible to order PROB 11 volumes through the usual document-ordering channels.

Historians in the last two decades have had to become more adept at navigating the complexities of the digital landscape. Jon Coburn's study of historians' digital practices suggests that, despite Tim Hitchcock's earlier warnings, many are cognisant of the limitations of archival databases and are mindful that the biases of keyword searching and algorithms can influence research in unintended ways. Those whom Coburn interviewed suggested that accessing digital surrogates should not be a substitute for viewing the original manuscript and indeed that sometimes a hybrid approach would be adopted: viewing some of a collection online could help a researcher decided whether to make a trip to the archive itself.[69] One of the key issues raised by Coburn's respondents about digital surrogates and keyword searching is that they remove the chance for 'serendipitous finds' – useful discoveries that are stumbled across only when one is browsing through a box or volume in an archive, or flicking through the papers adjacent to the ones that had actually been identified and requested through the catalogue. These are findings that cannot be captured by keyword searching and this in turn has an indirect effect upon the type of historical research that is produced. There is growing

---

[66] Hitchcock, 'Confronting the Digital', 14.

[67] Van Lit, *Among Digitized Manuscripts*, 71.

[68] https://www.nationalarchives.gov.uk/about/visit-us/researching-here/how-to-order-view-and-copy-documents/ (accessed 10 July 2024).

[69] Jon Coburn, 'Defending the Digital: Awareness of Digital Selectivity in Historical Research Practice', *Journal of Librarianship and Information Science*, 53 (2021), 398–410.

awareness within the historical discipline, and beyond it, of the limitations of consulting digital surrogates in isolation, but also of the benefits of using digital surrogates alongside viewing original manuscripts in person. The microfilming and digitisation of PROB 11 has made these sources accessible to a global community of researchers and has had a profound impact upon the forms of historical and genealogical research that can be produced. But in using the digital surrogates, researchers have a duty to consider the loss of archival context and materiality and how the purely pragmatic decision to microfilm the registered copies, and not the originals, has shaped and will continue to shape the forms of research that can be carried out. So too do researchers need to be mindful of how they are directed to search these digital surrogates: through interfaces that prioritise genealogical research, keyword searching for individual people and metadata that captures names, dates and places, but not other aspects of wills as a source. The PCC wills are an example of a fairly well-documented digital collection. The potential pitfalls we have identified in their case are all substantially more severe in the wider landscape of digital historical sources where, as we have seen, information on methods of digitisation and cataloguing are often worse or entirely absent.

Conclusions: towards the future of digitisation and archival materiality

Faced with these challenges, how can scholars and institutions reconcile digitisation efforts with the recognition of the materiality of their holdings? TNA itself has grappled with how best to digitally image and represent the materiality of its wax seal mould collection. After experimenting with different forms of colour photography and 3D scanning, it opted for greyscale scanning using a flat-bed scanner, alongside recording detailed metadata on colour and size.[70] Aengus Ward has pointed to how data encoding could be used 'to represent or recreate the physical dimension of manuscripts'.[71] Bill Endres's work has produced interactive 3D renderings of pages from the St Chad Gospels, allowing users to 'rotate' the book, and moving beyond the representation of pages as flat surfaces.[72] Other digital approaches to materiality have not only replicated the three-dimensional aspects of manuscript sources, but have been used to conduct further research on them. The 'Letterlocking' project has not only created three-dimensional scans of sealed seventeenth- and eighteenth-century letters, but has used X-ray

---

[70] Amy Sampson, 'TNA Wax Seal Moulds – from Drawer to Discovery', 18 Mar. 2019, https://blog. nationalarchives.gov.uk/wax-seal-moulds-drawer-discovery/ (accessed 10 July 2024).

[71] Ward, 'Of Digital Surrogates and Immaterial Objects', 43.

[72] Bill Endres, *Digitizing Medieval Manuscripts: The St. Chad Gospels, Materiality, Recoveries, and Representation in 2D and 3D* (Leeds, 2019); and Bill Endres, 'More than Meets the Eye: Going 3D with an Early Medieval Manuscript', in *Proceedings of the Digital Humanities Congress 2012*, ed. Clare Mills, Michael Pidd and Esther Ward (Sheffield, 2012), available online at https://www.dhi.ac.uk/ books/dhc2012 (accessed 10 July 2024).

microtomography to 'virtually unfold' and read their contents for the first time (without opening the letters or breaking their seals).[73]

Limitations of cost and other practicalities mean it is unlikely that PROB 11, or indeed PROB 10, would be re-digitised in light of developments in 3D digital technology. It is also unlikely that the metadata of either series will be updated to account for material features. But it is possible for future digitisation projects to comprise documentation and metadata that comprehensively accounts for material features, even when those sources, like the registered will copy volumes of PROB 11, have traditionally been used for textual rather than material analysis. We cannot predict the ways in which future researchers will approach sources such as these. While most researchers have little influence over future digitisation projects, there are other modes of best practice that we can all follow. We can follow the call of Hitchcock, Van Lit and others that we be honest in our citation practices and honest when we have viewed a digital surrogate rather than an original manuscript. This is true even of sources drawn from PROB 11, and in cases where the interest is primarily in a will's content, such as for genealogists, or social or economic historians, digital surrogates are entirely satisfactory. We also need to be more consistent in reporting methodologies, how material was identified, what biases or lacunae such methodologies may have introduced into the work and how we have sought to overcome them. And throughout our use of digital surrogates, we need to be ever mindful of their archival context, the reasons why these manuscripts were microfilmed or digitised (and other manuscripts overlooked) and the ways in which archival websites and other interfaces direct us towards certain forms of research and away from others.

Digital resources are of profound importance to the way that history is written today and that importance is likely only to increase in the future. Much of this article has been concerned with the limitations and problems arising from the way such sources are produced and accessed, yet we do not mean to give the impression that we are dubious of the value of digitisation, not least in terms of allowing access to material that for reasons of distance, cost or format is difficult to engage with and with regard to allowing other scholars to check others' published accounts directly. Indeed, it would be foolish of us, given the nature of our careers, to make such an argument. However, we have seen in this article the difficulties faced by scholars using these digitised resources: subscription costs, library or university access, poor or uncertain transcription practices, historical artefacts shaping the format of the resulting digital material, dead links, substandard or entirely absent documentation and metadata. All of these issues reflect the particular nature of the data/digital infrastructure in the United Kingdom, and, just as individual scholars need to adopt and push for better practices in using and citing such material, the historical profession

---

[73] https://letterlocking.org/ (accessed 10 July 2024); J. Dambrogio, A. Ghassaei, D. S. Smith *et al.*, 'Unlocking History through Automated Virtual Unfolding of Sealed Documents imaged by X-ray Microtomography', *Nature Communications*, 12 (2021), https://doi.org/10.1038/s41467-021-21326-w.

as a whole needs to push for improvements in the infrastructure which will ensure that future digitisation projects produce material that is easier to use with confidence and that can be employed for a wider range of historical enquiries.[74]

Acknowledgements. The authors would like to thank Mark Bell, Tim Hitchcock, Jan Michielsen, Laura Sangha, Ruth Selman, Jane Whittle and the readers at *TRHS* for their constructive feedback on this article.

Financial support. This research was conducted as part of Leverhulme Trust Research Project Grant, RPG-2023-07, 2023-27.

---

[74] The sorry state of data infrastructure in the United Kingdom is surveyed in Ahnert *et al.*, *Collaborative Historical Research*, 23–32. The country's weakness in this area is epitomised by the much-lamented discontinuation of the Historical Texts service in July 2024, which brought together several important digital resources: EEBO, ECCO, UK Historical Medical Library, British Library Nineteenth Century Collection; the impending retirement of this service makes it hard to cite, but see (hopefully) https://web.archive.org/web/20240513075051/https://historicaltexts. jisc.ac.uk/news#2024-02-29 (accessed 5 June 2024).

Cite this article: Smith H, Vine E (2024). Material and Digital Archives: The Case of Wills. *Transactions of the Royal Historical Society* 2, 441–470. https://doi.org/10.1017/S0080440124000094

Transactions of the RHS (2024), **2**, 471–489
doi:10.1017/S0080440124000082

COMMENT

Promoting Well-being through History Teaching

David Stack

Department of History, University of Reading, Reading, UK
Email: d.a.stack@reading.ac.uk

(Received 18 June 2024; revised 30 July 2024; accepted 30 July 2024;
first published online 18 September 2024)

Abstract

This article explores the potential for the greater infusion of well-being concerns into the teaching of history in UK HEIs. Drawing upon results from a survey of over 100 current undergraduates in one UK History department, alongside a scoping study of well-being provision provided by history departments or their equivalent in about ninety UK HEIs, this article considers ways in which well-being can be promoted through the teaching and learning strategies of historians. The article discusses the meaning of the term 'well-being' and asks why historians have sometimes been reluctant participants in the 'eudaemonic turn'. The negativity bias of history as an endeavour, and the potential for understanding the past to enhance or diminish an individual's sense of well-being is discussed, as is the value of historicising the concept of well-being itself. The case for integrating well-being as a key element in the degree-level study of history is made, and the article concludes by urging all HEI history practitioners to consider the value of curricular infusion and mapping the design and delivery of their modules onto the New Economics Foundation's 'five ways to well-being'.

Keywords: well-being; teaching and learning; curricular infusion; happiness

Introduction

There is a widespread recognition of the challenge of mental health and well-being among young people internationally, and facing UK students in particular. The most recent *World Happiness Report*, which draws on evidence from 140 nations, suggests that those aged between 15 and 24 in the UK, Europe, North America and Australia are experiencing declining well-being scores, and that attendance at university is no guarantee of psychological well-being.[1] Action to address this problem in UK HEIs has ranged from the creation of a sector-wide University Mental Health Charter, supported by the Office for Students (OfS), through to more local, departmental and disciplinary initiatives to embed well-being within teaching delivery.[2] Historians have participated in these initiatives, at all levels. The museum and heritage sectors have led the way in social prescribing and other well-being programmes, and many colleagues have developed modules and teaching resources that have built upon the obvious potential for historical study to help promote a sense of place, connection and belonging that can form powerful elements in an individual's well-being.[3] Moreover, the recent publication of the edited collection *History and Human Flourishing* (2023), which *Historical Transactions* highlighted in a blog series, represents a further step forward in professional historians reflecting upon how well-being concerns relate directly to our discipline and how our research, teaching and practices might contribute to addressing the challenges facing our students.[4]

In many ways, however, we are still in the early stages of the conversation about history and well-being.[5] In surveying the secondary literature around pedagogy and well-being it is relatively easy to find illustrative examples of attempts to integrate well-being at subject level in a range of disciplines, including anthropology, business studies, communications, computer studies, health, human sciences, law, nursing, philosophy, psychology and theology, but history is noticeably less prominent.[6] This does not mean that historians are unusually insensitive to student well-being; colleagues struggling to assist their personal tutees with pastoral concerns would certainly testify to the contrary. It might, however, suggest a certain hesitancy when it comes to discussing a more systematic integration of well-being concerns into our teaching. This, in turn, perhaps reflects the generally practical – critics would say undertheorised – way in which many historians tend to approach

---

[1] J. F. Helliwell, R. Layard., J. D. Sachs., J.-E. De Neve., L. B. Aknin and S. Wang (eds.), *World Happiness Report 2024* (Oxford, 2024). Full text and supporting documentation can be downloaded from the website: worldhappiness.report.

[2] Office for Students, 'Funding boost to support Student Minds' Mental Health Charter', 28 Feb. 2024. https://www.officeforstudents.org.uk/news-blog-and-events/press-and-media/funding-boost-to-support-student-minds-university-mental-health-charter/.

[3] These include initiatives aimed at students, such as the University of Edinburgh Museum's *Prescribe Culture* scheme. See https://www.ed.ac.uk/students/health-wellbeing/social-prescribeed/prescribe-culture.

[4] D. M. McMahon (ed.), *History and Human Flourishing* (Oxford, 2023). For the supporting blogs see https://blog.royalhistsoc.org/2023/06/28/history-and-human-flourishing/.

[5] Many of the most interesting contributions have come from those with a literature, rather than a straight history, background. See R. Solnit, *Wanderlust: A History of Walking* (2014); T. Lutz, *Crying: A Natural and Cultural History of Tears* (New York, 2001); A. Potkay, *Hope: A Literary History* (Cambridge, 2022).

[6] See T. A. Olson, T. A. and J. B. Riley, 'Weaving the Campus Safety Net by Integrating Student Health Issues into the Curriculum', *About Campus*, 14 (2009), 27–9.

problems and, I would suggest, owes something to a certain scepticism about the whole well-being agenda within the profession.[7]

In what follows, I want to address some of the doubts and questions about well-being, as a way of opening-up a broader conversation about promoting well-being through history teaching at university. Hitherto, the evidence from our scoping study suggests, where a well-being agenda has been consciously pursued within history departments, it has been on an ad hoc, unsystematic, individual basis. My argument is that well-being is too important to be left to the chance interests of particular members of staff; an approach which, in any case, runs the risk of producing unhealthy, dependence relationships in which students fixate on particular modules or teachers. Instead, well-being needs to become integral to the way in which we *all* teach our modules. If this article encourages readers to reflect upon their own practices and share their experiences, so that others might benefit from them, then it will have fulfilled its task.

Method and structure

As part of a Royal Historical Society Jinty Nelson Fellowship exploring how a well-being agenda might enrich history teaching, I undertook a survey of just over 100 current undergraduate students, enrolled on the History BA and related joint degree programmes at the University of Reading, and a scoping study of well-being practices in about ninety UK HEI history departments (or their equivalent).

The survey, which was conducted anonymously and online, asked fifteen questions, with a mixture of set and open text answers. The areas covered included: a well-being self-assessment (on a scale of 1 to 10); a ranking of concerns and areas in which students felt they needed help; awareness of departmental and central university support systems; and student views on the potential for a well-being module as part of a history degree programme. The participants were all full-time students, overwhelmingly aged 18–21 years old, and made up of first year (43), second year (39) and third year (21) undergraduates.[8]

The scoping study looked at the websites of about ninety UK HEIs which offer history degrees. It sought to establish a main point of contact, with responsibility for the well-being of history students, and evidence of well-being concerns and initiatives, on both the history pages and the university website. Once identified, each point of contact was asked to provide further details, and

---

[7] According to James Banner, 'the entire discipline of history is undertheorized in comparison with many of its kindred disciplines in the humanities and social science'. J. M. Banner, *The Ever-Changing Past: Why All History is Revisionist History* (New Haven, NJ, 2021), 240.

[8] Without making any unwarranted claims to be representative of history undergraduates nationally, there are no reasons for assuming that results drawn from Reading will be wildly out of line with what we might expect elsewhere. History at Reading occupies a mid-table position on most tabulated rankings; makes a BBB A-level offer; and scored 93.1% (national average 91.1%) for the theme one, 'Teaching on my Course' section of the 2023 NSS.

any reflections they wished to share. Representatives from eleven institutions responded.

In writing this article, insights from the survey, scoping study and further information provided have been combined with a review of the broader well-being literature, to help to answer the following questions:

- What is well-being?
- Does history teach and promote well-being?
- Should history promote well-being?
- How can historians teach with well-being?

The article concludes by making the case for historians to embrace an agenda which can simultaneously enrich our teaching and benefit our students.

What is well-being?

The term well-being, and the idea that it might form a key component in education, is not new. Jeremy Bentham in his *Chrestomathia* (1816) could not have been more direct: 'The proper end of education is no other than the proper end of life – wellbeing.'[9] But although the term is well established its meaning is notoriously unclear. As one recent review put it: 'a clear and useful definition and conceptualisation of well-being remains elusive.'[10] Almost every published article and piece of research on well-being begins by acknowledging that it remains 'a nebulous term' and goes on to discuss its contested meaning. This is a serious problem for anyone interested in integrating a theoretically valid concept of well-being into their work. As a recent exploration of the use of the term by doctors observes: 'In the absence of an agreed definition, many synonyms, descriptions, lists of well-being components or determinants, are used interchangeably when well-being is discussed, making it hard to compare well-being research studies.'[11] How then, one might reasonably ask, can we discuss well-being, let alone pursue it in an educational context, if we cannot agree on what it means?

One answer, I would suggest, lies in acknowledging that well-being is not – and can never be – a fixed, eternal, objective entity; it must instead be understood as a set of context-specific qualities. 'The research literature suggests significant differences in conceptualisations of wellbeing across different cultures, ages, and population groups', and rather than ignore this or attempt to smooth down distinctions, our starting point must be an

---

[9] J. Bentham, *Chrestomathia: being a collection of papers, explanatory of the design of an institution, proposed to be set on foot under the name of the chrestomathic school for the extension of the news system of instruction to the higher branches of learning, for the use of the meddling and higher ranks in life* (1816), 606.

See, also D. Collard. 'Research on Wellbeing: Some Advice from Jeremy Bentham', *WeD Working Paper 02*, ESRC April 2003.

[10] A. Jarden and A. Roache, 'What is Wellbeing?', *International Journal of Environmental Research and Public Health*, 20 (2023), 5006.

[11] G. Simons and D. S. Baldwin, 'A Critical Review of the Definition of 'Wellbeing' for Doctors and their Patients in a Post Covid-19 Era', *International Journal of Social Psychiatry*, 67 (2021), 984–91.

acknowledgement that we are concerned with a specific group and with enhancing specific (educationally favourable) aspects of their well-being.[12] As historians we are not seeking to promote well-being per se – as a societal wide, let alone an ahistorical, entity – but the well-being of history students *as history students* in UK HEIs in the third decade of the twenty-first century. If we return to the 'what is well-being?' question with this in mind, we can begin to build a workable definition.

Well-being from this perspective is immediately understood as something richer than a noun indicating a state of being comfortable, healthy or happy. Most of those working on the concept emphasise that beyond immediate happiness, well-being encompasses ideas of fulfilment, purpose and control in one's life.[13] This multidimensional definition is rooted in Abram Maslow's hierarchy of needs, and was given its current form by the positive psychology movement, which is said to have begun with Martin Seligman's 1998 presidency of the American Psychological Association, and has inspired initiatives such as the *World Happiness Report* (2012).[14] Positive psychology has been defined as 'the scientific study of positive human functioning and flourishing on multiple levels', in which the strengthening of positive character traits is encouraged.[15] The underlying idea can be traced back to the Aristotelian concept of *eudaemonia*, but its proximate roots lie in a later twentieth century reaction against psychological approaches, particularly Freudianism, which focused on dysfunction. In broad terms, positive psychology sought to reorientate the discipline so that it foregrounded positive emotions and the development of talents.[16]

As well as defining well-being, we also need to consider how it is measured. For the past forty years, the main method employed has been the Subjective Well-Being (SWB) model, pioneered by Ed Diener.[17] SWB surveys provide the core underlying material for all major well-being studies, including the annual *World Happiness Report*, the OECD's *How's Life?* survey, and the UK Office for National Statistics' *Measures of National Well-being*. Diener's SWB model includes both affective and cognitive components, asking participants to evaluate Positive Affects (PA), Negative Affects (NA) and an integrated, global Life Satisfaction (LS) score. The LS score, which is essentially cognitive, is usually measured by asking respondents to rate their overall satisfaction with life

[12] Jarden and Roache, 'What is Wellbeing?', 5006.

[13] See R. P. Dodge *et al.*, 'The Challenge of Defining Wellbeing', *International Journal of Wellbeing*, 2 (2012), 222–35.

[14] A. H. Maslow, 'A Theory of Human Motivation', *Psychological Review*, 50 (1943), 370–96.
For an uncritical and wholly sympathetic summary of Seligman's career see his page on his Positive Psychology Center site: https://ppc.sas.upenn.edu/people/martin-ep-seligman.

[15] M.E.P. Seligman and M. Csikszentmihalyi, 'Positive Psychology: An Introduction', *American Psychologist*, 55 (2000), 5–14.

[16] The practice of positive psychology by Dr Laurie Santos (Yale) and others, especially on her 'The Science of Well-being' course, has encompassed a fuller spectrum of emotions, including sadness. See https://www.drlauriesantos.com/science-well-being.

[17] E. Diener, 'Subjective Well-being', *Psychological Bulletin*, 95 (1984), 542–75.

Table 1. Seligman's five components of Wellbeing Theory

P	Positive Emotions	Satisfaction, awe, contentment
E	Engagement	The opportunity for 'flow'
R	Relationships	Quality and quantity of social connections in and out of group
M	Meaning	Sense of purpose
A	Accomplishment	Achievement and progression

on a scale of 0 (not at all satisfied) to 10 (completely satisfied) with a question such as: 'Overall, how satisfied are you with your life as a whole these days.'[18]

It perhaps needs to be emphasised, especially for those of us primed in positivism, that self-evaluation is a valid methodology. For immediate assessments a subjective judgement can be more meaningful than an observed one: 'I am enjoying myself' is a more reliable statement than 'You are enjoying yourself'. The balance perhaps shifts with a greater range of evidence and a longer-term perspective – 'My life is good' and 'Your life is good' might both be valid – but the idea that well-being can be ascertained without a subjective element is doubtful. Moreover, although measurement of LS is inherently individual and subjective, the frameworks in which LS is experienced are social and constructed. LS scores themselves are the endpoint, a balancing of Positive and Negative Affects, and a representation of the extent to which PA outweighs NA. The key to enhancing them, therefore, and what must sit at the heart of a definition of well-being with which historians designing curricula can engage, is the extent to which a history degree allows and encourages students to develop, thrive and flourish.

Well-being in an educational setting, that is, is eudaemonic rather than hedonistic. It is concerned with the extent to which development and fulfilment can be achieved through challenging tasks and meaningful activities associated with positive moods and elevated PA. To what extent do our degree programmes provide this? Do they enhance or detract from well-being defined in this way? Do our students enjoy opportunities for fulfilment, purpose, and control?

One way to think about this might be to consider the checklist of PERMA characteristics developed by Seligman (see Table 1).[19]

Do our programmes and modules promote these five characteristics? Do we induce Positive Emotions and provide opportunities for Engagement? Does a history degree foster Relationships and provide our students with Meaning? Are we certain that we impart a sense of Accomplishment? The evidence from our student survey, in which over half of those who responded said

---

[18] Slightly different wording is employed in different countries. See *OECD Guidelines on Measuring Subjective Well-being* (2013).

[19] See M. Seligman, *Flourish: A New Understanding of Happiness and Well-being and how to achieve Them* (2017).

that they struggled with 'Motivation' would suggest that we might do more to promote PERMA among our undergraduates.

Does history teach and promote well-being?

History is not a happy subject. Whether or not we accept Suzanne Marchand's judgement that the discipline took a wrong turn with Thucydides, it is certainly true that the birth of its modern incarnation came with dire tidings.[20] For Gibbon, history – by which he meant the recorded past, rather than the past in totality – was 'little more than the register of the crimes, follies, and misfortunes of mankind'.[21] Hegel was, if anything, even less jolly: 'The History of the World is not the theatre of happiness,' he wrote, 'Periods of happiness are blank pages in it.'[22] The discipline, of course, has expanded markedly in the past two centuries. War, statecraft and diplomacy have been joined by social, cultural, environmental, and a host of other histories, filling in some of the blank pages on women, children and subaltern populations. But despite this, and an admittedly more limited broadening of the profession in terms of race, gender and class, relatively little has happened to brighten history's content. A brief review of the module options on offer to students in my own department reveals titles replete with words such as Dystopia, Nuclear Disaster, Genocide, Rape, Anti-Semitism, War, Hunger, Famine, Fascist, Empire, Slavery, Death Camps and Hostile Environment. The only impact of the broadening of the profession's interests and profile, it is tempting to conclude, has been to expose swathes of previously neglected misery.

History as a subject undoubtedly suffers from what positive psychologists call negativity bias: a human tendency to remember unresolved and bad situations more clearly and with more frequency than happy outcomes.[23] Does this matter? Is the mental well-being of our students negatively impacted by the content we teach them? Positive psychology encourages its patients to become content with their past, as an element of being happy in the present and to enable them to look to the future with optimism. It is premised, *contra* Freud, on the notion that 'excessive focussing on the past had the framing effect of giving it excessive salience, making it more difficult to make progress'.[24] This is a critique not just of psychoanalysis but of all dwelling on unhappy histories. Debriefing after accidents, for example, can be seen as re-traumatising and negative, and we might extend this to historical investigations which entail a collective rehearsing of past traumas, with the potential to engender a vicious circle of depressive and disabling thoughts. Psychologists measuring brain activity with a PET scanner have detected how exposure to different information and images creates different reactions

---

[20] S. Marchand, 'Flourishing with Herodotus', in *History and Human Flourishing*, ed. McMahon,140–54.

[21] E. Gibbon, *History of the Decline and Fall of the Roman Empire* (1782), ch. 3, 43.

[22] G. W. F. Hegel, *The Philosophy of History* (Kitchener, ON, 2001), 41.

[23] See A. Vaish, T. Grossmann, A. Woodward, 'Not all emotions are created equal: the negativity bias in social-emotional development', *Psychological Bulletin*, 134 (2008), 383–403.

[24] R. Layard, *Happiness: Lessons from a New Science* (2005) 195.

and moods, and judging by our module titles most history degrees are the equivalent to being shown three continuous years of horrendous pictures.

This, however, is far from the whole story. Even if one accepts the critique of Freudian methods, it is still possible to reject any simplistic parallel between individual psychology and societal level questions. Foregrounding well-being, moreover, does not – as is sometimes assumed – preclude, or even discourage the teaching of difficult topics. What it does ask of us is to recognise when material might be challenging and to introduce it to students self-consciously and framed within appropriate supporting structures. To take an extreme example, a concern with well-being is not an argument against teaching the history of sexual violence. Such histories are vital in addressing injustice and challenging contemporary attitudes in ways that can enhance well-being for all in the longer term. It is even possible to make the argument that any short-term distress can create a 'stress inoculation' effect, which facilitates a deeper long-term sense of well-being.[25] Teaching with well-being, that is, does not demand that we forego the dark side of history, but that we show care and consideration when teaching it.

There is no evidence that the *content* of what we teach is inherently detrimental to student mental health. But nor is there much to suggest that our programmes *enhance* well-being. The average LS score for students participating in our survey was 6.9. This compares with a recent UK average across the whole population of 6.8 and an OECD average of 6.7.[26] The results, that is, are broadly in line with what we might expect, although perhaps a little on the low side, as those aged under 30 and better educated have, until relatively recently, tended to produce more markedly higher than average scores.[27] We need, of course, to keep in mind that the sample size is small, and this becomes an even more important consideration when we break down the results by year group, an exercise that points to LS declining marginally across the three years of a history degree. Without overstating the preciseness of these results, the tentative conclusion we might draw is that history undergraduates are no more and no less happy than the national average, and that the overall impact on well-being of studying for a history degree is probably no better than neutral.

This is a slightly disappointing conclusion. In theory, history degrees provide ample opportunities to fulfil Seligman's PERMA characteristics: Positive Emotions, induced by a past rich in awe-inspiring content; Engagement, found in deep reading techniques; Relationships, forged in seminar teaching; Meaning, established in working to a defined end; and Accomplishment, experienced at each semester staging post. In their studies history students ought to enjoy an opportunity to reach the highest level in

[25] D. Meichenbaum and R. Novaco, 'Stress Inoculation: A Preventative Approach', *Issues in Mental Health Nursing*, 7 (1985), 419–35.

[26] OECD, *How's Life? 2020: Measuring Well-being*: https://www.oecd-ilibrary.org/sites/9870c393-en/index.html?itemId=/content/publication/9870c393-en.

[27] R. Hall, 'University students more at risk of depression than non-students – study', *The Guardian*, 29 Sept. 2023.

Maslow's hierarchy of needs and to feel, even if only fleetingly, a state of self-actualisation.[28] Moreover, many of the skills we train our students in as historians might be thought to enable them simultaneously to manage their own well-being better. For example, the historian's skills for interpreting evidence and probing competing narratives form an interesting parallel with some Cognitive Behavioural Theory (CBT) techniques, which are similarly concerned with the ways in which we tell (ourselves) stories and learn to acknowledge subjectivity as an inherent part of being human. Why then are our students not happier?

It is, of course, important to keep in mind that history students do not exist hermetically sealed qua history students. They are subjected to the same external pressures – including the cost-of-living crisis and social media engagement – as others in their age group. Digging deeper into our survey results shows that 60 per cent of respondents claimed to be suffering 'stress' and 40 per cent 'mental health concerns', with a similar proportion worried about 'finance'. It is noticeable that these top three concerns relate to being a student generally rather than being a historian specifically, and the same is true of the top three areas in which respondents wanted help: 'motivation' (over 50 per cent); essay writing (40 per cent); and 'time management' (around a third). One conclusion we might draw from this is that even if the content of history teaching does not harm student well-being, some of the pedagogic practice which surrounds its delivery might. Class presentations, essay deadlines and examinations are established causes of stress, especially among neurodiverse students. More broadly, many of our teaching practices – weekly classes, large lectures, online delivery, individual assessment – do little to counteract problems of non-clinical mental health needs, such as anxiety, loneliness and isolation.

Should history promote well-being?

History departments should promote the well-being of their students because it aids their study of history. The claim that increased '*well-being is synergistic with better learning*' makes intuitive sense and explains why those who teach, at all levels, 'are being increasingly challenged to centre wellbeing' in their programmes of learning.[29] Demonstrating a direct connection between an individual's well-being and their academic performance, however, it should be acknowledged, is not always possible. Naysayers can point to some limited evidence that the attributes historians need to develop – including critical and analytic thinking – might actually be better produced by negative moods, but more studies suggest the benefits of well-being in promoting a virtuous circle of performance. There is evidence that well-being at earlier stages of life is

---

[28] Maslow's hierarchy of needs progressed through physiological needs, safety needs, love and belonging, and esteem, up to self-actualisation: a sense of fulfilment of one's potential.

[29] M. E. P. Seligman, R. M. Ernst, J. Gillham, K. Reivich and M. Linkins, 'Positive Education: Positive Psychology and Classroom Interventions', *Oxford Review of Education*, 35 (2009), 293–311, at 294; S. Carter and C. Andersen, *Wellbeing in Educational Contexts* (Davis, CA, 2024), 16.

predictive of future well-being, and that by raising awareness of well-being we are helping our students to become better at managing their own mental health in the future.[30] There are, in short, good grounds for championing well-being as an aid to our students' broader development, and for supposing that a successful well-being strategy would have a positive impact on the various metrics, including the NSS and Graduate Outcomes, by which history departments are judged.

The results of our scoping study suggest that there already exists an imperfect understanding of this within UK HEI history departments. Almost all departments framed student well-being in one or more of three overlapping ways: teaching activities; pastoral support; and the wider culture of learning. In terms of teaching, well-being concerns were expressed in relation to questions of group size; variety of assessment; hands-on experiences; and timetabling. Pastoral support centred on the Personal Tutor system, finance and opportunities to socialise. Wider cultural well-being considerations around learning focused primarily on the transition to university and provision of study skills, alongside attendance and engagement monitoring, and, more rarely, what one institution described as the need for a 'growth mindset'. It was interesting to note that the overwhelming focus of reflections on well-being in history departments was on entry-year students.

This emphasis on the challenge of transitioning to university needs unpacking. It might simply reflect an understanding of the value of good habits imbibed early on, but it might also speak to an unacknowledged desire to create a more uniform student body. The frequent mention of Foundation programmes in this regard is particularly interesting. Does this indicate a deficit model approach, in which well-being is regarded as a tool to help make up for supposed academic shortcomings? Or, given that many Foundation programmes cater disproportionately for students from socio-economic backgrounds who are under-represented in university, is the primary concern acculturation? Whatever the case, we need to move beyond any tendency to regard well-being as a stage to be achieved, or a one-off entry and transition task. One respondent to the scoping study reflected on how their department had begun to consider extending induction activities across the first half of the term, rather than overwhelming incoming students in a tsunami of induction week information. This is a step forward in understanding transition as an ongoing process, but we also need a further acknowledgement that to be meaningful well-being needs to form part of the student experience across the three years of a history degree programme.

One reason why this does not happen now, or at least happens only in an *ad hoc*, inconsistent way, is that very few history departments have a member of staff with overall responsibility for well-being. While Personal Tutors are often

---

[30] D. D. Danner, D. Snowdon and N. V. Friesen, 'Positive Emotions in Early Life and Longevity: Findings from the Nun Study', *Journal of Personality and Social Psychology*, 80 (2001), 804–13; S. Colleen, J. Conley, J. A. Durlak and D. A. Dickson, 'An Evaluative Review of Outcome Research on Universal Mental Health Promotion and Prevention Programs for Higher Education Students', *Journal of American College Health*, 61 (2013), 286–301.

charged, in general terms, with well-being responsibility for their individual tutees, there is rarely any assigned academic with responsibility for ensuring that the department maintains a collective well-being focus. In contrast to areas including research, impact, employability and social media, for which identifiable leads can be found, few history departments have a named well-being lead. Our scoping survey showed that where overall responsibility for well-being is assigned at all, it is packaged as a subsidiary concern in other administrative tasks. Even within this a surprising range of office-holders were identified. Many departments settled responsibility on the Programme Director (or equivalent), but other roles identified as leading on well-being included: Head of Department, Skills module coordinator, Senior Admissions Office, Associate Head, Senior Departmental Administrator, Director of EDI, Head of Welfare, Student Experiences Manager, Executive Dean, and Part One Coordinator. This absence of any clear consensus on where well-being should sit within the administrative framework of history departments is perhaps symptomatic of the more general lack of clarity about what well-being is and how it relates to historical study.

It may also reflect a residual hostility both to the concept of well-being and to the idea that the promotion of well-being is the responsibility of historians and history departments.

Historians' doubts about well-being

It was obvious when researching this topic that many practising historians are suspicious of well-being initiatives, on both intellectual and practical grounds. Some sympathise with the objections of those such as Kim Ecclestone who have characterised the integration of well-being into academic curricula as undermining subject knowledge and prompting an escape from 'hard study'.[31] Judging by conversations I have had I would suggest that a misleading belief in an opposition between (masculinised) 'hard work' and a 'soft' (feminised) well-being agenda is deep-rooted in the profession. More than one interlocutor was dismissive, with one making a disparaging reference to UCL's 'famous wellbeing alpacas' – an engaging but easily mocked initiative to help students 'de-stress' in the exam period – in order to clinch their case.[32] Well-being, that is, is seen by some as just too comfortable and reassuring to be compatible with a discipline built upon posing and probing discomforting questions.

Underlying this attitude are legitimate concerns that well-being can be used as a form of corporate performance – well-being washing – by universities and that the concept often aligns all too easily with ideological perspectives that

---

[31] K. Ecclestone, 'Are Universities encouraging Students to believe Hard Study is Bad for their Mental Health?', *Times Higher Education*, 2 Apr. 2020; K. Ecclestone and D. Hayes, 'Changing the Subject: The Educational Implications of Developing Emotional Well-being', *Oxford Review of Education*, 35 (2009), 371–89. See also K. Ecclestone and D. Hayes, *The Dangerous Rise of Therapeutic Education* (2008).

[32] See https://www.ucl.ac.uk/students/events/2024/apr/ssw-exam-season-toolkit-wellbeing-alpacas.

encourage conformity and underplay systemic injustice.[33] For example, initiatives that encourage individuals to reconcile themselves to existing circumstances, such as Covey's Circles of Influence, Concern and Control might be read as inherently palliative, and thereby conservative in undermining longer-term struggles for reform.[34] The suspicion many historians harbour on this point is deepened both by the general profile of those advocating a well-being agenda – white, western and privileged by existing structural inequalities – and the false universalism implicit in some of their arguments.[35] Others may be concerned by the 'lightly de-theologised terms' in which well-being is too often discussed, and the dominance of the Templeton Foundation, an organisation with an openly ideological agenda, as the dominant funder of well-being initiatives in the humanities.[36]

Acknowledging these concerns, however, is not in itself an argument against the integration of well-being into historical study; it is an argument against an *uncritical* integration. Just because much of the work on well-being has been ahistorical, individualistic and culturally insensitive does not mean that it must be so. For one thing, not all work on well-being replicates these failings: Lynne Segal's *Radical Happiness: Moments of Collective Joy* (2018), for example, looks beyond the individual to understand happiness in the structure and context of political economy. For another, any history of well-being can usefully highlight and explore these failings, just as any discussion of well-being in a specific historical period can highlight the context of exploitation and oppression in which notions of well-being are constructed and contested. As a recent piece by Mia Bay has highlighted, an African American history of well-being provides insights with which 'few works of positive psychology engage'.[37] History, as Peter Stearns has argued, has the potential to deepen and enrich the well-being agenda.[38] This will prove doubly valuable if, simultaneously, it can benefit our students. To do so successfully, however, will require some rethinking of how we teach, and our students learn, history.

It is here that we run into the practical objections of those who argue that the promotion of well-being is not the responsibility of history departments. This view, which was partially articulated in the detailed responses to the scoping study, consists of two overlapping objections concerning capacity and capability. The first is that it is unrealistic to expect historians and history departments to resolve issues of student well-being. This point is, in a limited sense, unanswerable: we cannot resolve all the travails of our students. Many

---

[33] W. Davies, *The Happiness Industry: How the Government and Big Business Sold us Happiness* (2015).

[34] S. Covey, *The 7 Habits of Highly Successful People* (2004), 83.

[35] N. Eustace, '"Beauty is Universal": Virtue, Aesthetics, Emotion, and Race in James Logan's Atlantic Moral Sense Philosophy', in *History and Human Flourishing*, ed. McMahon, 174.

[36] D. Graham Burnett, 'History, Humanities and the Human', in *History and Human Flourishing*, ed. McMahon, 30. The Templeton Foundation is the major funder of the Humanities and Human Flourishing initiative: https://www.humanitiesandhumanflourishing.org/.

[37] Mia Bay, 'Toward a History of Black Happiness', in *History and Human Flourishing*, ed. McMahon, 184–97.

[38] P. N. Stearns, 'Well-being and a Usable Past: The Role of Historical Diagnosis', in *History and Human Flourishing*, ed. McMahon, 100.

of the so-called 'Big Seven' factors affecting personal happiness, including family relations, finance and (physical) health, lie beyond the influence of any academic department.[39] And this feeds into the second objection: historians are overworked and ill-equipped to take on tasks that are more properly performed by the central university. Why should an expert on seventeenth-century agrarian reform or twelfth-century Papal letters concern themselves with issues that are more properly the province of the university's professional and welfare services?

The answer, of course, is that they should not. It is never appropriate for historians to provide surrogate support services or make good a shortfall in counselling provision. But framing the question in this way reinforces a misunderstanding of what well-being in education means. It should not be thought of as substituting or even supplementing professional and welfare services, which will continue to have their own specialist role to play. It means, rather, creating the conditions in which our students can best learn, flourish and thrive, and this needs to happen at the level of the individual discipline.

The results of our survey make clear the extent to which student engagement is overwhelmingly discipline-, indeed module-, based. Over a third of respondents indicated that they had never had any contact with central services, and those who had usually initiated contact to help resolve issues relating to individual modules, including assessment submission and adjustment, and timetable clashes. The centrality of modules to the student experience was further confirmed by the contrasting responses to questions about Academic Tutors and module tutors. Almost 40 per cent said that they had never engaged with their Academic Tutor, whereas almost 60 per cent identified module tutors as someone they would approach with a problem. The point here is that well-being initiatives will only reach (and have a chance of success with) most students through modules. All the alternative potential modes of transmission, such as student services, student counselling, or the Student Union sit outside the immediate learning environments in which students directly engage with the university. Academic staff and the curriculum are the only guaranteed points of contact between the university and its students, and 'the curriculum is the one consistent element in students' lives in which universities can influence behaviour and learning'.[40] To be successful, a well-being agenda needs to operate at the point at which students primarily exist and function: their discipline.

How can historians teach with well-being?

The question of 'how can historians teach with well-being?' might be more appositely phrased as 'how can historians teach with *more* well-being?' There are, and have always been, elements of well-being in history teaching and

---

[39] Layard, *Happiness*, 62–3.
[40] G. Hughes, 'Support Student Wellbeing Through Curriculum Design and Delivery', *The Watt Works Quick Guide*, 20 (n.d.), 1–3.

delivery. To make an only slightly facetious point, Leopold von Ranke would never have considered bringing an alpaca onto campus, but by pioneering seminar teaching and developing close source-reading techniques, he might be said to have delivered two of Seligman's five-part PERMA: Engagement, through deep reading, and Relationships, forged in class work. Just because this was not conceptualised or expressed in the language of positive psychology, does not mean that Ranke's teaching did not enhance well-being. What follows then is less about innovation per se, and more about increasing self-awareness and reflexivity, as part of a more systematic and self-conscious attempt to enhance existing practices so that we teach with *more* well-being. The best way to achieve this is through an ongoing process of curricular infusion.

The term curricular infusion refers to the practice of embedding discipline-specific materials and activities into the curriculum, in order to encourage discussion and reflection on a particular issue.[41] Rather than demand new structures or content, a curricular infusion approach would build upon existing module content in ways which foreground well-being. A philosophy module on existentialism, for example, would build out from readings from Dostoevsky, Sartre, Kierkegaard and Nietzsche into a discussion of loneliness, alienation, stress, anxiety and depression.[42] History modules are replete with similar opportunities. These might be direct (a module on J. S. Mill might discuss adolescent depression) or indirect (a module on medieval anti-Semitism might provoke reflections on the experience of discrimination today). A module on monasticism could help students to think about friendship; one on the First World War could encourage them to contemplate separation and fear; a module on the witch craze might be an opportunity to ponder paranoia and misogyny.

It is worth emphasising that what we are advocating here is the pursuit of a well-being agenda *through* existing modules. Although there might be some advantages in creating new, explicitly well-being-focused, history modules – for example, inviting students to reflect upon the history of the concept would, implicitly, provide them with an opportunity to reflect upon their own well-being – this would also entail downsides. Our scoping study suggests that no UK HEI history department runs a dedicated well-being module at present, and there is no evidence of enthusiasm for introducing one. Our survey revealed a large degree of uncertainty about what such an initiative would look like: 40 per cent of respondents answered 'Maybe' to the question whether a dedicated well-being module was a good idea. And those history departments that have experimented with well-being drop-in sessions reported very low levels of engagement. Making participation compulsory, in the form of a module, would risk alienating the very students we are seeking

---

[41] Union of Students in Ireland and National Forum for the Enhancement of Teaching and Learning in Higher Education, *Embedding Wellbeing across the Curriculum in Higher Education*, Oct. 2021.

https://usi.ie/wp-content/uploads/2021/10/Supporting-Wellbeing-in-Practice-October-2021.pdf.

[42] Olson and Riley, 'Weaving the Campus Safety Net', 28.

to aid. The other risk in creating a dedicated module is that it would tend to silo well-being into one spot in the curriculum and reinforce the tendency to see well-being as a one-off, transitional stage. This is unlikely to achieve enduring gains: there is cross-disciplinary evidence that the benefits of stand-alone psycho-educational modules teaching positive psychology are not sustained beyond the period of the module.[43] All this suggests that to be successful well-being initiatives need to be integrated into modules across the curriculum.[44]

The first step to making this happen is for every history department to have an assigned advocate, with a brief to promote well-being both within the overall programme *and* within individual modules.[45] Although we have argued that well-being concerns are not alien or extrinsic to the study of history, it is also the case that the discipline rarely foregrounds them. There is, for example, no explicit mention of well-being in the most recent QAA *Subject Benchmark Statement* (March 2022) for history.[46] An assigned advocate in every history department is needed, therefore, to perform two functions. First, the advocate must to review the programme overall in the light of Seligman's PERMA characteristics. The increasing awareness across HEIs of the need for coherent programme level design needs to embrace well-being. In particular, we need to review the balance of different PERMA characteristics at different stages of the degree, for example the importance of relationships in the first term, and the need to build a sense of accomplishment at key stages. Second, curricular infusion will only succeed with the widest possible buy-in from the staff who deliver modules, and this will be best achieved when championed *within* the department, by individuals who are sensitive to disciplinary concerns, and who can guide and reassure colleagues.

Remaking history modules

The key to promoting well-being through history teaching lies at the modular level, and the key innovation we can all make is to reflect on the extent to which our existing module content and teaching might be enhanced. This is an incremental agenda for change, which builds on existing practices, but which could have a transformative effect on the student experience. In the first instance, change will be, by necessity, teacher-led, but reforms that develop in a collaborative, co-constructive dialogue with students themselves are likely to be most effective. This can take different forms. Co-construction

---

[43] C. Hobbs, S. Jelbert, L. R. Santos and B. Hood, 'Long-Term Analysis of a Psychoeducational Course on University Students' Mental Well-being', *Higher Education*. Published online 8 Mar. 2024. https://doi.org/10.1007/s10734-024-01202-4.

[44] A.-M. Houghton and J. Anderson, *Embedding Mental Wellbeing in the Curriculum: Maximising Success in H. E.* (York, 2017).

[45] History departments are structured differently in different institutions, and it may not always be possible to create new roles. In these instances, student well-being should be made an explicit responsibility of an existing senior role.

[46] *Quality Assurance Agency for Higher Education, Subject Benchmark Statement: History*, 5th edn (Gloucester, 2022).

might occur within the module: on one Foundation level module which I convened students were able to vote to determine the subject content of the second half of the course each year. Or it might occur at the design stage. For example, I have been involved in the design of a new Part One module, 'Making History and You', where we worked with the university's Inclusion Consultants – current students from a range of disciplines who are paid to advise staff on how to make their courses and services more accessible and inclusive – to help build a module with well-being at its heart.[47] Some colleagues will be more comfortable with this level of co-construction than others. But what all module convenors can do, in consultation with a departmental well-being advocate, is to consider how the design and delivery of their modules map onto the 'five ways to well-being' template, developed by the New Economics Foundation.[48] This provides five simple tests through which we can all consider the extent to which our teaching contributes to student well-being.

Connect

Our first responsibility is to ensure that our students feel a direct connection to the module they are studying, and the initial focus for that is through the module tutor. Something as simple as remembering and using students' names in class, and taking a moment to learn correct pronunciations, can help deepen a personal connection and was mentioned as important by respondents to our scoping study. Specifically, as historians we can also help deepen connections by telling stories about the past and providing a space for students to reflect upon how an aspect of their own life – or their family history – might connect to the module content. We should also aim to humanise and demystify our subject matter. When discussing the approaches taken by different historians, for example, why not have slides with their photographs on, rather than just their names or book jackets? Those who are comfortable discussing their own experiences – what first drew you to the subject? what problems did you encounter? – can also help students to understand that their own difficulties are a necessary stage to work through. Personalising one's teaching in this way can be done to different extents. Few will match the bravura performance of Sarah Chaney's outstanding *Am I Normal? The 200-year Search for Normal People and Why they Don't Exist* (2022), which frames an exploration of modern thinking about normality in the tale of her own personal development as an undergraduate, but even sharing snippets of who we are, and how this relates to our research, can be valuable.

---

[47] On Reading's Inclusion Consultant scheme see https://www.reading.ac.uk/essentials/Diversity-and-Inclusion/Get-Involved/Inclusion-Consultants.

[48] These were outlined in the report by Foresight, *Mental Capital and Wellbeing: Making the Most of Ourselves in the 21st Century* (Government Office for Science, 2008). See also: https://neweconomics.org/uploads/files/five-ways-to-wellbeing-1.pdf.

Be active

The benefits of physical movement in learning were another theme that emerged strongly in the scoping study. One institution laid great stress on the importance of field trips; another had a rule that at least two sessions per module were delivered outside the classroom. For most, however, there was no systematic approach, and existing initiatives, such as visiting archives and museums, had developed in an *ad hoc*, unstructured way. We all instinctively understand that ten- or twelve-week modules, in which students take the same seats in the same classrooms for two or more hours at a time, session after session, can induce intellectual torpor. But breaking this cycle can be difficult, especially with large-sized groups, and study trips can create their problems in terms of cost and health and safety risks. At the very least, however, the injunction 'be active' might mean exploring different parts of a campus, or students simply moving around different breakout groups or considering information sheets pinned to different parts of the classroom.

For the more ambitious the recent upsurge of interest in the history of pedestrianism provides an opportunity to link an increasingly vibrant area of history with the established mental health benefits of walking.[49] A good example of how this might be done could be seen in the Goldsmiths, University of London module 'Walking through London's History', in which students used urban walking as a means to explore the city's history, and produced public-facing blogs charting their experiences.[50] Similar modules, with an urban or rural, landscape-focus, might be developed in almost any location. More broadly, there is also an opportunity to build upon the profession's growing interest in outdoor praxis – including the archive of the feet – as a means to explore ways in which walking simultaneously aids well-being and helps history connect to ecological and post humanist agendas.[51]

Keep learning

History demands an unusually high proportion of independent learning. Judging by the module descriptions at my own institution, there is an expectation that *c.* 85 per cent of a history student's study time is conducted independently outside the classroom. Our design and planning of modules ought to do much more to reflect this. At present there is a disproportionate focus on the content of contact hours – what will I say in the lecture? what materials will I discuss in class? – and far less on how students spend their learning hours outside class, or how the two connect , but this is vital in history. We need to acknowledge that independent learning is often

---

[49] See, for example, K. Andrews, *Wanderers: A History of Women and Walking* (2021). For research specifically exploring the benefits of walking for students see J. Ma, J. M. Williams, P. G. Morris and S. W. Y. Chan, 'Effectiveness of a Mindful Nature Walking Intervention on Sleep Quality and Mood in University Students during Covid-19: A Randomised Control Study' *Explore*, 19 (2022), 405–16.

[50] See https://wtlh.wordpress.com/about/.

[51] For example, D. Gange, 'Retracing Trevelyan? Historical Practice and the Archive of the Feet', *Green Letters*, 21 (2017), 246–61.

disorienting for students who, prior to university, have almost certainly only experienced a more rigid and directed learning environment. There are some tried and tested mechanisms that can help, including Weekly Learning Plans, which set clear expectations, and Worksheets, which help to structure individual learning. More ambitiously, many universities operate Peer-Assisted Learning (PAL) programmes in which students in an older cohort facilitate supplementary group study sessions. This is a well-established scheme, which research suggests has a dual benefit, for the students on module and for those who act as PAL leaders.[52] Both groups of students gain in terms of social connectedness, self-development and self-efficacy. However individual departments set about addressing this problem, the central point is that we want our students to have independence and self-direction, but this will not happen automatically; we need to help them to find ways to develop these attributes.

Take notice

One aspect of this might be found in the fourth of the New Economics Foundation's 'five ways to well-being'. *Take notice* is an invitation to relate module learning to what is going on in the wider world. The crucial point is to make a space within our modules for students to consider and express how they feel about the material under consideration. The well-being benefit of this is premised on the principle that we feel better about ourselves when we link our learning to other aspects of our lives, and when we are encouraged to relate it to those things we care about. In studying history, this can work either at a broad political level, in which we relate historic events and movements to contemporary parallels: what we might think of as a 'long view' approach. Or it can be much more personal and individual, where students explore the experiences of historical actors in relation to their own feelings and emotions. For the latter, the recent interest evinced by historians in questions of empathy offers some rich supporting soil, but it is perhaps worth emphasising that this *Take notice* approach can be made to work for almost any area, from the history of warfare to the history of emotions.[53]

Give

The fifth of the ways to well-being might be the most difficult to achieve for history students. Opportunities to *give* – in terms of sharing information, insight and understanding – are comparatively limited in history degrees. The proportion of time spent on independent study means that there is nothing comparable to the collective lab culture of natural sciences, and the extent of optionality in the second and third years of most history degrees militates against the kind of cohort identity which programmes with more

---

[52] S. Bailey, 'The Meaning Making Journey of Peer Assisted Learning (PAL) Leaders in HE', *International Journal of Evidence Based Coaching and Mentoring*, 15 (2021), 55–69.

[53] S. Fox, 'Archival Intimacies: Empathy and Historical Practice', *Transactions of the Royal Historical Society*, 1 (2023), 241–65.

compulsory elements can foster. History degrees, moreover, culminate in the (potentially isolating) experience of the dissertation. There are also broader forces that tend against a culture of giving, including tuition fees, which strengthen a transactional (or perhaps even mercantilist) attitude to degree-level study. Together these factors mean that we cannot expect a collaborative approach to be automatic or immediate for our students. That said, PAL schemes and group work can both help, and at the heart of the study of history at university sits the seminar which, when it functions as it should, is a giving experience. To facilitate this, we need to develop more open and inclusive environments – real and virtual – for our students, from day one in their degree programmes, to help them overcome engrained images of education as competition and to build their confidence in collaborating.

Conclusion

A conversation centred on how we can better integrate well-being into the teaching of history in UK HEIs is overdue. The suspicions and anxiety with which the term has sometimes been regarded need to be addressed and allayed, as a first step towards a fuller, more systematic integration of the well-being agenda into the design and delivery of our history modules. This is a task that we all need to share. The challenge of well-being among young people is societal, and even within universities action to address it needs to be supported at an institutional level. But a recognition of these wider contexts does not obviate the need for us to act directly, as historians, for our students. We have an opportunity to do more to promote well-being through history teaching, and we have a responsibility to discuss more widely how we might achieve this.

Acknowledgements. I would like to thank the two anonymous reviewers and Dr Dina Rezk for their comments on an earlier draft of this piece, and Abbie Tibbott for conducting the scoping study and survey which inspired this article.

Cite this article: Stack D (2024). Promoting Well-being through History Teaching. *Transactions of the Royal Historical Society* **2**, 471–489. https://doi.org/10.1017/S0080440124000082

Transactions of the RHS (2024), **2**, 491–507
doi:10.1017/S0080440124000033

COMMENT

Emerging Scholars Researching Black British Histories (mid-Eighteenth to mid-Nineteenth Centuries)

Kristy Warren[1] , Annabelle Gilmore[2] and Montaz Marché[2]

[1]Humanities and Heritage, University of Lincoln, Lincoln, UK and [2]University of Birmingham, Birmingham, UK
Corresponding author: Kristy Warren; Email: kwarren@lincoln.ac.uk

(Received 19 June 2023; revised 17 May 2024; accepted 18 May 2024; first published online 1 October 2024)

Abstract

Recent years have seen a vast expansion of scholarly interest in eighteenth- and nineteenth-century Black British histories, and increasing calls to support the work of early-career scholars (ECRs) in this field. Yet ECRs continue to face several specific challenges in conducting this crucial research. This section consists of a brief introduction and two case studies based on the research and experiences of Ph.D. students Annabelle Gilmore and Montaz Marché. Gilmore aims to amplify the connections between the lives and labour of enslaved people on plantations in Jamaica and the wealth and art collection of William Thomas Beckford, now held at Charlecote Park, from the mid-eighteenth to the mid-nineteenth centuries. Marché seeks to trace the presence of Black women in eighteenth-century London, drawing on archival documents that provide traces of who these women may have been, and confronting the limitations of the traditional archive. Together, these pieces offer a glimpse into how these ECRs are positioning themselves within the historiography as well as considering how they hope to contribute to the field.

Keywords: Black History; enslaved people; Caribbean; country houses; historiography; London; methodology; Warwickshire

Introduction

This section seeks to draw out the historiographical resonances between the research of two Ph.D. students, Annabelle Gilmore and Montaz Marché, and the field's broader body of work. It examines how they see their work fitting within the current shape and contributing to the direction of the field going forward. As a result, it also useful for considering the present and future state of Black British histories of the eighteenth and nineteenth centuries. The field of Black British history has grown significantly in the past fifteen years, but the work has a much longer history. It has seen the development of research concerning the African presence conducted with little institutional support, both within and outside of the academy. The early 1980s saw contributions in this vein from Paul Edwards, Peter Fryer, Edward Scobie, Folarin Shyllon and James Walvin.[1] In addressing this long-disregarded area of British history, they provided a wide framework for other researchers to build upon. More recently, the field has expanded to include a range of contributions that have stretched the field's methodology, critical lens, and periods and subjects of focus.[2] For the purposes of this section, key interests included research concerning the urban presence of Black people, particularly Black women in Georgian London, as well as studies which show the connections between the development of British wealth and influence, the Black presence in rural Britain and the labour and death of those based throughout the British empire.[3]

The work of Gilmore and Marché responds to and builds on the historiography. They engage with existing scholarship on the Black British past in Britain and the Caribbean and methodological approaches to the archives. Additionally, they are conducting research using a range of sources, some of which have not been analysed previously, while also reapproaching sources that have in the past been used to reinforce a national narrative that does not include the presence of those of African descent. In this work they see themselves contributing to the field by helping to shape the direction that study will take in the future with particular reference to their periods and geographies of focus. Thus, their engagement with the existing work is shaped by their research interests and education to date.

---

[1] Edward Scobie, *Black Britannia: A History of Blacks in Britain* (Chicago, 1972); James Walvin, *Black and White: The Negro and English Society 1555-1945* (1973); Folarin Shyllon, *Black People in Britain 1555-1833* (Oxford, 1977); Paul Edwards and James Walvin, *Black Personalities in the Era of the Slave Trade* (1983); Peter Fryer, *Staying Power: The History of Black People in Britain* (1984).

[2] For recent outlines of the development of Black British histories over time as well as some of the key debates in the field see Hakim Adi, *The History of the African and Caribbean Communities in Britain* (2020); Hakim Adi (ed.), *Black British History: New Perspectives* (2019); Caroline Brassey, Meleisa Ono-George, Diana Paton, Kennetta Hammond Perry and Sadiah Qureshi, 'Introduction: Reflections on Black British Histories in History Workshop Journal', *History Workshop Journal* (2021). Virtual Special Issue: Black British Histories; and Gretchen H. Gerzina (ed.), *Britain's Black Past* (Liverpool, 2020). For research concerning approaches to the archives see Saidiya Hartman, 'Venus in Two Acts', *Small Axe*, 12 (2008), 1-14; Jeannette A. Bastian, John A. Aarons and Stanley H. Griffin (eds.), *Decolonizing the Caribbean Record: An Archives Reader* (Sacramento, CA, 2018); and Marisa J. Fuentes, *Dispossessed Lives: Enslaved Women, Violence, and the Archive* (Philadelphia, PA, 2016).

[3] For example, see Madge Dresser and Andrew Hann (eds.), *Slavery and the British Country House* (Swindon 2013); Catherine Hall, Nicholas Draper, Keith McClelland, Katie Donington and Rachel Lang, *Legacies of British Slave-Ownership: Colonial Slavery and the Formation of Victorian Britain* (Cambridge, 2014); Sheryllynne Haggerty and Susanne Seymour, 'Imperial Careering and Enslavement in the Long Eighteenth Century: The Bentinck Family, 1710-1830s', *Slavery and Abolition*, 39 (2018), 642-62; and Sally-Anne Huxtable, Corinne Fowler, Christo Kefalas and Emma Slocombe, *Colonialism and Historic Slavery Report* (Swindon, 2020).

Gilmore and Marché's research spans from the mid-eighteenth to the mid-nineteenth centuries. Geographically, their work encompasses urban and rural spaces located in the British Isles and Jamaica. The focus is on the connections between spaces and unearthing little-studied narratives in the archives. Both draw on primary sources traditionally used to tell stories that centred on the experiences and accomplishments of wealthy white men. In some cases, the records completely ignore the presence and labour of Black people; in other cases, traces of Black people are evident but have often been either ignored by previous researchers or approached primarily through a wide lens. There are a number of reasons for this, including the nature of the archives and the way the field of history has been impacted by, for instance, a broadening of who is entering the archives, the ability to use databases and other digital tools to ask new questions. Their research, along with that of a range of other scholars, focused on this area of study and asks us to consider how British attitudes regarding race and gender impacted the experiences of specific individuals and small groups of Black people; this led to the erasure of their contributions to the much-celebrated wealth gained from the British empire.

Drawing on records located both in the United Kingdom and in Jamaica, Gilmore explores the connections between material culture in England and the lives of those whose labour fuelled the wealth that underpinned the purchases of objects and country houses. In her research, she centres the enslaved labourers who fuelled the wealth that enabled absentee enslaver William Thomas Beckford (1760–1844) to amass a collection of art objects. These objects are held at Charlecote Park, a National Trust property in Warwickshire. Additionally, she considers the presence of Africans within this English West Midlands county. Gilmore aims to show the links between two localities on either side of the Atlantic by exploring their connections to the global trade in trafficked Africans and the collection of objects made possible by the wealth created by enslavement. In order to do this, she engages with existing work on public histories concerning enslavement, the Black presence in Britain and the wealth of enslavers in museum exhibitions and other heritage sites to consider how the narrative is being altered through the intervention of researchers (both in and outside of the academy), curators and a 'curious' public. Gilmore is also learning about the nature of heritage sites through work placement and training that are not traditionally offered within a Ph.D. programme but have been made possible due to the collaborative nature of her project.

Meanwhile, Marché has compiled a database of 500 Black women who lived in London during the mid to late eighteenth century. Using a range of archival material, she aims to unearth the lived experience of such women during this period. This centring of individual everyday Black people in Georgian London has been limited. As Marché shows in her work, most existing research into questions of the impact of race, gender, age and class on everyday lives focuses on the nineteenth and twentieth centuries. Meanwhile, those histories concerned with the eighteenth century tend to focus on prominent figures within the Abolition movement. By focusing on working-class women in the eighteenth century, Marché is faced with several issues implicit in the records, such as the question of how to approach records such as run-away servant advertisements, which describe individuals with the aim of identifying them to recapture them. She thus examines the extent to which these descriptions align with how the women saw themselves and how they were seen by neighbours, family, friends and society more generally. Marché also explores the question of how these women may have masked their identity while on the run to avoid capture. Additionally, she considers what information is missing that would help historians better understand their lived experiences. Ultimately, Marché is asking us to not avoid difficult engagements with the archives and to understand how asking new questions is part of the role of the historian.

This brief intervention will give insight into how new research that includes the eighteenth century can help expand the field of Black British histories and how doing so can help us further interrogate the place of historical research in better understanding the nature of Blackness and Britishness then and now. It will also provide insight into how we can consider Black British histories moving forward. As those of us in this field grapple with these questions in our research and lived experience in the academy, we aim to help build a more equitable future for Black British histories. This is not something researchers can do alone. Reports, such as those conducted by the Royal Historical Society, offer key insights concerning the limitations experienced by those conducting this kind of research – especially those of African descent.[4] The push for more equitable forms of research within the academy is recognised; however, support for Black researchers and further consideration of methods that centre marginalised groups are needed to ensure nuanced, complex and equitable histories.

The enslaved labour behind art objects at Charlecote Park

Annabelle Gilmore

My doctoral project is in collaboration with Charlecote Park in Warwickshire, a National Trust property. It looks at how the narratives of imperialism and slavery are held within the specific art objects displayed at Charlecote that once belonged to William Thomas Beckford (1760–1844), an absentee enslaver whose plantations were in Jamaica. As an absentee enslaver, Beckford did not live in the same country as the plantations where his money was made; instead, he remained in England with some time spent living in Europe. While at first this project would appear to focus on the material aspect of the finely crafted art objects, many of which were made in Asia, and on the lives of the white people who owned the objects, firstly Beckford and then George Hammond Lucy (1789–1845) and his wife Mary Elizabeth Lucy

---

[4] Hannah Atkinson, Suzanne Bardgett, Adam Budd, Margot Finn, Christopher Kissane, Sadiah Qureshi, Jonathan Saha, John Siblon and Sujit Sivasundaram, *Race, Ethnicity and Equality in UK History: A Report and Resource for Change* (2018).

(1803–89), this is not the entirety of the work. Beckford made his wealth from the labour of enslaved Black people in Jamaica. It is their labour that is ultimately represented in the objects now displayed at Charlecote. I seek to bring into the light the unknown Black enslaved people whose efforts provided the fortune that led to the purchase of these art objects now displayed at Charlecote. Furthermore, the project is also linked to the presence of a small number of Black people in the county of Warwickshire and the absentee enslavers in the county. This highlights the connection between the local and the global, that there was no capacity for ignorance among the local Warwickshire population in regard to Blackness in Britain.

It has been very interesting working with a National Trust property that has indirect links to slavery and imperialism. The Trust's 2020 Interim Report highlights that twenty-nine properties 'have links to successful compensation claims for slave-ownership and somewhere in the region of one-third are directly connected to colonial histories'.[5] Sally-Anne Huxtable, Head Curator of the Trust, writes of the twentieth-century view of country houses as the epitome of 'Englishness' and most recently the '*Downton Abbey* effect' which has shifted the focus from the things in the houses, to the events and personal histories of the people who lived in them. She remarks that 'Neither of these views of the country house considers it as a dynamic site, in which global and national histories played out in a local setting.'[6] Huxtable continues that they also omit the origins of wealth that funded the spaces and collection as well as the general transnational influences of collections and properties.

In the section dedicated to research, Sophie Chessum, Senior Curator for London and the South East Region, notes that the interpretation at the houses has followed the histories of the families, based on the social standing of elite families and significant events.[7] Conversely, the histories of slavery and imperialism embedded in these country houses were minimised and erased because of the negative associations such histories may cause. As a result, the many global lives that led to the luxuries present in these homes were also ignored. Chessum also suggests that the new millennium brought a shift in how heritage is viewed due to increased academic interest, archive digitisation and visitor curiosity. She states that this change is 'vital to a better understanding of the properties and places in the care of the National Trust'.[8]

Through my collaboration with the Trust, I am working with the property team at Charlecote to investigate these hidden histories. My research looks beyond the borders of Charlecote Park to analyse how the narratives of slavery attached to the art objects from Fonthill Abbey were quieted over time and overpowered by presentations of taste and wealth. The team at Charlecote have provided me with access to items and knowledge that would not have readily been available to me. I have attended workshops only available to

---

[5] Sally-Anne Huxtable *et al.*, *Interim Report on the Connections between Colonialism and Properties now in the Care of the National Trust, Including Links with Historic Slavery* (Swindon, 2020), 5.
[6] Huxtable *et al.*, *Colonialism and Historic Slavery Report*, 7.
[7] *Ibid.*, 59.
[8] *Ibid.*

National Trust staff and volunteers and I have had opportunities to discuss my work with professionals in connection to the Trust. I will soon be working on a placement to gain a better understanding of how such heritage sites work and begin to insert my own research into their knowledge database to help develop new interpretations for the house.

As such, my project, spanning from the mid-eighteenth to mid-nineteenth century, infers that Black British history should also include the Black population that was resident in the anglophone Caribbean under British rule. While this is not a new idea (Paul Gilroy wrote an article thinking about nationalism and Black British history which discusses Caribbean inclusion in 1990), it can often be overlooked in favour for what is more readily defined as Black British history.[9] Hakim Adi notes that 'the history of Africans in Britain cannot be correctly understood without viewing it in the context of Britain's relationship with Europe, Africa and the Americas, especially the exploitive and colonial relationship that began in the sixteenth century'.[10] Christienna Fryar's forthcoming book *Entangled Lands: A Caribbean History of Britain* aims to explore further the relationship between the Caribbean and Britain. Similarly, Imaobong Umoren's forthcoming project *Empire Without End: A New History of Britain and the Caribbean* looks to analyse the impact of 400 years British Caribbean history on today's systemic racism. Furthermore, the IHR's seminar series 'Black British History: Geographies, Concepts, Debates' has acted as a space to discuss new scholarship and evolving perceptions of Black British histories. These works highlight the growing scholarship surrounding the idea of expanding what is Black British history.

In crossing the Atlantic to analyse such histories of the enslaved people working the plantations, my own research brings together the perceived separate spheres of activities of Black enslaved workers in the Caribbean and the collection and display of art in country houses. The plantations under Beckford's ownership were spread across the island of Jamaica; they varied in size but reached 600 acres. So far, I have been able to find the names of over 2,000 people enslaved on Beckford's many plantations. For one of the plantations, Esher, I have been able to identify people from two different lists approximately eight years apart.[11] This has allowed me to develop a continuity for some of these people. This includes Black Bess, a midwife in 1781; she was aged fifty-five and noted as infirm. In 1789 she is named as Old Bess and is no longer a midwife; instead, she has been superannuated, meaning that she is perceived to longer be of use. While the demarcation of useless is a particularly dehumanising act, Bess's skills can still be inferred within the document. By 1789 there is another midwife, Diana. Although it is unclear whether this Diana is Old Diana or Young Diana from the 1781 list, both are listed as working in the field. Diana would have probably learned her skills

    [9] Paul Gilroy, 'Nationalism, History and Ethnic Absolutism', *History Workshop*, 30 (1990) http://www.jstor.com/stable/4289014; Paul Gilroy, *The Black Atlantic: Modernity and Double Consciousness* (Cambridge, MA, 1993).

    [10] Hakim Adi (ed.), 'Introduction', in *Black British History: New Perspectives* (2019), 10.

    [11] National Archive c 107/143; Hull History Centre CDD1/2/7.

from Bess. Understanding Diana's journey to becoming a midwife is just one example of how the objects at Charlecote Park contain a much richer history. These histories should be included in the displays at Charlecote to connect to a global history through a personal narrative. Undertaking this fine-tuned analysis of the enslaved people creates a strong foundation for destabilising the thought that country houses are spaces exclusively for whiteness.

My research serves as a continuation of the analysis started by institutions such as the National Trust and English Heritage, particularly Corinne Fowler's work on the 'Colonial Countryside' project, and builds on work by scholars like Stephanie Barczewski and Catherine Hall, who argue that imperialism and slavery are woven into the foundations of so many country house estates.[12] In analysing Charlecote Park as a case study for the influence of slavery within country house displays, my research highlights how the history of enslaved people in the Caribbean impacts British history, thus emphasising how Black Caribbean history is, at the same time, Black British history. To use Stuart Hall's work, identity has often been a construction of splitting between what is and what is not Other. Hall describes the Other as histories we have depended upon, but which have not been spoken. In this instance, the identity constructed by country house elites relies on the silent histories of the Caribbean. To view these as two separate histories that do not speak to each other is absurd. As Hall remarks, Black people have been in Britain for centuries; their presence has been there for centuries. He states, 'I am the sugar at the bottom of the English cup of tea.'[13]

It is a significant issue for many historians studying Black British history prior to the twentieth century, but particularly for those researching the eighteenth century and before, that so often the resources concerning enslaved people which can be found in the archives provide only quantitative information. This includes simply names, ages, sometimes whether they were African or Creole, and occasionally their role on the plantation. Further complicating research is the difficulty in navigating the archives themselves. The major Black British history archives, such as the Black Cultural Archives in London and the Nottingham Black Archive, are heavily focused on the twentieth century. For historians researching earlier periods, it is often necessary to travel great distances to consult and collate dispersed material. Another issue I have faced with archival research concerns the databases themselves. While I applaud every effort of the hard-working archival staff, at times the databases can be very unclear about what the archive actually holds, and some of my discoveries in archives have been found through secondary reading or stumbling across them. Moreover, I was very unlucky during my research trip, because the trove of information held at the Jamaica Archives and Records Department in Jamaica eluded me due to a weather event, closing the archive

---

[12] Sally-Anne Huxtable *et al.* (2020); Madge Dresser and Andrew Hann, *Slavery and the British Country House* (Swindon, 2013); Stephanie Barczewski, *Country Houses and the British Empire, 1700-1930* (Manchester, 2014); Catherine Hall *et al.*, *Legacies of British Slave-Ownership: Colonial Slavery and the Formation of Victorian Britain* (Cambridge, 2014)

[13] Stuart Hall, 'Old and New Identities, Old and New Ethnicities', in *Culture, Globalization and the World-System: Contemporary conditions for the representation of identity*, ed. Anthony D. King (Basingstoke, 1991), 47–8.

to the public. This experience highlighted the troubles faced when working with a globalised history and the wider accessibility disadvantages faced by others in my situation or even for those who cannot readily travel outside their home country. However, by using what is available to me within this scope, a skeleton framework can be developed for a deeper understanding of the Black lives that, in the case of my work, led to my studying the profiteering and financial wealth of William Beckford. It also starkly contrasts with the wealth of archival evidence that exists for Beckford and the Lucy family at Charlecote. Yet, as historians such as Marisa Fuentes and Simon Newman have shown, from such quantitative data, rich narratives can be inferred from a wider understanding of the world.[14] Thus, the aim for my work is to topple Beckford as the pinnacle of the narrative for the art objects displayed at Charlecote. This would give a distinctively nuanced perspective that accurately connects Black enslaved labour in Jamaica to the artistic display at Charlecote that has otherwise only had a brief mention of Beckford as an enslaver. His presence is necessary to the telling and recognising that his part is significant for the narrative in connecting to the Black enslaved people. The aim is to decentralise William Beckford as art connoisseur of the collection. Instead, shifting the focus to the enslaved people pays tribute to an otherwise forgotten people whose forced labour provided the means for Beckford to purchase the art objects.

Local History

One of the elements that has shaped my work is the drive to look outside London for Black British history and its influence in the long eighteenth century. There has been work of such kind for places like Liverpool, Bristol and Lancaster, which as port cities have strong ties to slavery.[15] While working on aspects of country house history, I became more aware of the interconnected relationship between provincial great houses and the presence of Black people away from coastal areas and London. This has therefore led to the exploration of more provincial and countryside presence of Black British history, particularly in Warwickshire. This presents challenges as archival information is severely limited in comparison to port cities, particularly in comparison to London. My research so far has drawn on some of the elements found in Imtiaz Habib's *Black Lives in the English Archives*, in which a chapter is dedicated to the English provinces.[16] While this work is dedicated to the sixteenth and seventeenth centuries – before the transatlantic slave trade was

---

[14] Fuentes, *Dispossessed Lives*; Simon P. Newman, *Freedom Seekers: Escaping from Slavery in Restoration London* (2022).

[15] Ray Costello, *Black Liverpool: The Early History of Britain's Oldest Black Community 1730-1918* (Liverpool, 2001); Madge Dresser, *Slavery Obscured: The Social History of the Slave Trade in an English Provincial Port* (2016); Alan Rice, 'Ghostly Presences, Servants and Runaways: Lancaster's Emerging Black Histories and their Memorialization 1687-1865', in *Britain's Black Past*, ed. Gretchen H. Gerzina (Liverpool, 2020), 179–96.

[16] Imtiaz Habib, *Black Lives in the English Archives, 1500-1677: Imprints of the Invisible* (2020).

fully underway – it nevertheless is a useful tool in understanding the practical aspect of researching Black history in the British countryside.

However, the very existence of the few Black people living in the British countryside is enough to interrogate the information surrounding their lives, because their experience would differ greatly from those living in places with larger Black communities. This experience is worth exploring within the wider social history framework of countryside living. The evidence so far has placed the Black individuals found in Warwickshire either in country estates of the landed gentry, or within very close proximity to them. Through exploring how they would have experienced life amidst all the systemic societal prejudices of the eighteenth century provides a more detailed look at the wider Black British experience at the time.

This rural approach also strongly connects to the Caribbean, as part of my wider inclusive approach to Black British history. Not only were the Black individuals in the countryside living in country houses, but many members of the white gentry class were also absentee enslavers, connecting rural Britain to Caribbean life for financial gain through forced labour by Black bodies. This is seen with figures like Myrtilla, who was brought to Warwickshire from the Caribbean island of Nevis in the very early eighteenth century, possibly to work as a maid where she could be used, conspicuously objectified, as a show of wealth for the country house owners.[17]

Unfortunately, this method does bring its own challenges to researching Black British history. I recognise that the indirect approach does necessitate studying the white people who either enslaved, or held in service, the few Black individuals resident in Britain's countryside. It also leans on understanding the absentee enslaver in their country seat instead of focusing entirely on the enslaved people on the overseas plantations. However, this is all a necessary context to give voice to a population that would otherwise be dismissed as quantitative information in ledgers, or names in parochial records. While my research builds on the established foundation of whiteness, it is part of an effort to instil a richer and more thorough narrative for Warwickshire's Black British history. Following this approach, my research also emphasises the complexity of country houses as spaces that exist beyond their physical confines, because the contents and sometimes even the house itself embody the narratives of Black British history.

My plans for future projects include further exploration of Warwickshire's Black British history, inclusive of the Caribbean. This would build on my current research and understanding of the individuals who have been identified in the archival records of the Warwickshire County Record Office, and to build upon the names of individuals found, perhaps following the same methodological framework as Fuentes and Newman. This would involve looking into the gentry family of the area, such as the Earls of Warwick at Warwick Castle, who had connections to plantations in Tobago, and investigating Vice-Admiral Lord Hugh Seymour of Ragley Hall, who spent much of his

---

[17] Warwickshire County Records Office DR0024, 'Parish Records of St Lawrence, Oxhill' and Myrtilla's grave in St Lawrence churchyard.

naval career in the Caribbean and is noted as enslaving John Sutcliffe Fletcher, a man from Antigua.[18] This would be part of an effort to highlight the hidden connections between Warwickshire, the Caribbean and the Black people living there in the long eighteenth century. The objective for this would be to provide a nuanced approach to how places like Charlecote Park, Ragley Hall and Warwick Castle are viewed by the public today. It would not be a celebration of the diverse history of Warwickshire, due to the nature of the Black presence within its borders, but instead an opportunity to recognise and perhaps memorialise the Black British history of these places. Such a project would most likely require a collaborative effort with local authorities and heritage institutions to achieve this.

Ideas for the project were inspired by public exhibitions like the Birmingham Museum and Art Gallery exhibition 'Birmingham: Its People, Its History', which opened in October 2012, and which represented all aspects of life in Birmingham and its involvement with slavery and abolition of that institution. While Birmingham is now a major city with a significant Black population, the Birmingham Museum and Art Gallery shows the historic impact of slavery in a place outside London and the major cities often associated with slavery. Katie Donington, who was then part of the Legacies of British Slave-Ownership project team, visited the exhibition in its first few weeks; she highlighted that the aim of the exhibition was to reflect 'how the people of Birmingham and its industries have shaped not only the city but the world as we know it today'.[19] Donington's main interest was how the museum represented Birmingham's involvement in slavery, noting that Historians Advisory Group member Catherine Hall argued for material on slavery to be included. Donington wondered whether 'a display which is still in many ways rooted in a narrative of civic pride [should] allow itself to confront this uncomfortable history?'[20] Donington remarked that the gallery rightfully acknowledged Birmingham's role in slavery as well as in abolition; a key point was the explicit title of 'Birmingham and the Slave Trade'. The guns and metalwork, produced by Birmingham's famed industry, were displayed as objects of trade that 'stand in for the transatlantic human relationships which facilitated Britain's imperial and commercial ambitions'.[21] The presentation of this history to the public, within the central location of Birmingham city centre, allowed for a more direct method of transmitting academic histories to a wider and curious audience.

---

[18] Vere Langford Oliver, *Caribbeana*, I (1910), 24; Barbara Willis-Brown and David Callaghan (eds.), *History Detectives: Black People in the West Midlands 1650-1918* (Birmingham, 2010), 4.

[19] Kate Donington, '"Birmingham: its People, its History": Representing Slavery in a Civic Museum – Part 1', *Centre for the Study of the Legacies of British Slavery*, 22 (2013). Donington is quoting from a now inaccessible article.
https://lbsatucl.wordpress.com/2013/11/22/birmingham-its-people-its-history-representing-slavery-in-a-civic-museum-part-i/.

[20] Donington, 'Birmingham: its People, its History'.

[21] Kate Donington, '"Birmingham: its People, its History": Representing Slavery in a Civic Museum – Part 2', *Centre for the Study of the Legacies of British Slavery*, 6 Dec. 2013
https://lbsatucl.wordpress.com/2013/12/06/birmingham-its-people-its-history-representing-slavery-in-a-civic-museum-part-ii/.

Stuart Burch, at the time a lecturer in museum studies, commented that the exhibition showed a 'far from neutral treatment of history', in regard to the presentation of multicultural history.[22] However, Sara Wajid and Rachael Minott, members of Museum Detox, a network of Black, Asian and Minority Ethnic museum workers in the UK, declared the concept of 'neutral history', particularly when pertaining to histories of enslavement and the eradication of cultures, as an enactment of macro and micro aggressions. Such aggressions come in the form of 'the constant demand made to People of Colour to be grateful for the things that their white counterparts are allowed to complain about'.[23] Wajid and Minott developed the temporary exhibition 'The Past is Now: Birmingham and the British Empire', which opened in 2018 at the Birmingham Museum and Art Gallery. This exhibition was co-curated with six external activists, alongside Wajid and Minott as 'insider activists' to enact decolonial practices within a museum space. Minott expressed how decolonial work 'fundamentally challenges white supremacy and the centralising of Eurocentric views on morality, civilisation and knowledge' and referred to enacting political positioning within the museum space, which has often not been seen as the place for museum curators.[24] The decolonial approach to museum curation by Wajid, Minott and the outside activist-curators highlights the changes that have occurred since the opening of 'Its People, Its History' as well as the different approaches and methods that could be adopted when developing exhibitions around Coventry and Warwickshire's Black British history.

Looking outside the British framework, the government of Barbados, a new republic, announced the development of the Barbados Heritage District; the site is 'dedicated to accurately recounting the historic and contemporary impact of slavery on Barbados'.[25] This direct action in dedicating a public institution to researching and displaying the difficult histories of slavery is an important element of what I wish to achieve in my future work: representing the harsh realities of Warwickshire's Black history in a thoughtful and balanced manner, including connecting the people on Beckford's plantations in Jamaica to the Warwickshire countryside. While I do not yet consider myself an active decolonial historian, I hope to learn from the growing methodology and work to transform historical pedagogies in my future projects.[26] In

---

[22] Stuart Burch, 'Birmingham: Its People, its History, Birmingham Museum and Art Gallery', *Museum Association*, 4 Jan. 2013, https://www.museumsassociation.org/museums-journal/reviews/2013/01/02012013-birmingham-museum-art-gallery/

[23] Sara Wajid and Rachael Minott, 'Detoxing and Decolonising Museums', in *Museum Activism*, ed. Robert R. Janes and Richard Sandell (2019), 25; see also La Tanya S Autry, 'Changing the Things I Cannot Accept: Museums Are Not Neutral', Artstuffmatters blog, 15 Oct. 2017, https://artstuffmatters.wordpress.com/2017/10/15/changing-the-things-i-cannot-accept-museums-are-not-neutral/.

[24] Rachael Minott, 'The Past is Now: Confronting Museums' Complicity in the Imperial Celebration', *Third Text*, 33 (2019), 567.

[25] Barbados Government Information Services, 'Prime Minister Announces Creation of Barbados Heritage District', 3 Dec. 2021, https://gisbarbados.gov.bb/blog/prime-minister-announces-creation-of-barbados-heritage-district/.

[26] See also, Amanda Behm, Christienna Fryar, Emma Hunter, Elisabeth Leake, Su Lin Lewis and Sarah Miller-Davenport, 'Decolonising History: Enquiry and Practice', *History Workshop Journal*, 89 (2020), 169–91.

following this movement of decolonising histories and spaces where histories are told, and taking inspiration from places like Barbados, I aim for my method of exhibition to take on ideas from outside the academic institution and present the histories from the perspective of those who have been marginalised.

I also wish to consider further how William Thomas Beckford is remembered in connection to his overseas plantations and the people he enslaved. The work on my thesis so far has highlighted that Beckford's connection to slavery is often dismissed in favour of his art collecting. Alongside the work with the National Trust at Charlecote, I would like to work on how the art objects associated with Beckford can be seen from the perspective of a Black audience when considered as part of the legacy of slavery. I would like to work on answering questions of how to develop interpretations of the art objects that would appeal to a Black audience without evoking a traumatic history, while fully acknowledging such realities.

A case of Two Sylvias: contemplating gender and historical practice

Montaz Marché

In my research, I ask: 'what was it like to be a Black woman walking the streets of London in the eighteenth century?'[27] To examine this question, I first excavate and identify the presence of individual Black women in London within a range of historical material across several archives, including parish records, newspaper records, criminal records, family papers, hospital records, wills and more. I collate these recorded instances into a database of over 500 Black women in London between 1700 and 1800. I break down the brief, sporadic recorded instances of Black women often written by third-person commentators according to themes/categories: for example, name, age, physical description, origins and location. I use the database to comprehend patterns and answer quantitative and qualitative questions about the population of Black women.

Next, it was essential to evaluate, as much as possible, the contexts of each woman's life, for example, where they lived and the spaces and individuals with which they would have interacted. I argue that understanding these contexts will aid in extracting Black women's experiences in London, particularly when cross-referenced with other contemporary Black women of similar location and social standing. I also examine how Black women moved within London communities and how navigations, interactions and relationships impacted their lives. This examination of contexts constructs a composite image of Black women's lives in London while beginning to identify how London's micro-spaces engage daily with ideas of race, identity and empire.

---

[27] This reflection stems from my Ph.D. research

My research considered the possibility of examining the life histories of Black women through archival recovery. As Ibrahim argues, gender histories 'exclude variant considerations of gendered experience by not considering age'.[28] Within my research, I seek to shift historical perceptions of Black women from 'timeless' one-dimensional concepts to 'economic thinkers' and rational, evolving women positioned within geographies, infusing our thinking of the microhistories of London's spaces with themes of race, gender and class.[29] For some women in my research, it was possible to see archival traces of their lives across time. Yet, for many, it was not. Below, I present the cases of two Black women, Sylvia and Silvia, who challenged me to think creatively about examining women's lives to expand traditional social history methodologies. I consider if and how I could utilise historical imagination to examine the life histories of the women I could not directly trace through the archives.

On 11 November 1763, Sylvia, a 'Negro Woman' 'of the Island of Jamaica' ran away from her master, Samuel Gregory, a silk weaver from a notable family in Bishopsgate.[30] The advertisement format implies Sylvia's position in service. Despite the economic language of 'property' used in the advertisement, it is difficult to confirm if Sylvia was an enslaved woman. However, the record does state that Sylvia was of 'middle stature', 'about 25 years old' and spoke 'tolerable good English'. She also ran with her possessions, some clothing and linen. Although the details are few, the source places Sylvia, as a runaway servant to a silk weaver, in the Bishopsgate area on and before 11 November. Additionally, the advertisement was published on 23 November. Therefore, Sylvia had been missing for twelve days, meaning she probably fled through Bishopsgate, and engaged with its people and trade while escaping.

Silvia Woodcock, the wife of William Woodcock, was a 'mulatto' woman who had previously been a servant to Mr Lane but married out of his house and wed her husband in Cheshunt in January 1779.[31] The couple lived in Enfield for five years and were separated for two years when William left for London to be a servant. In October 1788, William lured Silvia to London to 'find her new lodgings in Holborn'. Arriving in Chelsea in the early morning of 27 October, William attacked Silvia with a wooden stick and delivered blows to the head 'of the length of three-quarters of an inch and the depth

---

[28] Habiba Ibrahim, *Black Age: Oceanic Lifespans and the Time of Black Life* (New York, 2021), 203.

[29] Jennifer Morgan, *Reckoning with Slavery: Gender, Kinship and Capitalism in the Early Black Atlantic* (Durham, NC, 2021), 3.

[30] *Public Advertiser*, 23 Nov. 1763.

[31] Other historians briefly reference Silvia Woodcock and the attack. Kathleen Chater references Silvia as a Black woman, recalling the events of the murder and trial in her research on Black lives in Old Bailey records. Additionally, Lyndon J Dominque references Silvia, as a representation of Black women in eighteenth-century Britain, in his introduction to *A Woman of Colour: A Tale*, 'Silvia Woodcock, whose murder led to the execution of her husband William in 1789'. See Kathleen Chater, *Untold Stories: Black People in England and Wales during the period of the British Slave Trade 1660-1807* (Manchester, 2011), 123. Lyndon Dominque (ed.), *The Woman of Colour: A Tale* (Plymouth, 2008 [1808]), 17.

of three-quarters of an inch'.[32] Silvia was found in the street and taken to St Luke's Chelsea workhouse.[33] A surgeon attended to her, but she died of her wounds on 31 October. Before her death, Silvia testified of her husband's attack. Prosecutors used this witness statement to convict her husband, who was executed for his crime in January 1789.[34]

When investigating the contexts of Sylvia/Silvia's lives, circumstantial evidence arose that posited exciting links between the two women. Firstly, there is a commonality in personal details. Superficially, their names are the same, despite the variations.[35] They would have been the same age. In 1763, Sylvia was about twenty-five years old and in 1788, Silvia was about fifty. As there were twenty-five years between the two records, the two women were probably of similar or the same age. Sylvia and Silvia were also highlighted as migrant women, although from different places. Sylvia's runaway advertisement stated that she was 'from the island of Jamaica'. A newspaper record highlighted that Silvia had served a family in the East Indies for ten years.[36]

Additionally, Silvia's master Mr Lane is a linchpin in confirming Silvia's story and connecting Silvia to London. Silvia Woodcock maintained a relationship with her ex-employer, Mr Lane; she would visit him in Hampton Court after he moved there.[37] Hampton Court tax records identify the only 'Mr Lane' in the area after Silvia's marriage as Mr John Lane, a tenant of Mrs Coggs House in Hampton Court.[38] He recently moved to the area in 1788, corroborating Susanna Brace's testimony that Silvia's last master had recently moved to Hampton Court. This Mr John Lane was made the secretary to the Commissioner of Public Accounts in August 1788.[39] Before this, he was a

---

[32] Trial of William Woodcock, Jan. 1789, Old Bailey Proceedings Online, reference: t17890114-1. Accessed 6 Mar 2022. https://www.oldbaileyonline.org/browse.jsp?id=t17890114-1-defend45&div= t17890114-1#highlight.

[33] St Luke's Workhouse Registers: Workhouse Admissions and Discharges Registers 28 –31 Oct. 1788, *London Lives 1690-1800: Crime, Poverty and Social Policy,* Reference No. sldswhr_30_3003 (accessed 6 March 2022). https://www.londonlives.org/browse.jsp?id=persNamesldswhr_30_3003&div=sldswhr_ 30_3003#highlight.

[34] 'Information of Sylvia Woodcock taken before one Edw. Read Esqr...' Old Bailey Sessions:

Sessions Papers - Justices' Working Documents, *London Lives* ..., reference no. LMOBPS450340479 (accessed 6 March 2022). https://www.londonlives.org/browse.jsp? id=LMOBPS45034_n2037-1&div=LMOBPS45034PS450340479#highlight; a copy of this statement is transcribed in William Woodcock's trial transcript.

[35] Silvia Woodcock is also called Sylvia in the original witness statement scribed by Edward Read, a magistrate. Silvia signed the statement with an X. Old Bailey Sessions Papers – Justices' Working Documents, 1788, *London Lives,* reference no. LMOBPS450340479 (accessed 18 May 2019). https://www.londonlives.org/browse.jsp?id=LMOBPS45034_n2037-1&div=LMOBPS45034PS450340479 #highlight.

[36] 'News', *World,* 6 Nov. 1788.

[37] According to Brace's testimony, Silvia's husband used her visits to her old master to explain her absence when returning to Enfield the day after the attack. The implication is that her visits were known to friends and William.

[38] Enfield Land Tax Records, 1767–75, *London Metropolitan Archives,* reference no: CLC/525/ MS05285.

[39] *London Gazette,* 5 Aug. 1788.

solicitor in Middlesex and became a commissioning magistrate for the Middlesex Sessions House. We can plausibly connect Mr John Lane as Silvia's master as he had a home in Ponders End, Enfield, in the 1760s and then in Cheshunt, Hertford, in the 1770s. This record corroborates the details stated in the Old Bailey trial.

Interestingly, John Lane also rented a home in Bloomsbury and worked in Hick's Hall in Clerkenwell at the Middlesex Quarter Sessions until 1780. Clerkenwell is just over a mile from Samuel Gregory's household in Bishopsgate. Therefore, Sylvia could have obtained work with Mr Lane. Firstly, we do not know when Silvia's service with Mr Lane began, but it was enough time to build a meaningful relationship. Secondly, evidence of runaway Black women servants in my database proves that Black women could run away from their posts and remain concealed within London. For example, in 1748, Christmas Bennett absented her master's house in Queens Square, Holborn and was 'suppos'd to be conceal'd somewhere about Whitechapel'.[40] Similarly, Jane Mower, who ran away from her master in Lincoln's Inn Field, was found in an inn in St Giles in the Field with her lover, John Kelly.[41] This concealment in urban spaces was possible because of London's local communities' socio-political and cultural fragmentation.[42] Thus, London's fluctuating local spaces concealed Black women's flights rather than distance. Sylvia could have run from Bishopsgate to Clerkenwell or Bloomsbury and found new employment. Finally, in the same tax record that records Sylvia's master, Samuel Gregory's residence at Cherubim Court in 1763 (Sylvia's likely residence), there are records of a William Woodcock paying rent to a property on Bottle Alley, a few streets over, since 1761.[43]

From this evidence, it was tempting to make a case that these two women could be the same woman and that I could construct the narrative of a labouring Black woman in 'service' over twenty-five years. However, this evidence is circumstantial. Silvia/Sylvia were migrants from different places. I contest that the William Woodcock I found was the right one, as newspaper reports indicated that William Woodcock was about '24 years of age' when the arrest warrant was issued after the attack.[44] The issues with constructing this narrative or uncovering details on Sylvia's life highlight the challenges of recovering the histories of ordinary working people, women and minority communities in the

---

[40] *Daily Advertiser*, 29 Feb. 1748, *Runaway Slaves in Britain Database*, reference no: r0565, Accessed 7 Jun. 2021. https://www.runaways.gla.ac.uk/database/display/?rid=565.

[41] Advertisements and Notices, *London Gazette*, 11–15 Oct. 1715. Jane Mower and Thomas Kelly were later indicted for theft at a trial in the Old Bailey, where Jane was found guilty. However, being with child, her sentence was respited. Old Bailey Proceedings: Accounts of Criminal Trials, 7 Dec. 1715, reference no. t17151207-40 (accessed 24 October 2021). https://www.oldbaileyonline.org/browse.jsp?id=t17151207-40-defend205&div=t17151207-40#highlight.

[42] Peter Clark, 'The Multi Centred Metropolis: The Social and Cultural Landscapes of London: 1600- 1840', in *Two Capitals: London and Dublin 1500-1840*, ed. Peter Clark and Raymond Gillespie (Oxford, 2001), 239.

[43] Bishopsgate Tax Records, 1763, London Land Tax Records, *London Metropolitan Archives*, reference no: CLC/525/MS11316/312.

[44] Advertisements and Notices, *World*, 6 Nov. 1788.

archives. Nevertheless, this circumstantial link between Sylvia and Silvia was the closest I had come to uncovering such a detailed and lengthy lifespan of a labouring Black woman. Therefore, I wondered if there was a way to combine the evidence of the two Sylvias and think about/examine Black life histories and experiences. As Lewis Gaddis writes, in the absence of conductible experiments, 'historians must use logic and imagination' to overcome difficulties of historical recovery, conducting 'their own equivalent of thought experiments'.[45] I employ historical imagination to breach the lines of theory and evidence.

Following the lead of Saidiya Hartman's critical fabulation, which combines historical and archival research with critical theory and fictional narrative, in this case of two Sylvias, I engage historical imagination to their lives as one labouring Black woman in service.[46] My research thus far presented me with two women of similar backgrounds (as migrants), working backgrounds (as once in service) and statuses (labouring people) in London, whose paths overlap by way of circumstantial evidence. I use Sylvia/Silvia's similar contexts and circumstantial evidence to imagine the bridge between the two women's lives. I merge their similar contexts and repurpose the circumstantial links to imagine the two Sylvias' lives as one and create a representative lifespan of a labouring Black woman. Speculation is inevitable, with many questions about Black women's lives. In this format, I forefront a more precise speculation based upon evidence of lived experiences.

As the earliest, Sylvia could represent the present, highlighting a recent experience in service. Contextualising Sylvia's experience using historical inference illuminates important themes, for example, the experience of working under a silk weaver within a middle-class household, her daily functions within that role or the possibility of her enslavement when comparing her life with similar runaway cases and the paradigms of service in the industrial East End of London. Through Silvia, on the other hand, I observe Black women's marriages from service, their marriage experiences, marital breakdown and the integration of migrant women into various London communities as a bare minimum. However, as Sylvia's prospective future, Silvia raises important questions. For example, little is known about Silvia's history. Her marriage record does not list her parish, unlike her husband. Furthermore, when asked if she knew what country Silvia came from in the trial, Brace, Silvia's friend of seven years, said, 'I cannot rightly say the part she came from'.[47] Only after Silvia's death do details emerge of her history from the East Indies and in newspaper reports specifically (although I have found no details to corroborate this). From this, one can speculate a conscious or unconscious silence around Silvia's history within the local space. How intentional was this silence if one were to consider Silvia's past as a runaway? Using this exercise, I can explore likely future prospects, the motivations and results of a subject's actions using imagination and the evidence of two women's lives as a representation of past, present or future.

---

[45] John Lewis Gaddis quoted in David J Staley, *Historical Imagination* (2021), 5.
[46] Saidiya Hartman, 'Venus in Two Acts', *Small Axe*, 12 (2008), 1-14.
[47] Trial of William Woodcock, *Old Bailey Proceedings*.

I do not present this exercise as the history of an individual, nor do I state that this is Silvia's or Sylvia's history. This exercise combines two individual histories and utilises them as an analytical tool to conceive ideas of experiences over time. Still, there are drawbacks to this exercise, the most significant being its position as a mental exercise rather than an excavation of actual historical narratives. However, this exercise has been helpful for me, adjacent to the historical narratives I have uncovered, to consider Black women's lives beyond a single event, to imagine diverse Black women's histories and articulate Black women's lives as whole lives lived. Here, I take advantage of the wealth of information my research has afforded and the historian's capacity to perceive remnants of the past and fill in that which is absent.[48]

[48] Staley, *Historical Imagination.*

Cite this article: Warren K, Gilmore A, Marché M (2024). Emerging Scholars Researching Black British Histories (mid-Eighteenth to mid-Nineteenth Centuries). *Transactions of the Royal Historical Society* **2**, 491–507. https://doi.org/10.1017/S0080440124000033

UNIVERSITY
OF LONDON
PRESS

NEW HISTORICAL PERSPECTIVES

ALL TITLES AVAILABLE OPEN ACCESS

New Historical Perspectives (NHP) is a book series for early career scholars (within ten years of their doctorate), commissioned and edited by the Royal Historical Society, in association with University of London Press and the Institute of Historical Research. To purchase the titles in print, use **RHSNHP30** for a 30% discount on the UoL Press site.

u o l p r e s s . c o . u k